P9-BBP-046

ROBERT LOUIS STEVENSON:
THE CRITICAL HERITAGE

THE CRITICAL HERITAGE SERIES

GENERAL EDITOR: B. C. SOUTHAM, M.A., B.LITT. (OXON.)
Formerly Department of English, Westfield College, University of London

For a list of books in the series see the back end paper

ROBERT LOUIS STEVENSON

THE CRITICAL HERITAGE

Edited by
PAUL MAIXNER

Late Professor of English
Rhode Island College

ROUTLEDGE & KEGAN PAUL
LONDON, BOSTON AND HENLEY

First published in 1981
by Routledge & Kegan Paul Ltd
39 Store Street, London WC1E 7DD,
9 Park Street, Boston, Mass. 02108, USA, and
Broadway House, Newtown Road,
Henley-on-Thames, Oxon RG9 1EN
Printed in Great Britain by
Redwood Burn Ltd, Trowbridge & Esher
Compilation, introduction, notes, bibliography and index
Copyright © the Estate of Paul Maixner 1981
No part of this book may be reproduced in
any form without permission from the
publisher, except for the quotation of brief
passages in criticism

British Library Cataloguing in Publication Data

Robert Louis Stevenson. – (The Critical
heritage series)

I. Maixner, Paul   II. Series
828'.8'09   // PR5496 ℞ 80–42296

ISBN 0–7100–0505–9

General Editor's Preface

The reception given to a writer by his contemporaries and near-contemporaries is evidence of considerable value to the student of literature. On one side we learn a great deal about the state of criticism at large and in particular about the development of critical attitudes towards a single writer; at the same time, through private comments in letters, journals or marginalia, we gain an insight upon the tastes and literary thought of individual readers of the period. Evidence of this kind helps us to understand the writer's historical situation, the nature of his immediate reading-public, and his response to these pressures.

The separate volumes in the *Critical Heritage Series* present a record of this early criticism. Clearly, for many of the highly productive and lengthily reviewed nineteenth- and twentieth-century writers, there exists an enormous body of material; and in these cases the volume editors have made a selection of the most important views, significant for their intrinsic critical worth or for their representative quality—perhaps even registering incomprehension!

For earlier writers, notably pre-eighteenth century, the materials are much scarcer and the historical period has been extended, sometimes far beyond the writer's lifetime, in order to show the inception and growth of critical views which were initially slow to appear.

In each volume the documents are headed by an Introduction, discussing the material assembled and relating the early stages of the author's reception to what we have come to identify as the critical tradition. The volumes will make available much material which would otherwise be difficult of access and it is hoped that the modern reader will be thereby helped towards an informed understanding of the ways in which literature has been read and judged.

B.C.S.

To
J. Thomson King
whose gift led me to reconsider Stevenson

Contents

Contents

'Catriona' (1893)

'The Ebb-Tide' (1894)

'Weir of Hermiston' (1896)

Contents

Acknowledgments

I should like to thank the following for permission to use materials: Associated Newspapers Group Ltd for reviews in the 'Daily Chronicle' and the 'Daily News'; the editors of the 'Contemporary Review', the 'Glasgow Herald', the 'Nation' (New York), 'Punch', the 'Scotsman', the 'Spectator', and 'The Times' for articles and reviews from their pages; the editors of the 'New Statesman' for reviews from the 'Athenaeum'; William Blackwood & Sons Ltd for M.O.W. Oliphant's reviews in 'Blackwood's Magazine'; Joan M. Ling for Sir James Barrie's essay in 'The Edinburgh Eleven'; A. & C. Black Ltd for an excerpt from 'The Letters of Dr John Brown', edited by his son and D.W. Forrest; Mrs C.S. Evans for an excerpt from an unpublished letter by Dr John Brown; Miss D.E. Collins for an article by G.K. Chesterton; Jennifer Gosse for extracts from 'The Life and Letters of Sir Edmund Gosse', ed. Evan Charteris, for an essay from Gosse's 'Questions at Issue', and for extracts from unpublished letters by Gosse; Oxford University Press for extracts from 'The Correspondence of G.M. Hopkins and R.W. Dixon',ed. C.C. Abbott, and 'The Letters of G.M. Hopkins to Robert Bridges', ed. C.C. Abbott, published by Oxford University Press by arrangement with the Society of Jesus; The Bodley Head Ltd for an extract from Vernon Lee's 'The Handling of Words'; Charles Scribner's Sons and John Farquharson Ltd for numerous extracts from 'The Letters of Henry James', ed. Percy Lubbock; The Society of Authors as the literary representative of the Estate of Richard Le Gallienne for reviews by Le Gallienne in 'Retrospective Reviews'; The Clarendon Press for extracts from 'The Letters of George Meredith', ed. C.L. Cline, © 1970 Oxford University Press; J.C. Medley and R.G. Medley, owners of the copyright in George Moore, for an extract from 'The Confessions of a Young Man' and for reviews printed in the 'Hawk' and the 'Daily Chronicle';

Foy F. Quiller-Couch for reviews by Sir Arthur Quiller-Couch printed in the 'Speaker' and, with G.P. Putnam's Sons, for reviews in 'Adventures in Criticism'; George L. Saintsbury for two unsigned reviews in the 'Pall Mall Gazette' by George Saintsbury; Charles Scribner's Sons and Associated Book Publishers Ltd for the extensive quotations from 'The Letters of Robert Louis Stevenson', ed. Sir Sidney Colvin; Frank Swinnerton and Doubleday & Co., Inc., for the extract from Swinnerton's 'R. L. Stevenson: A Critical Study'; Wayne State University Press for extracts from 'The Letters of John Addington Symonds', ed. Herbert M. Schueller and Robert L. Peters, Copyright 1967, 1968, 1969 by Herbert M. Schueller, Wayne State University, Detroit, Michigan, and Robert L. Peters, University of California at Riverside, California; the author's Literary Estate and The Hogarth Press Ltd for the essay by Leonard Woolf from 'Essays in Literature, History, Politics, etc.'; Mrs Elinor Finley for articles and reviews by William Archer that appeared in the 'Pall Mall Gazette' and 'Time' (London); A.D. Peters & Co. for an article by Maurice Hewlett in 'The Times'; Professor O.L. Zangwill for a review by Israel Zangwill in the 'Critic' (New York); Michael Balfour for an extract from an unpublished letter by Sir Graham Balfour; the Society of Antiquaries of London for an unpublished letter by William Morris; E.Q. Nicholson for unpublished letters by F.W.H. Myers; Alan Osbourne for excerpts from unpublished letters by R.L. Stevenson, Thomas Stevenson, and Fanny van de Grift Stevenson. While in certain cases it has been difficult to locate the proprietors of copyright material, all possible care has been taken to trace ownership of the items in the volume and to make a full acknowledgment.

I wish to thank the Trustees of the National Library of Scotland, the Huntington Library, San Marino, California, and the Beinecke Rare Book and Manuscript Library, Yale University, for permission to use the materials in their holdings. I should also like to express my deep appreciation for the courtesy and helpfulness of Mr Alan Bell, Assistant Keeper, Department of Manuscripts, National Library of Scotland; Miss Marjorie G. Wynne, Research Librarian, Beinecke Rare Book and Manuscript Library; and Mr Robert Reese, State Park Historian, Monterey, California. Furthermore, I wish to acknowledge my debt to Miss Marion Fleisher for the identification of reviews in the 'Athenaeum'; to Mr C.A. Seaton for the same service with regard to reviews in the 'Spectator'; and to numerous friends and acquaintances for checking information in libraries in Scotland, England, and the United States. For grants in support of my research I should like to

thank the American Philosophical Society and the New York
University Graduate Arts and Science Research Fund. I wish'
also to acknowledge an extensive debt to George L. McKay
for the information contained in 'Some Notes on Robert
Louis Stevenson, His Finances and His Agents and
Publishers' (1958).   Finally, I take this occasion to
express my profound gratitude to Mr Ernest J. Mehew, who
has so often and so willingly drawn on his extensive
knowledge of Stevenson to answer my various queries.   I
owe a very special debt to him for the dating of letters
(in Nos 10, 12, 16, 39, 77, 91) and for the identification of unsigned reviews (Nos 23, 28, 29, 49, 57, 67,
115).

Note on the Text

The items printed in this volume, whether from books,
periodicals, or unpublished materials, follow the
originals in every important respect. All omissions have
been clearly indicated; in the reviews these consist for
the most part of summaries or lengthy quotations from
Stevenson's work. Typographical errors, unless they have
some special significance, have been corrected without
remark and titles have been made uniform. The following
abbreviations have been used throughout:

B	Unpublished materials in the Beinecke Collection, Yale University Library. Items are indicated by their catalogue number in George L. McKay's 'The Stevenson Library of Edwin J. Beinecke', 6 vols, 1951–64.
LS	'The Letters of Robert Louis Stevenson', South Seas Edition, ed. Sir Sidney Colvin, 1925. The four volumes of letters (xxix–xxxii of the edition) are numbered separately; references are to the volume number in respect to the letter series rather than the edition. The South Seas Edition of the letters is the most complete to date.
Balfour, 'Life'	Sir Graham Balfour, 'The Life of Robert Louis Stevenson', 2 vols, 1901.
Furnas, 'Voyage'	J. C. Furnas, 'Voyage to Windward: The Life of Robert Louis Stevenson', 1952.

Chronology of Works

1886 (continued)	'Kidnapped' (July). Periodically in 'Young Folks', 1 May - 13 July 1886.
1887	'The Merry Men' (February). Stories published earlier in 'Cornhill', 'The Broken Shaft', the 'Court and Society Review', 'Longman's'.
	'Underwoods' (July). Some verses published earlier in 'Magazine of Art', 'Cornhill', 'Atlantic Monthly', etc.
	'Memories and Portraits' (November). Essays published earlier in 'Cornhill', 'Longman's', 'Edinburgh University Magazine', etc.
1888	'Memoir of Fleeming Jenkin' (January).
	'The Black Arrow' (June). Periodically in 'Young Folks', 30 June - 20 October 1883.
1889	'The Wrong Box' (June).
	'The Master of Ballantrae' (September). Periodically in 'Scribner's Magazine', November 1888 - October 1889.
1890	'Father Damien' (July). Published earlier in 'Scots Observer', 3 and 20 May 1890, and in the 'Australian Star', 24 May 1890.
	'Ballads' (December). Several ballads published earlier in 'Scribner's' and 'Scots Observer'.
1892	'Across the Plains' (April). Essays appeared earlier in 'Longman's', 'Fraser's', 'Magazine of Art', 'Scribner's'.
	'The Wrecker' (June). Periodically in 'Scribner's', August 1891 - July 1892.
	'A Footnote to History' (August).
1893	'Island Nights' Entertainments' (April). Stories published earlier in 'Illustrated London News', 'Black and White', 'National Observer'.
	'Catriona' (September). Periodically as 'David Balfour' in 'Atalanta', December 1892 - September 1893.
1894	'The Ebb-Tide' (September). Periodically in 'To-Day', 11 November 1893 - 3 February 1894; 'McClure's Magazine' (USA), February-July 1894.
	Edinburgh Edition, vol. i (November). Remaining twenty-seven volumes appeared at intervals to June 1898.
	[Stevenson dies, 4 December.]
1895	'Amateur Emigrant' (January). Text of 1880 extensively revised.
	'Vailima Letters' (October).

1896	'Fables' (March). Periodically in 'Longman's', August–September 1895. 'Weir of Hermiston' (May). Periodically in 'Cosmopolis', January–April 1896. 'Songs of Travel' (August). Verses previously printed in 'Pall Mall Gazette', 'New Review', 'Scots Observer', etc. The collection first printed in book form in vol. xiv of the Edinburgh Edition (December 1895). 'In the South Seas' (September). Published earlier in full in the New York 'Sun' between February and December 1891; published in part in 'Black and White' during the same period. First printed in book form in vol. xx of the Edinburgh Edition (June 1896).
1897	'St Ives' (October). Periodically in 'Pall Mall Magazine', November 1896 – November 1897.
1899	'Letters to Family and Friends', ed. Sidney Colvin (November).
[1901	Graham Balfour, 'Life of Stevenson'.]
1895[–1912]	Thistle Edition (New York).
1906[–1907]	Pentland Edition (London).
1908[–1912]	Biographical Edition (New York).
1911	Swanston Edition (London).
1922	Vailima Edition (London).
1924	Tusitala Edition (London).
1924[–1926]	Skerryvore Edition (London).
1925	South Seas Edition (New York).

Introduction

It requires an uncommon effort of the imagination to see
Stevenson as his more sympathetic and perceptive contemporaries saw him. Until recently few readers - at least
among those who gave much thought to the rise and fall of
critical reputations - would have been inclined to make
the effort because of the view of him that was current.
The view, which dated from the appearance of Frank
Swinnerton's study of Stevenson in 1914, was a reaction
against the uncritical adulation of him, especially in
the decade following his death, and against certain
values and attitudes he was seen to represent. Had this
view of him been patently false or had it discredited him
altogether, it would more easily have been gainsaid; but
it acknowledged a talent on his part, though essentially
a minor one, and it contained an ingredient of truth
adequate to satisfy readers whose knowledge of him was
limited. This view was not of course the only view of
Stevenson. He continued to have his followers and among
them were mature and intelligent readers. But he was not
a subject of serious critical discussion; indeed he was
on the whole better received by general readers, and practising writers, than by literary critics.
    According to the view which derived from Swinnerton and
which prevailed among readers who gave thought to critical
standards, Stevenson's achievement as a writer of children's books was never challenged. 'Treasure Island',
'Kidnapped', and 'A Child's Garden of Verses' were felt to
deserve their perennial popularity and their status as
classics. Nevertheless, his success along this line
served really to define and emphasize his limitations.
The essays, which had been regarded as charming and original, were now considered commonplace in thought and

1

contrived in expression. Indeed both the writing style
and the personality were seen as a collection of poses.
In the various roles he played - bohemian, vagabond,
adventurer, teller of tales, head of the clan at Vailima -
he was caught glancing at his mirrored image out of the
corner of his eye. He had admittedly faced ill health
with cheerful bravery and optimism, but the bravery was
forced and the optimism thin: both were supported by a
simplicity of belief as open to ridicule as the phrase in
which he expressed it - 'keep your pecker up'. He had
admittedly an immense appeal, but it was basically an
appeal to the simple-minded, the Philistine, or those who
had - like Leonard Bast in 'Howards End', a fervent
admirer of 'R.L.S.' - a spotty education, imperfectly
formed taste, and were culturally on the make.

   Henry James, writing just after the turn of the century
to Graham Balfour, Stevenson's official biographer, deplored the unfortunate effects of the popularity of
Stevenson as a personality. Because of the 'so complete
exhibition of the man and the life', James said, the works
were deprived of much of their 'supremacy and mystery'.
'The achieved legend and history that has *him* for subject
has made ... light of their subject and their claim to
represent him.'(1) It remains true even today that a disproportionate measure of the interest in Stevenson is
directed at the man and the reputation rather than the
works, and the effect has been to reduce rather than
increase the power and appeal of those works. But
Stevenson's popularity has had other unfortunate effects.
Exaggerated praise and the excessive reaction against it
describe the pattern of his reception. This was true even
in the early stages of his career. Sympathetic friends
and reviewers made extravagant claims and predictions that
provoked a reflex of antagonism on the part of readers or
led them to approach Stevenson with the wrong expectations. These readers were disappointed when they failed
to find what they had been led to expect and they overlooked qualities they might have found appealing had their
expectations been more modest. Stevenson was also hin-
dered by admirers in a more direct way. He was put in the
uncomfortable position of having to live up to their idea
of what he should accomplish. As a result he came into
his own later than otherwise he might, and was obliged to
expend too much of his limited energy trying to placate
supporters by doing work they would approve or by trying
to justify work he knew they would not. When Stevenson
did free himself from their influence and followed his own
inclinations (which he often justified on grounds of
financial need), he produced several extremely successful

works. Shortly after the appearance of these works, he
found himself faced with another adversary in addition to
his original circle of admirers - the monster of public
infatuation. It was essentially infatuation with the personality detached from the works and Stevenson was himself
in a degree responsible for it, if only by his willingness
to be interviewed and to share his personal affairs with
the public. Certainly Stevenson was not altogether displeased at the sudden and unexpected appearance of the
monster. Its appetite was huge and by supplying it he
could meet his growing expenses at Vailima. Furthermore,
while Stevenson scorned some segment of the hungry public,
it did not appear a monster to him in truth because no
concessions in his art beyond those he was naturally disposed to make were required to feed it. It is probably
true to say then, in spite of certain claims to the contrary by Stevenson himself, that his art paid little for
his popularity. It was rather his reputation, especially
his posthumous reputation, that paid - has paid and still
pays dearly.

The present volume offers a reasonably full selection
of opinions concerning Stevenson's work throughout his
writing career - from 1878 to 1894 - and for the two
decades following, namely, up to the time of Swinnerton's
study in 1914. Swinnerton's work, as I suggest, marks a
significant change of attitude towards Stevenson and,
following its appearance, and in part as a direct consequence of it, there was a sharp decline of interest in
him, at least among serious readers and critics. From
this time his 'fall' is to be dated, and comment, whether
it be favourable or not, is concerned with a figure
diminished in stature and significance. The two final
items, which follow the Swinnerton extract, date from the
early 1920s, but they express the negative sentiments
that have remained more or less unchanged up to the
recent past. Limitations of space have prohibited the
inclusion of comment beyond that date, but such comment
in any case is readily available elsewhere.

It should be said that this volume is not comprised of
the fond recollections, the legends, the exercises in
hagiography that fill J. A. Hammerton's 'Stevensoniana'
(1903, 1907, 1910); material of that nature has been
excluded except for a few examples to give the reader
some idea of what the subsequent reaction is against.
Until we have experienced these materials directly, the
attacks against Stevenson seem unnecessarily fierce and
bad tempered. It should be said, too, that much of the
comment in this volume may well be disappointing to a
reader who expects to find close and careful treatment of

Stevenson's works. This is certainly not the case,
though the items collected here do have, I believe, a
value that goes beyond their mere usefulness as a record
of superficial and out-of-date opinions about Stevenson.
Many of the items do contain overstated claims or denials,
but this is by no means always the case. If Stevenson was
the victim of his admirers, he also had the remarkable
good fortune to find during his life a sizeable readership
capable of a more or less full appreciation of his work
and a just and reasoned estimate of his achievement. The
result is that in brief and fugitive remarks and in reviews often written with no intention to be reprinted,
Stevenson's contemporaries have left a body of material
worth preserving and especially useful as a basis for further critical study, the result of which might be to re-
store to his writings something of the 'supremacy and mystery' Henry James and other figures of his stature found
in them.

The items collected here are ordered chronologically
under the title by Stevenson to which they pertain. The
titles selected are those which were significant in determining his reputation - the travel writings, essays,
poetry, and the fiction, including his collaborations with
Fanny Stevenson and Lloyd Osbourne. Grouped under these
works are first of all Stevenson's own remarks, if they
are available, made while he was engaged in writing or at
least prior to the time when reviewers delivered their
judgments. These are included on the grounds that the
reader is better able to gauge Stevenson's reaction to the
judgments of others when something is known of his intentions and his own assessments of a particular work.
Following Stevenson's remarks are the judgments of others
in the form of letters, reviews, journal entries, etc.,
with Stevenson's response or rejoinder - if it survives -
following directly the item to which it relates, unless
the comment is brief enough to appear in a headnote or is
more appropriate to the account in the Introduction. In
selecting materials for the volume I have given special
regard to items which are related in some way one to
another and gain in interest by being placed side by side,
and to those which reveal some interaction between Stevenson and his readers and critics.

II

How did Stevenson see himself in relation to his readers?
At the beginning of his career he held two different but
not irreconcilable views. At times he regarded himself as

an artist working without any immediate awareness of the
public at all, either as a specialized craftsman who
derives pleasure from working in his medium to produce a
highly finished object; or, at other times, though less
often, as a sort of husbandman who stands by patiently and
more or less passively while the miracle of creation takes
place - 'I can do but little; I mostly wait and look out'
(LS, i, 214) - and at length the essays and stories mature
and fall from the tree like ripe fruit. In neither case
is any emphasis placed upon his relationship with an audience (LS, i, 206).

More often, however, Stevenson thinks of his art as a
means of fulfilling obligations to others. As a young
man, the first obligation was to his father, who supported
him financially long beyond the time when both felt he
should be independent. In a curious way Stevenson conceived of the obligation or debt as extending beyond his
father to mankind at large, to 'civilization and my
fellowmen'. He was determined to settle the debt; if it
were not possible 'to get well and do good work yet and
more than repay my debts to the world', he would, he says,
'invest an extra franc or two in laudanum' and put an end
to himself. But he was determined: 'I *will* repay it'
(LS, i, 126). When Stevenson regards his writing as a
means of answering an obligation he is of course anxious
for the approval of his audience and his debt to them is
paid when he wins it, chiefly by offering entertainment or
solace.

In spite of his dependence upon the approval of an
audience, there are reasons for his deriving a greater
comfort and security from this view than from the other.
For one thing, being less ambitious, having less exalted
intentions, he is free of the artist's vanity and so less
sensitive to adverse criticism (LS, i, 104). Then too,
writing understood in this way is a more or less steady
occupation and means of financial support. Work can be
done in times of ill health or low energy, or when inspiration flags. This is an important consideration since
'occupation is the great thing; so that a man should have
his life in his own pocket and never be thrown out of work
by anything' (LS, i, 309). Also, according to this way of
looking at matters, a writer of even modest talents can
perform a noble service, at least for certain readers.
Genius is not required; it might even disqualify a writer
for such a service in so far as it implies energies incompatible with a sympathy for readers who have a tenuous
hold on life. For such an audience - those Stevenson felt
himself especially qualified to address - even a few good
paragraphs might give 'rest and pleasure' (LS, i, 169) (2).

Stevenson maintained these two views more or less throughout his career. The first was uppermost when he felt robust and able to entertain high ambitions as an artist. When he had doubts about his powers and his energies were reduced and his health bad, he inclined towards the latter view. From time to time it seems to have been his hope to discover a method – he was never to be very explicit on the matter nor even very clear in his own mind about it – to bring the two views together. When he exercised what he thought were his best talents, he kept before him the standard of George Meredith and, after the mid-1880s, Henry James. Sidney Colvin was the close friend and advisor in literary matters who encouraged Stevenson throughout his career to take himself seriously and to attempt to secure some kind of lasting reputation; Colvin was candid and persistent in his criticism, even to the point of being bothersome when he felt Stevenson was compromising his gifts or doing less than his best.

At the same time, however, Colvin gave Stevenson practical advice about the requirements of editors and publishers and recommended his work to them – to P. G. Hamerton and Richmond Seeley of the 'Portfolio' (where Stevenson's first essay, Roads, appeared, having been rejected by the 'Saturday Review'), to George Grove of 'Macmillan's Magazine', Dr Charles Appleton of the 'Academy', and Leslie Stephen of the 'Cornhill'. It was in the 'Cornhill' that Stevenson's best early work was published – sixteen of the twenty-four essays in 'Virginibus Puerisque' and 'Familiar Studies of Men and Books', as well as a number of short stories. Stevenson considered himself fortunate to appear in the 'Cornhill' and to be able, as many other contributors were not, to initial his work. Through his initials (R.L.S. was first thought by readers to stand for the 'Real Leslie Stephen'), he established his identity as a writer and became known to a comparatively small but important circle of readers. Stevenson's early work appeared also in a far less successful and prestigious periodical – the short-lived 'London, A Conservative Weekly Journal' (1877-9), which was founded by Glasgow Brown, a friend and associate of Stevenson from their days on the 'Edinburgh University Magazine'. Besides Stevenson and Henley, who became the editor after Brown's death, the chief contributors to the paper were Andrew Lang, George Saintsbury, Grant Allen, and James Runciman, its sub-editor. Stevenson's contributions included hastily written occasional pieces, many of which were unsigned and some of which even now remain unidentified (3).

We can gather something of the way Stevenson was regarded at this early stage of his career from the brief notices and occasional tributes of article length in newspapers and periodicals of the time. (4) Clearly one source of appeal was the special quality of the voice that spoke in the essays. Readers recognized that his essays, compared to many of those that stood beside them in the periodicals, treated common, even at times trivial matters; they were sometimes referred to as 'filler'. But his observations were vivid and exact and he spoke with a directness and familiarity that readers found rare and attractive. His ideas were not startlingly original; they were the ideas perennially discussed, but, as with Montaigne and other great essayists, they were freshly conceived and immediately experienced. Colvin, writing years later of his first impressions of Stevenson's work, recalled having admired above all a 'moderation of statement and lenity of style'. Colvin found the early essay Notes on the Movements of Young Children (1874) representative of that early work; it was

> an extraordinarily promising effort at analytic description half-humorous, half-tender - and promising above all in so far as it proved how well, while finding brilliantly effective expression for the subtlety of vital observation which was one part of his birthright, he could hold in check the tendency to emotional stress and vehemence which was another. This was in itself a kind of distinction in an age when so many of our prose-writers, and those the most attractive and impressive to youth, as Carlyle, Macaulay, Ruskin, Dickens, were men who, for all their genius, lacked or did not seek the special virtues of restraint and lenity of style, but were given, each after his manner, to splendid over-colouring and over-heightening: dealers in the purple patch and the insistent phrase, the vehement and contentious assertion. ('Memories and Notes' (1921), 123-4)

III

EARLY WORKS TO 'NEW ARABIAN NIGHTS' (1878-82)

Stevenson engaged a wider public with 'Inland Voyage' (1878) and 'Travels with a Donkey in the Cévennes' (1879). Accounts of travel were then in vogue and judged against other examples these volumes were clearly superior, though they did not rank high in Stevenson's own opinion, having been written according to him chiefly because they could

be turned out easily and might be profitable. They earned
little for him, but he was surprised and pleased at the
attention they were given by readers and reviewers.
P. G. Hamerton wrote a long and genial review of 'Inland
Voyage' (No. 5) which was quoted and echoed by other
reviewers, especially his remark that Stevenson was 'in
his own way (and he is wise enough to write simply in his
own way), one of the most perfect writers living, one of
the very few who may yet do something that will become
classical'. Stevenson's cousin, Robert Alan Mowbray
Stevenson, reported to him that a society at Oxford chose
'Inland Voyage' as the 'best specimen of the writing of
English of this century' (B, 5700). Charm was the foremost quality found in 'Inland Voyage'; the term appears
again and again in the reviews and only rarely with any
hint of condescension. The quality was discovered above
all in the disarming personality of the writer. Critics
admitted that because of the nature of that personality
not every reader would find the book to his taste.
Certain things in particular would not sit well with
readers of a conservative bent, namely, Stevenson's
'waywardness' and 'social rebelliousness', his tendency
to follow instinct and impulse rather than be bound to
the narrow responsibilities of a settled life, especially
life conforming to the dull procedures of the 'office' -
'his symbol', as Colvin said (No. 2), 'for all intolerable
routine and sterile death in life'. The reviewer for
'London' (No. 1), who was in all likelihood Henley, also
stressed the individual and inconoclastic nature of the
traveller, who

> flatly declines to look at the world as it is used to
> be looked at.... he dares (and his audacity is uncon-
> scious: a quite remarkable circumstance) to stand on
> his own legs, to decline precept and example from any
> and everybody, to keep his heart and his intelligence
> for that alone which interests him, to be as much of a
> sensualist as an exquisite intellect will let him, to
> make as much case of his humours as of his beliefs, to
> take life frankly and cheerfully.... There is none of
> the mim-mouthed austerity about him that passes with us
> for wisdom, and none of the niminy-piminy melancholy
> that does duty with us for a sign of the poetic temper-
> ament. He is almost a pagan in his fine indifference
> for dogma and tradition, no less than his freshness of
> spirit, his vigorous elasticity of temper, his pleasant
> open-heartedness, his sincerity in the matter of
> trifles, his genial catholicity as to opinions, his
> enjoyment of what is near and likeable.... Culture and

the natural element in man went never better hand-in-
hand; the artist in words and the artist in life would
seem to be equal in him; his head is full of thoughts,
and his heart is as a child's.... Rightly considered
[the book] has in it the elements of a sort of liberal
education; for none will read it without learning that,
for some men at least, the world is a thing to be
accepted, and life is a thing to be grateful for, without stint or reserve, that poetry lies everywhere, and
that our own instincts are oftentimes as well worth
following as anything else.

It is worth quoting at length because this review and
the passage quoted above from Colvin's 'Memories and
Notes' offer us in unusually explicit terms an idea of
what Stevenson's contemporaries thought of the nature and
significance of his talent; they also offer us some idea
of the burden placed on him by the expectations of two
close friends and advisors.

Not all readers and reviewers agreed with Henley's
estimate of 'Inland Voyage'. Instead of a refreshing
independence, a freedom from conventionality, dogma, and
cant, some found in it an egotism and a 'Bohemianism ...
too determined and ostentatious' ('Examiner', 25 May 1878);
instead of an ease and directness in style, some found a
'disturbing affectation' and 'perverted ingenuities of
expression' (No. 3). Even George Meredith, in a letter
that otherwise would have flattered any beginning writer,
objected to the 'Osric's vein' evident in the volume (No.
4).

Stevenson took the criticism of Meredith and others to
heart and carefully avoided the 'Osric's vein' in
'Travels with a Donkey'. By doing so he won over several
critics. The unsigned reviewer for the 'Saturday' (21
June 1879) expressed the opinion that in both works
Stevenson's aim was to 'run exactly counter to the florid
eloquence now in fashion' and to win us 'back to the
modulated beauties of a simple prose, and the quiet
humour of a generation that knew not Dickens'. In
'Inland Voyage' however he had not been altogether
successful; the attempt was strained and 'the good things
seemed occasionally like nuggets in a mass of clay'. In
'Travels' the style was natural without any loss of eloquence. In addition there was the same 'strong sympathy
with humanity', the same 'happy flight of quaint and original fun', but the view of natural life was even
'sweeter and healthier'. Grant Allen and other critics
were again impressed with Stevenson's lack of a palpable
design upon his readers; Allen, writing in the

'Fortnightly' (No. 13), praised Stevenson's ability to
divest himself of any 'restless consciousness of the moral
burden laid upon him as a preacher and teacher'. He is
content merely 'to please and amuse us, as though he had
been born in the easy eighteenth century, before the rise
of earnestness and intense thinkers'. He admired too his
'lightness of touch' - the phrase was to be William
Archer's point of attack in the first general assessment
of Stevenson (No. 52) - which he noted was more reminiscent of a Frenchman than a Scotsman. He belongs, Allen
said, to the 'great world of literature', and he 'smiles
a kindly smile at our petty discussions and differences'
while he and Modestine 'move in philosophic indifferentism
up and down the Cévennes, and the remainder of the moral
and material universe, with no other determination than to
enjoy life themselves, each after his kind, and help
others by telling the story of their enjoyment'. The
reviewer for 'Fraser's' (No. 14), in a lengthy and perceptive review, commented among other things on the 'natural
flow of a style as superior in grace as it is in spontaneousness and ease, to the big mouthings of that talk
which we call "tall" in these days', yet he expressed his
doubts that style alone would 'suffice to build a great
and permanent reputation upon'. Dr John Brown, author of
'Rab and His Friends', felt style was a basis for greatness that required neither qualification nor apology; it
was a complement to the substance of his art, not a sign
of its absence: 'besides thought and feeling, virtuosity
and keen-cutting you have as few have ever had and I fear
now fewer than ever - the charm and faculty of style -
that is the crystal that laughs at time' (No. 11).

In 1879 Stevenson entered a phase of his career that
deserves a word. By this time he had written most of the
essays and stories that were to fill his next three books
- 'Virginibus Puerisque' (1881), 'Familiar Studies of Men
and Books' (1882), and 'New Arabian Nights' (1882). In
the late summer of 1879 he went to the USA to join Fanny
Osbourne whom he was to marry the following May. Knowing
that his parents would approve neither of the trip nor
the marriage, he left without informing them and cut himself off from his father's financial help. Though Stevenson had not, to this time, been able to support himself, he
now undertook the responsibility to support Fanny and at
least one of her two children. Considering his uncertain
health, he was taking an extraordinary risk. He knew he
must attempt to write more and to reach a wider audience.
Those to whom he showed work written with this aim were
critical of it, but it is difficult to know in all cases

if the objections were not part of a strategy to discourage Stevenson from the marriage and to persuade him to return home. 'The Amateur Emigrant', his account of the journey to the USA, was judged harshly by critics at home. It was simpler in expression and more directly observant than anything he had written before and, strange to say, bore in certain ways a resemblance to Dickens's 'American Notes'. Stevenson's father, who had admired 'Inland Voyage' and 'Travels with a Donkey', was especially critical, judging it 'not only the worst thing you have done, but altogether unworthy of you' (B, 5770).

Although Stevenson fulfilled the first aim of his trip by marrying Fanny, it had otherwise every appearance of failure. He was unable to increase his income by his writing, he was broken in health, and in the end he returned home, accepted an annual allowance from his father of £250 and agreed to let him pay £100 to have the manuscript of 'Amateur Emigrant' withdrawn from the publishers. Yet from the point of view of his own development the trip served an important purpose and there may have been a motive behind it of which Stevenson himself was not fully aware. He had placed himself in circumstances that forced a change in his method, helped to justify the change to those who would otherwise not approve it and to excuse any failure that might result. Stevenson knew his future work would differ from what family and friends regarded as his most promising work of the past. He had a growing confidence that he would discover his 'true method' (LS, i, 384) through a freer and looser production and by addressing a popular audience – any by being paid a decent wage for his services. These services were entertainment and relief to the hard-pressed and the care-worn.

> When I suffer in mind stories are my refuge ... and I consider one who writes them as a sort of doctor of the mind. And frankly ... it is not Shakespeare we take to, when we are in a hot corner; nor, certainly, George Eliot – no, nor even Balzac. It is Charles Reade, or Old Dumas, or the 'Arabian Nights', or the best of Walter Scott; it is stories we want, not the high poetic function which represents the world.... We want incident, interest, action: to the devil with your philosophy. When we are well again, and have an easy mind, we shall peruse your important work....
> (LS, i, 383)

Stevenson does not rule out for himself altogether the high poetic or literary role; he implies that he may turn

to that (as the reader with whom he identifies may turn
to Shakespeare and George Eliot) when, if ever, he is less
hard-pressed. What he has offered is a justification of a
kind of fiction that his friends and perhaps he himself at
times felt to be unworthy of him.

Stevenson's next three books, 'Virginibus Puerisque',
'Familiar Studies', and 'New Arabian Nights', were on the
whole favourably reviewed, but their earnings were still
far from sufficient to make him independent of his father.
Style was again a main issue to reviewers of 'Virginibus
Puerisque'. Some thought the attention given to it was
not matched by any serious moral or intellectual concern.
E. Purcell, one of Stevenson's most humourless and
narrowly moralistic critics (second after the reviewer for
the 'Pioneer' (No. 6), who called Stevenson a 'faddling
hedonist'), charged him, as he would several times again
in the future, with a want of any fixed principles. All
that Stevenson had to offer, when all was said and done,
was 'merely superior fustian' (No. 21). A related objection was that Stevenson lacked originality; he borrowed
from writers of the past whatever offered him an opportunity to use his knack of expression. The 'Pall Mall
Gazette' (No. 17) voiced a majority opinion, however,
when it argued that if Stevenson's ideas were not altogether new, they were none the less 'felt and realized so
freshly' that they 'cease to appear commonplace and come
home to us with new meaning and conviction'. Furthermore,
Stevenson did not talk at his readers; he held them in
conversation; they felt invited to participate, and to
accept the invitation would be

> a refreshment to every one who can enjoy holding con-
> versation on the daily and vital facts of life with a
> writer who, accepting nothing at second-hand, brings
> to bear on the facts of experience a gift of singularly
> luminous and genial insight, and perceptions both
> poignant and picturesque.

The 'Spectator' (No. 19), in attempting to explain the
unity underlying the diverse and apparently unrelated
essays in the volume, expressed remarkably well, though in
terms Stevenson would have found inappropriate - he
referred to the 'Spectator' as his 'grandmamma' (No. 15) -
the leading idea in his work: 'As joy and peace are heavenly gifts, so is it the devil's work to show people how
little real foundation they have for enjoyment.'

A repeated objection to 'Familiar Studies' was that
while Stevenson's treatment of men was satisfactory, the
treatment of books was less so. The 'St James's Gazette'

(17 March 1882) noted that the essays were essentially
biographical, the books serving only as a 'medium through
which we discern the character of men'. George Saintsbury, in an unsigned review in the 'Pall Mall Gazette'
(No. 23), noted that Stevenson's real ability was in the
'criticism of life', not books, as did the reviewer for
the 'Athenaeum' (1 April 1882), who suggested that with
Stevenson's subjective turn of mind he was more at home
'telling his readers how the immediate objects of sense
affect him than when he is trying to estimate other people
who have in their own way done the same'. In spite of
objections of this nature, the book was well received.
It was by no means widely popular - nor was 'Virginibus
Puerisque' - but both books became better known as Stevenson increased his readership through other works and, by
the turn of the century, they became established as classics, even to the extent of being used as school texts.

    'New Arabian Nights' contained a variety of Stevenson's
early experiments in fiction. It consisted of two separate volumes very different in nature, and reviewers were
often content to do little more than choose their favourite volume and point out in a superficial way some of its
characteristic merits. Once again there were differing
opinions about Stevenson's manner of expression; the
'British Quarterly Review' (October 1882) found a 'want
of spontaneity and naturalness' in the stories, whereas
the 'Spectator' (No. 30) thought the style 'so finished
and so admirable that it constitutes a distinct enjoyment
in itself. So told, we seem to feel, any story would be
worth reading'. D. C. Lathbury and Mrs Lathbury, who
wrote the unsigned review in the 'Spectator', offered an
interesting, if brief, defence against charges made in the
'Athenaeum' (12 August 1882) and the 'Saturday Review'
(No. 29) that the stories were spoiled by carelessness
evident in the many improbabilities of circumstance, the
inconsistencies of character, and the lack of an overall
design. They argued that, rightly considered, these were
not flaws, but the characteristics of a form of 'grotesque
romance', as they chose to call it, which was a fresh
departure from the romance as it was represented by Dumas.
One regrets that their suggestions were not developed further. Judging from a wide range of personal testimony,
readers found pleasure in the volumes, and those who knew
Stevenson only through his essays were not disappointed.
P. G. Hamerton told Stevenson he had 'the story teller's
natural gift and I see with pleasure that you preserve the
lightness and elegance of your style even in incident
narrative, which must be very difficult' (B, 4511). John
Addington Symonds, writing to Horatio F. Brown, the

historian of Venice and later Symonds's biographer, said
his family found the stories 'marvellously brilliant and
light'. Will E. Low, the American artist whom Stevenson
met in France and with whom he was to correspond for the
rest of his life, wrote to Stevenson of the strong appeal
of Providence and the Guitar and urged that it be 'printed
as a tract for the conversion of the bourgeoise'
(B. 5141). Arthur Conan Doyle, writing to Stevenson some
years later, recalled his first impression of Pavilion on
the Links: 'Shall I ever forget the enthusiasm with which
I read [it]? I look on it as the first story in the
world' (B, 4455); and in Mr. Stevenson's Methods in Fiction ('National Review', January 1890), Doyle referred to
the story as 'so complete in itself, and so symmetrically
good, that it is hardly conceivable that it should ever be
allowed to drop out of the very first line of English
literature'. (5)

IV

FIRST POPULAR SUCCESS: 'TREASURE ISLAND' (1883)

'Treasure Island' was the first book by Stevenson known to
a wide general audience, and though the financial returns
from it were nowhere near what might have been expected
considering its reception, it was the first that brought
sufficient income to make him feel in some degree independent. What the book also meant to Stevenson, owing partly
to its profit, but more to its popularity, especially with
a number of highly placed readers, was a new confidence in
the face of those he would come to refer to as his
'purist' critics. He felt no such confidence, however, in
the course of writing the book. He spoke of it to Henley
(No. 34) as a playful diversion by which he might earn
money; he avoided mentioning it at all to John Addington
Symonds (who was at the time urging him to undertake a
scholarly work on the 'Characters' of Theophrastus), feeling certain Symonds would have accused him of 'capitulations of sincerity and solecisms of style' (My First Book:
'Treasure Island', 'Idler', August 1894).
    The genesis of the story is well known: it bore at
first the title of 'The Sea Cook' and was written with
what was for Stevenson extraordinary ease and speed, at
the rate of a chapter a day, at least through chapter fifteen. The style was less calculatedly artful than it had
been in his earlier fiction and would be again in 'Prince
Otto', to which he turned shortly after completing
'Treasure Island'. Stevenson's purpose was simple and

straightforward and his audience and their needs were
clearly defined: he was to entertain his family, kept
indoors during a wet and dreary holiday in Braemar.
They were greatly taken by the story and waited expect-
antly for a new chapter each afternoon. Stevenson's
father in particular was attracted to it: 'he caught fire
at once with all the romance and childishness of his
original nature'. It was, significantly enough, Stevenson
tells us, just the sort of story Thomas Stevenson himself
was in the habit of inventing at bed time to reduce his
anxieties and induce sleep. He entered so fully into the
son's enterprise that he was eager to help, which he did
by supplying such details as the list of items in Billy
Bones's chest; unfortunately however he also offered some
suggestions that were certainly not prompted by the
'romance and childishness of his original nature' and
were in fact altogether inappropriate to the spirit of
the work ; namely, that a 'kind of religious *tract*' be
introduced when Ben Gunn tells of his past (No. 35).

Stevenson was committed to finishing the book when
Dr Alexander Japp arranged for its serial publication in
'Young Folks'. Though Stevenson was led to expect as much
as £100 for serialization, payment was calculated by the
page and he received only £37 7s. 6d., though under this
arrangement he retained copyright. When the story
appeared (10 October 1881 - 28 January 1882) under the
pseudonym of Captain George North, the youthful readers
were not especially impressed. According to a later
report in the 'Academy' (3 March 1900), circulation was
not increased by a single copy and on at least one occasion the editor was obliged to defend the story against
a dissatisfied reader. Stevenson was not disturbed by
the reaction of the readership of 'Young Folks'; that was
one set of critics he was prepared to ignore. When
Stevenson proposed to publish the story in book form under
his own name, Fanny Stevenson attempted to dissuade him.
In March 1882 she wrote to Mrs Edmund Gosse,

> I am glad W. Gosse likes 'Treasure Island'. I don't.
> I liked the beginning, but after that the life seemed
> to go out of it, and it became tedious. Louis wants
> to publish it in book-form, under his own name, in
> order to get a better price for it. I am very noble
> about it, and don't like Louis' name to go before the
> public with any but the best work. What does the Poet
> [Gosse] think, honestly? Would he do it? Louis'
> friends are so fond of him and so prejudicial in his
> favour, that they seem blinded to his bad work. I am
> more keenly alive to his faults than if they were
> those of a stranger, and possibly aim the other way.(6)

Gosse urged publication but others besides Fanny did
not, judging by an angry letter Stevenson wrote Henley at
about this time:

> To those who ask me (as you say they do) to do nothing
> but refined, high-toned, bejay-bedamn masterpieces, I
> will offer the following bargain: I agree to their pro-
> posal if they give me £1000, at which I value *mon pos-*
> *sible*, and at the same time effect such a change in my
> nature that I shall be content to take it from them
> instead of earning it. If they cannot manage these
> trifling matters, by God, I'll trouble them to hold
> their tongues.... I will swallow no more of that
> gruel. Let them write their damn masterpieces for
> themselves and let me alone.... I am ever yours, the
> infuriated victim of his early books, who begs clearly
> to announce that he will be so no longer, that he did
> what he has done by following his nose to the best of
> his ability, and, please God Almighty, will continue to
> pursue the same till he die. (Furnas, 'Voyage', 180-1)

It was through Henley's negotiations that agreement was
reached with Cassell & Co. and Stevenson, at least at the
time, was delighted with the terms, which he felt were 'a
sight more than it is worth': 'A hundred jingling, ting-
ling, golden, minted quid. Is not this wonderful?' (5 May
1883; LS, ii, 123). The book was published on 14 November
1883, in time for the Christmas buying, and its success
was immediate. Stevenson wrote to his parents on 15 November that

> 'T.I.' has made a great flutter, as you perceive; it is
> in Mudie's List, and is advertised in the last 'Punch';
> and generally goes on in a triumphal manner. This
> gives one strange thoughts of how very bad the common
> run of books must be; and generally all the books that
> Fanny, our father, Colvin and the wiseacres think too
> bad to print, are the very ones that bring me praise
> and pudding.... 'Prince Otto', now hard upon com-
> pletion ... has received the fatal award of Fanny's
> approval! (B, 3406)

On 25 November Henley reported to Stevenson that their
friends were eager to do reviews: 'Lang is after it for
the "P.M.G."; I for the "S.R."; a friend for the
"Academy"; Runciman for the "Standard". I think it will
hit' (B, 4772; see Nos 36, 38, 40). A month later he
wrote 'The "Island" ... is a monstrous success. Booksellers are raging for it. Bain, the great Bain, smiles

when he hears its name. Gell, the faithful G---, blushes
and admits it's a good thing' (B, 4774). Henley also
reported the current word that 'Gladstone sat up all night
over "Treasure Island"' (B, 4822). In a letter to his
mother Stevenson reported rumours that Gladstone talked
'all the time about it', adding, peevishly, that he
should instead 'attend to the imperial affairs of England'
(15 December 1884; LS, ii, 236). Andrew Lang wrote to
Stevenson that the prominent barrister Fitzjames Stevens
and a group of his friends read the novel by turns aloud,
'the readers relieving each other as they dropped off
hoarse' (B, 5053). Lang's own opinion was that with the
exception of '"Tom Sawyer" and the "Odyssey" I never
liked any romance so' (B, 3405). Meredith called it 'the
best of boys' books and a book to make one a boy again,
without critical reserve as to the quality of composition'
('Letters of George Meredith' (1970), ed. C. L. Cline, ii,
730).
    Almost without exception the reviewers were enthusias-
tic. They testified to their own extraordinary delight
in reading the novel and often cited instances of individuals (besides Gladstone), high placed and serious minded,
who were unable to put the book aside once they had taken
it up, even to the neglect of weighty affairs. Above all
else perhaps, the reviewers praised Stevenson's vivid
delineation of character. The 'Graphic' (No. 41) declared
that his characters were as different from those of
Marryat and Ballantyne 'as any suit of clothes from a
breathing man'. The character they felt to be most interesting was Silver, yet an occasional reviewer expressed
some uneasiness over what the 'Athenaeum' (No. 37) regarded as the 'too philosophic rejection of poetic justice
in allowing the arch-scoundrel to escape the fate which
overtakes all his accomplices. In real life John Silver
would hardly have got off; he certainly ought not to do
so in fiction'. Stevenson's unusually sharp and memorable
description was also given high marks; time and again
reviewers referred to Pew's tapping stick and Silver's
eye - 'a mere pin-point in his big face, but gleaming like
a crumb of glass'. By the tributes given the book and the
way in which it was compared on equal terms with the best
work of Defoe, Dickens, Thackeray, Poe, and others of
similar stature, it was clear that reviewers were confident, from the very first, that it would be a classic.

V

A CRUCIAL PHASE: 'PRINCE OTTO' (1885)

Unlike other works to appear shortly after 'Treasure
Island' - 'More New Arabian Nights: The Dynamiter', which
was written in collaboration with Fanny Stevenson, 'The
Black Arrow', which Stevenson regarded, as did most of the
reviewers, as inferior 'tushery', and 'A Child's Garden of
Verses', 'a ragged regiment of verses', as Stevenson said,
that he worked at piecemeal and even during bouts of serious illness - unlike these works, 'Prince Otto' was 'long
gestated' and 'wrought with care'. It is first mentioned
in Stevenson's letters in 1880, but was conceived in a
different form even earlier (LS, i, 384-5); he laboured
over the writing as he did with no other work except 'Weir
of Hermiston' and portions of 'The Ebb-Tide'. George
Meredith, whom Stevenson spoke of in the early 1880s as
'the only man of genius of my acquaintance', inspired it
and set the standard.

In the course of writing the novel, however, Stevenson
realized it would fall short of his expectations. At times
the conception seemed trivial and the style artificial.
His disappointment was no doubt in his mind when he wrote
to Henley in June 1883 (and Will H. Low in the same frame of
mind in October) expressing dismay over his output to date:

> I sleep upon my art for a pillow; I waken in my art;
> I am unready for death, because I hate to leave it....
> I *am* not but in my art; it is me; I am the body of it
> merely.... And yet I produce nothing, am the author of
> 'Brashiana' and other works: tiddy-iddity - as if the
> works one wrote were anything but 'prentice's experi-
> ments. (LS, ii, 134)

Disappointment with 'Prince Otto' was by no means so great
that he considered abandoning the book. It was difficult
to write but there were successes along the way that kept
him going and, more importantly, by completing the work he
could give the purist critics what they wanted, or at
least show them that he was making an attempt to produce
distinguished work.

The situation changed with the success of 'Treasure
Island'. Stevenson was not suddenly led to exaggerate the
merits of that novel, but his regard for it was increased
and he was pleased that he now had strong justification
for devoting time to work that could be written easily and
naturally. The result of the success was that he gained a
new self-assurance and with it some relief from the burden

of obligation he felt towards his admirers. We are witness to an expression of his independence from them in a
letter to Colvin in March 1884 outlining a new scheme of
production which he seems more or less to have followed
for the remainder of his career. The scheme amounted to
producing works 'with a definite and not too difficult
artistic purpose; and then, from time to time, drawing
oneself up and trying, in a superior effort, to combine
the facilities thus acquired and improved' in the writing
of those easier works. Stevenson implies that if he is
ever to produce a masterpiece it will follow from a conception not too artistically ambitious and exalted. He
goes on to ask who, after all, can declare with absolute
authority what is or is not a masterpiece? When he
answers his own question, he expresses his imperfectly
suppressed antagonism and impatience towards Colvin and
the purists by an exaggerated scorn towards the public:
What is a masterpiece - 'no man can tell; only the brutal
and licentious public, snouting in Mudie's wash trough,
can return a dubious answer' (No. 54f). Still it is an
answer and, Stevenson implies, it may well be as reliable
as any Colvin and the others might return. Later, in outlining the same regimen for Gosse, he goes on to emphasize
two contrary dangers for the artist: to produce, on the
one hand, 'cheap replicas', works written to formula to
gain or to hold a wide body of readers, or - and this is
far worse - to devote oneself exclusively to artistic concerns and to believe that 'no triumph or effort is of
value, nor anything worth reaching except charm' (No.
54g).

    Considering Stevenson's own doubts about 'Prince Otto',
it should not have surprised him that the book was neither
a great critical nor a great popular success. The reviews
were not as enthusiastic as those for 'Treasure Island',
but they were favourable, in spite of Stevenson's remarks
to the contrary. Certainly no reviews were hostile to a
degree that they would have discouraged him if he had had
any great faith in the merits of the novel or any strong
inclination to develop his art along these lines. A
favourable letter from Meredith, which he mentioned to
Henley but which, to my knowledge, has not survived - only
an unfavourable comment survives (No. 56) - would have
been in itself enough to support him if his own belief in
the work had been strong. One of the oddest reviews
Stevenson was ever to receive was the ambiguous performance by Henley (No. 59).

    Far more unsettling than the reviews of 'Prince Otto'
was the first general assessment of his work by William
Archer: Robert Louis Stevenson: His Style and His Thought

(No. 52). This appeared just shortly before the reviews
of 'Prince Otto', and while it made no explicit judgment
on that novel it condemned it by implication. No review
or article on his work throughout his career disturbed
Stevenson so much. Archer was the first to express in
detail and with authority a number of objections that
would be made again and again. He characterized Stevenson
as a 'lover of literature for its own sake' and quoted
against him his own remark that 'there is indeed only one
merit worth considering in a man of letters - that he
should write well; and only one damning fault - that he
should write ill'. Stevenson's masterful 'lightness of
touch', according to Archer, was the perfect stylistic
correlate of his shallow beliefs and convictions - the
jaunty optimism, the 'happy-go-luckyism'. Stevenson, in
answering Archer (No. 53), did not deny his optimism, but
he insisted that it was achieved only after a hard look at
the grim conditions of our existence. Didn't the fact
that he held on to life by a thread prove the authenticity
of his beliefs? And since Archer knew the conditions of
his life, why did he omit to mention them? Or how, at
least, could he conclude what he did? Stevenson felt the
assessment to be unjust and inaccurate. Yet Archer was a
critic who was unquestionably intelligent and perceptive
and had earlier shown himself capable of appreciating his
work (No. 49). Stevenson charged Archer with having wilfully overlooked his recent work; that his objections
might in some ways apply to early work he admitted, but
not to work of recent years. Stevenson must have realized, however, that some of Archer's criticism applied to
'Prince Otto'. Indeed Archer's article may have made even
clearer to Stevenson what he already suspected, that the
novel marked a retrogression rather than an advance in his
art. The article also made Stevenson cautious about
expressing his optimistic outlook on life, and it hastened
him along in the direction his own inclinations were
taking him - towards a more vigorous and direct expression.
    In spite of Stevenson's distress over the Archer
review, he seems not to have minded greatly the reception
given to 'Prince Otto'. When he wrote to Gosse in January
of 1886 (No. 63) remarking on the bad reviews of 'Otto',
he appears to have gained rather than lost any self-
assurance and to have had his opinions confirmed and
strengthened. He criticized the public - the 'bestiality
of the beast whom we feed' - more fiercely than he ever
had or would again. With them, he said, the carefully
wrought work was bound to fail; their preference is for
something 'loosely executed ... a little wordy, a little
slack, a little dim and knotless'. Once he had expressed

his impatience with the 'fatuous rabble of burgesses' however, he declared his contempt for writers who narrowly
pursue their art, ignoring any responsibility towards an
audience, and who yet, when they are in turn ignored,
claim for themselves martyrdom. Martyrdom can never be
the artist's lot, Stevenson argued, since by devoting
himself to his art he has devoted himself to pleasure; 'We
were full of the pride of life and chose, like prostitutes, to live by pleasure. We should be paid if we give
the pleasure we pretend to give, but why should we be honoured?' Stevenson would develop the comparison between
the prostitute and the artist in Letter to a Young Gentleman Who Proposes to Embrace the Career of Art (No. 103):
like one of the 'Daughters of Joy' the artist

> chose his trade to please himself, gains his liveli-
> hood by pleasing others, and has parted with something
> of the sterner dignity of man.... There should be no
> honours for the artist; he has already, in the practice
> of his art, more than his share of the rewards of life;
> the honours are pre-empted for other trades, less
> agreeable and perhaps more useful.

How well do these remarks represent Stevenson's considered opinion? We may believe that in defending himself
against Archer he is led to overstate the case. Or we may
believe him guilty of an excessive modesty, as he was with
his remark, so frequently quoted against him that Max
Beerbohm said the printers kept it always in type, that in
learning his art he played 'sedulous ape'. Generally we
expect art to serve some principle beyond pleasure and we
expect the artist to think better of himself. But according to a long and respectable tradition, pleasure itself
is an end of art. When Stevenson uses the word pleasure,
clearly he is speaking of something more than the gratification of the senses, something resembling what Wordsworth called the 'grand elementary principle' that constitutes the 'naked and native dignity of man', and by
which he 'knows, and feels, and lives, and moves'. And
what more apt comment could be made by Stevenson on the
fate of pleasure in his time than to designate the prostitute as its representative? In a dreary and oppressed
world the prostitute might offer a more important service
than a stern and upright wife, just as romance, or even
'skeltery' - a literature 'cheerful and brave-spirited'
that can help to make life a 'green place' (LS, ii, 184,
217) - might offer a more important service than what is
considered the highest art.

VI

INTERNATIONAL ACCLAIM: 'THE STRANGE CASE OF DR JEKYLL AND
MR HYDE' (1886)

Stevenson's increased confidence in his judgment and creative powers may explain the remarkable speed with which he
wrote the first draft of 'Jekyll and Hyde'. The main
details of the story were furnished him in a dream and in
three days' time a draft was completed. Fanny, however,
strongly objected to the draft on grounds that the allegory was undeveloped; as it stood, it was 'merely a story
- a magnificent bit of sensationalism - when it should
have been a masterpiece'. According to Lloyd Osbourne's
account of the episode, Stevenson strongly disputed her
judgment, then acquiesced and - to her horror - burnt the
entire manuscript to avoid, as he said, relying on it too
heavily in his revisions, though one suspects that his
design may have been to warn Fanny about her interference.
    There is no way of knowing exactly what revisions were
made in the story, but we are told in Balfour's 'Life'
(ii, 13) that in the early version 'Jekyll's nature was
bad all through, and the Hyde change was worked only for
the sake of a disguise'. This suggests that Fanny encouraged Stevenson to do more than merely heighten the
allegory, namely, to make basic changes in the character
and import of the story. Following the rewriting of the
story it was submitted to Longman's where the decision
was made not to publish it serially in 'Longman's Magazine', but to issue it both in paper covers, at the price
and in the format of a shilling shocker, and in a more
respectable cloth binding. The book was ready shortly
before Christmas but by then the booksellers were fully
stocked and refused it. It was offered again after
Christmas but even then, according to Charles Longman,
dealers were reluctant to carry it until a review appeared
in 'The Times' which 'gave it a start and in the next six
months close on forty thousand copies were sold in this
country' (Balfour, 'Life', ii, 14). The story was also
extraordinarily successful in the USA where Scribners'
authorized edition was followed by numerous pirated editions. (Balfour estimated that by the turn of the century
no fewer than a quarter of a million copies had been sold
in the USA.) Within a short time the names of Jekyll and
Hyde, if not Stevenson's own, were known everywhere in
the English-speaking world; the story became a popular
topic in the press and the subject of countless sermons,
one of which was delivered at St Paul's, and of serious

articles in religious periodicals; it was translated into a number of different languages and adapted for the stage in several countries.

Though the story was reviewed favourably before the appearance of 'The Times' review of 25 January 1886 (No. 70), Charles Longman was no doubt correct in saying that that particular review helped greatly to determine the early success of 'Jekyll and Hyde'. The reviewer praised the story without qualification; he expressed confidence that it would appeal to general readers as well as the 'most cultivated minds' and the 'most competent critics'. He suggested that while the story brought to mind the 'sombre masterpieces' of Poe, Stevenson had gone 'far deeper' than Poe in his explorations of the human mind. Furthermore, Stevenson had not only written the story in excellent prose, but had 'weighed his words and turned his sentences so as to sustain and excite throughout the sense of mystery and horror'. (Reviewers agreed in approving the style, though Andrew Lang, writing in the 'Saturday' (No. 67), noted that he had briefly at the threshold of the story yielded to *his* 'old Tempter, preciousness'.) The unique achievement of the story, according to 'The Times', was its portrayal of a character 'steadily and inevitably succumbing to the influence of besetting weaknesses'. And to this and other reviewers the prime motive of the story was to illustrate the 'essential power of Evil, which, with its malignant patience and unwearying perseverance, gains ground with each carnal yielding to temptation, till the once well-meaning man may actually become a fiend, or at least wear the reflection of the fiend's image'. This was, one assumes, the 'allegory' that Fanny thought should be developed in the story.

It served Stevenson in several ways that Fanny's opinion had prevailed. Readers of the age were able to respond to a story in which there was a single prominent motive and one that could, as it were, be detached for the purposes of discussion and illustration. There had been no such easily graspable motive, moral, or idea in Stevenson's earlier writings; and the idea the 'Spectator' had formulated - 'As joy and peace are heavenly gifts, so is it the Devil's work to show people how little real foundation they have for enjoyment' - was one that was, while the true basis of Stevenson's appeal to his age, far more difficult to discuss. It had led to the charge that he was a mere painter in words, a 'faddling hedonist', or facile optimist. 'Jekyll and Hyde' made any such charge seem absurd.

Whether or not the pessimism of outlook in the story was in some sense a reaction against Archer's charge,

Stevenson felt that it was a serious fault and not expressive of his essential view. When John Addington Symonds
complained of its unrelieved pessimism (No. 72), calling
it 'most dreadful because of a moral callousness, a want
of sympathy, a shutting out of hope', and suggested that
Stevenson look to the ending of 'Crime and Punishment' as
an example by which he might profit, Stevenson was in full
agreement. He said he shared Dostoyevsky's view of human
nature and that he himself found 'Jekyll and Hyde' a
'dreadful thing', though he specified that the 'thing I
feel dreadful about is the damned old business of the war
in the members. This time it came out; I hope it will
stay in, in future' (LS, ii, 292). Some light is shed on
this last remark in a letter Stevenson wrote to John Paul
Bocock (No. 77) in which he says he found the allegory
'too like the usual pulpit judge', but declared that the
real intention (the intention prior to Fanny's interference?) was not to dramatize the war in the members: the
real harm done to Jekyll was not owing to desires of the
flesh which he failed to resist, but rather to his hypocrisy. By these remarks Stevenson implies that Hyde was
- or was originally intended to be - the creation of
desires which were perverted because they were unacknow-
ledged and repudiated. Some hint of this is found in the
story as it stands and one reviewer, James Ashcroft Noble,
writing for the 'Academy' (No. 69), was perceptive enough
to detect it when he observed that the flaw in Jekyll's
character lay in his inability to admit to pleasures he
indulged in because of their 'felt inconsistency with the
visible tenor of his existence'.

But it was 'Jekyll and Hyde' understood as a struggle
between Good and Evil, the Flesh and the Spirit, that
fascinated readers. Considering their degree of fascination, however, the written comment on the story is
extremely disappointing. Readers and reviewers lost
sight of the story in their concern for the large issues
on the one hand or the more or less insignificant details
on the other. Rider Haggard (B, 4496) was only one among
many to point out the impossible terms of Jekyll's will.
Countless readers - Henry James included - objected to the
transformation by chemical means, which they felt was too
material an agency. Perhaps the most interesting commentary is contained in F. W. H. Myers's extensive notes to
Stevenson (No. 73). Myers's remarks offer us the fullest
record we have of a contemporary's response to the story
and they contain the sort of observations and perceptions
that never, unfortunately, because of the conventions that
governed reviews and critical essays, found their way into
print.

VII

'KIDNAPPED' (1886)

The year 1886 was remarkable for Stevenson. 'Kidnapped'
followed 'Jekyll and Hyde' by just six months and, while
it did not reach so wide an audience nor stir discussion
to an equal degree, it was received with extraordinary
favour, not to say affection, by readers and reviewers
and it brought even greater financial returns than
'Jekyll and Hyde' because of better terms with the
publisher. Furthermore, the story won the more or less
unqualified approval of Colvin, Henley, and Fanny; and
Stevenson himself was highly pleased with the work,
believing it to be, in spite of certain shortcomings, the
best that he had produced thus far: a 'far better story
and far sounder at heart than "Treasure Island"' (LS, ii
287) and 'far the most human of my labours' (LS, ii, 301).
    Like 'Treasure Island', 'Kidnapped' was developed from
intentions initially quite modest; it was to be an adventure story addressed to the readers of 'Young Folks',
where it was serialized from May to July of 1886. The
beginning chapters of the book were written with the same
ease as the early portions of 'Treasure Island'. Then,
in a way Stevenson had never experienced before, the
characters seemed to take matters into their own hands -
'became detached from the flat paper ... turned their
backs and walked off bodily'. This happy condition did
not last to the end, however; at some point the characters
again turned matters over to Stevenson who found it very
hard to carry the story forward to what he believed was
its proper end. Colvin offered the practical suggestion
that the book be brought to an abrupt end with the promise
of a sequel. Stevenson accepted the suggestion, ending
the book with David Balfour claiming his inheritance,
planning for Alan Breck's escape to France and determining
to give testimony in defence of James Stewart, who was to
be tried for the murder of Colin Roy Campbell.
    T. Watts-Dunton detected some of the effects of the
abrupt ending in his review in the 'Athenaeum' (No. 82).
It was his opinion, and a number of other critics agreed,
that the story began with a conventional situation -

    a manly young hero of the old type struggles with an
    uncle-usurper of the old type, and after many adven-
    tures and hairbreadth escapes by sea and land ... comes
    into his own through the good offices of Providence and
    the conventional stage lawyer of the Latin-quoting
    type.

This conventional beginning, however, served to frame a
drama of an altogether different quality. When David is
free from the *Covenant* and the threat of kidnap, the novel
passes into a new artistic phase; the central chapters,
with their vivid picture of the Highlands after the '45
are fully and 'organically' *imagined*, rather than merely
'invented' or 'excogitated'. These chapters are equal to
Scott; indeed, in the opinion of Watts-Dunton, there is
'nothing in history and nothing in fiction equal to these
remarkable chapters'.

The reviewers generally agreed that the middle section
of the novel depicting the flight in the Highlands was
superior to the rest, and on the basis of it Stevenson was
referred to as Scott's successor. It was also agreed that
the primary interest in the novel lay in the interplay between Alan and David, representatives of the Highland and
Lowland, Jacobite and Covenanting character, though no
critic saw fit to elaborate at any length. Alan was
especially admired by almost all reviewers; only the
'Saturday Review' found him a 'trifle wearisome'. Critics
praised Stevenson's humour, especially in the scenes with
Cluny McPherson and Robin Oig, and also his vivid depic-
tion of states of physical fatigue. Gosse was especially
taken with this; the characters, he said, unlike the typical characters in romance, had sore throats and stomach
aches; this helped make the novel 'one of the most human
books I ever read' (No. 78). Andrew Lang expressed to
Stevenson his pleasure in the book, saying that in his
opinion 'Treasure Island' and 'Kidnapped' were his best
work and that the latter contained 'more of the spirit of
Scott than any other in English fiction' (Balfour,
'Life', ii, 17). Lang also reported to Stevenson how much
Matthew Arnold thought of 'Kidnapped'. 'He said *voila en
fin du vrai roman*, or words perhaps more grammatical, to
that effect' (B. 5088).

Critics were not inclined to slight 'Treasure Island'
when comparing it with 'Kidnapped'. We sense from the reviews that by this time 'Treasure Island' was as firmly
established a classic as 'Robinson Crusoe'. 'Kidnapped',
however, was seen to have a greater interest for adults.
As R. H. Hutton wrote in the 'Spectator' (No. 80), 'Kidnapped' was not so unique as 'Treasure Island', but it had
'more of the qualities proper to all true literature'.
These qualities that Hutton and other reviewers prized
constituted what Stevenson himself cherished in the novel -
its 'humanity'. It is not always easy to know precisely
what Stevenson and others meant by humanity, but it was
what Stevenson was proudest to achieve in his work and
what many of his contemporaries most valued in it. As we

have seen, they discovered this quality in the special
human timbre of the voice that spoke to the reader, not *at*
him. It was the voice of someone who was resolutely himself yet, for all his occasional assertiveness, disavowed
a stance of authority. He was tentative, self-critical,
and capable of a wide range of responses. His observations - which Colvin termed 'vital' - were marked by sympathy and detachment, humour and tenderness. His powers
of imagination were remarkable, and through them the
imaginative powers of the reader were stirred and height-
ened as they had not been since childhood or adolescence.
The restored imagination offered the reader more than an
avenue of escape. It did afford diversion and relief from
tedium, restraint, and anxiety, but even more it led to a
revitalization of his sense of the values and possibilities of life. A reawakening of his humanity.

This brings us to Henry James's essay on Stevenson (No.
102), written shortly after the appearance of 'Kidnapped'.
James answered Archer's charge that Stevenson's overriding
concern was style by arguing that it was a means only:
however much he 'cares for his phrase', said James, 'he
cares more for life'. What James found unusual in Stevenson was his capacity to grasp fully and imaginatively certain aspects of life - to *feel* them: 'He feels, as it
seems to us, and that is not given to everyone....' That
area of life he most cherished and was best able to grasp
imaginatively was youth:

> the direct expression of the love of youth is the
> beginning and the end of his message. His appreciation
> of this delightful period amounts to a passion; and a
> passion, in the age in which we live, strikes us, on
> the whole, as a sufficient philosophy.

James realized that in his time the concern for youth had
a special significance. This, unfortunately, he does not
choose to explore in the essay, but he does note that (what
makes Stevenson's work especially rare - something quite
different from the ordinary fare for children - was that
it not only offered a record of the conditions and sentiments of youth, but that it 'judges them, measures them,
sees them from the outside, as well as entertains them',
and all with a 'singular maturity of expression'. This
was especially the case with 'Kidnapped', which James
regarded as 'the highest point that Mr. Stevenson's talent
has reached' in spite of its abrupt and unsatisfactory
ending and the conventionally wicked uncle. Among its
achievements were the 'extraordinary pictorial value' of
the central section and the vivid 'imagination of physical

states', especially the 'wonderfully exact notation of the miseries of his panting Lowland hero'. The greatest achievement was the characterization of Alan and David, who were drawn with just the right 'mixture of sympathetic and ironical observation'. Stevenson's treatment was 'of the most truthful, genial, ironical kind, full of penetration, but with none of the grossness of moralizing satire'. Nothing, James said, speaking of both Alan and David, is more striking than the way in which he manages at once to admire and to see through a character. For James the dramatic triumph of the novel was the playing off of one representative character against another, especially in their quarrel, which was, he said, a 'real stroke of genius' that has to it 'the very logic and rhythm of life'.

While these particular virtues added up to a more spectacular success than Stevenson had achieved before, 'Kidnapped' was not different in purpose from his earlier work. All of his productions, James observed, 'constitute an exquisite expression, a sort of whimsical gospel of enjoyment', which is clearly something more, however, than 'pure high spirits and the gospel of the young man rejoicing in his strength and his matutinal cold bath', which Archer found to be the sum of his philosophy. James, in his rebuttal of Archer, turns - as did Stevenson in his own defence - to the personal circumstances of Stevenson's life to support his view that Stevenson's gospel is hard-won and is asserted with a gallant and heroic defiance of circumstance. His 'make believe' is an affirmation of human value:

> He would say we ought to make believe that the extra-
> ordinary is the best part of life, even if it were not,
> and to do so because the finest feelings - suspense,
> daring, decision, passion, curiosity, gallantry, elo-
> quence, friendship - are involved in it, and it is of
> infinite importance that the tradition of these pre-
> cious things should not perish.

We have in James's essay the high-water mark of criticism on Stevenson. Nothing else approaches it for eloquence or perception. And in this last remark James puts his finger on the motive behind Stevenson's work and his significance to his own and any subsequent age. James also makes clear to us here the basis of the strong affinity between Stevenson and himself, and his special importance to his brother William (No. 84).

Something should be said at this juncture about Stevenson's

reception in the USA on his second visit there in 1887-8.
When he arrived in New York he was surprised to find himself a celebrity. Column-long articles in the prominent
papers were devoted to him and to the successful production of T. R. Sullivan's version of 'Jekyll and Hyde',
which had just opened at the Madison Square Theatre star-
ring the popular actor Richard Mansfield. Stevenson was
startled - and certainly pleased - to see how his new position changed his relations with publishers. His work had
by this time already been published in the USA. Roberts
Brothers had issued 'Travels with a Donkey' (1879),
'Inland Voyage' (1883), 'The Silverado Squatters' (1884),
and 'Treasure Island' (1884); Henry Holt & Co. had published 'New Arabian Nights' (1882) and 'The Dynamiter'
(1885). Earnings from all these editions had been negligible; it was only when Scribners began handling his work,
starting with 'A Child's Garden of Verses' (1885), that
he gained even moderate earnings. Profits on all these
editions had been greatly reduced because inexpensive
pirated editions were readily available. The pirates had
indeed been active in plundering Stevenson; for example
five different unauthorized editions of 'Treasure Island'
and seven of 'Jekyll and Hyde' had appeared. (7) Because
unauthorized editions made it so difficult for the honest
publisher to earn a profit on his investment, Stevenson
was even more surprised at the enormous sums now offered
him. According to S. S. McClure, who was himself a
bidder, Stevenson commanded higher prices in the USA than
any other British author. We can better grasp what the
sums involved meant to Stevenson if first we know that he
had once estimated the income from his first six books at
something slightly over £600, £400 of which were earnings
from magazines; and that shortly before coming to the USA
he had expressed the opinion that if his yearly earnings
reached £250 (then approximately $1,200), he would con-
sider himself doing well. Now McClure, speaking for
Joseph Pulitzer, offered $10,000 (approximately £2,000)
for a weekly essay throughout the year to be published in
the New York 'World', and $8,000 for the serial rights of
his next book-length story. Stevenson rejected the offer
for the weekly essays, feeling it impossible to produce
them at such a rate. He did, however, accept $3,500 from
Scribners for twelve essays to be published monthly in
'Scribner's Magazine', though he expressed his uneasines
when he wrote to E. L. Burlingame, editor of the magazine,
to say I 'dislike this battle of the dollars. I feel sure
you all pay too much here in America; and I beg you not to
spoil me any more' (LS, iii, 44). Stevenson managed, however, to accommodate himself to his earnings in short

order and future complaints to Burlingame concerned other
things than overpayment.

The acclaim Stevenson received in the USA was to have
unfortunate effects on his reputation, in spite of the
immediate advantage of greatly increasing his income.
What happened, with the help of an ambitious press and a
credulous public, was the creation - perhaps it would be
better to say the 'creative' promotion - of a popular
myth, legend or fable out of the admittedly interesting
circumstances of his life. Judging by the wide assortment
of articles, notices, and reviews, gathered in Mrs Stevenson's scrapbooks, this phenomenon, especially the fascination with his physical appearance, dress, state of health,
place of abode, domestic arrangements, and travels, does
first begin with the American visit. A passage from the
New York 'Sunday World' (11 September 1887), quoted at
some length to give the full effect, will serve as an
example:

> What a striking face his was, as it looked over the
> folds of a poncho that enveloped his arms and chest in
> its warm red folds, and through the hole in its center
> gave play to the lithe neck under its burden of heavy
> brown hair, parted on the right side. Nobody could
> have foreseen the apparition of a great English novel-
> ist in an American blanket with a hole in its middle
> for his head. The fact is that this poncho, or Navajo,
> as we call it, is almost perfect protection from cold,
> and guards the lungs and throat closely from the
> slightest draught of air....
> Unconsciously the attention of the visitor has
> already been fixed on his host's hands and eyes. The
> latter are very wide apart and look as if they could
> see to one side as well as ahead. Their deep brown has
> nothing mournful in it, they are too active-looking for
> that; and yet they do not flash, but move slowly and
> seem all the while to be reading something - not neces-
> sarily a book, but a shadow, perhaps, or a storm on
> the Scottish coast, or a shipwreck or a temptation in a
> human soul.

Who could survive this undamaged?

Before long an increasing interest in Stevenson as a
personality was apparent in Britain as well. It is uncertain whether it spread from the USA by way of the press
or whether, which is more likely, it arose when news of
his travel to the South Seas captured the public imagination. In any case, a general reaction against the personal interest in the USA and Britain is apparent in the

reviews of 'Underwoods', published just before, and
'Memories and Portraits', published just after Stevenson's
arrival in the USA. Both books were highly personal in
nature and reviewers, who would probably have thought
little of the matter had there been less publicity, now
reacted by accusing Stevenson of arrogance and presumption
for assuming on the part of readers an interest in himself
and his friends. Mrs Oliphant went further and directly
accused him of exploitation of the personal (No. 98) and,
later, in a review of 'The Wrong Box' ('Blackwood's Magazine', August 1889), of playing up to an American audience
whose applause, 'though it is sweet', had a 'certain
idiocy in its roar'. 'American taste, in the cultivated
classes,' Mrs Oliphant wrote, 'is perhaps the very finest
thing going of its kind; but the caterers for the American
literary market do not belong to these high circles, and
the overtures and incitements which they offer to a
successful author are, when he is moved by them, too apt
to lead to folly.' It is certainly inaccurate to say that
Stevenson's work was fashioned to take advantage of the
American market, though it was to undergo certain changes
as a result of his awareness that his audience included a
sizeable number of Americans; it is also inaccurate to say
that he sought publicity as a means of promoting the sale
of his books. It was in his nature to be open before
reporters and the public and he may well, too, remembering
Archer's charges, have wanted to publicize the conditions
of his health to make clear that his generally optimistic
outlook on life was not too easily won. His fault was to
identify the public at large, and the press as its representative, with some ideal readership he imagined for himself.

VIII

'THE MASTER OF BALLANTRAE' (1889)

With the four works published after 'Kidnapped' -
'Underwoods' (1887) 'Memories and Portraits' (1887),
'The Black Arrow' (1888), and 'The Wrong Box' (1889) -
Stevenson neither extended his public nor increased his
prestige. All these books were judged to be below the
level of his best work, certainly below the level of
'Treasure Island' and 'Kidnapped'; and 'The Wrong Box',
his first collaboration with Lloyd Osbourne, provoked
more adverse reviews than any book he would publish. With
these works, it is true, he continued to surprise readers
by his versatility, by the capacity to explore new forms.

Opinion was divided over the value to be placed on such an ability, however. Perhaps more readers then than now would have valued it in a degree equal to Stevenson and would have agreed with his judgment on Henry James in this regard. In an interview in the New York 'Herald' (8 September 1887) Stevenson expressed his pleasure over what he regarded as James's determination to make a new start with his recent works, 'The Princess Casamassima' and The Author of Beltraffio. Stevenson had feared that James lacked the necessary power to 'break out in a fresh place', that he was to be numbered among that order of authors possessing 'only a halfing talent which can but do one thing, and which requires to repeat itself *ad infinitum*'. James was to answer Stevenson indirectly some time later when he wrote to him to say, regarding his 'Ballads', that they showed a certain cleverness, but 'they don't show your genius'; and he urged Stevenson to stick to prose, saying 'Things are various because we do 'em. We musn't do 'em because they're various' ('Letters of Henry James', ed. Percy Lubbock, ii, 178).

James found that the 'Master of Ballantrae' did show Stevenson's genius. He wrote to his brother William that he had read the novel with 'breathless admiration' and characterized it as 'wonderfully fine and perfect - he is a rare, delightful genius' ('Letters of Henry James', i, 140). To Stevenson himself he wrote, 'The intensest throb of my literary life, as of that of many others, has been "The Master of Ballantrae" - a pure hard crystal, my boy, a work of ineffable and exquisite art' (i, 157). And reporting to Stevenson on its reception, since the reviews were delayed in finding their way to him in the South Seas, James said its fate 'has been glittering glory - simply; and I ween - that is I hope - you will find the glitter has chinked as well' (i, 159-60).

In describing the fate of the novel with reviewers, James had not in this instance greatly exaggerated. When 'The Master' appeared, following 'The Wrong Box', readers felt Stevenson had redeemed himself and were assured, for the time at least, that he could continue to produce work of quality even though he was away from the literary centres of the world. The new novel was judged to be up to the level of his best earlier work and, in certain ways, to mark a distinct advance in his art. In an unsigned review in the 'Pall Mall Gazette' (No. 114), possibly by Archer, 'The Master' was characterized as 'by far his finest achievement in the way of fiction' and a work by which he has 'shown himself a truly tragic artist.' Mrs Oliphant (No. 121) praised its tragic power as well, saying it would disprove any claim henceforth

that Stevenson's books are only for boys: 'It is strong
meat for men.... Here all is uncompromising, tragic,
terrible, a deadly struggle all through.' 'The Times'
(28 Septemebr 1889), in a superior review, brief as it
was, went far towards convincing the reader of the soundness of its claim that the novel surpassed all Stevenson's
earlier work and that 'there are very few novels which so
nearly approach perfection'. George Saintsbury
('Academy', 2 November 1889) (8) believed the power displayed in the novel to be greater than in any of Stevenson's previous works; admittedly there were flaws - the
'huddled denouement, the prevailing gloom, the hints and
borrowings' and the 'excessive, sometimes intrusive
"elaboration" of style' - but in spite of these its
greatness was attested to by its capacity to 'enfist' the
reader, to hold his attention in a lasting way: 'There is
no possibility of forgetting "The Master of Ballantrae".'
    As we would expect, reviewers remarked on what was
recognized as perhaps the most distinctive achievement
of his art - his ability to 'print a scene in the mind's
eye forever' ('St James's Gazette', 10 October 1889).
'No living writer', said the critic for the 'Bradford
Observer' (29 October 1889), 'has to such an extent the
gift of enabling his reader to realize the scenes
described.' 'Little incidents', said Lang in an unsigned
review in the 'Daily News' (No. 115), 'are living before
the eyes.' The night duel was the scene most often
singled out for comment, though comment never goes beyond
a sentence or two. Reviewers also praised again Stevenson's ability to conceive and vividly delineate characters
that were striking and unusual. The Master was given high
honours; as the 'Bradford Observer' put it, 'he has not
yet been approached by any of the villains of romance ...
for sheer malignity, avarice and cruelty'. 'The Times'
also thought him successful as a portrait of consummate
evil and compared him to Milton's Belial - 'a fairer
person lost not heaven' - and later as his life draws
towards its end to Satan - 'with faded port and wasted
splendor wan'. It was also noted ('John Bull', 5 October
1889) how skilfully Stevenson dramatized the evolution of
character, especially Henry Durie's 'gradual deterioration
under the sense of the impotency of his struggle against
the more powerful and unscrupulous personality of his
brother'.
    In spite of all the merits they discovered in the
novel, however, a number of reviewers and readers expressed reservations about it on two points. The first -
which Stevenson himself recognized and judged even more
severely than his reviewers (No. 113b) - was the

startling and seemingly contrived dénouement. 'The Times'
expressed the view that it 'rather revolts our sense of
the probable'; J. M. Barrie, writing under the signature
of Gavin Ogilvy ('British Weekly', 1 November 1889), felt
that the novel by its ending was reduced to a 'shocker'.
E. T. Cook, in an unsigned review in the 'Athenaeum' (19
October 1889), remarked quite perceptively that the failure was part of a pattern in Stevenson's work:

> His great gift lies in the power of inventing and
> thoroughly grasping all the possibilities of his origi-
> nal and ingenious design, and while he is working at
> the full presentation of his thought he is at his best;
> but ... his energy begins to flag at the point where
> success has been made certain, and yet a stop is impos-
> sible.

In addition, readers found the novel unwholesomely gloomy
and morbid. Lang, in the review mentioned above, expressed the opinion that it was 'more akin to the temper of M.
Zola than of Scott', and suggested affinities with the
naturalistic novel in its manner of drawing characters
with a 'curious care and minuteness', and in its oppres-
sive atmosphere: 'The air is always heavy and charged with
storm ... there is no relief.' It was, in sum, a 'remarkable, elaborate, melancholy and almost hopeless book'.
The 'Glasgow Herald' (No. 118) objected to the absence of
any 'relieving gleam of humour in the whole narrative';
one feels as a result 'oppressed with the atrabiliar
atmosphere'. The 'Bradford Observer' noted that the
reader 'longs at times for a little glimmer of cheerful
sunshine', C. L. Graves, in an unsigned review in the
'Spectator' (5 October 1889), wrote that the theme is a
'painful and repellent one, and Mr. Stevenson's handling
of it, though supremely artistic, only enhances its pain-
fulness. One feels the want of a congenial character
amongst the *dramatis personae* on whom one's sympathies can
be legitimately bestowed'. For this reason Graves did not
predict any 'abiding popularity' for the novel. Though it
was full of 'interest and surprise', in the end 'it fat-
igues rather than refreshes one' and to set aside the book
is 'like awakening with relief from a painful dream'. The
'Literary World' (11 October 1889) complained that there was
no 'personage that stirs the heart with noble admiration, no
character that we entirely love'. Shakespeare 'gives us Des-
damona to balance the badness of Iago', but Stevenson
'affords us hardly a pretence of a foil to the malignity
of James Durie'. 'It is not a book to dwell upon and live
with', Lady Taylor wrote to Stevenson, 'because you have

evidently not loved any one of your *dramatis personae*'
(B, 5843). Balfour reported ('Life', ii, 65) that Sir
Henry Yule found the novel insupportable when S. R.
Crockett read it to him on his deathbed: 'I'm not strong
enough to stand writing of that kind', said Sir Henry;
'it's grim as the road to Lucknow.' (9)

    W. E. Henley, in a curious review (No. 117), character-
ized the book as 'a masterpiece in grime'. Stevenson was
puzzled by the word 'grime', as are we, and we sense, as
Stevenson no doubt did, more than a hint of animosity in
its use. This review was, however, the first of Stevenson's work by Henley following the break in their relations after Henley's charge that Fanny had, in effect,
plagiarized a story written by Stevenson's cousin,
Katharine de Mattos (Furnas, 'Voyage', 247-61). In spite
of the evidence of animosity in the review, however,
Henley's judgment of the book did not differ greatly from
that of other reviewers. A book of 'villainy and gloom
all complete can never rank with the highest works of art.
There should be light as well as shadow in a tale'. Indeed
Stevenson himself agreed with Henley and others in this
judgment and he later declared that the book was 'imperfect in essence' on grounds that it 'lacked all pleasurableness' (LS, iv, 111).

IX

'CATRIONA' (1893)

The year 1892 was especially productive for Stevenson.
'Catriona' (entitled 'David Balfour' in the USA), completed in only four months, was one of a number of works
written during the year. The serial rights to the book
had been sold to S. S. McClure in 1887 for £1,600.
McClure was resourceful in getting all the profit he could
from these rights, arranging for its serialization in
'Atalanta' (London) and its syndication in various newspapers, so many in fact that Cassell & Co., who were to
publish it in book form in Britain, complained that pro-
spective sales would be unfairly reduced. Before the
publication of 'The Wrecker' Stevenson had an arrangement
with Scribners whereby he received royalties of 10 per
cent on sales; this percentage was increased by 5 per cent
from the time the US Copyright Act came into effect in
1891. Because of the initially poor return on 'The
Wrecker', Stevenson demanded from Scribners a substantial
payment for the rights on delivery of his manuscript; for
'Catriona' he received a sum of £1,200. Owing both to the

sales and to the favourable arrangements, the book was a great financial success; its combined earnings, according to Charles Baxter, who was now acting as Stevenson's agent as well as his business manager, made it 'the best paying thing you have had as yet' (B, 4045).

Stevenson had intended, on the advice of Colvin, to make a number of revisions in 'Catriona' between the time of its serialization and its appearance in book form. When the time came, however, he found revision impossible, pleading as an excuse exhaustion and 'fiction-phobia' following his struggles with the second half of 'Ebb-Tide' (LS, iv, 188). None the less, even though he knew 'Catriona' was not altogether satisfactory as a sequel to 'Kidnapped', which it was intended to be, and that there was room for improvement in details, he was highly pleased with it. He regarded the Tod Lapraik tale (ch. xv), in which he was following the lead of Scott, a fine stroke, a 'piece of living Scots'. He also believed he had succeeded at last in writing a love story, though he realized that certain readers would have wished for a more direct treatment of sexual matters and would have little use for David and his 'innocent but real love affairs'. He believed, too, that in Catriona and Barbara he had drawn two reasonably full and satisfactory portraits of women. Furthermore, he was proud of the memorable little gallery of Scots types in the novel: 'there has been no such drawing of Scots character since Scott; and even he never drew a full length like Davie, with his shrewdness and simplicity, and stockishness and charm' (No. 140d). Above all, however, the book was 'alive', had vitality and spirit, and possessed the quality 'The Master of Ballantrae' had lacked which made it, for all its other merits, 'imperfect in essence'. 'Pleasurableness' was the quality 'Catriona', and 'Kidnapped', possessed in a supreme degree and which made them, on the other hand, 'nearer what I mean by fiction' than 'anything I have ever done' (LS, iv, 111) and 'much the best of my work and perhaps of what is in me' (LS, iv, 234).

Friends and sympathetic reviewers expressed relief, as they had with 'The Master', that Stevenson could produce work of high quality once he was away from Europe. There had certainly been no question of his ability to produce: between 'Master' and 'Catriona' he had published 'Father Damien' (1890), 'Ballads' (1890), 'Across the Plains' (1892), 'The Wrecker' (1892), 'A Footnote to History' (1892), and 'Island Nights' Entertainments' (1893). 'The Wrecker', in spite of being a collaboration, had been praised by a number of reviewers (see below p. 396), as

had 'Island Nights' Entertainments'. But these works
represented a departure from the most admired work of the
past, and while they might lead to a fiction wider in
range and more realistic, still, in themselves, they did
not measure up to his best work, did not compel affection
as did 'Treasure Island' and 'Kidnapped', nor bear the
marks of a classic. Many thought 'Catriona' did.

Reviewers were struck by Stevenson's power to evoke the
atmosphere of Scotland. Even reviewers for some of the
Scottish newspapers and periodicals, who usually are
reserved in their praise of Stevenson, especially with
respect to national qualities, expressed their pleasure
and satisfaction. The 'Scotsman' (4 September 1893)
declared that 'Catriona' had an unmistakable 'Edinburgh
accent' and would be especially enjoyable to any reader
with knowledge of Edinburgh and its environs. The
unsigned reviewer for the 'Elgin Courant' (5 September
1893), sounding very much like S. R. Crockett addressing
a 'Bookman' audience, saw the novel as essentially a nos-
talgic vision of the homeland by one of her wandering
sons: 'There in Samoa is the Scottish laddie ... and his
head is full of old Scotland and Old Edinburgh, and he
makes us see them.' Reviewers were quick to acknowledge
that Stevenson had successfully broken new ground with the
characters of Barbara Grant and Catriona and with the love
relation between Catriona and David. Barrie wrote to
Stevenson to express his admiration for the love story in
the novel, calling it 'the best thing you have done' and
'just about the only thing I thought you could never do'
(B, 3960), though he still did not regard 'Catriona' as
the great book that he felt Stevenson was long over-due
in producing (No. 108). Archer, in an unsigned review in
the 'Westminster Gazette' (2 September 1893), expressed
the view that Stevenson had 'enriched our literature with
a love-story of something very like classic texture'; the
relation between David and Catriona was 'purely idyllic,
a piece of impenitent romance, a tale of unsophisticated
minds and simple hearts', but it is 'saved from all maw-
kishness by the strong infusion of humour which permeates
it, and it is warmed by a touch of genuine passion, beneath all its reticence and unconsciousness, which we
have scarcely discovered hitherto in all Mr. Stevenson's
writings'. By far the most frequent objection that
reviewers raised was that 'Catriona' did not form a perfect sequel to 'Kidnapped', chiefly because David had
undergone more changes than any short passage of time
could account for. Reviewers also objected that the work
was divided into two more or less separate parts, the
first of which concerned the Appin murder trial and the

second David's relations with Catriona and her father.
Quiller-Couch (No. 141), who was, along with James and
Archer, one of Stevenson's most perceptive critics,
defended the organization of the novel and its sequel,
claiming that they constituted a single work which was
successfully unified though loose in structure.

When Stevenson read the reviews of 'Catriona' once
they had reached him in the South Seas, he must surely
have been gratified. They confirmed in nearly every
regard his own estimate of the strength and weakness of
the novel and they were also on the whole more interesting, more informative, less perfunctory than earlier
reviews. One wonders if novel reviewing had noticeably
improved in the span of a few years or if 'Catriona' is
responsible by having inspired a warmer and fuller
response. Certainly what is conspicuous in the reviews
is that they offer, to a greater degree than before,
testimony that the book possessed the quality of *pleasurableness*. A. B. Walkley in the 'Morning Leader' (13 September 1893) spoke more explicitly than others of that
quality when he said the book created a 'sort of physical
essence of pleasure which, if it were not for fear of
offending the weaker brethren, I would call sensual'.
He attempted within the limits of his brief review to
show how the effect was achieved, pointing to, among
other things, the vivid description of reaction and surprise on the part of Stevenson's characters, the extraordinary effect of Stevenson's style, especially the
vivid expression or description which appears with a
'suddenness', an 'unexpectedness' that leaves the reader
breathless. The chief source of pleasure in Stevenson,
Walkley felt, had to do with an aspect of the style that
could not be analysed and defined - 'a certain austere
rhythm, attained with a rigid economy of words, studious
brevity of sentence, an undercurrent of melody frugal and
spare like a piece of Sebastian Bach'.

X

'WEIR OF HERMISTON' (1896)

'Catriona' was written during a period of sound health,
buoyant spirits, and remarkable productivity. Since 1887
Stevenson's yearly income had been high, somewhere in the
vicinity of £4,000. Expenses at Vailima were, however,
also high and seemed to increase each year. Stevenson
was not following his own advice in Letter to a Young
Gentleman: 'if a man be not frugal, he had no business in

the arts'. Yet he was pleased with the scale of his
household and proud he could support it with an active
pen. He even liked to compare himself with Scott and to
refer to Vailima as Subpriorsford (LS, iv, 23). (10)
    After the taxing work on 'Ebb-Tide', which was com-
pleted in the early summer of 1893, Stevenson found himself ill, exhausted, depressed, and incapable of applying
himself to fiction at all, regardless of its merit. In
this situation he did with good reason become acutely
worried about money. He also began to survey his past
work and to assess it with as much dissatisfaction as he
had earlier when working on 'Prince Otto', in spite of
what he had produced in the interval: 'I wonder exceedingly if I have done anything at all good', he wrote
Colvin (LS, iv, 186). And to Low:

> I think 'David B' a nice little book, and very artis-
> tic, and just the thing to occupy the leisure of a busy
> man; but for the top flower of a man's life it seems to
> me inadequate. Small is the word; it is a small age
> and I am of it. I could have wished to be otherwise
> busy in this world. I ought to have been able to build
> lighthouses and write David Balfours too. (LS, iv,
> 263)

And again to Colvin:

> My skill deserts me, such as it is, or was. It was a
> very little dose of inspiration, and a pretty little
> trick of style, long lost, improved by the most heroic
> industry. So far, I have managed to please the jour-
> nalists. But I am a fictitious article and have long
> known it. I am read by journalists, by my fellow-
> novelists, and by boys; with these, *incipit et expli-
> cit* my vogue.... I cannot take myself seriously, as an
> artist; the limitations are so obvious. (LS, iv, 327)

In the late summer of 1894 the situation improved.
Stevenson returned to 'Weir' with energy and confidence.
It would seem to have offered him a happy compromise between the two methods and aims he had earlier described
to Colvin and Gosse (No. 54) - the method something between 'strain' and 'play'; the result the wished for
union between entertainment and art. He believed it
would be superior to anything he had done.
    Unfortunately, neither Stevenson nor the world was to
know. At the time of his death on 3 September 1894 the
novel was only into its ninth chapter. The fragment was
published serially in 'Cosmopolis' from January to April

1896 and in book form a month later, and was accompanied
on both occasions by an editorial note by Colvin claiming
for it the highest place among Stevenson's works. Most
later critics have agreed, seeing in it, compared to his
other works, a greater force in the style, a theme of
greater intensity and human interest, and characters of
greater psychological complexity. Those who reviewed the
book when it appeared, however, even those previously
sympathetic to Stevenson, were surprisingly unenthusias-
tic. Again we are faced with a reaction - against the
popular panegyrics which appeared everywhere following the
death and, even more, against the efforts of Colvin and
others to place on the work an authoritative seal of
approval.

Purcell, in his review in the 'Academy' (No. 160),
reacted specifically against the adulation of Stevenson's
countrymen: 'Caledonia, stern and wild enough upon occasions to little sinners like Keats and Byron, has ever
been to each poetic child of her own not only a fit nurse,
but a most partial, indulgent and boastful one.' To whom
does Purcell refer? The Scottish newspapers and journals
had not been in the habit of praising Stevenson. Purcell
cannot have been thinking of Lang, who had reviewed
Stevenson favourably from the first, but not from any
exclusively Scottish point of view. It was several months
too early to react to the tributes given at the memorial
gathering in Edinburgh over which Lord Rosebery presided
('The Times', 11 December 1896). Perhaps Purcell had in
mind the sentimental outpourings of S. R. Crockett and
Ian Maclaren in the London 'Bookman' (January 1895).

Certain reviewers reacted directly against Colvin's
note - perhaps against the tone of it more than anything
else. Joseph Jacobs in an unsigned review in the
'Athenaeum' (No. 157) and Quiller-Couch in the 'Speaker'
(No. 158) challenged Colvin's judgment and both made similar objections to the fragment. Jacobs granted it was a
'masterly torso', but pointed out how uncertain it was,
given its present weakness and all the difficulties still
facing Stevenson, to assume the novel could have been
brought to a successful conclusion. The one nearly in-
surmountable difficulty was to make plausible Hermiston's
sentence of death on his own son. In addition, the intended villain was an impossibly weak character: 'too facile
and flimsy a rogue to impart tragic intensity to any part
of the plot hinging on him'; had he seduced the heroine,
as was proposed, 'it would have taxed all Stevenson's
ingenuity to have preserved our respect for her'. Jacobs
remained unconvinced, in spite of 'Catriona', that Stevenson was able to portray women successfully. The elder

Kirstie remained a failure in spite of all of Stevenson's attention. As Jacobs pointed out, nearly fifty pages were devoted to the first glances and meeting of the lovers: 'This does not look like mastery. A greater artist would have produced his effects with fewer lines.' Jacobs concluded that Stevenson could only portray a woman when the 'fires of her woman-hood had burnt down'. Quiller-Couch made similar objections and also perceived that Stevenson was clearly experimenting with a different narrative form than he had used before and one of dubious merits: here the narrator intruded on occasion to make moral judgments and characters were now introduced with a lengthy history and description rather than being brought to life 'in the rush of talk and incident'. But the real interest of Quiller-Couch's review is what it tells us about a sensitive reader's response to Colvin's services on Stevenson's behalf. Quiller-Couch's opinion of Stevenson had always been favourable; his sympathy was almost complete and his response to 'Weir' was essentially positive. Yet Colvin's remarks awakened a resentment in Quiller-Couch which he felt others must share who 'had not received a course of critical instruction at Mr. Colvin's feet' and were not prepared to be 'lifted so complacently on Mr. Colvin's avuncular knee'. (11)

Essentially this was a reaction against Colvin's refusal to admit or to entertain the possibility that Stevenson's aesthetic achievement might not be commensurate with his appeal and his significance to his age. (Quiller-Couch undertook to define his appeal and significance in a brief article in the 'Speaker' a short time later (5 September 1896).) The failure to acknowledge this had the effect of giving a false impression to discriminating readers and has otherwise done Stevenson a disservice by placing him in company where he could only show to disadvantage. It is best to admit that Stevenson did not produce fully realized works of art. Perhaps he lacked the energy to do so, but it is also the case that it was not in his nature nor his deepest intention to do so. On the contrary, a genuine but limited and qualified concern for the realization of his art according to certain aesthetic standards of unity, wholeness, consistency was an essential of its nature; the tentative, the exploratory, the incomplete and unfinished quality of his undertakings was one main source of their power and appeal. It would have been a better strategy for critics supporting Stevenson to have acknowledged this and to have defended him on the grounds of his special motives and purposes.

XI

REACTION SINCE 1900

Stevenson was, as Gosse said, the author to whom 'above
all his contemporaries, was given the quality of seeming
lovable alike to those who knew him and to those who did
not know him' ('St James's Gazette', 5 December 1895).
But regrettably, only a short time after his death, it
became increasingly difficult for readers of taste and
discrimination to see Stevenson as lovable, owing to the
ambitious efforts of family and friends, admirers and
chance acquaintainces, to promote him, to remove all blemishes from the portrait, purge him of human dross, and enshrine every utterance, however fragmentary or jejune,
within the impressive covers of the Edinburgh Edition - by
doing everything, in short, within their power to hasten
immortalization.

The first widely publicized reaction against Stevenson
was Henley's fierce review of Balfour's official life (No.
166). While the review contains an intense personal antagonism against Stevenson - an antagonism that, as we
have seen, had been imperfectly suppressed in a number of
his reviews of Stevenson's work - the main object of the
attack was the sentimental Stevenson, the 'Seraph in Chocolate'. It was unfortunate that Balfour's biography
became the occasion of Henley's attack. Balfour attempted
to present as strong a case as possible for Stevenson to
be sure, but he realized, as few of his followers seemed
to, that to attempt to transform Stevenson into something
he was not was to do him serious injustice. The limitations and blemishes lent to the interest and appeal of
the personality as well as the work. Balfour's biography
is an intelligent and balanced study and it is to his
credit that he could remain detached and preserve critical
standards when working under the eye of Fanny Stevenson.
Balfour's life, supplemented by the comment in Colvin's
edition of the letters, presents a far more accurate picture of Stevenson than do the later biographies of Steuart
('Robert Louis Stevenson, A Critical Biography', 1924) and
Hellman ('The True Stevenson: A Study in Clarification',
1925), which were presented as correctives.

The first clear and unmistakable sign of an important
change in attitude towards Stevenson was Frank Swinnerton's study in 1914 - 'R. L. Stevenson, A Critical Study'
(No. 168). It was to some extent a reflex action against
excessive promotion, but it went beyond that to express
the response of a generation with different values, sensibilities, and critical attitudes. To some degree it was

an attack on Stevenson and his followers as representatives of the past. Swinnerton had what we think of as a
'modern' concern to apply critical standards and to
direct attention to the works rather than the personality
- on these points he was in full agreement with James.
These concerns are so rare in Stevenson studies that we
are obliged to him even if his treatment was often less
than objective. Swinnerton's book has held up well. It
offers the most detailed and thoughtful case we have
against Stevenson and anyone intent upon restoring Stevenson is obliged to face Swinnerton, especially his comment
on the novels and romances. At the time the book appeared
it provoked comment, most of it indignant, but little in
the way of serious discussion, probably because readers
sympathetic to Stevenson felt it so unjust that it did not
require an answer, and those who were sympathetic to Swinnerton felt he had said the final and definitive word.
Swinnerton's view of Stevenson has been, so far as I can
judge, the view shared until recently by the majority of
readers who claim a serious interest in literature. This
was certainly the case in the USA, where the negative
response to Stevenson has often been, since the general
decline in his reputation, more extreme than in Britain.
    What of critical significance has been written on
Stevenson since Swinnerton's work? It is hard to point
to anything until recently that has had a truly important
effect on the reputation or has to any extent altered our
perception of him. Chesterton's 'Robert Louis Stevenson'
(1927), which answered Swinnerton and other hostile critics, offered a number of insights, especially in respect
to Stevenson's work as a response to the Puritanism with
which he was surrounded in his early years and to the
pessimism which was pervasive in his age. But it is, as
T. S. Eliot remarked ('Nation and Athenaeum', 31 December
1927), 'diffuse' and 'dissipated', and it wastes so much
time attacking misconceptions that it fails to develop
adequately any line of thought of its own. 'What we
should have liked', Eliot said, is a 'critical essay
showing that Stevenson is a writer of permanent importance, and why'.
    The same might still be said. Articles and books have
appeared without abatement; most have dealt primarily
with the life and their essential aim - a lingering reaction - has been to humanize Stevenson further, most often
through the identification of some Jekyll-Hyde split
within him. This has been carried so far that the ultimate effect is often dehumanization. We do have, however, comment of value on Stevenson. Janet Adam Smith's
brief general study comes to mind ('R. L. Stevenson',

1937), as does David Daiches's critical examination of the
works ('Robert Louis Stevenson', 1947), and J. C. Furnas's
'Voyage to Windward' (1952), which will stand as the
authoritative biography for some time to come, certainly
until after the appearance of a new and more complete edition of the letters. In addition, we have the suggestive
essay by Leslie Fiedler, R.L.S. Revisited, published first
as an introduction to 'The Master of Ballantrae' (1954),
and reprinted in 'No! in Thunder' (1960). The argument of
Fiedler is that a 'single felt myth gives coherence, individually and as a group, to several of Stevenson's long
fictions - and it is the very myth explicitly stated in
Jekyll and Hyde'. The long fictions Fiedler has in mind
are 'Treasure Island', 'Kidnapped', 'The Master', and
'Weir of Hermiston'. The mythic concept, to quote Fiedler, 'might be called the Beloved Scoundrel or the Devil
as Angel, and the books make a series of variations on the
theme of the beauty of evil - and conversely the unloveli-
ness of good'. Whether or not we agree with Fiedler or
think he has turned Stevenson topsy-turvy, the essay has
reawakened an interest among professional critics and
academicians some of the results of which are to be seen,
if only indirectly, in Robert Kiely's 'Robert Louis
Stevenson and the Fiction of Adventure' (1964), Edwin
Eigner's 'Robert Louis Stevenson and Romantic Tradition'
(1966), the chapters on Stevenson in Masao Miyoshi's 'The
Divided Self: A Perspective on the Literature of the Vic-
torians' (1969), and Irving S. Saposnik's 'Robert Louis
Stevenson' (1974). One hesitates to speak of a Stevenson
revival, but one is entitled to say with confidence that
the reaction against him dating from Swinnerton's study
has finally run its course and that the man and the works
can now be looked at afresh.

NOTES

1 This letter is quoted in full in Michael Balfour, How
   the Biography of Robert Louis Stevenson Came to be
   Written - II, TLS, 22 January 1960, 53.
2 Certain of these views are expressed in the early
   poem To Sydney ('Robert Louis Stevenson: Collected
   Poems', ed. Janet Adam Smith (1971), 72-4, 458), which
   presumably dates from the summer of 1872 and is
   addressed to Stevenson's cousin, Robert Alan Mowbray
   Stevenson.
3 The circulation of 'London' could never have been very
   large and its chances of survival were always uncertain. It is doubtful that Stevenson's stories titled

'Latter-Day Arabian Nights' - published later as 'The
New Arabian Nights' - were in any way responsible for
the failure of the paper, in spite of a later report
by L. Cope Cornford that the stories were 'supposed by
more than one of the proprietors ... sufficiently to
account for the unpopularity of the paper' ('Robert
Louis Stevenson' (1900), 51). The report no doubt had
its origin in W. E. Henley, whom Cornford identifies
in his preface as his main source of information on
Stevenson. Later reviews of the volume suggest that
the stories, though perhaps not widely known, had
been well received by readers who encountered them in
'London'.

4 In the scrapbooks kept by Stevenson's mother we have
an extensive collection of notices, articles, and reviews dating from the beginning of his career to the
time of his death; these are among the holdings of the
Stevenson Memorial House, Monterey, California, and
the Stevenson Society, Saranac Lake, New York.

5 Conan Doyle's article in the 'National Review' was
reprinted with changes in 'Through the Magic Door'
(1907), 260-71.

6 Quoted from an unpublished letter by Gosse to Graham
Balfour dated 7 March 1900 (National Library of Scotland).

7 For a full account, see George L. McKay, 'Some Notes
on Robert Louis Stevenson, His Finances and His Agents
and Publishers' (1958), 21-3.

8 Reprinted in 'A Saintsbury Miscellany' (1947), 208-10.

9 Deathbed testimony on a work, as we might suppose,
would have been important to Stevenson. W. B. Yeats
assured Stevenson of his high regard for 'Treasure
Island' by saying it was the only book his sea-faring
grandfather enjoyed reading and that even on his
deathbed he read it 'with infinite satisfaction'
(Furnas, 'Voyage', 181).

10 To what extent, one wonders, did Stevenson exaggerate
his financial stress to forestall criticism? And did
he prefer to remain in a position in which he had to
write to meet his immediate financial needs, feeling
that if he were once released from that obligation he
would be faced with the more difficult obligation to
produce a masterpiece?

11 Colvin was, up to the time of his death in 1927, the
most faithful and energetic defender of Stevenson's
reputation. His efforts to do battle against the
growing number of adversaries, especially during his
last years, were often touching (see headnotes to Nos
169 and 170). To what extent Stevenson's reputation

suffered from the association with Colvin - and for
that matter with Gosse and Lang as well - is a matter
for conjecture. In any event, however, his loyalty,
which he saw as loyalty not only to a man of rare
worth, but to a better age, was in many ways admirable
and Stevenson would have been the last to scorn it.

'An Inland Voyage'

April 1878

1. FROM AN UNSIGNED REVIEW, 'LONDON'

25 May 1878, iii, 403-4

This enthusiastic review may have been by W. E. Henley
(see headnote to No. 16).

Originality is rare everywhere; rarest of all, perhaps,
in literature. In literature, therefore, it is doubly
acceptable. Intelligence is gregarious, and where and how
the bell-wether wills to go the rest of the flock are quite
too apt to follow. It follows, then, that an original
book is to be received with honour always, if sometimes
with criticism dissentient and austere.
   'An Inland Voyage' is a book among ten thousand;
charming in itself, and charming in an even greater
degree by reason of the glimpses it affords of its
author's personality. It is apparently not much. Two
young Englishmen elect to go a-canoeing on Belgian
rivers and French, and one of them sits down afterwards
to tell the story of their trip. It is not the first time
that such a thing has been done, nor will it be the last.
Man is a writing animal, and his instinct comes never so
strongly on him as when he has been on travel. Hence, it
need hardly be added, a whole cloud of booklets; gay,
austere, pensive, picturesque; treating of God's universe
and man's from the points of view of the romp, the sta-
tist, the economist, the critic, the poet; and most of
them withal as dull and uninteresting as their several
developments of the Commonplace can be. Most of them,

too, of little inherent vitality and less interest, human,
or scientific, or divine. Those who take up 'An Inland
Voyage' with an idea that it may chance to approve itself
of these will be disappointed; not disagreeably.

For it is a book apart and of no style save its own.
In certain ways it is comparable with the 'Sentimental
Journey' itself, for it contains no single word of evidence that the author is subservient to the conventionalities, but an abundance of proof that he has views of his
own on most things, that he flatly declines to look at the
world as it is used to be looked at, and that he has something to say about things which your wide-eyed, philosophical traveller is wont to ignore altogether. While your
tourist is perspiring inquiringly about with his Murray
and his binocular, poking his nose into altar-pieces and
cricking his neck in efforts of architectural intelligence,
this young man is smoking a pipe on the ramparts, or talking to the people in the inn-parlour. While your athletic
oarsman is breaking his heart over the question of pace,
while your aesthetic person is pumping up sentiment over the
scenery or its associations, this young man is listening
serenely to the music of Pan, and gladdening down a dance
to the tune of his own bright thoughts. We have had
travellers a-many, but since the days of Laurence Sterne
we have had no such traveller as this. For he dares (and
his audacity is unconscious: a quite remarkable circumstance) to stand on his own legs, to decline precept and
example from any and everybody, to keep his heart and his
intelligence for that alone which interests him, to be as
much of a sensualist as an exquisite intellect will let
him, to make as much case of his humours as of his beliefs,
to take life frankly and cheerfully, and in questioning
nothing to be master of everything. There is none of the
mim-mouthed austerity about him that passes with us for
wisdom, and none of the niminy-piminy melancholy that does
duty with us for a sign of the poetic temperament. He is
almost a pagan in his fine indifference for dogma and tradition, no less than his freshness of spirit, his vigorous
elasticity of temper, his pleasant open-heartedness, his
sincerity in the matter of trifles, his genial catholicity
as to opinions, his enjoyment of what is near and like-
able. The motes in the sunbeam, one would say, are all
sunbeam to him. Culture and the natural element in man
went never better hand-in-hand; the artist in words and
the artist in life would seem to be equal in him; his head
is full of thoughts, and his heart is as a child's. If
'An Inland Voyage' gave us no more than a half idea of
such a creature as this, it would, in all conscience, be
pretty valuable. But more than that it does actually

bestow. For it is a proof - necessary perhaps, and perhaps not - that artificiality is a thing to be excluded,
and that those who rely on affectation and fine writing
for the production of a kind of interest are in error.
Rightly considered, it has in it the elements of a sort of
liberal education; for none will read it without learning
that, for some men at least, the world is a thing to be
accepted, and life a thing to be grateful for, without
stint or reserve, that poetry lies everywhere, and that
our own instincts are oftentimes as well worth following
as anything else....

The book is a small one; you can read it in an hour; but
that hour must be for you so full and varied and sweet,
that it's odds but you are the better and happier for it,
and it's odds but you will thank your stars for having
brought you into contact with such a clear, humane,
delightful spirit as is his who gives it you.

He is humorous, philosophical, picturesque by turns:
but he is never sentimental; and he is always human. And
his English, which has a savour about it as of exquisite
homespun - the delicate linen woven of fine, white, high-
bred fingers - enables him to be all this with a quite
beautiful ease and directness. There are one or two pro-
vincialisms and several misprints. But the book's great
fault is that it is too short. That reflection, and that
only, prevents us from quoting one of the many pages
marked for citation. It is all so good, and there is
comparatively little of it, that it would be unfair to
anticipate a single line.

2. SIDNEY COLVIN, FROM AN UNSIGNED REVIEW, 'ATHENAEUM'

1 June 1878, 2740, 694-5

According to 'Athenaeum' files this review is by Sidney
Colvin (1845-1927), critic of art and literature, Slade
professor of fine art at Cambridge from 1873 to 1885;
director of the Fitzwilliam Museum from 1876 to 1884; and
keeper of the department of prints and drawings in the
British Museum from 1884 to 1912. Aside from his critical
studies on art, he wrote 'Landor' (1881) and 'Keats' (1887)
for the English Men of Letters Series and, later, the more
ambitious work on Keats entitled 'John Keats, His Life and
Poetry' (1917). Colvin was one of Stevenson's most

important advisors in literary matters and certainly one
of his most demanding critics; he edited Stevenson's
correspondence and was to have written the official biography until, owing presumably to his delays, Fanny Stevenson and Lloyd Osbourne appointed in his stead Stevenson's cousin, Graham Balfour.

The excursion related in these pages is neither remote
nor, in the ordinary sense of the word, remarkable. It
is that of two friends, who took their canoes and made a
round in the late summer of 1876 - in deplorable weather,
as it seems - on some canals and rivers of Belgium and
Northern France, beginning at Antwerp, and ending at
Pontoise, near the junction of the Oise and Seine. But
the interest of a book of travels depends in all cases on
the character of the traveller much more than on the
extent of his travels, and the most trivial journey related by one man will be better worth reading than the most
perilous explorations and hair-breadth escapes of another.
We have here to do with a traveller whose impressions,
and the fancies and reflections with which they are mixed
up, are so vivid and so much his own, and whose manner in
telling them is in general so happy and taking, that we
read and remember his inconsiderable adventures with more
pleasure than many others of much greater importance.
Since the 'Log of the Water-Lily', (1) there has been no
book of the kind so much above the level of an ordinary
narrative of a holiday tour. In spite of occasional airs
and caprices, the result of a self-consciousness which
now and then, for instance in the Preface, betrays itself
awkwardly enough - the self-consciousness, it appears, of
a young writer publishing his first book - in spite of
these, the 'Inland Voyage' is admirably readable. With
its emblematic title-page, from a design by Mr. W. Crane,
(2) the little volume has about it both in form and matter
a touch of the classical and the ideal. It contains passages of feeling, humour, insight, description, expressed
with fluency and finish in the best manner of English
prose. These descriptions are not in the nature of an
inventory of facts; it is a landscape-writing like the
landscape-painting of the Japanese, setting down this or
that point that happens to have made itself vividly felt,
and leaving the rest; so that another traveller might go
the same journey and scarcely notice any of the same
things....
    [Furthermore] that acute self-consciousness of the
writer, which leads him, as we have said, to unbosom

himself now and again in a manner somewhat embarrassing,
on the other hand is the secret of his singular gift of
realizing and expressing the transitions of physical and
intellectual mood through which a traveller passes during
such travels as these....
   But neither glimpses of scenery, however vivid and
poetical, nor moods of the mind and body, however well
observed and recorded, are enough of themselves to give
substance and variety to a narrative so slight as this.
The substance and variety are furnished by two other
elements which we naturally look for in such a book - the
element of human incident and the element of moralizing
reflection. The human incidents and encounters of Mr.
Stevenson's voyage are excellent. From the members of the
canoeing club at Brussels, whose fraternal enthusiasm compels our own *dilettanti* canoeists to a premature escape,
down to the travelling showman and his wife at Précy, we
have a series of typical sketches, some simple or tender,
and others extremely comical, but all living and genuine,
and taken down with a thoroughly quick and sympathetic
observation. The omnibus conductor at Maubeuge, the pedlar's family at Pont-sur-Sambre, the floating population
of the barges, the graces of Origny, the inhospitable
landlady of La Fère, these and several others are personages that we shall not forget. The writer has one qualification indispensable for his undertaking, a natural
liking for and fellow-feeling with the French character,
in all classes of the population; and of such transitory
human revelations, such light dramatic contacts between
man and man, or man and woman, as travelling brings about,
it is hardly possible to read reports of more insight,
kindliness, and liveliness than these.
   In his moralizing, the author has a more uncertain
vein. He is wayward and socially rebellious, with a
rebelliousness much tempered by humour, but reposing upon
one or two positive tenets about which he is plainly in
earnest; such as, that men are bound to find out and
follow their own real preferences, instead of adopting the
preferences ready made and dictated to them by society;
and that the 'gipsily-inclined among men', if they will
but follow their inclinations, will lead lives much more
worth living that those who gather grist in 'offices' -
an 'office' being our author's abomination in chief, and
his symbol for all intolerable routine and sterile death
in life. Paradoxical, according to ordinary standards,
in the conclusions, he is often still more paradoxical
in the processes of his thinking; as when his own unwork-
manlike rashness, in tying the sheet of his sail on the
open Scheldt, suggests the reflection how much better and

braver we commonly find ourselves when we try than we knew
beforehand; or as when the mention of a coarse, semi-
English chambermaid at Boom leads on to the praise of the
Greek ideal of Artemis the chaste. Paradoxical, then, yet
from time to time striking out a flash both new and true -
humorously or cordially rebellious, but never sour or
puling - material, animal even, in his philosophy, but anon
full of fancies the most chivalrous or tender - this brilliant and entertaining writer may at one moment show himself too raw in youth, and at another his words may seem to
carry in them an echo of Heine, or at another of Sterne;
but we shall acknowledge that he has both gifts and promise, and one inestimable gift in especial - charm.

Notes

1 By Robert Blachford Mansfield (1824-1908), published in
   1851.
2 Walter Crane (1845-1915), the well-known illustrator,
   also did the frontispiece for Stevenson's 'Travels with
   a Donkey'.

3.   FROM AN UNSIGNED REVIEW, 'SATURDAY REVIEW'

1 June 1878, xlv, 701-2

Mr. Stevenson's 'Inland Voyage' is more full of moralizing
than of incident. The type and the paper, and the eccen-
tricities of printing where proper names and various other
words are arbitrarily emphasized with italics, give one
the impression that the author affects the quaint and original. We doubt not that considerable thought and care
went to the opening sentence of the elaborate little preface: - 'To equip so small a book with a preface is, I am
half afraid, to sin against proportion.' And the 'equip,'
for no obvious reason, is impressed upon us with the very
largest capitals. In short, the 'Inland Voyage' seems to
be a compound of the styles of Sir Philip Sidney and
Bacon, George Herbert, Sterne, and Mr. Blackmore's rural
characters of the last century. Mr. Stevenson, like the
sailor's famous parrot, has an unfathomable profundity of
thought; and he has devoted most painstaking study to perverted ingenuities of expression. Looking at English

composition from his very peculiar point of view, nothing can be more creditable than the extreme trouble he takes to go out of his way to pick circumlocutory phrases when there are short and simple words that would apparently answer his purpose. It is true that his drift becomes sometimes so ambiguous that possibly we may be misled as to his meaning; but this, on the whole, is in happy harmony with the dreamy mysticism of his philosophical speculations. He lets his mind follow its wayward impulses as he lets his canoe glide downwards with the eddies of the streams. We have no wish to be uncharitable or ungrateful, and we admit that he often amuses us with a clever thing; and not unfrequently we come on a novel idea among a crowd of platitudes rather prettily expressed. But a little of his mannerism goes a long way, and we frankly confess that he has now and then put us out of temper. The more so because, if he had been less pompously formal, he would have written a more entertaining little book. As it is, now and then, when he appears to forget himself, he has flashes of unaffected liveliness; he dashes off telling little sketches of character, and has graceful touches of vivid landscape-painting. He makes himself thoroughly at home with the natives, and has a knack of drawing out their ideas; so that by the time we have accompanied him through the Low Countries and down the Oise, we are aware that we have had some new lights and experiences....

Altogether, with all its faults and affectations, the little book is very lively and pleasant reading, especially if the reader chances to fall in with the writer's peculiar vein.

4.   GEORGE MEREDITH, FROM A LETTER TO STEVENSON

4 June 1878

_____

From 'Letters of George Meredith' (1970), ed. C. L. Cline, ii, 559-61.

Stevenson met Meredith at Box Hill in March 1878. He was long an admirer of his work, especially 'The Egoist', and spoke of him - at least in the early 1880s - as 'the only man of genius of my acquaintance' (LS, ii, 80).

_____

My dear Stevenson,

I had not time to write to you immediately after reading the book, but my impressions are fresh. My wife has gained possession of it at last, so I should have to run down to the house to quote correctly. She fell on the book, I snatched it, she did the same, but I regaining it, cut the pages, constituting an act of ownership. I leave this to her to do invariably, so she was impressed and abandoned the conflict. - I have been fully pleased. The writing is of the rare kind which is naturally simple yet picked and choice. It is literature. The eye on land and people embraces both, and does not take them up in bits. I have returned to the reading and shall again. The reflections wisely tickle, they are in the right good tone of philosophy interwrought with humour.

My protest is against the Preface and the final page. The Preface is keenly in Osric's vein - 'everything you will, dear worthy public, but we are exceeding modest and doubt an you will read us, though exquisitely silken-calvely we are, and could say a word of ourselves, yet on seeing our book, were we amazed at our littleness, indeed and truly, my lord Public?' (1) As for the closing page, it is rank recreancy. 'Yes, Mr. Barlow,' said Tommy, 'I have travelled abroad, under various mishaps, to learn in the end that the rarest adventures are those one does not go forth to seek.' 'My very words to him,' said Mr. Barlow to himself, at the same time presenting Tommy with a guinea piece. (2) - This last page is quite out of tone with the spirit of the book.

I remember On the Oise [The Oise in Flood], you speak of the river hurrying on, 'never pausing to take breath' ['the river never stopped running or took breath']. This, and a touch of excess in dealing with the reeds, whom you deprive of their beauty by overinforming them with your sensations, I feel painfully to be levelled at the Saxon head. It is in the style Dickens.

But see what an impression I have of you when these are the sole blots I discover by my lively sensations in the perusal....

Adieu. I trust you are well. Look to health. Run to no excess in writing or in anything. I hope you will feel that we expect much of you. I beg you to remember me to your father and mother. Yours very faithfully,

George Meredith

Notes

1   Thomas Hardy remarked that Henry James and Stevenson

were 'the Polonius and Osric of novelists', Florence E.
Hardy, 'The Later Years of Thomas Hardy', 1892-1928
(1930), 8.
2 Mr Barlow is the tutor to Tommy and Harry in Thomas
Day's 'History of Sanford and Merton' (1783-9).

5. P. G. HAMERTON, FROM A REVIEW, 'ACADEMY'

22 June 1878, xiii, 547-8

Philip Gilbert Hamerton (1834-94) was an artist, essayist,
and critic who first gained recognition with 'A Painter's
Camp in the Highlands' (1862). He contributed to the
'Fortnightly' and other periodicals and succeeded F. T.
Palgrave as art critic on the 'Saturday Review'. In 1869
he founded with Richmond Seeley the 'Portfolio', where
Stevenson's first regularly paid contribution to a periodi-
cal appeared, the essay entitled Roads. Following a visit
to Hamerton's home in Autun, France, in October 1878,
Stevenson wrote to his mother

> I have seen Hamerton; he was very kind, all his family
> seemed pleased to see 'An Inland Voyage', and the book
> seemed to be quite a household word with them. P.G.
> himself promised to help me in my bargains with pub-
> lishers, which, said he, and I doubt not very truth-
> fully, he could manage to much greater advantage than
> I. He is also to read 'An Inland Voyage' over again,
> and send me his cuts and cuffs in private, after having
> liberally administered his kisses *coram publico*. I
> liked him very much. Of all the pleasant parts of my
> profession, I think the spirit of other men of letters
> makes the pleasantest. (LS, i, 331)

Mr. Stevenson belongs to a class of writers which has
never been numerous, and which is now singularly small in
proportion to the enormous literary production of the day.
We live in a time when minds are jaded by mere quantity in
everything, and ask, in consequence, when they ask for
anything at all, for some new stimulant strong enough to
awaken their deadened powers of perception. One of the
principal publishers in London said to me not very long

ago, that, in his opinion, the English public was completely *blasé* by this time, quite incapable of any enthusiastic delight in literature, and in the highest degree
difficult to move. In such a condition of the public
mind, what is to become of an author whose principal
quality is delicacy of perception? He is like some flower
with a very faint but very exquisite odour in a room
already perfumed with strong essences. I wonder how many
people there are in England who know that Robert Louis
Stevenson is, in his own way (and he is wise enough to
write simply in his own way), one of the most perfect
writers living, one of the very few who may yet do something that will become classical? It is just the writers
of this small class who are most exposed to the neglect of
vulgar people, and even to the contempt of those who are
at the same time coarse and energetic. Mr. Stevenson it
is true, does not tell the story of his inland voyage in
what may be called the athletic manner: he does not tell
us how strong his muscles were after a thirty miles'
paddle, and how boldly he dashed at a rapid, for, though
the book is a narrative of a canoe voyage, the canoeing
occupies a subordinate place in the narrative; but may
there not be as much real manliness in the complete
absence of pretension as in any amount of self-glorifica-
tion? This absence of pretension is one of the great
charms of Mr. Stevenson's manner....

6. FROM AN UNSIGNED REVIEW, 'PIONEER' (ALLAHABAD)

27 June 1878

Stevenson was aware of this review. In 'Travels with a
Donkey' he wrote 'I am afraid I must be at bottom what a
cheerful Indian critic has dubbed me, "a faddling hedonist"'; and in a letter to William Archer (see headnote to
No. 50) he mentions the Indian 'friend' who thus characterized him.

... ['Inland Voyage'] is decidedly brilliant, but not
free from some serious faults: a large amount of affectation founded on the faddling hedonism of the day - by
which young men choose to represent themselves as the

effeminate egotists English young men will never really
become - being the worst.   Then there is a far too easy
use of the name of the Supreme Being;   and what surprised
me in so very superior a person, a foolish habit of laughing at religious ceremonies - on the ground that they were
unintelligible.   Now, in such a case there are clearly
only two courses - a sensible man should pursue: when a
ceremony takes place, either pass it over as a matter concerning which Gallio need not concern himself, or, if
curiosity is felt, look it up in the 'Missale Romanum'....

[Following a brief summary of 'Voyage', the reviewer
quotes the two concluding paragraphs of the chapter titled
La Fère of Cursed Memory.]

If Mr. Stevenson will only write in this vein, he will
never want readers.   I sincerely hope he will and not
again describe an old woman passing along the shrines of
a cathedral, as 'having nothing better to do with her
mornings than come into the cold church and juggle for a
slice of heaven.'   But for all the faults of taste and
inanities of hedonism, I can sincerely say I was very
sorry when the 'Inland Voyage' came to an end.

7.   HENRY JAMES, FROM A LETTER TO T. S. PERRY

14 September 1879

From Virginia Harlow, 'l. S. Perry, A Biography' (1950),
303.
    Thomas Sergeant Perry (1845-1928), American educator
and literary historian, taught at Harvard and was for
several years editor of the 'North American Review'.
Perry was a friend and correspondent of James from the
time of their boyhood together in Newport, Rhode Island,
in the late 1860s.   Of the beginnings of the relationship
between Stevenson and James, Furnas says '[It] had not
begun auspiciously when ... Lang had introduced James to
Louis and Gosse at lunch....   Louis thought James "a mere
club fizzle," saw little more than "a supreme knack of
neatness" in his work, and presently found "Washington
Square" unpleasant' (Furnas, 'Voyage', 212).   A close
friendship between Stevenson and James began following the
former's response in 'Longman's' to James's The Art of

Fiction (see No. 44). The fullest record of their relationship is found in Janet Adam Smith, 'Henry James and
Robert Louis Stevenson' (1948).

I have seen R. L. Stevenson but once - met him at lunch (&
Edmund Gosse) with Lang. He is a pleasant fellow, but a
shirt-collarless Bohemian & a great deal (in an inoffen-
sive way - of a *poseur*. But his little 'Inland Voyage'
was, I thought, charming. I haven't read the other
['Travels with a Donkey'].

8.   STEVENSON ON THE RECEPTION GIVEN TO 'INLAND VOYAGE',
FROM LETTERS TO HIS MOTHER

1878

It was Mrs Thomas Stevenson's habit to collect notices and
reviews regarding her son and his work; the surviving
scrapbooks in which these were kept are now in possession
of the Stevenson Memorial House in Monterey, California,
and the Stevenson Museum, Saranac Lake, New York.

(a) June 1878

About criticisms, I was more surprised at the tone of
the critics than I suppose any one else. And the effect
it has produced in me is one of shame. If they liked that
so much, I ought to have given them something better,
that's all. And I shall try to do so. Still, it strikes
me as odd; and I don't understand the vogue. It should
sell the thing. (LS, i, 325-6)

(b) September 1878

I read 'Inland Voyage' the other day: what rubbish these
reviewers did talk! It is not badly written, thin,
mildly cheery, and strained. *Selon moi.* (LS, i, 328)

'Edinburgh: Picturesque Notes'

December 1878

9. FROM AN UNSIGNED REVIEW, 'SCOTSMAN'

21 January 1879

It is difficult to tell how offended the citizens of
Edinburgh were by Stevenson's sketch of the city. He
was, however, soon to anger a number of his fellow
countrymen with Some Aspects of Robert Burns ('Cornhill',
October 1879).

Edinburgh is the most bewritten of modern cities. Not to
speak of the countless allusions to its characteristic
features in biography and romance, there are hundreds of
formally historical and descriptive works about it; and
it is rediscovered, and described afresh - if such a word
may be used - by touring Cockney litterateurs at least
every autumn. It requires some courage, therefore, in a
young author to give to a work on Edinburgh the title of
'Picturesque Notes;' but in whatever quality Mr Robert
Louis Stevenson fails, it is not in what, to borrow a
French phrase, may be called the courage of his convictions, one of the most cherished of which is evidently a
thorough - and to a large extent just - belief in himself.
He sets himself to write picturesquely, and he does it;
his air is lofty as his theme; or loftier, for on his
native city and all its belongings, its society, its
sects, its arts and institutions, he looks down with a
sort of divine complacency. The complacency is not without
admiration and affection; but these are deeply veiled in
the cynical humour which he cultivates. It is not, we

believe, 'good form' now-a-days for youths to be earnest
or enthusiastic about anything under the sun; yet Mr
Stevenson has not so well tutored himself but that some
hearty feeling of admiration and warm praise occasionally
escapes him.   Usually, however, his tone is that of a
well-bred lounger, a *flaneur*, not deeply interested in
anything, sympathising with well-bred languor in the
misery or the welfare of the people he observes and
describes, but not much moved by either, or, if moved at
all, showing emotion lightly, as becomes a philosopher and
a man of the world.   Philosophers and men of the world
admire this method, and they like it - except, perhaps,
when it touches themselves.   The risk, therefore, that
professors of cynical humour run is that they are apt to
offend every class in its turn, and to this risk Mr Stevenson freely, and at every turn, lays himself open....

One of his pretty descriptions has already, it appears,
brought down the wrath of men upon him, and shaken two
cities.   Dwelling upon the contrasts of old and new that
Edinburgh displays, he writes: -

[Quotes a lengthy passage from Introductory, ending with
the following description of the common citizens of Edinburgh.]

'Chartered tourists, they make free with historical local-
ities, and rear their young among the most picturesque
sites with a grand human indifference.   To see them
thronging by in their neat clothes and conscious moral
rectitude, and with a little air of possession that verges
on the absurd, is not the least striking feature of the
place.'

It seems that when this clever and effective if somewhat strained paragraph appeared, as it did originally, in
the 'Portfolio', Edinburgh was profoundly moved, though
the commotion was not, we are bound to say, observed or
chronicled by the daily paper - whichever it may be - for
which the citizens pay so heavily.   To speak for ourselves, we confess that we now obtain the important information for the first time from the following foot-note
appended to the peccant passage: -

[Quotes Stevenson's footnote in Introductory: 'These sentences have, I hear, given offence' to '*I have not yet
written a book about Glasgow.*']

If Mr Stevenson had duly remembered the maxim that a prophet or poet has no honour in his own country - especially
when writing sarcastic, if poetic, descriptions of it - he

would have been spared alike the pain he refers to, and
the merriment in which he profanely indulged; and he would
perhaps have refrained from adding insult to insult, if
not to injury, as he here does. And had he been humane
and tender-hearted, as poets and prophets ought to be, he
would have refrained from turning Glasgow's pleasure to
mourning by the utterance of that terrible threat, in consideration of the present already humiliated position of
that Western Nineveh. Seriously, this sort of thing may
be passed over, and smiled at coming from a Ruskin or a
Carlyle - by either of whom, of course, each in his own
especial way, it would be rather better done - but from
Mr Robert Louis Stevenson? Happily Mr Stevenson is yet a
young writer, as well as a young man; and if he eschews
such errors of youth, he may make his mark in letters.
The faculty is in him; he has a gift of style; style with
a distinct individuality in it, which would be altogether
charming if the individuality were less obtrusive. He has
great cleverness of phrase; not a little power of observation; and he can light up worn and commonplace topics with
very pleasant touches of fancy. The writing of 'picturesque notes' is to a man of his peculiar powers decidedly
a snare; that he has not escaped the snare is not wonderful. With a less outworn subject, he would no doubt rise
to a more manly and less egotistical treatment; and we
trust to see him soon more worthily occupied than he is
here in laboriously spinning pretty sentences on his own
romantic town. He has it in him even to add to the
already grand repute of this most prolific birthplace and
dwelling-place of authors....

'Travels with a Donkey in the Cévennes'

June 1879

10. STEVENSON, FROM A LETTER TO R. A. M. STEVENSON

April 1879, Balfour, 'Life', i, 160

Robert Alan Mowbray Stevenson was Stevenson's cousin (see
No. 163b). 'Protestations to F' are presumably Stevenson's protestations at the absence of Fanny van de Grift
Osbourne, who had left him nearly a year before this to
return to California; she was eventually to gain a divorce and to marry Stevenson in May 1880.

['Travels with a Donkey'] has good passages. I can say no
more. A chapter called The Monks, another A Camp in the
Dark, a third A Night among the Pines. Each of these has,
I think, some stuff in it in the way of writing. But lots
of it is mere protestations to F, most of which I think
you will understand. That is to me the main thread of
interest. Whether the damned public - But that's all one,
I've got thirty quid for it and should have had fifty.

11.   DR JOHN BROWN, FROM LETTERS TO STEVENSON AND LADY MINTO

1879, 1880

Dr John Brown (1810-82), was a medical practitioner in Edinburgh and the author of 'Horae Subsecivae' (3 vols, 1858, 1861, 1882) and 'Rab and His Friends' (1859).

(a) From a letter to Stevenson dated 14 June 1879

I once had the pleasure of seeing you in this room and would like to see you here again - were it only to tell you how delighted I have been and am with you and the 'Donkey' and with 'Picturesque Notes' ['Edinburgh: Picturesque Notes', 1878] which I have just finished with much admiration and envy - besides thought and feeling, virtuosity and keen-cutting you have as few have ever had and I fear now fewer than ever - the charm and faculty of style - that is the crystal that laughs at time.

What else have you written? I know the uncanny Miller [Will o' the Mill] and some other things - you should put them into a volume - and do 'do' Glasgow - forgive all this you are yourself to blame. (B, 4107)

(b) From a letter to Lady Minto dated 14 November 1880

I don't wonder you like the 'Travels with a Donkey'; it is just what you say of it, true genius, a new liquor, fresh and aromatic.... He wrote in the 'Cornhill' some time ago the wisest and best words, since Carlyle, on Burns [Some Aspects of Robert Burns, October 1879], on whom of late far too much has been written; and he has a clever little book, 'An Inland Voyage in France in a Canoe', which he made with Sir James Simpson's son Walter; and he has a paper on the old Capital of California in this month's 'Fraser' [The Old Pacific Capital], full of charm in feeling and description. ('Letters of Dr John Brown' (1907), ed. by his son and D. W. Forrest, 266)

12. THOMAS STEVENSON, FROM A LETTER TO HIS SON

8 June 1879, B, 5765

I think your book a very bright one but I almost think
second to the 'Inland Voyage' though it has one advantage
over it in having a stronger core of facts. There can be
no doubt that the best part is the night among the pines
[from the chapter A Night Among the Pines]. The next best
is, I think, the scene with the Plymouth brother [from In
the Valley of the Tarn]. The book has the same fault as
the 'Inland Voyage' for there are some three or four
irreverent uses of the name of God which offend me and
must offend many others. They might have been omitted
without the slightest damage to the interest or merit of
the book. So much for your absurdity in not letting me
see your proof sheets. The only other fault in the book
is, I think, a superfluity in the way of description of
scenery. Had there been a great variety of scenery the
objection would not have been justifiable but when the
scenery is so generally the same I think some of it might
have been spared. On the whole however I think it is a
very successful volume of travel and I believe that your
two volumes are unique in point of style.

13. GRANT ALLEN, FROM A REVIEW, 'FORTNIGHTLY REVIEW'

July 1879, xxvi n.s., 153-4

Allen (1848-99) reviewed widely and wrote essays and
studies in various fields, including the sciences. His
best known work of fiction was 'The Woman Who Did' (1895).
The following extract is from a review treating, along
with Stevenson's work, George Eliot's 'Impressions of
Theophrastus Such' and Browning's 'Dramatic Idyls'. In a
review of Stevenson's 'Footnote to History' in the 'Illustrated London News' (17 September 1892), Allen was to
write: 'I admired the "Arethusa" ages before the Stevenson
boom, and got laughed at in my time, a dozen years since,
for an enthusiastic "Fortnightly" notice of "Through the
Cévennes with a Donkey"; but I have lived since, thank
heaven! to see the laughers blush.'

Of late years, literature pure and simple has perhaps been
somewhat at a discount in England. Every writer, whatever
his form of writing, has been too laudably anxious to in-
struct and improve us. Our novelists have indited novels
with a purpose, and our young men have made their poetry
ancillary to their political, social, or religious opinions. But Mr. Robert Louis Stevenson is a brilliant
exception. He is not pursued by a restless consciousness
of the moral burden laid upon him as a preacher and teacher: he is amply content to please and amuse us, as
though he had been born in the easy eighteenth century,
before the rise of earnestness and intense thinkers. His
'Inland Voyage' struck the key-note of his literary gamut;
and the new volume of travel with which he now favours us,
has the self same happy ring, the self-same light and
graceful touch, as if Mr. Stevenson were rather a Frenchman born out of due place, than a Scotsman of the Scots.
I shall not attempt to quote any specimen passage from his
delightful travels, because, as in all such work, the
setting is everything, and the intrinsic worth a minor
consideration. Mr. Stevenson is a stylist who lays himself out for the mastery of style. He has succeeded in
placing himself high among those whose object it is rather
to say well than merely to say. Mr. Walter Crane contri-
butes a frontispiece which aptly prepares one for the work
it introduces. Indeed, Mr. Stevenson's manner may be regarded as one among the many products of the Queen Anne
revival. His writing is a phase of that reaction which is
everywhere making itself felt against the formless solidity of the age wherein we live. The quaint use of italics for proper names, the little tricks of Georgian locution, the mere mechanical repetition of 'tis and it's, all
bring back in a thousand ways the pleasant memories of
that idealised classical England which Mr. Crane and Mr.
Caldecott delight in reproducing. (1) We hear echoes of
Sterne and even of Addison in every page. (2) But, as is
always the case in genuine literary revivals, we find
touches of the modern spirit everywhere interwoven with
the older style. This it is which gives the picture its
truest grace. Without a passing allusion to Mr. Herbert
Spencer, or the Plymouth Brethren, the restoration would
sink to the level of mere wooden imitation: it is the
union of the earlier manner with the latter-day ideas
which gives us such a keen sense of literary enjoyment.
Mr. Stevenson wanders with his mouse-coloured donkey
Modestine through the midst of our burning political and
religious questions, like one who has no part or interest
in these small mundane concerns. He belongs to the great
world of literature, and he smiles a kindly smile at our

petty discussions and differences, apparently reflecting
that they would have mattered but little to Aristophanes,
or Rabelais, or Jean Paul. He and his donkey move in
philosophic indifferentism up and down the Cevennes, and
the remainder of the moral or material universe, with no
other determination than to enjoy life themselves, each
after his kind, and help others by telling the story of
their enjoyment. Nevertheless, since one cannot wholly
divorce oneself from the ethical feeling of one's age, I
must confess that I should have liked Mr. Stevenson
better if he had beaten his donkey less unmercifully, and,
above all, if he had not used that wooden goad, with its
eighth of an inch of pin. This is not the place to discuss the broad question of 'no morality in art:' but most
Englishmen will perhaps feel pained rather than amused by
the description of poor Modestine's many stripes, or of
her forelegs 'no better than raw beef on the inside.'

Notes

1 On Walter Crane, see No. 2, n. 2. Randolph Caldecott
   (1846-86) was the well known illustrator chiefly
   remembered for his series of children's books. Stevenson thought highly of Caldecott's work and in 1880
   hoped that he might illustrate a collection of his
   stories (LS, i, 387); this was not to be, but Caldecott
   did illustrate Stevenson's The Character of Dogs
   ('English Illustrated Magazine', February 1884).
2 On 26 December 1879 Stevenson wrote to Colvin, 'I have
   tried to read the "Spectator", which they all say I
   imitate, and - it's very wrong of me, I know - but I
   can't. It's all very fine, you know, and all that, but
   it's vapid' (LS, i, 371).

14. FROM AN INSIGNED REVIEW, 'FRASER'S MAGAZINE'

September 1879, xx, 404-11

...   The expedition of Mr. Stevenson recorded in the charming little book which he has been pleased to call 'Travels
with a Donkey', is as admirable an example of disgust with
the ordinary conditions of pleasure-rambling, as it is of
graceful writing, and the original and delicate vein of
fancy which this young gentleman has developed. In its

key-note, however, we find still something more than the
mere fastidious dislike of over-refinement for the pleasures which the rabble share, and desire after a sensation
more delicate; in the superiority of that new-fangled old-
fashionedness which is the very height of the mode nowadays. The traveller in this case goes a step further.
He is a young man of letters, one of those who, standing
on the very apex of culture and the nineteenth century,
find nothing better to do than to topple over and begin
again on the other side; and he is at the same time, we
presume, one of those darlings of fortune, who, having no
natural hardships of their own, find a piquant gratification in inventing a few artificial ones, that they may
know how it feels to be weary, and cold, and footsore, and
belated, with the option at any moment of returning to
their ordinary life.... So Mr. Stevenson turns from life,
which is too soft and indulgent, to try how it feels to be
a vagabond. It is a caprice like another. 'Why any one
should desire to visit either Luc or Cheylard is more than
my much-inventing spirit can suppose,' he says, with
ingenuous frankness, while discussing his own itinerary;
and we are obliged to agree with him fully. No madder
expedition could well have been; and it does not seem to
have had the usual pretence of fine scenery or historical
interest. 'For my part,' he says, 'I travel not to go
anywhere, but to go. The great affair is to move; to feel
the needs and hitches of our life more nearly, to come
down off this feather-bed of civilisation, and find the
globe granite underfoot and strewn with cutting flints.'
This is so wonderful a counter-proposition to our innocent
assumption that pleasure-travel was an amusement and
refreshment for hard-working people, that we cannot but
laugh even in the midst of our gasp of surprise. In our
day we say, with that half-irritated sense of contrast
which is one of the symptoms of age coming on - in our day
hardships were not voluntary. We had them without the
asking. What a thing it is to be young, to be super-
refined, to load a donkey with all one's belongings, and
to start out upon the barest of hill-sides at the moment
when all the fiddles are tuning up, and feasting and
merry-making in full progress over all the world! This is
the last whim of exquisite youth. The reader can imagine
the supreme satisfaction with which the young monarch of
civilisation discards it and all its comforts, and contem-
plates himself in the cunning disguise of a pedlar, exulting vastly in the practical joke which he is playing upon
mankind. It is a still more piquant version of the prince
travelling incognito, with always an amused wonder that
nobody recognises him. To be sure, our young traveller

does not hesitate to tell that he is a writer travelling
with the purpose of bookmaking; but a maker of books is
but a sort of pedlar, or wandering raconteur to the out-
of-the-way French peasant, who attaches no importance to
the title. And probably none of the people he met in the
way had any real idea what an amusing thing it was to see
an English author leading a donkey over the bleak pathways
of the Cévennes.

Having said this, however, we are bound to admit that a
prettier book than that which contains the history of this
journey we have not met with for a long time. Nothing
particular happens to the traveller; he has nothing much
to tell us. But he tells us that nothing in detail, hour
by hour of his not very long journey, with a happy grace
of narrative and lucid flow of musing, which among all the
vulgarities and commonplaces of print are singularly
refreshing. It is all about himself, but it is not egotistical in the evil meaning of the word. We never feel
that we are hearing too much of him, or find his details
impertinences - or at least *hardly* ever, to use the
guarded language of the popular poet. Though the idea of
the expedition is altogether over-fine and superior in its
very rudeness, our young author is never priggish. He is
perfectly unaffected in his affectation. The innocent
vanity of his satisfaction in doing something no one has
thought of doing before *is* quite innocent and pleasant,
and in no way harms the impression produced on our minds
that he is a charming companion, full of good feeling and
good taste, as well as of sense and spirit, and with a
quite exceptional gift of literary expression. If here
and there a passing temptation towards fine writing cros-
ses his mind, it is speedily brushed aside by the natural
flow of a style as superior in grace as it is in spontaneousness and ease, to the big mouthings of that talk which
we call 'tall' in these days. Mr. Stevenson will think
but poorly of us when we say that this little book is the
first, bearing his name, that has fallen into our hands;
but this fact will not disturb the reader, who probably,
like ourselves, has not found out the new name which, in
all likelihood, will make itself very well known ere long.
We say 'in all likelihood,' with a doubt in our minds as
to whether the graceful art of writing about nothing will
suffice to build a great and permanent reputation upon.
Perhaps it is because we ourselves belong to a more positive age that this doubt affects us. At the present
moment it is a delightful gift, and, while our author is
young, gives such an air of promise, and of that easy
play of nascent power which 'may do anything,' that it is
perhaps more attractive than a more solid performance.

But - . Nothing can be more charming than those sketches
of Mr. Henry James, for instance, which are as near as
possible stories about nothing - a breath, a passing sentiment, a problem unsolved. They are the very flower and
perfection of literature in its superlative mood, written
for those to whom a suggestion is enough, and requiring
that combination of mutual sentiment and fancy in writer
and reader which carries intellectual intercourse in the
airier regions to the very highest point of which it is
capable - the point, in fact, from which that also must
topple over and get back to common earth again. 'So-and-
So,' says a musical friend, in perfect good faith, 'has
carried so far his studies in pure sound that he is impatient of music.' There is a vulgarity in execution of all
kinds, which jars upon these delicate souls. The artist's
highest gift is to elude the appearance of doing anything,
and to secure his effect as by magic, by a suggestion, the
airiest touch, a light and fine indication of meaning.
But - . It is all delightful; yet, as in life, so in
literature, we must feel, as Mr. Stevenson himself says,
'the granite underfoot.' And we think it probable that,
after a while, these young exquisites of genius will have
to commit themselves to a recognition of the obstinate
solidity of old earth, and the flesh and blood that in-
habit it. We speak with precaution, not at all sure
whether it may not be a lingering prejudice from a more
positive age, a middle-aged incapacity to understand how a
musician should so cultivate himself as to be independent,
nay intolerant, of music, and feel every note jar
upon the perfection of sound - which alarms us! In the
meantime it is very delightful fooling - if it does but
last....

15. FROM AN UNSIGNED REVIEW, 'SPECTATOR'

27 September 1879, lii, 1224-5

Stevenson was in the USA when this review appeared; in a
letter to Henley from Monterey, California (dated by
Colvin October 1879), he asks, 'Why did you not send me
the "Spectator" which slanged me?' (LS, i, 358); and
later, in a letter to Professor John Meiklejohn (1 February 1880): 'I have not seen the "Spectator" article;
nobody sent it to me. If you had an old copy lying by

you, you would be very good to despatch it to me. A
little abuse from my grandmamma would do me good in
health, if not in morals' (LS, i, 383). Stevenson likewise refers to the 'Spectator' as his 'grandmamma' in the
verses of dedication to her intended presumably, at the
time of writing, to stand at the head of 'Virginibus
Puerisque':

Dedication

To her, for I must still regard her
As feminine in her degree,
Who has been my unkind bombarder
Year after year, in grief and glee,
Year after year, with oaken tree;
And yet between whiles my laudator
In terms astonishing to me:
To the Right Reverend THE SPECTATOR
I here, a humble dedicator,
Bring the last apples from my tree.

In tones of love, in tones of warning
She hailed me through my brief career;
And kiss and buffet, night and morning,
Told me my grandmamma was near;
Whether she praised me high and clear
Through her unrivalled circulation,
Or, sanctimonious insincere
She damned me with a misquotation –
A chequered but a sweet relation,
Say, was it not, my granny dear?

Believe me, granny, altogether
Yours, though perhaps to your surprise.
Oft have you spruced my wounded feather,
Oft brought a light into my eyes –
For notice still the writer cries.
In any civil age or nation,
The book that is not talked of dies.
So that shall be my termination:
Whether in praise or execration,
Still, if you love me, criticise!
        'Collected Poems', ed. Janet Adam Smith (1970),
                                              336-7, 541

In a letter to Colvin dating from August 1880, Stevenson
wrote that the poem was 'occasioned by that delicious
article in which the "Spectator" represented me as going
about the Cévennes roaring for women, and only disquieted

at the monastery because it was not a bawdy house, for
which more congenial scene, I accordingly aspired'.

It is evident that the depression which exists in other
branches of trade has not yet reached that of book-making.
Books are written on the smallest provocation. It is
taken for granted that whatever other luxuries are given
up, in these hard times, there will be no lack of money to
buy anything in the shape of a book. There are certain
circles of society, moreover, where a man is not considered to have won his spurs until he has put pen to paper.
However immature may be his views of life, and however
little he may feel himself that he has anything to write
that is worth the reading, if his lot is cast among the
aesthetic or the intense, he loses repute - at least, with
his women friends - if he modestly shuns the field of
literature. It is no wonder, under these circumstances,
that a young man who has a few holiday-weeks to fill
thinks he cannot employ them better than by writing a
book. He must be original, of course; young men of promise always aim at that. But with so much literature
abroad, originality is a difficult mark to hit. People
who can travel, and who can describe the country they
travel over in graceful language, abound. Something more
than this is required, before a book of the kind can hope
to be distinguished from its hosts of neighbours. Mr.
Stevenson shows his wisdom in 'Travels with a Donkey', in
providing for the necessary originality in the outset, by
the choice of his travelling companion. A four-footed
friend was required to carry the unwieldy sleeping accom-
modation that Mr. Stevenson shows so much pride in. As a
child of his own invention, he purrs loudly over its capabilities, and we might add, its inconveniences; and
finally elects to buy a donkey, for the purposes of carriage. Donkeys are such proverbially tiresome animals,
that no one who was not in search of notoriety at any
cost to himself would have thought of deliberately choosing one as his sole travelling companion. The early part
of the book is taken up by the account of how this donkey
was purchased, how it was over-laden, and how much the
writer had to beat it. Pages are devoted to his struggles
with the unwieldy pack, which was apparently far too large
for the small animal, and which was arranged with great
lack of skill on the impromptu pad. Nothing can be less
amusing than to hear how he was obliged to carry his own
packages, after fruitless efforts to overload his donkey,
unless it is the vivid description he gives of each blow,

as it descended on the creature's back. Mr. Stevenson in
other works has shown so refined a taste, that it is
strange how he can dwell with such placid content on the
sufferings that he owns to have inflicted on his companion. Raw legs and bleeding skin do not move him in the
least. He stifles any feelings of remorse that may
occasionally arise, by dwelling on the exquisite, 'Quaker-
ish elegance' of the poor brute. No doubt, donkeys are
exasperating animals, but Mr. Stevenson though young,
might have known that before undertaking such an expedition some technical knowledge of driving a donkey would
have been advisable. It is with relief we hear that,
after a few lessons given him by a passing peasant and
the purchase of a goad, he becomes more learned in the
art, and it is to be hoped the creature suffered less in
consequence.

The part of the world chosen for his wanderings is the
Cevennes Mountains. After a month spent in an animated
highland valley, where the inhabitants 'all hate, loathe,
decry, and calumniate each other,' Mr. Stevenson must
have been fully prepared to enjoy the pleasure of his own
company. The sojourn in such an exciting atmosphere had,
no doubt, taught him that solitude is often preferable to
society though, as we have seen, it had not taught him
the beauty of gentleness. Mr. Stevenson especially looked
forward to his nights, which, as often as he can, he
passed out of doors. The unusual serenity and stillness
surrounding nights spent in the open air make them fitting
occasions for assimilating the beauties of the day gone
by, and help Mr. Stevenson to weave in the delicate vein
of sentiment that he introduces into so much of his writing. These little threads of sentiment are very pretty
and evidently genuine and give a charm to travels that are
otherwise exceedingly thin. Seldom has any book of the
kind been woven out of slighter materials. No adventures
happened to our traveller, no exciting incidents fell to
his lot. His journeying was as peaceful as the country he
travelled over. Still, by the help of a graceful style of
writing, he has given us a very readable volume. His mus-
ings over the natural beauties that surround him, if not
specially striking, are pleasant and natural. It is possible to read a good deal about setting suns and jewelled
stars, the 'blue-black' of the sky at night, and the
'mild, gray blue of the early morn,' without realising too
clearly that we have heard it all before. It is easy also
to sympathise with the enthusiasm of youth, which finds
that nature does not grow less attractive when enjoyed in
the company of 'a pretty, engaging' young hostess. Mr.
Stevenson takes no pains to conceal his susceptibility

towards the softer sex. When his feelings are most
wrought upon, he remembers them with longing or remorse.
After a more than ordinarily severe chastisement of his
donkey, he recognises with sorrow the resemblance she
bears to a lady friend of his. He dwells with self-
complacency upon his kindly encouragement of a middle-aged
lady at a table d'hôte. 'A poor, timid thing of forty' is
better than none. Neither were charms found wanting in the
'heavy, placable, nochalance' of the waitress at that same
table d'hôte. Though reminding him of a 'performing cow,'
he describes with gusto the 'amorous' and 'interesting
lines' in her physical bearing. Evidently the sensation
of finding himself once more in the company of women is
one of great delight to Mr. Stevenson. It is pardonable
if it should somewhat warp an otherwise keen aesthetic
judgment. All this is amusing enough, but Mr. Stevenson's
literary ambition is not to be contented without breaking
a lance in the cause of his own particular form of religion. Though he tells us candidly that he 'has never been
able, even for a moment, to weigh seriously the merits of
this or that creed,' he gives his opinion on each and all
that he comes across as if it were of the greatest weight.
A visit to a Trappist monastery, and an attempt made to
convert him, afford him the fitting opportunity of showing
the height of open-minded detachment at which he has
arrived. It is in the words of the pretty French song
that comes back to his memory, and which, to him, tells
'of the best of our mixed existence,' that he discloses
his true worship, -

    Que t'as de belles filles,
        Giroflé,
        Girofla,
    Que t'as de belles filles,
    L'Amour les comptera.

Until a man has passed out of the stage when women, with
their love and their charms, make up all religion to him,
his judgment upon the intellectual bearing of different
creeds is worth as little as his love. It would not be
fair, however, to leave an impression that Mr. Stevenson
is flippant, - he is only young; and in the present day it
is thought a graceful tribute to old and 'effete' beliefs,
for youth to discuss them sentimentally, from its own
superior intellectual stand-point. It is a fashion which
will probably quickly pass, as the serious work of ignoring creeds, with their inconvenient trammels, becomes more
engrossing.
    His religious criticism apart, however, the account

Mr. Stevenson can give of life in the Trappist monastery, is the most interesting part of the book. The rule is apparently a wise one, breaking up the day into infinitesimally small portions, and encouraging the monks to employ their hours of recreation on the most varied secular occupations. Bookbinding, photography, literature, all have their disciples, and Mr. Ruskin's heart would be gratified by one of the fathers choosing road making as his special pursuit. The unexciting tenour of their lives seems to suit the monks. In spite of their rule of silence, their cheerfulness and health astonish Mr. Stevenson, though he sees a certain policy, not only in the exclusion of women, but in this vow of silence. On the whole, he approves of the existence of such a retreat, - for others; and knows 'many persons, worth several thousands in the year, who are not so fortunate in the disposal of their lives.'

The ending of the travels is a fitting consequence of their beginning. After twelve days, his four-footed companion becomes unfit to proceed further without rest, while the delights of social life and the prospect of letters become too alluring for Mr. Stevenson to bear further delay. Throughout the volume we have felt that the charms of a solitary journey in the company of a donkey would have not been so attractive to the author, if he had not desired to write a book. It was a pardonable and in the main successful ambition.

'Virginibus Puerisque and Other Papers'

April 1881

All the essays in the volume except Some Portraits by
Raeburn had appeared previously in the following periodicals:

Virginibus Puerisque, I, II ('Cornhill Magazine', August
1876)
On Falling in Love ('Cornhill Magazine', February 1877)
Truth of Intercourse ('Cornhill Magazine', May 1879)
Crabbed Age and Youth ('Cornhill Magazine', March 1878)
An Apology for Idlers ('Cornhill Magazine', July 1877)
Ordered South ('Macmillan's Magazine', May 1874)
AEs Triplex ('Cornhill Magazine', April 1878)
El Dorado ('London', 11 May 1878)
The English Admirals ('Cornhill Magazine', July 1878)
Child's Play ('Cornhill Magazine', September 1878)
Walking Tours ('Cornhill Magazine', June 1876)
Pan's Pipes ('London', 4 May 1878)
A Plea for Gas Lamps ('London', 27 April 1878)

16. W. E. HENLEY, FROM A LETTER TO STEVENSON

April 1881, B, 4743

William Ernest Henley (1849-1903), poet, critic, and
dramatist, was introduced to Stevenson by Leslie Stephen
in 1875 when Henley was under Joseph Lister's treatment
for tuberculosis of the bone in the Edinburgh Infirmary.
In the following years Stevenson and Henley were close
friends and in Stevenson's dedication to Henley of

'Virginibus Puerisque', which Henley here acknowledges, he
speaks of Henley's constant 'advice, reproof or praise'.
In 1877 Henley became the editor of 'London', then, subsequently, the 'Magazine of Art' (1882-6), the 'Scots Observer' - later the 'National Observer' - (1889-94), and the
'New Review' (1894-8). He collaborated with Stevenson in
the writing of four plays and served from time to time as
Stevenson's unpaid literary agent. Relations between the
two men grew strained in the late 1880s following Henley's
accusation that Fanny Stevenson had published a story
without adequately acknowledging her debt to Katharine de
Mattos (see Furnas, 'Voyage', 247-61).

The dedication has pleased and moved me much. I am really
very grateful to you and very proud of it. I think the
better of myself for having inspired such an evidence of
regard; and I always shall....
   I have read some of the essays. They have made me
heartily ashamed of my own style. That's effect number
one. Number two is that they are about the best things of
their kind I know. I think they'll live: as Charles Lamb
lives, if in no other way. Another impression I seem to
have is, that I like the style of the new essays better
than that of the others - the earlier ones. It is
clearer, more sufficient, less foppish or rather less
tricksy (not tricky, mind) and more like Style; has more
distinction, in fact, and less personality. It's an
admirable piece of writing. In Pan [Pan's Pipes] - an
excellent piece of matter - and the Lamps [A Plea for Gas
Lamps] - I get wafts of Carlyle. Here and there too -
passim - I came upon odds and ends of verse: chiefly
inserted to round off sentences! My practice with the
Jenk. (1) has given me a nose for verse-in-prose, you know.
Truly, I think, à *la fin des fins*, that you are a tip-top
artist. You have Style, dear lad - the great quality, the
distinguishing sign of the Artist, the Amateur's unattainable thing. You are eclectic, reflective, constructive in
it: but by God, you've got it. Your writing is - as it
seems to me - a creation: an example of that union of the
Personal with the Absolute in art which is only to be
triggered [?] in the work of the very good men. *Va, mon
fils*, I am proud of thee. I used to doubt; but of late I
have got wiser, and I doubt no more. I have learned, and
I am fresh from my lesson. You are a Writer and you are a
Stylist - or, to be more correct, a Master of Style.
Little or big, I care not; but a Master certainly. I
would I could think half as much of myself, or speak one

half as well of - well, of most of them.
    I agree, *du reste*, with Colvin. The book's your best
by a long way. And it's a privilege to have my name
associated with it. It will take me far.

Note

1 Fleeming Jenkin (1833-85), engineer and electrician,
   amateur actor and dramatic critic, was Stevenson's
   teacher at Edinburgh University and later his close
   friend. After Jenkin's death Stevenson wrote the book-
   length 'Memoir of Fleeming Jenkin' (1887).

17. AN UNSIGNED REVIEW, 'PALL MALL GAZETTE'

16 April 1881, xxxiii, 11

Essays and discursive reflections on morals and society
form so considerable a part of current newspaper and
magazine literature in England, and are written in many
quarters with so fair a measure of shrewdness and com-
petence, that when exceptional excellence in this kind of
writing occurs its recognition is apt to be less prompt
and certain than would be the case in times relatively of
dearth. The 'papers' collected in the little volume
before us have been originally printed for the most part
in ephemeral shape, but are of a character and quality
above the ephemeral. Mr. Stevenson is already well known
as the writer of two books of slight and unadventurous
travel, made fascinating by the vivid personality of the
traveller, by his impressionable eye both for character
and scenery, by his vein of fanciful and genial medita-
tion, and by a style which, although full to a fault of
colour and vivacity, yet in the main adheres scrupulously to the traditions of sound, simple, and genuine
English. The contents of the present volume furnish evidence of a graver, although not on that account a less
brilliant or taking gift than either 'The Inland Voyage'
or 'The Travels with a Donkey'. They consist for the
most part of reflections humorous, didactic, or both at
once, on the conduct and issues of life, diversified with
side-lights upon literature, art, and travel, and illustrated with an ingenious profusion of images and

instances. It is the abundance and coruscation of these
which give to Mr. Stevenson's writing its peculiar charm,
and which at the same time, but for the soundness of his
style and diction, would bring it occasionally within a
measurable distance of the faults of affectation and
fancifulness. Mr. Stevenson shows himself in the present
volume certainly one of the most readable of recent writers, even if he were nothing more. To say that since the
days of Charles Lamb there has appeared nothing in the way
of personal essays so spirited and so engaging as these
would be to invite comparisons of the kind which are
always unsafe in judging the works of contemporary literature, and at the same time perhaps to suggest ideas of
imitation which in the present instance are altogether out
of place. Mr. Stevenson, both in his strong and in his
weak points, is nothing if not original, in the sense of
having spontaneously and for himself conceived the ideas
and experienced the emotions in which he invites us to
participate. To accept his invitation will be a refreshment to every one who can enjoy holding conversation on
the daily and vital facts of life with a writer who,
accepting nothing at second-hand, brings to bear on the
facts of experience a gift of singularly luminous and
genial insight, and perceptions both poignant and picturesque.

The experiences avowed by Mr. Stevenson include those of
sickness and the anticipation of death, but his temper is
the reverse of morbid. He is, indeed, equally far removed
from pining feebleness and from the opposite and more grotesque condition of the blatantly and affectedly robust.
His mood is at once gallant and humorously meditative.
His sympathies are all with stirring deeds and hearty sayings. His cherished ideal of life wears a roving, vivid,
somewhat gipsy complexion, and he is the sworn opponent of
the precepts of elderly prudence, of the apathetic virtues
of routine, conformity, and mercantile regularity. He
holds a brief on the side of youth and its impulses *versus*
age and its calculations. To the pleading of this suit,
indeed, his book, as he tells us in its preface, was
intended to be entirely addressed. But circumstances, and
the slipping away from under the writer of his own
vantage-ground of boyish years, have prevented the completion of the plan. Other considerations and other materials have been introduced, so that the volume as it now
appears bears a somewhat fragmentary and disconnected
character. One or two of its essays, especially the criticism on Raeburn's gallery of Scotch portraits, might
perhaps have been left out with advantage to the congruity
of the whole. The chapters in which the author most
explicitly unfolds his banner, carrying the war into the

enemy's camp, and skirmishing against the accepted maxims
of worldly prudence with his light artillery of generous
and suggestive paradox, are the two entitled respectively
Crabbed Age and Youth, and An Apology for Idlers. The
longest essay in the book, and that which gives it its
name, contains reflections, almost always happy and
entertaining, and sometimes only needing the touch of
dulness in order to be recognized at once as both vital
and profound, on love-making, marriage, and the management
of domestic relations. It is a result of the vivid personality of Mr. Stevenson's work that he is as interesting, and has the air of being as original, in his platitudes as in his paradoxes. Platitudes, in the fundamental
sense, he sometimes commits. Thus, the text expounded in
the paper called El Dorado, to the effect that life is
only worth having in so far as it is animated by ideal
aims, and as the view is fixed upon unattainable horizons,
has in itself nothing of novelty. Neither, again, has
that which forms the theme of the stirring and nobly written essay headed *Aes Triplex*. These views about the reasons for which life is to be cherished, and the way in
which death is to be regarded, are essentially as old as
Plato and Aristotle at least. But they have been felt
and realized so freshly by the present writer for himself,
and are enforced with so much vivacity and felicity of
illustration, that they cease to have anything, formally
speaking, of the character of commonplace, and come home
to us with new meaning and conviction. Where Mr. Stevenson, as it seems to us, best unites in the present volume,
the characters of fundamental and of formal originality
is in one of the divisions of his first essay - that,
namely, on Truth of Intercourse; and in the paper called
Child's Play. The former deals with the difficulties and
ambiguities which beset a human creature in the endeavour, upon which so much of his daily happiness depends,
to explain to those dearest to him, by means of the imperfect instrument of words, his hourly states and shades of
feeling. The latter invites us to extend a more intelligent sympathy than we are commonly capable of to the
moods and imaginations of children, and to forbear applying to their visionary narratives the matter-of-fact standard of adult veracity. Both of these essays seem to us
as new and just in substance as they are certainly attractive and almost approaching the classical in form. And,
indeed, there are few pages in this brilliant volume which
are not marked by enough of one or another of these qualities, or of all together, to claim for its author a place
of very high promise in contemporary literature.

18.   ARTHUR JOHN BUTLER, FROM AN UNSIGNED REVIEW,
'ATHENAEUM'

30 April 1881, 2792, 589-90

Butler (1844-1910), an Italian scholar whose chief work
was on Dante, contributed to the 'Athenaeum' for many
years; this particular review is identified as Butler's by
the 'Athenaeum' files.

...   The danger to which writers of Mr. Stevenson's class
- those who are strongly impressed with the artistic value
of literature - are liable is ... that of making style the
first object, of thinking how they are to say it before
they have made sure that they have anything to say: a most
insidious snare, because it is hard to believe that a
well-turned sentence may really be nothing but twaddle
after all. Most of us, whether as writers or readers, are
apt to reverse the maxim laid down by one of the natives
of Wonderland, and to say, 'Take care of the sounds and the
the sense will take care of itself.' From this fault Mr.
Stevenson is on the whole commendably free. Still the
attentive reader will find examples of it, especially in
the earlier essays: so will the author when he has lived
long enough to see the 'entrancing age' of twenty-five and
his present maturity merged together in one dim haze of
youth. Probably the essays he will then write will serve
as standards of composition in that kind as long as the
English language lasts....
   Mr. Stevenson's remarkable power of composition is
more often employed, either to put old thoughts in such
a way as to set one thinking afresh ... or else to pro-
pound others original even to the verge of paradox, but
stated in a way to set an archdeacon revising his convictions. Here are a few random specimens: -

   I hate questioners and questions, there are so few
   that can be spoken to without a lie. 'Do you forgive
   me?' Madam and sweetheart, so far as I have gone in
   life I have never yet been able to discover what forgiveness means. 'Is it still the same between us?'
   Why, how can it be? It is eternally different, and
   yet you are still the friend of my heart. 'Do you
   understand me?' God knows; I should think it highly
   improbable. [From Truth of Intercourse]

I have always suspected public taste to be a mongrel
product, by dogmatism out of affectation. [From Virginibus Puerisque, I]

It is to be noticed that those who have loved once
or twice already are so much the better educated to a
woman's hand; the bright boy of fiction is an odd and
most uncomfortable mixture of shyness and coarseness,
and needs a deal of civilizing. Lastly (and this is,
perhaps, the golden rule), no woman should marry a tee-
totaller or a man who does not smoke. [From Virginibus Puerisque, I]

Times are changed with him who marries; there are no
more by-path meadows where you may innocently linger,
but the road lies long and straight and dusty to the
grave. [From Virginibus Puerisque, II]

'Of making books there is no end,' complained the
Preacher; and did not perceive how highly he was praising letters as an occupation. [From El Dorado]

As a matter of fact, although few things are spoken
of with more fearful whisperings than this prospect of
death, few have less influence on conduct under healthy
circumstances. [From Aes Triplex]

Is this borrowed from Spinoza? All our extracts thus far,
whether their substance be sarcastic or pathetic, have
contained a touch of irony, as is natural to the school of
the master whom Mr. Stevenson follows. We will conclude
with one in which the essayist allows his readers for once
to see into his heart. He is speaking of persons cut off
by death 'in mid-career, laying out vast projects, flushed
with hope': -

When the Greeks made their fine saying that those
whom the gods love die young, I cannot help believing
they had this sort of death also in their eye. For
surely, at whatever age it overtakes the man, this is
to die young. Death has not been suffered to take so
much as an illusion from his heart. In the hot-fit of
life, a-tiptoe on the highest point of being, he
passes at a bound on to the other side. The noise of
the mallet and chisel is scarcely quenched, the trum-
pets are hardly done blowing, when, trailing with him
clouds of glory, this happy, full-blooded spirit shoots
into the spiritual land. [From Aes Triplex]

Both for its own thoughts and for the charming manner
in which it leads the reader's mind back to two of the
noblest passages of all literature, ancient and modern,
this may be pronounced as good a paragraph as could be
found to exemplify the modern essay at its best. It is
worth noting that where Addison, say, would probably have
referred to Thucydides and Wordsworth, could he have
quoted him, by chapter and verse, the writer of to-day
depends on the education of his readers for his full
effect. So far he reduces the number of his public; on
the other hand, he has the satisfaction of feeling that
few of those to whom he speaks find out all he has to say
at once; the most, if they are pleased with his work at
first, may turn to it again and again, with the hope that
it will please at the tenth visit.

The essay entitled Pan's Pipes, though the author does
not think so, is the least satisfactory in the book - not
in expression, for there it is one of the best, but in the
thought expressed. It may be strictly true, for example,
that 'to distrust one's impulses is to be recreant to
Pan'; but if we take the author's meaning correctly, in
recreancy to Pan lies the secret of greatness, and by it
men have become great and done great things for the world,
from the days of Heracles to those of the admirals whom
Mr. Stevenson rightly admires. It should be remembered
that where Pan is, Silenus is usually not far off.

19.   AN UNSIGNED REVIEW, 'SPECTATOR'

11 June 1881, liv, 775-6

Mr. Stevenson has given us a charming collection of essays
in 'Virginibus Puerisque.' Like all his work, it is suggestive, piquant, and full of graceful exaggeration. In
his preface he says for what purpose these essays were
written. 'I was to state temperately the beliefs of
youth, as opposed to the contentions of age; to go over
all the field where the two differ, and produce at last
a little volume of special pleading, which I might call,
without misnomer, 'Life at Twenty-five.' After this frank
statement, all who read the book must read it with the
light and sympathy of twenty-five upon them. That Mr.
Stevenson could seize upon the essence that makes that age
one of such keen delight, is very evident. Live in the

present, this is the key-note of it all. Youth follows
childhood, age follows manhood; gather of all as you go,
and between them they will build up an edifice whose foundations are upon eternal youth, and whose summit reaches
to wisdom throned among the clouds. The advice of the
whole book may be summed up in this: As joy and peace are
heavenly gifts, so it is the Devil's work to show people
how little real foundation they have for enjoyment. To
have a hobby, to ride it hard, assures a man at least as
much of downright pleasure as there are hours that he
spends upon it.

The series of essays that give its name to the book
have love and marriage for their subject. With just a
shade of cynicism, Mr. Stevenson approaches his fascinating subject. He has studied it from the outside, he has
touched it from within. It is the 'Great Perhaps,'
around which mystery throws a veil; while possible shipwreck only adds to it a keener zest. He points out how
inevitable is the choice between two possibilities, 'The
fact is, we are much more afraid of life than our ancestors, and cannot find it in our hearts either to marry, or
not to marry. Marriage is terrifying, but so is a cold
and forlorn old age.' It will not do to live entirely on
friendship. 'The friendships of men are vastly agreeable,
but they are insecure. You know all the time that one
friend will marry, and put you to the door; a second
accept a situation in China, and become no more to you
than a name, a reminiscence, and an occasional crossed
letter, very laborious to read.... So that, in one way
or another, life forces men apart, and breaks up the
goodly fellowship for ever.' But on the other side, marriage has its dangers, its very virtues giving birth to
evils. 'Marriage, if comfortable, is not at all heroic.
It certainly narrows and damps the spirits of generous
men. In marriage, a man becomes slack and selfish, and
undergoes a fatty degeneration of his moral being.... The
air of the fireside withers out all the fine wildings of
the husband's heart. He is so comfortable and happy, that
he begins to prefer comfort and happiness to everything
else on earth, his wife included.' Mr. Stevenson makes
some exception to this view of marriage, in the case of
women. An unmarried life with them is necessarily limited in its openings, at least until first youth is no
longer there to need the protection of guarding conventionalities. After that period, single life may be the
freer one; but Mr. Stevenson misses in it the true
motherly touch that comes to women in happy married life.
He is right in the main, but happy married life even to
women brings much of necessary selfishness. The happiness

that is centred in a husband inevitably rebounds upon the
wife. Devotion to his concerns, ambition for his ends, is
implied in the perfect wifely ideal, and can rarely be
accomplished without the sacrifice of larger sympathies.
That the highest wifely ideal can be attained, and yet
the character not be cramped, is possible, no doubt; but,
like all complex undertakings, it needs something more
than the mere following-up of the instincts that lie
deepest in the nature of women. That the reconciliation
of the conflicting duties is rarely accomplished, the
narrow sympathies and mere personal outlook of the gener-
ality of women go to prove. How seldom can wives and
mothers view with impartiality any change in circumstances or laws which, while giving greater happiness to
the multitude, tend to restrain or alter the chances that
might lie before husband or children. There are many men
willing to sacrifice their private hopes to the good of
the multitude, but the women are rare who as willingly
could see the interests of the individuals they love
merged in the larger gain.

In the course of these essays, Mr. Stevenson suggests
some crucial tests to those who would risk their happiness
in matrimony. There must be 'some principle to guide
simple folk in their selection.' Speaking of the choice
of a wife, he says: - 'She must know her *métier de femme*,
and have a fine touch for the affections. It is more
important that a person should be a good gossip, and talk
pleasantly and smartly of common friends and the thousand
and one nothings of the day and hour, than that she should
speak with the tongues of men and angels.' If any question arises of the profession that a wife may follow, Mr.
Stevenson strongly deprecates that of letters. 'The
practice of letters is miserably harassing to the mind'..
.. To find the right word is so doubtful a success and
lies so near to failure, that there is no satisfaction in
a year of it.' Music as a profession is also to be avoided, but painting is allowed. Perhaps it is the soothing
harmony of form and colour that helps to allay the anxiety
of heart, when the end attained falls short of the ideal.
The qualities to be looked for in a husband are of the
same type. 'Whatever keeps a man in the front garden,
whatever checks wandering fancy and all inordinate ambition, whatever makes for lounging and contentment, makes
just so surely for domestic happiness.'

One of the most attractive of the essays is Crabbed Age
and Youth. While reading it, the sternest censor of
youthful follies must grow indulgent over the lost possibilities of youth, when it is cramped and confined by the
staider judgment of age. Perhaps the doctrine tends

towards a dangerous laxity, but it does not matter much,
if we do deal a little over-tenderly with the foibles of
the young. They will have their foibles, whatever their
elders may say. Mr. Stevenson is not speaking of real
errors, when he pleads for the vagaries of youth.   'To
love playthings well as a child, to lead an adventurous
and honourable youth, and to settle when the time arrives
into a green and smiling age, is to be a good artist in
life, and deserves well of yourself and your neighbour.'
But unfortunately the artist spirit is often wanting, both
in those who spend and those who judge. In youth, ten to
one our adventures are neither adventurous nor strictly
honourable; while in age, our judgment is apt to be
warped by what is convenient to us in the conduct of our
more youthful friends. To be an artist means that we have
the artistic temperament in its truest sense, and have
hearts large enough to appreciate good, honest completeness, whether of physique, intellect, or morality. The
power of living one's life completely and artistically is
at least as rare as the power of being an artist in any
particular branch of it. Mr. Stevenson specially enforces
the lesson of allowing life to develop naturally in childhood. The joys of children are outside our world altogether. Truth is beyond their power, for they live in a
fairyland of romance and adventure; and our cold world of
fact is outside their understanding. He compares the
castles in the air of childhood and middle-life, and
leaves us uncertain which is the most enticing. But we
doubt if true castle-building is possible in later life.
Grown people can compose stories; but to build a castle,
we need the possibilities of life to be in front of us.
Of course, our childish romances dealt largely in impos-
sibilities; but life had not shown its hand, and in the
future *something* would come, if that something were not
the exact fulfilment of our childish dreams. No wonder
childhood's stories are so fascinating. We are our own
heroes and heroines then, while others take their places
in age. We could afford to act the grand tragedies of
life, before their reality had left a mark upon our
countenance. The absence of any memory only quickened
our inspirations. So unhelpful is memory in all real
romances, that those in whom it is keenest are rarely
capable of writing a story that is anything but their
own experience. To write objectively, both memory and
passion must be stilled, and although we may be deeply
touched by a novel that bears throughout the mark of personal experience, it is not seldom that it absorbs so
completely the whole identity of its author as to leave
no reserve force behind for future creations.

The essays, of course, vary in interest, and the later
ones are less fresh than the earlier, but special pleading
for life at twenty-five is apt to die away on the lips of
a later age. Slight, however, as they are, they show a
rare insight into the subtler reasons that give rise to
action which apparently is only fragmentary and superficial. They lay bare the network of motive and desire,
and in them we have a key that can open many secrets, both
in ourselves and others. They are not metaphysical,
because Mr. Stevenson has drawn his conclusions from the
positive side of experience, and thereby appeals to a like
experience in the reader, but intellectually they are of
a high order. It is, perhaps, unfortunate that we cannot
find more fault with the book. As Mr. Stevenson says,
amusement lies in differing, not in agreeing. But whether
it is that youth lingers, and the glow of twenty-five is
with us still, or that in mature years the illusions of
youth still arouse our sympathies, we cannot tell. Anyhow, Mr. Stevenson's essays must be reckoned as one of
the pleasures that both young and old will alike enjoy.

20.   AN UNSIGNED REVIEW, 'BRITISH QUARTERLY REVIEW'

July 1881, lxxiv, 219-20

Mr. Stevenson's contributions to essay literature are
marked by acuteness, and occasionally by tender and quaint
fancy. To say that every sentence that drops from his pen
is of great value would be a profound mistake, or even to
say that the essays are of equal value. He is too fond of
disguised paradox, of half-statements, where half-statements are hardly justified, to be quite successful. We
understand Charles Lamb's allusiveness: it was part of
himself, altogether native to him; Mr. Stevenson's allusiveness is often intentional and affected, and with all
his facility and grace of style, we feel sometimes as if
the matter was thin, as if he were carving cherry-stones
when he fancies he is constructing something fitted to be
useful. And this notwithstanding that he affects the
Bohemian and does not disguise his dislike of set engage-
ments. It is all very well to sneer in a subdued way, and
to run a tilt against the man who goes with unvarying
regularity to his office in the City; but certainly in
many ways Mr. Stevenson profits by the City man's

steadiness, else his easy Bohemianism might sit less
lightly on him. We confess we like Mr. Stevenson best
when he is least ambitious, and is not greatly concerned
to surprise us by edging-in paradoxes on the mind as if
they were verified truths of his own experience. Child's
Play, Aes Triplex, Pan's Pipes, and a Plea for Gaslight
are far more to our taste than the *pièce de résistance* of
the volume, which he names Virginibus Puerisque, and
adopts as its title. Here we have a discourse on marriage
of the most disconcerting kind. The redeeming point is
that Mr. Stevenson is not even half in earnest. He is,
after all, only a wistful inquirer, and yet he cannot help
being dogmatic on a turn or two. He is quite sure that,
in marrying, man 'undergoes a fatty degeneration of the
heart,' which is a good point set in an apt figure; that
though women are generally made better by marriage, it is
because of their defects; that your wise man is your ripe
old bachelor; that one woman will do for wedlock quite as
well as another if you only make up your mind to it, and
after a good deal of 'craning,' which seems inseparable
from the process, the only advantage is in getting the
thing well over. It will thus be seen that Mr. Stevenson
is too intensely sarcastic to be quite playful, and too
self-conscious to be quite innocently amusing. We cannot
imagine that men of much experience, and detached from
interest in literary charm as such, would care much for
these essays, and we are not sure that it will do 'vir-
gins' and 'young men' much good to read them. However
there is always an audience for what is original and
finished, what is piquant, suggestive, full of fancy, and
marked by delicate ·perception; and honesty compels us to
admit the claim of Mr. Stevenson's Essays to the possession of some of these qualities. While therefore we accord
to this volume high praise for its clear and graceful
literary style, its ease, its restrained satire, we cannot
say of it that it has the fulness, the calm air of experience of our earlier essayists, while in true humour it is
very deficient, and makes up for it by a kind of affected
wit which too often recalls Sterne and sometimes Heine.

21.   E. PURCELL, FROM A REVIEW, 'ACADEMY'

9 July 1881, xx, 21-2

Edmund Sheridan Purcell was for a time editor of the
'Westminster Gazette' and author of the controversial
'Life of Cardinal Manning' (1896); he followed Stevenson's
career closely and was one of his sharpest critics.

Mr. Stevenson's new book will scarcely cool the ardour of
any who passionately loved his earlier work; but those who
have hitherto admired him more soberly will see little
cause to regret the first misgivings to which each
succeeding volume gives a more definite and less favourable colour.   In justice both to Mr. Stevenson and to
ourselves, it should be conceded that any estimate of his
genius must be perforce a purely individual one.   The real
question - far more important and interesting than any
enquiry as to style or method - is surely this: Are his
books in the strict sense genuine? - are they, as they
profess to be, the spontaneous, careless pastime of a
philosopher, or the studied, artificial, practised work
of a man of letters?   If the latter, it is well; if the
former, it were far better.   For then we should gladly
confess that the man who, urging his donkey over the
stony Cévennes, or slipping down the flood in his canoe,
could, with each passing change of sun or cloud, philoso-
phise in spite of himself, so lazily, so carelessly, so
unaffectedly, and yet so well, and in words always so apt
and poetical, must stand upon a little pinnacle of fame
far above the heads of such as we who cannot even now and
then be at once perfectly natural and perfectly elegant.
   But whether he really did all this, or only pretended,
or persuaded himself afterwards that he did so, each
reader must judge for himself, according to his own sentimental experiences, his own knowledge of men and books,
and still more by noting how far he feels as he reads
that undefinable but surely unmistakable feeling of
affectionate *cameraderie*, that strong sense of a peronal-
ity whom one would like to know in the flesh as well as in
the book, and, knowing, would find to be not other than
his book, and yet something far better.   It is thus that
we know Montaigne and Walton, and even Bacon, Browne, and
Sterne, for what they were and still are for us; it may be
thus that some have traced in these essays a friendly

revelation of virgin genius, wayward, unconscious, and unpremeditated. But, for ourselves, far different are the conclusions to which these tests have led us. For if these books turned out to be the joint production of two or three ingenious pens, we know not whether we should not admire them the more nor like them the less. And saying this is to say all. For is it not to say in other words that they have not the faintest shadow of a claim to be added to that too short list of books which have been the pastime of fine writers, and will ever remain the infinite delight of fine readers?

Regarding, then, these essays as elaborate studies in the literary art - and, after all, Mr. Stevenson may himself view them in no other light - one cannot be deaf to the praises which his refined and flexible style has so fully deserved, and which may here be endorsed without repetition. The many instances of strained metaphor, forced illustration, and obscure extravagance which we might quote are due not to defects of style, but to barrenness of matter. For, cloudy in purpose and confused in execution, these papers were fore-doomed to comparative failure. No hint is now given to remind us of the fact that many of them have already appeared in a magazine; but from the Preface it would seem that they were commenced some years ago as a plea for youth against age, and that, in deference to friendly advice, the title 'Life at Twenty-five' has been droppped, and apparently some other things with it. Hence, possibly, the page of orthodox morality which winds up many of the earlier essays, and lends to them so singular an air of vagueness and insincerity. Other papers have been added. 'Upon these,' he says, 'rests the shadow of the prison-house,' but in truth not much more gloomily than upon the others. The author here accuses in order to excuse himself, but in vain. For if, at forty, one has grown beyond what one idly scribbled at twenty-five, why sow broadcast one's unripe notions on matters of all others the most momentous? And if at twenty-five we felt and thought and wrote as we can never hope to do again, if 'the old convictions have deserted us, and with them the style that fits their presentation and defence,' it were surely better to offer to the world our summer fruits just as they grew, a little garish it may be in tint, and unsound perhaps at core, without vainly trying to blend the worse of to-day with the better of yesterday. One alternative we must choose, for fine writing and many metaphors will not help us to be young and old, wise and foolish, at the same time. The only resource is pathetic platitude and shifty double-facedness. Mr. Stevenson could not avoid the inevitable.

Yet when he has really anything to say, it is as thoroughly worth saying as it is sure to be well said. The isolated paper on Raeburn's Portraits shows him at his best, not as a *dilettante* essayist, but as a sympathetic critic skilled alike to read men and their likenesses. Some charming conceits in his Plea for Gas-lamps are peculiarly timely just now when citizens are going forth nightly to gape at the rival stage-moons....

Nor are bright thoughts and wise saws wanting in the first five papers which come under the title 'Virginibus Puerisque,' as, for instance, the quaint argument whereby he proves that, 'if you wish the pick of men and women, you must take a good bachelor and a good wife.' But these, after all, are few, scattered, and isolated, not bound together by any abiding principles of purpose and action firm enough to live by, but embedded in an ooze of platitudes....

It is impossible not to treat the book thus seriously, and so with apparent severity; for nothing can well be more serious than the subjects which it handles with play-ful dexterity and fantastic wantonness. To complacently ignore its implied claims or its probable influence upon certain readers would be a poor compliment. To them its confident maxims and playful audacity will seem to imply some background of solid opinion. Such, at least, was the inference naturally suggested by Mr. Stevenson's first books. Were his earlier moralisings, so light yet earn-est, so fluent yet so inconsistent, but reticent whispers of an uncandid epicureanism, or were they the playful tinkling of some more massive forge whose full ring we must wait to catch? Each succeeding book only proves that they were neither. For if at first the gentle stroke but disguised the latent strength of a self-gained and well-rounded philosophy, right or wrong, it must before now have made itself felt. But what have we here beyond the same clever conceits and ingenious sallies furbished up and re-set in freshly gilt commonplace? In truth, very little. Mr. Stevenson has nurtured his beautiful gifts with rare cultivations. His pen is well worthy - and this praise he at least would feel means much - to describe the heaving tints of a sunset river, or the transient emotions of an artistic soul; but a philosopher or a moralist we cannot allow him to be. And yet at least half of this book consists of moralising upon Death, or, rather, of pathetic mumblings, graceful whimpers, and seductive little shrieks, in which the changes are rung upon every metaphor and simile which ever has been, or ever can be, applied to this new grisly pet of drawing-rooms given over

to the infernal amusement of wondering whether life is
really worth living. Some of this is merely superior fustian, much of it has been read before, none of it would
one desire to read again. This endless fantasia upon the
theme of the charnel house is the more profoundly depress-
ing because it is written in no particular key. Does Mr.
Stevenson believe, or does he doubt, or does he reject the
doctrine of a future state? Unless he will make this
plain he can hardly hope to amuse any man who has himself
adopted any one of these alternatives by the ingenuity
with which he mingles dirge and carol - one moment sobbing
in the procession, the next dancing merrily over the
graves. Death is a fashionable subject, but, if one must
write for the mere sake of writing, it were more seemly to
write of Tar-water.

22.   J. A. SYMONDS ON STEVENSON AS AN ESSAYIST

1881, 1882

John Addington Symonds (1840-93) was a long-time resident
at the health resort of Davos-Platz, where Stevenson spent
two successive winters, 1880-2. While they enjoyed one
another's friendship and conversation, neither was highly
appreciative of the other's work. In writing to H. F.
Brown in February 1881, Symonds said, 'I have apprehensions about his power of intellectual last. The more I
see of him, the less I find of solid mental stuff. He
wants years of study in tough subjects. After all a
University education has some merits. One feels the want
of it in men like him' ('Letters of J. A. Symonds' (1968),
ed. Herbert M. Schueller and Robert L. Peters, ii, 664).
Stevenson, on the other hand, according to Symonds,
'hardly disguises his opinion that I cannot write poetry
at all, and am a duffer at prose' ('Letters of J. A.
Symonds', ii, 717). On the whole Symonds had a higher
opinion of Stevenson's fiction than of his essays.

(a) Symonds to H. F. Brown, from a letter dated 1 September 1881

I hear from Stevenson now and then. Did I tell you he has

taken the Tschuggen Chalet for next winter?   I do not
greatly like 'Virginibus Puerisque' in spite of its brilliancy.   It is always to me a little forced and flashy.
('Letters of J. A. Symonds', ii, 690-1)

(b) Symonds to Stevenson, letter dated 5 April 1882.
Although the first part of Stevenson's essay Talk and
Talkers ('Cornhill', April 1882), in which Symonds figures
under the name of Opalstein, offers the occasion for this
letter, Symonds speaks also of the essays in 'Virginibus
Puerisque':

My dear Louis
    I think it may amuse you to look at an annotated copy
of your article on Talk.   I therefore send it.   This is
what Opalstein sometimes does, where he reads, but is too
often too indolent to do it.   If we did this oftener, we
should oftener through literature, get the echo in our own
soul's cavern of talk.
    I find the former qualities of your mind and style
strong here.   I hold this to be up to the mark of what
delights the amateur of 'Virginibus Puerisque'.   It is the
singularly clear, outspoken, naiveté of the writer - his
artless self-revelation crystallized in purest literary
art - wh makes the paper so stimulative....   Given that
that amateur chimes in with you, or that he has been
obsessed by you, his utterance is just.   So far as I perceive, with far blunter artistic sensibilities, with perhaps wider though dimmer intuitions into the possibilities of talk, I should say that you have discoursed upon
the species as though it were the genus.
    But this is just the speciality of your genius - God
save the mark so near a pun!   In your Individuality, combined with your rare power of condensation by the might
of style, you hold a potent fructifying instrument.   It is
of course double-edged, cutting some folk to the quick
with its truth, others on the surface with its limitations.
    The great quality of this force in you is that it comes
fresh from self and from personal experiences.   Its defect is that it has not absorbed into itself a hundred
things wh have occurred to men of other selves and other
experiences.
    To my mind, this is what the essayist should have -
this acute trenchant personality.   But we sometimes meet a
Pope or Horace who took more up into his solution.
    I give this as a hint for growth, for the next Manner.
Possibly, deeper reading; possibly, more omnivorous

sympathies might make the brilliance of the art still more
imposing.

Everyrs

JAS

It is self-portraiture more than science. Hence attractiveness. Hence limitation. ('Letters of J. A. Symonds',
ii, 742-3)

'Familiar Studies of Men and Books'

February 1882

The volume contained the following essays, all of which had appeared earlier in periodicals:

Victor Hugo's Romances ('Cornhill Magazine', August 1874)
Some Aspects of Robert Burns ('Cornhill Magazine', October 1879)
Walt Whitman ('New Quarterly Magazine', October 1878)
Henry David Thoreau: His Character and Opinions ('Cornhill Magazine', June 1880)
Yoshida-Torajiro ('Cornhill Magazine', March 1880)
'Francois Villon, Student, Poet, and House-breaker ('Cornhill Magazine', August 1877)
Charles of Orleans ('Cornhill Magazine', December 1876)
Samuel Pepys ('Cornhill Magazine', July 1881)
John Knox, and His Relations to Women ('Macmillan's Magazine', September and October, 1875)

23. GEORGE SAINTSBURY, FROM AN UNSIGNED REVIEW, 'PALL MALL GAZETTE'

18 March 1882, xxxv, 5

Saintsbury (1845-1933), the literary critic and historian, perhaps first met Stevenson as a fellow-contributor to 'London'. He reviewed for the 'Academy' and the 'St James's Gazette', but chiefly for the 'Saturday Review', where he was assistant editor from 1883 to 1894. Saintsbury succeeded David Masson as holder of the chair in English at Edinburgh University. E. J. Mehew has identi-

fied this review as Saintsbury's from an unpublished
letter (British Museum) Stevenson sent Saintsbury thanking
him for it and signing himself 'An Author Definitely
Young', a reference to the opening line of the review.

There is probably no author of the present day who may be
definitely called young in regard to whom opinions are so
much divided as is the case with regard to Mr. Louis
Stevenson. His only parallel in this respect is the
author of 'The New Republic;' (1) but the cases are different. Mr. Mallock has for the most part the vulgar on
his side and the non-vulgar against him, except in his now
almost forgotten quality of epigrammatist. Mr. Stevenson
divides both classes in a curious fashion. The secret of
the division is, however, not very difficult to make out.
There are some persons who are attracted and others who
are offended and bored by an extremely personal attitude.
Now, Mr. Stevenson is nothing if not personal.... The
climax of this style is reached in an essay on John Knox,
respecting which Mr. Stevenson quaintly enough remarks in
the preface that McCrie is 'unreadable.' (2) Now McCrie
is not unreadable; at least, he has been read by persons
not very tolerant of dulness. He is not unreadable because he has the good sense to talk about Knox, who is
interesting, and not about McCrie, who is not. Mr.
Stevenson's essays positively bristle with 'you see,' 'you
remember,' 'I say,' 'I fancy,' and the rest of it. 'Do,
my good Sir, leave my buttons alone; and don't whisper in
comany' is the inevitable cry of the natural man. And yet
the said natural man, if he has any literary knowledge and
taste whatever, knows that Mr. Stevenson is almost invariably worth reading, and that pretty Fanny's way must be
taken with pretty Fanny. As a mere literary critic Mr.
Stevenson does not take a very high place. He confesses
with characteristic ingenuousness that he has a habit of
writing about books when his heart is hot within him from
their perusal. Now, this is about the worst moment possible for criticising a book, though it is the best moment
possible for criticising a man. It is, in fact, in the
criticism of life, not of books, that Mr. Stevenson is
strong. The few persons who happen to be in the secret
know that there are, lurking about in uncollected and forgotten print, tales of his which for strangeness, vividness, and unfamiliar truth of imagination are the equal of
Poe or of Gérard de Nerval, and that he lets them lurk
while he republishes essays of sprightly thought, mixed
with audacious platitudes and criticisms, in which the not

rare jewels of expression hardly atone for the insuffi-
ciency of the total on any properly literary estimate.
     There probably never was a writer more entirely free
from humbug than Mr. Stevenson, and his transparent sincerity could not be better shown than in the preface to
this book.   Never, perhaps, did a man in reprinting a
handful of magazine papers take such pains to indicate his
own state of mind at the time of their conception and production.   The brutal and bearish critics before mentioned
will probably pass over all this clinical information
about the author's soul, and go straight to the work.
They will find one paper than which nothing much better
has been published for years; another hardly inferior to
it; and half-a-dozen make-weights of varying merit; among
the last class, and at the bottom of it, must rank the
'Knox Papers' already mentioned.   An essay on Victor
Hugo's novels is enthusiastic and pleasant to read.   One
on Walt Whitman, without being enthusiastic, and indeed
without having any very definite characteristic, is sensible, moderate, and useful.   In two essays on Villon and
Charles d'Orléans Mr. Stevenson shows a certain incapacity
which we have noticed in him on other occasions - an
incapacity to appreciate poetry as such.   Both are excellent examples of his faculty of building up out of dry-as-
dust details a living presentment of a man.   He has this
faculty in a most remarkable degree, and it is this which
makes him so excellent a tale-teller; but for any comment
that his main pictures give as to the works of Villon and
the works of Charles D'Orléans they might as well not have
been written.   Mr. Stevenson's Villon and the Villon of
the poems agree not together.   The essayist's 'sorriest
figure on the rolls of fame' certainly did not write the
rondeau 'Mort,' or the famous ballades.   If Mr. Stevenson
is right the Villon Society must follow the examples of
certain elder societies, and prove that Louis XI. wrote of
them, or Coquillart, or the Hangman, or Charles d'Orléans
himself in his old age.   These poems contain an explanation of the whole matter, and Mr. Stevenson has not
grasped it.   As for Charles, the essayist himself admits
in his preface that he has probably made a man of straw or
snow there.   It may be added that he is weak in his
facts....
     But the two essays we have reserved - that on Pepys and
that on Burns - to which may be added one on Thoreau, do
far more than redeem the book.   The Thoreau essay is the
least interesting of the three, simply because Thoreau
was infinitely the least interesting man of the three.
As a piece of interpretation - not, let it be remembered,
of books, which in Thoreau's case are worth very little
indeed, but of the man who, in his priggish, unhealthy,
cross-grained fashion, was worth something - it is excel-

lent. Better still is the paper on Burns, in which Mr.
Stevenson, following up, though on a different track, the
outspokenness of Mr. Carlyle, has destroyed another part
of the Burns legend and reconstructed great part of the
Burns history and the Burns man. The man was not, indeed,
bad (that Mr. Stevenson indignantly and justly denies that
he was), but spoiled and warped by his very virtues as
well as by his vices. A good literary essay on Burns
remains to be written, but with Mr. Stevenson's to supple-
ment and correct Carlyle's, not much more is wanted in the
way of moral comment. Again better, and this time almost
perfect, is the paper on Pepys. It is so discriminating,
so acute, so entirely adequate, that we could almost let
Mr. Stevenson say 'You see' on every page of it. The
Clerk of the Acts of the Navy is there, and there for the
first time. Mr. Stevenson's picture of him as a kind of
middle-class humanist, a bourgeois with an almost poetical
aspiration after things pleasant and beautiful, is perfectly justified by the facts, perfectly composed in
itself, only we are not sure that he is quite fair to Mrs
Pepys in calling her 'a vulgar woman.' However, this
shall not part us....

Notes

1 'The New Republic; or, Culture, Faith and Philosophy in
   an English Country House' (1877) by William Hurrell
   Mallock (1849-1923).
2 Rev. Thomas McCrie (1772-1835); Stevenson refers to his
   'Life of John Knox' (1812).

24. W. E. HENLEY, REVIEW, 'ACADEMY'

1 April 1882, xxi, 224

In this collection of reprinted pieces - from the 'Cornhill,' from 'Macmillan,' and from the 'New Quarterly' -
there is included not a little very admirable work. Mr.
Stevenson is not less himself - is not less humorous, per-
spicuous, original, engaging - when he is critical of
character and literature than when he takes to discoursing
to bachelors and maids, or playing at travel on Flemish
rivers, or trudging, whimsical and adventurous, behind a
she-ass in the Cévennes. He has most of, if not all, the
qualities that make the critic: an impartial, yet sympa-

thetic, intelligence; a fresh and liberal interest in
life and art and man; a student's patience; an artist's
fine perceptiveness; a passion for all forms and aspects
of truth; a frank, whole-hearted courage; a good method of
analysis; rare distinction of style; and singular powers
of felicitous and appropriate expression. That this is so
the present volume proves abundantly. It is not of equal
and unbroken excellence. In places it seems mistaken, and
in places it is tedious; it is capable of making you nod,
and it is capable of making you swear. But its good matter is good indeed; its bad is only bad in comparison with
its best. Its purpose is serious and critical; and it
achieves its purpose admirably. But, for all that, it
has something of the chief characteristics of its author,
it is touched with something of the fresh and happy grace,
the bright, humane fancy, the engaging originality, that
made such pleasant reading for so many of the 'Inland
Voyage,' of the 'Travels,' and - as I like to think - of
the 'Virginibus Puerisque.'

The 'Studies' are nine in number. They are sufficiently varied in manner and matter. They range from the
fifteenth century to the present time, from the France of
Villon to the Japan of Yoshida-Torajiro, from Knox at
Holyrood to Pepys at Whitehall, from Hugo's novels to the
love-letters of Sylvander and Clarinda. It is much the
same with the style in which they are written and the
spirit of their utterance. Something of the heaviness and
sententiousness of John Knox's prelections seems to have
crept into Mr. Stevenson's accounts of them. In his
charming note on Charles of Orleans he now and then seems
trifling with his subject, much as that subject trifled
always with the Muse. The Yoshida-Torajiro is merely a
piece of plain story-telling; the principal quality of the
Gospel According to Walt Whitman is a kind of luminous
thoroughness; the manner of the study on Villon is one of
picturesque and intelligent contempt, not without hints
and suggestions of an acquaintance with Carlyle. In his
discourse on Hugo's romances, Mr. Stevenson is young, and
as yet not altogether a man of letters; in his essay on
Thoreau he carries mere literary skill - mere mastery of
diction, phrase, and sentence - to a higher point, I
think, than he reaches elsewhere in any one of his works.
Variety indeed is a principal attribute of the book. It
appears not only in the material and style, but in the
temper and tone. Mr. Stevenson's regard for those 'qualities of human dealing' with which he has chosen to concern
himself is uniformly clear-eyed and independent; in honesty of purpose, in sincerity of insight, he seems incapable of change; he is at all times equable and temperate.
But he appropriates his humour to his theme; he alters his
tone as he changes his subject. He is scornful with

Villon and genial with Pepys; he is happily generous with
Whitman as he is sorrowfully just with Burns. He thinks
critically and dispassionately; he writes as his thoughts
have made him feel. He is solemn, or sententious, or
cheerful, just as the study of his author has left him.
Each of his essays is the expression of a fitting and
peculiar mood of morality and intellect. He reproduces
his impressions in effects. He is a critic in method and
intelligence, and an advocate in manner and temperament;
and he makes you glad or sorry as - with his reflections
and conclusions - he has made himself before you. If his
criticism were less acute and methodical than it is, the
accent and the terms in which it is conveyed would sometimes get it mistaken for an outcome of mere aesthetic
emotion. As it is, the critic is equally apparent in it
with the man; you can see that the strong feeling has come
of clear thinking, and what is purely intellectual is
rendered doubly potent and persuasive by the human sentiment with which it is associated. It is possible that
this fact will ultimately militate against the success of
Mr. Stevenson's 'Studies' as criticism; for criticism - a
science disguised as Art - is held to be incapable of passion. I cannot but think, however, that it will always
count for a great deal in their favour as literature, and
that meanwhile it clothes them with uncommon interest and
attraction.

Of the 'Studies' individually, I have left myself no
space to speak. The least interesting - out of Scotland
at all events - are certainly the two essays on John Knox
in his Relations to Women; the least literary is probably
the note on Victor Hugo's Romances; the least strikingly
satisfactory, the story of Yoshida-Torajiro. Better than
any of these, I think, is the critical biography of
Charles of Orleans, which is charming as reading and
unexceptionable as criticism. The note on Some Aspects of
Robert Burns is one of the most powerful and original of
all; it can hardly be neglected by anyone who is interested in its subject; it is worthy (to say the least of
it) of association with Carlyle's famous essay. The paper
on Walt Whitman is, in its way, as good as the Aspects;
that on Thoreau, admirable as a piece of writing, is cold
and negative in its effect, mistaken in its conclusions
(as Mr. Stevenson, in his pleasant and ingenious Preface
by Way of Criticism, has taken care to own), and somewhat too obviously elaborate in method. The Pepys, on the
other hand, is not less admirable than it is delightful;
while as for the Villon, it is in some way the most
remarkable work of all. Mr. Stevenson's Villon is not by
any means the 'Postlethwaite with a jemmy,' (1) with whom
we have got to be familiar. He is - with the addition of
genius and an admirable gift of style - the *mauvais*

pauvre of Hugo, a variant on the Rogue Riderhood of
Dickens; a man utterly heartless, miserably depraved, and
absolutely insincere. He is said to sit 'in the narrow
dungeon of his soul, mumbling crusts and picking vermin;'
and his 'Large Testament' is described as 'one long-drawn
epical grimace, pulled by a merryandrew, who has found a
certain despicable eminence over human respect and human
affections by perching himself astride upon the gallows.'
He is a fearful creature indeed; and he is so horribly
like his poems that it is not easy to disbelieve in him,
or to doubt that he is in very deed the Villon of Noël de
Joly and Colin de Cayeux, the poet of Fat Maggie and the
gibbet, the greatest singer and the sorriest scoundrel of
mediaeval France.

Note

1 George Du Maurier's caricature (which appeared in
   'Punch') of the aesthetic poet, imitator of Swinburne
   and Rossetti.

25. AN UNSIGNED REVIEW, 'BRITISH QUARTERLY REVIEW'

July 1882, lxxv, 212-13

Mr. Stevenson has here given us a book of varieties,
marked by genial insight, humour, and an occasional careless grace peculiar to himself. He writes with great
freedom, and his keenly individual views impart piquancy
to the essays which, perhaps, deeper and more consistent
thought would hardly have sufficed to give, or would at
any rate have failed to aid. For though Mr. Stevenson is
always incisive and clever, full of ingenious hints and
quaint reflections, he is not always consistent - in some
slight degree, as it would seem, acting on the recommendation of Emerson, to speak the feelings of to-day faithfully, and, if necessary, to contradict it flatly to-
morrow. The book consists of nine essays reprinted from
the 'Cornhill' and other magazines. They are pretty well
contrasted in character, and yet all are really treated
in one manner. It is in reality the manner of the satirist who isolates traits that he may find full scope for
the play of his peculiar powers. Victor Hugo, Robert
Burns, Walt Whitman, Thoreau, Francois Villon, Charles of

Orleans, Samuel Pepys, John Knox and Women, Joshida-
Torajiro - a Japanese hero - are the subjects; and as
regards four of them, Mr. Stevenson has found it convenient to make confession in his characteristic Preface
by way of Criticism to the effect that they are admirable
instances of what is oftentimes inevitable in the Essay -
the 'point of view forced throughout, and of too earnest
reflection on imperfect facts.' The Preface is a good
illustration of literary *nonchalance*; but it is withal so
sunshiny and frank that we are fain to accept it for what
it is worth, and to pardon its assumption for the sake of
its ingenuity. A prosaic person might very well argue
that it would have been better in Mr. Stevenson to have
amended his Essays than to have written his Preface; but
then we fear that Mr. Stevenson would, if he liked,
speedily raise the laugh at such a serious, simple-minded
critic's expense. (1) In a word, Mr. Stevenson is *not* a
critic; he is a satirist and humourist of a special type,
so rich in reserve that he does not always know when he is
joking. He tries to deceive himself on very important
matters, and then laughs at his own self-deceptions, so
that he does no despite to the golden rule when he laughs
a quiet little laugh at others. It is of no use being
severe with such a writer, even though he writes on themes
that should demand seriousness: he is sure to discern some
loose and *outré*-looking thread even in the most decorous
garment. The odd thing is that where we should expect him
to be funny he is severe, and not seldom severe where we
should fancy he would be funny. He has little patience
with Villon's blackguardism, and hungry envy, and cynical
philosophizing, always looking back with an air of pretended carelessness to his past enjoyments, but really, as
Mr. Stevenson says, with a grudge of those who could still
find enjoyments in life. We have ourselves, in noticing
Mr. Payne's translation, &c., (2) modestly suggested the
same view. This essay will cause Mr. Stevenson's book to
be viewed with jaundiced eyes by some who might have
puffed it; but still we are grateful to him for having
reprinted it. He sees clearly where Whitman follows
Thoreau and where he departs from him; but he is hardly
fair even yet - even with the modifications of the Preface
by way of criticism - to Thoreau, and is guilty of some
almost unpardonable errors as to facts: one where he puts
a 'he' instead of a 'she,' and thus loses both the superficial and the subtle point of the anecdote. Samuel Pepys
is a delicious bit in its way, and every historical student should read the Essay on John Knox in his Relations
to Women. With Charles of Orleans we are not so well
satisfied, and as to Robert Burns - why! after having discredited Principal Shairp, (3) Mr. Stevenson simply

proceeds to re-erect, in intention, the very structure he
had impugned. Burns's utter cowardice and failure to act
with decision in the testing matter of Jean Armour is the
most fatal charge that can be raised against him from the
moral point of view of Principal Shairp. But Mr. Stevenson sets out by protesting against this point of view, and
finally ends, as it seems to us, by adopting it. But Mr.
Stevenson's book is simply sui generis, and will, no
doubt, find its own way whatever critics may say of it.
The whimsical, paradoxical outré air imparted to it by the
Preface only whets the appetite of the reader.

Notes

1 The reviewer appears to have in mind E. Purcell's
   review of 'Virginibus Puerisque'; see No. 21.
2 John Payne's 'Poems of Master Francois Villon' (1878).
3 Principal Shairp's 'Burns' (1878) in the English Men of
   Letters Series.

26. AN UNSIGNED NOTICE, 'WESTMINSTER REVIEW'

July 1882, lxii, 276-7

Mr. Stevenson is beginning to write too much. He has made
some very bright and pleasant books, and unfortunately he
seems to have become convinced that it is his duty to keep
on making bright and pleasant books indefinitely. He has
been overpraised by enthusiastic friends and reviewers; he
deserved, and still deserves, great praise for his easy
literary style and his fresh quaint fancy; but he is young
enough to take advice, and let us hope not young enough to
consider that he is quite fallible. He has brought
together now some nine essays that have already appeared
in magazines. In the pages of such serial publications
these papers had their fitting place. They were better by
a good deal than the ordinary run of magazine articles.
They were refreshing, for they had ideas, and they were
well written; but there was little or no reason, beyond
the mere pitiful reason of book-making, for binding them
together and sending them out into the world to sham at
being an honest contribution to literature. A volume of
essays may be very delightful reading, much for example as

Mr. Stevenson's 'Virginibus Puerisque' was very delightful
reading. But this is not quite a volume of essays. It is
a volume of magazine articles, each of which is good
enough by itself, while the whole set taken together are
not particularly valuable. Mr. Stevenson seems to suffer
in three ways: First, because he appears to consider that
his judgment of most men and most matters is final;
secondly, because he entertains the impression that his
style is akin to that of Thackeray; thirdly, because he
conceives it as his duty to regard everything from some
new and startling point of view; to take up one side of
every question simply because the other is the more
generally accepted. There is an unpleasant affectation
of laying down the law running through all these pages,
which would make not a few readers inclined to quarrel
with him out of sheer weariness at his eternal swagger.
When he writes of Robert Burns and Robert Burns's faults,
Mr. Stevenson affects a cheap tone of superiority towards
the Ayrshire singer which is rather absurd. Mr. Stevenson
is quite right when he points out that 'Marcus Aurelius
found time to study virtue, and between whiles to conduct
the Imperial affairs of Rome' while Thoreau 'was so busy
improving himself that he must think twice about a morning
call,' and he does well to censure him for venturing in
his theory of life 'not one word about pleasure, or
laughter, or kisses or any quality of flesh and blood.'
But we should like also some readier, or at least some
more obvious, acceptance of the greatness that was in
Thoreau. Mr. Stevenson undoubtedly admires him, but it
is his trick to dwell more on those points wherein he
depreciates than those wherein he appreciates his subject.
The article on Francois Villon does not greatly please its
author, because he considers it to be 'too picturesque.'
It does not greatly please us, but for a different reason.
We find no fault with it for being too picturesque. This
is its most agreeable quality. In the pathetic, melancholy, poetically fanciful paper on Master Samuel Pepys,
we have Mr. Stevenson, if not at his best, at least in
very good form indeed, and we are glad of it, and wish
the volume had been all of a piece with this. But we must
pronounce the volume, as a whole, tiresome and lengthy.
Expectations which were inspired by any book bearing the
name of the author of the story of The Pavilion on the
Links have not been gratified here, and we close the book
with some pleasure at its being finished, and some regret
to find we think so.

27.   GRAHAM BALFOUR, FROM A LETTER TO STEVENSON ON WHITMAN
AND 'FAMILIAR STUDIES'

25 February 1887, B, 3929

Sir Graham Balfour (1858-1929) first met Stevenson, his
cousin, in Samoa in 1892; he lived with the Stevensons
at Vailima until a short time before Stevenson's death
in December 1894. Balfour was requested to undertake the
official biography when the privilege was withdrawn from
Colvin. Aside from his biography of Stevenson, Balfour
was known for his administrative work in education and his
'Educational Systems of Great Britain and Ireland' (1898),
which became a standard work in its field; he was knighted
in 1917. In the following extract Balfour tells of a
visit made to Whitman's house in Camden, New Jersey, in
November of 1885.

Several comments by Whitman on Stevenson are found in
Horace Traubel, 'With Walt Whitman in Camden' (1905, 1959,
1964). On 18 May 1888, when questioned on Stevenson: 'I
never met him, but his wife has been here in Camden -
visited me. I do not think I would have cared for him,
all in all, for a companion: he was rather morbid and
more than a bit whimsical - lacking, I am sure, in guts -
guts: a man, a sure man, must have guts. Stevenson was
friendly to me - has rare gifts: I do not dispute his
powers: considering his persistent illness, his rather
black background, is rather sunny, rather cheerful. Yes,
he was complimentary to the "Leaves": not outrightly so -
saying yes with reservations: but being a man in whom I
dare not waits upon I would he does not state his conviction unequivocally. You have seen what he has written
about the "Leaves" - his first view, the after-
qualifications. His wife assured me that he felt far more
strongly on the subject than he wrote. I have read
Stevenson - some, not much. I tried "Dr. Jekyll and Mr.
Hyde" but did not get along with it: I tried some of the
short stories: I felt that I should know about them: but
the thing wouldn't work: I couldn't make a connection, so
I gave up trying' (vol. 1, 145-6). On 30 December 1888
Whitman comments on Stevenson's popularity: 'Stevenson
appears to be famous: all the things of the world that
go to make a man famous seem to be his: I confess I do not
enthuse in the slightest degree myself' (vol. 3, 422). On
5 April 1889 Whitman again remarks on Stevenson's popularity: 'Stevenson is the man on top these days - most in
vogue: popular, sellable, accepted' (vol. 4, 491).

On the table, among piles of papers and several of the
well-known grey hats, was lying open your 'Familiar
Studies'. Whitman, after talking of America, and of himself, asked what I could tell him of the fellows over in
England, the literary men, and if I knew them. Humbly I
made the most of you, and he said that only the day before
he had received the 'Studies' with Messrs. Chatto and
Windus' compliments, but he had only read the Burns. He
did not seem to have read the preface, as he complained
that the Essay was too depreciatory. Carlyle's to him
seemed still the best word on Burns, though he admitted
that Carlyle might require a corrective. But the critic's
function was to see, (as Heine said, and as Heine practised), 'What does the author mean, what would he be at?'
and not to point out that he ought to have done something
entirely different. I argued, but, no doubt, a more complete reading of your book brought fuller conviction, but
unfortunately on the way back I did not see Whitman
again.... Did you, by the way, ever hear of the London
bookseller's clerk, for whom the title of 'Virginibus
Puerisque' proved altogether too much, so that he entered
it in my bill as 'V. Peerage'?

'New Arabian Nights'

July 1882

The first volume of 'New Arabian Nights' contained stories
that had appeared in 'London' (8 June - 26 October 1878)
under the title Latter-Day Arabian Nights. The second
volume contained four stories, Pavilion on the Links
('Cornhill', September 1880), A Lodging for the Night
('Temple Bar', October 1877), The Sire de Maletroit's
Door ('Temple Bar', January 1878), and Providence and the
Guitar ('London', 2-23 November 1878).

28. GEORGE SAINTSBURY, FROM AN UNSIGNED REVIEW 'PALL MALL
GAZETTE'

4 August 1882, xxxvi, 4

On Saintsbury see headnote to No. 23. E. J. Mehew has
identified this review as Saintsbury's from two unpublished letters Stevenson sent Henley (National Library of
Scotland). In the first Stevenson refers to the 'Athenaeum' review (an unsigned review by E. T. Cook which
appeared on 12 August) as a 'confused intelligence in
revolt against Saintsbury's exaggerations'. In a second
letter he mentions 'Saintsbury's plaining cry for the
"Nights" in "P.M.G."'.

Whether any of the admirers of Mr. Stevenson's previous
works will shake their heads over this we cannot say, and
do not care to guess; but it may be said that if the

publication does not gain him a new and goodly contingent,
why then the public must confess its inability to appreciate the purely fantastic in literature. Many of the
characteristics of the author's better known work are conspicuously absent here. There is no buttonholing of the
reader, no attempt at moralizing, no conceits of phrase,
or at least very few, most of which are simple Gallicisms.
The chief characteristic which reappears is Mr. Stevenson's
excellent faculty of description, which is here thoroughly
in place. For the 'New Arabian Nights,' at least the
first volume, which alone originally bore and now properly
bears the title, are fantastic stories of adventure, with
the scene pitched in contemporary London or Paris, but
with a noble disregard of probability, not to say possibility, in the facts which is worthy of Poe or Balzac or
of the authors of the 'Thousand and One' themselves, and
with not a little of the imaginative force of these masters. We have used the word 'originally' because these
stories are not now published for the first time, though
it is exceedingly improbable that one in a hundred of
their readers will know where they appeared before. The
original form Mr. Stevenson does not seem, as far as
memory serves us, to have altered in any material degree.
Perhaps he was right; for the things are so obviously
written in a jet of humorous fancy that to alter them in
cold blood might have spoiled them. As it is, we deliberately consider them to be, with considerable faults,
exceedingly good and original things in fiction. They
have been called fantastic, but they are more than that -
they are extravagant. As far as they have any common subject, that subject is the adventures and experiences of
Prince Florizel of Bohemia - a gentleman who, probably
finding the Seven Castles dull and yachting on the coast
of his native country tedious, abides chiefly in London
and Paris and sees life therein. There are two subdivi-
sions, each of which is independent of the other, but each
of which is in its turn subdivided; these are The Suicide
Club and The Rajah's Diamond.
    We shall not attempt to give the faintest hint of the
subject of the various tales - The Story of the Young Man
with the Cream Tarts, The Story of the Physician and the
Saratoga Trunk, The Adventure of the Hansom Cabs, The
Story of the Bandbox, Of the Young Man in Holy Orders, Of
the House with the Green Blinds, The Adventure of Prince
Florizel and a Detective. The last two are distinctly
inferior to the others, and The Rajah's Diamond as a whole
is not equal to The Suicide Club. But, as great part of
the attraction of the story consists in the preposterous
character of the incidents, to indicate these would simply

be to spoil the reader's pleasure. That pleasure (it is
necessary to define it for the sake of some good people
to whom the book will probably be a simple mystification)
consists in the contrast of the fertility of extravagant
incident, grim or amusing or simply bizarre, with the
quiet play of the author's humour in the construction of
character, the neatness of his phrase, the skill of his
description, the thoroughly literary character of his
apparently childish burlesque. The stories are by no
means faultless. More than one of them is hastily and
inartistically wound up. In more than one, also, are
there slips - which, indeed, no writer in this kind, save
perhaps Poe, has ever avoided - in the introduction of
irrelevant details which are neither explained nor con-
tribute in any way to the explanation of the story. But
after making every allowance for this and for minor de-
merits, we must place the 'New Arabian Nights' very high
indeed, almost *hors concours*, among the fiction of the
present day.

The second volume also contains reprinted stories, but
from much better known sources, and, as we think, of much
less interest. The longest, The Pavilion on the Links,
has merits of its own, but it is of a much more ordinary
kind than The Suicide Club or The Rajah's Diamond; and,
indeed, partakes, as do all the stories in this part of
the book, rather of the 'Household-Words'-Christmas-number
character, though of course Mr. Stevenson's pen imbues
the style with a distinction which it has not always
possessed. A Lodging for the Night, in which Mr. Stevenson's very unfavourable notion of Francois Villon finds
concrete expression; The Sire de Malétroit's Door,
another mediaeval French story with pretty passages and a
pleasant ending; and Providence and the Guitar, likely to
be the most generally popular of all, complete the book.
But these many men might have written, and others like
them many men have. Of the 'Arabian Nights' proper this
can hardly be said. We cannot call them masterpieces, for
that word is not lightly to be used, and they have, as has
been noted, not a few defects; but they show, in our
opinion, a much more original talent, and one much better
worth cultivating, than anything else that Mr. Stevenson
has done. The few and easy strokes with which he builds
up characters; the skill with which they play their parts
in a condition of things preposterous, indeed, but never
actually impossible or calculated to pull the reader up
with the reflection, 'This is nonsense;' and the cool
determination with which Mr. Stevenson carries off his
topsy-turveyfications - all these things are admirable....

29. W. H. POLLOCK, FROM AN UNSIGNED REVIEW, 'SATURDAY REVIEW'

19 August 1882, liv, 250-1

William Herries Pollock (1850-1926), author and journalist, was sub-editor, then editor (1883-94) of the 'Saturday Review'. E. J. Mehew has identified this review as Pollock's on the basis of an unpublished letter from Stevenson to Henley dated around 21 August 1882 in which Stevenson says: 'Pollock, I must say, has written a handsome and discriminating notice; he thinks too well of the Pavilion; but most of what he says is good as criticism and very kindly said. I warmed to him like fun' (National Library of Scotland).

Since the days of Athos, Count de la Fère, and of the other Count of Monte Cristo, we have not met in fiction a more attractive personage than Prince Florizel of Bohemia, who is the central figure of Mr. Stevenson's 'New Arabian Nights.' He combines the dauntless courage and the *grand seigneur* ways and views of life of Athos with the boundless wealth and resource of Monte Cristo, while he has also a princely gaiety and good humour which belonged to neither of the illustrious persons to whom we have compared him. The stories in which he figures, and of which we may try to give such an account as will not spoil their interest for readers, are some of the most thrilling and inventive that we have read. They have indeed, and in this we pay their author a very high compliment, not a little of the magnificent extravagance that lent so great a charm to the stories written by the creator of Athos and Monte Cristo. Their faults are faults which are the more irritating because they could have been so easily removed. They lack finish and care. One is annoyed in the middle of an exciting tale to come upon such a slip on the part of the author as his representing a lieutenant in the British army as being introduced and addressed with 'Lieutenant' prefixed to his name; or, again, at finding that a person living on one side of a canal has seemingly crossed over to the other side and swum back again with a knife in his mouth, for no other reason than that he may appear dripping wet before the people who are waiting concealed for him. In the same story we hear of 'a very tall black man with a heavy stoop' who refuses to accede to a

certain extravagant proposition with a weight and impressiveness of manner and speech that lead us to suppose he
knows something of what is going on and is going to play
an important part in the action. One turns page after
page in the expectation of hearing something more of the
very tall black man with the heavy stoop, and he never
appears again. Such slips as these, however, we can forgive far more easily than the curiously ill-judged burlesque ending which Mr. Stevenson has put to the adventures of Prince Florizel and Colonel Geraldine, who
corresponds to the Vizier in 'The Thousand and One Nights.'
The reader has followed the fortunes and the amazing and
stirring adventures of the Prince with unwavering interest
which suffers but little from such pieces of carelessness
as are above referred to. He reads anxiously up to the
last line of the last adventure, and he might be content
to rest there, wishing indeed for more, but thankful for
the enjoyment which he has got, and free to form his own
conclusions as to the secret of the Prince's mysterious
influence and power and as to his future fortunes. Then
Mr. Stevenson turns round upon the reader with a statement
that 'as for the Prince, that sublime person having now
served his turn, may go, along with the *Arabian Author*,
topsy-turvy into space.' This is, at least in the original sense of the word, impertinent enough; not to the purpose, since no reader of intelligence can wish to be
reminded that Prince Florizel is merely a device of Mr.
Stevenson who has 'served his turn.' But the statement
which follows for the benefit of those imaginary persons
who 'insist on more specific information' is much worse.
Nothing could well be more inartistic, or more calculated
to offend a reader whose admiration for the Prince and for
the invention to which he and his delightful adventures
are due has been so long aroused, than to suddenly find
him disposed of with such a feeble and facetious conclusion as one might expect to find given by an unwise imitator of Mr. Gilbert's style of humour. We could wish
indeed that this last paragraph of Mr. Stevenson's first
volume could be blacked out like articles supposed to be
dangerous in English newspapers sent to Russia. However,
until one comes to this last paragraph, there is little
but pleasure to be got out of the 'New Arabian Nights,'
with their striking fertility of invention, their charming
touch of a chivalry which is by no means too common either
in real life or in fiction, and that other quality of the
author's, also by no means too common, of making his
readers sup full with horrors and yet putting no offence
in it. Even another quality, in itself a fault, that of
a seeming disinclination to be at the trouble of

unravelling various threads in the stories, is not without
its attraction, since it leaves an additional element of
mystery for the reader's mind to play with. Yet the
author has not shrunk, in the paragraph above referred to,
from pulling down the whole fabric of splendour and
knightly valour which he has raised for our delight, and
suddenly turning the dazzling figure of a hero who in the
thick of modern life meets with adventures, and does deeds
not less startling than those of the *Mousquetaires*, into
the common type of foreign refugee with which we are only
too familiar in the pages of many would-be comic writers.
However, this unpleasant surprise comes at the very end of
the 'New Arabian Nights,' and therefore in no way injures
the enjoyment of reading the stories through straight on
end, as they are certain to be read by any one who once
takes the book up.

The first story in the series, a series which up to the
very end is constantly full of new surprises and of daring
and successful touches of character, is called The Suicide
Club, with the sub-title of Story of the Young Man with
the Cream Tarts. Prince Florizel and his Master of the
Horse, Colonel Geraldine, each disguised, are walking
about near Leicester Square in search of adventures, and
turn into an oyster bar, where their attention is caught
by the strange eccentricity of the Young Man with the
Cream Tarts. They carry him to dinner at a restaurant in
Soho, and the speech with which the Prince addresses him
after dinner is at once attractive and characteristic both
of the author and of the traits which he assigns to Prince
Florizel: - 'You will, I am sure, pardon my curiosity.
What I have seen of you has greatly pleased but even more
puzzled me. And though I should be loth to seem indiscreet, I must tell you that my friend and I are persons
very well worthy to be entrusted with a secret. We have
many of our own, which we are continually revealing to
improper ears. And if, as I suppose, your story is a
silly one, you need have no delicacy with us, who are two
of the silliest men in England. We pass our lives
entirely in the search for extravagant adventures; and
there is no extravagance with which we are not capable of
sympathy.' Thus adjured by the Prince, who passes under
the name of Mr. Godall, while Colonel Geraldine assumes
that of Major Hammersmith, the Young Man proceeds to
recount his history.

The story of the Young Man in its essence is ordinary
enough, though it is told with great brevity in a manner
which is far from ordinary, but its telling is the first
link in the chain of wonderful things which befall Prince
Florizel and his associates. In the first place it leads

to the Prince vowing vengeance against the infamous President of this Club, a vengeance which he proposes to attain with the chivalry which is part of his nature, and it is the pursuit of this vengeance which serves in the most natural way to introduce us to the extravagant and charming events and characters that fill the stories....

Not less startling than the first series is the second series of the Nights, which has the general title of The Rajah's Diamond, and not less instinct with a noble, yet reckless, justice is its conclusion. Through all the stories there runs a vein of exaltation, which is more than enough to carry off their extravagance and to make a reader both believe and delight in them, and all of them are full, underneath the extravagance, of true and happy turns of thought and expression. In The Pavilion on the Links, which occupies a considerable part of Mr. Stevenson's second volume, we get upon slightly different grounds. Extravagance is here replaced by wild but serious adventures, which are so told as to carry with them a complete air of probability. Nothing could be more exciting in its way than the dangers which Northmour and his friends run while they live prepared for a siege from their mysterious enemies in a house on the Links. But the story has rarer qualities than skilful management of exciting incidents to recommend it. The characters of Northmour, of Cassilis, of Clara, and of the repulsive, canting, fraudulent banker are all, from the nature of the case, little more than sketches in extent; but the touch is at once so bold and fine that the characters are anything rather than sketchy in the ordinary sense of the word. We get an impression of knowing them, as in real life one may know certain people of marked personality after but few and brief meetings. The story has yet another quality - pathos - which is very seldom put forth by writers of fiction, as it here is, with perfect taste. Throughout the story of Clara and Cassilis there runs an exquisite and dignified tenderness....

Of the shorter stories which help to make up the volume, of which the greater part is given to The Pavilion on the Links, it is difficult, for want of space, to speak adequately. All have originality and, it is hardly too much to say, a touch of genius; in some ways, perhaps, the story of Villon, called A Lodging for the Night, is the most remarkable. The general effect of the two volumes is to make us wish for more of the same kind, but more carefully finished, from the same pen.

30.   D. C. LATHBURY AND MRS LATHBURY, UNSIGNED REVIEW,
'SPECTATOR'

11 November 1882, 1v, 1450-2

Mrs Bertha Lathbury remains unidentified except as the
author of 'Thoughts and Fancies' (1913) and the wife of
Daniel Connor Lathbury (1831-1922), journalist and joint-
editor of 'The Economist' (1878-81); editor of the
'Guardian' (1883-99); and of the 'Pilot' (1900-4).
Lathbury likewise edited Gladstone's 'Correspondence on
Church and Religion' (1910). The reviewers answer charges
made in the 'Athenaeum' (12 August 1882) and the 'Saturday
Review' (No. 29) that Stevenson's stories were carelessly
designed and executed.

The first thing that strikes the reader of Mr. Stevenson's
'New Arabian Nights,' is that he is tasting two pleasures
at once. Every great novelist has a style of his own, and
we soon learn to think each appropriate to the use to
which it is turned. But Mr. Stevenson tells a story in a
style so finished and so admirable, that it constitutes a
distinct enjoyment in itself. So told, we seem to feel,
any story would be worth reading. There is no need to
give ourselves this assurance, because the matter of the
stories here collected is singularly original and effective. But though original and effective stories are sufficiently uncommon, they are less uncommon than the excellent English in which these are conveyed. The title
properly belongs to the first volume only. In this, the
form of the 'Arabian Nights' is fairly preserved. The
Caliph Haroun Alraschid has his representative in Prince
Florizel of Bohemia, and in the first story the very cream
tarts of the original are reproduced in the copy. But the
resemblance goes no farther. The 'New Arabian Nights'
deal with adventures, wild enough, indeed, for the far-
thest East and a distant century, but supposed to take
place in London and Paris, amidst the most modern surroundings. The incidents are as strange and startling as
in the best of Mr. Wilkie Collins's stories, but improbable or impossible as they are, they do not seem so,
because the actors in them behave with perfect consistency. The draft on our credulity is made once for all,
and when it has been duly honoured, we are never reminded
how large it was in the first instance.

In the first, or Arabian, volume, the most telling
story is the Suicide Club. Prince Florizel, of Bohemia,
and his attendant, Colonel Geraldine - who represent, for
Mr. Stevenson's purpose, the Caliph and the Grand Vizier -
are introduced by a young man, whom they find selling
cream tarts in Leicester Square, into the secrets of a
society organised for the easy accomplishment of suicide
by means of mutual murder. All that is demanded of the
neophyte is weariness of life, and £40 in money. The
Prince and the Colonel profess the one and produce the
other, and they promptly find themselves in a room, of
which the 'single tall window looked out upon the River
and the Embankment; and by the disposition of the lights,
they judged themselves not far from Charing Cross Station.'
Here assemble each night a little band of members pledged
to decide, by the fall of the cards, which shall kill and
which be killed. The Club exists for the benefit of a
president, who pockets the money and provides the entertainment. Various members of the Club are drawn with
great spirit, and the excitement attaching to the fatal
deal which conveys the signal of death and murder is fully
shared by the reader. The succeeding chapters, although
complete tales in themselves, link themselves on to the
first story; while the adventures of Prince Florizel are
brought to a close in another series of tales, called The
Rajah's Diamond. If one or two of these hang fire a
little, the interest revives again in The House with the
Green Blinds; and the closing chapter of the volume is a
particularly happy specimen of the author's grace of
style and expression. When the diamond finds its final
resting-place, we can wish for no better conclusion to a
series of adventures which have kept our interest alive to
the last.
In the second volume, the tales are less distinctive,
and in becoming less fanciful they lose, perhaps, a little
of their charm. But in one, at least, of them, if the
originality is not so striking, the word-painting can
hardly be surpassed. The story of a night in the life of
Francois Villon is a drama of remarkable power. The very
atmosphere itself bespeaks the story. 'It was late in
November, 1456. The snow fell over Paris with rigorous,
relentless persistence; sometimes, the wind made a sally,
and scattered it in flying vortices; sometimes, there was
a lull, and flake after flake descended out of the black
night air, silent, circuitous, interminable.' What night
could be more fitted as a background to the scene where
Villon and his thievish companions are gambling, and pre-
paring the way for the murder which was to send the poet
out on his quest for A Lodging for the Night. 'A great

pile of living embers diffused a strong and ruddy glow
from the arched chimney. Before this straddled Dom
Nicolas, the Picardy monk, with his skirts picked up and
his fat legs bared to the comfortable warmth. His dilated
shadow cut the room in half.... On the right, Villon and
Guy Tabary were huddled together over a scrap of parch-
ment, Villon making a ballade, which he was to call the
Ballade of Roast Fish, and Tabary spluttering admiration
at his shoulder. The poet was a rag of a man, dark,
little, and lean, with hollow cheeks and thin, black,
locks.... Greed had made folds about his eyes, evil
smiles had puckered his mouth.... It was an eloquent,
sharp, ugly, earthly countenance. His hands were small and
prehensile, with fingers knotted like a cord; and they
were continually flickering in front of him, in violent
and expressive pantomime.' This was Villon, at the age of
twenty-four. As the scene is described, the reader seems
to be watching the various players in that far-off tragedy
- each absorbed in his own mean interest, but all united
in a confraternity of evil. Two of the party, Montigny
and Thevenin Pensete, are playing a game of chance; while
Villon is stringing rhymes together, and picturing the
storm without, after his own wild fashion: -

Thevenin was just opening his mouth to claim another
victory, when Montigny leaped up, swift as an adder,
and stabbed him to the heart.... The four living
fellows looked at each other in rather a ghastly
fashion, the dead man contemplating a corner of the
roof with a singular and ugly leer. 'My God!' said
Tabary, and he began to pray in Latin. Villon broke
out into hysterical laughter. He came a step forward,
and ducked a ridiculous bow at Thevenin, and laughed
still louder. Then he sat down suddenly, all of a
heap, upon a stool, and continued laughing bitterly, as
though he would shake himself to pieces. Montigny recovered his composure first. 'Let's see what he has
upon him,' he remarked, and he picked the dead man's
pocket with a practical hand, and divided the money
into four equal portions on the table.

The spoil divided, and Villon unwittingly robbed of his
share by the Picardy monk, the party slip out one by one,
to try and lose their identity until the affair should be
blown over. After all, a dead man was not such an
unusual customer in a Paris tavern of the fifteenth century. The snow made the city light through its whiteness.
Where are the guilty spirits to hide themselves? Villon
is the first to depart, and try his fortune in the great

city that lies asleep before him. His own vivid pictures
arise before him. He sees the gallows of Montfaucon, upon
which he had so lightly rallied his companion but a short
half-hour before. His nervous memories quicken his steps.
Along the deserted street comes the patrol, and Villon
stumbling under a ruined hotel to keep himself from their
notice, finds himself once more in the presence of death.
This time it is a woman frozen to death in the pitiless
snow of that November night, with her whole substance
summed up in two small coins, which she had not lived long
enough to spend. The poet's heart can still be touched by
the sense of pathos which the woman's hard fate awakes in
him. But the softened mood gives way to mad rage, when
he discovers that he has been robbed of his own ill gotten
gains: -

> Suddenly, his heart stopped beating; a feeling of cold
> scales passed up the back of his legs, and a cold blow
> seemed to fall upon his scalp. He stood petrified for
> a moment; then he felt again, with one feverish move-
> ment; and then his loss burst upon him, and he was
> covered at once with perspiration. To spendthrifts,
> money is so living and actual, - it is such a thin veil
> between them and their pleasures. There is only one
> limit to their fortune, - that of time; and a spend-
> thrift with only a few crowns, is the Emperor of Rome
> until they are spent.

Driven to despair, where is he to turn for the night's
lodging which stands between him and a possible death
through starving cold? His adopted father, the Chaplain
of St. Benoit, drives him from his door, well knowing his
applicant, and deaf to his entreaty for help. Once more
Villon turned into the inhospitable streets, to break, if
need be, into a lodging, if none offered itself peaceably
to him. The freezing cold began to play its part, and the
pictures of inviting food and warmth that his artistic
imagination conjured up did not add comfort to the desperate man. A glimmer of light at last announced that in one
house its inhabitants were on the move. Villon knocked
boldly at the door, and, to his own surprise, met with a
courteous reception at the last from a perfect stranger.
In the person of the old French knight, Mr. Stevenson
catches the spirit of the century. The large apartment was
lighted 'by a great lamp, hanging from the roof. It was
very bare of furniture, only some gold plate on a sideboard, some folios, and a stand of armour between the windows.' 'I am alone in my house,' said the old man, 'and
if you are to eat, I must forage for you myself.' His

host gone to find him food, the Devil once more awakes in
Villon. The furniture, if scanty, was rich in quality.
The gold plate on the sideboard might help to supply the
purse which his companion of the evening had robbed him
of. How subtly Mr. Stevenson draws the calculating spirit
of the poet-thief. 'Seven pieces of plate,' he said. 'If
there had been ten, I would have risked it.' These words
give us the key to the whole situation, - the patrician
host, calm in his dignified courtesy; the poet himself
calculating closely the chances of success, if he made a
daring robbery. At one moment, his courage seems equal to
his avarice; at the next, he quails before the question
the blood upon his shoulder gives rise to. This strange
medley of conflicting purposes runs through the conversation which follows. Both saw life from their own point of
view, and no sympathy could spring up between them. Then,
as now, the contest was unequal. The pillage which the
old man called honourable in war, the poet justified in
himself when he practised it for a livelihood in times of
peace. Such reasoning is always ready, when the discussion is between two fearless spirits of unequal rank. Mr.
Stevenson, however, has managed to make it fresh to his
readers, from the originality of the surroundings, but it
adds, possibly, a little too much weight to an otherwise
perfect work of art.

Stories like those which Mr. Stevenson has written
naturally suggest the question as to what place such writing holds in literature. They are not novels, and they
hardly pretend to describe real life. Strictly speaking,
they are grotesque romances, in which the author has
allowed himself a considerable licence as to probability
of incident. To compare him with another writer of something of the same kind, Mr. Stevenson's treatment of the
impossible is bolder than that of Bulwer Lytton, who
shelters himself behind the supernatural as soon as
probability ceases. He bears more resemblance to the
elder Dumas, than to any English author; but in Dumas,
the intensity of writing is stronger, and the excitement
of the reader far more stimulated, than in the slighter
sketches of the 'New Arabian Nights.' We can imagine
Dumas losing himself in his characters, and believing in
his stories, while Mr. Stevenson gives us the impression
of being outside both. He is the stage manager skilfully
directing his actors, while he never ceases to regard them
from the point of view of pure art. He has the advantage,
however, of Dumas in the subtle humour which pervades
everything he writes. As a collection of grotesque romances, the 'New Arabian Nights' are perfect in form and
finish; and such an aim is not only legitimate in itself,

but constitutes a fresh departure in romance-writing.

31.   AN UNSIGNED NOTICE, 'WESTMINSTER REVIEW'

January 1883, lxiii, 284

In opening a new book by so popular an author as Mr.
Stevenson, one naturally expects to be charmed, and
especially as in the present case the book has, in a few
months, reached a second edition; we must confess, however, that 'The New Arabian Nights' fails to realize our
anticipations.   The stories seem to us far-fetched and
improbable, without ever rising above commonplace; some of
them are even silly and frivolous ; e.g., The story of the
young man with the cream tarts.   In all of them there is a
straining of the sensational effect which sometimes
attains to ghastliness, but never to romance.   The style,
too, is frequently forced and affected; one pervading
affectation being the use of French idioms literally
translated into English.   Quite un-French, however, is a
certain haziness of expression which in its milder form
dimly shadows forth the writer's meaning, leaving much to
the ingenuity and goodwill of the sympathetic reader;
while in more aggravated cases it expresses something
which the writer assuredly did not intend.   A somewhat
amusing instance of this latter kind is to be found in the
story entitled The Adventure of the Hansom Cabs, where one
of the characters is in such poignant suspense that he
breaks out into a sweat of agony, or, according to Mr.
Stevenson, 'an agony of sweat,' a form of words more suggestive of the Turkish bath than of intensity of emotion.
If, however, Mr. Stevenson has a slight tendency to amphi-
bology, he may comfort himself with the reflection that it
is a thorough English defect.   Has not Mr. Arnold told us
that we 'want lucidity'?   A graver fault than any mere
defect of style is the morbid tone which more or less runs
through all the stories.   They are feverish, unwholesome
reading.   The original 'Arabian Nights' no doubt left much
to be desired on the score of moral edification, but they
possess in an extraordinary degree the merit of local
colouring.   Perhaps no other book, whether of fiction or
of travels, ever brought the East so clearly and fascin-
atingly before the eyes of European readers.   In that
sunny land of mirage and unreality, peopled by Genii, and

where everything is brought about by enchantment, a
stringent moral code could hardly be expected to obtain,
but Mr. Stevenson's tales are Arabian only in name, the
suicides, robberies and murders, which form their subject
matter are perpetrated in our own day, not further off
than London or Paris, and the treatment and colouring are
essentially modern and realistic. Consequently in our
opinion they much too nearly resemble glorified and mundane 'Penny dreadfuls' - with royal princes, general
officers, physicians, and clergymen for *dramatis personae*
- to be regarded as legitimate successors of 'The Arabian
Nights.'

32. H. C. BUNNER, UNSIGNED REVIEW, 'CENTURY MAGAZINE'

February 1883, xxv, 628-9

Henry Cuyler Bunner (1885-96) was a New York journalist
and writer. Stevenson, writing to W. H. Low on 23 October
1883, asked him to

> thank Mr. Bunner (have I the name right?) for his
> notice, which was of that friendly, headlong sort
> that really pleases an author like what the French
> call a 'shake-hands.' It pleased me the more coming
> from the States, where I have met not much recognition,
> save from the buccaneers, and above all from pirates
> who misspell my name. I saw my book advertised in a
> number of the 'Critic' as the work of one R. L.
> Stephenson; and, I own, I boiled. It is so easy to
> know the name of the man whose book you have stolen;
> for there it is, at full length, on the title-page of
> your booty. But no, damn him, not he! He calls me
> Stephenson. These woes I only refer to by the way, as
> they set a higher value on the 'Century' notice.
> (LS, ii, 160-1)

A few months ago an English book made its appearance in
this country, handicapped with the name of 'New Arabian
Nights.' It was, for a time, no more warmly welcomed than
might have been the 'New Rabelais,' or 'A Nineteenth Century Nibelungen Lied,' or 'Robinson Crusoe' with all the

modern improvements. Then, by and by, one or two of the
chorus of indolent reviewers glanced at the first page,
read the second, and of a sudden found themselves *bolting*
the rest of the book, and finding stomach for it all, even
as in boyhood they swallowed whole the indigestible
'Radcliffe.' But this new feast had a fine literary smack
to it, and it assimilated readily to the mental system.
These reviewers found a chance to say of the book a good
word in a general way to the public, and a good word in a
particular way to their friends, and 'New Arabian Nights'
passed from hand to hand until it came about that a large
and steadily widening circle of readers was asking if Mr.
Robert Louis Stevenson had written any more books like
this, or if he were likely to write more. For the 'New
Arabian Nights' turned out to be no new 'Arabain Nights'
at all; but a very different and surprising something
which is much more easily read at full length than
described in a few words.

On the face of it, the book is a collection of short
stories, each differing from each, every one distinct and
singular, yet all linked together by the adventures of one
central character, who is half Monte Cristo and half
Haroun Al Raschid up to the last page, where in an unexpected fashion he leaves you laughing at him, laughing at
yourself, and wondering how long his inventor has been
laughing at you both.

This is the book on the face of it. But then, in fact,
you cannot speak of the book on the face of it, for under
the face is a fascinating depth of subtleties, of ingenuities, of satiric deviltries, of weird and elusive forms of
humor, in which the analytic mind loses itself. It would
be possible to give a synopsis of the series; to tell how
Prince Florizel of Bohemia, accompanied by his Master of
the Horse, Colonel Geraldine, wander in disguise about
London, meeting with many strange haps and mishaps; how
from being a mere spectator, the Prince becomes an all-
important agent in the affairs of others, always super-
naturally successful, ubiquitous, all-powerful, brave,
gracious, wise, and kingly, - the ideal prince, the charming, incredible, cavalier apology for the monarchical
principle. It would be possible to give an idea of the
many delicate touches by which this character is created
and vivified before the reader's very eyes. It would be
possible to show how the flavor of the original 'Arabian
Nights' is caught and kept by the mere suggestion of an
imitation of the style and language. It would not be
difficult to show how the Story of the Young Man with the
Cream Tarts leads into the Story of the Physician and the
Saratoga Trunk, and that in turn into the Adventure of the

Hansom Cabs, the three together introducing us to the
Suicide Club and gratifying us with its complete and final
dissolution; how the Rajah's Diamond glitters through the
Story of the Band-box, the Story of the Young Man in Holy
Orders, the Story of the House with the Green Blinds, and
the Adventure of Prince Florizel and a Detective; how it
exerts a baleful influence upon the lives of many people
who in the ordinary course of things would have no single
interest in common; how Florizel appears at just the moment he is wanted, and puts all things right by virtue of
his royalty and his conversational powers, and how, in the
end, having served his turn, as the author remarks, he is
hurled by a revolution from the throne of Bohemia, 'in
consequence of his continued absence and edifying neglect
of public business,' and now keeps a cigar store in Rupert
street, London, much frequented by other foreign refugees.
'He has an Olympian air behind the counter,' says Mr.
Stevenson, 'and although a sedentary life is beginning to
tell upon his waistcoat, he is probably, take him for all
in all, the handsomest tobacconist in London.'

But were all this told at far greater length, it would
give but a vague notion of the characteristic power and
charm of the work. Of course, the passage just quoted is
clearly a piece of exquisite fooling - a piece of keen
satire, too, this upsetting of one's *deus ex machina* when
one has done with him. But there is more behind it than
fooling or satire. Any one who reads the 'Nights' and the
four stories that are bound with them must be struck by
the author's versatility, his power of picturesque
description, his skill in drawing character with half a
touch, and his all-pervading humor.

Yet it seems to us that the qualities we have indicated
do not give the key-note of Mr. Stevenson's genius, or
whatever one may please to call a faculty one of the most
original that we have met since the appearance of Bret
Harte. The new author has a power that is strongly akin
to the dramatic. He juggles with his readers and with his
characters. He dresses up a puppet and tells you it is a
man, and you believe it, and hold your breath when the
sword is at the puppet's breast. Then he holds up the
stripped manikin and smiles maliciously. With him, men
and ideas are but literary properties, to be used as he
sees fit, for this or that effect. In The Pavilion on the
Links he offers you an ordinary English magazine story of
the 'sensation' sort, very well done. And if one's blood
must be curdled, 'twere well the curdling were done
secundum artem. A Lodging for the Night gives an episode
in the life of Francois Villon, told with a realism that
is at once brutal and poetic; it is the strongest piece

of work in the book.   It is followed by The Sire de Malétroit's Door, - another mediaeval French theme, handled,
this time, in the pure romantic style.   And then there is
an odd little conceit, where laughter comes near the line
of tears, to end one of the brightest, boldest, most
stimulating books that modern fiction has given us.

It is worth noting here that the two French stories
mentioned above seemingly owe their being to Théodore de
Banville's 'Gringoire.'   They are not thefts; they imply
merely a reversion to the fundamental ideas of the Frenchman's work, and a re-creation from those bases.   This is
neither blameworthy nor unnatural, for Mr. Stevenson is,
as we all have found out now that we have made his
acquaintance, a critic and a scholar, an essayist and a
traveler, whose brilliant and original work has made him
only a local reputation these many years.   'An Inland
Voyage,' 'Travels with a Donkey in the Cévennes,' 'Virgin-
ibus-Puerisque,' 'Edinburgh, Picturesque Notes,' and a
volume called 'Familiar Studies of Men and Books,' which
has a pungent flavor to the jaded palate of the most
wearied student of over-biographed writer-folk and their
over-criticised works, - all these, with a delightful
and suggestive little Gossip on Romance, in the first
number of Longman's new English magazine, are to be had by
those who, having read the 'New Arabian Nights,' will want
something more by Mr. Stevenson.

33.   G. M. HOPKINS, FROM A LETTER TO R. W. DIXON

15 August 1883

From 'The Correspondence of G. M. Hopkins and R. W. Dixon'
(1935), ed. C. C. Abbott, 114.

Gerard Manley Hopkins (1844-89) was a Jesuit priest and
poet whose small body of remarkable poetry remained unpublished during his lifetime.   When editions of Hopkins's
work appeared in this century (in 1918 and 1930), the
poetry was to exercise a strong influence on modern poets.
Richard Watson Dixon (1833-1900) was a historian, a poet,
and a divine.

A friend recommended me if I met with them to read

L. Stevenson's stories, the 'New Arabian Nights' and
others since. I read a story by him in 'Longman's', I
think, and a paper by him on Romance [A Gossip on Romance,
'Longman's', November 1882]. His doctrine, if I apprehend
him, is something like this. The essence of Romance is
incident and that only, the type of pure Romance the
'Arabian Nights': those stories have no moral, no
character-drawing, they turn altogether on interesting
incident. The incidents must of course have a connection,
but it need be nothing more than that they happen to the
same person, are aggravations and so on. As history consists essentially of events likely or unlikely, consequences of causes chronicled before or what may be called
chance, just retributions or nothing of the sort, so
Romance, which is fictitious history, consists of event,
of incident. His own stories are written on this principle: they are very good and he has all the gifts a
writer of fiction should have, including those he holds
unessential, as characterisation, and at first you notice
no more than an ordinary well told story, but on looking
back in the light of this doctrine you see that the persons illustrate the incident or strain of incidents, the
plot, *the story*, not the story and incidents the persons.
There was a tale of his called the Treasure of Fourvières
[the Treasure of Franchard, 'Longman's', April and May
1883] or something like that; it is the story of an old
treasure found, lost, and found again. The finding of
the treasure acts of course and rather for the worse upon
the finder, a retired French doctor, and his wife; the
loss cures them; you wait to see the effect of the refind-
ing: but not at all, the story abruptly ends – because its
hero was, so to say, this triplet of incidents. His own
remarks on the strength and weakness of the Waverleys are
excellent. But I have been giving my own version of the
doctrine (which is, I think, clearly true) rather than his
for I do not remember well enough what he says.

'Treasure Island'

November 1883

34. STEVENSON ON 'TREASURE ISLAND', FROM LETTERS TO
W. E. HENLEY

August, September 1881

(a) From a letter dated by Colvin 25 August 1881. By
'crawlers' Stevenson means the bogey stories or ghost
stories he was at the time working on with his wife.

... See here - nobody, not you, nor Lang, nor the devil
will hurry me with our crawlers. They are coming. Four
of them are as good as done, and the rest will come when
ripe; but I am now on another lay for the moment, purely
owing to Lloyd, this one; but I believe there's more coin
in it than in any amount of crawlers: now, see here, 'The
Sea Cook, or Treasure Island: A Story for Boys'.
    If this don't fetch the kids, why, they have gone
rotten since my day. Will you be surprised to learn that
it is about Buccaneers, that it begins in the 'Admiral
Benbow' public-house on the Devon coast, that it's all
about a map, and a treasure, and a mutiny, and a derelict
ship, and a current, and a fine old Squire Trelawney (the
real Tre, purged of literature and sin, to suit the infant
mind), and a doctor, and another doctor, and a sea-cook
with one leg, and a sea-song with the chorus 'Yo-ho-ho and
a bottle of rum' (at the third Ho you heave at the capstan
bars), which is a real buccaneer's song, only known to the
crew of the late Captain Flint (died of rum at Key West,
much regretted, friends will please accept this intima-
tion); and lastly, would you be surprised to hear, in this
connection, the name of *Routledge*? (1) That's the kind of
man I am, blast your eyes. Two chapters are written, and

124

have been tried on Lloyd with great success; the trouble
is to work if off without oaths. Buccaneers without oaths
- bricks without straw. But youth and the fond parent
have to be consulted.

And now look here - this is next day - and three chapters are written and read.... All now heard by Lloyd,
F[anny Stevenson], and my father and mother, with high
approval. It's quite silly and horrid fun, and what I
want is the *best* book about the Buccaneers that can be
had....

A chapter a day I mean to do; they are short; and perhaps in a month 'The Sea Cook' may to Routledge go,
yo-ho-ho and a bottle of rum! My Trelawney has a strong
dash of Landor, as I see him from here. No women in the
story, Lloyd's orders; and who so blythe to obey? It's
awful fun boys' stories; you just indulge the pleasure of
your heart, that's all; no trouble, no strain. The only
stiff thing is to get it ended - that I don't see, but I
look to a volcano. O sweet, O generous, O human toils.
You would like my blind beggar [Pew] in Chapter III I
believe; no writing, just drive along as the words come
and the pen will scratch! (LS, ii, 51-2)

(b) Extract from a letter dated September 1881. The £100
refers to the amount Alexander Japp thought 'Young Folks'
would be willing to pay for serialization rights; they
paid Stevenson by the page, however, and he received
£37 7s. 6d. 'Jerry Abershaw: A Tale of Putney Heath' was
the title of a highway story that for a time Stevenson
seriously considered writing.

.... The £100 fell through, or dwindled into somewhere
about £30. However, that I've taken as a mouthful, so
you may look out for 'The Sea Cook, or Treasure Island:
A Tale of the Buccaneers', in 'Young Folks'. (The terms
are £2, 10s. a page of 450 words; that's not noble, is it?
But I have my copyright safe. I don't get illustrated -
a blessing; that's the price I have to pay for my copyright.)

I'll make this boy's business pay; but I have to make a
beginning. When I'm done with 'Young Folks', I'll try
Routledge or some one. I feel pretty sure the 'Sea Cook'
will do to reprint, and bring something decent at that....

I propose to follow up 'The Sea Cook' at proper intervals by 'Jerry Abershaw: A tale of Putney Heath' (which is
its site I must visit), 'The Leading Light: A Tale of the
Coast', 'The Squaw Men: or the Wild West', and other
instructive and entertaining work. 'Jerry Abershaw' should

be good, eh? I love writing boys' books. This first is
only an experiment: wait till you see what I can make 'em
with my hand in. I'll be the Harrison Ainsworth of the
future; and a chalk better by St. Christopher; or at least
as good. You'll see that even by 'The Sea Cook'.

Jerry Abershaw - O what a title! Jerry Abershaw: d——n
it, sir, it's a poem. The two most lovely works in English; and what a sentiment! Hark you, how the hoofs ring!
Is this a blacksmith's? No, it's a wayside inn. Jerry
Abershaw. 'It was a clear, frosty evening, not 100 miles
from Putney,' etc. Jerry Abershaw. Jerry Abershaw.
Jerry Abershaw. 'The Sea Cook' is now in its sixteenth
chapter, and bids for well up in the thirties. Each three
chapters is worth £2, 10s. So we've £12, 10s. already.

Don't read Marryat's 'Pirate' anyhow; it is written in
sand with a salt-spoon: arid, feeble, vain, tottering production. But then we're not always all there. *He* was *all*
somewhere else that trip. It's *damnable*, Henley. I don't
go much on 'The Sea Cook'; but, Lord, it's a little
fruitier than the 'Pirate' by Cap'n. Marryat.

Since this was written 'The Cook' is in his nineteenth
chapter.... (LS, ii, 53-5)

Note

1 Cassell & Co. was the eventual publisher, following
   serialization of the story in 'Young Folks'.

35. THOMAS STEVENSON, FROM A LETTER TO R. L. STEVENSON
ON BEN GUNN AND THE OPPORTUNITY TO 'INTERJECT A LONG
PASSAGE ... OF A RELIGIOUS CHARACTER'

26 February 1882, B, 5771

The character Ben Gunn appears in ch. xv, The Man of the
Island. It is clear from the chapter in its finished
form that Stevenson followed some of his father's advice.
Ben Gunn has been on the island for three years; he mentions his pious mother and her predictions of his down
fall, which began 'with chick-farthen on the blessed
gravestones'; he is attired in 'tatters of old ship's
canvas and old sea cloth' (though later in the chapter
Stevenson erroneously refers to the 'marooned man in his

goatskins'). While Ben Gunn says 'it were Providence that
put me here' and promises that he has returned to pious
ways, the chapter contains nothing approaching a religious
tract.

The character painting which is so well done in the early
chapters drops a good deal after getting to the island and
necessarily must for you pass from that kind of work into
blood and thunder and this cannot be altered. But I think
you should intermit this tragic work if possible and I
think you have a good opportunity with Ben Gunn. I would
interject a long passage then of a religious character. I
would have him ask if Jim had ever been at some little
port [?] village, say Mousehole near Penzance [?] and
whether he had ever seen or heard of his father or mother.
The want of such an inquiry strikes me as unnatural. Then
I would have him regret the fatal day on which he had run
away from his home and some pathetic passage should follow
as to what he had lost and what troubles he had passed
through and something about his misspending of Sundays and
something about the Minister of the place and the sayings
of his father or his mother and so forth. So far as I can
see this is the only way of harking back to something
higher than mere incident. Perhaps some story of his
going with a companion and netting or nutting in the woods
on Sunday and his mother's objurgations. In short you
might have here a striking and pathetic passage to relieve
the more bloody work which goes after. I object to the
goatskin dress and hat which is merely R. Crusoe and his
running down goats which is the same. He ought to have
some tattered naval uniform for a coat and ragged canvas
trousers. You must not have him left for more than 3
years on the island. I want you to make a real point of
his breaking away from home and this should be a kind of
religious *tract* and should be fully done but all in the
Defoe style.

Stevenson's answer to his father appears in an undated
letter in the National Library of Scotland:

I highly and thoroughly agree with you as to Ben Gunn. I
had meant to dwell on Benjamin later on, and never had
room for him; but as you say, we'll put a whole religious
tract in that very place. I cannot give up the goats: the
phrase 'they're all mast-headed on them mountings for the
fear of Benjamin Gunn' amuses me so much. My own feeling

is to re-write most of it from the beginning of the story,
or say Chapter III and Chapters VII to XV inclusive.
After Chapter XV, there is I think a marked improvement;
and Silver at the end is all my fancy painted him. But
I'll have your views on this.

36. AN UNSIGNED NOTICE, 'ACADEMY'

1 December 1883, xxiv, 362

The reviewer is unidentified, but in a letter to Stevenson
dated 25 November (B, 4772) Henley remarks that a 'friend'
hopes to write the 'Academy' review.

Mr. Stevenson has treated a well-worn theme with freshness. His story is skilfully constructed, and related
with untiring vivacity and genuine dramatic power. It is
calculated to fascinate the old boy as well as the young,
the reader of Smollett and Dr. Moore and Marryat as well
as the admirer of the dexterous ingenuity of Poe. It
deals with a mysterious island, a buried treasure, the
bold buccaneer, and all the stirring incidents of a merry
life on the Main. Mr. Stevenson's buccaneers are not of
the heroic age that Kingsley sang; they know nothing of
pleasant isles in the glowing tropic seas; their traditions are not of good Queen Bess and the hated Spaniard;
they do not swagger in picturesque attire and drink
canary; they belong, in short, to the more prosaic era of
the Georges. But they are not less individual and rather
more entertaining. They are, for the most part, superlative and consistent villains. They cannot inspire the
most enthusiastic youth with a desire for the return of
the glorious age of buccaneering. Their profession is not
set forth in a dangerous halo of romance, nor are their
deeds made alluring through a familiar moral process by
which crimes are mitigated with the milk of sophistry.
Mr. Stevenson deserves praise not alone for this. He has
dared to depict an island the sole attraction of which
lies in its hidden treasure. With a healthy realism he
has avoided that false and specious luxuriance which
denaturalises the action of a story by placing its actors
out of harmony with their surroundings. His island is no

garden of Eden, where all the products of all the zones
thrive in happy ignorance, and where the modern representatives of the Swiss Family Robinson may find all to their
liking and life certainly worth living. It has its draw-
backs as well as its piratical hoard, but it is portrayed
in several vivid pictures with the truth and precision of
nature. In the opening chapters only may be detected a
discordant touch. Here the events are a little too melodramatic and the narrative somewhat strained. The affray
with the revenue officers and the discovery of the chart
of the island are cleverly managed and form an ingenious
prelude. The blind sailor, Pew, is an exception to the
author's otherwise excellent delineations. After we have
recovered from the thrilling shudder he causes, we feel
that he is an anomaly, monstrous, irrelevant - a transitory spasm of nightmare in a coherent story. This, however, is a slight matter. The dramatic verse of the
narrative is not less striking than its unflagging spirit.
The invention is rich and ready, the dialogue abounds in
pith and humour, while the characters - particularly the
sailors - are drawn with great force and distinction.
Among these is one who stands out with the prominence of
one of Cooper's or Marryat's heroes. Long John Silver
is a creation. There is not so much of the salt about
him as might be desired, but there is no gainsaying his
merit. We may long to hang him, or wish him a bad end,
in the final chapter, but it is impossible not to be
interested in him. With all our knowledge of this abandoned ruffian, of his treachery, his craft, and his abominable wickedness, it is surprising how his humour and
cynicism move us to admiration. There is not a false
touch in the portrait; the character has all the complexity of a humorist, and is painted with unerring consistency. The scheme by which this cold-blooded villain
seduces the crew to mutiny is detailed with admirable
irony and humour. The owner of the ship treats his men
with a leniency that almost parallels that of Capt. Reece,
commander of the *Mantelpiece*. How their ingratitude and
criminal designs are divulged - how the island is reached,
and becomes the theatre of the most exciting events - and
how Long John eventually comes off - the book must tell.
We can only add that we shall be surprised if 'Treasure
Island' does not satisfy the most exacting lover of perilous adventures and thrilling situation; he can scarcely
fail to share in the anticipations of Jim Hawkins, the
relater of this sea yarn, when he finds himself on board
the *Hispaniola*, 'with a piping boatswain and pig-tailed
singing seamen, bound for an unknown island and to seek
for buried treasure.'

37.   ARTHUR JOHN BUTLER, UNSIGNED REVIEW, 'ATHENAEUM'

1 December 1883, 2927, 700

See headnote to No. 18. 'Treasure Island' was the first
of nine volumes reviewed in a section entitled Christmas
Books. The 'Athenaeum' files identify Butler as the
reviewer.

Any one who has read 'The New Arabian Nights' will recognize at once Mr. Stevenson's qualifications for telling a
good buccaneer story. The blending of the ludicrous with
the ghastly, the commonplace with the romantic, of which
that book offered examples in plenty, is just what a tale
of the search for a pirate's treasure demands. Mr.
Stevenson's genius is not wholly unlike that of Poe, and
one might almost suspect that the germ of 'Treasure
Island' is to be found in the Gold Beetle, and especially
in its last sentence; but it is Poe strongly impregnated
with Capt. Marryat. Yet we doubt if either of those
writers ever succeeded in making a reader identify himself with the supposed narrator of a story, as he cannot
fail to do in the present case. As we follow the narrative of the boy Jim Hawkins we hold our breath in his
dangers, and breathe again at his escapes. The artifice
is so well managed that when, for a few chapters, Jim
disappears, and the story is taken up by a shrewd doctor,
who is never in much danger, the change is felt as a sensible relief. And yet, artistic as the book is, one cannot help feeling that the art is a little too patent.
Partly, no doubt, this arises from the fact of the story
being laid in the last century. It is given to very few
people so to throw themselves into a past age as to avoid
all appearance of unreality. In the heroic style this
does not matter; but the more real the characters, the
more does the difference between the views of one age and
another show itself. To take an author already named,
'Snarleyvow' is one of the feeblest of Marryat's novels.
In the common phrase, a story of this kind is seldom
wholly free from the 'smell of the lamp.' To a reader who
can discount this (if one can discount a smell!) it matters little; but it may be doubted whether Mr. Stevenson
will succeed as well as inferior artists in pleasing the
public whom his story might seem best adapted to reach -
the boys. Even if they do not feel the difficult already

indicated, they will demur to his too philosophic rejection of poetical justice in allowing the arch-scoundrel
to escape the fate which overtakes all his accomplices.
In real life John Silver would hardly have got off; he
certainly ought not to do so in fiction.

38. W. E. HENLEY, UNSIGNED REVIEW, 'SATURDAY REVIEW'

8 December 1883, lvi, 737-8

This review is tentatively identified as Henley's on the
basis of his letter to Stevenson of 25 November (B, 4772):
'Lang is after it for the "P.M.G."; I for the "S.R."; a
friend for the "Academy"; Runciman for the "Standard".'

Buried treasure is one of the very foundations of romance.
To our thinking, there are no such enchanting passages in
the 'Arabian Nights' themselves as those in which the
hero, alone in the mysterious desert, comes suddenly, even
promiscuously, on an iron ring in the earth, and, lifting
the trapdoor to which it is attached, descends by a neat
stone staircase into a subterranean chamber chastely furnished with brazen jars, which on examination prove to be
filled to the brim with sequins, or gold-dust, or diamonds
and emeralds of the largest size and the purest water.
Aladdins's lamp and ring are, after all, no more than
talismanic introductions to the hoard of the djinns, which
is an example of buried treasure on the largest and cost-
liest scale; the secret of the cave where Ali Baba
spoiled the forty robbers of their ill-gotten gains is but
a variation on the same delightful theme - at the back of
it there is buried treasure in its most romantic shape.
What is El Dorado itself but an ideal of discovery and
hidden wealth? To many of us The Gold Beetle is Poe's
best story. To many of us the interest of 'Monte Cristo'
culminates in the discovery of the hoards of Caesar
Borgia. To many of us Facino Cane lighting on the secret
bank of the Venetian Republic is one of the most striking
of Balzac's many wonderful and moving inventions. The
scheme looks noble and adventurous which has for its
object the rescue of doubloons and ingots from between the
ribs of tall galleons, sunk long ages back in mysterious

nooks of ocean. The pirate who so far respected himself
as to deal in treasure-hiding becomes at once heroic. To
have buried moidores and pieces-of-eight in islets off the
Spanish Main is to have deserved well of romance and the
arts. Kidd is a hero by virtue of his buried gold; and
the memory of Execution Dock itself is powerless to break
the spell and ruin the tradition.

    This is the theory on which Mr. Stevenson has written
'Treasure Island.' Primarily it is a book for boys, with
a boy-hero and a string of wonderful adventures. But it
is a book for boys which will be delightful to all grown
men who have the sentiment of treasure-hunting and are
touched with the true spirit of the Spanish Main. It is
the story of the monstrous pile which Flint, the great
pirate, buried, with extraordinary circumstances of
secresy and ferocity, on an unknown islet; and it sets
forth, with uncommon directness and dexterity, the adventures of certain persons who went in search of the cache,
and returned to Bristol city with seven hundred thousand
pounds in all the coinages of the world. It contains a
delightful map (a legacy from Flint himself), a hoard that
will bear comparison with Monte Cristo's own, a fort, a
stockade, a maroon, and one of the most remarkable
pirates in fiction. Like all Mr. Stevenson's good work,
it is touched with genius. It is written - in that
crisp, choice, nervous English of which he has the
secret - with such a union of measure and force as to be
in its way a masterpiece of narrative. It is rich in
excellent characterization, in an abundant invention, in
a certain grim romance, in a vein of what must, for want
of a better word, be described as melodrama, which is
both thrilling and peculiar. It is the work of one who
knows all there is to be known about 'Robinson Crusoe,'
and to whom Dumas is something more than a great *amateur*;
and it is in some ways the best thing he has produced.

    Mr. Stevenson deals but sparingly in landscape and the
emotional analysis of emotion. He makes his personages
explain themselves. (What he is most interested in is his
story.) In his very first paragraph he gives us a foretaste of all the many delights of the book. 'I take up my
pen,' says Jim Hawkins, the boy-hero, 'in the year of
grace 17—, and go back to the time when my father kept
the "Admiral Benbow" inn, and the brown old seaman with
the sabre cut first took up his lodgings under our roof.'
The brown old seaman is a tremendous and ferocious rascal;
'a tall, strong, heavy, nut-brown man,' Jim Hawkins
writes, with a 'tarry pigtail,' hands 'ragged and scarred,
with black, dirty nails,' and 'the sabre cut across his
face a dirty, livid white.' He consumes immense

quantities of rum; he settles his score in blasphemies
and threats; he is always singing, to himself or the
'Admiral Benbow's' guests, in 'a high old tottering voice
that seemed to have been tuned and broken at the capstan
bars,' a certain reckless and desperate shanty –

> Fifteen men on the dead man's chest,
>   Yee–ho–ho and a bottle of rum,
> Drink and the Devil had done for the rest –

and so forth; he is full of oaths and wicked stories –
'about hanging, and walking the plank, and storms at sea,
and the Dry Tortugas, and wild deeds and places on the
Spanish Main.' What is more, he is in daily and nightly
terror of men of his own profession; he is always looking
out to sea through a brass telescope; and he engages Jim
Hawkins at fourpence a month (the only debt he ever pays)
to keep his 'weather' eye open for a seafaring man with one
leg.' For some time the captain (so he dubs himself) pur--
sues his wicked way unchecked; he roars, he swaggers, he
bullies the company, he takes down unlimited rum, he even
ventures on a brash with Dr. Livesey, the village physician, and is severely worsted. But at last, though not in
the shape he had feared, his fate swoops down upon him.
One day there comes to the 'Admiral Benbow' a leering,
evil-looking mariner, with two fingers slashed from his
left hand. This gentleman, who answers to the name of
Black Dog, beards the captain, though with visible reluc-
tance. He is presently put to flight by that awful ship-
man, who gashes him badly on the shoulder, and, after
pursuing him for some little distance, comes back to the
inn and has a fit on the parlour floor. When Dr. Livesey,
of whom he is much afraid, strips his arm to bleed him, he
find it neatly tattooed with piratical devices – a gallows, 'Billy Bones his Fancy,' and such like; and when,
restored to something like his right mind and threatened
with death if he persists in his habit of rum, he finds he
is too weak to get away, as he is wild to do, he breaks
into strange and tremendous confidences: –

[Quotes ch. iii, from '"Jim," he said, "you saw that seafaring man today?"' to '"But you won't peach unless they
get the black spot on me, or unless you see that Black Dog
again, or a seafaring man with one leg, Jim – him above
all"'.]

As it falls out, these confidences are more or less useless. Jim's father, who is ailing, dies that same night;
and the next day the pirate comes downstairs, and goes to

work on the rum. He gets weaker and angrier and more
drunken than ever; but his time is up, and he has death
and terror on every hand of him. The day after the fun-
eral Jim is standing at the inn door, when he sees 'some
one drawing slowly near along the road. He was plainly
blind, for he tapped before him with a stick, and wore a
great green shade over his eyes and nose; and he was
hunched, as if with age or weakness, and wore a huge old
tattered sea cloak with a hood, that made him appear
positively deformed.' Addressing him in the true blind
man's whine, this dreadful apparition implores to be led
into the 'Admiral Benbow.' No sooner, however, does Jim
take hands with him than 'the horrible, soft-spoken, eye-
less creature' grips him as in a vice, playfully wrenches
his joints for him, and, in a voice 'so cruel and cold and
ugly' that he never heard the like of it, commands him to
take him in to the captain. That mariner is absolutely
overwhelmed by the visit. He allows the black spot -
'that's a summons, mate' - to be put upon him without
resistance; and, as soon as his guest has withdrawn
(which he does 'with incredible accuracy and nimbleness'),
he falls 'from his whole height face foremost to the
floor.' That is the end of old Flint's first mate, the
redoubtable Billy Bones. Of course Jim Hawkins knows
that there is worse than death behind, that the black
spot has been passed, and that in a very little while all
Flint's crew will be down at the inn after Billy Bones's
chest. He tells his mother all he knows; and she, after
vainly asking help of her neighbours, determines to search
the chest, and pay the pirate's score with whatever she
may find. By the pirate's corpse they pick up the
dreaded spot - 'a little round of paper blackened on one
side,' and on the other, 'written in a very good, clear
hand,' the words, 'You have till ten to-night.' Tied to
the dead man's neck they find the key of the chest. It
is only six o'clock, and they have a good four hours
before them; so they at once proceeded to make an inventory of Billy Bones's assets. Among these are a very
good suit of clothes, 'carefully brushed and folded - they
had never been worn, my mother said; 'a quadrant, a tin
canikin, several sticks of tobacco, two brace of very
handsome pistols, a piece of bar silver, an old Spanish
watch and some other trinkets of little value and mostly
of foreign make, a pair of compasses mounted with brass,
and five or six curious East Indian shells'; 'an old boat
cloak, whitened with salt on many a harbour bar', with 'a
bundle tied up in oil-cloth and looking like papers,' and
'a canvas bag that gave forth, at a touch, the jungle of
gold.' Mrs. Hawkins is obstinate to take no more than her

due; and while she is hunting out the English coins in
Billy Bones's very miscellaneous savings something happens. 'I suddenly put my hand upon her arm,' says Jim,
'for I had heard in the silent frosty air a sound that
brought my heart into my mouth - the tap-tapping of the
blind man's stick upon the frozen road.' What follows
shall be told by none but Mr. Stevenson himself. It is
too good and alarming to be paraphrased; and, besides, to
take it out piecemeal would spoil the excitement and
interest of the book.

As yet, it will be noted, the terrible seafaring man
with one leg has not yet put in an appearance. When he
does, he is so fascinating, and looks so innocent, that
Jim Hawkins fails to recognize him. He turns up in
Bristol, in the person of a certain John Silver, landlord
of the 'Spyglass,' a tavern frequented by seamen. He is
a big fellow, 'very tall and strong, with a face as big as
a ham; plain and pale, but intelligent and smiling'; his
left leg is cut off at the hip, and he carries a crutch,
which he manages with 'wonderful dexterity, hopping about
on it like a bird.' He has travelled all the world over;
he has a black wife; he is master of a parrot named Captain Flint; he is so helpful and clever, so smooth-spoken
and powerful and charming, that everybody is deceived in
him, and that to have him as cook aboard the *Hispaniola*,
searching for Treasure Island and Flint's hoard, is to
the leaders of the expedition the greatest piece of luck
imaginable. Of course he makes himself the most useful
of men while the ship is fitting out, and of course a
considerable proportion of the crew are of his discovery
and recommendation. The consequences are plain to the
meanest capacity. There is a mutiny and they hoist the
black flag, the noble Jolly Roger; there are fights and
murders and adventures; only a few of the expedition
escape with their lives; and it is all John Silver's
doing. John Silver, in fact, is Flint's old quarter-
master, and the bloodiest and most dangerous villain of
all Flint's crew of villains. His wickedness is the
wickedness of a man of genius; he has no heart, but he
has any amount of character and brains; he is a desperado
of the worst type, but entirely passionless - a kind of
buccaneering Borgia; in victory and defeat alike he main-
tains a magnificent intellectual superiority - to himself,
his comrades, and his circumstances; and when at last he
disappears from the story, you are glad that he has not
gone the way of his companions (shot, drowned, stabbed,
marooned), but has got off to his old negress with a
whole skin and a bagful of pieces-of-eight. There are
many good characters and sketches of character in the

book - Dr. Livesey, Squire Trelawney, Captain Smollett,
Billy Bones, Ben Gunn the maroon (a study of singular
freshness and originality), the horrible blind pirate,
Jim Hawkins himself; but Long John, called Barbecue, is
incomparably the best of all. He, and not Jim Hawkins,
nor Flint's treasure, is Mr. Stevenson's real hero; and
you feel, when the story is done, that the right name of
it is not 'Treasure Island,' but 'John Silver, Pirate.'

39.   STEVENSON, LETTER TO W. E. HENLEY

December 1883, LS, ii, 162-3

Stevenson's opening remarks answer Henley's objections to
his seamanship in 'Treasure Island'. Presumably Henley
expressed these in an earlier letter to Stevenson; there
are certainly no such objections in No. 38. Stevenson
says below, 'I'm glad to think I owe you the review that
pleased me best of all the reviews I ever had.' If No. 38
is indeed the review referred to, then this letter would
date from December rather than November, the date assigned
it by Colvin. (E. J. Mehew dates the letter from mid-
December.)

My Dear Lad,
    .... Of course, my seamanship is jimmy; did I not be-
seech you I know not how often to find me an ancient
mariner - and you, whose own wife's own brother is one of
the ancientest, did nothing for me? As for my seamen, did
Runciman (1) ever know eighteenth century Buccaneers? No?
Well, no more did I. But I have known and sailed with
seamen too, and lived and eaten with them; and I made my
put-up shot in no great ignorance, but as a put-up thing
has to be made, i.e. to be coherent and picturesque, and
damn the expense. Are they fairly lively on the wires?
Then, favour me with your tongues. Are they wooden, and
dim, and no sport? Then it is I that am silent, otherwise not. The work, strange as it may sound in the ear,
is not a work of realism. The next thing I shall hear is
that the etiquette is wrong in Otto's Court! With a warrant, and I mean it to be so, and the whole matter never
cost me half a thought. I make these paper people to

please myself, and Skelt, (2) and God Almighty, and with
no ulterior purpose. Yet am I mortal myself; for, as I
remind you, I begged for a supervising mariner. However,
my heart is in the right place. I have been to sea, but I
never crossed the threshold of a court; and the courts
shall be the way I want 'em.

I'm glad to think I owe you the review that pleased me
best of all the reviews I ever had; the one I liked best
before that was ── 's on the 'Arabians.' (3) These two are
the flowers of the collection, according to me. To live
reading such reviews and die eating ortolans - sich is my
aspiration.

Whenever you come you will be equally welcome. I am
trying to finish 'Otto' ere you shall arrive, so as to
take and be able to enjoy a well-earned - 0 yes, a well-
earned - holiday. Longman fetched by 'Otto': is it a
spoon or a spoilt horn? Momentous, if the latter; if the
former, a spoon to dip much praise and pudding, and to
give, I do think, much pleasure. The last part, now in
hand, much smiles upon me. - Ever yours,

R.L.S.

Notes

1   James Runciman (1852-91), a journalist and teacher
    associated with Stevenson and Henley as sub-editor of
    the 'London'. His review of 'Treasure Island', if
    indeed he wrote one, has not been identified, though
    Henley (B, 4772) reported to Stevenson that he sought
    to review it for the 'Standard'.
2   The illustrator of popular figures from drama and
    melodrama. Skelt's Juvenile Drama was the subject of
    Stevenson's A Penny Plain and Twopence Coloured, the
    'Magazine of Art', April 1884.
3   W. H. Pollock's review (No. 29).

40.   AN UNSIGNED REVIEW, 'PALL MALL GAZETTE'

15 December 1883, xxxviii, 4-5

This review is probably by Andrew Lang; Henley's letter to
Stevenson dated 25 November 1883 (B, 4772) indicates that
Lang wanted to review 'Treasure Island' for the 'Pall

Mall Gazette'.

A book for boys which can keep hardened and elderly
reviewers in a state of pleasing excitement and attention
is evidently no common Christmas book. No one but Mr.
Stevenson could have written 'Treasure Island,' for no one
else has his vivid imagination combined with his power of
drawing character, his charm of style, and his grave,
earnest, perfectly boyish delight in a storm, a shipwreck,
a sword combat for two or more. Mr. Stevenson probably
wrote 'Treasure Island' for his diversion; it has the ease
and fluency of work that is done in play. Certainly he
has contributed more to the diversion of one critic than
all the serious and laborious novelists of the year have
done. The question may be asked, will 'Treasure Island'
be as popular with boys as it is sure to be with men who
retain something of the boy? Our opinion of boys will
fall considerably if 'Treasure Island' is not their perennial favourite. Of all things boys enjoy chapters about
boys from the pens of really great writers. What can be
so thrilling and moving as 'the Little Boy's Dance,' in
'Vanity Fair,' the fight between Cuff and old Figs, the
spirited rally between Berry and Biggs, the boyhood of
David Copperfield, the infancy of Pip in 'Great
Expectations'? To the last narrative, especially to the
splendid scenes between Pip and the convict, we would
liken the beginning of 'Treasure Island.' When the hero
of that volume is a small boy at the lonely seaside inn,
during the last century, when the bullying, robbing sea
captain comes and bids the lad warn him if a one-legged
man makes his appearance, we are carried back to the
youth of Pip. And why does the braggart captain, with
his endless song -

   Drink and the Devil had done for the rest,

why is he as afraid of the one-legged man as the tyrant
was of the man with one shoe? That is the secret, which
is not solved when first another bully comes for the captain, and then a cruel blind beggar, his staff tapping on
the frozen roads, comes, and tortures the boy, and fright-
ens even bold bad Captain Bones into an apoplexy. But
before dying the captain has warned the boy, 'If they tip
me the black spot, it's my old sea-chest they're after.'
Unluckily we have not Captain Johnson's 'Lives of Eminent
Pirates' (1) at hand. But, apparently, the 'black spot'
is the sign which a pirate crew show their captain when

they mean to revolt against his authority. The inn-
keeper's son and his mother, on the captain's death, pay
his bill out of his loose cash, and the boy secures an
oilskin-covered parcel. Just in time they secure it, for,
says the hero, 'I had heard in the silent frosty air a
sound that brought my heart into my mouth - the tap,
tapping of the blind man's stick upon the frozen road.'
The buccaneers search the inn, cannot find the parcel, and
are routed by the revenue officers, the awful blind beggar
being killed in the affray. Then the boy shows his parcel
to the doctor and the squire; they recognize the chart of
an isle where treasure is hidden - of course 'in the
Spanish main' - and off they set to secure the moidores.
The squire being a talkative man, his object gets known,
and the buccaneers (the dreaded one-legged man and all)
form the greater part of his crew. This one-legged man is
a perfect hero of crime, and clearly a great favourite of
the author's. A cold-blooded murderer, he has yet such
excellent manners, is such a clever 'opportunist,' such an
ingenious, plausible, agreeable double-dyed traitor, that
one can hardly help siding with him in his plots and
treasons, and rejoicing when, after all, he escapes clean
away from poetical justice. Out of Thackeray we scarcely
know where to find John Silver's parallel, and he might
have appeared with credit in the gallery of Barry Lyndon.
It were too long to tell all the adventures of the
treasure-seekers, and, besides, it would spoil the fun.
Of course, the boy-hero performs wonderful exploits; safe
in an empty apple-barrel overhears mutineers plotting;
defeats their plans on the island, and (a delightful
horrible scene, this) boards and captures the ship, where
the two drunken guards have fought to the death of one of
them and the wounding of the other. The fight in the
rigging between the boy and the wounded pirate holds the
reader breathless, as does the scene when the boy is captured by the one-legged man, and is in danger of torture.
The skeleton which holds the secret of the treasure is,
however, too like an idea of Poe's. The reticence in the
matter of 'word-painting' is most praiseworthy, and the
description of the island - a horrible, commonplace,
foggy, yet haunted island - is eminently original. It is
clear that fiction is a field in which Mr. Stevenson is
even stronger than in essay and in humorous and sentimental journeying. After this romance for boys he must give
us a novel for men and women.

Note

1   Captain Charles Johnson, 'A General History of the
    Robberies and Murders of the Most Notorious Pirates,
    etc.' (*c*.1724).

41.   UNSIGNED REVIEW, 'GRAPHIC'

15 December 1883, xxxviii, 599

The warmest admirer of Mr. Robert Louis Stevenson would
probably find it difficult to say what precise quality in
his writings it is which gives them such keen and peculiar
pleasure.   It is not only his perfect mastery of style, -
a mastery which entitles Mr. Stevenson almost alone among
living writers to be called classic, - it is something
more than his unique imaginative power.   These are things
one can name; but in their combination something further
suggests itself to the mind, something for which it would
almost appear criticism has yet to find a name.   There is
no need to inquire why, after giving us such a rare piece
of fiction as 'The New Arabian Nights,' Mr. Stevenson
should choose to present us with a story for boys.   It
seems whimsical- but it would be grudging to resent an
apparent decline in choice of subject when the story for
boys is such a one as 'Treasure Island,'   It is a tale,
says Mr. Stevenson, in his introductory stanzas 'To The
Hesitating Purchaser,' of 'storm and adventure, heat and
cold, of schooners, islands, and maroons, and buccaneers
and buried gold, and all the old romance, retold exactly
in the ancient way,' and further on he suggests a comparison between himself and 'Kingston and Ballantyne the
Brave, or Cooper of the Wood and Wave.'   Needless to say
there is no resemblance between Mr. Stevenson and any
other boys' writer, and this romance is told in anything
but the ancient way.   In 'Treasure Island' there is combined with an imagination far stronger than that of any
of the writers named, a power of expression unique in the
literature of our day, and an insight into character, and
a capacity to depict it, unsurpassed, and almost unsurpas-
sable.   This was a bold experiment, this resuscitation of
tales of buried treasure in the Spanish Main, the mutiny,
the buccaneer, the stockade, and the miraculous boy who
does everything and always succeeds.   Yet under Mr.

Stevenson's masterly touch everything becomes new. We can
think of no other writer who possesses such an extraordinary power of filling the reader with a sense of coming
danger. As in 'The Pavilion on the Links' the air seemed
thick with Italians, so in the opening of 'Treasure
Island' it seems thick with buccaneers. Pew, the horrible
blind man, whose stick came tap-tapping along the frosty
road; Billy Bones, the captain 'who blew through his nose
so loudly that you might say he roared;' Ben Gunn, the
marooned sailor, whose heart was 'sore for Christian diet,'
who many a long night on his lonely island 'dreamed of
cheese - toasted mostly - and woke up again;' and Long
John Silver, the wooden-legged miscreant, 'his eye,' at
certain times, 'a mere pin-point in his big face, but
gleaming like a crumb of glass' (an ordinary writer would
have said a bead) - these are all creations, living,
lying, swearing, murderous miscreants, as different from
the sailors of Marryat and Ballantyne as any suit of
clothes from a breathing man. There are passages in this
romance surpassing in power anything that Mr. Stevenson
has yet done; there are characters that deserve to live
among literary creations; there are adventures as rapid
and breathless as any ever imagined or experienced; for
all this we must be thankful. Yet we want no more boys'
books from Mr. Stevenson. We want him to employ his
unique gifts in the highest department of literature now
open to him - contemporary fiction.

42. W. E. HENLEY, FROM A LETTER TO STEVENSON ON
'BEESLEY - THE PROFESSOR ... SUNK TO THE THROAT IN
"TREASURE ISLAND"'

21 February 1884, B, 4779

In all likelihood Henley here refers to Edward Spencer
Beasly (1831-1915), professor of Latin at Bedford College
(1860-93), translator of Comte, and a fervent positivist.

I must tell you of Beesley. You know of Beesley - the
Professor? Well, Beesley has a wife, and she a son.
Beesley junior procured a copy of 'Treasure Island' and
read it through three times on end. He then consented

to hand it over to his mama and his mama went at it and
downed it at a gulp. Last of all, the book was mislaid.
They hunted for it high and low, for it was dear to their
hearts, and they suspected the servants. In their distress
they went into Beesley's study to complain to Beesley; and
there was Beesley, his history books thrown by, his Comte,
his Prudhon, his Herbert Spencer all forgotten, sunk to the
throat in 'Treasure Island'! He had a magnifier at his
eye, and through that magnifier he was (historian-like)
a-studying the map of Captain Flint, tracking the bloody
course of John Silver, much as he would have studied one
of Hannibal's campaigns.

Is not the picture sweet? Does not your heart warm for
this once to Beesley? Mine does, I confess.

... The thing is that 'Treasure Island' has sent your
name sky high and tripled the value of your work; ... [it]
will make more commissions for you than I know how to
handle.

43. AN UNSIGNED NOTICE, 'DIAL' (CHICAGO)

May 1884, v, 19

Mr. Stevenson's romance of 'Treasure Island' is a tissue
of highly improbable incidents which do not for a moment
throw the spell of reality around the reader, and yet con-
strain him to acknowledge the skill with which they are
worked up. The author shows considerable strength of
invention in unfolding the plot and delineating the
characters, which are life-like and well-sustained. But
beyond this exhibition of his power in the line of fiction, there is no appreciable good accomplished by the
book. It is a picture of the roughest phases of sea-life.
The effort to recover a pirate's buried treasure from a
desolate island in the mid-ocean, by a couple of gentlemen
whose followers comprise cutthroats, mutineers, and a
sprinkling of honest mariners, is neither dignified nor
edifying. It will be relished by adventure-loving boys,
but whether it will be wholesome reading for them is more
than doubtful.

44. HENRY JAMES, LETTER TO STEVENSON ON A HUMBLE
REMONSTRANCE

5 December 1884

From 'The Letters of Henry James' (1920), ed. Percy
Lubbock, i, 110-11.
    See headnote to No. 7.   Stevenson's A Humble Remon-
strance was a response to James's The Art of Fiction.
Both essays appeared in 'Longman's' - James's in September
and Stevenson's in December 1884. As James says, his
essay was a rejoinder to a lecture by Sir Walter Besant
(1836-1901), the author and philanthropist whose most
ambitious work was the 'Survey of London', 10 vols
(1902-12). In his lecture Besant urged that writers of
fiction be given greater recognition and he also attempted
to set down some rules for the aspiring novelist to
follow. It was against any such rules that James made his
'plea for liberty'.

My dear Robert Louis Stevenson,
    I read only last night your paper in the December
'Longman's' in genial rejoinder to my article in the same
periodical on Besant's lecture, and the result of that
charming half-hour is a friendly desire to send you three
words. Not words of discussion, dissent, retort or remonstrance, but of hearty sympathy, charged with the assurance of my enjoyment of everything you write. It's a
luxury, in this immoral age, to encounter some one who
does write - who is really acquainted with that lovely
art. It wouldn't be fair to contend with you here;
besides, we agree, I think, much more than we disagree,
and though there are points as to which a more irrepressible spirit than mine would like to try a fall, that is
not what I want to say - but on the contrary, to thank
you for so much that is suggestive and felicitous in your
remarks - justly felt and brilliantly said. They are full
of these things, and the current of your admirable style
floats pearls and diamonds. Excellent are your closing
words, and no one can assent more than I to your proposition that all art is a simplification. It is a pleasure
to see that truth so neatly uttered. My pages, in
'Longman's', were simply a plea for liberty: they were
only half of what I had to say, and some day I shall try
and express the remainder. Then I shall tickle you

a little affectionately as I pass. You will say that my
'liberty' is an obese divinity, requiring extra measures;
but after one more go I shall hold my tongue. The native
gaiety of all that you write is delightful to me, and when
I reflect that it proceeds from a man whom life has laid
much of the time on his back (as I understand it), I find
you a genius indeed. There must be pleasure in it for you
too. I ask Colvin about you whenever I see him, and I
shall have to send him this to forward to you. I am with
innumerable good wishes yours very faithfully,

Henry James.

45. STEVENSON, FROM A LETTER TO HENRY JAMES

8 December 1884, LS, ii, 232-4

My dear Henry James,
    This is a very brave hearing from more points than one.
The first point is that there is a hope of a sequel. For
this I laboured. Seriously, from the dearth of information and thoughtful interest in the art of literature,
those who try to practise it with any deliberate purpose
run the risk of finding no fit audience. People suppose
it is 'the stuff' that interests them; they think, for
instance, that the prodigious fine thoughts and sentiments
in Shakespeare impress by their own weight, not understanding that the unpolished diamond is but a stone. They
think that striking situations, or good dialogue, are got
by studying life; they will not rise to understand that
they are prepared by deliberate artifice and set off by
painful suppressions. Now, I want the whole thing well
ventilated, for my own education and the public's, and I
beg you to look as quick as you can, to follow me up with
every circumstance of defeat where we differ, and (to prevent the flouting of the laity) to emphasise the points
where we agree. I trust your paper will show me the way
to a rejoinder; and that rejoinder I shall hope to make
with so much art as to woo or drive you from your threatened silence. I would not ask better than to pass my life
in beating out this quarter of corn with such a seconder
as yourself.
    ... I am rejoiced indeed to hear you speak so kindly
of my work; rejoiced and surprised. I seem to myself a
very rude, left-handed countryman; not fit to be read, far

less complimented, by a man so accomplished, so adroit, so craftsmanlike as you. You will happily never have cause to understand the despair with which a writer like myself considers (say) the park scene in 'Lady Barbarina'. Every touch surprises me by its intangible precision; and the effect when done, as light as syllabub, as distinct as a picture, fills me with envy. Each man among us prefers his own aim, and I prefer mine; but when we come to speak of performance, I recognise myself, compared with you, to be a lout and slouch of the first water....

Yours sincerely,
Robert Louis Stevenson.

P.S.   I reopen this to say that I have re-read my paper, and cannot think I have at all succeeded in being either veracious or polite. I knew, of course, that I took your paper merely as a pin to hang my own remarks upon; but, alas! what a thing is any paper! What fine remarks can you not hang on mine! How I have sinned against proportion, and with every effort to the contrary, against the merest rudiments of courtesy to you! You are indeed a very acute reader to have divined the real attitude of mind; and I can only conclude, not without closed eyes and shrinking shoulders, in the well-worn words,

Lay on, Macduff!

'A Child's Garden of Verses'

March 1885

The verses collected in this volume were begun in 1882
after Stevenson came upon Kate Greenaway's 'Birthday Book
for Children' (1880) and decided he could equal or better
with little effort the verses in it by Mrs Sale Barker.
He worked on the rhymes intermittently, especially during
times of illness when he was unable to apply himself to
'Prince Otto'. In 1883 he had forty-eight of the verses
privately printed under the title 'Penny Whistles' and
copies were sent to Colvin, Gosse, and other friends.
Only thirty-nine of these forty-eight verses appeared
among the sixty-four published two years later under a new
title. Henley negotiated with publishers on Stevenson's
behalf and wrote to him of a proposal by Longman's Green
& Co. to pay £30 for the first 1,000 copies of the volume
and £20 for each subsequent 500 copies up to a total of
2,500 copies, whereupon a new agreement would be discussed
(B, 4811). These terms were apparently revised since
shortly afterwards Andrew Lang rather than Henley was
carrying on negotiations with Longman's (B, 5022, 5058).
Will H. Low negotiated on Stevenson's behalf with Scribners, the firm that was soon to become Stevenson's chief
publisher in the USA. The volume was published in England
on 6 March and in the USA on 16 April 1885 and was sympa-
thetically, if not enthusiastically received. The
reviewer for the 'Saturday' (No. 47) thought the collection fell short of complete success because it did not
appeal equally to children and adults. Henley's fear
that this review might 'hurt the book damnably' (B, 4617)
was apparently groundless. H. C. Bunner wrote a warm
review (No. 51) that no doubt pleased Stevenson, as had
his review of 'New Arabian Nights' (No. 32), but it was
William Archer's unsigned review in the 'Pall Mall
Gazette' (No. 49) that most attracted his attention and
prompted him to write, to Archer's surprise, a letter of
thanks (No. 50).

46. STEVENSON ON 'CHILD'S GARDEN', FROM A LETTER TO
EDMUND GOSSE

12 March 1885, LS, ii, 247-8

On Gosse see headnote to No. 61.

I have now published on 101 small pages 'The Complete
Proof of Mr. R. L. Stevenson's Incapacity to Write Verse',
in a series of graduated examples with table of contents.
I think I shall issue a companion volume of exercises:
'Analyse this poem. Collect and communicate the ugly
words. Distinguish and condemn the *chevilles*.   State Mr.
Stevenson's faults of taste in regard to the measure.
What reasons can you gather from this example for your
behalf that Mr. S. is unable to write any other measure?'
    They look ghastly in the cold light of print; but there
is something nice in the little ragged regiment for all-
the blackguards seem to me to smile, to have a kind of
childish treble note that sounds in my ears freshly; not
song, if you will, but a child's voice.

47. AN UNSIGNED REVIEW 'SATURDAY REVIEW'

21 March 1885, lix, 394

To write good verse for children where children are the
only readers written for is no easy feat; to write such
children's verse as may delight adults also is more difficult still. Mr. Robert Louis Stevenson, as much of his
prose work has shown, is more than commonly well equipped
with the qualities which make for success in either of
these endeavours; yet we cannot say that in the volume
before us he has been entirely successful. That simplicity of diction which is essential to such writing he has
nearly always at command; the 'force of statement' - we
can find no less prosaic phrase to describe what we mean -
which is characteristic of so much children's talk when it
is at once intelligent and unaffected, in this also he is
not wanting. Again, he has a quick and vivid fancy, with

much power of picturesque description, and he can be humorous and tender, not only by turns, which is common
enough, but at the same time. Nor can he be said to have
neglected or inexpertly used the various gifts which he
possesses. In this volume there is an abundance of graceful fancy, much of it admirably expressed. Some of its
lyrics would undoubtedly delight any child old enough to
take delight in such things at all; while others, again,
will undoubtedly be read with pleasure by its elders.
What we look for, however, in a book of this sort, though
perhaps it is putting our requirements too high, is the
combination of the two kinds of attraction in the same
pieces. The highest point attainable in writing of this
description is only attained when what may be called the
surface-motive of the lyric or the prose-story is sufficient in itself to charm the child, while the adult sense
of humour can enjoy the undercurrent of thought or meaning
with a relish proportioned to the completeness of its concealment from the younger reader. This point, however, is
rarely attained in Mr. Stevenson's verse. He has added to
his difficulties - if also to his opportunities - by writing throughout in the person of the child. It is the
child's thoughts, fancies, pleasures, ambitions - in
short, the child's record of impressions and criticism of
life - as given from its own lips; and it is, of course,
extremely hard to maintain the requisite tone of *naïveté*
in these touches, which are meant to appeal to the appreciation of its elders. The infantile humour or pathos
cannot help appearing at times to be too conscious of
itself.

We regret that considerations of space forbid us to
illustrate with any fulness the points we have noted, but
they are of the kind which at once strike any critical
reader. No such reader, we imagine, can fail to observe
how this faint undertone of self-consciousness just mars
the effect of such an otherwise exquisite little piece as
My Kingdom or of the closing stanzas of the Dumb Soldier.
We get it in -

> I called the little pool a sea,
> The little hills were big to me,
>   For I am very small.
>   [From My Kingdom]

And we get it again in -

> Alas! and as my home I neared,
> How very big my nurse appeared.
>   [From My Kingdom]

This is not the child, but the 'grown-up' speaking through
the mouth of the child. Sometimes, indeed, the youthful
voice is made to talk 'old' with humour and appropriateness, as -

> The child that is not clean and neat,
> With lots of toys and things to eat,
> He is a naughty child, I'm sure -
> Or else his dear papa is poor.
>   [From System]

It is easy to imagine a child picking up the idea conveyed in this last line from his elders, among whom the
conversation has perhaps turned more often upon the
worldly circumstances of 'papas' in general than the
philosophic mind would approve; and the sudden clash of
the mystical and rationalistic theories of human unhappiness, without any suspicion of their incongruity, is
delightfully fraught with the unconscious humour of
childhood. Foreign Children, again, is good, though the
lines, 'You must often as you trod, Have wearied *not* to
be abroad,' meaning, 'You must often have felt bored at
being abroad,' is unfortunately ambiguous, and would
equally apply to a foreign child languishing under exile
in England, which, of course, as the whole context shows,
is the very reverse of what Mr. Stevenson means. Perhaps
the most successful of all the poems in maintaining the
child-attitude throughout is The Gardener, which, in
order to illustrate that particular merit, we must of
course quote entire: -

> The gardener does not love to talk,
> He makes me keep the gravel walk,
> And when he puts his tools away
> He locks the door and takes the key.
>
> Away behind the currant row,
> Where no one else but cook may go,
> Far in the plots I see him dig,
> Old and serious, brown and big.
>
> He digs the flowers, green, red, and blue,
> Nor wishes to be spoken to;
> He digs the flowers and cuts the hay,
> And never seems to want to play.
>
> Silly gardener! summer goes,
> And winter comes with pinching toes,
> When in the garden bare and brown
> You must lay your barrow down.

Well now, and while the summer stays,
To profit by these garden days,
O how much wiser you would be
To play at Indian wars with me!

Even here, no doubt, a hypercritical taste may detect
blemishes. 'Far in the plots' might be altered with
advantage; 'nor wishes' is hardly a child's locution
(surely 'he'd rather not' is the natural phrase, and one
wonders at its not having suggested itself to, or, if so
it did, at its being rejected by, the author); and 'to
profit by these garden days' sounds, too, a little 'old.'
But these are comparatively trifling points; and, as a
whole, the little poem is a thoroughly humorous expression
of childhood's contemptuous wonder at the follies of the
adult. My Treasures, the enumeration of the nuts, the
whistle, the stone, and last and most precious -

The chisel both handle and blade,
Which a man who was really a carpenter made -

is another thoroughly successful piece. But Mr. Stevenson
would have done well to have rejected such trivialities as
Auntie's Skirts and Rain, which are unworthy of any but a
very young child indeed. And generally we should be disposed to say that the book would have been the better for
being shortened. Sixty-four flower-beds are too many for
a 'Child's Garden of Verses'; we can hardly help tiring of
such often-repeated specimens of what from the nature of
the case must be a very limited order of horticulture.
We are unwilling, however, to take leave of a volume in
many respects so attractive as this with words of faultfinding. Considered merely as verse, and without any
reference to its special claim upon the young, one may
linger with pleasure upon many of its pages. For picturesque touches of observation, and for spirited workmanship, the five stanzas of Summer Sun surpass anything
perhaps in the volume; Night and Day has merit enough to
atone almost for the barbarous rhyme ('valleys' and
'allies') with which it concludes; and the Envoys at the
end of the book are full of grace and pathos, that To
Minnie in particular possessing indescribable tenderness
and charm. On the whole, and despite the shortcomings we
have felt obliged to notice, Mr. Stevenson's book deserves
to have plenty of readers, both young and old.

48. R. H. HUTTON, UNSIGNED REVIEW, 'SPECTATOR'

21 March 1885, lviii, 382-3

Hutton (1826-97), theologian, journalist, and man of
letters, was a close friend of Walter Bagehot and for a
time editor with him of the 'National Review'; from 1861
until shortly before his death he was joint editor of the
'Spectator'. According to the 'Spectator' files, Hutton
wrote five other reviews of Stevenson's work: 'Kidnapped'
(No. 80), 'The Merry Men' (No. 89), 'The Black Arrow'
(11 August 1888), 'Ballads' (No. 122), and 'Fables'
(7 September 1895).

Mr. R. L. Stevenson has as good an idea of children and
their favourite notions as any English writer of our time.
His 'Treasure Island' is the delight of all children, big
and little, who love adventure in its simplest and most
vivid forms; and he has just proved, in his 'Child's
Garden of Verse' that he understands equally well the
imaginative world of children still smaller than those for
whose delight 'Treasure Island' was probably written.
Nevertheless, he seems to us to fall into some confusion
between two very different things indeed, - the verse
which children might be supposed to write, and the verse
which they would delight to read. In his 'Child's Garden
of Verse' he gives us a good many specimens of verses, of
which the best you could say would be that a bright child
might have written them, but which for that very reason
no bright child would value, except indeed as his own
productions. For example, the following Happy Thought
(to which, by the way, a separate page is devoted) is
hardly a thought which would make any child happy, unless
from triumph at having given birth to a rhyme: -

    The world is so full of a number of things,
    I'm sure we should all be as happy as kings.

That is merely puerile, and you will never find children
pleased with what is merely puerile. It is the same with
Looking Forward (which also fills a page): -

    When I am grown to man's estate
    I shall be very proud and great,
    And tell the other girls and boys
    Not to meddle with my toys.

That, again, expresses a very common puerile feeling in a
decidedly puerile manner, and therefore it is not the
sort of verse in which children would take pleasure. And
of this puerile verse, though Mr. Stevenson knows better
than to give us nothing else, there is a great deal too
much for so small a volume as this, - a great deal too
much that might really have been written by such a child
as Mr. Stevenson himself once was, and which expresses
nothing but frank, childish thoughts. Now, we are far
from saying that children condemn verse because it is not
poetry. On the contrary, they often take a great fancy to
the prosaic verses written for them by older people, -
witness the popularity a generation or two ago of the
'Original Poems,' by Jane Taylor, of Ongar. (1) But then
bad as most of the 'Original Poems' were, considered as
poems, they contained lively delineations of incident and
character such as no child could have written. The well-
known picture of the greedy boy, beginning, -

> I've got a plum-cake,
> And a rare feast I'll make,
> I'll eat, and I'll stuff, and I'll cram;
> Morning, noontime, and night,
> It shall be my delight;
> What a happy young fellow I am!

was not precisely poetical, but it was a very vigorous
sketch of greediness, such as no child could have drawn.
And it was this strong delineation which made it popular
with children, while the rhymes only served to impress it
on their recollection. Now, in the verses in Mr. R. L.
Stevenson's volume, which we have described as verses
which a smart boy might have written, there is no such
force of graving. Like the specimens we have given, they
have the mark of the child's experience without anything
at all but the rhyme to distinguish them in form from the
language in which a lively boy would have been apt to
express that experience. But to find favour with children, verse needs a good deal more than this. Undoubtedly
it must embody the child's feeling, but it must embody it
in a form far beyond the reach of a child's power of expression, - in other words, in a form to give no less, or
even more, vividness to the mere record of that feeling
than the original feeling itself would have carried with
it at the time it was present in all its force to the
child's mind. Mr. Stevenson himself gives us ample opportunity of illustrating what we mean. Take, for example,
this admirable little poem on the Wind

[The Wind quoted in full.]

That is not only a true poem, but a poem that expresses
the child's wonder at the invisible force of the wind in
words which though simple enough, are far beyond the compass of a child's imagination. The burden, taken alone,
is a whole world above the range of the child's thought.
Again, the very form of the question, -

    O you that are so strong and cold,
    O blower, are you young or old?

is a form that would never occur to a child. He would
never address the wind merely in the second person, nor
without giving it the name of 'wind' by which he knows
it; and the mere fact of this direct address to an invisible and unknown power into the nature of which the ques-
tioner is inquiring, carries a sense of mystery which
would excite the child's sense of wonder, and lift him
above the puerile level. Or, again, take this admirable
little poem on a child's march to bed in the winter
night, and notice how far beyond the child's power of
expression is the verse, though it exactly touches the
heart of an imaginative child's feeling: -

[Part 2 of North-West Passage quoted.]

What a force of vision there is in the lines: -

    All round the candle the crooked shadows come
        And go marching along up the stair.

How vividly that crookedness of the shadows, as they
leaped from the wall to the ceiling, or from the floor to
the wall, as the light changed its position, used to impress us as children, and yet how impossible it would have
been for us to give to that half-shivering sense of the
fearfulness of shadows, a voice so lively and yet so sensitive as this. Or, again, take this bright little picture of the advantages of birds over boys, conveyed in
verses of almost birdlike simplicity and buoyancy: -

[Nest Eggs quoted in full.]

What child could have written that? and, indeed, we may
well ask what child could have written any sort of verse
in which children would delight? What the child looks
for to rouse his imagination, is some extension of his
own experience, either in the direction of more living

detail, or in the direction of a more buoyant imagination.
No child would think of calling the songs of the birds
'musical speeches;' and the very use of that expression
widens his enjoyment of the bird's song, and brings it
nearer to his heart.   This is what Mr. Stevenson can do
for the child when he will.   But it is not by simply fitting a child's thought with rhymes that he can do it, but
rather by fitting a child's feelings with wings.   And when
he does this he is delightful.   For example, how he lifts
the child's inarticulate thought into the heavens, when he
sings of the dumb soldier whom the child is supposed to
have buried in the grass: -

[The Dumb Soldier quoted from 'He has seen the starry
hours' to the end.]

But the child, though he might have made-up the tale himself, could never have made it up in that language of the
heart which betrays the nice discernment at once what to
say and what to omit.   The child could never have spoken
of 'the forests of the grass,' or have realised the lonely
rapture of listening to 'the talking-bee and ladybird,'
though that is what he might have tried dimly to express.
No, Mr. Stevenson may be sure that those of his rhymes -
and they are too many, - which a lively boy might have
made, will never seize hold of children, while those of
his poems which give the force of mature vision and emotion to childish feelings, will be as popular with children as even his romance of piracy itself.

Note

1 'Original Poems for Infant Minds' (1804-5) was the
   joint work of Jane Taylor (1783-1824) and her sister
   Ann (1782-1866).

49. WILLIAM ARCHER, FROM AN UNSIGNED REVIEW, 'PALL MALL
GAZETTE'

24 March 1885, xli, 5

Archer (1858-1924), the well-known drama critic and
early advocate and translator of Ibsen.   This review is

identified in Charles Archer, 'William Archer: Life, Work, and Friendships' (1931), 137.   Answering Stevenson's inquiries about Archer, Henley wrote: 'He's a very clever fellow indeed with a good gift of style and a great deal of guts and insight as a dramatic critic.   He's the W.A. of the "World"' (National Library of Scotland).   For Stevenson's warm response to this review see No. 50.

The child is father to the man, and the Robert Louis Stevenson of to-day clearly takes after his father as figured for us in this delightful little book.   It is autobiographical rather than dramatic.   Mr. Stevenson does not attempt a many-sided view of child life, does not seek to depict varieties of child character, but sets himself to reflect the moods of one particular child, well known to him.   He takes an Inland Voyage up the river of Memory, and sketches with his clear, crisp, vivid touch a few of his adventures and experiences.   He draws with charming simplicity, yet in the selection of his subjects we trace the irony of self-conscious manhood, and here and there we find a touch in which the artist does not quite conceal his art.   This is merely repeating in other words that he does not care to be consistently dramatic.   'These are my starry solitudes,' is a literary phrase, and so is

> I saw the dimpling river pass,
> And be the sky's blue looking-glass.
>   [From Foreign Lands]

A child might conceivably say 'dimpled river,' or if the idea occurred to him at all would probably invent an adjective and say 'dimply;' but the participial epithet is a verse-writer's trick.   Little disputable turns of this sort occur now and then; but, as Mr. Stevenson makes no professions, we can at worst maintain that they are inconsistent with his general practice.

In 'Virginibus Puerisque' there is an essay on Child's Play which should be read as a preface to this booklet. Its first line explains what many readers of the 'Garden' must find noteworthy, if not absolutely strange, the persistent dwelling on the sunny aspect of childhood, with scarcely a hint of its night side.   'The regret we have for our childhood is not wholly justifiable,' says Mr. Stevenson, assuming as universal a feeling which in many minds is non-existent.   He admits further on that 'innocence, no more than philosophy, can protect us from the sting of pain,' but this sting sends no discordant cries

through his 'Songs of Innocence.' The child is the very
same cheerful stoic whom we admire in the man - a philosopher who does not attempt to bring pain and evil into
harmony with any system, but simply disregards and ignores
them. On looking up a little poem which dwelt in our
memory as illustrating this frame of mind, we find,
curiously enough, that it is headed System: -

> Every night my prayers I say,
> And get my dinner every day;
> And every day that I've been good
> I get an orange after food.
>
> The child that is not clean and neat,
> With lots of toys and things to eat,
> He is a naughty child, I'm sure -
> Or else his dear papa is poor.

That is enough; to inquire further were to inquire too
curiously; a good child will be satisfied with proximate
causes, and not rack his brains and worry his elders with
questions as to the ultimate reasons of things. A few
pages more and we come to the following Happy Thought into
which is compressed the whole of Mr. Stevenson's gospel: -

> The world is so full of a number of things,
> I'm sure we should all be as happy as kings.

For the better enforcement of this maxim he has written
several volumes which are not the least among the 'number
of things' we Englishmen of to-day may be happy over.
Were we not a perverse generation we should no doubt dance
with a will to such resolutely cheerful piping; but, alas!
even in this 'brave gymnasium, full of sea-bathing and
horse exercise, and bracing, manly virtues,' the best we
can do is to be about as happy - as kings.

Thoughts of Blake will inevitably intrude themselves
upon readers of Mr. Stevenson's verses, but they should at
once be banished as impertinent. The two men are on different planes. Their ends are different, their means are
different. Blake is a poet who now and then rises to a
poignant note beyond Mr. Stevenson's compass as it is
above his ambition. Mr. Stevenson is a humourist and an
artist in words, a man of alert, open-eyed sanity, unconcerned as to the mystery of childhood, but keenly alive
to its human grace and pathos, its fantastic gravity, its
logical inconsequence, its exquisite egoism. Moreover,
Mr. Stevenson's child, unlike Blake's children, is distinctly an agnostic. He says his prayers, but it is with

no 'petitionary vehemence.' He does not seem even to
indulge in the fetishism which is the first spiritual
experience of so many children. It is the unhappy child
who is a metaphysician, and is 'cradled into scepticism
by wrong,' or into fetish worship, as the case may be.
Mr. Stevenson knows nothing of the fierce rebellions, the
agonized doubts as to the existence of justice, human or
divine, which mar the music of childhood for so many; or
if he realizes their existence, he relegates them to that
other life, the life of pain, and terror, and weariness,
into which it is part of his philosophy to look as seldom
as possible....

50.   STEVENSON, LETTER TO WILLIAM ARCHER

29 March 1885, LS, ii, 254-5

Archer was surprised to receive this letter from Stevenson:

>   It took me aback almost as much as it gratified me,
>   for it had never occurred to me that the review was
>   anything but a rather second-rate production even for
>   me.... But R.L.S. has given me so much pleasure that
>   I am glad to have paid him back a little.... I'm
>   afraid he wouldn't appreciate so much an elaborate
>   article on his style and thought [No. 52] which I
>   have had knocking about for some time - praising the
>   former, of course, but pitching into him hot and
>   strong as an aggressive optimist, or what an Indian
>   friend of his own (he says) calls a 'faddling hedon-
>   ist'. (Letter to Charles Archer, 'William Archer'
>   (1931), 140-1)

The reviewer of 'Inland Voyage' in the 'Pioneer' (Allahabad) (No. 6) had called Stevenson a 'faddling hedonist'.

Dear Mr. Archer, - Yes, I have heard of you and read some
of your work; but I am bound in particular to thank you
for the notice of my verses. 'There,' I said, throwing
it over to the friend who was staying with me, 'it's worth
writing a book to draw an article like that.' Had you
been as hard upon me as you were amiable, I try to tell

myself I should have been no blinder to the merits of your
notice. For I saw there, to admire and to be very grateful for, a most sober, agile pen; an enviable touch; the
marks of a reader, such as one imagines for one's self in
dreams, thoughtful, critical, and kind; and to put the top
on this memorial column, a greater readiness to describe
the author criticised than to display the talents of his
censor.

I am a man *blasé* to injudicious praise (though I hope
some of it may be judicious too), but I have to thank you
for THE BEST CRITICISM I EVER HAD; and am therefore, dear
Mr. Archer, the most grateful critickee now extant.

                                    Robert Louis Stevenson.

P.S. - I congratulate you on living in the corner of all
London that I like best. *À propos*, you are very right
about my voluntary aversion from the painful sides of life.
My childhood was in reality a very mixed experience, full
of fever, nightmare, insomnia, painful days and interminable nights; and I can speak with less authority of gardens
than of that other 'land of counterpane.' But to what end
should we renew these sorrows? The sufferings of life may
be handled by the very greatest in their hours of insight;
it is of its pleasures that our common poems should be
formed; these are the experiences that we should seek to
recall or to provoke; and I say with Thoreau, 'What right
have I to complain, who have not ceased to wonder?' and,
to add a rider of my own, who have no remedy to offer.

                                                    R.L.S.

51. H. C. BUNNER, FROM A REVIEW, 'BOOK BUYER'

May 1885, ii, 103-4

On Bunner see headnote to No. 32.

It is rather hard, when once a man's youth has been
renewed for him like the eagle's, and he has been led into
green pastures such as cows and children only enjoy to the
full - it is rather hard to snatch him back by the ear to
this dull grown-up world, and to explain to him that it
wasn't true after all, that he has only been making

believe, under the guidance of an able adult magician –
that he is no child, but a dull, mechanic, responsible
man, and that he must sit down and write a notice commen-
datory of the skill of the able magician.

We know the magician of old. Under his spell we have
seen the life of mediaeval France awaken for us, growing
as warm, as real, as true, as – well, as our mosaic-working
novelists and story-tellers don't make the life of to-day.
And we have seen him turn this staid nineteenth century
into a time of wild intrigue and mad adventure and high-
hearted chivalry....

But we never suspected that he had the power to unseal
the tender springs of childhood's inborn poetry, and set
them flowing in the sight of all men to tell to the world
that secret which we each one of us, once upon a time,
guarded so jealously: the secret of our dear playfellow
who could not be seen or heard or felt of with our hands;
but only be *thought* and *dreamed*: and whom, since then, we
have learned to call Fancy. What a secret it was! It
made the whole world glad and fair and desirable to us.
And yet we scarcely dared whisper it to the older people,
or even to the best of our comrades. You see, other
people were likely to laugh, and nothing scared our play-
mate away like laughing at him.

But here is this Scotch magician making a child of himself for our benefit. And at first we look on, and smile
at his childlike antics and oddities of expression, and
say: 'How true! very accurate, indeed.' And pretty soon
we have ceased smiling and commenting, and before long we
are children too, doing it all, thinking it all, being it
all; and we know that it is true with a truth of which we
do not often get glimpses....

We should all be grateful to our magician. But, like
all true magicians, he has something more to do than
merely to make us laugh and wonder. His art has a stronger hold on nature. Were he only the bright and clever
man of talent, who does the bright and clever thing that a
man may do with his talent, it would be easy enough to
dismiss him with a hatful of thanks and compliments. But
we who have read the half dozen books which he has given
us must see clearly that we have to deal, not with talent,
but with that strange and precious thing which we call
genius. If he does no more than he has done – and he
gives every sign and promise of doing more – Robert Louis
Stevenson is one of these men whom we have to label with
the name of genius. And the mission of genius, however it
reveal itself, is sad at bottom. There is much in this
book that we may teach to the children, at our side; there
is much that we may smile over, remembering the childhood

from which we grew; but there is also something there that
hints of the stifled childhood in us that never grew up;
something that touches us with a deep, half-understood,
wholly unspeakable grief.

52.   WILLIAM ARCHER, FROM ROBERT LOUIS STEVENSON: HIS
STYLE AND HIS THOUGHT, 'TIME' (LONDON)

November 1885, ii, 581-91

See headnote to No. 49. This is the first important
general assessment of Stevenson's work. Stevenson is
represented as standing at the head of a trivial company -
'our new school of stylists'. Granted, he is a master of
'lightness of touch' (see No. 13), but a writer of significance - Dickens is offered as the example - has at
his command emphasis as well as light grace, the sombre
and grand tones as well as the lighter harmonies.
Whatever we may say of Stevenson's style, however, it is
the perfect expression of his thought, which amounts to an
optimism indifferent or blind to the stern conditions of
life and those less fortunate and robust than ourselves.
The extent to which Stevenson was distressed by this
article may be seen in the several letters that follow
(No. 53). The relations between Stevenson and Archer
were to become cordial following the latter's visit to
Skerryvore, Stevenson's home in Bournemouth. For Archer's
more favourable attitude towards Stevenson, see Nos. 100
and 129. See Introduction, p. 19.

I.

... In the front rank of our new school of stylists, Mr.
Robert Louis Stevenson holds an undisputed place. He is a
modern of the moderns both in his alert self-consciousness
and in the particular artistic ideal which he proposes to
himself. He is popular, not, perhaps, with that puff-bred
vogue which draws elbowing crowds to Mudie's counters, but
with the better popularity which makes his books familiar
to the shelves of all who love literature for its own
sake. Now, to love literature for its own sake implies a
mental habit, which is, perhaps happily, unknown to the

many, even to the educated many. To be less concerned
about what a man says than how he says it is unutilitar-
ian, unprogressive, not to say reactionary; for the world
is not to be regenerated by a nice arrangement of epithets. Mr. Stevenson, however, is not only philosophically content, but deliberately resolved, that his readers
shall look first to his manner, and only in the second
place to his matter. He has committed himself to the
explicit assertion that 'there is indeed only one merit
worth considering in a man of letters - that he should
write well; and only one damning fault - that he should
write ill.' Shakespeare is not more unconcerned about the
advancement of humanity. As we shall see in the sequel,
Mr. Stevenson sometimes inclines to the opinion that an
ardent reformer is, as Charles Reade said of a flippant
novelist, 'impertinent to his Creator.' He professes himself an artist in words, and thinks only those thoughts,
tells none but those tales, paints those pictures alone,
which adapt themselves to his peculiar manner. An
impressionist on occasion, he is always an expressionist.
    There are fashions in style as in everything else, and,
for the moment, we are all agreed that the one great
saving grace is 'lightness of touch.' Of this virtue Mr.
Stevenson is the accomplished model. He keeps it always
before his eyes, and cultivates in everything a buoyant,
staccato, touch-and-go elasticity. In description he
jots effects rather than composes pictures. He has a
Dickens-like knack of giving life and motion to objects
the most inanimate.... By instinct or design he eschews
those subjects which demand constructive patience in their
describer. It is in touches like the following that he
excels - touches which, 'light' as they are, seem to
quicken the imagination, and pass into the reader's store
of remembered experiences: -

    I have never seen such a night. It seemed to throw
    calumny in the teeth of all the painters that ever
    dabbled in starlight. The sky itself was of a ruddy,
    powerful, nameless, changing colour, dark and glossy
    like a serpent's back. The stars, by innumerable mil-
    lions, stuck boldly forth like lamps. The milky way
    was bright, like a moon-lit cloud; half heaven seemed
    milky way. The greater luminaries shone each more
    clearly than a winter's moon. Their light was dyed
    in every sort of colour - red, like fire; blue, like
    steel; green, like the tracks of sunset; and so
    sharply did each stand forth in its own lustre that
    there was no appearance of that flat, star-spangled
    arch we know so well in pictures, but all the hollow of

heaven was one chaos of contesting luminaries - a
hurly-burly of stars. Against this the hills and
rugged tree-tops stood out redly dark. [From A Starry
Drive, 'The Silverado Squatters']

Is there not a magnetism in the lightness of this
touch?

In character-drawing, or rather sketching, Mr. Stevenson's effort is the same. Here he forswears analysis as
in description he has forsworn synthesis. A few crisp,
clean strokes and a wash of transparent colour, and the
oddity stands before us as though fresh from the pencil
of Mr. Caldecott. For Mr. Stevenson's characters are all
oddities. It is to the quaintly abnormal that this method
of presentation applies. To draw the normal, to make a
revelation of the commonplace, is a task which demands insight quite other than Mr. Stevenson's, labour quite foreign to his scheme. Richardson knew nothing of lightness
of touch; it was at some sacrifice of this supreme quality
that George Eliot made Rosamond Vincy live not only as a
phantasm before the mind's eye, but as a piece of flesh
and blood, solid in three dimensions, to whose reality
every fibre of our moral being bears witness with a thrill.
All Mr. Stevenson's personages have hitherto been either
wayside silhouettes taken in the course of his wanderings,
or figures invented to help out the action of tales whose
very essence lies in their unreality. 'Long John Silver'
is perhaps his most sustained effort in character-drawing,
brilliantly successful as far as vividness of presentation
is concerned, but conceived outside of all observation, a
creature of tradition, a sort of nautical were-wolf. To
apply analysis to such a character would merely be to let
out the sawdust.

As a narrator Mr. Stevenson marks the reaction against
the reigning ethical school. He has somewhere given in
his adhesion to a widespread heresy which proclaims narrative to be the consummate literary form, from which all
others have been evolved, towards which, in their turn,
they all tend. Put it never so speciously, this theory
resolves itself in the last analysis into an assertion
that incident is more important than character, action
than motive, the phenomenon than the underlying cause; yet
Mr. Stevenson explains, if he does not justify, the faith
that is in him, by proving himself endowed in a high
degree with the gift of mere story-telling. Here again
the last work of his secret is lightness of touch. He
plunges into the midst of things. He is direct, rapid,
objective. His characters have always their five senses
about them, to record those minutely trivial impressions

which, by their very unexpectedness, lend an air of reality to a scene. Who can forget the tap-tap-tap of the
blind man's stick on the frosty road, in the opening scene
of 'Treasure Island'?   If Mr. Stevenson has a leaning towards the horrible, he presents his horrors frankly, not
crudely. As an inventor and interweaver of incidents he
has the great advantage of not being over-particular in
making them dovetail, but feeling with a just instinct
what the reader will demand to know clearly, what he will
be content to accept without explanation. His chief
efforts in fiction having hitherto been parodies, so to
speak, of antiquated narrative forms, - the eastern tale
and the romance of piracy - he has been able to throw a
veil of light humour over their mere sensationalism, which
we miss in such a story as The Pavilion on the Links.
Here he is on the confines of the penny-dreadful, or
rather over the border-line of the half-crown dreadful
after the good old style of 'Tales from "Blackwood."'
How, in his future work, he may succeed in introducing
the requisite seasoning of humorous fantasy, we need not
try to guess; but he will assuredly have to get it in
somehow, or else to compound his fiction after a totally
different formula.

    To protest against any fashion not positively vicious
is to show a fussy forgetfulness of the flow of time. And
indeed lightness of touch is in no sense a fashion to be
protested against. It is entirely good so far as it goes;
only it may not, perhaps, go quite so far as its modern
devotees believe. We are asked to regard it as the watchword of a new dispensation, consummating and superseding
all the law and the prophets. This it assuredly is not.
It is only one, and not the highest of a hierarchy of
virtues recognized wherever and whenever the art of
expression has been cultivated. Let us isolate it, exalt
it, and bow down before it as much as we please, since it
happens to chime with our temperament and tone of thought;
but let us not despise and reject as vices other qualities
which have their own due place and function. The current
criticism of the day opposes to its one saving grace a
deadly sin called 'emphasis,' conceived as the evil habit
of gibbering barbarians without the pale of articulate-
speaking culture. Mr. Stevenson confesses how 'in a fit
of horror at his old excess' he cut out from the first
draft of his essay on Whitman 'all the big words and emphatic passages.' Perhaps this is not to be regretted,
since much study of Whitman might deceive the very elect
into false emphasis but the writer who cuts out a true
and just emphasis simply because it is emphatic, performs
an act, not of wise temperance, but of affectation or

cowardice. Mr. Stevenson himself quotes from Thoreau the
saying that 'no truth was ever expressed but with this
sort of emphasis, that for the time there seemed to be no
other'; and if this is itself an over-emphatic statement,
it at least contains a moiety of the truth. Mr. Stevenson
has no lack of theories to express, but his beliefs are
not weighty enough, his truths are not true enough, to
demand emphasis. Not that he is sceptical of them or
regards them from Pilate's point of view; on the contrary,
he gives them forth with great confidence, which may be
defined as emphasis without enthusiasm. Occasionally he
forgets himself and lets slip an emphatic utterance; and
sometimes, be it noted, the emphasis is false. When he
calls some page of Thoreau's 'the noblest and most useful
passage I remember to have read in any modern author,' he
indulges in a hyperbole. However noble and useful the
passage in question, such a sweeping superlative is essentially untenable; unless, indeed, we suppose Mr. Stevenson's memory to be very short, in which case the assertion
becomes a mere forcible-feeble circumlocution. But such
slips are rare. As a rule, Mr. Stevenson gossips along as
lightly as need be. His is healthy human speech, sane and
self-contained. We can listen to it long without either
irritation or tedium, until suddenly there vibrates across
our memory an echo of some other utterance compared with
which this light-flowing discourse 'is as moonlight unto
sunlight, is as water unto wine.' Then we reflect that
there is a time for everything; a time for lightness and
a time for emphasis; a time for speech and a time for
song; a time for rippling melody and a time for rich-
woven, deep-toned harmony; and we remember that in English
prose there is room for all these different forms of
strength and beauty. Lightness of touch is good, but so
are power and passion and multitudinous music. The
countrymen of Milton need not sneer at majesty of rheto-
ric; the contemporaries of Ruskin should know that
subtlety and splendour may go hand in hand.

II.

The world is so full of a number of things,
I'm sure we should all be as happy as kings.
                                             Stevenson.

When we come to look at Mr. Stevenson as a teacher, we
find that in his case, at least, the style is the man himself. He may possibly deny at the outset that he is, or
aspires to be, a teacher, and, in fact, the process of

teaching implies in the popular conception a certain
emphasis, foreign, by our hypothesis, to Mr. Stevenson's
manner. But every writer, unless his paper-staining be so
futile as to constitute a positive social misdemeanour,
has a message to deliver, or at least some echo or semblance of a message. Let us say, then, that on examining
the message which Mr. Stevenson makes it his business to
promulgate, we find that his style chimes with his philosophy as the cantering anapaests of Bonnie Dundee chime
with its martial spirit; for is not the ever-recurring
burden of Mr. Stevenson's wisdom an exhortation to cultivate lightness of touch upon the chords of life?

'I wish sincerely,' he says, 'for it would have saved
me much trouble, that there had been some one to put me in
a good heart about life when I was younger; to tell me how
dangers are most portentous on a distant sight; and how
the good in a man's spirit will not suffer itself to be
overlaid, and rarely or never deserts him in the hour of
need.' And again: - 'A happy man or woman is a better
thing to find than a five-pound note.... We need not care
whether they could prove the forty-seventh proposition;
they do a better thing [than] that, they practically
demonstrate the great Theorem of the Liveableness of
Life.' This is the theorem to the demonstration of which
all Mr. Stevenson's writings are devoted. He is, in a
word, an aggressive optimist, than whom, to some of us,
there can scarcely be a more bewildering phenomenon.

The commonplace optimism, which has its basis in stupidity, is by no means bewildering, however pathetic. It
is, moreover, the only genuine article, for the optimism
which knows its own name, which has become self-conscious
and self-assertive is already tinctured with its opposite.
So soon as we go about to persuade ourselves that life is
worth living, we have left our coign of vantage in crass,
inert, unreasoning habit. In excusing life we accuse it;
and what is bewildering is that a mind so acute as Mr.
Stevenson's should fail to perceive this. We are either
arguing about words, or pitting mutually destructive
experiences against each other, and in either case admitting that existence does not carry its own justification.
We bring forward elaborate pleas in mitigation of sentence, and then toss our caps and huzza as though we had
secured a triumphant acquittal. Having proved that things
might be worse, we pass at one bound to the corollary that
they could not be better.

Mr. Stevenson - and this is the key to the enigma - is
an artist in life as he is in words. From a hundred hints
and half-confessions in his writings, we learn that he
has, at an early period, formed for himself a sort of

eclectic stoic-epicurean ideal, and that he considers
himself to have been at least moderately successful in
carving his life in accordance with that ideal. He has
determined to be, and has been, 'a man, acting on his
own instincts, keeping in his own shape that God made him
in; and not a mere crank in the social engine-house,
welded on principles that he does not understand, and for
purposes that he does not care for.' These are his own
words, not, of course, applied directly to himself, but
evidently describing a personal ideal. Hence his keen
sympathy with Thoreau and Whitman, two brother-artists in
life, though each with a somewhat different technical
method. Hence his denunciation of the commercial spirit,
which forgets that money has to be bought at the expense
of life, and can be paid for at infinitely more than its
worth. Hence his apologies for idlers, his eulogies of
the state in which 'the great wheels of intelligence turn
idly in the head, like fly-wheels, grinding no grist.'
Hence, too, the exactness with which his style corresponds with his character; for the style, as we have seen,
always reveals the artist in a man's nature, and Mr.
Stevenson is all artist.

As half the pleasure of art lies in the sense of difficulty overcome, in the feeling of power to combine, mould,
or carve the most obstinate materials in obedience to the
plastic will, so the artist in life finds a not unnatural
pleasure in the very hardness of the substance with which
he has to deal. The sculptor loves the cold, hard
marble, because he knows that out of it he can create
delicate forms, shadows and surfaces, which would be
unattainable in sandstone or soapstone. Moreover, the
sense of exclusive possession adds zest a hundredfold to
the pleasure arising from mere skill. If the art of
carving statues were 'as easy as lying,' or even if, like
carpentering, it could be learned by every one with moderate perserverence, how little should we envy Phidias,
and how little would Phidias himself glory in his calling!
It is the nature of man to take pride in his fortuitous
advantages, the beauty and genius which raise him above
his fellows by no merit of his own, rather than in the
personal qualities of temperance, industry, and so forth,
whereby he has retained his beauty and developed a genius
which would otherwise have lain fallow. In the same way,
if all men were, or could be, artists in life, the 'Art of
Living' (thus Mr. Stevenson styles it in so many words)
would afford much less gratification to its professors.
All the qualities which constitute the artist in life -
and some of them are suspiciously like mental limitations
- are born with him. The opportunities for their

cultivation and development almost always exist independently of any effort or volition on his part. Nevertheless - or perhaps we should rather say on that very account - he glories in them with a sense of personal merit, and regards with contemptuous wonder the thousand would-be artists or bunglers who minister by contrast to his sense of mastery, and the million no-artists but toilers and sufferers in the depths who render possible his free art-life upon the heights. 'Times change,' says Mr. Stevenson, 'opinions vary to their opposite, and still this world appears a brave gymnasium, full of sea-bathing, and horse-exercise, and bracing manly virtues.' There are some people on whom even sea-bathing and horse exercise are apt to pall, and who fail to find a joy for ever in the practice of manly virtue; these, let us admit for the sake of the argument, are despicable persons, unworthy of regard. But what of those whose wishes are their only horses, who know more of sweat-baths than of sea-baths, and who are shut out from the exercise of any manly virtue, save that of renunciation? They, too, demonstrate the theorem of the liveableness of life, and that much more conclusively than the 'happy man or woman' who affords Mr. Stevenson more gratification than a five-pound note. The happiness *must* be temporary, for under the best of circumstances it tends to wear itself out; the misery *may* be permanent, since it has no inherent tendency to decrease. If, then, the cancer-eaten pauper is as tenacious of existence as the horse-riding, sea-bathing, virtuous athlete, is not he the true proof positive of the liveableness of life, which simply means the tenacity of our earliest, most mechanical habit? It is not Apollo-Goethe but Prometheus-Heine who demonstrates the liveableness of life.

'Although it' ('An Inland Voyage') 'runs to considerably upwards of two hundred pages,' says Mr. Stevenson in his preface to that delightful book, 'it contains not a single reference to the imbecility of *God's* universe, nor so much as a single hint that I could have made a better one myself.' It is a characteristic of such optimism as Mr. Stevenson's to do homage to God in capitals and italics, while refraining from any too curious consideration as to what is meant by that convenient term. Mr. Matthew Arnold expresses himself grateful to the Eternal-not-ourselves ' for the boon of this glorious world to be righteous in.' For 'to be righteous in' read 'to go canoeing in,' and you have Mr. Stevenson's doxology. It is hard to say which formula is the more aptly designed to make the very angels - laugh.

Mr. Stevenson has a perfect right to practise and take

pleasure in the Art of Life, and to celebrate the efficacy
of his methods. There are men who come beaming and rosy-
gilled from a seven-o'clock cold shower-bath in mid-
January, and proclaim winter to be the only school of
bracing manly virtue. For once in a way it is pleasant,
and even instructive, to listen to them; but when they
go about professing that the whole philosophy of life is
summed up in the word 'shower-bath,' and hinting that whoever cannot procure or endure a morning douche must be a
Philistine or dullard, we begin to find their pose irritating, and to wonder whether a turn of rheumatic fever
might not leave them wiser, if sadder, men. For aggressive optimism, let Mr. Stevenson remember, is just as
distinctly a pose as Wertherism, or Byronism, or Heine-
ism, or Musset-ism, and is in the long run quite as
offensive. It has not even the title to respect possessed
by that idealism which, in George Eliot's phrase, is
actively 'meliorist' in the present, and optimist as
regards the future. Granted certain conditions of purse
and physique a man may easily get hold of the half-truth
that from an athletico-aesthetic point of view this is a
reasonably satisfactory world; but when we find him con-
fidently propounding this as the whole truth, and going
on his way with an 'Allah bismillah!' in athletico-
aesthetic content, it is charitable to suspect him of
affectation, since the only alternative would be to accuse
him of egoistic callousness.

'It is not at all a strong thing,' so Mr. Stevenson
philosophizes, 'to put one's reliance upon logic; and our
own logic particularly for it is generally wrong. We
never know where we are to end if once we begin following
words and doctors. There is an upright stock in a man's
heart that is trustier than any syllogism; and the eyes
and the sympathies and appetites know a thing or two that
have never yet been stated in controversy.' It would be
hard to find in an equally small space a more flourishing
crop of sophisms. Because the compass does not always
point true, we are to throw it overboard, and trust to the
good old rule which recommends us to follow our nose. It
is the function of logic, though Mr. Stevenson evidently
does not know it, to teach us when we are arguing about
words and confuting our opponents by disproving what they
never asserted. But Mr. Stevenson's disdain is not really
directed against logic in the scholastic sense of the
word; he uses it, consciously or unconsciously, as a
synonym for science; and in so doing he formally chooses
his side in the great strife which is dividing the world.
It is becoming clearer every day that this fundamental
difference must absorb and sum up all other differences of

human opinion, and that the antagonistic factions, whether
in politics, religion, literature, or art, will soon be
found to resolve themselves into two great parties, whom
we may call, for the moment, scientists and anti-
scientists. The former are those who accept loyally and
consistently the belief that the success and at least the
relative happiness of the human race, depends upon its
knowledge and observance of the vast system of natural
laws, mental as well as physical, which is being gradually
revealed to us; the latter are those who reject this faith,
and take their stand on supernaturalism, pure inert egoism,
or (as in Mr. Stevenson's case) on a form of opinion which
puts its trust in 'the eyes and the sympathies and appetites,' and may be called happy-go-lucky-ism. On the
ground that 'we never know where we are to end if once we
begin following words' (for 'words' please read 'ideas'),
they spend their strength in the vain endeavour to remain
where they are. Vain indeed! for the only choice is between stumbling onward in the darkness, and marching forward in the light. It is sad to find a man of Mr. Stevenson's genial talent posing as a wilfully blind leader of
the blind.

53. STEVENSON ON ARCHER'S ASSESSMENT: LETTERS TO ARCHER,
THOMAS STEVENSON, AND HENRY JAMES

October-November 1885

(a) Stevenson to Archer, letter dated 28 October 1885

Dear Mr. Archer, - I have read your paper with my custom-
ary admiration; it is very witty, very adroit; it contains a great deal that is excellently true (particularly
the parts about my stories and the description of me as
an artist in life); but you will not be surprised if I do
not think it altogether just. It seems to me, in particular, that you have wilfully read all my works in terms of
my earliest; my aim, even in style, has quite changed in
the last six or seven years; and this I should have
thought you would have noticed. Again, your first remark
upon the affectation of the italic names; a practice only
followed in my two affected little books of travel, where
a typographical *minauderie* of the sort appeared to me in
character; and what you say of it, then, is quite just.

But why should you forget yourself and use these same
italics as an index to my theology some pages further on?
This is lightness of touch indeed; may I say, it is almost
sharpness of practice?

Excuse these remarks.   I have been on the whole much
interested, and sometimes amused.   Are you aware that the
praiser of this 'brave gymnasium' has not seen a canoe nor
taken a long walk since '79? that he is rarely out of the
house nowadays, and carries his arm in a sling? Can you
imagine that he is a backslidden communist, and is sure he
will go to hell (if there be such an excellent institution) for the luxury in which he lives? And can you
believe that, though it is gaily expressed, the thought is
hag and skeleton in every moment of vacuity or depression?
Can you conceive how profoundly I am irritated by the
opposite affectation to my own, when I see strong men and
rich men bleating about their sorrows and the burthen of
life, in a world full of 'cancerous paupers,' and poor
sick children, and the fatally bereaved, ay, and down even
to such happy creatures as myself, who has yet been
obliged to strip himself, one after another, of all the
pleasures that he had chosen except smoking (and the days
of that I know in my heart ought to be over), I forgot
eating, which I still enjoy, and who sees the circle of
impotence closing very slowly but quite steadily around
him?   In my view, one dank, dispirited word is harmful, a
crime of *lèse-humanité*, a piece of acquired evil; every
gay, every bright word or picture, like every pleasant air
of music, is a piece of pleasure set afloat; the reader
catches it, and, if he be healthy, goes on his way rejoicing, and it is the business of art so to send him, as
often as possible,

For what you say, so kindly, so prettily, so precisely,
of my style, I must in particular thank you; though even
here, I am vexed you should not have remarked on my
attempted change of manner: seemingly this attempt is
still quite unsuccessful! Well, we shall fight it out on
this line if it takes all summer.

And now for my last word: Mrs. Stevenson is very
anxious that you should see me, and that she should see
you, in the flesh. If you at all share in these views, I
am a fixture. Write or telegraph (giving us time, however, to telegraph in reply, lest the day be impossible),
and come down here to a bed and a dinner. What do you
say, my dear critic? I shall be truly pleased to see
you; and to explain at greater length what I meant by
saying narrative was the most characteristic mood of
literature, on which point I have great hopes I shall persuade you. - Yours truly,

Robert Louis Stevenson.

P.S. - My opinion about Thoreau, and the passage in the
'Week,' is perhaps a fad, but it is sincere and stable.
I am still of the same mind five years later; did you
observe that I had said 'modern' authors? and will you
observe again that this passage touches the very joint of
our division? It is one that appeals to me, deals with
that part of life that I think the most important, and
you, if I gather rightly, so much less so? You believe in
the extreme moment of the facts that humanity has acquired
and is acquiring; I think them of moment, but still of
much less than those inherent or inherited brute principles and laws that sit upon us (in the character of
conscience) as heavy as a shirt of mail, and that (in the
character of the affections and the airy spirit of pleasure) make all the light of our lives. The house is,
indeed, a great thing, and should be rearranged on sanit-
ary principles; but my heart and all my interest are with
the dweller, that ancient of days and day-old infant man.
                                                    R.L.S.

     An excellent touch is p. [161 above]. 'By instinct or
design he eschews what demands constructive patients.'
I believe it is both; my theory is that literature must
always be most at home in treating movement and change;
hence I look for them. (LS, ii, 264-6)

(b) From a letter to Thomas Stevenson dated 28 October
1885

My dearest Father, - Get the November number of 'Time',
and you will see a review of me by a very clever fellow,
who is quite furious at bottom because I am too orthodox,
just as Purcell [No. 21] was savage because I am not
orthodox enough. I fall between two stools. It is odd,
too, to see how this man thinks me a full-blooded fox-
hunter, and tells me my philosophy would fail if I lost
my health or had to give up exercise! (LS, ii, 266)

(c) From a letter to Henry James dated 28 October 1885

Pray see, in the November 'Time' (a dread name for a
magazine of light reading), a very clever fellow,
W. Archer, stating his views of me; the rosy-gilled
'athletico-aesthete'; and warning me, in a fatherly
manner, that a rheumatic fever would try my philosophy
(as indeed it would), and that my gospel would not do for
'those who are shut out from the exercise of any manly

virtue save renunciation.' To those who know the rickety
and cloistered spectre, the real R.L.S., the paper,
besides being clever in itself, presents rare elements of
sport. The critical parts are in particular very bright
and neat, and often excellently true. Get it by all
manner of means.

I hear on all sides I am to be attacked as an immoral
writer; this is painful. Have I at last got, like you, to
the pitch of being attacked? 'Tis the consecration I
lack - and could do without. Not that Archer's paper is
an attack, or what either he or I, I believe, would call
one; 'tis the attacks on my morality (which I had thought
a gem of the first water) I referred to. (LS, ii, 268)

(d) Stevenson to Archer, letter dated 30 October 1885

Dear Mr. Archer, - It is possible my father may be soon
down with me; he is an old man and in bad health and
spirits; and I could neither leave him alone nor could we
talk freely before him. If he should be here when you
offer your visit, you will understand if I have to say
no, and put you off.

I quite understand your not caring to refer to things
of private knowledge. What still puzzles me is how you
('in the witness box' - ha! I like the phrase) should
have made your argument actually hinge on a contention
which the facts answered.

I am pleased to hear of the correctness of my guess.
It is then as I supposed; you are of the school of the
generous and not the sullen pessimists; and I can feel
with you. I used myself to rage when I saw sick folk
going by in their Bath-chairs; since I have been sick
myself (and always when I was sick myself), I found life,
even in its rough places, to have a property of easiness.
That which we suffer ourselves has no longer the same air
of monstrous injustice and wanton cruelty that suffering
wears when we see it in the case of others. So we begin
gradually to see that things are not black, but have their
strange compensations; and when they draw towards their
worst, the idea of death is like a bed to lie on. I
should bear false witness if I did not declare life
happy. And your wonderful statement that happiness tends
to die out and misery to continue, which was what put me
on the track of your frame of mind, is diagnostic of the
happy man raging over the misery of others; it could never
be written by the man who had tried what unhappiness was
like. And at any rate, it was a slip of the pen: the
ugliest word that science has to declare is a reserved

indifference to happiness and misery in the individual; it
declares no leaning towards the black, no iniquity on the
large scale in fate's doings, rather a marble equality,
dread not cruel, giving and taking away and reconciling.

Why have I not written my 'Timon'? Well, here is my
worst quarrel with you. You take my young books as my
last word. The tendency to try to say more has passed
unperceived (my fault, that). And you make no allowance
for the slowness with which a man finds and tries to learn
his tools. I began with a neat brisk little style, and a
sharp little knack of partial observation; I have tried to
expand my means, but still I can only utter a part of what
I wish to say, and am bound to feel; and much of it will
die unspoken. But if I had the pen of Shakespeare, I have
no 'Timon' to give forth. I feel kindly to the powers
that be; I marvel they should use me so well; and when I
think of the case of others, I wonder too, but in another
vein, whether they may not, whether they must not, be like
me, still with some compensation, some delight. To have
suffered, nay, to suffer, sets a keen edge on what remains
of the agreeable. This is a great truth, and has to be
learned in the fire. - Yours very truly,

Robert Louis Stevenson.

We expect you, remember that. (LS, ii, 269-70)

(e) Stevenson to Archer, 1 November 1885

Dear Mr. Archer, - You will see that I had already had a
sight of your article and what were my thoughts.

One thing in your letter puzzles me. Are you, too,
not in the witness-box? And if you are, why take a wilfully false hypothesis? If you knew I was a chronic
invalid, why say that my philosophy was unsuitable to
such a case? My call for facts is not so general as
yours, but an essential fact should not be put the other
way about.

The fact is, consciously or not, you doubt my honesty;
you think I am making faces, and at heart disbelieve my
utterances. And this I am disposed to think must spring
from your having not had enough of pain, sorrow, and
trouble in your existence. It is easy to have too much;
easy also or possible to have too little; enough is
required that a man may appreciate what elements of con-
solation and joy there are in everything but absolutely
overpowering physical pain or disgrace, and how in almost
all circumstances the human soul can play a fair part.
You fear life, I fancy, on the principle of the hand of

little employment. But perhaps my hypothesis is as unlike
the truth as the one you chose. Well, if it be so, if you
have had trials, sickness, the approach of death, the
alienation of friends, poverty at the heels, and have not
felt your soul turn round upon these things and spurn them
under - you must be very differently made from me, and I
earnestly believe from the majority of men. But at least
you are in the right to wonder and complain.

To 'say all'? Stay here. All at once? That would
require a word from the pen of Gargantua. We say each
particular thing as it comes up, and 'with that sort of
emphasis that for the time there seems to be no other.'
Words will not otherwise serve us; no, nor even Shakespeare, who could not have put 'As You Like It' and 'Timon'
into one without ruinous loss both of emphasis and substance. Is it quite fair then to keep your face so
steadily on my most light-hearted works, and then say I
recognise no evil? Yet in the paper on Burns, for
instance, I show myself alive to some sorts of evil. But
then, perhaps, they are not your sorts.

And again: 'to say all'? All: yes. Everything: no.
The task were endless, the effect nil. But my all, in
such a vast field as this of life, is what interests me,
what stands out, what takes on itself a presence for my
imagination or makes a figure in that little tricky
abbreviation which is the best that my reason can conceive. That I must treat, or I shall be fooling with my
readers. That, and not the all of some one else.

And here we come to the division: not only do I believe
that literature should give joy, but I see a universe, I
suppose, eternally different from yours; a solemn, a
terrible, but a very joyous and noble universe, where
suffering is not at least wantonly inflicted, though it
falls with dispassionate partiality, but where it may be
and generally is nobly borne; where, above all (this I
believe; probably you don't: I think he may, with cancer),
any brave man may make out a life which shall be happy for
himself, and, by so being, beneficent to those about him.
And if he fails, why should I hear him weeping? I mean if
I fail, why should I weep? Why should *you* hear *me*? Then
to me morals, the conscience, the affections, and the
passions are, I will own frankly and sweepingly, so
infinitely more important than the other parts of life,
that I conceive men rather triflers who become immersed
in the latter; and I will always think the man who keeps
his lip stiff, and makes 'a happy fireside clime,' and
carries a pleasant face about to friends and neighbours,
infinitely greater (in the abstract) than an atrabilious
Shakespeare or a backbiting Kant or Darwin. No offence

to any of these gentlemen, two of whom probably (one for certain) came up to my standard.

And now enough said; it were hard if a poor man could not criticise another without having so much ink shed against him. But I shall still regret you should have written on an hypothesis you knew to be untenable, and that you should thus have made your paper, for those who do not know me, essentially unfair. The rich, fox-hunting squire speaks with one voice; the sick man of letters with another. - Yours very truly,

Robert Louis Stevenson.
(Prometheus-Heine in minimis)

P.S. - Here I go again. To me, the medicine bottles on my chimney and the blood on my handkerchief are accidents; they do not colour my view of life, as you would know, I think, if you had experience of sickness; they do not exist in my prospect; I would as soon drag them under the eyes of my readers as I would mention a pimple I might chance to have (saving your presence) on my posteriors. What does it prove? what does it change? it has not hurt, it has not changed me in any essential part; and I should think myself a trifler and in bad taste if I introduced the world to these unimportant privacies.

But, again, there is this mountain-range between us - that you do not believe me. It is not flattering, but the fault is probably in my literary art. (LS, ii, 270-3)

'Prince Otto'

November 1885

54. STEVENSON ON 'PRINCE OTTO', FROM LETTERS TO HENLEY,
W. H. LOW, COLVIN, AND GOSSE

1883, 1884

(a) Stevenson to Henley, from a letter dated by Colvin
April 1883

I have no idea whether or not 'Otto' will be good. It is
all pitched pretty high and stilted; almost like the
Arabs, at that; but of course there is love-making in
'Otto', and indeed a good deal of it. I sometimes feel
very weary; but the thing travels - and I like it when I
am at it. (LS, ii, 120)

(b) Stevenson to Henley, from a letter dated by Colvin
May 1883

'Otto' is, as you say, not a thing to extend my public on.
It is queer and a little, little bit free; and some of the
parties are immoral; and the whole thing is not a romance,
nor yet a comedy; not yet a romantic comedy; but a kind of
preparation of some of the elements of all three in a
glass jar. I think it is not without merit, but I am not
always on the level of my argument, and some parts are
false, and much of the rest is thin; it is more a triumph
for myself than anything else; for I see, beyond it,
better stuff. I have nine chapters ready, or almost
ready, for press. My feeling would be to get it placed
anywhere for as much as could be got for it, and rather in
the shadow, till one saw the look of it in print. (LS, ii,
127)

(c) Stevenson to Henley, from a letter dated by Stevenson
'May or June, 1883'

'... ['Otto'] has, I do believe, some merit: of what
order, of course, I am the last to know; and, triumph of
triumphs, my wife - my wife who hates and loathes and
slates my women - admits a great part of my Countess to
be on the spot.... As a story, a comedy, I think 'Otto'
very well constructed; the echoes are very good, all the
sentiments change round, and the points of view are continually, and, I think (if you please), happily contrasted. None of it is exactly funny, but some of it is
smiling. (LS, ii, 130-2)

A year after these remarks were written, in the spring of
1884, Fanny Stevenson wrote to her mother-in-law that
'Prince Otto' was almost completed:

Louis and I fighting the path of one character inch by
inch: it is she alone waits to be finished. I am not
sure whether it is well or ill but in the combats I
generally come off victorious, so I hope this poor countess will be all right. I wish often for Mr. Stevenson's
opinion. I believe I don't care much for anybody else's.
(B, 3797)

(d) Stevenson to Henley, from a letter dated by Colvin
October 1883

I am now deep, deep, ocean deep in 'Otto': a letter is a
curst distraction, about 100pp. are near fit for publication; I am either making a spoon or spoiling the horn of a
Caledonian bull, with that airy potentate. God help me, I
bury a lot of labour in that principality; and if I am not
greatly a gainer, I am a great loser and a great fool.
However, *sursum corda*; faint heart never writ romance.
(LS, ii, 151)

(e) Stevenson to Will H. Low, from a letter dated 13 December 1883. Will Hickok Low (1853-1932), a well-known
American artist, was a close friend of Stevenson from the
time of their meeting in France in the 1870s. Low's recollections of Stevenson are found in his 'Chronicle of
Friendships' (1908).

I was much pleased with what you said about my work. Ill-
health is a great handicapper in the race. I have never

at command that press of spirits that are necessary to
strike out a thing red-hot. 'Silverado' is an example of
stuff worried and pawed about, God knows how often, in poor
health, and you can see for yourself the result: good pages,
an imperfect fusion, a certain languor of the whole. Not,
in short, art.... My brief romance, 'Prince Otto' - far my
most difficult adventure up to now - is near an end. I have
still one chapter to write *de fond en comble*, and three or
four to strengthen or recast. The rest is done. I do not
know if I have made a spoon, or only spoiled a horn; but I
am tempted to hope the first.... There is a good deal of
stuff in it, both dramatic and, I think, poetic; and the
story is not like these purposeless fables of to-day, but
is, at least, intended to stand firm upon a base of philosophy - or morals - as you please. It has been long gestated,
and is wrought with care. *Enfin, nous verrons*. My labours
have this year for the first time been rewarded with upwards of £350; that of itself, so base we are! encourages
me; and the better tenor of my health yet more. (LS, ii, 172)

(f) Stevenson to Colvin, from a letter dated 9 March 1884

Two chapters of 'Otto' do remain: one to rewrite, one to
create; and I am not yet able to tackle them. For me it
is my chief o' works; hence probably not so for others,
since it only means that I have here attacked the greatest
difficulties. But some chapters towards the end: three in
particular - I do think come off. I find them stirring,
dramatic, and not unpoetical. We shall see, however; as
like as not, the effort will be more obvious than the
success. For, of course, I strung myself hard to carry it
out. The next will come easier, and possibly be more
popular. I believe in the covering of much paper, each
time with a definite and not too difficult artistic purpose; and then, from time to time, drawing oneself up and
trying, in a superior effort, to combine the facilities
thus acquired or improved. Thus one progresses. But,
mind, it is very likely that the big effort, instead of
being the masterpiece, may be the blotted copy, the gymnastic exercise. This no man can tell; only the brutal
and licentious public, snouting in Mudie's wash trough,
can return a dubious answer. (LS, ii, 181)

(g) Stevenson to Edmund Gosse, from a letter dated 17
March 1884

I am at a standstill; as idle as a painted ship, but not

so pretty. My romance, which has so nearly butchered me
in the writing, not even finished; though so near, thank
God, that a few days of tolerable strength will see the
roof upon that structure. I have worked very hard at it,
and so do not expect any great public favour. *In moments
of effort, one learns to do the easy things that people
like*. There is the golden maxim; thus one should strain
and then play, strain again and play again. The strain is
for us, it educates; the play is for the reader, and
pleases. Do you not feel so? We are ever threatened by
two contrary faults: both deadly. To sink into what my
forefathers would have called 'rank conformity', and to
pour forth cheap replicas, upon the one hand; upon the
other, and still more insidiously present, to forget that
art is a diversion and a decoration, that no triumph or
effort is of value, nor anything worth reaching except
charm. (LS, ii, 188)

55. W. E. HENLEY ON 'PRINCE OTTO' AND THE 'IAMBIC PULSE',
FROM A LETTER TO STEVENSON

29 April 1885 (National Library of Scotland)

Henley's comments here are on a manuscript version of
'Prince Otto'. The lines he quotes to illustrate the
'iambic pulse' were changed when the story appeared in
'Longman's Magazine' and, more extensively, in the final
version in book form.

The style is generally very good - particularly in the
bits of landscape, where you seem to me to go sometimes
beyond praise. With that of the dialogue I am not (as
yet) so greatly taken. It beats too often with the iambic
pulse; it feels too often a little Stevensonian, a little
mannered and dry. The iambic pulse, by the way, is more
audible all over the shop than I like to remember: e.g.

In a few white-hot words he bade adieu.
Dubbed desperation by the name of love,
And called his wrath forgiveness; cast one look
Of leave taking upon the place that was
No longer to be his and hurried forth,
Love's prisoner or pride's!

This from the accomplished stylist that used to look
down on his Dickens - the early Dickens; the Dickens of
'Barnaby Rudge' and 'Little Nell' - is steep.   Thus the
whirligig of Time!

56.   GEORGE MEREDITH ON 'PRINCE OTTO', FROM A LETTER TO
STEVENSON

13 November 1885

From 'Letters of George Meredith' (1970), ed. C. L. Cline,
ii, 799.
     'Prince Otto' was inspired by Meredith's work and his
favourable judgment would no doubt have meant a great deal
to Stevenson.   During the time of its serialization in
'Longman's', Meredith wrote to Stevenson (26 September
1885) saying only: 'I have read pieces of "Prince Otto",
admiring the royal manner of your cutting away of the
novelist's lumber.   Straight to the matter is the secret'
('Letters of George Meredith', ii, 791).   The letter below
was written shortly after publication of the novel in book
form.   It surely is not the letter Stevenson reported on
to Henley: 'I had yesterday a letter from George Meredith,
which was one of the events of my life.   He cottoned (for
one thing), though with differences, to Otto; cottoned
more than my rosiest visions had inspired me to hope;
said things that (from him) I would blush to quote'
(Balfour, 'Life', ii, 12).

My dear Stevenson,
     Another look at 'Prince Otto', as you have exposed him
[i.e. in book form].
     Oh! but he is too masterful in his limpness.   'Feel my
heart,' says she.   And he talks on crisply of business.
- And is morally limp, and has been kept physically fast-
ing.   And you abstain from telling us that he does *not*
feel her heart.
     Now virtue is possible for men, surely so (in some)
under the spell of love.   Critically if you had it in
design at all to humanize your Otto, there was an error of
omission in not showing us previously impressively the
charm of Seraphina's character for him.   She stamped

herself on him at one time - and had the stuff to do so.
But when?   Or when did the aggregate of her charms affect
him in a manner to make him lay hand on another woman's
heart, and continue discoursing like a professional
gentleman with client? -
     Till further, and for the moment, with my salute to
your wife, adieu.

Warmly yours,
George Meredith

57.   ANDREW LANG, AN UNSIGNED REVIEW, 'PALL MALL GAZETTE'

6 November 1885, xlii, 5

Lang claims authorship of this review in an unpublished
letter to Stevenson dated 17 December (B, 5076).

Those who like ourselves, have refrained from sipping at
'Prince Otto' in its periodical driblets, can now enjoy
their reward.   It is a book to be drunk in one long
breath, like a draught of sunny Moselle from a tapering,
iridescent Venetian goblet.   Iridescent is just the word
to describe Mr. Stevenson's fantasy in this, its latest
expression.   Its colours flit and flash and flow into each
other, and will not bear enumeration, much less analysis.
We must bring to it the light of imaginative sympathy, or
its hues will not show.   The ordinary novel-reader, and
even the reader of Mr. Stevenson's previous fiction, must
be warned not to expect a story of sensational incident.
If we were required to docket the book with Polonius-like
accuracy we should call it a philosophical-humouristical-
psychological fantasy.   Of recent English books, Mr.
Shorthouse's 'spiritual romances' - is not that the name
he gives them? - are perhaps those which, in externals,
'Prince Otto' most nearly resembles. (1)   In style and
spirit, we hasten to add, Mr. Stevenson and Mr. Shorthouse
have fortunately nothing in common.   Admirers of either
author may interpret 'fortunately' as they please.
     In dealing with modern fiction the reviewer's duty (so
we understand it) is too often that of sparing his reader
the trouble of essaying the book itself.   In the case of
'Prince Otto' his duty is just the reverse; consequently

we do not discount the effect of Mr. Stevenson's combinations by any outline of their nature.   In their unexpected-
tedness lies their chief charm.   We ask ourselves how this
turn of fancy ever found its way into the writer's mind,
how that touch of palpitating reality managed to pass from
his memory into his imagination so exactly at the right
time.   Indeed, it is the unexpectedness of the whole conception which renders it so irresistible.   It might have
come in a dream, like the rhythms of 'Kubla Khan.'   Where
are we to look for its germs?   They exist, doubtless,
since nothing comes from nothing, but they elude our
search.   Did some psychological or ethical concept suggest
the parable?   If so, we have missed Mr. Stevenson's meaning; for we take his work to be a free invention, not a
parable at all.   Did some external stimulus, some incident
in history or fiction, set his imagination to work?   It
does not appear so.   Did the character of Prince Otto –
the man of fine instincts in a false position – give the
initial impulse?   If so, the difficulty is only thrown a
step further back.   Was it the scene – the little German
principality, with its pine-clad hills and 'sable vales
of forest between' – that cried aloud to be peopled with
the quaint and graceful creatures of Mr. Stevenson's
fancy?   That one can scarcely suppose.   A second reading
might possibly throw light on the genesis of the work.
Meanwhile we are content to treat it as Campbell would
fain have treated the rainbow, rejoicing in its beauty,
not 'asking proud philosophy' to teach us what it is.
Mr. Stevenson calls it a 'romance' – we should rather
describe it as a comedy in the purest sense of the word.
For an ideal theatre it might be dramatized, though
heaven forbid that it should be for any real theatre!
It is somewhat akin to Alfred de Musset's plays, quite as
dramatic, much less evanescent, much more healthy.
Another ingenious writer, of whom we are frequently
reminded in reading 'Prince Otto,' is Mr. George Meredith;
and it must be said that if Mr. Stevenson does not take us
to the heights which we now and then attain under Mr.
Meredith's guidance, we are at least spared the rough
places of the ascent.
    The style of this book is masterly beyond that of its
predecessors; sometimes, perhaps, a trifle overbold, but
generally as sober as it is strong and concentrated.   In
the way of sustained description Mr. Stevenson has done
nothing so powerful as the night and morning scenes in the
pine forest through which 'Princess Cinderella' takes her
flight: and there are many other nature-pictures rich in
colour yet deliciously fresh and cool.   The wit of the
dialogue is matched by the imaginative vigour of epithet

and illustration where the author speaks in his own
person.   Here are some touches from the portrait of Mdme.
von Rosen: 'She was a good vocalist; and, even in speech,
her voice commanded a great range of changes, the low
notes rich with tenor quality, the upper ringing, on the
brink of laughter, into music.   A gem of many facets and
variable hues of fire; a woman who withheld the better
portion of her beauty, and then, in a caressing second,
flashed it like a weapon full on the beholder.'   Again,
of the same lady: 'When a man has been embraced by a woman
he sees her in a glamour, and at such a time, in the baffling glimmer of the stars, she will look wildly well.   The
hair is touched with light; the eyes are constellations;
the face sketched in shadows - a sketch, you might say, by
passion.'   How vividly the following few words describe a
mental feat we have all attempted in our time: 'Hastily
she trod the thoughts out like a burning paper.'   How
delicate are these reflections: 'Of all injured vanities,
that of the reproved buffoon is the most savage;' and 'It
is ourselves we cannot forgive, when we refuse forgiveness
to our friend.   Some strand of our own misdoing is
involved in every quarrel.'   Such quotations might be
multiplied indefinitely; but they will be sought for in
their context by all who care for graceful invention,
fresh thought, and fine expression.

Note

1   Joseph Henry Shorthouse (1834-1903); his 'John Ingle-
    sant' (1880) and 'Little Schoolmaster Mark' (1883) had
    wide vogue.   Edmund Gosse wrote to Stevenson (25 Decem-
    ber 1885): 'I have been staying in Birmingham with
    Shorthouse, who always stimulates me.   We were talking
    of you; he fancies that there are relations not of
    resemblance but of sympathy between "Prince Otto" and
    "Little Schoolmaster Mark".   I see what he means: I
    should like to know whether you see also.   I hope you
    are not one of those who stiffen the nape-muscle
    against Shorthouse, because he is beloved of deans
    and premiers.   You are beloved of premiers also...'
    ('Life and Letters of Edmund Gosse' [1931], 183).

58.   FROM AN UNSIGNED REVIEW, 'SATURDAY REVIEW'

21 November 1885, lx, 691

This review dealt with 'Prince Otto' and three other
novels.   For Stevenson's comments on the review, see Nos
60 and 63.

When we are given, as in 'Prince Otto,' an impossible
prince ruling over an impossible territory at an indeter-
minate time we naturally expect a fairy tale, and nobody
can write fairy tales in modern form so well as Mr. Stevenson can when he chooses.   But the Prince of Grünewald is
not a fairy prince like Prince Giglio, or a funny prince
like Prince Bulbo, or an entrancing prince like Prince
Florizel.   The author calls his book a romance, but the
story deals with persons who have no high or romantic
aspirations, no lofty ideals, no longing to perform
doughty deeds.   None of the princes, or princesses, or
great lords or ladies, soar; they all grovel.   Tales of
unsavoury court intrigue are not pleasant to read even
when the facts are real and the historian is bound to tell
them.   In a work of imagination, and especially in a
'romance,' which should always have high and noble aims,
they seem oddly out of place.
    The Prince of Grünewald is a fool and a wittol who
leaves affairs of State to his wife and her alleged para-
mour, Baron Gondremark.   He is fond of acknowledging that
he is a 'mere plexus of weakness.'   He tries by fits and
starts, however, to pluck up a little manhood, and he
actually challenges an English baronet to fight a duel.
But the Grunewalders are tired of him and the Princess,
and they proclaim themselves a Republic.   Then the Prince
says to his wife, who, for aught we are told, may or may
not have been the Messalina folks thought her, 'My love
is changed.   It is purged of any conjugal pretension.   It
does not ask, does not hope, does not wish for a return in
kind.   You may forget for ever that part in which you
found me so distasteful, and accept without embarrassment
the affection of a brother.'   This sort of thing is as
distasteful to us as Prince Otto can have ever been to the
Princess Seraphina.
    The author's descriptions of scenery and some of his
passing expressions seem to us laboured and affected.   A
burn 'set and tended primrose gardens and made a favourite

of the silver birch.... Through all these friendly features the path, its human acolyte, conducted our two wan-
derers downwards.... Gaily the pure water, air's first
cousin, fleeted along the rude aqueduct.' Again we are
told that the touch of Baron Gondremark's skin 'revolted
the Princess to her toes.' A bright fire is called 'an
eating blaze.' We are assured that a woodman was visibly
'commoved' when the author means that his feelings were
touched. We read, too, in these pages of a *partie carré*'
and of a 'chaperone.' Would the author write a cornichone?

It is painful to have no words of praise to say of a
book by Mr. Stevenson. But it is precisely because he is
what he is that he can afford to have his faults brought
home to him. 'On ne jette pas de pierres aux arbres qui
ne portent pas de fruits.'

59. W. E. HENLEY, UNSIGNED REVIEW, 'ATHENAEUM'

21 November 1885, 3030, 663-4

See No. 60 for Stevenson's response to this review. The
reviewer is identified as Henley by two letters from
Henley to Stevenson (B, 4847 and 4848).

Mr. Stevenson's new book is so plainly an essay in pure
literature that to the average reader it may be something
of a disappointment. It has none of the qualities of an
ordinary novel. Means, atmosphere, characters, effects –
everything is peculiar. Mr. Stevenson has worked from
beginning to end on a convention which is hardly to be
paralleled in modern literature. The ordinary material of
the novel he throws aside; in half a dozen sentences he
gives the results of a whole volume of realism; he goes
straight to the quick of things, and concerns himself with
none but essentials. That his work is perfectly successful it would be rash to assert. But in some respects – in
certain qualities of other than verbal form – it may be
taken as a model by anybody with an understanding of art
in its severer and more rigid sense, and a desire to excel
in the higher ranges of literary achievement.

The author's theme is the morals of marriage. The hero
is a delightful trifler, with views concerning life, and a

secret passion for his wife, the Princess Seraphina; the
heroine a young woman with ambition, a strong sense of
duty, an incomparable ignorance of men and things, and
withal unconsciously in love with her husband, Prince
Otto.   Their dominion is the principality of Grünewald,
which marches with the duchy of Gerolstein, and, in
another direction, with that 'seaboard Bohemia' which is
known to students of the 'Winter's Tale.'   To bring
together these young people (Otto is six-and-thirty,
but as young as most lads of two-and-twenty) is the task
that Mr. Stevenson has set himself.   Their story, as
imagined and set forth by him, is delightful.   Dumas would
have told it with a more truly human feeling and a more
general and taking sympathy than Mr. Stevenson has been
able to compass; Alfred de Musset with a rarer note of
passion, a touch of humour that would have appealed to a
wider public.   But neither Musset nor Dumas could have
written 'Prince Otto' as we have it.   It is possible that
in their several ways they might have proved their case
more convincingly; it is probable enough that they would
have been a trifle less fantastic, less individual and
peculiar, and for that reason in some measure more persuasive.   But when all is said, Mr. Stevenson has little
or no reason to avoid such a comparison or to dread its
results.   Here and there - in the turn of his dialogue,
the pregnant brevity of his descriptions - he reminds the
reader of Mr. George Meredith; here and there he appears
to be slightly too personal to be wholly acceptable, a
little too histrionic to be quite effective.   But his book
has a real organic completeness.   It lives with its own
life, and succeeds by virtue of an inspiration to be found
nowhere else.   It will scarcely be so popular (it may be)
as 'Treasure Island' or 'The Dynamiter.'   But it has been
produced as a 'classic,' so to speak; it may be called the
author's diploma piece; and as a 'classic,' if in no other
capacity, it is tolerably certain to endure.   Of course,
to some extent, it is open to criticism.   Otto is, perhaps, a trifle too histrionic, especially in his relations
with Madame von Rosen, and Seraphina too priggish and un-
amiable; it may be that Gondremark - who seems to be a
kind of prose sketch of the German Chancellor - requires
more energy, a more vigorous humanity than Mr. Stevenson
can wield.   But, on the other hand, Madame von Rosen is
an admirable character in conception and in execution.
In the style there are notes of blank verse which afflict
the reader with a sense of chill unknown to those who
have delighted in the verbal felicity of 'Virginibus
Puerisque' and 'Travels with a Donkey.'   Yet the vocabulary is choice and full, the form varied, the manner

elegant and distinguished. The chapter called 'Princess
Cinderella' as a piece of romantic prose will bear comparison with the best work of its kind. This is high
praise no doubt, but no one who reads it will assert that
it is too high - perhaps, indeed, it is scarcely high
enough. And it is possible to say almost as much of the
book, considered as a whole. For 'Prince Otto' is a protest against the existence of most of that which is unworthy in the theory and practice of modern literature,
and is plainly the work of a man who writes, not for the
public of Mudie, but with a constant respect for the principles of art, and an unalterable sense of the excellence
of beauty, in life and literature alike.

60. STEVENSON, LETTER TO HENLEY

November (?) 1885, LS, ii, 262-3

Henley had expressed in earlier letters his displeasure
with the editor of the 'Athenaeum' for shortening his
review and the hope that Stevenson would not regard it as
unfavourable (B, 4847, 4848). Clearly he was uneasy about
how Stevenson would receive it and not without cause. The
review was a curious performance; the effort not to offend
is so apparent, so ill-concealed (except perhaps to Henley
himself) that the praise seems insincere. It is hardly
surprising when Stevenson says the praise 'stops my
throat', 'chokes me'. The name suppressed by Colvin was
perhaps that of Norman MacColl, at the time editor of the
'Athenaeum'. The notice in the 'Saturday Review' on
'Otto' is No. 58 above.

Dear Lad, - If there was any more praise in what you
wrote, I think [the editor] has done us both a service;
some of it stops my throat. What, it would not have been
the same if Dumas or Musset had done it, would it not?
Well, no, I do not think it would, do you know, now; I am
really of opinion it would not; and a dam good job too.
Why, think what Musset would have made of Otto! Think how
gallantly Dumas would have carried his crowd through! And
whatever you do, don't quarrel with - . It gives me much
pleasure to see your work there; I think you do yourself

great justice in that field; and I would let no annoyance,
petty or justifiable, debar me from such a market. I think
you do good there. Whether (considering our intimate relations) you would not do better to refrain from reviewing
me, I will leave to yourself: were it all on my side, you
could foresee my answer; but there is your side also, where
you must be the judge.

As for the 'Saturday.' Otto is no 'fool,' the reader
is left in no doubt as to whether or not Seraphina was a
Messalina (though much it would matter, if you come to
that); and therefore on both these points the reviewer has
been unjust. Secondly, the romance lies precisely in the
freeing of two spirits from these court intrigues; and here
I think the reviewer showed himself dull. Lastly, if
Otto's speech is offensive to him, he is one of the large
class of unmanly and ungenerous dogs who arrogate and
defile the name of manly. As for the passages quoted, I
do confess that some of them reek Gongorically; they are
excessive, but they are not inelegant after all. However,
had he attacked me only there, he would have scored.

Your criticism on Gondremark is, I fancy, right. I
thought all your criticisms were indeed; only your praise
- chokes me. - Yours ever,

R.L.S.

61.   EDMUND GOSSE, LETTER TO STEVENSON

22 November 1885

From 'Life and Letters of Sir Edmund Gosse' (1931), ed.
Evan Charteris, 180-1.
    Gosse (1849-1928), poet, critic, and man of letters,
was a long-time supporter of Stevenson; their friendship
began in the mid-1870s when they both frequented the Savile
Club. At the time of this letter Gosse had succeeded
Leslie Stephen as Clark lecturer at Trinity College,
Cambridge, a post Gosse held until 1890.

My dear Louis, -

I was very grateful to you for the gift of 'Prince
Otto', which arrived just when my college work for the
term was beginning. It is the only book I have allowed

myself to read outside my range of labour.

Of course I read it right through at a rush, and then I read it slowly. My opinion about it is expressed with such surprising exactitude by a gentleman in last night's 'Athenaeum' [Henley's review, No. 59] that I feel as if he must be me or I must be he - though this is not so.

The book has given me intense pleasure, and it will take a high place among your works. I suppose it was written in a time of suffering and weakness, but there is no sense of this, it is bubbling with energy and fullness of life, and its faults, where it has faults, are those of youth.

I hope it is not impertinent of me to allude to these faults, or rather to the one I have noted. That is a lack of simplicity. Perhaps I should limit down my accusation to the particular passage of the Flight of Seraphina. I don't know whether you have already been upbraided for this piece of fine writing. Forgive me for saying that it is not worthy of you. It is a wilful and monstrous sacrifice on the altar of George Meredith, whose errors you should be the last to imitate and exaggerate. In this passage you inflate your chest and toss back your hair, and are, in fact, devilish brilliant and all that, by Gad. The reader that has followed you all entranced, and who has forgotten you entirely, in the excitement of the narrative, becomes conscious of you again, and is amazed to find you so offensively clever and original. And then back you go to the beautiful old simplicity that makes you so easily the master of us all.

There are many things, I believe, that could be said about your ethics. I find myself, however, after some inward argument, inclined to believe that you know best. You are a great magician, and not least in this that you make one acquiesce in what is naturally unpleasant to one. The gentlemanliness of the Prince is intended, I take it, to be rather the reverse of real gentility sometimes? He is delightfully exasperating and Scotch.

You will not gather from these few foolish words how much I have enjoyed the book or how much it has occupied my thoughts. I hear you are simply breaking out on all sides into penny dreadfuls. They are sure to send me with a gooseskin to bed. It is one of the great advantages of a married life that one can go to bed after a soul-devouring tale of blood without the awful solitude of darkness around one.

It is so long - this is not a reproach - since you wrote to me that I do not know the name of your new house. Pray remember me very kindly to Mrs. Stevenson - to either Mrs. Stevenson, please - and believe me,

Very sincerely yours,
                                        Edmund Gosse.

Your dedication to Otto is a masterpiece of tenderness
and delicate grace.

62.   AN UNSIGNED REVIEW, 'ST JAMES'S GAZETTE'

1 January 1886, xii, 7

'Yes, sir, by six-and-thirty,' says the old farmer Killian
in Mr. Louis Stevenson's new romance, 'if a man be a fol-
lower of God's laws he should have made himself a home and
a good name to live by; he should have got a wife and a
blessing on his marriage; and his works, as the Word says,
should begin to follow him.' The same sentiment has been
put into the mouths of several other personages whom Mr.
Stevenson has introduced to us on previous occasions. The
ideal thus indicated is confronted in the author's fancy
with another, which is seemingly its direct opposite – the
ideal, namely, of unshackled adventure, an independent
outlook, and poetic impulse. But it is in Mr. Stevenson's
view only the poorer conventionalities of society, the
slavery to mechanism, which lead people to regard these
ideals as incompatible.
   The outward dress of 'Prince Otto' is very different
from that of the author's modern and realistic fantasies.
No place is assigned to the action except the State of
Grünewald, which borders on 'Maritime Bohemia;' and the
period is left to the conjecture of the reader. It is, in
fact, several periods at once; though the predominant
atmosphere is that of last-century Courts, as they are
reflected in the didactic tales of Prince Charming and
the like, which were composed for the instruction of
youthful monarchs. Very skilfully has Mr. Stevenson
seized the tone of light irony, of vanity, and intrigue
which are familiar to us from so many volumes of Memoirs
and Correspondence. The figure of Gondremark, on the
other hand, is an embodiment of modern statecraft, with
its 'bold piratical dishonesty, which it would be calum-
nious to call deceit.' And now and again, especially in
the last scene, there breathes upon it that atmosphere of
the 'golden world,' of Arden, or of 'Seaboard Bohemia,'
which is more welcome than the ingenuities of courtly wit

or extravagant invention.

By far the best parts of the book, to our thinking, are
the chapters which relate the adventures of the Countess
von Rosen. That lady, who is certainly 'imperfect,' has
notwithstanding the undeniable merit of real existence.
She is alive and a personage, where some of the other
figures are merely abstract or typical. It is very
noticeable that Mr. Stevenson has hitherto succeeded best
in such parts of his stories as follow step by step the
expeditions or escapes of some single character. The best
thing in 'Treasure Island' was the adventure of the boy
Hawkins in the coracle. The management of that strange
little revolving craft and the momentous tug at the
schooner's cable are really things to 'to stir the heart
like a trumpet.' And the flight of the chicken-hearted
caitiff M'Guire, with his cruel and futile bag, was
worthy to compare in its way with the flight of Sikes.
Here also Mr. Stevenson follows the various embassies and
escapades of the unscrupulous adventuress with a wonderfully keen sympathy for her shifting impulses of generosity and self-interest, till he has justified his
description of her as a Providence. Thoroughly awakened
by the breathless suspense of the Countess's situation,
Mr. Stevenson is at his best in the scene where she brings
the Prince her bag of money for the purchase of Killian's
farm. The moonlight, the 'Mercury' of Gian Bologna, the
Countess's male disguise, the skill with which she plays
on the Prince's mobile nature - the wildness, the wit,
and yet the charm of it all - give the scene that very
unusual and delightful air, the air of Romantic Comedy.
In a different vein the flight of the Princess is a piece
of well-sustained narrative. But it is marred by a fault,
which it is curious to find in Mr. Stevenson - the fault
of 'preciosity': 'dish-shaped houses in the fork of giant
arms' is a triumph of euphuism, only one word being
employed in its usual sense. We leave our readers to
interpret. We guessed it pretty soon ourselves; but that
was only because, like Lamb's friend, George Dyer, when he
found himself in the New River, 'We knew where we were.'
There are other instances. But where Mr. Stevenson is
thoroughly inspired his style may be left to himself. It
is peculiarly plastic to the vigour of his conceptions.
Here, as we have said, the greatest vigour is displayed in
a subordinate character. For this reason we must pronounce regretfully that 'Prince Otto' is not a masterpiece. The Suicide Club was a masterpiece in its own way.
But here the author has aimed higher. Against every temptation, Mr. Stevenson has essayed resolutely the steeper
and the harder path. 'I still purpose,' he says in his

dedication, 'by hook or crook, this book or the next, to
launch a masterpiece.' And if it is not the next, we
exhort him cordially to let it be the one after.

63.   STEVENSON, FROM A LETTER TO GOSSE ON THE RECEPTION OF
'OTTO' AND THE 'BESTIALITY OF THE BEAST WHOM WE FEED'

2 January 1886, LS, ii, 280-1

Stevenson's letter was prompted by the review in the 'St
James's Gazette' of 1 January (No. 62), which he thought
was by Gosse; however, in a letter dated 4 January, Gosse
denies having written the review ('Life and Letters of
Edmund Gosse' (1931), 186).

My dear Gosse, - Thank you for your letter, so interesting
to my vanity. There is a review in the 'St. James's,'
which, as it seems to hold somewhat of your opinions, and
is besides written with a pen and not a poker, we think
may possibly be yours. The 'Prince' has done fairly well
in spite of the reviews, which have been bad; he was, as
you doubtless saw, well slated in the 'Saturday' [No. 58];
one paper received it as a child's story; another (picture
my agony) described it as a 'Gilbert comedy.' It was
amusing to see the race between me and Justin M'Carthy:
the Milesian has won by a length. (1)
   That is the hard part of literature. You aim high, and
you take longer over your work, and it will not be so
successful as if you had aimed low and rushed it. What
the public likes is work (of any kind) a little loosely
executed; so long as it is a little wordy, a little slack,
a little dim and knotless, the dear public likes it; it
should (if possible) be a little dull into the bargain.
I know that good work sometimes hits; but, with my hand on
my heart, I think it is by an accident. And I know also
that good work must succeed at last; but that is not the
doing of the public; they are only shamed into silence or
affectation. I do not write for the public; I do write
for money, a nobler deity; and most of all for myself, not
perhaps any more noble, but both more intelligent and
nearer home.
   Let us tell each other sad stories of the bestiality of

the beast whom we feed. What he likes is the newspaper;
and to me the press is the mouth of a sewer, where lying is
professed as from an university chair, and everything prurient, and ignoble, and essentially dull, finds its abode
and pulpit.   I do not like mankind; but men, and not all of
these - and fewer women. As for respecting the race, and,
above all, that fatuous rabble of burgesses called 'the
public,' God save me from such irreligion! - that way lies
disgrace and dishonour. There must be something wrong in
me, or I would not be popular.

     This is perhaps a trifle stronger than my sedate and
permanent opinion. Not much, I think. As for the art
that we practise, I have never been able to see why its
professors should be respected. They chose the primrose
path; when they found it was not all primroses, but some
of it brambly, and much of it uphill, they began to think
and to speak of themselves as holy martyrs. But a man is
never martyred in any honest sense in the pursuit of his
pleasure; and *delirium tremens* has more of the honour of
the cross. We were full of the pride of life, and chose,
like prostitutes, to live by a pleasure. We should be
paid if we give the pleasure we pretend to give; but why
should we be honoured?... (2)

R.L.S.

Notes

1 McCarthy's 'Camiola: A Girl with a Fortune' was one of
   the three other books reviewed with 'Prince Otto' in
   the 'Saturday'.
2 Stevenson expresses these views at greater length in
   Letter to a Young Gentleman (No. 103).

64. STEVENSON, FROM A LETTER TO C. W. STODDARD ON
'PRINCE OTTO' AND THE 'DIFFICULTY OF BEING IDEAL IN AN
AGE OF REALISM'

13 February 1886, LS, ii, 290

Stevenson first met Charles Warren Stoddard (1843-1909) in
San Francisco during his stay there in 1880. Stoddard had
travelled widely in the south seas and wrote 'South-Sea
Idyls' (1873), 'The Lepers of Molokai' (1885), and other

accounts of travel. It was through him that Stevenson
first became acquainted with Melville's 'Typee' and
'Omoo'. Stoddard was teaching at Notre Dame University in
Indiana at the time this letter was written.

How does your class get along? If you like to touch on
'Otto', any day in a by-hour, you may tell them - as the
author's last dying confession - that it is a strange
example of the difficulty of being ideal in an age of
realism; that the unpleasant giddy-mindedness, which
spoils the book and often gives it a wanton air of unreality and juggling with air-bells, comes from unsteadiness
of key; from the too great realism of some chapters and
passages - some of which I have now spotted, others I dare
say I shall never spot - which disprepares the imagination
for the cast of the remainder.
    Any story can be made *true* in its own key; any story
can be made *false* by the choice of a wrong key of detail or
or style: 'Otto' is made to reel like a drunken - I was
going to say man, but let us substitute cipher - by the
variations of the key. Have you observed that the famous
problem of realism and idealism is one purely of detail?
Have you seen my Note on Realism in Cassell's 'Magazine of
Art' [November 1883]; and Elements of Style in the Contemporary' [On Style in Literature, April 1885]; and
Romance [A Gossip on Romance] and Humble Apology [A Humble
Remonstrance] in 'Longman's' [November 1882 and December
1884]? They are all in your line of business; let me know
what you have not seen and I'll send 'em.

65.   E. PURCELL, FROM A REVIEW, 'ACADEMY'

27 February 1886, xxix, 140-1

On Purcell see headnote to No. 21.

... I have succeeded in unearthing a number of the
'Academy,' five years old, in which I reviewed Mr. Stevenson's Essays [No. 21]. As his genius has been more widely
revealed that review has lain upon my conscience. But, on

reading it to-day, there seems little to repudiate,
except a few pompous or gushing expressions. Severe it
was, and one-sided - but at that time unavoidably so.
He had not then attempted romance; and upon his exquisite
little tours and essays some admirers were then trying to
build up a claim of original and profound philosophy.
Against that claim I protested, perhaps too seriously.
He had not - he never will have - any new gospel of life
to give us. He has developed precisely as I hoped and
prophesied that he would. There still, however, remains
that strange mixture of audacious candour and audacious
reticence on the great issues of morality which attracted
and distressed from the first. On this much might be
written interesting to Mr. Stevenson and a few more, but
to most others neither acceptable nor helpful. We have no
right to demand his scheme of human life; but this is certain, that his puzzling enigmatic ethics, whether they be
individual, or whether they are a true reflection of a
present transitional state of society, are the real hindrance to his aim of producing a great romance worthy of
his genius. In 'Prince Otto' he tried and owns his failure. It seems to me that, if we are to deal at length
with men and motives, we must lay a good foundation of
ethical principles and repose comfortably upon them. Is
not this restful solidity the secret of most works of the
imagination of sustained interest? A friend - no mean
critic - brings back my 'Prince Otto' in a rage - he
cannot read it - a vicious style, cannot explain why, but
does not like it. Yet he again and again plods through
Scott's ponderous stories, not sparing himself a line.
This instance is suggestive. Sir Walter's mind was quite
made up about the right and wrong of most things and persons. He could afford to describe and judge them steadily, without excitement or misgiving; and the reader,
soothed and reassured, resigns himself with confidence to
the prolonged spell of the great magician. Not that Scott
is a greater, or Stevenson a lesser genius for all that.
It is but their fate. Equal in imagination, the one is
strengthened and disciplined to prolonged flights by his
perfect assimilation of conventional principles; the
other's course, rapid, erratic, and interrupted, displays
far deeper insight, far keener perception, far bolder
genius - a genius brilliant but seemingly troubled,
because it ventures into a world ignored by Scott, where
all is doubt and difficulty.
What, then, is the position to which Mr. Stevenson has
so far attained? Not, I still think, beside the great
masters, whose profound and simple humanity commands universal and perpetual sympathy. May he not be regarded as

the author's author, just as Keats has been called the
poet's poet? Widely read his tales will perforce be, if
only for the weird and morbid interest which has lately
marked them, but read with imperfect appreciation. Even
thus, only an author or critic can appreciate the consummate art by which he has handled worse horrors than Poe's,
by means of a fantastic burlesque setting, just strong
enough to redeem their repulsiveness, without marring
their fascination. That he should have dropped this
sportive tone in 'Dr. Jekyll' amazes me. If we are bound
to take this cruel tale seriously, I see not how to defend
it. Life is already so full of doubts and miseries, that
all such sacrileges on human credulity as this or the
'Peau de Chagrin', cannot but do harm. Manicheism is a
contagious disease. It may be ridiculed, or preached
sincerely, but should not be preached gravely just for
fun.

But in the 'New Arabian Nights,' and still more in the
'Dynamiter,' the art is phenomenal. It is not the old-
fashioned *ars celare artem*, but art so carelessly,
roguishly exposed, that it charms by its very audacity.
The author seems to say: 'Now you need not agitate yourself so much over these horrors - they are only made-up
rubbish, and I am laughing at you all the time. I don't
mind telling you this, because you know in spite of it,
you won't go to bed till you have finished the book.'
Probably there is nothing else quite like this in literature, though it is one of the many aspects of Rabelais.
Indeed, no modern English book contains such a profusion
and superfluity of talent as this little 'Dynamiter.' It
is a masterpiece, upon which 'Prince Otto' has not
improved, and no novelist can read it without gnawing
envy. This - on two grounds. One, the insolent prodi-
gality of its invention. Mr. Trollope once spun out a
six-line story about a mustard plaster into a weary
novelette. Mr. Stevenson flushes a regular three-volume
covey of incident, pursues it awhile - for a chapter, a
page, a few lines - and then gaily tosses it aside. The
novelist must be horrified to see all these valuable
plots and promising openings bandied about, instead of
being hoarded and doled out to the world in expensive
volumes. The 'Dynamiter' contains a whole library of
possible novels. Its charm lies in this wanton profusion
of a spendthrift whose resources seem inexhaustible. The
other ground of envy is most interesting, and may not yet
have been adequately noticed. Space precludes more than
a reference to it. Mr. Stevenson is a perfect adapter.
I have traced so many of his happiest conceptions to other
books, that still more might probably be traced by other

readers. No one, unless inspired, can evolve ideas and
incidents, without some peg of suggestion. It is delightful to notice how Mr. Stevenson hits upon some unlikely
material in a book, sees its capabilities, turns it upside
down, inside out, transforms it, builds upon it a graceful
creation of his own. I wondered how anyone could invent
the Story of the Fair Cuban. I wonder still more, since I
lit on a certain heavy book about Hayti, how such prose
could be sublimated into such fiction.

Much more could be said about Mr. Stevenson's peculiar
genius and methods, but, after all, it would be premature.
His later works have revised the criticism of their predecessors; final judgment must be suspended till his
labours - may they be long and prosperous! - are
completed.

Hitherto I have written not about 'Prince Otto,' but
about its author, since the less is included in the
greater; for really there is little to be said. It is too
late to analyse the plot or characters, or point out
beauties or defects. The only useful or interesting
remark that occurs is a caveat as to the lukewarmness of
the public. The book is not a failure at all - it is a
success. It is not uninteresting - it is most fascinating. It is confessedly a wild, rambling, nondescript
book; but it contains some things of rare beauty and
sweetness, and overflows with cleverness and originality.
It refines the odours of Auerbach's pine woods and the
splendour of Ruskin's skies. But it is disappointing.
That is the true verdict. And why? Because we, and the
author too, are bent upon his producing something more
sustained, more suited to be placed beside, and compared
with, and preferred to, other great fictions; and we all
expected that 'Prince Otto' was to prove the *magnum opus*.
Well, we were wrong. It is not even equal to its predecessors; but it still towers above its rivals. Faults
it has - exasperating ones - and a certain wrong-
headedness which is a new feature. What reader does not
wish that he could have stood at the author's elbow with
a few suggestions? For my part, I would have said - give
me either less or more delicacy in regard to marriage,
tone down Mdme. de Rosen, alter the closing scene, define
the Prince rather clearer, and tell us more about the
princess, work out Roederer's Authoritarian system - and
so on. So between us we should all have made a strange
jumble of it. It cannot please us all - only mild commonplace can - and it displeases some. In disparaging
'Prince Otto' we praise the author; for, after all, who
else could have written it?

66. STEVENSON, FROM A LETTER TO HARRIET MONROE IN DEFENCE
OF THE CHARACTER OF PRINCE OTTO

25 May 1886, LS, ii, 303-4

Harriet Monroe (1860-1936) was a Chicago writer and the
founder and editor of 'Poetry: A Magazine of Verse'.

... I must lose no time in thanking you for a letter
singularly pleasant to receive.... You are not pleased
with Otto; since I judge you do not like weakness; and no
more do I. And yet I have more than tolerance for Otto,
whose faults are the faults of weakness, but never of
ignoble weakness, and who seeks before all to be both kind
and just. Seeks, not succeeds. But what is man? So much
of cynicism to recognise that nobody does right is the
best equipment for those who do not wish to be cynics in
good earnest. Thing better of Otto, if my plea can
influence you; and this I mean for your own sake - not
his, poor fellow, as he will never learn your opinion;
but for yours, because, as men go in this world (and
women too), you will not go far wrong if you light upon so
fine a fellow; and to light upon one and not perceive his
merits is a calamity. In the flesh, of course, I mean;
in the book the fault, of course, is with my stumbling
pen. Seraphina made a mistake about her Otto; it begins
to swim before me dimly that you may have some traits of
Seraphina.
     With true ingratitude you see me pitch upon your
exception; but it is easier to defend oneself gracefully
than to acknowledge praise. I am truly glad that you
should like my books; for I think I see from what you write
that you are a reader worth convincing.

'The Strange Case of Dr Jekyll and Mr Hyde'

January 1886

67. ANDREW LANG, AN UNSIGNED REVIEW, 'SATURDAY REVIEW'

9 January 1886, lxi, 55-6

E. J. Mehew attributes this review to Andrew Lang, who was
a reader for Longman's and must have seen the story in
manuscript and written to Stevenson commenting on similarities between 'Jekyll and Hyde' and Poe's William
Wilson and Gautier's Le Chevalier Double. Stevenson, in
his reply, admitted to knowing William Wilson but said,
'I now hear for the first time (and with chagrin) of The
Chevalier Double. Who in hell was he?' Some years later,
in a letter to the 'Athenaeum' (9 February 1895), Lang
recalled that 'After the success of the book, Mr. Stevenson told me that he had mentioned the *idea* of the man who
was two men to me before (I think it was long before), and
that I had said that it was impracticable, and not new.
I think I gave the instance of Poe's William Wilson.'
Commentators on the story saw similarities between it and
a wide range of earlier works; William Wilson and Le
Chevalier Double were by no means obvious choices for
comparison.

Mr. Stevenson's 'Prince Otto' was, no doubt, somewhat disappointing to many of his readers. They will be hard to
please if they are disappointed in his 'Strange Case of
Dr. Jekyll and Mr. Hyde.' To adopt a recent definition of
some of Mr. Stevenson's tales, this little shilling work
is like 'Poe with the addition of a moral sense.' Or
perhaps to say that would be to ignore the fact that Poe

was extremely fond of one kind of moral, of allegories
in which embodied Conscience plays its part with terrible
efficacy. The tale of William Wilson, and perhaps that of
the Tell-Tale Hearts, are examples of Poe in this humour.
Now Mr. Stevenson's narrative is not, of course, absolutely original in idea. Probably we shall never see a
story that in germ is absolutely original. The very rare
possible germinal conceptions of romance appear to have
been picked up and appropriated by the very earliest masters of fiction. But the possible combinations and possible methods of treatment are infinite, and all depends
on how the ideas are treated and combined.
    Mr. Stevenson's idea, his secret (but a very open
secret) is that of the double personality in every man.
The mere conception is familiar enough. Poe used it in
William Wilson and Gautier in Le Chevalier Double. Yet
Mr. Stevenson's originality of treatment remains none the
less striking and astonishing. The double personality
does not in his romance take the form of a personified
conscience, the *doppel ganger* of the sinner, a 'double'
like his own double which Goethe is fabled to have seen.
No; the 'separable self' in this 'strange case' is all
unlike that in William Wilson, and, with its unlikeness
to its master, with its hideous caprices, and appalling
vitality, and terrible power of growth and increase, is,
to our thinking, a notion as novel as it is terrific.
We would welcome a spectre, a ghoul, or even a vampire
gladly, rather than meet Mr. Edward Hyde. Without telling
the whole story, and to some extent spoiling the effect,
we cannot explain the exact nature of the relations between Jekyll and Hyde, nor reveal the mode (itself, we
think, original, though it depends on resources of pseudo-
science) in which they were developed. Let it suffice to
say that Jekyll's emotions when, as he sits wearily in the
park, he finds that his hand is not his own hand, but
another's; and that other moment when Utterson, the
lawyer, is brought to Jekyll's door, and learns that his
locked room is haunted by somewhat which moans and weeps;
and, again, the process beheld by Dr. Lanyon, are all of
them as terrible as anything ever dreamed of by Poe. They
lack, too, that quality of merely earthly horror or of
physical corruption and decay which Poe was apt to introduce so frequently and with such unpleasant and unholy
enjoyment.
    It is a proof of Mr. Stevenson's skill that he has
chosen the scene for his wild 'Tragedy of a Body and a
Soul,' as it might have been called, in the most ordinary
and respectable quarters of London. His heroes (surely
this is original) are all successful middle-aged

professional men. No woman appears in the tale (as in
'Treasure Island', and we incline to think that Mr. Stevenson always does himself most justice in novels without a
heroine. It may be regarded by some critics as a drawback
to the tale that it inevitably disengages a powerful lesson
in conduct. It is not a moral allegory, of course; but you
cannot help reading the moral into it, and recognizing
that, just as every one of us, according to Mr. Stevenson,
travels through life with a donkey (as he himself did in
the Cévennes), so every Jekyll among us is haunted by his
own Hyde. But it would be most unfair to insist on this,
as there is nothing a novel-reader hates more than to be
done good to unawares. Nor has Mr. Stevenson, obviously,
any didactic purpose. The moral of the tale is its natural
soul, and no more separable from it than, in ordinary life,
Hyde is separable from Jekyll.

While one is thrilled and possessed by the horror of the
central fancy, one may fail, at first reading, to recognize
the delicate and restrained skill of the treatment of
accessories, details, and character. Mr. Utterson, for
example, Jekyll's friend, is an admirable portrait, and
might occupy a place unchallenged among pictures by the
best masters of sober fiction.

> At friendly meetings, and when the wine was to his
> taste, something eminently human beaconed from his eye;
> something indeed which never found its way into his
> talk; but which spoke not only in these silent symbols
> of the after-dinner face, but more often and loudly in
> the acts of his life. He was austere with himself, but
> tolerant to others, sometimes wondering, almost with
> envy, at the high pressure of spirits involved in their
> misdeeds.

It is fair to add that, while the style of the new romance
is usually as plain as any style so full of compressed
thought and incident can be, there is at least one passage
in the threshold of the book where Mr. Stevenson yields to
his old Tempter, 'preciousness.' Nay, we cannot restrain
the fancy that, if the good and less good of Mr. Stevenson's literary personality could be divided like Dr.
Jekyll's moral and physical personality, his literary Mr.
Hyde would greatly resemble - the reader may fill in the
blank at his own will. The idea is capable of development.
Perhaps Canon McColl is Mr. Gladstone's Edward Hyde, a
solution of historical problems which may be applauded by
future generations. This is wandering from the topic in
hand. It is pleasant to acknowledge that the half-page
of 'preciousness' stands almost alone in this excellent

and horrific and captivating romance, where Mr. Stevenson
gives us of his very best and increases that debt of gratitude which we all owe him for so many and such rare
pleasures.

There should be a limited edition of the 'Strange Case'
on Large Paper. It looks lost in a shilling edition - the
only 'bob'svorth,' as the cabman said when he took up Mr.
Pickwick, which has real permanent literary merit.

68. E. T. COOK, UNSIGNED NOTICE 'ATHENAEUM'

16 January 1886, 3038, 100

(Sir) Edward Tyas Cook (1857-1919) was editor of the 'Pall
Mall Gazette' (1890-2), the 'Westminster Gazette' (1893-5),
and the 'Daily News' (1895-1901). With Alexander Wedder-
burn he edited Ruskin's works (1903-11); and he himself
wrote the standard biography of Ruskin (1911), a 'Life of
Florence Nightingale' (1917), and 'John Delane of The
Times' (1915). Cook was not the only reader to object to
the terms of Jekyll's will. On 26 January, Rider Haggard
wrote to Stevenson that the will was the one 'blot upon an
otherwise perfect story'; he .pointed out that

  probate would not have been allowed to issue for a
  period of years. It would have been necessary to produce overwhelming evidence in support of the presumption of Jekyll's death.... I point this out in case
  you should care to alter it in future editions. As it
  stands the story is to the best of my belief really
  based upon a misconception of the law. (B, 4496)

Mr. R. L. Stevenson's proved ability in the invention of
exciting stories is by no means at fault in his 'Strange
Case of Dr. Jekyll and Mr. Hyde.' It is certainly a very
strange case, and one which would be extremely difficult
to see through from the beginning. It has also the first
requisite of such a story - it is extremely clearly narrated, and it holds one's interest. It overshoots the mark,
however, by being not merely strange, but impossible, and
even absurd when the explanation is given. So good an
artist in fanciful mysteries as Mr. Stevenson should have

avoided the mistake of a lengthy rationalization at all.
In the effective part of the story two points strike the
reader as weak: the first incident which is meant to show
the diabolical character of Mr. Hyde is inadequate, and
the terms of Dr. Jekyll's will would have been inoperative. Mr. Stevenson has overlooked the fact that a man's
will does not come into force until he is dead, and that
the fact that he has not been heard of for three months
would not enable his executor to carry out his testament-
ary directions.

69.   JAMES ASHCROFT NOBLE, FROM A REVIEW, 'ACADEMY'

23 January 1886, xxix, 55

Noble (1844-96) was a regular contributor to the 'Spectator', the 'New Age', and the 'Academy', as well as the
author of 'Morality in English Fiction' (1887), 'The
Sonnet in England and Other Essays' (1893), and 'Impressions and Memories' (1895). 'Jekyll and Hyde' was the
first of nine works dealt with in this review.

'The Strange Case of Dr. Jekyll and Mr. Hyde' is not an
orthodox three-volume novel; it is not even a one-volume
novel of the ordinary type; it is simply a paper-covered
shilling story, belonging, so far as external appearance
goes, to a class of literature familiarity with which has
bred in the minds of most readers a certain measure of
contempt. Appearances, it has been once or twice
remarked, are deceitful; and in this case they are very
deceitful indeed, for, in spite of the paper cover and the
popular price, Mr. Stevenson's story distances so unmistakably its three-volume and one-volume competitors, that
its only fitting place is the place of honour. It is,
indeed, many years since English fiction has been enriched
by any work at once so weirdly imaginative in conception
and so faultlessly ingenious in construction as this
little tale, which can be read with ease in a couple of
hours. Dr. Henry Jekyll is a medical man of high reputation, not only as regards his professional skill, but his
general moral and social character; and this reputation
is, in the main, well-deserved, for he has honourable

instincts and high aspirations with which the greater part
of his life of conduct is in harmony. He has also, however, 'a certain impatient gaiety of disposition,' which
at times impels him to indulge in pleasures of a kind
which, while they would bring to many men no sense of
shame, and therefore no prompting to concealment, do bring
to him such sense and such prompting, in virtue of their
felt inconsistency with the visible tenor of his existence. The divorce between the two lives becomes so complete that he is haunted and tortured by the consciousness
of a double identity which deprives each separate life of
its full measure of satisfaction. It is at this point
that he makes a wonderful discovery, which seems to cut
triumphantly the knot of his perplexity. The discovery is
of certain chemical agents, the application of which can
give the needed wholeness and homogeneity of individuality
by destroying for a time all consciousness of one set of
conflicting impulses, so that when the experimenter
pleases his lower instincts can absorb his whole being,
and, knowing nothing of restraint from anything above
them, manifest themselves in new and quite diabolical
activities. But this is not all. The fateful drug acts
with its strange transforming power upon the body as well
as the mind; for when the first dose has been taken the
unhappy victim finds that 'soul is form and doth the body
make,' and that his new nature, of evil all compact, has
found for itself a corresponding environment, the shrunk-
en shape and loathsome expression of which bear no resemblance to the shape and expression of Dr. Jekyll. It is
this monster who appears in the world as Mr. Hyde, a
monster whose play is outrage and murder; but who, though
known, can never be captured, because when he is apparently tracted to the doctor's house, no one is found there
but the benevolent and highly honoured doctor himself.
The re-transformation has, of course, been affected by
another dose of the drug; but as time goes by Dr. Jekyll
notices a curious and fateful change in its operation. At
first the dethronement of the higher nature has been difficult; sometimes a double portion of the chemical agent
has been found necessary to bring about the result; but
the lower nature gains a vitality of its own, and at
times the transformation from Jekyll to Hyde takes place
without any preceding act of volition. How the story ends
I must not say. Too much of it has already been told; but
without something of such telling it would have been impossible to write an intelligible review. And, indeed,
the story has a much larger and deeper interest than that
belonging to a mere skilful narrative. It is a marvellous
exploration into the recesses of human nature; and though

it is more than possible that Mr. Stevenson wrote with no
ethical intent, its impressiveness as a parable is equal
to its fascination as a work of art.   I do not ignore the
many differences between the genius of the author of 'The
Scarlet Letter' and that of the author of 'Dr. Jekyll and
Mr. Hyde' when I say that the latter story is worthy of
Hawthorne.

70.   AN UNSIGNED REVIEW, 'THE TIMES'

25 January 1886, 13

According to Charles Longman, who headed the firm that
published 'Jekyll and Hyde', this review marked the beginning of the great popularity of the book.

Nothing Mr. Stevenson has written as yet has so strongly
impressed us with the versatility of his very original
genius as this sparsely-printed little shilling volume.
From the business point of view we can only marvel in
these practical days at the lavish waste of admirable
material, and what strikes us as a disproportionate
expenditure on brain-power, in relation to the tangible
results.   Of two things, one.   Either the story was a
flash of intuitive psychological research, dashed off in
a burst of inspiration; or else it is the product of the
most elaborate forethought, fitting together all the parts
of an intricate and inscrutable puzzle.   The proof is,
that every connoisseur who reads the story once, must
certainly read it twice.   He will read it the first time,
passing from surprise to surprise, in a curiosity that
keeps growing, because it is never satisfied.   For the
life of us, we cannot make out how such and such an incident can possible be explained on grounds that are intelligible or in any way plausible.   Yet all the time the
seriousness of the tone assures us that explanations are
forthcoming.   In our impatience we are hurried towards the
denouement, which accounts for everything upon strictly
scientific grounds, though the science be the science of
problematical futurity.   Then, having drawn a sigh of
relief at having found even a fantastically speculative
issue from our embarrassments, we begin reflectively to

call to mind how systematically the writer has been working towards it. Never for a moment, in the most startling
situations, has he lost his grasp of the grand ground-
facts of a wonderful and supernatural problem. Each
apparently incredible or insignificant detail has been
thoughtfully subordinated to his purpose. And if we say,
after all, on a calm retrospect, that the strange case is
absurdly and insanely improbable, Mr. Stevenson might
answer in the words of Hamlet, that there are more things
in heaven and in earth than are dreamed of in our philosophy. For we are still groping by doubtful lights on the
dim limits of boundless investigation; and it is always
possible that we may be on the brink of a new revelation
as to the unforeseen resources of the medical art. And,
at all events, the answer should suffice for the purposes
of Mr. Stevenson's sensational *tour d'esprit*.

The 'Strange Case of Dr. Jekyll' is sensational enough
in all conscience, and yet we do not promise it the wide
popularity of 'Called Back.' The *brochure* that brought
fame and profit to the late Mr. Fargus was pitched in a
more commonplace key, and consequently appealed to more
vulgar circles. But, for ourselves, we should many times
sooner have the credit of 'Dr. Jekyll,' which appeals
irresistibly to the most cultivated minds, and must be
appreciated by the most competent critics. Naturally, we
compare it with the sombre masterpieces of Poe, and we may
say at once that Mr. Stevenson has gone far deeper. Poe
embroidered richly in the gloomy grandeur of his imagination upon themes that were but too material, and not very
novel - on the sinister destiny overshadowing a doomed
family, on a living and breathing man kept prisoner in a
coffin or vault, on the wild whirling of a human waif in
the boiling eddies of the Maelstrom - while Mr. Stevenson
evolves the ideas of his story from the world that is
unseen, enveloping everything in weird mystery, till at
last it pleases him to give us the password. We are not
going to tell his strange story, though we might well do
so, and only excite the curiosity of our readers. We
shall only say that we are shown the shrewdest of lawyers
hopelessly puzzled by the inexplicable conduct of a familiar friend. All the antecedents of a life of virtue and
honour seem to be belied by the discreditable intimacy that
has been formed with one of the most callous and atrocious
of criminals. A crime committed under the eyes of a witness goes unavenged, though the notorious criminal has
been identified, for he disappears as absolutely as if
the earth had swallowed him. He reappears in due time
where we should least expect to see him, and for some
miserable days he leads a charmed life, while he excites

the superstitious terrors of all about him. Indeed, the
strongest nerves are shaken by stress of sinister circumstances, as well they may be, for the worthy Dr. Jekyll -
the benevolent physician - has likewise vanished amid
events that are enveloped in impalpable mysteries; nor can
any one surmise what has become of him. So with over-
wrought feelings and conflicting anticipations we are
brought to the end, where all is accounted for, more or
less credibly.

Nor is it the mere charm of the story, strange as it
is, which fascinates and thrills us. Mr. Stevenson is
known for a master of style, and never has he shown his
resources more remarkably than on this occasion. We do
not mean that the book is written in excellent English -
that must be a matter of course; but he has weighed his
words and turned his sentences so as to sustain and excite
throughout the sense of mystery and of horror. The mere
artful use of an 'it' for a 'he' may go far in that respect, and Mr. Stevenson has carefully chosen his language
and missed no opportunity. And if his style is good, his
motive is better, and shows a higher order of genius.
Slight as is the story, and supremely sensational, we
remember nothing better since George Eliot's 'Romola' than
this delineation of a feeble but kindly nature steadily
and inevitably succumbing to the sinister influences of
besetting weaknesses. With no formal preaching and without a touch of Pharisaism, he works out the essential
power of Evil, which, with its malignant patience and
unwearying perseverance, gains ground with each casual
yielding to temptation, till the once well-meaning man
may actually become a fiend, or at least wear the reflection of the fiend's image. But we have said enough to
show our opinion of the book, which should be read as a
finished study in the art of fantastic literature.

71. A PARODY OF 'DR JEKYLL AND MR HYDE', 'PUNCH'

6 February 1886, xc, 64

THE STRANGE CASE OF DR. T. AND MR. H.
Or Two Single Gentlemen rolled into one.

CHAPTER I. - *Story of the Bore.*

MR. STUTTERSON, the lawyer, was a man of a rugged countenance, that was never lighted by a smile, not even when
he saw a little old creature in clothes much too large for
him, come round the corner of a street and trample a
small boy nearly to death. The little old creature would
have rushed away, when an angry crowd surrounded him, and
tried to kill him. But he suddenly disappeared into a
house that did not belong to him, and gave the crowd a
cheque with a name upon it that cannot be divulged until
the very last chapter of this interesting narrative. Then
the crowd allowed the little old creature to go away.
    'Let us never refer to the subject again,' said Mr.
STUTTERSON.
    'With all my heart,' replied the entire human race,
escaping from his button-holding propensities.

CHAPTER II. - *Mr. Hidanseek is found in the Vague Murder
Case.*

    Mr. **STUTTERSON** thought he would look up his medical
friends. He was not only a bore, but a stingy one. He
called upon the Surgeons when they were dining, and generally managed to obtain an entrance with the soup. 'You
here!' cried Dr. **ONION**, chuckling. 'Don't speak to me
about **TREKYL** - he is a fool, an ass, a dolt, a humbug,
and my oldest friend.'
    'You think he is too scientific, and makes very many
extraordinary experiments,' said **STUTTERSON**, disposing of
the fish, two *entrées* and the joint.
    'Precisely,' replied **ONION**, chuckling more than ever -
'as you will find out in the last Chapter. And now, as
you have cleared the table, hadn't you better go?'
    'Certainly,' returned the Lawyer, departing (by the
way, *not* returning), and he went to visit Mr. **HIDANSEEK.**
He found that individual, and asked to see his face.
    'Why not?' answered the little old creature in the
baggy clothes, defiantly. 'Don't you recognise me?'
    'Mr. R. L. **STEVENSON** says I mustn't,' was the wary

response; 'for, if I did, I should spoil the last chapter.'

Shortly after this Mr. HIDANSEEK, being asked the way by a Baronet out for a midnight stroll, immediately hacked his interrogator to pieces with a heavy umbrella. Mr. STUTTERSON therefore called upon Dr. TREKYL, to ask for an explanation.

'Wait a moment,' said that eminent physician, retiring to an inner apartment, where he wrote the following note: -

'Please, Sir, I didn't do it.'

'TREKYL forge for a murderer!' exclaimed STUTTERSON; and his blood ran cold in his veins.

CHAPTER III. - *And any quantity of Chapters to make your flesh creep.*

AND so it turned out that TREKYL made a will, which contained a strange provision that, if he disappeared, HIDANSEEK was to have all his property. Then Dr. ONION went mad with terror, because, after some whiskey-and-water, he fancied that his old friend TREKYL had turned into the tracked and hunted murderer, HIDANSEEK.

'Was it the whiskey?' asked STUTTERSON.

'Wait until the end!' cried the poor medical man, and, with a loud shriek, he slipped out of his coat, leaving the button-hole in the bore's hand, and died!

CHAPTER THE LAST. - *The Wind-up.*

I AM writing this - I, TREKYL, the man who signed the cheque for HIDANSEEK in Chapter I., and wrote the forged letter a little later on. I hope you are all puzzled. I had no fixed idea how it would end when I began, and I trust you will see your way clearer through the mystery than I do, when you have come to the imprint.

As you may have gathered from ONION'S calling me 'a humbug, &c., &c.,' I was very fond of scientific experiments. I was. And I found one day, that I, TREKYL, had a great deal of sugar in my composition. By using powdered acidulated drops I discovered that I could change myself into somebody else. it was very sweet!

So I divided myself into two, and thought of a number of things. I thought how pleasant it would be to have no conscience, and be a regular bad one, or, as the vulgar call it, bad 'un. I swallowed the acidulated drops, and in a moment I became a little old creature, with an acquired taste for trampling out children's brains, and hacking to death (with an umbrella) midnight Baronets who had lost their way. I had a grand time of it! It was all the grander, because I found that by substituting sugar for the drops I could again become the famous doctor, whose chief employment was to give Mr. **STUTTERSON** all my dinner. So much bad had been divided into the acidulated **HIDANSEEK** that I hadn't enough left in the sugary **TREKYL** to protest against the bore's importunities.

Well, that acidulated fool **HIDANSEEK** got into serious trouble, and I wanted to cut him. But I couldn't; when I had divided myself into him one day, I found it impossible to get the right sort of sugar to bring me back again. For the right sort of sugar was adulterated, and adulterated sugar cannot be obtained in London!

And now, after piecing all this together, if you can't see the whole thing at a glance, I am very sorry for you, and can help you no further. The fact is, I have got to the end of my '141 pages for a shilling.' I might have made myself into four or five people instead of two, - who are quite enough for the money.

72. J. A. SYMONDS, LETTER TO STEVENSON ON THE 'MORAL CALLOUSNESS' OF 'JEKYLL AND HYDE'

3 March 1886

From 'Letters of J. A. Symonds' (1968), ed. Herbert M. Schueller and Robert L. Peters, iii, 120-1.
     On Symonds and Stevenson see headnote to No. 22.

My dear Louis
     At last I have read Dr Jekyll. It makes me wonder whether a man has the right so to scrutinize 'the abysmal deeps of personality.' It is indeed a dreadful book, most dreadful because of a certain moral callousness, a want of sympathy, a shutting out of hope. The art is burning and intense. The 'Peau de Chagrin' disappears; Poe is as water. As a piece of literary work, this seems to me the finest you have done - in all that regards style, invention, psychological analysis, exquisite fitting of parts, and admirable employment of motives to realize the abnormal. But it has left such a deeply painful impression on my heart that I do not know how I am ever to turn to it again.
     The fact is that, viewed as an allegory, it touches one

too closely. Most of us at some epoch of our lives have
been upon the verge of developing a Mr Hyde.

Physical and biological Science on a hundred lines is
reducing individual freedom to zero, and weakening the
sense of responsibility. I doubt whether the artist
should lend his genius to this grim argument. Your Dr
Jekyll seems to me capable of loosening the last threads
of self-control in one who should read it while wavering
between his better and worse self. It is like the Cave of
Despair in the 'Faery Queen.'

I had the great biologist Lauder Brunton (1) with me a
fortnight back. He was talking about Dr Jekyll and a book
by W. O. Holmes (2), in wh atavism is played with. I
could see that, though a Christian, he held very feebly to
the theory of human liberty; and these two works of fiction interested him, as Dr Jekyll does me, upon that point
at issue.

I understand now thoroughly how much a sprite you are.
Really there is something not quite human in your genius!

The denouement would have been finer, I think, if Dr
Jekyll by a last supreme effort of his lucid self had
given Mr Hyde up to justice - wh might have been arranged
after the scene in Lanyon's study. Did you ever read
Raskolnikow ['Crime and Punishment']? How fine is that
ending! Had you made your hero act thus, you would at
least have saved the sense of human dignity. The doors of
Broadmoor would have closed on Mr Hyde.

Goodbye. I seem quite to have lost you. But if I come
to England I shall try to see you.

Love to your wife.

Everyrs
J A Symonds

Notes

1 Sir Thomas Lauder Brunton (1844-1916), Scottish physician known for his studies on the physiological
   effects of certain drugs.
2 Oliver Wendell Holmes's 'Elsie Venner' (1861).

73. F. W. H. MYERS, CRITICISM AND PROPOSED REVISIONS OF
'JEKYLL AND HYDE', FROM LETTERS TO STEVENSON

1886, 1887

Students of literature know Frederick William Henry Myers
(1843-1901) chiefly from his account of a walk with George
Eliot in the Fellows' Garden of Trinity College, Cambridge
at the crepuscular hour:

> taking as her text the three words ... *God, Immortal-*
> *ity, Duty,* - [she] pronounced, with terrible earnest-
> ness, how inconceivable was the *first*, how unbelievable
> the *second*, and yet how peremptory and absolute the
> *third*.... I listened, and night fell; her grave,
> majestic countenance turned toward me like a sybil's in
> the gloom....

This often-quoted passage is from Myers's essay on Eliot
in the 'Century' (November 1881). Myers was a poet, classical scholar, and essayist; he published several volumes
of poetry and his 'Essays Classical' and 'Essays Modern'
(2 vols, 1883) were highly regarded; according to J. A.
Symonds the essay on Virgil was 'quite remarkable; among
the best critical products of this century' ('Letters of
J. A. Symonds', i, 254). Myers's interest turned to psychical research during the last twenty years of his life
and he was one of the founders of the Society for Psychical Research, the purpose of which was to investigate, in
as detached and scientific a fashion as possible, such
phenomena as dreams, hypnotism, hysteria, unconscious
cerebration, hallucinatory voices, clairvoyance, thought-
transference, etc. On Myers's contributions in this field
and on the significance of his concept of consciousness,
see William James's Frederic Myers' Services to Psychology, an address to the society after Myers's death,
published in the society's 'Proceedings', XLII (1901), 17,
and reprinted in 'Memories and Studies' (1911), 145-70.
    Myers was deeply moved by 'Jekyll and Hyde' and in his
first letter to Stevenson (a) on 21 February 1886 he
praised the story and proposed that certain corrections be
made to ensure its position among the masterpieces of
literature; he offered to elaborate on his suggestions if
Stevenson so desired. Stevenson apparently wrote request-
ing more extensive comment, for Myers wrote again on 28
February enclosing several sheets of notes (b) and again
urging Stevenson to make corrections. Stevenson answered

(c) on 1 March. Then Myers apparently sent more sheets
(d) entitled Further Meditations on the Character of the
Late Mr. Hyde, dated 17 March. Then on 17 April 1887,
exactly one year and one month later, Myers wrote again
(e) reminding Stevenson that 'your masterpiece remains
(so far as I know) without that final revision, the possible lack of which would be a real misfortune to English
literature'. Myers was to mention the need for revisions
one final time in a letter (29 April 1892) to Stevenson
prompted by his keen interest in Stevenson's Chapter on
Dreams, an essay that appeared in 'Scribner's' (January
1888) and was reprinted in 'Across the Plains' (1892).
Stevenson's final letter to Myers (14 July 1892) contained
a lengthy account of several personal experiences of his
own that he considered 'of a high psychological interest'.
Myers printed this letter as an appendix to the chapter on
Disintegrations of Personality in his 'Human Personality
and Its Survival After Bodily Death' (1903), i, 300-3.
Stevenson was never to make any of the revisions of
'Jekyll and Hyde' that Myers suggested; perhaps Stevenson's objections (No. 77) to readers who saw Jekyll's
problem as arising from his sexual desire rather than his
hypocrisy were in part directed at Myers. All Myers's
page references below are to the first edition of 'Jekyll
and Hyde'; the bracketed numbers following his citations
refer to the South Seas Edition, vol. x.

(a) Myers to Stevenson, from a letter dated 21 February
1886

My dear Sir,
    We have a common friend in Mr. J. A. Symonds, who has
often spoken of you to me - and I have often wished that
I might have the pleasure of meeting you. The present
letter is called forth by the extreme admiration with
which I have read and reread your 'Strange Case of Dr.
Jekyll and Mr. Hyde'. I should be afraid to say how high
this story seems to me to stand among imaginative productions; and I cannot but hope that it may take a place in
our literature as permanent as 'Robinson Crusoe'.
    But, owing part to the brevity which forms one of the
book's merits, partly perhaps to a certain speed in its
composition which also reflects itself - especially in the
style, there are certain points which I think that you
might expand or alter with advantage; and which are well
worth the slight trouble involved. These are specially
on pages (1st edition)

I think that I would select pp. 121 [77-8], 138 [87-8]
as instances of a mastery of language and imagination
which it would be hard to parallel in fiction.
    I do not know whether you will care to receive any of
these suggestions which have occurred to me. But I venture to say that [it] is primarily as the author of this
work that you will be known to posterity, and that pains
spent on perfecting it will be well repaid. If pushed, I
will explain the suggestions which I have thought of....
                          Yours sincerely,
                          Frederick W. H. Myers (B, 5260)

(b) Pages (dated 27 February 1886) enclosed in a letter
from Myers to Stevenson dated 28 February 1886

              NOTES ON 'DR. JEKYLL AND MR. HYDE'
                   pages from 1st edition

p. 6 [7-8]   Quite admirable. Some foolish review (I
              believe) missed this altogether and saw his
              act as [?] not sufficiently criminal.
9 [9-10]   After 'in my chambers' are not a few words
              like ' - a grisly time - ' needed? One has
              rather too vague an idea of the group. A
              word or two as to Hyde's demeanour would be
              valuable.
19 [16]   Admirable! 22-26 [17-20] Admirable!
              33 [24-5] *Admirable!*
35-38 [26-8] This is the weakest point, to my mind.
              The cruelty developed from *lust* surely never
              becomes of just the same quality as the
              cruelty developed from mere madness [?] and
              savagery. Hyde would, I think, have simply
              brushed the baronet aside with a curse, and
              run on to some long-planned crime. The
              ground is ticklish, but could you not hint
              at a projected outrage (not on the baronet)
              hurried into dangerous haste by his having

been long away from Soho and not made the
usual preparations? Page 6 [7-8] is the key-
note. If you think it needful to avoid a
female victim it might be a policeman or some
relation of a tacitly-understood victim. No
real temptation to make body of baronet jump
on roadway (p. 37 [27]). Jekyll was
thoroughly civilized, and his degeneration
must needs take certain lines only. Have you
not sometimes thought of incarnate *evil*
rather too vaguely? Hyde is really not a
generalized but a specialized fiend.
Minor objections. 1) Ambiguity as to house
where maid was. Was it in Westminster? How
did Baronet need to ask way to post close to
Parliament or to his own house? If house is
meant to be in a low district how did Baronet
come there? 2) Why did Hyde leave the
stick? Excitement too *maniacal* to make us
thoroughly enter into Hyde.

39-40[28-9]   Admirable! 42 [30 One would like to hear
more of this house. Would Jekyll have sent
a picture there? Would he not have concealed
the house from his servants? If picture
wanted you might try one or two small Jan
Steens (1) which he could have taken in a
cab.

43 [30-1]   'Other half of stick' Why not thrown away?

45 [32-3]   No obvious reason why Jekyll receives Utterson in *theatre*. (Not important, as he *must*
be made to do so, and *need not* give explicit
reason.)

52 [36-7]   Here I think you miss a point for want of
familiarity with recent psycho-physical discussions. Handwriting in cases of double
personality (spontaneous ... or induced, as
in hypnotic cases) *is not* and *cannot be* the
same in the two personalities. Hyde's writing might look like Jekyll's done *with the
left hand*, or done when partly drunk, or ill:
that is the kind of resemblance there might
be. Your imagination can make a good point
of this.

56 [39]   The effect of shock in Dr. Lanyon might be
more specified. At present it seems rather
unreal. It *might* induce diabetes, if there
were previous kidney weakness. Could some
slight allusion be made to this on p. 57
[39-40]?

62-65 [43-4]	*Admirable!*
74 [49-50]	Admirable!
83 [54-5]	Surely not a true point - tidiness of room. When had the housemaid been in? Who had removed cinders from under grate? Surely coals were left at door and only the empty coal scuttle put out. Who washed cups? Sugar in tea-cup p. 86 [56] seems to me a false point. Neither J. nor H. would prepare in that minute way for comfort.
99-100 [64-5]	Excellent.
102 [66]	Objections to this page stated later: on page 131 [83-4].
103 [66-7]	Two objections. (1) Style too elevated for for Hyde. (Of this further on p. 138 [87-8].) These are not remarks that fit the husky broken voice of Hyde - they are Jekyllian. Surely Hyde's admirable style (p. 24 [19]) should be retained for him. (2) He would have been more unwilling to show the transformation. Lanyon should show, I think, more resolve (hint at pistol?) to make him do it.
106-110 [69-71]	Excellent.
111 [71-2]	I suppose the agent must be a drug. But the description of the process surely needs more substance and novelty. For one thing, there must have been a loss of consciousness. (This point admirable when we come to the spontaneous reversions into Hyde during sleep.) The first time the loss of consciousness might last for some hours.
112 [72-3]	*Admirable* - but I think there should be more physical exhaustion the first time. Then he might revive himself by wine placed nearby: his new body would be specially sensitive to stimulants. You perhaps purposely make *few* (but admirable) points as to the new body.
114 [73-4]	Excellent! excellent!
115 [74]	The return to Jekyll should surely be more insisted on - the doubt whether possible, and doubt whether taking drug again might not be *fatal*. A little more too about subsequent shrinkings from the pain etc. - overcome by restless impulse. I don't understand the phrase 'kept awake by

ambition.' I thought the stimulus was a different one.

116 [74-5]   We should understand already that he hadn't yet conquered his aversion. Surely the motive for the change was this. And, by the way, I think that it might somewhere be hinted that Jekyll was a good deal more licentious in early life than he avows. I don't want him to be prematurely aged but might there not be something more of flabbiness in his portliness? And some hint of his desiring *variety*? And a word or two more of Utterson's? Or a *thought* of Utterson's? How had Jekyll come across the housekeeper whom he placed in Soho? (What led you to specify Greek street?)

118 [75-6]   Excellent, but needs expansion. 'They soon began to turn towards the monstrous' is almost the only hint in the book of the process by which the thoroughly sympathetic and gently apolaustic Jekyll becomes the ruffianly Hyde. This is one of the great moral nodes of the book, and while I thoroughly admire your rapidity of manner and absence of didactic preoccupation, I nevertheless feel that this is a point on which Jekyll's memory would have dwelt: which he would have insisted on. He would not have liked that his friends should think that he had *fiendish* qualities in him at all to begin with: he would rather have laid all that on the continually expanding desires and insatiable enterprise of Hyde - 'That insatiability which is attached to inordinate desires as their bitterest punishment.'

120 [77]   'Sloping my own hand backward': see on p. 52 [36-7]. (Note that Hyde would have to make great effort to simulate Jekyll's signature - be long about it - signature would look odd, but unmistakably Jekyll's.)

121 [77-8]   *This is genius.*

123 [78-9]   Excellent! But correspondingly Jekyll's body should have got flabbier. See also p. 55 [38] where Jekyll, I think, regains vigour and cheerfulness far too rapidly. There should be something deprecative [?]

	rather than complacent about him after the murder.
124 [79]	An admirable page but 'begun to pamper' might be stronger and we here also begin to note a slight uncertainty in the psychical relationship of the two person-alities. Here Hyde is (bandit simile) hardly at all Jekyll; later on (and on p. 120 [77]) he is much more Jekyll and see p. 103 [66-7].
127 [81]	Here I again feel a false note. See on p. 36 [26-7] mauled the unresisting body' - no, not an elderly MP's!
129 [82]	'the hands of all men would be raised' Surely the one servant maid and his few acquaintances were not so dangerous. Hyde might have escaped from England easily enough. Why does Jekyll not think of a trip to Brussels?
131 [83-4]	An admirable page! But here one asks why, after the metamorphosis in bed, take the risk of separation from the drug? At any time even before the spontaneous metamor-phosis it might have been extremely desir-able to change back into Jekyll. If the drug was portable and manageable anywhere he would likely have taken it with him: - and after the murder certainly. Can you suppose that a Bunsen burner or some means of producing intense heat was necessary to effect a chemical combination? Or an electrical machine (which Lanyon also might possess) to assist change of body?
136-138 [86-8]	Genius!
138 [87-8]	But Hyde was in very little danger. Who could identify him? Probably almost any acquaintance that he had could have been bought off. And what chance of their seeing him if he went to an unfamiliar quarter of London? Or why does he not think of Paris or New York? For he is now so psychically separate from Jekyll (and I think something should be said as to growing psychical separation, if you determine to take that line) - he would surely have thought 'I will give up the Jekyll life, which can't really be re-tained, and will start fresh in New York.' (Even Liverpool would have tempted him,

if you say that he was not [?] enough for
New York.)

141 [89]   How would it be if Jekyll committed suicide and we were left to infer, from the
finding of Hyde's body, that the death-
agony had so transformed him? (B, 7271)

(c) Stevenson, letter to Myers dated 1 March 1886

My dear Sir, - I know not how to thank you: this is as
handsome as it is clever. With almost every word I agree
- much of it I even knew before - much of it, I must confess, would never have been, if I had been able to do what
I like, and lay the thing by for the matter of a year.
But the wheels of Byles the Butcher drive exceeding
swiftly, and 'Jekyll' was conceived, written, re-written,
re-re-written, and printed inside ten weeks. Nothing but
this white-hot haste would explain the gross error of
Hyde's speech at Lanyon's. Your point about the special-
ised fiend is more subtle, but not less just: I had not
seen it. - About the picture, I rather meant that Hyde had
brought it himself; and Utterson's hypothesis of the gift
(p. 42 [30]) an error. - The tidiness of the room, I
thought, but I dare say my psychology is here too ingenious to be sound, was due to the dread weariness and horror
of the imprisonment. Something has to be done: he would
tidy the room. But I dare say it is false.

I shall keep your paper; and if ever my works come to
be collected, I will put my back into these suggestions.
In the meanwhile, I do truly lack words in which to express my sense of gratitude for the trouble you have
taken. The receipt of such a paper is more than a reward
for my labours. I have read it with pleasure, and as I
say, I hope to use it with profit. - Believe me, your
most obliged,

                    Robert Louis Stevenson. (LS, ii, 294-5)

(d) Additional notes from Myers to Stevenson, dated 17
March 1886

FURTHER MEDITATIONS ON THE CHARACTER OF THE LATE MR. HYDE
        'We could have better spared a better man'

I.   Would Hyde have brought a picture? I think - and
friends of weight support my view - that such an act
would have been altogether unworthy of him. What are
the motives which would prompt a person in his situation to that act?

1. There are jaded voluptuaries who seek in a special
    class of art a substitute or reinforcement for the
    default of primary stimuli. Mr. Hyde's whole
    career forbids us to insult him by classing him
    with these men.

2. There are those who wish for elegant surroundings
    to allure or overawe the minds of certain persons
    unaccustomed to luxury or splendour. But does not
    all that we know of Mr. Hyde teach us that he dis-
    dained these modes of adventitious attractions?
    When he is first presented to us as 'stumping
    along eastward at a good walk' (I have mislaid my
    copy and must quote from memory) does not this
    imply the gait of one who aimed at energy but not
    at grace? And when we read that he was 'very
    plainly dressed,' don't we know that his means
    were such that he might have permitted himself
    without extravagance an elegant costume, - does
    not this show us the man aiming only at simple
    convenience, direct sufficiency? not anxious to
    present himself as personally attractive to
    others, but relying frankly on a cash nexus, and
    on that decision of character which would startle
    - almost terrify into compliance in cases where
    the blandishments of the irresolute might have
    been lavished in vain?

3. There are those, again, who surround their more
    concentrated enjoyments with a halo of mixed
    estheticism; who even if blameably adventurous in
    action are gently artistic in repose. Such, no
    doubt, was Dr. Jekyll: such, no doubt, he *expected*
    that Mr. Hyde would be. But was he not deceived?
    Was there not something unlooked for, something
    Napoleonic, in Hyde's way of pushing aside the
    aesthetic as well as the moral superfluities of
    life? Between the conception of some lawless
    design and its execution do we suppose that Jekyll
    himself could look at his pictures with tranquil
    pleasure? Did not his inward state 'suffer with
    the likeness of an insurrection'? And was not
    Hyde's permanent state this stabler and intenser
    reproduction of such absorbed and critical moments
    in Jekyll's inward history? We do not imagine the
    young Napoleon as going to concerts or taking a
    walk in a garden. We imagine him as now plunged
    in gloomy torpor, now warmly planning crimes to
    be. I cannot fancy Hyde looking in at picture
    shops. I cannot think that he ever even left his
    rooms, except on business. And in these rooms I

fancy that there would be a certain look as of
lower tenancy supervening [?] on a high-class
outfit; a certain admixture of ill-chosen with
handsome things; an unhomelike bareness along
with provision for ready ease.

II.   I have thought of how you could alter the murder
with least trouble. Perhaps it might do if the servant maid looked out of the window when the murderous assault had just begun and mentions that there
was no one else in the street except 'a shabbily
dressed johnny just a-scampering around the street
corner.' The girl need never appear again; but
Jekyll might speak of the Baronet as having inter-
fered to baulk what (in his way of speaking of Hyde)
he would probably call 'an enterprise too hastily
conceived.'

III. A very small point. I think that the housekeeper
says 'What's he been doing?' If 'now' were added,
it might imply that in her view he had already been
fortunate in escaping the interference of the Law.

IV.   A criticism of Mr. Gladstone's (to whom my sister-
in-law took the book while he was forming a minis-
try[?] which is now, I hope, splitting up more
irretrievably than Dr. Jekyll's personality) may
introduce my next suggestion. He said that while
he much admired and enjoyed the book, he felt that
the ethical retransference of Hyde into Jekyll was
made too easy a thing; - that he could not fancy so
profound and sudden a *backward* change. This, as
you perceive, bears out what I ventured to hint as
to the progressive effect which the repeated changes
must needs operate on the Jekyllian phase. And it
suggests, I think, the need of dealing with the subject of community of memory. At first I think such
community would be very imperfect; gradually the two
memories would fuse into one; and in the last stage
you might make an effective contrast of the increasing *fusion* of the two personalities in all except
ethical temper, joined with the increasing revulsion
in all except ethical temper, joined with the
increasing revulsion of Jekyll against the ethical
temper of Hyde; a revulsion maintained, no doubt, at
great cost of nervous exhaustion - like the prolonged attention needed down an ice-slope which gets
steeper and steeper; till the suicide (of Jekyll in
my view, not of Hyde) would represent the kind of

despairing spring with which the thoroughly exhausted climber leaps to a point where he could not in
his right senses have expected to find foothold,
misses and falls.

F. W. Myers.   (B, 7272)

(e) Myers to Stevenson, letter dated 17 April 1887

My dear Sir,
   I do not want to be importunate, but I cannot but help
reminding you that time is going on, and your masterpiece
remains (so far as I know) without that final revision,
the possible lack of which would be a real misfortune to
English literature. The works, even of the most fertile
and brilliant authors, which can hope for *permanent* pre-
servation must needs be few. Is it not well worth while
to make them as perfect as possible? I have heard the
views of many other persons on 'Dr. Jekyll and Mr. Hyde'
since I last wrote. I have not found any competent person
who does not think it your best work, or who did not also
feel it contained obvious, and removable, blots.
   I will not trouble you with further words; but may I
add how perfectly I admire the story called The Merry Men,

I remain, etc.
F. W. H. Myers.   (B, 5262)

Note

1 Dutch painter of the eighteenth century known for his
   historical and genre pictures.

74. JULIA WEDGWOOD, NOTICE, 'CONTEMPORARY REVIEW'

April 1886, xlix, 594-5

Frances Julia Wedgwood (1833-1913), who also wrote under
the pseudonym of Florence Dawson, was the author of 'John
Wesley and the Evangelical Reaction of the Eighteenth Century' (1870), 'The Moral Ideal' (1888), 'Nineteenth Century Teachers, and Other Essays' (1909), as well as other
books; her contributions to periodicals appeared chiefly in
the 'Contemporary' and 'Macmillan's'. She was to deal

briefly with Stevenson in Ethics and Literature, 'Contemporary Review' (January 1897).

By far the most remarkable work we have to notice this
time is 'The Strange Case of Dr. Jekyll and Mr. Hyde,' a
shilling story, which the reader devours in an hour, but
to which he may return again and again, to study a profound allegory and admire a model of style. It is a perfectly original production; it recalls, indeed, the work
of Hawthorne, but this is by kindred power, not by imitative workmanship. We will not do so much injustice to any
possible reader of this weird tale as to describe its
motif, but we blunt no curiosity in saying that its motto
might have been the sentence of a Latin father - 'Omnis
anima et rea et testis est.' Mr. Stevenson has set before
himself the psychical problem of Hawthorne's 'Transformation,' (1) viewed from a different and perhaps an opposite
point of view, and has dealt with it with more vigour if
with less grace. Here it is not the child of Nature who
becomes manly by experience of sin, but a fully-developed
man who goes through a different form of the process, and
if the delineation is less associated with beautiful imag-
ery, the parable is deeper, and, we would venture to add,
truer. Mr. Stevenson represents the individualizing
influence of modern democracy in its more concentrated
form. Whereas most fiction deals with the relation between man and woman (and the very fact that its scope is
so much narrowed is a sign of the atomic character of our
modern thought), the author of this strange tale takes an
even narrower range, and sets himself to investigate the
meaning of the word *self*. No woman's name occurs in the
book, no romance is even suggested in it; it depends on
the interest of an idea; but so powerfully is this interest worked out that the reader feels that the same material might have been spun out to cover double the space,
and still have struck him as condensed and close-knit
workmanship. It is one of those rare fictions which make
one understand the value of temperance in art. If this
tribute appears exaggerated, it is at least the estimate
of one who began Mr. Stevenson's story with a prejudice
against it, arising from a recent perusal of its predecessor, his strangely dull and tasteless 'Prince Otto.' It
is a psychological curiosity that the same man should have
written both, and if they were bound up together, the
volume would form the most striking illustration of a
warning necessary for others besides the critic - the
warning to judge no man by any single utterance, how

complete soever.

Note

1 Hawthorne's 'The Marble Faun' first appeared in England
   under the title 'Transformation'.

75. FROM AN UNSIGNED REVIEW, SECRET SIN, 'ROCK'

2 April 1886, 3

'Jekyll and Hyde' became a popular topic in the pulpit.
The following review gives some idea of what sermons based
upon it must have been like. The 'Rock' (London) was an
organ of the Unified Church of England and Ireland.

A very remarkable book has lately been published, which
has already passed through a second edition, called
'Strange Case of Dr. Jekyll and Mr. Hyde'.... It is an
allegory based on the two-fold nature of man, a truth
taught us by the Apostle **PAUL** in Romans vii., 'I find then
a law that, when I would do good, evil is present with me.'
We have for some time wanted to review this little book,
but we have refrained from so doing till the season of
Lent had come, as the whole question of temptation is so
much more appropriately considered at this period of the
Christian year, when the thoughts of so many are directed
to the temptations of our Lord.
    Our readers, however, must not understand us to mean
that this is a religious book. The name of **CHRIST** we do
not remember to have seen, and the name of **GOD**, we think,
only appears once. As for texts, or quotations from the
Word of **GOD**, such are conspicuous by their absence.
Nevertheless, the book is calculated to do a great deal of
good, not only to those who profess and call themselves
Christians, but to those who are, in every sense of the
word, true believers. Though there is nothing distinct-
ively Christian about it, we hope none will suppose that
we mean to imply that there is anything antagonistic to
Christianity. The truth taught us by the Apostle, to
which we have referred above, is one recognised by those

outside Christian Churches. Every thoughtful Hindoo,
Mahommedan, Buddhist, or Parsee recognises the fact of the
dual nature of his composition - the higher and the lower.
Among the heathen in all ages have ever been found some
who, like one well-known classical writer, confessed that
he approved of that which is good, though he followed that
which was evil.

In the allegory with which we are dealing we are introduced to a Dr. JEKYLL, who was a well-to-do medical man of
a very respectable type, pleasant and genial, but somewhat
weak and yielding. Of the best of men it can always be
said that there is about them an element of evil, whereas
with the worst of men there is, if we can only discover
it, an element of good - doubtless a relic of primitive
man 'made in the image of God' before the fall of our
ancestors. Dr. JEKYLL is no exception to the general
rule, and he finds that mixed up with much that was good
there was in his character a certain amount of evil. He
discovers a medicine which is capable of separating his
two natures into two distinct identities. By taking one
dose he completely throws off all traces of his better self,
and his lower nature asserts itself without any of the con-
straining influences of his higher nature being left. Not
only was this the case with regard to his moral nature,
but even his very appearance became so changed that no one
could possibly recognise him. Consequently he assumes another name when the evil nature predominated, and called
himself Mr. HYDE. Even the worst of men have something good
in them, and consequently they do not appear to us so
repulsive as Mr. HYDE, who had not a single trace of the
better nature.

The allegory is good. How many men live out two distinct characters? To the outer world they are the honourable, upright men, with a good professional name, holding a respectable position in society, looked up to and
spoken well of by all their neighbours. Within, however,
the inner sanctum of their own hearts they are conscious
of another self, a very different character. So far this
is more or less common to all. It is a result of the Fall
of Man that we have ever present a lower nature struggling
to get the mastery. So conscious was the Apostle of this
second self that he cried out, 'O wretched man that I am!
Who shall deliver me from the body of this death?' The
metaphor here, is, doubtless, borrowed from an ancient
cruel custom of binding together a living captive with a
corpse. The dead body must of necessity be repugnant to
the living man, and to the living Christian the very
existence of the lower nature must be abhorrent. Unfortunately, however, some act the part played by Dr. JEKYLL.
They live the respectable life 'to be seen of men,' and

then, when away from the public gaze, they give way to
the lower nature. Our **SAVIOUR** says of them, 'For every
one that doeth evil hateth the light, neither cometh to
the light, lest his deeds should be reproved.'
There are two strange scenes brought before us in the
allegory. The first is, Mr. **HYDE** trampling over the body
of a child in the street, treading down, as it were,
innocence. In the second scene, Mr. **HYDE** commits a
murder. Both scenes take place at night, both bring a
penalty. The first one was comparatively easily atoned
for, as the child, no thanks to Mr. **HYDE**, was not permanently injured. The second scene, however, results in a
price being set on the head of the murderer, which finally
leads to his committing suicide. Immediately after the
crime of murder, however, Mr. **HYDE** takes his dose of
chemicals, and he becomes again Dr. **JEKYLL**, the respectable member of a scientific profession, about the last man
in the town to be suspected of such a crime. We need
hardly say that, though no one could recognise in Dr.
JEKYLL the foul villain who had trampled down innocence
and committed a murder, his memory was keenly alive and
his sorrow was intense. In the words of the author 'the
pangs of transformation' had not done tearing him, before
HENRY JEKYLL, with streaming tears of gratitude and
remorse, had fallen upon his knees and lifted his clasped
hands to **GOD**. The veil of self-indulgence was rent from
head to foot, 'I saw my life as a whole; I followed it up
from the days of childhood, when I walked with my father's
hand, and through the self-denying toils of my professional life, to arrive again and again, with the same
sense of unreality, at the damned horrors of the evening.
I could have screamed aloud; I sought with tears and
prayers to smother down the crowd of hideous images and
sounds with which my memory swarmed against me; and still,
between the petitions, the ugly face of my iniquity stared
into my soul.... But I was still cursed with my duality
of purpose, and, as the first edge of my penitence wore
off, the lower side of me, so long indulged, so recently
chained down, began to growl for licence. Not that I
dreamt of resuscitating **HYDE**, the bare idea of that would
startle me to frenzy; no, it was in my own person that I
was once more tempted to trifle with my conscience, and it
was as an *ordinary secret sinner* that I at last fell before
the assaults of temptation.'
We regret that our limited space prevents us going more
into the details of the book which we are considering.
The most thrilling part is that in which Dr. **JEKYLL**, to
his horror, discovers that from having so frequently
assumed the form of Mr. **HYDE**, that nature gradually begins

to assert itself in him. To such an extent is this the
case that, though he retires to rest at night as Dr.
JEKYLL, he finds that when he wakes up in the morning he
is Mr. HYDE. At first this discovery does not trouble
him so much, as a dose of his chemicals effects a transformation back again. But, by degrees, he finds that from
frequent interchange of character the chemicals lose their
power. He doubles the strength of the ingredients, but
all to no avail. The better man has gone, the lower and
the viler nature gains the ascendancy. Mr. HYDE is the
murderer - he, if discovered, will be hanged - so that the
conviction grows on his mind that the day of reckoning is
coming, the penalty will, sooner or later, have to be
paid. After a very graphic description of the appalling
horrors of his position, we find Dr. JEKYLL has disappeared, but that Mr. HYDE has taken his place and, with a
view to escape his impending fate, dies by his own hand.

How many there may be who will read this book, and, if
they rightly understand it, will recall the words of
NATHAN the prophet to DAVID the King, 'Thou art the man.'
At first they trifle with their lower nature, always conscious that they can, at any time, reassume their better
self. By degrees, however, the unfortunate victim finds
that he is losing his better self, and that the lower
nature acquires more and more power. The jovial man does
not mean to become a drunkard, though he yields now and
then in secret. The man whose passions are strong has no
intentions of becoming a sensualist, though he, too, gives
way to the fascinating power of temptation. The fashionable lady of the world does not mean to become insincere,
though she, too, with a view of pleasing those around her,
does not always strictly adhere to the path of truth.
We might enumerate many other different forms of sin.
But enough: *ex une omne discit*. The appalling truth
bursts on the victim that the will, which once was so
powerful, has lost its strength, and that the lower
nature, which every one should seek to bring into subjec-
tion, has gained the ascendancy. That which has hitherto
been done in secret is at last proclaimed upon the house-
tops; all restraints are thrown aside. May GOD grant that
this book may be a warning to many who are trifling with
sin, unconscious of its awful power to drag them down to
the lowest depths of hell. We need hardly say even to the
most guilty, even to those who have sunk lowest, that we
believe that there is a Divine power in CHRIST to enable
us to become more than conquerors through Him that loved
us, and washed us in His own most precious blood.

76.   G. M. HOPKINS IN DEFENCE OF 'TREASURE ISLAND' AND
'JEKYLL AND HYDE', FROM A LETTER TO ROBERT BRIDGES

28 October 1886

From 'The Letters of G. M. Hopkins to Robert Bridges'
(1935), ed. C. C. Abbott, 236-9.
   Bridges wrote at the bottom of the manuscript copy of
the following letter:

> Wishing to keep this letter I have made a few notes in
> justification of my criticisms, which were no doubt
> ill expressed - to give rise to such misrepresentation.
> The letter gives a true picture of G.M.H.'s views of
> English literature & his judgement of modern writers.
> About Louis Stevenson I may add that my chief 'objec-
> tion' to his works is merely a want of sympathy. I
> admire his art much, but he is constantly offending
> my feelings.

This note appears in Abbott's edition of the letters, as
well as Bridges's interlinear comments in the letter,
which are given in the notes at the end.

...   I have at much length remonstrated with Canon
Dixon (1) for slighting Wordsworth's Ode on the Intima-
tions, at which he might have taken offence but on the
contrary he took it with his usual sweetness; and I beg
you will with my remonstrances with you about Barnes (2)
and Stephenson; of both of whom, but especially S., you
speak with a sourness which tinges your judgment....
   I have not read 'Treasure Island'. When I do, as I
hope to, I will bear your criticisms in mind.... Nevertheless I mean to deal with two of these criticisms now,
for it is easy to do so on the face of them.
   One is that a boy capable of a brave deed would be incapable of writing it down - well *that* boy. Granting
this, still to make him tell it is no fault or a trifling
one. (3) And the criticism, which ignores a common convention of romance or literature in general, is surely
then some 'αγροικία [boorishness] on your part. Autobiography in fiction is commonly held a hazardous thing and
few are thought to have succeeded in it on any great
scale: Thackeray in 'Esmond' is I believe held for one of
the exceptions. It is one of the things which 'O Lord,

sir, we must connive at.' The reader is somehow to be informed of the facts. And in any case the fault is removable without convulsing the structure of the whole: like a bellglass or glass frame over cucumbers or flowers it may be taken off, cleansed, and replaced without touching them. So this criticism I look on as trifling.

The other criticism is the discovery of a fault of plot about the whereabouts of some schooner: (4) I take your word for it. One blot is no great matter, I mean not a damning matter. (5) One blot may be found in the works of very learned clerks indeed. 'Measure for Measure' is a lovely piece of work, but it was a blot, as Swinburne raving was overheard for hours to say, to make Isabella marry the old Duke. 'Volpone' is one of the richest and most powerful plays ever written, but a writer in a late 'Academy' points out a fault of construction (6) (want of motive, I think, for Bonario's being at Volpone's house when Celia was brought there); it will stand that one fault. True you will say that in Stevenson's book there are many such: but I do not altogether believe there are.

This sour severity blinds you to his great genius. 'Jekyll and Hyde' I have read. You speak of the 'gross absurdity' of the interchange. (7) Enough that it is impossible and might perhaps have been a little better masked: it must be connived at, and it gives rise to a fine situation. It is not more impossible than fairies, giants, heathen gods, and lots of things that literature teems with - and none more than yours. (8) You are certainly wrong about Hyde being overdrawn: my Hyde is worse. The trampling scene is perhaps a convention: he was thinking of something unsuitable for fiction.

I can by no means grant that the characters are not characterised, though how deep the springs of their surface action are I am not yet clear. But the superficial touches of character are admirable: how can you be so blind as not to see them? e.g. Utterson frowning, biting the end of his finger, and saying to the butler 'This is a strange tale you tell me, my man, a very strange tale.' And Dr. Lanyon: 'I used to like it, sir[life]; yes, sir, I liked it. Sometimes I think if we knew all' etc. These are worthy of Shakespeare. Have you read the Pavilion on the Links in the volume of 'Arabian Nights' (not one of them)? The absconding banker is admirably characterised, the horror is nature itself, and the whole piece is genius from beginning to end.

In my judgment the amount of gift and genius which goes into novels in the English literature of this generation is perhaps not much inferior to what made the Elizabethan drama, and unhappily it is in great part wasted. How

admirable are Blackmore and Hardy! Their merits are much
eclipsed by the overdone reputations of the Evans - Eliot
- Lewis - Cross woman (poor creature! one ought not to
speak slightingly, I know), half real power, half imposi-
tion. Do you know the bonfire scenes in the 'Return of
the Native' and still better the sword-exercise scene in
the 'Madding Crowd', breathing of epic? or the wife-sale
in the 'Mayor of Casterbridge' (read by chance)? But
these writers only rise to their great strokes; they do
not write continuously well: now Stevenson is master of a
consummate style, and each phrase is finished as in
poetry. It will not do at all, your treatment of him.

Notes

1 R. W. Dixon; see No. 33
2 William Barnes (1801-86), Dorset poet and student of
   language.
3 Bridges wrote: 'My objection was not to his telling,
   but to his narration being sometimes in a vein untrue
   to his character as required by his actions, the two
   being incompatible & bad as art.'
4 Bridges: 'This I gave as an instance of the author's
   art [wh. is not disguised] breaking down.'
5 Bridges: 'There are others in plenty - '
6 C. C. Abbott identifies this as H. C. Beeching's
   review (16 October 1886) of J. A. Symonds's 'Ben
   Jonson'.
7 Bridges: 'No - of the means employed, wh. is physical
   & should have been magical.'
8 Bridges: '[but does not make chemistry of]'

77. STEVENSON, FROM A LETTER TO JOHN PAUL BOCOCK
(HUNTINGTON LIBRARY, HM 2414)

November 1887

John Paul Bocock (1856-1903) was a journalist and author
whose work appeard in 'Scribner's Magazine', New York
'World', New York 'Tribune', and New York 'Sun'; some of
his verses were collected and published posthumously in
'Book Treasures of Maecenas' (1904). The 'prominent
dramatic critic' is unidentified, but evidently he had

written a review of Richard Mansfield's production of
'Jekyll and Hyde' in which Mansfield played the leading
role.   That production opened in New York at the Madison
Square Theatre on 12 September 1887.   This letter is
printed with a few slight changes, in George S. Hellman's
'The True Stevenson' (1925), 129-30; Hellman apparently
copied it from an article written by Bocock in the New
York 'Sun'.

Your prominent dramatic critic, writing like a journalist,
has written like a braying ass: what he meant is probably
quite different and true enough - that the work is ugly
and the allegory too like the usual pulpit judge and not
just enough to the modesty of facts.   You are right as to
Mansfield: Hyde was the younger of the two.   He was not
good looking however; and not, great gods! a mere voluptuary.   There is no harm in a voluptuary; and none, with my
hand on my heart and in the sight of God, none - no harm
whatever - in what prurient fools call 'immorality.'   The
harm was in Jekyll, because he was a hypocrite - not
because he was fond of women; he says so himself; but
people are so filled full of folly and inverted lust, that
they can think of nothing but sexuality.   The hypocrite
let out the beast Hyde - who is no more sensual than
another, but who is the essence of cruelty and malice, and
selfishness and cowardice: and these are the diabolic in
man - not this poor wish to have a woman, that they make
such a cry about.   I know, and I dare to say, you know as
well as I, that bad and good, even to our human eyes, has
no more connection with what is called dissipation than it
has with flying kites.   But the sexual field and the business field are perhaps the two best fitted for the display
of cruelty and cowardice and selfishness.   That is what
people see; and then they confound.

'Kidnapped'

July 1886

78. EDMUND GOSSE, FROM A LETTER TO STEVENSON

15 July 1886

From 'Life and Letters of Sir Edmund Gosse' (1931), ed.
Evan Charteris, 187-8.

My dear Louis, -
    Thank you for the most welcome gift of 'Kidnapped.'
I consumed a great deal of the night in reading it, and
got up earlier than usual in order to finish it, reading
it very carefully, every word; so that you see it does
at least arrest the attention. I think on the whole it
is the best piece of fiction that you have done.
'Treasure Island' was more of a surprise, because we did
not expect it; but putting aside that first rapture which
you 'never can recapture,' I think 'Kidnapped' is more
strong throughout and better sustained. It is certainly
much more human and convincing. It is one of the most
human books I ever read. The only romance I know in which
the persons have stomach-aches and sore throats and have
not cast-iron physiques that feel nothing. There are passages that are quite superb - the attempted murder on the
tower-stair, the scene on Earraid, in all its details -
the scene in the cage (but this you should have made a
little more of, I think, because in that terrible journey
through the heather the reader would be glad of a longer
episode more picturesquely emphasized) - the scene in the
ale-house opposite Queensferry. The language is
exceedingly pure and true, sometimes the answers crack

like a whip. I feel sure that you have never done such
good dialogue before. Pages and pages might have come out
of some lost book of Smollett's. You are very close to
the Smollett manner sometimes, but better, because you
have none of the Smollett violence. Your 18th-century is
extraordinarily good; I read the whole book through, every
word, and although there were of course plenty of little
things in it not said exactly as Balfour would have said
them, there was only one phrase that actually shocked me.
That was in the Appin part, 'ferny dells.' This strikes
me as purely post-Wordsworthian....

I am your affectionate Friend,
Edmund Gosse

79. FROM AN UNSIGNED REVIEW, 'ST JAMES'S GAZETTE'

19 July 1886, xiii, 7

Mr. Stevenson is the Defoe of our generation. Since the
days when 'Robinson Crusoe' first delighted English readers, no book of adventure has appeared that can pretend
to rivalry with the story of 'Treasure Island.' Beside
the exquisite prose of Mr. Stevenson, his delightful
quaintness of humour and his fertile inventiveness, the
romances of Fenimore Cooper seem very poor performances.
The simplicity which is the highest art, a mastery of
language, and a subtle and sympathetic power of compelling attention, are all at the command of Mr. Stevenson.
He is rarely dull, he is often slily humorous, and he is
prone to weave into his narrative a fine and brilliant
thread of suggestive reflection which is alike characteristic and alluring. The wave of his magician's wand is
truly magical; but, while he draws his readers from a too
prosaic world to one of aerial fancy, he lets them know in
a sort of gravely jesting undertone that it is semblance
and not reality. His writings inspire a pleasure which
is all the more genuine and refreshing for their innocence; yet their fun, their effectiveness, their brilliancy would be much less striking were they not in part
the result of a grave experience and understanding of
human life, such as makes every man who is a man desire
once more to become as a little child.

It is high praise, therefore, of this new volume to say
that it is no unworthy companion of 'Treasure Island.'

Its incidents are not so uniformly thrilling; there is no
touch of art in it quite equal to the account of the blind
sailor's visit to the country inn in the former story; yet
'Kidnapped' is excellent from end to end. Two characteristics of Mr. Stevenson's last volume are in themselves
worthy of notice. The first, that, as in 'Treasure
Island,' he has succeeded in telling a story in which
women and feminine influence play positively no part.
There is no love-making in 'Kidnapped,' and, with one
exception, no woman takes any share in the action. There
are some pretty and touching passages illustrative of the
unspoken love of man for man which has been a finer side
of human intercourse since the days of David and Jonathan.
But of the conventional heroine and the yet more conventional love scene, which are wont to appear even in so-
called books for boys, Mr. Stevenson will have none. Not
but that he indulges in delicate incidental references to
the fair sex: as witness his ruffian sea-captain Hoseason,
who never sails by his aged mother's cottage on the sea-
shore of Fife without the compliment of a salute of guns.
The second observation is that Mr. Stevenson has boldly
and even wisely ventured into the field of Jacobite
romance which has already been occupied by the genius of
Sir Walter Scott. Different as is the character of his
book, we feel that indirectly Mr. Stevenson owes a little
of his general idea to the author of 'Rob Roy' and
'Waverley.' But although there is a perceptible parallel
between the adventures of David Balfour and those that
have immortalized the names of Osbaldistone and Bailie
Jarvie, the parallel is too slight to be insisted on.
The story of the Jacobite times is an inexhaustible mine
for the writer of fiction, and the originality and literary skill of Mr. Stevenson is doubly welcome for this
addition to the number of Highland stories. 'Rob Roy'
is inimitable; but it says much for Mr. Stevenson's
powers that 'Kidnapped' seems none the less charming for
the very reason that it recalls the masterpieces of the
greatest story-teller of our century.
     ... Mixed feelings of disappointed curiosity in the
present and pleasant hope for the future will contend in
the reader's breast when he finds that the matter is not
brought to a thorough conclusion, but that several important particulars are left incomplete; with more than a
hint that on some other day the further adventures of
David Balfour will be related. Of the two personages who
play the largest part in these pages, it is hard to say
which creates the keener interest: David Balfour, the
ostensible hero; or Alan Breck, most pugnacious and
attractive of Jacobites, whose views of his duty towards

his neighbours and hereditary foes the Campbells are expressed with a humour befitting our English apologists of
Irish agrarian outrage.... Alan, indeed, is incorrigible
on all matters of blood-feuds and fighting, but he is a
delightful creature. We shall say nothing of wicked Uncle
Ebenezer, or the perils and shipwreck of the brig *Covenant*, or of Mr. Stevenson's wonderfully vivid pictures of
physical fatigue and suffering as endured by the Jacobite
fugitives who 'took to the heather.' Those who have read
Mr. Stevenson know the grace and magic of his pen, and
they will need no solicitation to spend a few hours in the
delight of 'Kidnapped.'

80. R. H. HUTTON, UNSIGNED REVIEW, 'SPECTATOR'

24 July 1886, xliv, 5

On Hutton see headnote to No. 48.

We question whether Mr. Stevenson will ever again come
quite up to the freshness of 'Treasure Island,' a book
which may be said to have had more charm for boys than
even 'Robinson Crusoe' itself, though less for men.
Indeed, we should be disposed to regard the boys of England who lived before 'Robinson Crusoe' was written, as
boys without a literature, and the boys who lived between
'Robinson Crusoe' and 'Treasure Island,' as boys who had
only a foretaste of what was in preparation for them;
while boys who have lived since 'Treasure Island' was
published, are boys who have a right to look back on all
previous boyhoods with compassion, as boyhoods sunk in
comparative darkness, or touched only with the streaks of
dawn. 'Kidnapped' is not so ideal a story of external
adventures as 'Treasure Island.' On the other hand, it
has more of human interest in it for those who have passed
the age of boyhood. It touches the history of Scotland
with a vigorous hand. It gives a picture of Highland
character worthy of Sir Walter Scott himself. Its
description of the scenery of the Highlands in the old,
wild times, is as charming as a vivid imagination could
make it; and the description of the cowardly old miser
who plotted his nephew's death rather than give him up his

inheritance, is as vivid as anything which Mr. Stevenson's singular genius has yet invented for us. Nor is there in this delightful tale the least trace of that evil odour which makes 'The Strange Story of Dr. Jekyll and Mr. Hyde' so unpleasant a reminiscence, in spite of the originality and eeriness of the inconceivable and illogical marvel on which it is based.

The power of 'Kidnapped' consists chiefly in the great vivacity with which the portrait of the Highland chieftain is drawn, and with which the contrast is brought out between the frank vanity of the Highland character and the rooted self-sufficiency of the Lowland character in the relations between the Stewart of Appin and the Lowland hero of the adventures. So far as the mere story goes, though there is plenty of adventure, there is not that rush of danger and enterprise which transfigured 'Treasure Island.' The story depends far more for its interest on the realities of history and character than that of the earlier tale. The first striking effect in the book is the description of the hatred in which the uncle of the hero is held by the country-folk in the neighbourhood of his house, the desolation of the old miser's abode, and the struggle in his mind between his horror of his nephew, who may deprive him of his property, and his wish to keep him till some plan of finally ridding himself of the lad occurs. The description of his attempt to bring him to his death by sending him on a dark night up an unfinished staircase is very powerful: -

[Quotes ch. iv, from 'The tower, I should have said, was square ...' to 'My uncle gave a kind of broken cry like a sheep's bleat ... and tumbled to the floor like a dead man'.]

The next great success in the book introduces us to the Highlander, the Stewart chief of Appin, whose character is so skilfully drawn that Scott himself would, we think, have been glad to own the picture. The hero, David Balfour, has helped him in his fight against the crew of the *Covenant*, in which David Balfour had been kidnapped. The Highlander is as grateful as he is vain; but then, he is also as vain as he is grateful, and David Balfour, who is full of the self-sufficiency of the Lowlands, is not a little mortified at finding how little of the credit of the victory is set down to himself: -

[Quotation from ch. x: 'The round-house was like a shambles ... ' to 'But poets ... have to think upon their rhymes; and in good prose talk, Alan always did me more than justice'.]

In the relations between these two, the chief intellectual
interest of the story consists. These relations are very
powerfully drawn, and perhaps nothing is better told than
the great quarrel which results from Alan's borrowing
David's money to gamble with and lose, and the sulky
bitterness with which David Balfour resents the wrong.
The acount of the long days of estrangement, during which
the two flee together through the highlands, the one
sullenly nursing his wrath,and perhaps partly on that
account sickening for a long illness, while the other,
after a generous effort to clear away the cause of quarrel
by a candid acknowledgment of his fault, accepts the feud
with a malignant joy, is admirably effective, as also is
the close of the feud, when David breaks down altogether,
and Alan all but carries him to the house of one of the
Maclarens in the Braes of Balquidder. Perhaps, too, there
is nothing much better in the book than the account of the
contest between Alan Stewart and the Macgregor for victory
as rivals on the bagpipes. Nothing could have brought out
the petty vanity and the deep generosity of the Highland
character better than this spirited contest.

On the whole, while this book is not quite so unique as
'Treasure Island,' it has perhaps even more of the qualities proper to all true literature, and for the lovers of
Scotch scenery and Scotch character it is altogether
delightful. Mr. Stevenson has, so far as we know, written
nothing which is more likely to live, and to be a favourite with readers of all sorts and classes.

81. AN UNSIGNED REVIEW, 'SATURDAY REVIEW'

7 August 1886, lxii, 195-6

The fertility of Mr. Louis Stevenson's invention rarely
flags, and he seems quite incapable of writing himself
out. 'Kidnapped' is as fresh and strong, as thorough in
workmanship and well sustained in interest, as anything
which he has yet given to the world, 'Treasure Island'
itself not excepted. If the style should seem somewhat
laboriously precise, sufficient explanation may be found
in the fact that David Balfour's adventures are supposed
to be narrated by himself, who is something of a preci-
sian. They are, we need scarcely say, of a stirring
kind, and include a voyage, a shipwreck, and a good deal

of wandering through the Highlands, together with a
reasonable admixture of bloodshed. The author of David's
misfortunes is his uncle, who has robbed him of his property, and tries to put him out of the way. For this
purpose David is delivered at Queensferry to the very
villainous captain of a brig, who is charged to sell him
as a slave in the Carolinas. But the brig, after being
driven round Scotland, is wrecked off the coast of Mull,
and David eventually finds his way on foot, at the immi-
nent risk of his life, back to the place where he was kidnapped. How justice was finally done must be discovered
in the book itself. Apart from the force and vigour of
the narrative, which seldom falls below the highest level,
and the wonderful description of the Highlands just after
the last Jacobite rebellion, the chief interest of the
book lies in the characters of David Balfour, the hero,
and Alan Breck Stewart, whose life he saves on board the
Covenant, and with whom he painfully finds his way across
Scotland. David is a Lowlander and a Whig, Alan is a
Jacobite and a Highlander. The contrast is amusing,
though the points of resemblance are perhaps exaggerated
and the points of difference too much ignored. Alan, after
after all, is a plain type of the brave, reckless, impul-
sive, lawless 'Hieland shentleman,' whose pride in his
French clothes is, it must be confessed, a trifle wearisome. David Balfour is a distinct creation, and will
live. If Sir Walter could revisit the glimpses of the
moon, and read 'Kidnapped' by their light, that great man
would acknowledge, with his characteristic excess of
generosity, that David Balfour was worthy to rank with
Alan Fairford. It would be ridiculous to name Alan Breck
Stewart in the same breath as Rob Roy. The best scene
between David and Alan - perhaps the best scene in the
book - is that which follows the murder of Colin Campbell,
the 'Red Fox.' At first David believed that Alan had done
it, and on Alan solemnly denying the accusation upon 'the
holy iron,' there ensued a conversation which, as Mr. Stevenson would say, is worth setting down. '"Do you know
that man in the black coat?" "I have nae clear mind about
his coat," said Alan, cunningly; "but it sticks in my head
that it was blue." "Blue or black, did ye know him?" said
I. "I couldnae just conscientiously swear to him," says
Alan. "He gaed very close by me, to be sure; but it's a
strange thing that I should just have been tying my
brogues." "Can you swear that you don't know him, Alan?"
I cried, half in anger, half in a mind to laugh at his
evasions. "Not yet," says he; "but I've a grand memory
for forgetting, David." "And yet there was one thing I
saw clearly," said I, "and that was that you exposed

yourself and me to draw the soldiers." "It's very
likely," said Alan; "and so would any gentleman. You and
me were innocent of that transaction." "The better reason, since we are falsely suspected, that we should get
clear," I cried. "The innocent should surely come before
the guilty." "Why, David," said he, "the innocent have
aye a chance to get assoiled in Court; but for the lad
that shot the bullet, I think the best place for him will
be the heather. Them that havena dipped their hands in
any little difficulty should be very mindful of the case
of them that have. And that is the good Christianity.
For if it was the other way round about, and the lad whom
I couldnae just clearly see had been in our shoes, and we
in his (as might very well have been), I think we would be
a good deal obliged to him oursels if he would draw the
soldiers"' [ch. xviii]. No one can read this admirable,
and no doubt essentially truthful, dialogue without thinking of Ireland, and making his own reflections. We cannot
regard the voyage of the *Covenant* as by any means equal to
the account of David Balfour's travels by land. Mr. Stevenson describes with lucid power the worst sort of British sailor, a compound of rum, cruelty, and piratical
instincts. But he has performed this feat once for all in
'Treasure Island,' and even if the performance were worth
repeating, Captain Hoseason, or Mr. Shuan, pales before
the more consummate wickedness of John Silver. Marryat,
to whom Mr. Stevenson, especially in 'The Dynamiter,' is
much indebted, had more regard for the proper limitations
of art. On the other hand, for knavery of an uncanny
kind, commend us to the blind catechist whom David met on
his walk to Torosay. The portrait of Cluny Macpherson,
in whose 'cage' on Ben Alder David and Alan took refuge,
is a masterpiece, too, in its way. David, being completely prostrated by his travels, Cluny and Alan fall to
at 'the cartes,' and in the course of their game all the
money of the travellers, chiefly David's, disappears.
Cluny at once offers to return it, but David is at first
unwilling.

[Quotation from ch. xxiii: '"I am a young man ... and I
ask your advice."' to '"Upon my honest word, ye may take
this money ... and here's my hand along with it"'.]

David's endurance and pluck are at least equal to
Alan's, and the descriptions of his physical fatigue in
the flight through the heather are most heartrending.
Very vivid and graphic they are too, and in their less
distressing aspect they may be compared with the account
of Levine's amateur mowing in 'Anna Karénine.' There is

only one complete failure in 'Kidnapped,' and that is the
wicked old uncle, Ebenezer Balfour, the merest shadow and
simulacrum of a wicked uncle. There is no love in the
story, which will perhaps make it the more popular with
boys, helping them to tolerate the map and the geographi-
cal information. We hope that it will not be long before
Mr. Stevenson fulfils his conditional promise to continue
the history of David and Alan.

82.   T. WATTS-DUNTON, UNSIGNED REVIEW, 'ATHENAEUM'

14 August 1886, 3068, 197-8

Walter Theodore Watts-Dunton (1832-1914), critic, novelist, and poet, reviewed first for the 'Examiner', then,
from 1876 to the end of the century, for the 'Athenaeum';
he is perhaps best remembered for his association with
Swinburne.

It seems to be considered necessary that the schoolboy of
the period should be supplied with a new story of adventure for every day in the week. It also seems to be considered necessary that men of genius should be told off
to write them - men who, like Mr. Rider Haggard and Mr.
Stevenson, are sorely needed to produce stories for men
and women. The consequence is that some of the most
picturesque and vigorous imaginative writing that has been
produced of late years is to be found in such boys' books
as 'King Solomon's Mines,' 'Treasure Island,' and the tale
before us. We are not sure that this is entirely a fortunate circumstance. In novels written for adult readers
it is not enough to furnish a rapid succession of brilliant scenes; these scenes must be accounted for by that
severe logic of the imagination which is as inexorable as
the logic of the schools. But in stories written for boys
the action moves in entire freedom from those conditions
which are at once the trammel and the strength of true
art. Hence in fictive art no boys' story can hold a
very high place, no matter how powerful may be the imagination informing it. Perhaps we had better give an
illustration of our meaning. When the writer of a boys'
story wants, as in 'King Solomon's Mines,' to show how, in

a great battle between many thousands of savage combatants, two English heroes can display prodigies of strength
and valour equal to those of Achilles or Sigurd, and yet
come out of the fray unwounded, he can without hesitation
furnish his heroes with European chain-armour the moment
it is required - find it stowed away in the armoury of an
African tribe who are ignorant of firearms, and who, like
the ancient Mexicans and Peruvians, actually believe the
white man to have fallen from the stars. And when, as in
the book before us, the writer of a boys' story wants to
show the superhuman fighting powers of a hero, a Highland
soldier, he can depict him fighting and conquering an
entire ship's crew of reckless desperadoes and fire-eaters
- fighting and conquering them single-handed save for the
aid of a boy who knows not how to handle sword or pistol.
Such incidents as these, which are perfectly legitimate in
a boys' story, would be absurd in a story for adults, and
it is a first principle of criticism that no form of art
is very high if it can dispense with the logic of imagination.

This is seen plainly enough if we compare the prowess
of Mr. Stevenson's Alan Breck in the round-house with the
feats of Dandie Dinmont in the smugglers' cave. While in
the one case the very charm of the thing lies in its boyish freedom from the restraints of imaginative logic, in
the other every incident of the contest is explained and
accounted for as rigidly as though it were matter of
actual history. Of both 'Guy Mannering' and 'Kidnapped'
the main action was suggested by the Annesley case, that
marvellous romance of real life which, in The Wandering
Heir, not even Charles Reade could effectually vulgarize
and spoil for future use. And no doubt it may be said
that the true story of young Annesley is crowded with
adventures more wonderful and exploits more incredible
than those to be found in 'Kidnapped.' No doubt it may
be said that in Balfour's struggle with old Ebenezer
there is nothing so improbable as the real struggle of
Annesley with *his* wicked uncle, and that Annesley's
adventures in the plantations, the fight between the
Iroquois girl and the slave-owner's daughter for possession of the slave, Annesley's escape from the Indian
girl's brothers, and his subsequent more astonishing
escape from the gallows at Chester as an unconscious
accomplice in an elopement, surpass in wonderfulness any
of the chances, escapes, and disasters that befell
Balfour. But the saying that 'truth is stranger than
fiction' has an artistic as well as a moral application.
Fiction dares not be so strange as truth save in a boys'
story, where strangeness and exaggeration are, it seems,

not only tolerated, but demanded. But after the fight in
the round-house 'Kidnapped' passes, as we are going to
show, into a new artistic phase - the phase of true art,
where no exaggeration and no artistic insincerity can have
a place.

Unlike Annesley and unlike young Ellangowan, Mr. Stevenson's hero is not carried abroad after all, and here,
perhaps, the book as a story attractive to boys will be
found to fall behind 'Treasure Island' and 'King Solomon's
Mines.' What boys love above everything else is new
scenery, and to baulk the expectation of the scenery of
Wonderland aroused by the opening chapters of this story
is exceedingly dangerous. Having tasted the delight of
'Treasure Island' and 'King Solomon's Mines,' the boy
reader who follows David Balfour's adventures up to the
point of his landing at Mull will most likely be disappointed at finding that he not to be taken to the
plantations. And yet, as has been just indicated, it is
here where the story passes into literature. As a picture
of the state of Scotland immediately after 1745 we do not
hesitate to say that there is nothing in history and nothing in fiction equal to these remarkable chapters. It is
not only as vivid as a word-picture by Carlyle; it is true
and always true as a picture by Carlyle is false and
always false. When the hero has left the ship and the
kidnapping scheme is entirely frustrated, and not till
then, we come upon such really vital, really organic work
as Mr. Stevenson has never given us in his stories for
adults, such as 'Prince Otto,' 'The New Arabian Nights,'
and the striking novelette in the 'Court and Society
Review' called Olalla [17 December 1885]. While the
adventures in connexion with the wicked uncle, though unquestionably vigorous, are excogitated, the adventures in
the Highlands are imagined, and this makes us think that
it was merely in order to bring in these latter adventures
that the somewhat stale business of the kidnapping was
resorted to. For it should always be remembered in criti-
cizing fiction that in the mind of every true story-teller
the story passes through two stages - the stage when the
group of situations is conceived or, as we say, 'invented,' and the stage when they are really imagined, when
the inventor's mind has become as familiar with them as
though he had actually lived in them. Not till it has
reached the latter stage can imaginative work in any art
become vital and, so to speak, organic. This is why the
dramatic work of the novel of ingenious plot is almost
always excogitated, while that of stories allowed to grow
chapter by chapter, like the best of Scott's, is imagined.
This is why, in short, there is more imagination in a

single page of 'The Antiquary' than in an entire story by
Gaboriau. Scott, though a hasty writer, does not, as
Gaboriau does, depict a scene because a mechanically constructed plot has forced him to do so, but because the
scene - suggested to him originally by some local anecdote
or by some chapter of history - has lain in his mind for
so long a time that all the imaginative energy at his
command is called up as soon as he begins to write about
it. In other words the plot grows out of the scenes; the
scenes do not grow out of the plot. Hence, in the deepest
and truest sense, Scott, often called the most improvisatorial, is the least improvisatorial of writers.

'Monte Cristo' furnishes the most striking illustration of what we mean. Those portions of the romance which
precede the working out of the revenge are imagined,
while those portions which deal with the revenge are
excogitated. Why? The latter portions were written
first, before the story had taken root in the novelist's
imagination; the portions dealing with the imprisonment
and the finding of the treasure were written after the
story had taken root. Originally the narrative began with
the adventures of the count in Italy, when he was plotting
his revenge. The earlier portions of the work as we now
have it were rapidly glanced at for working purposes by
way of retrospective dialogue. But Maquet, in talking
over the story with Dumas, suggested that by this method
of structure the finest chances afforded by the plot were
missed, and advised that the narrative should begin, not
in Italy with the revenge, but in Marseilles, with the
conspiracy, the imprisonment, and the finding of the
treasure. Dumas acted upon this and found that, thanks
to his previous work upon the materials, his imagination
was now able to live in the situations, startling and
romantic as they were, though as a rule the strength of
Dumas lies in invention rather than in imagination. Now
of 'Kidnapped' the Highland portions alone are imagined.
Hence we cannot but think that for these portions the
entire story, such as it is, was invented: a story which
simply tells how a manly young hero of the old type
struggles with an uncle-usurper of the old type, and
after many adventures and hairbreadth escapes by sea and
land - adventures and escapes having nothing to do with
any proper *peripeteia* - comes into his own through the
good offices of Providence and the conventional stage
lawyer of the Latin-quoting type. In the Highland portions the imagination is of an exceedingly high and rare
kind. The scenes are flashed not only upon the mental
vision, but upon the actual senses of the reader. And
even in the earlier chapters, where there is but little

imagination in this narrow sense, we come across single
touches where there is imagination, but then it leaps up
in a short, sudden, dazzling flame, as where the cry
forced from the murderous uncle by superstitious terror
is likened in sound to a sheep's bleat.

In the perfect, the ideal story-teller imagination and
invention would, of course, be found in equipoise. Until
recent years the word 'imagination' had a meaning so wide
that it included both fancy and invention. Hence our
remarks may not be generally intelligible. It seems
strange that Coleridge was the earliest critic who gave
that special meaning to the word 'fancy' which it now
owns. But even now invention and imagination are often
confounded; critics are apt to use the two words as
loosely as did the critics of the eighteenth century – as
loosely, for instance, as did Alexander Pope in his
remarks upon the invention in the Homeric poems. The
truth is, however, as we have before pointed out when
writing of Homer, that it is these very same Homeric
poems which above everything else in literature afford
striking examples of the deep distinction between the inventive and imaginative faculties, and ... the strongest
of all arguments in favour of the separate authorship of
the 'Iliad' and the 'Odyssey' [is] the argument that while
the 'Odyssey' shows a very wonderful power of primary invention, the 'Iliad' shows almost none at all; and that
while in the 'Odyssey' imagination, though powerfully
active, is always ready to yield to invention, in the
'Iliad' the imaginative force is as unyielding to all
demands of invention, whether primary or accessory, as
Shakspeare's own.

Perhaps, however, could we pursue the subject here,
we should find the most remarkable instance of the difference between an imaginative and an inventive poet to be
furnished by the cases of Shakspeare and Spenser. But we
are concerned at the present moment with prose fiction
alone, and Charlotte Brontë affords us an example of a
writer in whom the imaginative faculty was very great, but
whose inventive faculty scarcely existed at all. After
'The Professor' was rejected on account of deficiency of
plot-interest she set to work to construct a plot of the
sensational kind, and gave us the ugly old situation of a
maniac hidden away in a country house. The entire plot
showing how the Lowood governess narrowly escaped committing bigamy with her 'master,' whose mad wife was secretly
imprisoned at Fieldhead, was as poor and banal as that of
any of those 'shilling dreadfuls' that add to the horrors
of the railway stations, and seem just now to threaten
the very existence of prose fiction. And yet 'Jane Eyre'

stands at the top of English romances for sheet imaginative strength. On the other hand, a writer like the
author of 'Called Back,' (1) while showing a very considerable power of invention, seems to have been absolutely
without the imaginative faculty - that faculty which is
seen at work in the story before us, and entitles it to
the attention it is now receiving from us.

The humorous portions of 'Kidnapped' are of a very high
order. The musical contest between Robin Oig and Alan
Breck is to be ranked with the finest humorous scenes of
Scott. Alan Breck is a great success, and the hero Davie
Balfour really lives and breathes. That he is a landsman
to the very marrow is well indicated by his mistaking a
tidal islet for a real Robinson Crusoe island, but it is
difficult to imagine the veriest land-lubber, gazing at
the sea from a lonely land, saying that it strikes the
soul 'with a kind of fear' [ch. xiv]. On the contrary,
it is from a ghostly flat or a range of spectral cliffs
that the sight of the sea seems to drive away the superstitious terrors conjured up by some landscapes. Amid
superstitious dreads on the loneliest coast on the dimmest
night a sense of companionship comes with the smell of
sea-weed.

Note

1 'Called Back' (1883) was a widely read novel by Hugh
   Conway, pseudonym of John Frederick Fargus (1847-85).

83. STEVENSON, LETTER TO T. WATTS-DUNTON

September 1886, LS, ii, 316-18

At this time Watts-Dunton had not yet added to his name
the surname of his mother.

Dear Mr. Watts, - The sight of the last 'Athenaeum'
reminds me of you, and of my debt, now too long due. I
wish to thank you for your notice of 'Kidnapped'; and
that not because it was kind, though for that also I
valued it, but in the same sense as I have thanked you

before now for a hundred articles on a hundred different writers. A critic like you is one who fights the good fight, contending with stupidity, and I would fain hope not all in vain; in my own case, for instance, surely not in vain.

What you say of the two parts in 'Kidnapped' was felt by no one more painfully than by myself. I began it partly as a lark, partly as a pot-boiler; and suddenly it moved, David and Alan stepped out from the canvas, and I found I was in another world. But there was the cursed beginning, and a cursed end must be appended; and our old friend Byles the butcher was plainly audible tapping at the back door. So it had to go into the world, one part (as it does seem to me) alive, one part merely galvanised: no work, only an essay. For a man of tentative method, and weak health, and a scarcity of private means, and not too much of that frugality which is the artist's proper virtue, the days of sinecures and patrons look very golden: the days of professional literature very hard. Yet I do not so far deceive myself as to think I should change my character by changing my epoch; the sum of virtue in our books is in a relation of equality to the sum of virtues in ourselves; and my 'Kidnapped' was doomed, while still in the womb and while I was yet in the cradle, to be the thing it is.

And now to the more genial business of defence. You attack my fight on board the *Covenant*: I think it literal. David and Alan had every advantage on their side - position, arms, training, a good conscience; a handful of merchant sailors, not well led in the first attack, not led at all in the second, could only by an accident have taken the round-house by attack; and since the defenders had firearms and food, it is even doubtful if they could have been starved out. The only doubtful point with me is whether the seamen would have ever ventured on the second onslaught; I half believe they would not; still the illusion of numbers and the authority of Hoseason would perhaps stretch far enough to justify the extremity. - I am, dear Mr. Watts, your very sincere admirer,

Robert Louis Stevenson.

84. WILLIAM JAMES ON 'KIDNAPPED', FROM A LETTER TO HIS
SISTER ALICE

27 September 1886

From Ralph Barton Perry, 'The Thought and Character of
William James' (1935), i, 394.
    James (1842-1910), the philosopher, psychologist, and
brother of the novelist Henry James, had the highest
regard for Stevenson. In another letter to Alice, written
around this time, he says Stevenson 'is simply to me the
most delightful of living writers'. Later in his essay
On a Certain Blindness in Human Beings, collected in
'Talks to Teachers on Psychology' (1899), he quotes at
length a passage from Stevenson's The Lantern Bearers
('these paragraphs are the best thing I know in all
Stevenson') in support of his own assertion that

    Wherever a process of life communicates an eagerness
    to him who lives it, there the life becomes genuinely
    significant.... [And] wherever it is found, there
    is the ... excitement of reality; and there is 'impor-
    tance' in the only real positive sense in which impor-
    tance ever anywhere can be.... Robert Louis Stevenson
    has illustrated this by a case, drawn from the sphere
    of imagination, in an essay which I really think
    deserves to become immortal, both for the truth of its
    matter and the excellence of its form. (234-40)

In another essay from this volume entitled What Makes a
Life Significant?, James quotes a passage from Pulvis et
Umbra as offering a significant expression of 'piety
toward the elemental virtue of mankind', of sympathy
'with the common life of common men', saying of it 'this
is as true as it is splendid, and terribly do we need
our ... Stevensons to keep our sense for it alive'
(281-3).

We have taken great delight in Stevenson's 'Kidnapped'.
So beautiful, so manly, such English! There is something
about the story that sings, from beginning to end, and I
shouldn't wonder if it lasted in our literature. I
wanted to write him a page of gush, but courage failed.
I hope he'll live to do more work.

85. WILLIAM MORRIS ON THE VIRTUES AND DEFECTS OF
'TREASURE ISLAND' AND 'KIDNAPPED', FROM A LETTER TO
G. B. SHAW

14 October 1886, B, 5253

William Morris (1834-96) was an English poet, painter,
craftsman and socialist.

I haven't written anything about Stevenson's books: I have
read 'Treasure Island' and 'Kidnapt' and was much pleased
by both: to be critical and disagreeable I thought that in
the first I could see the influence of three books, in
the first part 'Lorna Doon', in the second 'Arthur Gordon
Pym' mingles with 'Masterman Ready', but I see no harm in
that after all. 'Kidnapt' is a much more artistic work I
think; the defects (to be again nasty) being that he has
failed to interest one in the wicked uncle's scheme and
that the book don't end properly: however nobodies' books
do now-a-days. For the rest the book is full of admirable
pictures: there is one particularly of when they are
hiding on the big stone, and turn in with the Valley
solitary and wake up with it full of soldiers [ch. xx] - .
Then the cowardly revolutionist kinsman (James I think)
touched me home [ch. xix].

'The Merry Men and Other Tales and Fables'

February 1887

All six stories contained in this volume had been published earlier:

The Merry Men ('Cornhill Magazine', June and July 1882)
Will o' the Mill ('Cornhill Magazine', January 1878)
Markheim ('The Broken Shaft', Unwin's Annual, Christmas
    Number, 1885)
Thrawn Janet ('Cornhill Magazine', October 1881)
Olalla ('Court and Society Review', Christmas Number,
    1885)
The Treasure of Franchard ('Longman's Magazine', April and
    May 1883)

86. STEVENSON ON 'THE MERRY MEN', FROM LETTERS TO LADY
TAYLOR

January 1887

Sir Henry and Lady Taylor (née Theodosia Alice Spring-
Rice) were friends of the Stevensons at Bournemouth.
Stevenson had dedicated 'The Merry Men' to Lady Taylor.

(a) From a letter dated by Colvin 1 January 1887

I feel very sorry to think the book to which I have put
your name will be no better, and I can make it no better.
The tales are of all dates and places; they are like the

box, the goose, and the cottage of the ferryman; and must go floating down time together as best they can. But I am after all a (superior) penny-a-liner; I must do, in the Scotch phrase, as it will do with me; and I cannot always choose what my books are to be, only seize the chance they offer to link my name to a friend's. I hope the lot of them (the tales) will look fairly disciplined when they are clapped in binding; but I fear they will be but an awkward squad. I have a mild wish that you at least would read them no further than the dedication. (LS, ii, 325)

(b) From a letter dated by Colvin January 1887

I don't know but what I agree fairly well with all you say, only I like The Merry Men, as a fantasia or vision of the sea, better than you do. The trouble with Olalla is that it somehow sounds false; and I think it must be this that gives you the feeling of irreverence. Of Thrawn Janet, which I like very much myself, you say nothing, thus uttering volumes; but it is plain that people cannot always agree. I do not think it is a wholesome part of me that broods on the evil in the world and man; but I do not think that I get harm from it; possibly my readers may, which is more serious; but at any account, I do not purpose to write more in this vein. But the odd problem is: what makes a story true? Markheim is true; Olalla false; and I don't know why, nor did I feel it while I worked at them; indeed I had more inspiration with Olalla, as the style shows. I am glad you thought that young Spanish woman well dressed; I admire the style of it myself, more than is perhaps good for me; it is so solidly written. And that again brings back (almost with the voice of despair) my unanswerable: why is it false? (LS, ii, 326-7)

87.   STEVENSON, FROM NOTE FOR 'THE MERRY MEN'

1887

This Note stood as a preface to 'The Merry Men' volume.

The stories here got together are somewhat of a scratch lot. Three of them seem to me very good and, in the

absence of the public, I may even go to the length of
saying that I very much admire them; these three are
Will o' the Mill, Thrawn Janet, and Markheim.   Thrawn
Janet has two defects; it is true only historically, true
for a hill parish in Scotland in old days, not true for
mankind and the world.   Poor Mr. Soulis's faults we may
equally recognise as virtues; and feel that by his conversion he were merely coarsened; and this, although the
story carries me away every time I read it, leaves a painful feeling on the mind.   I hope I should admire Will o'
the Mill and Markheim as much if they had been written by
someone else; but I am glad no one else wrote them.

One is in a middle state; some persons of good taste
finding it pizzicato and affected to the last degree;
others finding in it much geniality and good nature.

88.   E. T. COOK, UNSIGNED REVIEW, 'ATHENAEUM'

5 March 1887, 3097, 318-19

On Cook see headnote to No. 68.

The extravagance of the praise sometimes bestowed upon
Mr. R. L. Stevenson's work makes a calmer estimate seem
almost a slight.   Yet it may be matter for sober doubt
whether any of the six tales called 'The Merry Men, &c.'
will live even twenty years.   Are they, indeed, when compared only with Mr. Stevenson's own previous work, really
first rate?   Taking The Merry Men, and accepting the view,
which the author no doubt rightly holds, that it is the
best of the collection, one cannot say that it is beyond
criticism.   It must be read twice in order that its scope
may be understood.   At a first reading its effect chiefly
depends on the abruptness of its conclusion.   Till within
a page or two of the end the story is perfectly clear and
circumstantial.   It is, in a few words, a story of a
Hebridean wrecker who has murdered the only survivor from
the wreck, and has become touched in the head by brooding
over his crime.   All this is told with great force; the
stormy Hebrides are described admirably, and without the
borrowing of a single touch from Mr. William Black; and
the dialect is so good that one is repaid for the trouble
of translating it.   One can see, too, easily enough that
the old man is a fine piece of character.   Avoiding the

common vices of explanation and analysis, the author
shows the working of the man's mind and the influence on
it of his life and circumstances. Here is a study which
deserves unqualified praise. But the narrator into whose
mouth the story is put does not make a particularly
definite impression, and the little bit of love-making
seems to have been thrown in because magazine readers
demand it. Next comes the crucial point in the story,
where the reader begins to ask how it is to end. Suddenly
a negro appears standing on the stranded wreck, and looking gigantic against the sky. It turns out that a considerable part of the story has been introduced in order
to account for the negro's appearance. Ultimately, after
a wild chase, the old wrecker and the negro are drowned
together. This is, of course, stating the facts too
baldly; but the disappointment of the final episode is
complete. The story, indeed, seems to collapse, and the
reader almost feels that he has been interested only to be
made a fool of. At a second reading he may take a better
measure of the author's object, and he may be right in
supposing that the negro is to stand for retribution, so
that the old Scotch belief in the devil's appearing as a
black man may add something to the legendary air of the
story. The Treasure of Franchard stands next in order of
merit. It is in a quite different style - humorous, and
not at all tragic. Nothing in it is better than the
description of a Frenchwoman of the middle class: 'She
had much of the placidity of a nun; with little of her
piety however; for Anastasie was of a very mundane
nature, fond of oysters and old wine, and somewhat bold
pleasantries, and devoted to her husband for her own sake
rather than for his. She was imperturbably good-natured,
but had no idea of self-sacrifice. To live in that pleasant old house, with a green garden behind and bright
flowers about the window, to eat and drink of the best,
to gossip with a neighbour for a quarter of an hour,
never to wear stays or a dress except when she went to
Fontainebleau shopping, to be kept in a continual supply
of racy novels, and to be married to Dr. Desprez and have
no ground of jealousy, filled the cup of her nature to the
brim.' Of the other stories one is Scotch, one Spanish,
and one may be said to be German. The remaining piece is
a horrible study of a murderer's mind immediately after
the murder. The volume therefore offers varied fare, and
one ought to add that all the stories are written with Mr.
Stevenson's precise attention to style, the only fault of
which is that he has not yet quite freed himself from
affectation.

89.   R. H. HUTTON, FROM AN UNSIGNED REVIEW, 'SPECTATOR'

12 March 1887, lx, 358-9

On Hutton see headnote to No. 48.

Some of Mr. Stevenson's shorter tales show, on the whole,
even higher indications of genius than his most successful
stories. At least, we can remember nothing in 'Treasure
Island' or 'The Dynamiter' quite so good as The Treasure
of Franchard, Olalla, and Markheim, in this volume. The
last we should call a study after Nathaniel Hawthorne, if
we had to describe it to any one who knew Hawthorne
thoroughly, and so successful a study in the school of
that great master, that if it had appeared among his
'Twice-Told Tales,' we should have selected it as one of
the best and most original of the series. The tale which
gives its name to the volume, The Merry Men, is also a
very striking production, being a wild tale of wreckers
in the West of Scotland, where a series of reefs which
send up in every gale a weird sound of laughter into the
air, are termed by the cynical imaginations of the inhabitants 'the Merry Men.' Partly by his vivid descriptive
powers, partly by virtue of his keen insight into the
gloomy religion and the sullen discontent of a Calvinist
who 'believes and trembles,' but who really hungers all
the time for the gratification of his avaricious passion,
Mr. Stevenson has made of The Merry Men a tale of lurid
power which might match in its way the best of those
impressive shorter tales which Sir Walter Scott has scattered through his works. But even The Merry Men is
hardly as striking as Markheim and Olalla, while none of
them can compare in vividness of dramatic feeling with
The Treasure of Franchard. The only tales in this volume
in which we cannot find much to admire, are Will o' the
Mill and Thrawn Janet, - the former being a kind of
parable wherein the disposition which prefers holding its
enjoyments in reserve to exhausting them, is painted without any very great skill or effectiveness; and the latter
a tale of Scotch superstition which wants the clearness
needful to make it thoroughly impressive. The delineation
of popular Spanish bigotry in Olalla is extremely powerful; yet even that effect, impressively as it is painted,
is less remarkable than the picture of deteriorated brain
in the exhausted family of the Spanish grandee whose

descendants had through so many generations abused their
physical gifts, that at last a sort of sensuous insanity
descended upon them, though it was unaccompanied by any
loss of physical beauty. An eerier and more powerful tale
than Olalla it would not be easy to discover.

After all, however, it is in The Treasure of Franchard
that Mr. Stevenson shows us how dramatic is his humour,
and how humorous his drama can be. Two more brilliantly
painted figures than Dr. Desprez and his wife our English
fiction could hardly produce, - two stranger mixtures of
selfishness and kindliness, of materialism and a gascon-
ading kind of idealism, of egotism and disinterestedness.
The flourishes of the atheistic French philosopher, - his
fantastic reveries, his indignation when he is expected
to be inconsistent with himself, his still greater indignation when he is expected to be consistent with himself,
his sudden loss of self-control, and his sudden recovery
of it, his theatrical gloom and childlike gaiety, his
ostentatious scepticism and his equally ostentatious display of wholesome feeling, his gratitude for small things
and his elasticity under great misfortunes, - are all
painted so vividly and within such small compass, that
one could fancy one had known him all one's life. And if
Madame Desprez is not quite so finished a picture, Jean-
Marie, the adopted son, with his perfect simplicity, the
deep convictions which take hold of him, and his slow,
undemonstrative ways, is an almost more original picture
still.... We do not think it would be easy ... to make
any figures live more truly than Mr. Stevenson makes
these live within the narrow limits of eighty not very
full pages. We shall say nothing of the course of the
story, except that it is admirably adapted to give us an
even more vivid conception of these three characters than
any dialogue, however skilful and dramatic, could give.
No man without the most definite genius could have written
this tale, or, indeed, for that matter, much the greater
part of this little volume.

90. ANNIE R. M. MORGAN, FROM AN UNSIGNED REVIEW,
'NATION' (NEW YORK)

19 May 1887, xliv, 429-30

Annie R. M. Morgan remains unidentified except as a

reviewer for the 'Nation' in the late 1880s. 'The Merry
Men' was reviewed along with several other works in a
section headed Recent Novels.

In the remarkable tales collected under the title 'The
Merry Men,' Mr. Stevenson has concentrated much observation and thought on the baffling problem, why sin is sin,
and why men are persistently sinful, when all would be so
much happier if all were good. The narrator of the first
story lies awake one night listening to a storm howling
over the Island of Aros, and to the voices of the Merry
Men as they raged across the reefs and broke against the
cliffs. Once in a while he hears a human cry piercing the
elemental din, and he knows it to be the cry of his
kinsman, Gordon Darnaway, crazed with the unconfessed sin
of murder on his soul. Then, he says, 'A great fear fell
upon me of God's judgments and of the evil in the world.'
    There, in few words, is the inspiration of the tales.
In not one is there any sophistical palliation or extenua-
tion of evil, not a scoff, or a doubt of the awful, inevitable judgment of God. No time or space is given to the
superficial man, the thing made up of artificial conventions, the 'botched mass of tailors' and cobblers'
shreds.' We have souls striving consciously or unconsciously to avert damnation in eternity. The forces are
tremendous, and the man who develops them in language of
the utmost simplicity and vigor necessarily writes with
full belief in the importance of the message which he is
called to deliver to the world. Mr. Stevenson has softened and humanized the stern Calvinistic creed - as he
calls it, 'the damnatory creed' - but it is nevertheless
the pivot of his genius. It is to the pith and marrow of
his work what 'deils, bogles, sea-spensters, and sic-
like' are to the embellishment. He probably does not
believe that the devil habitually takes shape of man or
beast or fish the better to work his wicked will; but if
he didn't come very near that, he couldn't make his reader
afraid to look over his shoulder lest he should see the
Prince of Darkness behind him.
    The personal and incarnate devil is a conspicuous
figure in most of the stories; he is the personage of
Thrawn Janet and of Markheim. His appearance in Thrawn
Janet is for purposes of sheer deviltry, and horrible
without relief. Told in broad Scotch, the tale is a complete exposition of that incongruous union of grotesque
superstition with the theology of John Knox which could
probably never have been arrived at by a people with less

imagination and a more generally diffused sense of humor
than the Scotch.   In Markheim the devil is akin to the
German *Doppelgänger*.   He is Markheim's worst self, or
represents in the flesh his worst possibilities, coming
at a crucial moment to tempt the man who has slipped away
from good to commit himself irrevocably to evil.   Here, in
half-a-dozen pages, is compressed the whole history of a
weak mortal's gradual descent from innocent youth,
highly aspiring, to most iniquitous manhood.   Markheim is
going, as thousands of Markheims infirm of purpose have
gone, morally straight to hell.   He is stayed at the last
moment by a flash of defiance, of revolt against the
malignant shape that would bind him fast for ever.   Only
George Eliot's Tito Melema is comparable in drawing to
Markheim, and Mr. Stevenson does not lose in force by
brevity.   For grip of the vitals of humanity he is George
Eliot's successor and only peer.   Untrammelled by her
pedantry, perhaps because he may not have her learning,
he bids fair to pass her as a teacher.   He seems to feel
that the modern world will really heed only the voice that
says what it has to say in a breath, no word weak or
superfluous; and he has so far been conscientious enough
never to lift his voice till the right word is springing
to his lips.   A deeper appreciation of his conscientious-
ness and of the fact that singularity of incident and
picturesqueness are with him secondary to meaning and
truth in character, might arrest the flow of talk about
his weird, fantastic, morbid imagination, his poetical
style, his likeness to Poe and other purveyors of literary
hashish dreams.
     His style is the nearest imaginable approach to perfect
prose narrative.   A man, clever enough, would tell these
tales almost exactly as they are written.   His sparingly
used metaphors and similes are matter-of-fact; his language is vivid and impressive, because it is accurate,
acutely descriptive of his scene or character, perfectly
elucidating his thought.   Every word of his tells.   Poets,
especially poets like Poe, whose kingdom is the supernatural, work their effects by delighting or appalling
the imagination to such a degree that the befogged reason
forgets about accuracy and does not care a snap about
truth.   Even when they fascinate the intellect, it is by a
brilliant display of invention, of constructive ingenuity,
not by sustained and acute reasoning.   They rarely concern
themselves with moral questions, and, when they do, their
views have generally more glitter than substance.   In the
art that appeals to the imagination alone, Poe towers
above Stevenson; in the art that stirs the soul, moving
men to stretch out feeble hands to good for good's sake,

Poe sinks beneath comparison with Stevenson.

In work which is largely the expression of human intellect groping for an answer to a riddle which human intellect may not read, there can be nothing very light or
amusing. Those who want relief from strains of melancholy
and horror must hasten to the last pages, devoted to The
Treasure of Franchard. Dr. Desprez fights his angel in a
buoyant, cheerful French way. He is an engaging old
humbug, whom, if the author had been familiar with the
word, he must have dubbed a 'blatherskite.' A good angel
who knew how to cook, and a succession of calamities,
barely sufficed to keep him in the narrow way. Yet, for
all his unworthiness, he must take hold of common affections, even as he wound himself round the heart of the
loyal Jean-Marie and of his placid Anastasie. The
delineation of Desprez exonerates the author from the
possible charge of being hard on the sinner. The mere
technical art of all these stories is so obvious that comment is superfluous. But we cannot refrain from commend-
ing the last to aspiring writers. By a thoughtful reading
they may learn a bit of the secret of making characters
stand on their own legs, and compelling them to lay bare
the heart upon the sleeve.

'Underwoods'

July 1887

Stevenson's claims for himself as a poet - or versifier -
were modest. 'Underwoods', like 'Child's Garden', was
written at intervals between more taxing labours, often
to commemorate some occasion of slender significance, to
thank a friend, to pay a personal tribute. The volume
was published in August 1887 by Chatto & Windus in England
and by Scribners in the USA. Reviewers were sympathetic
to the volume. They admired its directness and simplicity, its 'sane and straightforward human speech' ('Pall
Mall Gazette', 20 August 1887). In spite of the title,
they felt Herrick had priority over Jonson as a source of
inspiration. The fullest assessments were by William
Sharp in the 'Academy' (No. 93) and by Gosse in the
lengthy article, Mr. R. L. Stevevson as a Poet in 'Longman's' (No. 96). Sharp's conclusions were shared by other
reviewers: Stevenson was a 'man of fine poetic culture,
but not a poet'; his verses were 'the work of an accomplished writer and a cultivated student of literature, but
from first to last they carry no emblem of the royalty of
poetry'. Gosse argued that both 'Child's Garden' and
'Underwoods' achieved their effect because they offered a
vital record of 'memory of an extraordinarily vivid kind
patiently directed to little things, and charged with
imagination'. None the less, Gosse felt that Stevenson's
fame would rest on his prose rather than his poetry. He
defended Stevenson against the charge that he was too
personal in 'Underwoods', though he pointed out the absurdity of Stevenson's dedication of the volume to the eleven
separate physicians who had ministered to him. Henry
James was one of those disturbed by the personal nature of
some of the verse (No. 95), as was Mrs Oliphant (No. 98),
who accused Stevenson not only of immodesty, but of a
failure of taste and an aim to exploit the prurient curiosity of American readers.

91. STEVENSON ON 'UNDERWOODS', A LETTER TO HENLEY

8 April 1883, LS, ii, 132

The verses Stevenson speaks of here were later collected
in 'Underwoods'. 'Pollock' is Walter Herries Pollock
(see headnote to No. 29). E. J. Mehew has established the
correct date for this letter; Colvin dates it 'May or June
1883'.

Dear Henley, -
    You may be surprised to hear that I am now a great
writer of verses; that is, however, so. I have the mania
now like my betters, and faith, if I live till I am forty,
I shall have a book of rhymes like Pollock, Gosse, or whom
you please. Really, I have begun to learn some of the
rudiments of that trade, and have written three or four
pretty enough pieces of octosyllabic nonsense, semi-
serious, semi-smiling. A kind of prose Herrick, divested
of the gift of verse, and you behold the Bard. But I like
it.

                                                    R.L.S.

92. JOSEPH KNIGHT, FROM AN UNSIGNED REVIEW, 'ATHENAEUM'

10 September 1887, 3124, 333-4

Knight (1829-1907) was dramatic critic for the 'Athenaeum'
from 1869 to the time of his death. His criticism
appeared also in the 'Sunday Times', the 'Daily Graphic',
and the 'Globe'; his contributions to the 'Gentleman's
Magazine' were under the signature 'Sylvanus Urban'.

Upon his poetic firstlings Mr. Stevenson has bestowed the
name of 'Underwoods,' which in a modestly apologetic
introductory quatrain he owns to having stolen. It is
futile to cavil at a title, especially when, as in this
instance, it is intrinsically musical and beautiful, and

in a sense appropriate. There is moreover something in
this collection that recalls the lyrics on which 'rare
Ben Jonson' bestowed the graceful name of 'Underwoods.'
Herrick, however, Ben's loyal and devoted pupil, is suggested more frequently than his master, and the more fantastic title of 'Hesperides,' which Herrick chose for his
'numbers,' might, on the whole, be considered more appropriate than 'Underwoods' to these poems of a later day.

That Mr. Stevenson possesses a distinct lyrical gift is
revealed in his 'A Child's Garland [Garden] of Verses,' and
in the one or two short and tender poems included in his
'Travels with a Donkey.' His present volume will secure
him a place among the poets. His position in the Olympian
hierarchy may not easily be fixed. As first fruits his
unpretending volume cannot compare with the efforts of the
greatest of his predecessors. His language is well selected and beautiful, his thoughts are graceful and intellectually stimulating or satisfying, and the whole has a
music at once caressing and provocative, like ripples of
laughter which disturb without breaking repose. Alternately tender and playful, he pleases and does not weary.
On the other hand, his happiest phrases come short of full
inspiration, a thought is rarely crystallized into a gem,
a word still more rarely ennobled by employment. Here and
there a line is supremely happy in workmanship, and a compound epithet is admirably chosen. It comes, however, in
obedience to a summons. Add to this that the utterances
are individual rather than dramatic, that the moods and
fancies of the writer are clothed in poetic phrase, and
that there is little attempt to go far outside himself,
and less attempt to extort from nature a sympathetic
response to human aspiration or suffering, and the limits
of Mr. Stevenson's early efforts in verse are indicated.

No poem in the volume is prettier in fancy or more
careful in execution than that entitled The Canoe Speaks.
It is noteworthy moreover as revealing a feeling for
sensuous beauty which is not common in Mr. Stevenson's
work. Leaving to the ships the great stream, the canoe
loves to

                    Sleep
On crystal waters ankle-deep:
I, whose diminutive design,
Of sweeter cedar, pithier pine,
Is fashioned on so frail a mould,
A hand may launch, a hand withhold:
I, rather, with the leaping trout
Wind, among lilies, in and out.
*   *   *   *   *   *

                              I wend
    Beside the cottage garden-end;
    And by the nested angler fare,
    And take the lovers unaware.
    By willow wood and water-wheel
    Speedily fleets my touching keel;
    By all retired and shady spots
    Where prosper dim forget-me-nots;
    By meadows where at afternoon
    The growing maidens troop in June
    To loose their girdles on the grass.
    Ah! speedier than before the glass
    The backward toilet goes; and swift
    As swallows quiver, robe and shift
    And the rough country stockings lie
    Around each young divinity.

It cannot be denied that a series of attractive pictures
is here presented in verse of much beauty and of remarkable fluency. In the case of a poetling a poem such as
the above, of which we have quoted all but a few lines,
might safely be advanced as a credential. In the concluding picture, indeed, the homeliness and sincerity in
their combination with beauty are so delightful, the
qualm of modesty which subsequently arrests the picture
in the middle of a line is to be regretted. If, however,
single images provoke criticism, it is because from Mr.
Stevenson the best is expected. The 'pithier pine' of
which the canoe is built fails to commend itself; the
'nested angler' is a not too successful image; and the
two lines

    By willow wood and water-wheel
    Speedily fleets my touching keel

have nothing to commend them but a trick of alliteration.

    Where prosper dim forget-me-nots

is happy. Is it hypercriticism, however, to say that the
word 'prosper' is not happy enough? It arrests attention
and fails to satisfy. A more commonplace word, such as
'cluster,' is to be preferred. An instance of similar
daring is, we believe, from Emerson, who says - we quote
from memory: -

    And the untaught spring is wise
    In cowslips and anemonies.

In this case the assigning to the spring of absolute par-
ticipation in its own beauties is successful. The pros-
pering of the forget-me-nots is without themselves, and
the idea is rather of *bourgeois* success than of conscious
development of beauty. All that in our quotation follows
this line is worthy of Herrick at his best....

From the fault of obscurity which besets many of our
foremost poets Mr. Stevenson is free. More knowledge of
his personality than is probably possessed by the average
reader is necessary to wrest from certain poems their full
significance, but of intentional difficulty or perplexity
cast in the student's path there is no instance....

In A Visit from the Sea, lines addressed to a seagull
seen inland, Mr. Stevenson sings more clearly than is
common with him. His verse seems as a rule an outcome of
culture and effort - successful effort. In the lines to
N.V. de G.S. he proves his capacity to write blank verse
at once sinuous, powerful, and musical. In beauty of diction and in the idea they enshrine the following verses
reach a high mark: -

>   Thou to me
> Art foreign, as when seamen at the dawn
> Descry a land far off and know not which.
> So I approach uncertain; so I cruise
> Round thy mysterious islet, and behold
> Surf and great mountains and loud river-bars,
> *And from the shore hear inland voices call.*
> Strange is the seaman's heart; he hopes, he fears;
> Draws closer and sweeps wider from that coast;
> Last, his rent sail refits, and to the deep
> His shattered prow uncomforted puts back.
> Yet as he goes he ponders at the helm
> Of that bright island; where he feared to touch,
> His spirit reädventures; and for years,
> When by his wife he slumbers safe at home.
> Thoughts of that land revisit him; he sees
> The eternal mountains beckon, and awakes
> Yearning for that far home that might have been.

Exquisite throughout is this, and the line we have printed
in italics opens out to the imagination a vivid picture.
It is worthy to stand beside that lovely verse of Mr.
Arnold's in Thyrsis,

> And groups under the dreaming garden trees,

which contains in itself an idyl of youth and its rapture
of desire, and almost worthy to compare with the immortal
line

Lone sitting by the shores of Old Romance,
[Wordsworth, A Narrow Girdle of Rough Stones and Crags]

or with Milton's vision of

Faery damsels met in forest wide
By knights of Logres or of Lyones,
Lancelot, or Pelleas, or Pellenore.
            ['Paradise Regained', II]

Some of the poems were written in periods of illness,
and in most of those in English there is a remote suggestion of ache. Somewhat curiously, in the lyrics which
deal most intimately with thoughts of death the verse is
the lightest, and is most charged with something not far
removed from humour. The lines to H. F. Brown (written
during a dangerous sickness) begin: -

I sit and wait a pair of oars
On cis-Elysian river-shores.
Where the immortal dead have sate,
'Tis mine to sit and meditate;
To re-ascend life's rivulet,
Without remorse, without regret;
And sing my *Alma Genetrix*
Among the willows of the Styx.

In a different and more heroic spirit is the poem Not Yet,
My Soul, in which the poet presses on himself the duty to
'defend that fort of clay' the body, 'now beleaguered,'
and urges: -

Contend, my soul, for moments and for hours
Each is with service pregnant.

Like his predecessor in the composition of 'Underwoods,' Mr. Stevenson dedicates to friends many of his
short poems. Instead, accordingly, of A Vision on the
muses of his friend Michael Drayton, or lines To my truly
beloved Friend, master Browne, on his Pastorals, we have
poems to Andrew Lang - dear Andrew, 'with the brindled
hair,' to W. E. Henley, and to Henry James.
    The Scottish poems may be more rapidly dismissed. In
these the method of Burns in his satirical pieces seems
to commend itself to Mr. Stevenson, who in his English
poems shows no trace of imitation and scarcely any of
outside influence. In the former also the satire, though
playful, is not without a sting; The Scotsman's Return
from Abroad pokes some very effective fun at Scottish

puritanism. In Scottish, too, as experience shows, a man
may venture upon freedom of expression which is denied
the chaster Southern muse. Had the resource of broad
Scotch been denied Mr. Stevenson, it is to be feared we
should have lost the ripe, broad humour of The Blast and
The Counterblast. Some lines to Dr. John Brown are good
and vigorous. Of the Scottish poems the best is A Lowden
Sabbath Morn. This contains much admirable description.
In the procession to church is another of those pictures
of rustic feminity in which Mr. Stevenson is happy: -

    The lasses, clean frae tap to taes,
    Are busked in crunklin' underclaes;
    The gartened hose, the weel-filled stays,
        The nakit shift,
    A'bleached on bonny green for days,
        An' white's the drift.

Verse is the blossom of most minds from which a harvest
is to be expected. It is the fruit of the few, and it is
only, as a rule, in the case in which it comes as fruit
that the world is greatly and lastingly concerned with it.
That poetry will be the fruit of Mr. Stevenson's mind
remains doubtful. His blossoms are at least fair, and
full of perfume and promise.

93. WILLIAM SHARP, FROM A REVIEW,'ACADEMY'

1 October 1887, xxxii, 212-14

Sharp (1855-1905) wrote under his own name and under the
pseudonym Fiona Macleod. His writing career began with
contributions of verse to various periodicals in the
1880s. For a while he was art critic for the 'Glasgow
Herald.' He reviewed for the 'Academy', the 'Athenaeum',
the 'Literary World', and various other periodicals at the
time the present review was written. Sharp had dealt
briefly with 'The Merry Men' in an omnibus review in the
'Academy' (26 February 1887).

Even if 'Underwoods' had not been preceded by 'A Child's
Garden,' there would doubtless be many of Mr. Stevenson's

readers who would not be oblivious to the fact that he had
written some charming verses. Those who have read the
'Travels with a Donkey' can hardly fail to have been
allured from the direct stream of narrative by such
snatches of song as The Caravanserai or The Country of
the Camisards; while the author's House Beautiful and
other poems have won admirers prior to their inclusion in
the volume just published. But it is a different thing to
charm a reader by an occasional lyrical outflow, and to
win his loyalty by a collection of poems.

Mr. Stevenson has been complimented for his happy
adoption of the title which Ben Jonson gave to his collection of fugitive poems and versicles - I confess I fail to
see on what grounds. The title has no particular rele-
vancy to the contents of the book - certainly none, at
least, to the latter portion of it, that written in
'Scots.' If, instead of from Ben Jonson, Mr. Stevenson
had appropriated from Herrick the collective name which
that genial singer gave to his poetic offspring, there
would have been less objection to urge. The same blithe
spirit animates the poet of these new 'Underwoods' as
inspired the author of the 'Hesperides.' There is no
imitation of Herrick, yet this poet is more frequently
suggested than any other. It is significant, moreover,
that the best verses in Mr. Stevenson's volume are those
which positively or vaguely call to mind memories of the
delicate music, the bland graciousness, of him who so
long dwelt and lilted in 'miry Devon.' This Herrick-
strain is perceptible not only in the charming envoy:

Go, little book, and wish to all
Flowers in the garden, meat in the hall,
A bin of wine, a spice of wit,
A house with lawns enclosing it,
A living river by the door,
A nightingale in the sycamore! -

or in these opening lines of The House Beautiful:

A naked house, a naked moor,
A shivering pool before the door,
A garden bare of flowers and fruit,
And poplars at the garden foot:
Such is the place that I live in,
Bleak without and bare within -

or, again, in the poem To a Gardener, with its closing
quatrain:

And I, being provided thus,
Shall, with superb asparagus,
A book, a taper, and a cup
Of country wine, divinely sup –

not only in these, but even in such a paradoxical couplet
as

Dew, frost and mountains, fire and seas,
Tumultuary silences.
[From To K. de M.]

'Underwoods' consists practically of two books: the one
of poems in English, the other of poems in Scots. The two
portions are as distinct as if they were the productions,
say, of a contemporary Herrick and of a contemporary
Burns. The attempt to criticise them as a poetic whole is
absurd. This, of course, not because of the linguistic
distinction, nor on account of the different metrical
methods pursued in each; but because the dominant mental
mood of the second portion of the book entirely differs
from that of the first, because the aspects of life therein viewed are seen with other eyes, and are interpreted
for us in a manner absolutely alien to what we have grown
accustomed to ere we leave the English section.
Thirty-eight poems make up Book I. Of these, about a
third are addresses to friends and relatives. Most of
these rhymed epistles are touched with dainty grace,
though their inclusion is a mistake in so far that it
inevitably leads to the inference that the author's poetic
store must be meagre indeed if these are his choice
gatherings therefrom. It would be unfair to assert that
any one of them is too slight for publication. It would,
on the other hand, be unjust to state that they have any
poetic warrant for their insertion in a volume wherein we
naturally expect to find only the rarest flowering of a
writer's mind, selected with the most careful discrimination. The best (excepting one) of these dedicatory pieces
are those addressed to the author's father and to his
friend, Mr. H. F. Brown. The first affects us by its
filial reverence and by its graceful diction; the second
pleases even more by its dexterous simplicity. In
neither, however, is there a single noteworthy line – a
word or phrase so especially fortunate that the reader at
once recognises the coinage as the product of that occult
faculty which we call genius. The exception referred to
is the poem in admirable blank verse inscribed to N.V. de
G.S. Here Mr. Stevenson shows that he can make as well
as merely speak in verse.

>   And from the shore hear inland voices call

is one of the two, at most three or four, haunting lines
which remain when the volume is laid aside. To have
uttered even one or two lines memorable for their quintes-
sential poetry, their subtle, inexplicable magic, is
something in these days, when an infinitude of jargon
passes for poetry. But one or two really noteworthy lines
do not make a poem, much less many poems, any more than
one snowstorm makes a winter.

A curious uncertainty is apt to arise in the mind of
the critic while his ear is tickled with the delight of
some such line as that quoted above. If he be wary, he
will at once seek to determine whether the haunting words
do indeed, howsoever remotely, derive from some ancestral
line of potent music; or whether, in truth, they inherit
nothing of their magic, and are, like the first pieces of
a new coinage, fresh from the mint of their author's mind.
If, on the contrary, the critic allow himself to dally
with doubt, he will be apt either to make a sweeping
assertion of plagiarism or, more probably, to lose all
sense of haunting reminiscence. And it so happened,
during the perusal of 'Underwoods,' that now and again I
was aware of tantalising echoes of familiar verse. The
most noteworthy lines in the book seemed at once to call
to mind and to hold up a veil of obscurity before certain
words, phrases, or poems. The epistle to N.V. de G.S. -
is not Landor at once suggested, even though no single
line has its prototype in the poetry of the author of The
Hamadryad? Even the already quoted admirable line,

>   And from the shore hear inland voices call

strikes me as distinctly Landorian, in its concision even
more than in its balanced rhythm. In the same poem, does
not the opening line,

>   The unfathomable sea, and time, and tears,

contain an echo of Shelley's monumental lines on Time?
In the rhymed address to Mr. Andrew Lang (very charming in
its graceful ease and frank personalities) the reader
encounters the line:

>   Or of the old unhappy gods.

Probably he is at once perturbed by some vague feeling
that he has previously read this line. Then the mental
atmosphere grows clearer, and while he remembers that

Wordsworth's imagination was touched not by the olden
gods, but by a Highland reaper, who sang as she stood amid
the corn, he realises who it was that wrought such subtle
music out of the simple words 'old' and 'unhappy':

> For old, unhappy, far-off things.
>
> [Wordsworth, The Solitary Reaper]

On the opposite page, in an epistolary poem entitled Et Tu
in Arcadia Vixisti, there occurs this fine passage:

> And perilous lands thou sawest, sounding shores
> And seas and forests drear, inland and dale
> And mountain dark.

What lover of English poetry but would at once hear beneath these lines the deeper, the supreme music of one of
Keats's most exquisite lines? (1) Genius seems to have
the power to usurp the prerogative of using certain words,
so that any writers who adopt them thereafter run the risk
of designation as singers of borrowed strains. It is unfortunate for the bard who does not possess genius, and
it is, perhaps, illogical and foolish; but the fact
remains. Shakspere would seem to have a prescriptive
right to the word 'wrought,' since he used it so wonderfully of Othello when 'perplexed in the extreme.' None
can write of 'perilous' lands or seas without apparent
infringement of Keats's literary patent in that felicitous
adjective; nor can the contemporary verse-writer, howsoever dexterously, insert an 'immemorial' without tempting
his critics to remind him of Tennysonian echoes.
    It is significant that the finest lines in this volume
are so markedly reminiscent. They emphasise - to one
reader at any rate - the inference that the author of
'Underwoods' is a man of fine poetic culture, but not a
poet. I have a very strong admiration for Mr. Stevenson
as a story-teller and an essayist. His prose is virile,
flexible, delicate, and rhythmical. These qualities combine to form a style which has a vital charm not excelled
by that of any living writer. So fine an artist in words
can well afford to be content with prose - the prose of
the richest and most potent language in the world. No one
could read Mr. Stevenson's recently published collection
of stories ('The Merry Men,' &c.) without being struck by
his variety and resource of language. Four such radically
distinct yet thoroughly original tales as The Merry Men,
Olalla, Thrawn Janet, and The Treasure of Franchard,
could hardly have been written by any other English roman-
ticist of the day. They can be read again and again for

the mere pleasure afforded by their felicitous words and phrases. The writer, one feels, is a master of his art.

But in 'Underwoods' there is nothing of this. To begin with, the reader realises that he brings to the perusal something of the same pleasurable expectancy wherewith he would take up any new tale or essay by Mr. Stevenson. Former pleasure has produced an intellectual prejudice, as it were, whereby the author gains greater benefit than is his due. In the next place, there is in these poems little or nothing either of that originality or of that satisfying beauty which conjointly characterise Mr. Stevenson's best prose. They are the production of an accomplished writer and a cultivated student of literature; but from first to last they carry no emblem of the royalty of poetry. As verses by a prose writer they deserve high praise, and, for their author's sake, a gladsome welcome. As practically the first poetic fruits of a writer who has had long literary experience, they hold out no golden promise, nor have they in themselves that which will preserve them from the avarice of time.

When we turn from the English to the Scottish poems we have to reckon, as it were, with a new author. The delicate air, the dainty fancifulness, the pleasant personalities and individuality of the first half of 'Underwoods' belong to another sphere than the racy and vigorous vitality of the second section. In his admirable preface Mr. Stevenson, in acknowledging that he is no purist in his choice of Scottish, and while referring to his preference for the 'Lallan tongue,' admits that Burns has often appeared to him as a foreigner. Yet it is Burns rather than Scott whom he follows linguistically as well as in metrical methods. He speaks in good 'Lallan' indeed; yet he only occasionally rivals Scott's 'brave metropolitan utterance.' He has the secret of the force and point of good Scottish; but not, as in his prose, that of its magic pathos and extreme beauty. Yet how admirably delineative are these bucolics - despite the townsman's slip (2) in the second line of the second stanza:

Frae the high hills the curlew ca's;
The sheep gang baaing by the wa's;
Or whiles a clan o' roosty craws
    Cangle thegether;
The wild bees seek the gairden raws,
    Weariet wi' heather.

Or in the gloamin' douce an' gray
The sweet-throat mavis tunes her lay;
The herd comes linkin' down the brae;

>   An' by degrees
> The muckle siller müne maks way
>   Amang the trees.

[From Ille Terrarum]

It is in irony and satire, however, that Mr. Stevenson
most reveals his affinity to Burns. What caustic speech,
what happy freedom of expression - where English would be
blasphemous or vulgar - what keen incisiveness in poems
like The Blast, The Counterblast Ironical, and Embro' Hie
Kirk!...

Mr. Stevenson certainly deserves to see the fulfilment
of his modest wish - the wish to have his hour as a native
maker, and be read by his 'own countryfolk in our own
dying language; an ambition, surely, rather of the heart
than of the head, so restricted as it is in prospect of
endurance, so parochial in bounds of space.'...

Yet when I come to say a last word of 'Underwoods,' it
is to refer again to the first portion thereof. The House
Beautiful and Skerryvore - 'for love of lovely words' - I
recall with growing pleasure. But, to my mind, better
than any of its more ambitious neighbours, better than any
poem either of those in English or of those in Scots, is
the little piece called A Requiem. The haunting music of
this unvarnished, this simplest and homeliest of dirges,
is not for either praise. or blame. Some will feel all its
subtle charm; to others it will seem nothing else than the
fragment of a song; yet I believe it will outlive - it
assuredly deserves to outlive - the whole of 'Underwoods,'
and perhaps, so greedy is oblivion, the greater portion of
the author's prose.

> Under the wide and starry sky,
> Dig the grave and let me lie.
> Glad did I live and gladly die,
>   And I laid me down with a will
>
> This be the verse you grave for me:
> *Here he lies where he longed to be;*
> *Home is the sailor, home from sea,*
>   *And the hunter home from the hill.*

Notes

1 Ode to a Nightingale:

>   Charm'd magic casements, opening on the foam
>   Of perilous seas, in faery lands forlorn.

2   For Stevenson's reaction see No. 94.

94.   STEVENSON, LETTER TO WILLIAM SHARP

October (?) 1887

From 'William Sharp (Fiona Macleod)' (1910), compiled by
his wife Elizabeth A. Sharp, 138-9.
On the 'townsman's blunder' see above p. 269.

Dear Mr. Sharp,
    What is the townsman's blunder? - though I deny I am a
townsman, for I have lived, on the whole, as much or more
in the country: well, perhaps not so much. Is it that the
thrush does not sing at night? That is possible. I only
know most potently the blackbird (his cousin) does: many
and many a late evening in the garden of that poem have
I listened to one that was our faithful visitor; and the
sweetest song I ever heard was past nine at night in the
early spring, from a tree near the N.E. gate of Warriston
cemetery. That I called what I believe to have been a
merle by the softer name of mavis (and they are all turdi,
I believe) is the head and front of my offence against
literal severity, and I am curious to hear if it has
really brought me into some serious error.
    Your article is very true and very kindly put: I have
never called my verses poetry: they are verse, the verse
of a speaker not a singer; but that is a fair business
like another. I am of your mind too in preferring much
the Scotch verses, and in thinking Requiem the nearest
thing to poetry that I have ever 'clerkit.'
                                    Yours very truly,
                                    Robert Louis Stevenson

95.   WILLIAM AND HENRY JAMES ON 'UNDERWOODS'

September, October 1887

From Ralph Barton Perry, 'The Thought and Character of William James' (1935), i, 396, 399.

(a) William to Henry James, from a letter of 1 September 1887

I see that R. L. Stevenson is in this country, and I see by the papers that he has paid you a couple of handsome 'tributes' in his new volume of verses. I'm glad of it. I hope I may see him ere he leaves, for if there is an author I love 't is he; and I'm sure he'll be hereafter reckoned as one of our masters of good classic English.

(b) Henry to William James, from a letter dated 1-5 October 1887

I'm afraid you won't see Louis Stevenson, who is a most moribund but fascinating being, of whom I am very fond. If he were in health he would have too much 'side' as they say here, but his existence hangs but by a thread, and his almost squalid invalidism tones down the '"Ercles" vein' (1) in him, as well as any irritation that one may feel from it. He has a most gallant spirit and an exquisite literary talent; but don't read the verses to me in his new little volume of poems, as they happen, especially the first, to be the poorest things in the book. The second was occasioned by my giving his wife the little mirror he commemorates. Both were scribbled off at the moment, - the first put on my plate one day I went to dine with him at Bournemouth, and I never dreamed that he had kept copies of them and would publish them. Four or five other pieces in the little volume are perfect and destined, I think, to live. He and Howells are the only English imaginative writers today whom I can look at.

Note

1 Bottom's speech in 'A Midsummer Night's Dream' (I, ii, 420): 'This is Ercles' vein, a tyrant's vein.'

96.   EDMUND GOSSE, FROM MR. R.L. STEVENSON AS A POET,
'LONGMAN'S MAGAZINE'

October 1887, x, 623-31

This essay was reprinted in Gosse's 'Questions at Issue'
(1893), 237-54.

... Though Mr. Stevenson's prose volumes are more than
twelve in number, and though he had been thought of
essentially as a prose writer, the ivory shoulder of the
lyre has peeped out now and then. I do not refer to his
early collections of verse, to 'Not I, and other Poems,'
to 'Moral Emblems,' and to 'The Graver and the Pen.' (I
mention these scarce publications of the Davos press in
the hope of rousing wicked passions in the breasts of
other collectors, since my own set of them is complete.)
These volumes were decidedly occult. A man might build
upon them a reputation as a sage, but hardly as a poet.
Their stern morality came well from one whose mother's
milk has been the 'Shorter Catechism'; they are books
which no one can read and not be the better for; but as
mere verse, they leave something to be desired. *Non
ragionam di lor, ma guarda*, if you happen to be lucky
enough to possess them, *e passa*. (1) Where the careful
reader has perceived that Mr. Stevenson was likely to
become openly a poet has been in snatches of verse published here and there in periodicals, and of a quality
too good to be neglected. Nevertheless, the publication
of 'A Child's Garden of Verses' was something of a surprise, and perhaps the new book of grown-up poems,
'Underwoods' is more surprising still. There is no
doubt about it any longer. Mr. Stevenson is a candidate
for the bays.
     The 'Child's Garden of Verses' has now been published
long enough to enable us to make a calm consideration of
its merits. When it was fresh, opinion was divided, as
it always is about a new strong thing, between those who,
in Mr. Longfellow's phrase about the little girl, think
it very, very good, and those who think it is horrid.
After reading the new book, the 'Underwoods,' we come back
to 'A Child's Garden' with a clearer sense of the writer's
intention, and a wider experience of his poetical outlook
upon life. The later book helps us to comprehend the
former; there is the same sincerity, the same buoyant

simplicity, the same curiously candid and confidential
attitude of mind. If any one doubted that Mr. Stevenson
was putting his own childish memories into verse in the
first book, all doubt must cease in reading the second
book, where the experiences, although those of an adult,
have exactly the same convincing air of candour. The
first thing which struck the reader of 'A Child's Garden'
was the extraordinary clearness and precision with which
the immature fancies of eager childhood were reproduced
in it. People whose own childish memories had become
very vague, and whose recollections of their games and
dreams were hazy in the extreme, asked themselves how far
this poet's visions were inspired by real memory and how
far by invention. The new book sets that question at
rest....

We now perceive that it is not invention, but memory
of an extraordinarily vivid kind, patiently directed to
little things, and charged with imagination; and we turn
back with increased interest to 'A Child's Garden,'
assured that it gives us a unique thing, a transcript of
that child-mind which we have all possessed and enjoyed,
but of which no one, except Mr. Stevenson, seems to have
carried away a photograph. Long ago, in one of the very
earliest, if I remember right, of those essays by R.L.S.
for which we used so eagerly to watch the 'Cornhill Magazine' in Mr. Leslie Stephen's time, in the paper called
Child['s] Play, this retention of what is wiped off from
the memories of the rest of us was clearly displayed.
Out of this rarely suggestive essay I will quote a few
lines, which might have been printed as an introduction
to 'A Child's Garden':

'In the child's world of dim sensation, play is all in
all. "Making believe" is the gist of his whole life, and
he cannot so much as take a walk except in character. I
could not learn my alphabet without some suitable *mise-en-
scène*, and had to act a business-man in an office before I
could sit down to my book.... I remember, as though it
were yesterday, the expansion of spirit, the dignity and
self-reliance, that came with a pair of mustachios in
burnt cork, even when there was none to see. Children are
even content to forego what we call the realities, and
prefer the shadow to the substance. When they might be
speaking intelligently together, they chatter gibberish by
the hour, and are quite happy because they are making believe to speak French.

Probably all will admit the truth of this statement of
infant fancy, when it is presented to them in this way.
But how many of us, in perfect sincerity, not relying
upon legends of the nursery, not refreshed by the study of

our own children's 'make-believe,' can say that we clearly
recollect the method of it? We shall find that our memories are like a breath upon the glass, like the shape of a
broken wave. Nothing is so hopelessly lost, so utterly
volatile, as the fancies of our childhood. But Mr. Stevenson, alone amongst us all, appears to have kept
daguerreotypes of the whole series of his childish sensations. Except the late Mrs. Ewing, (2) he seems to be
without a rival in this branch of memory as applied to
literature.

The various attitudes of literary persons to the child
are very interesting. There are, for instance, poets like
Victor Hugo and Mr. Swinburne who come to admire, who stay
to adore, and who do not disdain to throw their purple
over any humble article of nursery use. They are so magnificent in their address to infancy, they say so many
brilliant and unexpected things, that the mother is almost
as much dazzled as she is gratified. We stand round, with
our hats off, and admire the poet as much as he admires
the child; but we experience no regret when he presently
turns away to a discussion of grown-up things. We have an
ill-defined notion that he reconnoitres infancy from the
outside, and has not taken the pains to reach the secret
mind of childhood. It is to be noted, and this is a
suspicious circumstance, that Mr. Swinburne and Victor
Hugo like the child better the younger it is....

To the real student of child-life the baby contains
possibilities, but is at present an uninteresting chrys-
alis. It cannot carry a gun through the forest, behind
the sofa-back; it is hardly so useful as a cushion to
represent a passenger in a railway-train of inverted
chairs.

Still more remote than the dithyrambic poets are those
writers about children - and they are legion - who have
ever the eye fixed upon morality, and carry the didactic
tongue thrust in the cheek of fable. The late Charles
Kingsley, who might have made so perfect a book of his
'Water-Babies,' sins notoriously in this respect. The
moment a wise child perceives the presence of allegory,
or moral instruction, all the charm of a book is gone.
Parable is the very antipodes of childish 'make-believe,'
into which the element of ulterior motive or secondary
moral meaning never enters for an instant. The secret of
the charm of Mrs. Gatty's 'Parables from Nature,' (3)
which were the fairest food given to the very young minds
in my day, was that the fortunate child never discovered
that they were parables at all. I, for one, used to read
and re-read them as realistic statements of fact, the
necessity of pointing a moral merely having driven the

amiable author to the making of her story a little more
fantastic, and therefore more welcome, than it would
otherwise be. It was explained to me one hapless day
that the parables were of a nature to instil nice principles into the mind; and from that moment Mrs. Gatty
became a broken idol. Lewis Carroll owed his great and
deserved succccess to his suppleness in bending his fancy
to the conditions of a mind that is dreaming. It has
never seemed to me that the 'Adventures in Wonderland'
were specially childish; dreams are much the same,
whether a child or a man is passive under them, and it is
a fact that Lewis Carroll appeals just as keenly to adults
as to children. In Edward Lear's rhymes and ballads the
love of grotesque nonsense in the grown-up child is mainly
appealed to; and these are certainly appreciated more by
parents than by children.

It would be easy, by multiplying examples, to drive
home my contention that only two out of the very numerous
authors who have written successfully on or for children
have shown a clear recollection of the mind of healthy
childhood itself. Many authors have achieved brilliant
success in describing children, in verbally caressing
them, in amusing, in instructing them; but only two, Mrs.
Ewing in prose, and Mr. Stevenson in verse, have sat down
with them without disturbing their fancies, and have
looked into the world of 'make-believe' with the children's own eyes. If Victor Hugo should visit the nursery,
every head of hair ought to be brushed, every pinafore
be clean, and nurse must certainly be present, as well as
mamma. But Mrs. Ewing or Mr. Stevenson might lead a long
romp in the attic when nurse was out shopping, and not a
child in the house should know that a grown-up person had
been there....

In publishing this autumn a second volume, this time of
grown-up verses, Mr. Stevenson has ventured on a bolder
experiment. His 'Underwoods,' with its title openly
borrowed from Ben Jonson, is an easy book to appreciate
and enjoy, but not to review. In many respects it is
plainly the work of the same fancy that described the
Country of Counterpane and the Land of Story-books, but it
has grown a little sadder, and a great deal older. There
is the same delicate sincerity, the same candour and simplicity, the same artless dependence on the good faith of
the public. The ordinary themes of the poets are un-
touched; there is not one piece from cover to cover which
deals with the passion of love. The book is occupied
with friendship, with nature, with the honourable instincts of man's moral machinery. Above all, it enters
with great minuteness, and in a very confidential spirit,

into the theories and moods of the writer himself. It
will be to many readers a revelation of the everyday life
of an author whose impersonal writings have given them so
much and so varied pleasure. Not a dozen ordinary inter-
viewers could have extracted so much of the character of
the man himself as he gives us in these one hundred and
twenty pages.

The question of admitting the personal element into
literature is one which is not very clearly understood.
People try to make rules about it, and say that an author
may describe his study, but not his dining-room, and his
wife, but not her cousin. The fact is that no rules can
possibly be laid down in a matter which is one of individual sympathy. The discussion whether a writer may speak
of himself or no is utterly vain until we are informed
in what voice he has the habit of speaking. It is all a
question which depends on the *timbre* of the literary
voice. As in life there are persons whose sweetness of
utterance is such that we love to have them warbling at
our side, no matter on what subject they speak, and others
to whom we have scarcely patience to listen if they want
to tell us that we have inherited a fortune, so it is in
literature. Except that little class of stoic critics
who like to take their books *in vacuo*, most of us prefer
to know something about the authors we read. But whether
we like them to tell it us themselves, or no, depends
entirely on the voice. Thackeray and Fielding are never
confidential enough to satisfy us; Dickens and Smollett
set our teeth on edge directly they start upon a career
of confidential expansion; and this has nothing to do with
any preference for 'Tom Jones' over 'Peregrine Pickle.'
There is no doubt that Mr. Stevenson is one of those
writers the sound of whose personal voices is pleasing to
the public, and there must be hundreds of his admirers
who will not miss one word of To a Gardener or The Mirror
Speaks, and who will puzzle out each of the intimate
addresses to his private friends with complete satisfaction.

The present writer is one of those who are most under
the spell. For me Mr. Stevenson may speak for ever, and
chronicle at full length all his uncles and his cousins
and his nurses. But I think if it were my privilege to
serve him in the capacity of Molière's old woman, or to
be what a friend of mine would call his 'foolometer,' I
should pluck up courage to represent to him that this
thing can be overdone. I openly avow myself an enthusiast, yet even I shrink before the confidential character
of the prose inscription to 'Underwoods.' This volume is
dedicated, if you please, to eleven physicians, and it is

strange that one so all compact of humour as Mr. Stevenson
should not have noticed how funny it is to think of an
author seated affably in an armchair, simultaneously
summoning by name eleven physicians to take a few words of
praise each, and a copy of his little book.

The objective side of Mr. Stevenson's mind is very rich
and full, and he has no need to retire too obstinately
upon the subjective. Yet I know not than anything he has
written in verse is more worthily dignified than the following little personal fragment, in which he refers, of
course, to the grandfather who died a few weeks before his
birth, and to the father whom he had just conducted to the
grave, both heroic builders of lighthouses:

Say not of me that weakly I declined
The labours of my sires, and fled the sea,
The towers we founded and the lamps we lit,
To play at home with paper like a child.
But rather say: In the afternoon of time
A strenuous family dusted from its hands
The sand of granite, and beholding far
Along the sounding coast its pyramids
And tall memorials catch the dying sun,
Smiled well content, and to this childish task
Around the fire addressed its evening hours.

[xxxviii]

This is a particularly happy specimen of Mr. Stevenson's blank verse, in which metre, as a rule, he does not
show to advantage. It is not that his verses are ever
lame or faulty, for in the technical portion of the art
he seldom fails, but that his rhymeless iambics remind
the ear too much now of Tennyson, now of Keats. He is,
on the contrary, exceedingly happy and very much himself
in that metre of eight or seven syllables, with couplet-
rhymes, which served so well the first poets who broke
away from heroic verse, such as Swift and Lady Winchilsea,
Green and Dyer. If he must be affiliated to any school of
poets it is to these, who hold the first outworks between
the old classical camp and the invacing army of romance,
to whom I should ally him. Martial is with those octo-
syllabists of Queen Anne, and to Martial might well have
been assigned, had they been in old Latin, the delicately
homely lines, To a Gardener. How felicitous is this
quatrain about the onion -

Let first the onion flourish there,
Rose among roots, the maiden fair,
Wine-scented and poetic soul
Of the capacious salad-bowl.

Or this, in more irregular measure, and enfolding a
loftier fancy -

>Sing clearlier, Muse, or evermore be still,
>Sing truer, or no longer sing!
>No more the voice of melancholy Jacques
>To make a weeping echo in the hill;
>But as the boy, the pirate of the spring,
>From the green elm a living linnet takes,
>One natural verse recapture - then be still. [xxxi]

It would be arrogant in the extreme to decide whether
or no Mr. R. L. Stevenson's poems will be read in the
future. They are, however, so full of character, so
redolent of his own fascinating temperament, that it is
not too bold to suppose that so long as his prose is
appreciated those who love that will turn to this. There
have been prose writers whose verse has not lacked accomplishment or merit, but has been so far from interpreting
their prose that it rather disturbed its effect and weak-
ened its influence. Cowley is an example of this, whose
ingenious and dryly intellectual poetry positively terri-
fied the reader away from his eminently suave and human
essays. Neither of Mr. Stevenson's volumes of poetry
will thus disturb his prose. Opinions may be divided as
to their positive value, but no one will doubt that the
same characteristics are displayed in the poems, the same
suspicion of 'the abhorred pedantic sanhedrim,' the same
fulness of life and tenderness of hope, the same bright
felicity of epithet as in the essays and romances. The
belief, however, may be expressed without fear of contradiction that Mr. Stevenson's fame will rest mainly upon
his verse and not upon his prose, only in that dim future
when Mr. Matthew Arnold's prophecy shall be fulfilled and
Shelley's letters shall be preferred to his lyrical poems.
It is saying a great deal to acknowledge that the author
of 'Kidnapped' is scarcely less readable in verse than he
is in prose.

Notes

1 Dante, 'Inferno', iii, 51: Speak not of them, but look
   and pass.
2 Juliana Horatia Ewing (1841-85), daughter of Mrs Gatty
   (see n. 3 below), was author of 'The Brownies and Other
   Tales' (1870), 'Jackanapes' (1883), 'Daddy Darwin's
   Dovecote' (1884), etc. Most of her work first appeared
   in 'Aunt Judy's Magazine', edited by Mrs Gatty from
   1866 to 1885.

3 Mrs Margaret Gatty (1809-73); her 'Parables of Nature'
   appeared in five volumes from 1855 to 1871.

97. STEVENSON, FROM A LETTER TO GOSSE

8 October 1887, LS, iii, 14-15

My dear Gosse, - I have just read your article twice, with
cheers of approving laughter. I do not believe you ever
wrote anything so funny: Tyndall's 'shell,' the passage
on the Davos press and its invaluable issues, and that on
V. Hugo and Swinburne, are exquisite; so, I say it more
ruefully, is the touch about the doctors. For the rest,
I am very glad you like my verses so well; and the qualities you ascribe to them seem to me well found and well
named. I own to that kind of candour you attribute to
me: when I am frankly interested, I suppose I fancy the
public will be so too; and when I am moved, I am sure of
it. It has been my luck hitherto to meet with no stagger-
ing disillusion. 'Before' and 'After' may be two; and
yet I believe the habit is now too thoroughly ingrained
to be altered. About the doctors, you were right, that
dedication has been the subject of some pleasantries that
made me grind, and of your happily touched reproof which
made me blush. And to miscarry in a dedication is an
abominable form of book-wreck; I am a good captain, I
would rather lose the text and save my dedication....
    I had some experience of American appreciation; I liked
a little of it, but there is too much; a little of that
would go a long way to spoil a man; and I like myself
better in the woods. I am so damned candid and ingenuous
(for a cynic), and so much of a 'cweatu' of impulse - aw'
(if you remember that admirable Leech) that I begin to
shirk any more taffy; I think I begin to like it too well.
But let us trust the Gods; they have a rod in pickle;
reverently I doff my trousers, and with screwed eyes await
the *amari aliquid* of the great God Busby.
    I thank you for the article in all ways, and remain
yours affectionately,

                                        R.L.S.

98. MRS OLIPHANT ON 'UNDERWOODS' AND STEVENSON'S
EXPLOITATION OF THE PERSONAL, 'BLACKWOOD'S MAGAZINE'

November 1887, cxli, 709-12

Margaret Oliphant (1828-97), the extremely prolific novelist, biographer, and historical writer, was long associated with the Blackwoods and wrote a history of the firm,
'Annals of a Publishing House: William Blackwood and His
Sons, Their Magazine and Friends', 2 vols (1897). Much of
her work appeared in the pages of 'Blackwood's Magazine',
including a great number of reviews. This present review
is taken from The Old Saloon series.

... We yield to none in our admiration for the delightful
style, the refined humour, the spontaneous and brilliant
fun of our countryman. He has had the honour of founding
a new school of fictitious literature, in which, though
there have been miraculous successors, no one, to our
liking, has ever come within a hundred miles of 'Treasure
Island.' And his later book, 'Kidnapped,' though perhaps
not so pleasing to the populace, has still higher and
more beautiful qualities. But - Mr Stevenson is still
young; in his own personality he is exceedingly interesting, we have no manner of doubt, to a large and varied
circle. Might we venture to hint, to suggest, that it
would be well to be content with that affectionate appreciation, and not allow himself to be deluded into thinking that his house, and his doctors, and his gardeners,
and the pretty presents he makes to his friends, are
equally absorbing in their interest to a large and already
much occupied public? Nobody who is in the habit of sitting with us from time to time in this Old Saloon, and
sharing in our literary diversions, will doubt, for instance, of our attachment to our distinguished contemporary, Mr Andrew Lang.... But with all our love for him,
we are conscious of a faint titillation in our throat - a
little excitement of the risible muscles - when we hear
him addressed in public as 'Dear Andrew of the brindled
hair' [from To Andrew Lang]. And we yield to no one in
our regard for Mr Henry James. His fine if sometimes
hesitating utterances are dear to us. When he leads upon
the stage a fantastic princess, though he takes a long
time, a very long time, in describing her, we listen to
him, every word, with a gravity equal to his own. (1) But

when we read in a printed book that the Venetian mirror
at Skerryvore, which is not a lighthouse but Mr Stevenson's house at Bournemouth - waits, as the climax of an
existence which has seen many pretty things in its native
palaces and elsewhere,

> Until the door
> Open, and the Prince of men,
> Henry James, shall come again,
>
> [From The Mirror Speaks]

we - well, not to put too fine a point upon it, we laugh.
We presume Mr James laughed too; and we can scarcely
doubt, though not perhaps given to blushing, felt a little
heat mounting to his ears [see No. 95b]. It is not permitted, even to a man of genius, to make his friends, even
when they too are men of genius, absurd. The world has
nothing to do with these little endearments. It is an
American fashion quite unworthy of importation, and, as
English authors may see, looking sadly ridiculous when
Mr Lowell, for instance, calls upon us to admire a number
of men of Harvard by their names which we never heard
before. Perhaps it rather adds than takes away from the
absurdity when they are names which we have heard. The
most Christian critic can scarcely refrain from a chuckle
of delight when he sees his friend opposite branded as
Prince of men. What did the Venetian mirror continue to
say when it reflected that bland image? It would rather
have had the Princess, we'll go bail.
    Let us address Mr Stevenson in a verse of his own, with
all the force of affectionate remonstrance: -

> Sing clearlier, Muse, or evermore be still!
> Sing truer or no longer sing!
> No more the voice of melancholy Jaques,
> To wake a weeping echo in the hill.
> But as the boy, the pirate of the spring,
> From the green elm a living linnet takes,
> One natural verse recapture - then be still. [xxxi]

These are precisely our sentiments, expressed in more
admirable language. We return the tuneful couplets to the
author with a respectful salutation.
    The following poem is still on the inexhaustible
subject of the author's own surroundings, being the house
(as we presume - if we are wrong, that no doubt accounts
in some measure for the superiority of the poetry) in
which the Venetian mirror hangs: -

[The House Beautiful is quoted in full.]

This is very charming and pretty, and sufficiently impersonal to command the general sympathy of all who have
houses and live therein, and find their homely roofs
glorified with sunrisings and sunsettings every day. We
are tempted also to quote an address to the poet's father,
in which there is all the honest pride of a good lineage
and a personal feeling more justifiable than that which
shines through his addresses to contemporary friends.

[Quotes from To My Father.]

We may indicate here, as worth the reader's while, a
striking little poem called The Celestial Surgeon, an
address to a mother, It is not yours, O Mother, to complain, and if he is polemically minded, Our Lady of the
Snows, and sundry of the poems called Skerryvore - but
advise him to leave out the more purely personal part,
unless he happens to have a stronger interest in Mr Louis
Stevenson than in poetry; in which case he will probably
like to know what that gentleman thinks of the onion, that
it is the

    Rose among roots, the maiden fair,
    Wine-scented, and poetic soul,
    Of the capacious salad-bowl,

                            [From To a Gardener]

and various other oddish things. All this, however, is
but the half of the volume. The second part is taken up
with verses - in Scots. Now be it far from us to say that
no man is to write in Scots, or what Mr Stevenson calls
'Lallan,' because Burns has made that language classic;
but we do feel that there is a rashness almost blasphemous
in the proceeding, when a new rhymester takes up the measure of the Second Epistle to Davie, and puts some very
commonplace sentiments into it, with a little lecture on
the pronunciation of vowels before it, and a fear in the
middle of it that somebody may take up the book in after-
ages -

    May find an' read me, an' be sair
        Perplexed, puir brither!

    What tongue does yon auld bookie speak?
    He'll speir, and I, his mon' to steik,
    No bein' fit to write in Greek,
                    I wrote in Lallan;

> Dear to my heart as the peat-reek,
>   Auld as Tantallon.

Few spak' it then, and noo there's nane –

Does Mr Stevenson really suppose that his address of The
Maker to Posterity will survive to puzzle the antiquaries
when the works of that ploughman whose life we are aware he
does not approve of have disappeared into the dust of ages?
Does he believe that any man in his senses, or woman
either, will find in these poetical exercises anything but
faint echoes of

> Him who walked in glory and in joy,
> Following his plough along the mountain-side?
>   [From Wordsworth's Resolution and Independence]

Let us not lose our temper with this rash young man. Much
applause has, we fear, turned his head. Having nothing in
the world to say in 'Lallan' which he could not say better
in his ordinary fine speech (pleasantly breathing a Scotti-
cism here and there, we are glad to say, much more characteristic than the 'Scots'), he has framed his verses very
nicely, and brought out the different *ow's* and *ou's* and
o's in a manner which does credit to his breeding. But Mr
Stevenson is no rival of Burns, who spoke his natural
tongue, and had a great many of the most lovely and
delightful things to say in it; and when he speaks of his
little pipings as likely to perplex a world which has the
works of that great poet before it, he says a very silly
thing, quite unworthy of any good sense he may happen to
possess, and highly injurious to his unquestionable genius.
Let us be done with this foolish self-opinion and disrespect. To be pious about the lighthouse is pretty, to
be impious about the fathers of one's tongue and thoughts
is detestable....
    It is America that is the cause of it all – America
which thrusts in her little reputations upon us, and so
swears they are of the first rank, that with a gasp, and
for the sake of peace, yet with wonderful searchings of
heart, we give a feeble assent. A living dog is better –
that big continent thinks – than a dead lion; and if Longfellow is as worthy of Westminster as Shakespeare himself –
or at least as Dryden and Pope and Coleridge – why should
not Mr Robert Louis Stevenson be better than Robert
Burns?...

Note

1 James's 'The Princess Casamassima' appeared serially in
   the 'Atlantic', September 1885 - October 1886; it first
   appeared in book form in October 1886.

99. STEVENSON ON THE '*PROSE* MERITS' OF 'UNDERWOODS', FROM
A LETTER TO J. A. SYMONDS

21 November 1887, LS, iii, 25

I wonder if you saw my book of verses? It went into a
second edition, because of my name, I suppose, and its
prose merits. I do not set up to be a poet. Only an all-
round literary man: a man who talks, not one who sings.
But I believe the very fact that it was only speech served
the book with the public. Horace is much a speaker, and
see how popular! most of Martial is only speech, and I
cannot conceive a person who does not love his Martial;
most of Burns, also, such as The Louse, The Toothache,
The Haggis, and lots more of his best.. Excuse this little
apology for my muse; but I don't like to come before
people who have a note of song, and let it be supposed I
do not know the difference.

'Memories and Portraits'

November 1887

All the essays in this volume except A College Magazine,
Memoirs of an Islet, and A Gossip on a Novel of Dumas's
had appeared earlier in periodicals:

The Foreigner at Home ('Cornhill Magazine', May 1882)
Some College Memories ('New Amphion', December 1886)
Old Mortality ('Longman's Magazine', May 1884)
An Old Scotch Gardener ('Edinburgh University Magazine',
    March 1871)
Pastoral ('Longman's Magazine', April 1887)
The Manse ('Scribner's Magazine', May 1887)
Thomas Stevenson ('Contemporary Review', June 1887)
Talk and Talkers: First Paper ('Cornhill Magazine', April
    1882)
Talk and Talkers: Second Paper ('Cornhill Magazine',
    August 1882)
The Character of Dogs ('English Illustrated Magazine', May
    1883)
A Penny Plain and Twopence Coloured ('Magazine of Art',
    April 1884)
A Gossip on Romance ('Longman's Magazine', November 1882)
A Humble Remonstrance ('Longman's Magazine', December
    1884)

100. WILLIAM ARCHER, FROM AN UNSIGNED REVIEW, 'PALL MALL
GAZETTE'

1 December 1887, xlvi, 3

Among the Graham Balfour papers at the National Library of
Scotland is a note from Archer identifying many of his un-

signed reviews and articles on Stevenson; this review is to
be on the list, as is No. 129.

As Mr. Stevenson has not been held worthy of a place in the
last edition of 'Men of the Time' we cannot state his age
to a year; but as he tells us in this book that in 1870 he
'thrilled and trembled on the brink of life, like a
childish bather on the beach,' we may pretty safely suppose him to be six or eight and thirty.   In an ordinary
man it would be reckoned presumption, not to say fatuity,
to publish a volume of 'Memories and Portraits' at such an
age, especially if 'the face of what was once himself'
proved to be the principal object portrayed.   As a rule,
we do not expect a man to unburden his memory until it has
become something of a marvel that he should have any
memory to unburden.   But Mr. Stevenson is not an ordinary
man.   He can talk delightfully about any subject under the
sun, and he could scarcely find a more entertaining subject than himself.   It is because we are all egoists that
we are so quick to cry out upon egoism, just as one coloured gentleman will revile another by calling him an
'habitual nigger.'   The man who assumes a privilege we
long for but dare not claim awakens malice, envy, and all
uncharitableness.   He must justify his audacity by using
the privilege with exceptional grace; and this Mr. Stevenson could scarcely fail to do.   It is the clumsy, the apologetic, the stolid, or the morbid egoist whom we detest.
The world has always delighted in its exquisite egoists,
for they have known how to transmute our original and besetting sin into something very like a virtue.
     The book opens with a delicately observant paper called
The Foreigner at Home, which no Scot who has ever crossed
the border will read without a thrill of sympathy.   What
can be truer, in the midst of its humour, than this remark:
'About the very cradle of the Scot there goes a hum of
metaphysical divinity; and the whole of two divergent
systems is summèd up, not merely speciously, in the two
first questions of the rival catechisms, the English
tritely inquiring, "What is your name?" the Scottish
striking at the very roots of life with, "What is the chief
end of man?" and answering nobly, if obscurely, "To glorify
God and to enjoy Him for ever."'   A paper of College
Memories, noteworthy for its charming portrait of the late
Professor Kelland, is followed by a more elaborate study of
the story and stress of youth, under the heading of Old
Mortality.   The essay called A College Magazine ... lets

us into some of the secrets of Mr. Stevenson's workshop.
It says much, in our opinion, for his inborn faculty that
it survived his early course of 'sedulous aping.' We may
perhaps trace to it one of the faults of his style, its
ever-present self-consciousness. When at its best it is
perfect in purity and variety of cadence, but not always
in choice of words. A word may become wrong by being too
right, or rather too obtrusively right. The perfection of
style, we conceive, is that it should delight without surprising; Mr. Stevenson often surprises while he delights.
He is a little too much of the conjurer with words, and
every now and then, after some feat of surpassing deft-
ness, we seem to see him smiling behind his page and mur-
muring, 'There is no deception!'...

One or two less important papers lead us up to the concluding Gossip on a Novel of Dumas's, Gossip on Romance,
and Humble Remonstrance, which may be taken as Mr. Stevenson's literary confession of faith. There is a fine
superiority to 'the poor little orthodoxies of the day' in
his resolute use of 'romantic' as a term of eulogy. This
is not the place for anything like a formal discussion of
Mr. Stevenson's many-sided critical doctrines. Before they
can be fruitfully discussed, indeed, he must be more explicit on one or two important points. In this book, as in
its predecessors, there is a portentous vagueness of statement on the ethical side of life and art. To take Mr. Stevenson at his word, 'there is no quite good book without a
good morality;' and his own work, he would have us understand, is nothing if not moral. Now, beyond the constant
exhortation to 'keep your pecker up,' and the ordinary
commonplaces which belong to good-breeding rather than to
morality, we should be puzzled to discover one solitary
ethical message in all Mr. Stevenson's writing which could
conceivably influence the conduct of any human being. He
has a vague way of alluding to some esoteric morality of
his own, which is as impressive as it is tantalizing. Not
that he is troubled by any doubts as to the absolute
rightness of his system; only he seems to despair of
explaining it to any one who does not understand it
already. This nebulous cocksureness, this dogmatism without dogma, at last becomes a little irritating. We tire
of waiting on tiptoe for a revelation which never comes,
and begin to suspect that Mr. Stevenson's morality is like
the Emperor's new clothes in Hans Andersen. It is as
though Moses, after going up with much pomp and circumstance into the Mount, had returned with no less solemnity
to exhibit a pair of blank tablets.

101.   E. T. COOK, FROM AN UNSIGNED REVIEW, 'ATHENAEUM'

24 December 1887, 3139, 860-1

On Cook see headnote to No. 68.

We have never been able to share the extravagant estimate
of Mr. R. L. Stevenson's powers which has been formed in
some quarters, and we have said that Mr. Stevenson himself
must have felt embarrassed by unmeasured eulogy. His
volume of collected magazine articles and others, called
'Memories and Portraits' shows for once a desire to offer
himself to the world in general at the price put upon him
by the select circle of his most enthusiastic admirers.
The title of the book claims too much, and the preface,
which peremptorily bids one to read the papers through
from the beginning rather than to dip into them at random,
is not an agreeable introduction. The papers, it is asserted, form something like an autobiography, and enable the
reader to trace through the grandfather and the father the
person designated by an unfortunate phrase as 'the person
of to-day.' The question, which would not otherwise have
arisen, is therefore forced upon one whether Mr. Stevenson
has yet achieved a position which makes it fitting for him
to present his autobiography to the world. He has written
two admirable boys' books, one of the best of shilling
dreadfuls, and a number of other works which have been
extremely successful, and he has been much 'interviewed'
in America; but he is still a young man, and it is sincerely hoped he has a brilliant future before him. Is he
yet entitled to issue his magazine articles with such a
flourish? In truth, after going through them from the
beginning an impartial reader cannot find it possible to
admit that they at all bear out the character claimed for
them. About half of them deal with Scotch life and manners; but the rest are as diverse as any other chance
collection - Talk and Talkers, The Character of Dogs, A
Gossip on a Novel of Dumas's, and A Gossip about Romance
being among the titles. It is difficult to discover what
quality should give them a permanent interest. Speaking
of them as a whole, they have an air of seriousness, and
even of sadness, lightened here and there by humorous
touches, but wanting that vivacity and that restrained
irony which mark the best of Mr. Stevenson's work. The
form in which they are cast, suitable enough no doubt to

their original purpose, gives them an appearance of egotism, a little fault from which Mr. Stevenson has been
otherwise entirely free hitherto. The matters dealt with
in the book being so various, it is impossible to criticize it in detail. The chapters on novel-writing are, for
the moment, the most inviting; but the fact that they are
in substance answers to Mr. Besant, Mr. Henry James, and
Mr. Howells only shows that they are ephemeral [see No.
44]. They are, indeed, excellently written, with great
beauty of style and with the vigour of a strong conviction;
but they are neither simple enough nor sufficiently close
in argument to be convincing to others. When Mr. Stevenson comes to sum up the whole matter by laying down his
advice to young novelists, it is obvious that an accomplished artist is not always the best person to teach the
rudiments....

102. HENRY JAMES, FROM ROBERT LOUIS STEVENSON, 'CENTURY
MAGAZINE'

April 1888, xxxv, 869-79

This essay first came into Stevenson's hands in the autumn
of 1887 when Will H. Low (No. 54e), a friend of the editor
of 'Century Magazine', Richard Watson Gilder, visited
Stevenson at Saranac Lake, New York, and brought with him
the manuscript or proofs for Stevenson to read. In a
letter to James dating from sometime in October Stevenson
writes,

    I have seen the article; and it may be from natural
    partiality, I think it the best you have written.
    O - I remember the Gautier, which was an excellent
    performance; and the Balzac, which was good; and the
    Daudet, over which I licked my chops; but the R.L.S.
    is better yet. It is so humorous, and it hits my
    little frailties with so neat (and so friendly) a
    touch; and Alan is the occasion for so much happy talk,
    and the quarrel is so generously praised. I read it
    twice, though it was only some hours in my possession;
    and Low, who got it for me from the 'Century', sat up
    to finish it ere he returned it; and, sir, we were all
    delighted. (LS, iii, 20-1)

The essay was reprinted in James's 'Partial Portraits'
(1888), 137-74.

While James is highly enthusiastic about Stevenson here,
as he is in a later review essay of 'Letters to Family and
Friends' ('North American Review', January 1900), and in
his remarks to Stevenson himself in his letters, it is not
easy to conclude what his exact assessment was of Stevenson's achievement. He sympathizes with Stevenson's concern for matters of form and expression, a concern James
found all too rare among writers in English. But clearly
his feelings of kinship with Stevenson went well beyond
this, in spite of their very great temperamental differences. The feelings seem to have had a basis in what
James below, speaking of Stevenson, calls a 'love of
brave words as well as brave deeds'. Both were equally
moved by this love, as men and artists, however differently each may have expressed bravery of deed and word.
Another remark of James here would also seem to suggest
the basis of their kinship:

> He would say we ought to make believe that the extra-
> ordinary is the best part of life, even if it were
> not, and to do so because the finest feelings - sus-
> pense, daring, decision, passion, curiosity, gallantry,
> eloquence, friendship - are involved in it, and it is
> of infinite importance that the tradition of these
> precious things should not perish.

Nevertheless, while James finds that Stevenson's works
represent an admirable success of sorts, he does not claim
for them the highest achievement nor does he actually try
to arrive at a final estimate of their value by submitting
them to judgment by the highest standards. See Introduction, p. 27.

In the first paragraphs of his essay, James remarks on
the fitness of Stevenson as a subject for literary portraiture.

... And if the figures who have a life in literature may
also be divided into two great classes, we may add that
he is conspicuously one of the draped; he would never, if
I may be allowed the expression, pose for the nude. There
are writers who present themselves before the critic with
just the amount of drapery that is necessary for decency,
but Mr. Stevenson is not one of these; he makes his
appearance in an amplitude of costume. His costume is
part of the character of which I just now spoke; it never
occurs to us to ask how he would look without it. Before
all things he is a writer with a style - a model with a
complexity of curious and picturesque garments. It is by
the cut and the color of this rich and becoming frippery -

I use the term endearingly, as a painter might - that he
arrests the eye and solicits the brush.

That is, frankly, half the charm he has for us, that he
wears a dress and wears it with courage, with a certain
cock of the hat and tinkle of the supererogatory sword;
or, in other words, that he is curious of expression, and
regards the literary form not simply as a code of signals,
but as the keyboard of a piano and as so much plastic
material. He has that vice deplored by Mr. Herbert Spencer, a manner - a manner for a manner's sake, it may sometimes doubtless be said. He is as different as possible
from the sort of writer who regards words as numbers and
a page as the mere addition of them; much more, to carry
out our image, the dictionary stands for him as a ward-
robe, and a proposition as a button for his coat. Mr.
William Archer, in an article [No. 52] so gracefully and
ingeniously turned that the writer may almost be accused
of imitating even while he deprecates, speaks of him as a
votary of 'lightness of touch' at any cost, and remarks
that 'he is not only philosophically content, but deliberately resolved, that his readers shall look first to his
manner and only in the second place to his matter.' I
shall not attempt to gainsay this; I cite it rather, for
the present, because it carries out my own sense. Mr.
Stevenson delights in a style, and his own has nothing
accidental or diffident; it is eminently conscious of its
responsibilities and meets them with a kind of gallantry -
as if language were a pretty woman and a person who proposes to handle it had, of necessity, to be something of
a Don Juan. This element of the gallant is a noticeable
part of his nature, and it is rather odd that, at the
same time, a striking feature of that nature should be an
absence of care for things feminine. His books are for
the most part books without women, and it is not women
who fall most in love with them. But Mr. Stevenson does
not need, as we may say, a petticoat to inflame him; a
happy collocation of words will serve the purpose, or a
singular image, or the bright eye of a passing conceit,
and he will carry off a pretty paradox without so much as
a scuffle. The tone of letters is in him - the tone of
letters as distinct from that of philosophy or of those
industries whose uses are supposed to be immediate. Many
readers, no doubt, consider that he carries it too far;
they manifest an impatience for some glimpse of his moral
message. They may be heard to ask what it is he proposes
to deduce, to prove, to establish, with such a variety of
paces and graces.

The main thing that he establishes, to my own perception, is that it is a delight to read him and that he
renews this delight by a constant variety of experiment.
Of this anon, however; and meanwhile it may be noted as

a curious characteristic of current fashions that the
writer whose effort is perceptibly that of the artist is
very apt to find himself thrown on the defensive. A work
of literature is a form, but the author who betrays a
consciousness of the responsibilities involved in this
circumstance not rarely perceives himself to be regarded
as an uncanny personage. The usual judgment is that he
may be artistic, but that he must not be too much so; that
way, apparently, lies something worse than madness. This
queer superstition has so successfully imposed itself that
the mere fact of having been indifferent to such a danger
constitutes in itself an originality. How few they are in
number and how soon we could name them, the writers of
English prose, at the present moment, the quality of whose
prose is personal, expressive, renewed at each attempt!
The state of things that would have been expected to be
the rule has become the exception, and an exception for
which, most of the time, an apology appears to be thought
necessary. A mill that grinds with regularity and with a
certain commercial fineness - that is the image suggested
by the manner of a good many of the fraternity. They turn
out an article for which there is a demand, they keep a
shop for a speciality, and the business is carried on in
accordance with a useful, well-tested prescription. It is
just because he has no specialty that Mr. Stevenson is an
individual, and because his curiosity is the only receipt
by which he produces. Each of his books is an independent
effort - a window opened to a different view. 'Dr. Jekyll
and Mr. Hyde' is as dissimilar as possible from 'Treasure
Island'; 'Virginibus Puerisque' has nothing in common with
'The New Arabian Nights,' and I should never have supposed 'A Child's Garden of Verses' to be from the hand of
the author of 'Prince Otto.'
   Though Mr. Stevenson cares greatly for his phrase, as
every writer should who respects himself and his art, it
takes no very attentive reading of his volumes to show
that it is not what he cares for most, and that he regards
an expressive style only, after all, as a means. It seems
to me the fault of Mr. Archer's interesting paper that it
suggests too much that the author of these volumes considers the art of expression as an end - a game of words.
He finds that Mr. Stevenson is not serious, that he neglects a whole side of life, that he has no perception, and
no consciousness, of suffering; that he speaks as a happy
but heartless pagan, living only in his senses (which the
critic admits to be exquisitely fine), and that, in a
world full of heaviness, he is not sufficiently aware of
the philosophic limitations of mere technical skill.
(In sketching these aberrations Mr. Archer himself, by
the way, displays anything but ponderosity of hand.) He
is not the first reader, and he will not be the last, who

shall have been irritated by Mr. Stevenson's jauntiness.
That jauntiness is an essential part of his genius; but, to
my sense, it ceases to be irritating - it indeed becomes
positively touching, and constitutes an appeal to sympathy
and even to tenderness - when once one has perceived what
lies beneath the dancing-tune to which he mostly moves.
Much as he cares for his phrase he cares more for life,
and for a certain transcendently lovable part of it. He
feels, as it seems to us, and that is not given to every
one; this constitutes a philosophy which Mr. Archer fails
to read between his lines - the respectable, desirable
moral which many a reader doubtless finds that he neglects
to point. He does not feel everything equally, by any
manner of means; but his feelings are always his reasons;
he regards them, whatever they may be, as sufficiently
honorable, does not disguise them in other names or col-
ors, and looks at whatever he meets in the brilliant
candle-light that they shed. As in his extreme artistic
vivacity he seems really disposed to try everything, he
has tried once, by way of a change, to be inhuman, and
there is a hard glitter about 'Prince Otto' which seems to
indicate that in this case, too, he has succeeded, as he
has done in most of the feats that he has attempted. But
'Prince Otto' is even less like his other productions than
his other productions are like each other.

The part of life that he cares for most is youth, and
the direct expression of the love of youth is the beginning and the end of his message. His appreciation of this
delightful period amounts to a passion; and a passion, in
the age in which we live, strikes us, on the whole, as a
sufficient philosophy. It ought to satisfy Mr. Archer,
and there are writers graver than Mr. Stevenson on whose
behalf no such moral motive can be alleged. Mingled with
his almost equal love of a literary surface it represents
a real originality. This combination is the key-note of
Mr. Stevenson's faculty and the explanation of his per-
versities. The feelings of one's teens, and even of an
earlier period (for the delights of crawling, and almost
of the rattle, are embodied in 'A Child's Garden of
Verses'), and the feeling for happy turns - these, in the
last analysis (and his sense of a happy turn is of the
subtlest), are the corresponding halves of his character.
If 'Prince Otto' and 'Dr. Jekyll' left me a clearer field
for the assertion, I should say that everything he has
written is a direct apology for boyhood; or rather (for
it must be confessed that Mr. Stevenson's tone is seldom
apologetic) a direct rhapsody on the age of little jack-
ets. Even members of the very numerous class who have
held their breath over 'Treasure Island' may shrug their
shoulders at this account of the author's religion; but

it is none the less a great pleasure - the highest reward
of observation - to put one's hand on a rare illustration,
and Mr. Stevenson is certainly rare. What makes him so is
the singular maturity of the expression that he has given
to young sentiments; he judges them, measures them, sees
them from the outside, as well as entertains them. He
describes credulity with all the resources of experience,
and represents a crude stage with infinite ripeness. In a
word, he is an artist accomplished even to sophistication,
whose constant theme is the unsophisticated. Sometimes,
as in 'Kidnapped,' the art is so ripe that it lifts even
the subject into the general air; the execution is so
serious that the idea (the idea of a boy's romantic adventures) becomes a matter of universal relations. What he
prizes most in the boy's ideal is the imaginative side of
it, the capacity for successful make-believe. The general
freshness in which this is a part of the gloss seems to
him the divinest thing in life; considerably more divine,
for instance, than the passion usually regarded as the
supremely tender one. The idea of making believe appeals
to him much more than the idea of making love. That
delightful little book of rhymes, the 'Child's Garden,'
commemorates, from beginning to end, the picturing, per-
sonifying, dramatizing faculty of infancy, the view of
life from the level of the nursery-fender. The volume is
a wonder, for the extraordinary vividness with which it
reproduces early impressions; a child might have written
it if a child could see childhood from the outside, for
it would seem that only a child is really near enough to
the nursery-floor. And what is peculiar to Mr. Stevenson
is that it is his own childhood he appears to delight in,
and not the personal presence of little darlings. Oddly
enough, there is no strong implication that he is fond of
babies; he doesn't speak as a parent, or an uncle, or an
educator - he speaks as a contemporary absorbed in his own
game. That game is almost always a vision of dangers and
triumphs; and if emotion, with him, infallibly resolves
itself into memory, so memory is an evocation of throbs
and thrills and suspense. He has given to the world the
romance of boyhood, as others have produced that of the
peerage, the police, and the medical profession.
    This amounts to saying that what he is most curious
of in life is heroism, - personal gallantry, if need be,
with a manner, or a banner, - though he is also abundantly
capable of enjoying it when it is artless. The delightful
exploits of Jim Hawkins , in 'Treasure Island,' are unaffectedly performed; but none the less 'the finest action
is the better for a piece of purple,' as the author remarks in the paper on The English Admirals, in 'Virginibus
Puerisque' - a paper of which the moral is, largely, that

'we learn to desire a grand air in our heroes; and such a
knowledge of the human stage as shall make them put the
dots on their own i's and leave us in no suspense as to
when they mean to be heroic.' The love of brave words as
well as brave deeds - which is simply Mr. Stevenson's
essential love of style - is recorded in this little paper
with a charming, slightly sophistical ingenuity. 'They
served their guns merrily, when it came to fighting, and
they had the readiest ear for a bold, honorable sentiment
of any class of men the world ever produced.' The author
goes on to say that most men of high destinies have even
high-sounding names. Alan Breck, in 'Kidnapped,' is a
wonderful picture of the union of courage and swagger; the
little Jacobite adventurer, a figure worthy of Scott at
his best, and representing the highest point that Mr. Stevenson's talent has reached, shows us that a marked taste
for tawdry finery - tarnished and tattered, some of it,
indeed, by ticklish occasions - is quite compatible with a
perfectly high mettle. Alan Breck is, at bottom, a study
of the love of glory, carried out with extreme psychological truth. When the love of glory is of an inferior
order, the reputation is cultivated rather than the opportunity; but when it is a pure passion, the opportunity is
cultivated for the sake of the reputation. Mr. Stevenson's kindness for adventurers extends even to the hum-
blest of all, the mountebank and the strolling player, or
even the peddler whom he declares that in his foreign
travels he is habitually taken for, as we see in the
whimsical apology for vagabonds which winds up 'An Inland
Voyage.' The hungry conjurer, the gymnast whose *maillot*
is loose, have something of the glamour of the hero, inasmuch as they, too, pay with their person.

> To be even one of the outskirters of art leaves a
> fine stamp on a man's countenance.... That is the kind
> of thing that reconciles me to life; a ragged, tippling
> incompetent old rogue, with the manners of a gentleman
> and the vanity of an artist, to keep up his self-
> respect! [From Précy and the Marionettes]

What reconciles Mr. Stevenson to life is the idea that
in the first place it offers the widest field that we know
of for odd doings, and that in the second these odd doings
are the best of pegs to hang a sketch in three lines or a
paradox in three pages.
As it is not odd, but extremely usual, to marry, he
deprecates that course in 'Virginibus Puerisque,' the collection of short essays which is most a record of his
opinions - that is, largely, of his likes and dislikes.

It all comes back to his sympathy with the juvenile, and
that feeling about life which leads him to regard women as
so many superfluous girls in a boy's game. They are almost
wholly absent from his pages (the main exception is 'Prince
Otto,' though there is a Clara apiece in The Rajah's Diamond and The Pavilion on the Links), for they don't like
ships and pistols and fights; they encumber the decks and
require separate apartments; and, almost worst of all,
have not the highest literary standard. Why should a
person marry, when he might be swinging a cutlass or looking for a buried treasure? Why should he go to the altar
when he might be polishing his prose? It is one of those
curious, and, to my sense, fascinating inconsistencies
that we encounter in Mr. Stevenson's mind that, though he
takes such an interest in the childish life, he takes no
interest in the fireside. He has an indulgent glance for
it in the verses of the 'Garden,' but to his view the
normal child is the child who absents himself from the
family-circle, in fact when he can, in imagination when
he cannot, in the disguise of a buccaneer. Girls don't do
this, and women are only grown-up girls, unless it be the
delightful maiden, fit daughter of an imperial race, whom
he commemorates in 'An Inland Voyage.'

A girl at school in France began to describe one of
our regiments on parade to her French schoolmates; and
as she went on, she told me the recollection grew so
vivid, she became so proud to be the countrywoman of
such soldiers, and so sorry to be in another country,
that her voice failed her, and she burst into tears.
I have never forgotten that girl, and I think she very
nearly deserves a statue. To call her a young lady,
with all its niminy associations, would be to offer
her an insult. She may rest assured of one thing,
although she never should marry a heroic general, never
see any great or immediate result of her life, she will
not have lived in vain for her native land. [From At
Compiègne]

There is something of that in Mr. Stevenson. When he
begins to describe a British regiment on parade (or something of that sort) he, too, almost breaks down for emotion, which is why I have been careful to traverse the
insinuation that he is primarily a chiseler of prose. If
things had gone differently with him (I must permit myself this allusion to his personal situation, and I shall
venture to follow it with two or three others), he might
have been an historian of famous campaigns - a great
painter of battle-pieces. Of course, however, in this

capacity it would not have done for him to break down for
emotion.

Although he remarks that marriage 'is a field of
battle, and not a bed of roses,' he points out repeatedly
that it is a terrible renunciation, and somehow, in
strictness, incompatible even with honor - the sort of
roving, trumpeting honor that appeals most to his sympathy. After that step

> there are no more by-path meadows where you may inno-
> cently linger, but the road lies long and straight and
> dusty to the grave.... You may think you had a con-
> science and believed in God; but what is a conscience
> to a wife?... To marry is to domesticate the Recording
> Angel. Once you are married, there is nothing left for
> you, not even suicide, but to be good.... How, then,
> in such an atmosphere of compromise, to keep honor
> bright and abstain from base capitulations?... The
> proper qualities of each sex are, indeed, eternally
> surprising to the other. Between the Latin and the
> Teuton races there are similar divergences, not to be
> bridged by the most liberal sympathy.... It is better
> to face the fact and know, when you marry, that you
> take into your life a creature of equal if unlike
> frailties; whose weak human heart beats no more tune-
> fully than yours. [From 'Virginibus Puerisque', II]

If there is a grimness in that, it is as near as Mr.
Stevenson ever comes to being grim, and we have only to
turn the page to find the corrective - something delicately genial, at least, if not very much less sad:

> 'The blind bow-boy' who smiles upon us from the end
> of terraces in old Dutch gardens laughingly hails his
> bird-bolts among a fleeting generation. But for as
> fast as ever he shoots, the game dissolves and dis-
> appears into eternity from under his falling arrows;
> this one is gone ere he is struck; the other has but
> time to make one gesture and give one passionate cry;
> and they are all the things of a moment. [From 'Vir-
> ginibus Puerisque', III, On Falling in Love]

That is an admission that though it is soon over, the
great sentimental surrender is inevitable. And there is
geniality too, still over the page (in regard to quite
another matter), geniality, at least, for the profession
of letters, in the declaration that there is

> one thing you can never make Philistine natures

understand; one thing which yet lies on the surface,
remains as unseizable to their wits as a high flight
of metaphysics - namely, that the business of life is
mainly carried on by the difficult art of literature,
and according to a man's proficiency in that art shall
be the freedom and fullness of his intercourse with
other men. [From 'Virginibus Puerisque', IV, Truth
of Intercourse]

Yet it is difficult not to believe that the ideal in which
our author's spirit might most gratefully have rested
would have been the character of the paterfamilias, when
the eye falls on such a charming piece of observation as
these lines about children, in the admirable paper on
Child's Play:

> If it were not for this perpetual imitation, we
> should be tempted to fancy they despised us outright,
> or only considered us in the light of creatures
> brutally strong and brutally silly, among whom they
> condescended to dwell in obedience, like a philosopher
> at a barbarous court.

II.

We know very little about a talent till we know where
it grew up, and it would halt terribly at the start any
account of the author of 'Kidnapped' which should omit to
insist promptly that he is a Scot of the Scots. Two facts,
to my perception, go a great way to explain his composition,
the first of which is that his boyhood was passed in the
shadow of Edinburgh Castle, and the second, that he came of
a family that had set up great lights on the coast. His
grandfather, his uncle, were famous constructors of lighthouses, and the name of the race is associated above all
with the beautiful and beneficent tower of Skerryvore. We
may exaggerate the way in which, in an imaginative youth,
the sense of the 'story' of things would feed upon the impressions of Edinburgh - though I suspect it would be difficult really to do so. The streets are so full of history
and poetry, of picture and song, of associations springing
from strong passions and strange characters, that for my
own part I find myself thinking of an urchin going and
coming there as I used to think - wonderingly, enviously -
of the small boys who figured as supernumeraries, pages,
or imps in showy scenes at the theater; the place seems
the background, the complicated 'set' of a drama, and the
children the mysterious little beings who are made free
of the magic world. How must it not have beckoned on

the imagination to pass and repass, on the way to school,
under the Castle rock, conscious acutely, yet familiarly,
of the gray citadel on the summit, lighted up with the
tartans and bagpipes of Highland regiments! Mr. Stevenson's mind, from an early age, was furnished with the
concrete Highlander, who must have had much of the effect
that we nowadays call decorative. I encountered somewhere
a fanciful paper of our author's (1) in which there is a
reflection of half-holiday afternoons and, unless my own
fancy plays me a trick, of lights red, in the winter
dusk, in the high-placed windows of the Old Town - a
delightful rhapsody on the penny sheets of figures for
the puppet-shows of infancy, in life-like position, and
awaiting the impatient yet careful scissors. 'If landscapes were sold,' he says in 'Travels with a Donkey,'
'like the sheets of characters of my boyhood, one penny
plain and twopence colored, I should go the length of
twopence every day of my life.'

Indeed, the color of Scotland has entered into him
altogether, and though, oddly enough, he has written but
little about his native country, his happiest work shows,
I think, that she has the best of his ability. 'Kidnapped' (whose inadequate title I may deplore in passing)
breathes in every line the feeling of moor and loch, and
is the finest of his longer stories; and Thrawn Janet, a
masterpiece in thirteen pages (lately republished in the
volume of 'The Merry Men'), is, among the shorter ones,
the strongest in execution. The latter consists of a
gruesome anecdote of the supernatural, related in the
Scotch dialect; and the genuineness which this medium - at
the sight of which, in general, the face of the reader
grows long - wears in Mr. Stevenson's hands is a proof of
how living the question of form always is to him, and what
a variety of answers he has for it. It never would have
occurred to us that the style of 'Travels with a Donkey,'
or 'Virginibus Puerisque,' and the idiom of the parish of
Balweary could be a conception of the same mind. If it is
a good fortune for a genius to have had such a country as
Scotland for its primary stuff, this is doubly the case
when there has been a certain process of detachment, of
extreme secularization. Mr. Stevenson has been emanci-
pated - he is, as we may say, a Scotchman of the world.
None other, I think, could have drawn with such a mixture
of sympathetic and ironical observation the character of
the canny young Lowlander David Balfour, a good boy but
an exasperating. 'Treasure Island,' 'The New Arabian
Nights,' 'Prince Otto,' 'Doctor Jekyll and Mr. Hyde,' are
not very directly founded on observation; but that quality
comes in with extreme fineness as soon as the subject is
Scotch.

I have been wondering whether there is something more
than this that our author's pages would tell us about him,
or whether that particular something is in the mind of an
admirer, because he happens to have had other lights upon
it. It has been possible for so acute a critic as Mr,
William Archer to read pure high spirits and the gospel
of the young man rejoicing in his strength and his matutinal cold bath between the lines of Mr. Stevenson's prose.
And it is a fact that the note of a morbid sensibility is
so absent from his pages, they contain so little reference
to infirmity and suffering, that we feel a trick has
really been played upon us on discovering by accident the
actual state of the case with the writer who has indulged
in the most enthusiastic allusion to the joy of existence. We must permit ourselves another mention of his
personal situation, for it adds immensely to the interest
of volumes through which there draws so strong a current
of life to know that they are not only the work of an
invalid, but have largely been written in bed, in dreary
'health resorts,' in the intervals of sharp attacks.
There is almost nothing in them to lead us to guess this;
the direct evidence, indeed, is almost all contained in
the limited compass of 'The Silverado Squatters.' In
such a case, however, it is the indirect that is the most
eloquent, and I know not where to look for that, unless
in the paper called Ordered South and its companion Aes
Triplex, in 'Virginibus Puerisque.' It is impossible to
read Ordered South attentively without feeling that it is
personal; the reflections it contains are from experience,
not from fancy....
   The second of the short essays I have mentioned has a
taste of mortality only because the purpose of it is to
insist that the only sane behavior is to leave death and
the accidents that lead to it out of our calculations.
Life 'is a honeymoon with us all through, and none of the
longest. Small blame to us if we give our whole hearts
to this glowing bride of ours'; the person who does so
'makes a very different acquaintance with the world,
keeps all his pulses going true and fast, and gathers
impetus as he runs, until, if he be running towards anything better than wildfire, he may shoot up and become a
constellation in the end.' Nothing can be more deplorable
than to 'forgo all the issues of living in a parlor with a
regulated temperature.' Mr. Stevenson adds that as for
those whom the gods love dying young, a man dies too
young at whatever age he parts with life. The testimony
of Aes Triplex to the author's own disabilities is, after
all, very indirect; it consists mainly in the general protest not so much against the fact of extinction as against

the theory of it. The reader only asks himself why the
hero of 'Travels with a Donkey,' the historian of Alan
Breck, should think of these things. His appreciation of
the active side of life has such a note of its own that we
are surprised to find that it proceeds in a considerable
measure from an intimate acquaintance with the passive.
It seems too anomalous that the writer who has most
cherished the idea of a certain free exposure should also
be the one who has been reduced most to looking for it
within, and that the figures of adventurers who, at least
in our literature of to-day, are the most vivid, should be
the most vicarious. The truth is, of course, that, as the
'Travels with a Donkey' and 'An Inland Voyage' abundantly
show, the author has a fund of reminiscences. He did not
spend his younger years 'in a parlor with a regulated
temperature.' A reader who happens to be aware of how
much it has been his later fate to do so may be excused
for finding an added source of interest - something,
indeed, deeply and constantly touching - in this association of peculiarly restrictive conditions with the vision
of high spirits and romantic accidents of a kind of honor-
ably picturesque career. Mr. Stevenson is, however, distinctly, in spite of his occasional practice of the gruesome, a frank optimist, an observer who not only loves
life, but does not shrink from the responsibility of
recommending it. There is a systematic brightness in him
which testifies to this and which is, after all, but one
of the innumerable ingenuities of patience. What is
remarkable in his case is that his productions should
constitute an exquisite expression, a sort of whimsical
gospel, of enjoyment. The only difference between 'An
Inland Voyage,' or 'Travels with a Donkey' and 'The New
Arabian Nights,' or 'Treasure Island,' or 'Kidnapped,' is,
that in the later books the enjoyment is reflective, -
though it stimulates spontaneity with singular art, -
whereas in the first two it is natural and, as it were,
historical.
    These little histories - the first volumes, if I mis-
take not, that introduced Mr. Stevenson to lovers of good
writing - abound in charming illustrations of his disposition to look at the world as a not exactly refined, but
glorified, pacified Bohemia. They narrate the quest of
personal adventure - on one occasion in a canoe on the
Sambre and the Oise, and on another at a donkey's tail
over the hills and valleys of the Cévennes. I well remember that when I read them, in their novelty, upward of ten
years ago, I seemed to see the author, unknown as yet to
fame, jump before my eyes into a style. His steps in
literature presumably had not been many; yet he had

mastered his form – it had in these cases, perhaps, more
substance than his matter – and a singular air of literary
experience. It partly, though not completely, explains
the phenomenon, that he had already been able to write the
exquisite little story of Will of the Mill, published previously to 'An Inland Voyage,' and now republished in the
volume of 'The Merry Men'; for in Will of the Mill there
is something exceedingly rare, poetical, and unexpected,
with that most fascinating quality a work of imagination
can have, a dash of alternative mystery as to its meaning,
an air – the air of life itself – of half inviting, half
defying, you to interpret. This brief but finished composition stood in the same relation to the usual 'magazine story' that a glass of Johannisberg occupies to a
draught of table d'hôte *vin ordinaire*.

> One evening, he asked the miller where the river
> went.... 'It goes out into the lowlands, and waters
> the great corn country, and runs through a sight of
> fine cities (so they say) where kings live all alone
> in great palaces, with a sentry walking up and down
> before the door. And it goes under bridges with stone
> men upon them, looking down and smiling so curious at
> the water, and living folks leaning their elbows on
> the wall and looking over too. And then it goes on
> and on, and down through marshes and sands, until at
> last it falls into the sea, where the ships are that
> bring parrots and tobacco from the Indies.'

It is impossible not to open one's eyes at such a
paragraph as that, especially if one has taken a common
texture for granted. Will of the Mill spends his life in
the valley through which the river runs, and through
which, year after year, post-chaises and wagons, and
pedestrians, and once an army, 'horse and foot, cannon and
timbrel, drum and standard,' take their way, in spite of
the dreams he has once had of seeing the mysterious world,
and it is not till death comes that he goes on his travels. He ends by keeping an inn, where he converses with
many more initiated spirits, and though he is an amiable
man, he dies a bachelor, having broken off, with more plain-
ness than he would have used had he been less untraveled,
– of course he remains sadly provincial, – his engagement
to the parson's daughter. The story is in the happiest
key, and suggests all kinds of things, but what does it in
particular represent? The advantage of waiting, perhaps –
the valuable truth, that, one by one, we tide over our
impatiences. There are sagacious people who hold that if
one doesn't answer a letter it ends by answering itself.

So the sub-title of Mr. Stevenson's tale might be The
Beauty of Procrastination. If you don't indulge your
curiosities your slackness itself makes at last a kind of
rich element, and it comes to very much the same thing in
the end. When it came to the point, poor Will had not
even the curiosity to marry; and the author leaves us in
stimulating doubt as to whether he judges him too selfish
or only too philosophic.

I find myself speaking of Mr. Stevenson's last volume
(at the moment I write) before I have spoken, in any
detail, of its predecessors, which I must let pass as a
sign that I lack space for a full enumeration. I may mention two more of his productions as completing the list
of those that have a personal reference. 'The Silverado
Squatters' describes a picnicking episode, undertaken on
grounds of health, on a mountain-top in California; but
this free sketch, which contains a hundred humorous
touches, and in the figure of Irvine Lovelands one of Mr.
Stevenson's most veracious portraits, is perhaps less
vivid, as it is certainly less painful, than those other
pages in which, some years ago, he commemorated the
twelvemonth he spent in America - the history of a journey
from New York to San Francisco in an emigrant-train, performed as the sequel to a voyage across the Atlantic in
the same severe conditions. He has never made his points
better than in that half-humorous, half-tragical recital,
nor given a more striking instance of his talent for
reproducing the feeling of queer situations and contacts.
It is much to be regretted that this little masterpiece
has not been brought to light a second time, as also that
he has not given the world - as I believe he came very
near doing - his observations in the steerage of an Atlantic liner. If, as I say, our author has a taste for the
impressions of Bohemia, he has been very consistent and
has not shrunk from going far afield in search of them.
And as I have already been indiscreet, I may add that if
it has been his fate to be converted in fact from the
sardonic view of matrimony, this occurred under an influence which should have the particular sympathy of American
readers. He went to California for his wife; and Mrs.
Stevenson, as appears moreover by the title-page of the
work, has had a hand - evidently a light and practiced
one - in 'The Dynamiter,' the second series, characterized
by a rich extravagance, of 'The New Arabian Nights.' 'The
Silverado Squatters' is the history of a honeymoon - prosperous, it would seem, putting Irvine Lovelands aside,
save for the death of dog Chuchu 'in his teens, after a
life so shadowed and troubled, continually shaken with
alarms, and the tear of elegant sentiment permanently in
his eye.'

Mr. Stevenson has a theory of composition in regard to
the novel, on which he is to be congratulated, as any
positive and genuine conviction of this kind is vivifying
so long as it is not narrow. The breath of the novelist's
being is his liberty; and the incomparable virtue of the
form he uses is that it lends itself to views innumerable
and diverse, to every variety of illustration. There is
certainly no other mold of so large a capacity. The doctrine of M. Zola himself, so meager if literally taken,
is fruitful, inasmuch as in practice he romantically departs from it. Mr. Stevenson does not need to depart, his
individual taste being as much to pursue the romantic as
his principle is to defend it. Fortunately, in England
to-day, it is not much attacked. The triumphs that are to
be won in the portrayal of the strange, the improbable,
the heroic, especially as these things shine from afar in
the credulous eye of youth, are his strongest, most constant incentive. On one happy occasion, in relating the
history of 'Doctor Jekyll,' he has seen them as they present themselves to a maturer vision. 'Doctor Jekyll' is
not a 'boys' book,' nor yet is 'Prince Otto'; the latter,
however, is not, like the former, an experiment in mystification - it is, I think, more than anything else, an
experiment in style, conceived one summer's day, when the
author had given the reins to his high appreciation of Mr.
George Meredith. It is perhaps the most literary of his
works, but it is not the most natural. It is one of
those coquetries, as we may call them for want of a better
word, which may be observed in Mr. Stevenson's activity -
a kind of artful inconsequence. It is easy to believe
that if his strength permitted him to be a more abundant
writer he would still more frequently play this eminently
literary trick - that of dodging off in a new direction -
upon those who might have fancied they knew all about him.
I made the reflection, in speaking of Will of the Mill,
that there is a kind of anticipatory malice in the subject
of that fine story; as if the writer had intended to say
to his reader, 'You will never guess, from the unction
with which I describe the life of a man who never stirred
five miles from home, that I am destined to make my greatest hits in treating of the rovers of the deep.' Even
here, however, the author's characteristic irony would
have come in; for - the rare chances of life being what he
most keeps his eye on - the uncommon belongs as much to
the way the inquiring Will sticks to his door-sill as to
the incident, say, of John Silver and his men, when they
are dragging Jim Hawkins to his doom, hearing, in the
still woods of Treasure Island, the strange hoot of the
Maroon.

The novelist who leaves the extraordinary out of his account is liable to awkward confrontations, as we are compelled to reflect in this age of newspapers and of universal publicity. The next report of the next divorce case - to give an instance - shall offer us a picture of astounding combinations of circumstance and behavior, and the annals of any energetic race are rich in curious anecdote and startling example. That interesting compilation, 'Vicissitudes of Families,' is but a superficial record of strange accidents; the family - taken, of course, in the long piece - is, as a general thing, a catalogue of odd specimens and strong situations, and we must remember that the most singular products are those which are not exhibited. Mr. Stevenson leaves so wide a margin for the wonderful - it impinges with easy assurance upon the text - that he escapes the danger of being brought up by cases he has not allowed for. When he allows for Mr. Hyde he allows for everything; and one feels, moreover, that even if he did not wave so gallantly the flag of the imaginary and contend that the improbable is what has most character, he would still insist that we ought to make believe. He would say we ought to make believe that the extraordinary is the best part of life, even if it were not, and to do so because the finest feelings - suspense, daring, decision, passion, curiosity, gallantry, eloquence, friendship - are involved in it, and it is of infinite importance that the tradition of these precious things should not perish. He would prefer, in a word, any day in the week, Alexandre Dumas to Honoré de Balzac; and it is, indeed, my impression that he prefers the author of 'The Three Musketeers' to any novelist except Mr. George Meredith. I should go so far as to suspect that his ideal of the delightful work of fiction would be the adventures of Monte Cristo related by the author of 'Richard Feverel.' There is some magnanimity in his esteem for Alexandre Dumas, inasmuch as in 'Kidnapped' he has put into a fable worthy of that inventor a fineness of grain with which Dumas never had anything to do. He makes us say, Let the tradition live, by all means, since it was delightful; but at the same time he is the cause of our perceiving afresh that a tradition is kept alive only by something being added to it. In this particular case - in 'Doctor Jekyll' and 'Kidnapped' - Mr. Stevenson has added psychology.

'The New Arabian Nights' offers us, as the title indicates, the wonderful in the frankest, most delectable form. Partly extravagant, and partly very specious, they are the result of a very happy idea, that of placing a series of adventures which are pure adventures in the

setting of contemporary English life, and relating them in
the placidly ingenious tone of Scheherezade. This device
is carried to perfection in 'The Dynamiter,' where the
manner takes on more of a kind of high-flown serenity in
proportion as the incidents are more 'steep.' In this
line The Suicide Club is Mr. Stevenson's greatest success;
and the first two pages of it, not to mention others, live
in the memory. For reasons which I am conscious of not
being able to represent as sufficient, I find something
ineffaceably impressive - something really haunting - in
the incident of Prince Florizel and Colonel Geraldine, who,
one evening in March, are 'driven by a sharp fall of sleet
into an Oyster Bar in the immediate neighborhood of Leicester Square,' and there have occasion to observe the
entrance of a young man followed by a couple of commis-
sionaires, each of whom carries a large dish of cream-
tarts under a cover - a young man who 'pressed these con-
fections on every one's acceptance with exaggerated courtesy.' There is no effort at a picture here, but the
imagination makes one of the lighted interior, the London
sleet outside, the company that we guess, given the local-
ity, and the strange politeness of the young man, leading
on to circumstances stranger still. This is what may be
called putting one in the mood for a story. But Mr. Stevenson's most brilliant stroke of that kind is the opening
episode of 'Treasure Island' - the arrival of the brown
old seaman, with the saber-cut, at the 'Admiral Benbow,'
and the advent, not long after, of the blind sailor, with
a green shade over his eyes, who comes tapping down the
road, in quest of him, with his stick. 'Treasure Island'
is a 'boy's book,' in the sense that it embodies a boy's
vision of the extraordinary; but it is unique in this, and
calculated to fascinate the weary mind of experience, that
what we see in it is not only the ideal fable, but, as
part and parcel of that, as it were, the young reader
himself and his state of mind: we seem to read it over
his shoulder, with an arm around his neck. It is all as
perfect as a well-played boy's game, and nothing can
exceed the spirit and skill, the humor and the open-air
feeling, with which the whole thing is kept at the critical pitch. It is not only a record of queer chances, but
a study of young feelings; there is a moral side in it,
and the figures are not puppets with vague faces. If Jim
Hawkins illustrates successful daring, he does so with a
delightful, rosy good-boyishness, and a conscious, modest
liability to error. His luck is tremendous, but it does
n't make him proud; and his manner is refreshingly provincial and human. So is that, even more, of the admirable John Silver, one of the most picturesque, and,

indeed, in every way, most genially presented, villains
in the whole literature of romance. He has a singularly
distinct and expressive countenance, which, of course,
turns out to be a grimacing mask. Never was a mask more
knowingly, vividly painted. 'Treasure Island' will surely
become - it must already have become, and will remain -- in
its way a classic; thanks to this indescribable mixture of
the prodigious and the human, of surprising coincidences
and familiar feelings. The language in which Mr. Stevenson has chosen to tell his story is an admirable vehicle
for these feelings; with its humorous braveries and
quaintnesses, its echoes of old ballads and yarns, it
touches all kinds of sympathetic chords.
      Is 'Dr. Jekyll and Mr. Hyde' a work of high philosophic
intention, or simply the most ingenious and irresponsible
of fictions? It has the stamp of a really imaginative
production, that we may take it in different ways, but I
suppose it would be called the most serious of the
author's tales. It deals with the relation of the baser
parts of man to his nobler - of the capacity for evil that
exists in the most generous natures, and it expresses
these things in a fable which is a wonderfully happy invention. The subject is endlessly interesting, and rich
in all sorts of provocation, and Mr. Stevenson is to be
congratulated on having touched the core of it. I may do
him injustice, but it is, however, here, not the profundity of the idea which strikes me so much as the art of
the presentation - the extremely successful form. There
is a genuine feeling for the perpetual moral question, a
fresh sense of the difficulty of being good and the bru-
tishness of being bad, but what there is above all is a
singular ability in holding the interest. I confess that
that, to my sense, is the most edifying thing in the short
short, rapid, concentrated story, which is really a
masterpiece of concision. There is something almost
impertinent in the way, as I have noticed, in which Mr.
Stevenson achieves his best effects without the aid of
the ladies, and 'Dr. Jekyll' is a capital example of his
heartless independence. It is usually supposed that a
truly poignant impression cannot be made without them,
but in the drama of Mr. Hyde's fatal ascendency they
remain altogether in the wing. It is very obvious - I do
not say it cynically - that they must have played an important part in his development. The gruesome tone of the
tale is, no doubt, deepened by their absence; it is like
the late afternoon light of a foggy winter Sunday, when
even inanimate objects have a kind of wicked look. I
remember few situations in the pages of mystifying fiction
more to the purpose than the episode of Mr. Utterson's

going to Dr. Jekyll's to confer with the butler, when
the doctor is locked up in his laboratory and the old
servant, whose sagacity has hitherto encountered successfully the problems of the sideboard and the pantry, confesses that this time he is utterly baffled. The way the
two men, at the door of the laboratory, discuss the identity of the mysterious personage inside, who has revealed
himself in two or three inhuman glimpses to Poole, has
those touches of which irresistible shudders are made.
The butler's theory is that his master has been murdered,
and that the murderer is in the room, personating him with
a sort of clumsy diabolism. 'Well, when that masked thing
like a monkey jumped from among the chemicals and whipped
into the cabinet, it went down my spine like ice.' That
is the effect upon the reader of most of the story. I say
of most rather than all, because the ice rather melts in the
sequel, and I have some difficulty in accepting the business of the powders, which seems to me too explicit and
explanatory. The powders constitute the machinery of the
transformation, and it will probably have struck many
readers that this uncanny process would be more conceivable (so far as one may speak of the conceivable in such a
case), if the author had not made it so definite.
    I have left Mr. Stevenson's best book to the last, as
it is also the last he has given, at the present speaking,* to the public - the tales comprising 'The Merry Men'
having already appeared; but I find that, on the way, I
have anticipated some of the remarks that I had intended
to make about it. That which is most to the point is that
there are parts of it so fine as to suggest that the
author's talent has taken a fresh start, various as have
been the impulses in which it had already indulged, and
serious the impediments among which it is condemned to
exert itself. There would have been a kind of perverse
humility in his keeping up the fiction that a production
so literary as 'Kidnapped' is addressed to immature minds;
and though it was originally given to the world, I believe, in a 'boy's paper,' the story embraces every occasion that it meets to satisfy the higher criticism. It
has two weak spots, which need simply to be mentioned.
The cruel and miserly uncle, in the first chapters, is
rather in the tone of superseded tradition, and the tricks
he plays upon his ingenuous nephew are a little like those
of country conjurers; in these pages we feel that Mr. Stevenson is thinking too much of what a 'boy's paper' is
expected to contain. Then the history stops without
ending, as it were; but I think I may add that this accident speaks for itself. Mr. Stevenson has often to lay
down his pen for reasons that have nothing to do with the

failure of inspiration, and the last page of David Balfour's adventures is an honorable plea for indulgence.
The remaining five-sixths of the book deserve to stand by
'Henry Esmond,' as a fictive autobiography in archaic
form.   The author's sense of the English idiom of the last
century, and still more of the Scotch, have enabled him to
give a gallant companion to Thackeray's *tour de force*.
The life, the humor, the color of the central portions of
'Kidnapped' have a singular pictorial virtue; these passages read like a series of inspired foot-notes on some
historic page.   The charm of the most romantic episode in
the world - though perhaps it would be hard to say why it
is the most romantic, when it was intermingled with so
much stupidity - is over the whole business, and the forlorn hope of the Stuarts is revived for us without evoking
satiety.   There could be no better instance of the
author's talent for seeing the actual in the marvelous,
and reducing the extravagant to plausible detail, than the
description of Alan Breck's defense in the cabin of the
ship, and the really magnificent chapters of The Flight
in the Heather.   Mr. Stevenson has, in a high degree (and
doubtless for good reasons of his own), what may be called
the imagination of physical states, and this has enabled
him to arrive at a wonderfully exact notation of the
miseries of his panting Lowland hero, dragged for days and
nights over hill and dale, through bog and thicket, without meat or drink or rest, at the tail of an Homeric Highlander.   The great superiority of the book resides, to my
mind, however, in the fact that it puts two characters on
their feet in an admirably upright way.   I have paid my
tribute to Alan Breck, and I can only repeat that he is a
masterpiece.   It is interesting to observe that, though
the man is extravagant, the author's touch exaggerates
nothing; it is, throughout, of the most truthful, genial,
ironical kind, full of penetration, but with none of the
grossness of moralizing satire.   The figure is a genuine
study, and nothing can be more charming than the way Mr.
Stevenson both sees through it and admires it.   Shall I
say that he sees through David Balfour?   This would be,
perhaps, to underestimate the density of that medium.
Beautiful, at any rate, is the expression which this unfortunate though circumspect youth gives to those qualities which combine to excite our respect and our objurgations in the Scottish character.   Such a scene as the
episode of the quarrel of the two men on the mountain-side
is a real stroke of genius, and has the very logic and
rhythm of life - a quarrel which we feel to be inevitable,
though it is about nothing, or almost nothing, and which
springs from exasperated nerves and the simple shock of

temperaments. The author's vision of it has a profundity
which goes deeper, I think, than 'Dr. Jekyll.' I know
of few better examples of the way genius has ever a surprise in its pocket - keeps an ace, as it were, up its
sleeve. And in this case it endears itself to us by making
us reflect that such a passage as the one I speak of is in
fact a signal proof of what the novel can do at its best
and what nothing else can do so well. In the presence of
this sort of success we perceive its immense value. It is
capable of a rare transparency - it can illustrate human
affairs in cases so delicate and complicated that any other
vehicle would be clumsy. To those who love the art that
Mr. Stevenson practices he will appear, in pointing this
incidental moral, not only to have won a particular triumph, but to have given a delightful pledge.

Notes

* Since the above was written, 'Underwoods,' as well-as
  'Memories and Portraits,' has been published.
1 A Penny Plain and Twopence Coloured, 'Magazine of Art',
  April 1884; the essay was to be reprinted in 'Memories
  and Portraits'.

103. STEVENSON ON THE ARTIST AND HIS PUBLIC FROM A LETTER
TO A YOUNG GENTLEMAN WHO PROPOSES TO EMBRACE THE CAREER OF
ART, 'SCRIBNER'S MAGAZINE'

September 1888, x, 623-31

Letter to a Young Gentleman was reprinted in 'Across the
Plains' (1892). The notions in this extract are in part
an elaboration of those expressed in letters to Colvin and
Gosse in March 1884 (No. 54 f and g) and in a letter to
Gosse dated January 1886 (No. 63). The extract begins
several pages into the essay. Stevenson has discussed a
true as against a false calling to a career of art, the
test of which lies chiefly in the pleasure derived from
the occupation itself: 'No other business offers a man his
daily bread upon such joyful terms.' See Introduction,
p. 21.

... Nor will the practice of art afford you pleasure only;
it affords besides an admirable training. For the artist
works entirely upon honour. The public knows little or
nothing of those merits in the quest of which you are condemned to spend the bulk of your endeavours. Merits of
design, the merit of first-hand energy, the merit of a
certain cheap accomplishment which a man of the artistic
temper easily acquires - these they can recognise, and
these they value. But to those more exquisite refinements
of proficiency and finish, which the artist so ardently
desires and so keenly feels, for which (in the vigorous
words of Balzac) he must toil 'like a miner buried in a
landslip,' for which, day after day, he recasts and
revises and rejects - the gross mass of the public must be
ever blind. To those lost pains, suppose you attain the
highest pitch of merit, posterity may possibly do justice;
suppose, as is so probable, you fail by even a hair's
breadth of the highest, rest certain they shall never be
observed. Under the shadow of this cold thought, alone in
his studio, the artist must preserve from day to day his
constancy to the ideal. It is this which makes his life
noble; it is by this that the practice of his craft
strengthens and matures his character; it is for this that
even the serious countenance of the great emperor was
turned approvingly (if only for a moment) on the followers
of Apollo, and that sternly gentle voice bade the artist
cherish his art.

And here there fall two warnings to be made. First,
if you are to continue to be a law to yourself, you must
beware of the first signs of laziness. This idealism in
honesty can only be supported by perpetual effort; the
standard is easily lowered, the artist who says '*It will
do*,' is on the downward path; three or four pot-boilers
are enough at times (above all at wrong times) to falsify
a talent, and by the practice of journalism a man runs
the risk of becoming wedded to cheap finish. This is the
danger on the one side; there is not less upon the other.
The consciousness of how much the artist is (and must be)
a law to himself, debauches the small heads. Perceiving
recondite merits very hard to attain, making or swallowing
artistic formulae, or perhaps falling in love with some
particular proficiency of his own, many artists forget the
end of all art: to please. It is doubtless tempting to
exclaim against the ignorant bourgeois; yet it should not
be forgotten, it is he who is to pay us, and that (surely
on the face of it) for services that he shall desire to
have performed. Here also, if properly considered, there
is a question of transcendental honesty. To give the
public what they do not want, and yet expect to be

supported: we have there a strange pretension, and yet not uncommon, above all with painters. The first duty in this world is for a man to pay his way; when that is quite accomplished, he may plunge into what eccentricity he likes; but emphatically not till then. Till then, he must pay assiduous court to the bourgeois who carries the purse. And if in the course of these capitulations he shall falsify his talent, it can never have been a strong one, and he will have preserved a better thing than talent - character. Or if he be of a mind so independent that he cannot stoop to this necessity, one course is yet open: he can desist from art, and follow some more manly way of life.

I speak of a more manly way of life, it is a point on which I must be frank. To live by a pleasure is not a high calling; it involves patronage, however veiled; it numbers the artist, however ambitious, along with dancing-girls and billiard-markers. The French have a romantic evasion for one employment, and call its practitioners the Daughters of Joy. The artist is of the same family, he is of the Sons of Joy, chose his trade to please himself, gains his livelihood by pleasing others, and has parted with something of the sterner dignity of man. Journals but a little while ago declaimed against the Tennyson peerage; and this Son of Joy was blamed for condescension when he followed the example of Lord Lawrence and Lord Cairns and Lord Clyde. The poet was more happily inspired; with a better modesty he accepted the honour; and anonymous journalists have not yet (if I am to believe them) recovered the vicarious disgrace to their profession. When it comes to their turn, these gentlemen can do themselves more justice; and I shall be glad to think of it; for to my barbarian eyesight, even Lord Tennyson looks somewhat out of place in that assembly. There should be no honours for the artist; he has already, in the practice of his art, more than his share of the rewards of life; the honours are pre-empted for other trades, less agreeable and perhaps more useful.

But the devil in these trades of pleasing is to fail to please. In ordinary occupations, a man offers to do a certain thing or to produce a certain article with a merely conventional accomplishment, a design in which (we may almost say) it is difficult to fail. But the artist steps forth out of the crowd and proposes to delight: an impudent design, in which it is impossible to fail without odious circumstances. The poor Daughter of Joy, carrying her smiles and finery quite unregarded through the crowd, makes a figure which it is impossible to recall without a wounding pity. She is the type of the unsuccessful

artist. The actor, the dancer, and the singer must appear
like her in person, and drain publicly the cup of failure.
But though the rest of us escape this crowning bitterness
of the pillory, we all court in essence the same humilia-
tion. We all profess to be able to delight. And how few
of us are! We all pledge ourselves to be able to continue
to delight. And the day will come to each, and even to
the most admired, when the ardour shall have declined and
the cunning shall be lost, and he shall sit by his deserted booth ashamed. Then shall he see himself condemned
to do work for which he blushes to take payment. Then (as
if his lot were not already cruel) he must lie exposed to
the gibes of the wreckers of the press, who earn a little
bitter bread by the condemnation of trash which they have
not read, and the praise of excellence which they cannot
understand.

And observe that this seems almost the necessary end at
least of writers. 'Les Blancs et les Bleus' (for
instance) is of an order of merit very different from 'Le
Vicomte de Bragelonne'; and if any gentleman can bear to
spy upon the nakedness of 'Castle Dangerous,' his name I
think is Ham: let it be enough for the rest of us to read
of it (not without tears) in the pages of Lockhart. Thus
in old age, when occupation and comfort are most needful,
the writer must lay aside at once his pastime and his
breadwinner. The painter indeed, if he succeed at all in
engaging the attention of the public, gains great sums and
can stand to his easel until a great age without dis-
honourable failure. The writer has the double misfortune
to be ill-paid while he can work, and to be incapable of
working when he is old. It is thus a way of life which
conducts directly to a false position.

For the writer (in spite of notorious examples to the
contrary) must look to be ill-paid. Tennyson and Montépin
make handsome livelihoods; but we cannot all hope to be
Tennyson, and we do not all perhaps desire to be Montépin.
If you adopt an art to be your trade, weed your mind at
the outset of all desire of money. What you may decently
expect, if you have some talent and much industry, is such
an income as a clerk will earn with a tenth or perhaps a
twentieth of your nervous output. Nor have you the right
to look for more; in the wages of the life, not in the wages
of the trade, lies your reward; the work is here the
wages. It will be seen I have little sympathy with the
common lamentations of the artist class. Perhaps they do
not remember the hire of the field labourer; or do they
think no parallel will lie? Perhaps they have never
observed what is the retiring allowance of a field
officer; or do they suppose their contributions to the

arts of pleasing more important than the services of a
colonel? Perhaps they forget on how little Millet was
content to live; or do they think, because they have less
genius, they stand excused from the display of equal virtues? But upon one point there should be no dubiety: if a
man be not frugal, he has no business in the arts. If he
be not frugal, he steers directly for that last tragic
scene of *le vieux saltimbanque*; if he be not frugal, he
will find it hard to continue to be honest. Some day,
when the butcher is knocking at the door, he may be tempted, he may be obliged, to turn out and sell a slovenly
piece of work. If the obligation shall have arisen
through no wantonness of his own, he is even to be commen-
ded; for words cannot describe how far more necessary it
is that a man should support his family, than that he
should attain to - or preserve - distinction in the arts.
But if the pressure comes through his own fault, he has
stolen, and stolen under trust, and stolen (which is the
worst of all) in such a way that no law can reach him.

And now you may perhaps ask me, if the débutant artist
is to have no thought of money, and if (as is implied) he
is to expect no honours from the State, he may not at
least look forward to the delights of popularity? Praise,
you will tell me, is a savoury dish. And in so far as you
may mean the countenance of other artists, you would put
your finger on one of the most essential and enduring
pleasures of the career of art. But in so far as you
should have an eye to the commendations of the public or
the notice of the newspapers, be sure you would but be
cherishing a dream. It is true that in certain esoteric
journals the author (for instance) is duly criticised, and
that he is often praised a great deal more than he
deserves, sometimes for qualities which he prided himself
on eschewing, and sometimes by ladies and gentlemen who
have denied themselves the privilege of reading his work.
But if a man be sensitive to this wild praise, we must
suppose him equally alive to that which often accompanies
and always follows it - wild ridicule. A man may have
done well for years, and then he may fail; he will hear of
his failure. Or he may have done well for years, and still
do well, but the critics may have tired of praising him,
or there may have sprung up some new idol of the instant,
some 'dust a little gilt,' to whom they now prefer to
offer sacrifice. Here is the obverse and the reverse of
that empty and ugly thing called popularity. Will any man
suppose it worth the gaining?

'The Black Arrow'

June 1888

104. STEVENSON ON 'THE BLACK ARROW', FROM LETTERS TO
HENLEY AND COLVIN

1883

Stevenson regarded 'The Black Arrow' as 'tushery', the
term used by himself and Henley to refer to romances of
the 'Ivanhoe' variety written for the market. In a letter
to Henley dated shortly after the one quoted below,
Stevenson writes an amusing poem on 'tushing': 'A lytle
Jape of Tusherie. By A. Tusher' (LS, ii, 128-9). The
office of 'Young Folks', the boys' magazine for which 'The
Black Arrow' was written, was located in Red Lion Square.

(a) From a letter to Henley dated by Colvin May 1883

... as my good Red Lion Counter begged me for another
Butcher's Boy - I turned me to - what thinkest 'ou? to
Tushery, by the mass! Ay, friend, a whole tale of
tushery. And every tusher tushes me so free, that may I
be tushed if the whole thing is worth a tush. 'The Black
Arrow: A Tale of Tunstall Forest' is his name: tush! a
poor thing! (LS, ii, 127)

(b) From a letter to Colvin dated by him October 1883

Your remarks on the 'Black Arrow' are to the point. I am
pleased you like Crookback; he is a fellow whose hellish
energy has always fixed my attention. I wish Shakespeare

316

had written the play after he had learned some of the
rudiments of literature and art rather than before. Some
day, I will re-tickle the Sable Missile, and shoot it,
moyennant finances, once more into the air; I can lighten
it of much, and devote some more attention to Dick o'
Gloucester. It's great sport to write tushery. (LS, ii,
152)

105. STEVENSON, DEDICATION OF 'THE BLACK ARROW' TO THE
'CRITIC ON THE HEARTH'

8 April 1888

The 'Critic on the Hearth' is, of course, Fanny Stevenson.

No one but myself knows what I have suffered, nor what my
books have gained, by your unsleeping watchfulness and
admirable pertinacity. And now here is a volume that goes
into the world and lacks your *imprimatur*: a strange thing
in our joint lives; and the reason of it stranger still!
I have watched with interest, with pain, and at length
with amusement, your unavailing attempts to peruse 'The
Black Arrow'; and I think I should lack humour indeed, if
I let the occasion slip and did not place your name in the
fly-leaf of the only book of mine that you have never
read - and never will read.
    That others may display more constancy is still my
hope. The tale was written years ago for a particular
audience and (I may say) in rivalry with a particular
author; I think I should do well to name him - Mr. Alfred
R. Phillips. (1) It was not without its reward at the
time. I could not, indeed, displace Mr. Phillips from his
well-won priority; but in the eyes of readers who thought
less than nothing of 'Treasure Island', 'The Black Arrow'
was supposed to mark a clear advance. Those who read
volumes and those who read story papers belong to different worlds. The verdict on 'Treasure Island' was reversed
in the other court: I wonder, will it be the same with its
successor?

Note

1 Phillips's work was highly popular with the readers of
   'Young Folks'. 'The Black Arrow' appeared there serially between 30 June and 20 October 1883.

106. R. H. HUTTON, UNSIGNED REVIEW, 'SPECTATOR'

11 August 1888, lxi, 1099-100

On Hutton see headnote to No. 48.

The 'critic on the hearth' to whom Mr. Stevenson dedicates
this very charming romance is certainly very hard to
please. We should ourselves prefer 'The Black Arrow' to
any story which Mr. Stevenson has published except 'Treasure Island.' It has not, perhaps, quite the overflowing
life and imaginative resource in it which gave the magic
to that buoyant book. The 'blind beggar' of 'Treasure
Island' was, perhaps, one of the most happy strokes of
fancy in English fiction, and the piratical cook, too, was
a villain of villains whose like we never hope to see
again. But we prefer 'The Black Arrow' both to 'Kidnapped' and to Mr. Stevenson's stories concerning the
dynamiters, - indeed, to anything else that he has
written. It is fresh, eager, and skilful. It contains
two charming sketches of women, better than any which Mr.
Stevenson has yet produced. And it has also a brilliant
portrait of the Richard Crookback of tradition, whether it
be true to the genuine Richard who was killed on Bosworth
field or not, a portrait reminding us of Sir Walter
Scott's vivid studies in the characters of Kings. And
that bright and rapid flow of the narrative so essential
to the reader's fascination, so impossible to imitate, so
difficult even to genius except of one rather rare kind,
is hardly to be surpassed in English literature. Nor is
there any obtrusion of the historical element. There is
enough, and only enough, of it to give a certain richness
and impressiveness to the background of the tale, but not
enough to encumber the story, or to inlay it with that
antiquarian study which the reader who is no antiquarian
resents. It is as easy to read as a story of to-day, and

that is more than one can say of some of the best historical romances in existence.

The 'Black Arrow' is the name given to an association
of yoemen who combine against the exactions and tyranny
of their feudal lords. It is an association not unlike
that of which Sir Walter Scott has given us so brilliant
a sketch in 'Ivanhoe,' in the picture of Locksley and his
followers, though Mr. Stevenson's story is supposed, of
course, to be a couple of centuries or more later. The
opening scene of the story introduces us to the flight of
one of these Black Arrows, and its latest scene concludes
with the flight of another of them, and during the course
of the narrative the Black Arrows fly, of course, whenever and wherever they are most wanted. But the art of
making outlaws impressive, and of so interweaving their
feats with the feats of feudal oppressors as to excite
sympathy for the outlaw without entirely destroying the
charm of the feudal order to which he was opposed, seems
to have been reserved for Scotchmen, and Mr. Stevenson
wields it with all the ease and freedom, though not, of
course, with the same massive effect of power, of Sir
Walter Scott himself. If 'Ivanhoe' be the most brilliant
tale for boys which genius ever penned, 'The Black Arrow'
certainly deserves to be mentioned next to it as one
which, without even suggesting an imitator, displays a
master-hand in the same field. What is somewhat new to
us in Mr. Stevenson's books, is his skill in the management of the love-story. Nothing can be more charming
than the boy-and-girl love-making of Richard Shelton and
Joanna Sedley, who meet first when the girl is disguised
as a boy, though she so acts her part as to raise the
feeling of tenderness in the real boy's heart without
betraying her sex or eliciting more than curiously perplexed emotions which prepare the way for love, though
they do not kindle it. There is real subtlety in this
part of the tale, as well as the most perfect simplicity
and healthiness of drawing. The adventures of the two
boys together in Tunstall Forest during the escape of the
heroine from her grasping and masterful guardian, is an
exquisite bit of literary art; and then, when the riddle
is explained, and Dick Shelton recognises his old comrade
in Joanna Sedley, the frank tenderness of the love between them is as freshly and poetically rendered as the
previously half-understood attraction of Shelton to the
disguised girl was subtly painted. Nor could the episode
of the alarm they receive from the supposed leper be
better imagined or more admirably told. The two companions, after losing their way in the forest, have passed
the night in a sandy pit, when they are awakened by the

sound of a bell: -

[Quotation from ch. vii: 'They awoke in the grey of the morning ...' to 'Next moment he had disappeared into a little thicket'.]

We must not extract the conclusion of the episode, but this much will be sufficient to give our readers an impression of the eager movement of Mr. Stevenson's delightful story, which runs on without even a momentary break in the interest from beginning to end.

We hardly know whether the book from which we have just quoted, and which gives the adventures of the two lads, as they appear at least to Shelton, or the book which tells the perils of Shelton in the Moat House, or the final fifth book, which gives us Mr. Stevenson's portrait of Richard, Duke of Gloucester, is the most brilliant; but we certainly incline to prefer those three to the third and fourth books, fascinating as these are. There is more of freshness in the first, more of excitement in the second, and more of art in the last; while the third and fourth have perhaps a little too much in them of the mere complexity of perilous adventure without adequate individual effects. On the whole, the three sketches which charm us most, and to which we return at the end of the story to renew the pleasure which they have given, are the sketches of Joanna Sedley, in disguise and in her own person; of Alicia Risingham, Joanna's tenderly impertinent and irrepressible friend; and of the traditionary Duke of Gloucester, who, though painted in the usual colours, is still so painted as to live more vividly than ever before the mind. Mr. Stevenson has written a new work of genius in which the historical background adds greatly to the effect of his tale, instead of in any way detracting from it.

107. WILLIAM ARCHER, UNSIGNED REVIEW, 'PALL MALL GAZETTE'

13 August 1888, xlviii, 3

See headnote to No. 100.

'Sirs, this knave arrow likes me not,' says Sir Oliver
Oates in Mr. Stevenson's resurrected story, and we fear
his readers of the maturer sort will be apt to echo the
phrase. The judgment of his boy admirers we cannot fore-
cast; but those who have followed with understanding the
adventures of Jim Hawkins and David Balfour will scarcely
place Dick Shelton on an equal footing in their affections. Mr. Stevenson tells us that the readers of the
story-paper for which it was written considered 'The Outlaws of Tunstall Forest' (as it was then called) 'a clear
advance' on 'Treasure Island.' Well, it is something to
be able to write down to your audience. It shows a species of literary suppleness in which some authors are
deficient. Yet one cannot but regret that Mr. Stevenson
should have thought it worth while to break a lance (note
the mediaeval metaphor) with the G. P. R. Jameses of Red
Lion-court. (1) Life is too short for such aimless
emprises. Mr. Stevenson has assured us that among the
penny-weekly publishers he has acquired the reputation of
'a reliable author.' Such good report is not to be despised, but it may be dearly bought if the public which is
more peculiarly his own should come to think of Mr. Stevenson as unreliable. He has hitherto succeeded in
breathing fresh life into every literary form he has
touched - the pirate story, the shilling shocker, and so
forth. There seems to be no reason why even the mediaeval
romance should not have become a new thing in his hands.
Without offending his penny patrons, he might surely have
tuned his imagination to an epic strain. Far from making
any such attempt, however, he seems merely to have
'whistled as he went for want of thought;' and it is this
incuria (as Mr. Saintsbury would say) that we hold unworthy of him.
  Let it not be understood that the peculiar qualities of
Mr. Stevenson's talent are absent from 'The Black Arrow.'
The story is spirited, vivid, and, in spite of its triviality, by no means unreadable. Here and there we come
across a touch in Mr. Stevenson's best manner. The hooded
leper with his bell haunts the memory almost as weirdly as
blind Pew with his tapping staff in 'Treasure Island.' Lawless, the Friar Tuck of the outlaws, is a character in his
way; infinitely superior to Long John Silver, indeed, yet
something more than a marionette. Moreover, there are little
bits of fresh and crisp description every here and there.
In the opening chapters we breathe the very air of the
woodland glades through which Dick and 'Matcham' pursue
their adventurous way, and the snow scenes of the wintry
close are no less happily touched. In short, we never
forget for many minutes together that it is Mr. Stevenson
we are listening to. On every page there is something to

remind us that this is not the ordinary 'reliable author'
of the penny-fiction factory. Yet the imitation is peri-
lously perfect. Except in a few isolated cases, Mr.
Stevenson has given his invention a holiday. The startling vicissitudes endured by his hero are managed in the
most patently mechanical fashion. As in the terrific
sword-bouts of the stage the combatants go through a pre-
arranged figure, each in turn gaining the upper hand with
rhythmic punctuality, so in 'The Black Arrow' the hero's
ups and downs recur at intervals of five pages or so
until the oscillation between triumph and despair becomes
positively ludicrous. When the worst comes to the worst
there is always an invisible archer somewhere around to
send a black arrow through the heart of the foeman. It is
true that the hair's-breadth 'scape forms the very essence
of all stories of adventure, and the god from the machine
is the presiding genius of the to-be-continued-in-our-next
school of fiction. But there are machines and machines,
and those which Mr. Stevenson uses in 'The Black Arrow'
are somewhat rusty. The lack of ingenuity in detail is
not redeemed by any structural merit in the general
design. The story is a mere string of incidents which
might stop at any moment or go on to all eternity. There
is an annoying break in the middle of it, at the end of
the second book. It cannot even be said that each individual episode is very carefully thought out. The adventure of the *Good Hope*, for instance, is told with great
spirit but with curiously imperfect vision. We do not
believe in it for a moment. The voyagers set off,
apparently without the smallest thought as to how they are
to get ashore, when lo! in the nick of time, a 'stone
pier,' of which we have hitherto heard nothing, looms up
through the darkness in the most conveniently impossible
spot. On such promiscuous piers as this our faith in the
story-teller is apt to go to wreck. It should be noted,
too, that in the matter of bloodshed, Mr. Stevenson enters
into animated competition with Mr. Rider Haggard. From
the first chapter to the last we wade in gore; and carnage
is somehow less shocking in Impossible Africa than in
Improbable England. Mr. Stevenson has recently declared
that he prefers open warfare to pestilence and profit-
grinding as a means of keeping down the population.
'Periods of bloodshed and periods of tedium appear to
follow each other,' he is represented to have said. 'Some
people have a natural taste for the tedium, which I seem
to lack.' But bloodshed and tedium are not mutually exclusive.
    A writer cannot complain of being judged by the stan-
dards he has himself established, and Mr. Stevenson would

probably be the last to deny that in 'The Black Arrow' he
has fallen, or at least descended, below his proper level.
He may allege, what is no doubt true, that he deliberately turned aside from his course to execute a *tour de
force*. But what is the use of a *tour de force* which
means, and must necessarily mean, a *tour de faiblesse*?

Note

1 George Payne Rainsford James (1799-1860) wrote historical novels and other popular historical works; he
   was parodied ('Barbazure') by Thackeray in 'Novels by
   Eminent Hands'. The magazine 'Young Folks' had its
   headquarters in Red Lion Square.

108. GAVIN OGILVY (J. M. BARRIE) ON STEVENSON, 'BRITISH
WEEKLY'

2 November 1888, v, 9

(Sir) James Matthew Barrie (1860-1937). In the mid-1880s
Barrie was beginning his career with contributions to a
number of periodicals including the 'British Weekly' where
his work appeared under the signature Gavin Ogilvy (Ogilvy
being his mother's maiden name). This article is one of
a series of brief portraits and assessments of Edinburgh
worthies that had first appeared in the 'British Weekly',
were brought together as a Christmas extra for that magazine entitled An Edinburgh Eleven, and were subsequently
published in book form the following year (1889). Stevenson was of course aware of this essay; see LS, iv, 142.

Some men of letters, not necessarily the greatest, have an
indescribable charm to which we give our hearts.
Thackeray is the young man's first love. Of living
authors none perhaps bewitches the reader more than Mr.
Stevenson, who plays upon words as if they were a musical
instrument. To follow the music is less difficult than
to place the musician. A friend of mine, who, like Mr.
Grant Allen, reviews 365 books a year and 366 in leap
years, recently arranged the novelists of to-day in order

of merit. Meredith, of course, he wrote first, and then
there was a fall to Hardy. 'Haggard,' he explained, 'I
dropped from the Eiffel Tower; but what can I do with
Stevenson? I can't put him before "Lorna Doone."' So
Mr. Stevenson puzzles the critics, fascinating them until
they are willing to judge him by the *magnum opus* he is to
write by and by when the little books are finished. Over
'Treasure Island' I let my fire die in winter without
knowing that I was freezing. But the creator of Alan
Breck has now published nearly twenty volumes. It is so
much easier to finish the little works than to begin the
great one, for which we are all taking notes.

Mr. Stevenson is not to be labelled novelist. He
wanders the byways of literature without any fixed address.
Too much of a truant to be classified with the other boys,
he is only a writer of fiction in the sense that he was
once an Edinburgh University student because now and again
he looked in at his classes when he happened to be that
way. A literary man without a fixed occupation amazes Mr.
Henry James, a master in the school of fiction which
tells, in three volumes, how Hiram K. Wilding trod on the
skirt of Alice M. Sparkins without anything coming of it.
Mr. James analyses Mr. Stevenson [No. 102] with immense
cleverness, but without summing up. That 'Dr. Jekyll and
Mr. Hyde' should be by the author of 'Treasure Island,'
'Virginibus Puerisque' by the author of 'The New Arabian
Nights,' 'A Child's Garland [Garden] of Verses' by the
author of 'Prince Otto,' are to him the three degrees of
comparison of wonder, though for my own part I marvel more
that the author of 'Daisy Miller' should be Mr. Stevenson's
eulogist. One conceives Mr. James a boy in velveteens
looking fearfully at Stevenson playing at pirates.

There is nothing in Mr. Stevenson's sometimes writing
essays, sometimes romances, and anon poems to mark him
versatile beyond other authors; I dread his continuing to
do so, with so many books at his back, lest it means
weakness rather than strength. He experiments too long;
he is still a boy wondering what he is going to be. With
Cowley's candour he tells us that he wants to write something by which he may be for ever known. His attempts in
this direction have been in the nature of trying different
ways, and he always starts off whistling. Having gone so
far without losing himself, he turns back to try another
road. Does his heart fail him, despite his jaunty bearing, or is it because there is no hurry? Though all his
books are obviously brothers, no living writer has come so
near fame from so many different sides. Where is the man
among us who could write another 'Virginibus Puerisque,'
the most delightful volume for the hammock ever sung in

prose? The poems are as exquisite as they are artificial.
'Jekyll and Hyde' is the greatest triumph extant in
Christmas literature of the morbid kind. The donkey on
the Cevennes (how Mr. Stevenson belaboured him!) only
stands second to the 'Inland Voyage.' 'Kidnapped' is the
outstanding boy's book of its generation. 'The Black
Arrow' alone, to my thinking, is second-class. We shall
all be doleful if a marksman who can pepper his target
with inners does not reach the bull's-eye. But it is
quite time the great work was begun. The sun sinks while
the climber walks round his mountain, looking for the
best way up.

Hard necessity has kept some great writers from doing
their best work; but Mr. Stevenson is at last so firmly
established that if he continues to be versatile it will
only be from choice. He has attained a popularity such
as is, as a rule, only accorded to classic authors or to
charlatans. For this he has America to thank rather than
Britain, for the Americans buy his books, the only honour
a writer's admirers are slow to pay him. Mr. Stevenson's
reputation in the United States is creditable to that
country, which has given him a position here in which only
a few saw him when he left. Unfortunately, with popularity has come publicity. All day the reporters sit on his
garden wall.

No man has written in a finer spirit of the profession
of letters than Mr. Stevenson, but this gossip vulgarises
it. The adulation of the American public and of a little
band of clever literary dandies in London, great in criticism, of whom he has become the darling, has made Mr.
Stevenson complacent, and he always tended perhaps to be a
thought too fond of his velvet coat. There is danger in
the delight with which his every scrap is now received.
A few years ago, when he was his own severest and sanest
critic, he stopped the publication of a book after it was
in proof - a brave act. He has lost this courage, or he
would have re-written 'The Black Arrow.' There is deterioration in the essays he has been contributing to an
American magazine ['Scribner's'], graceful and suggestive
though they are. The most charming of living stylists,
Mr. Stevenson is self-conscious in all his books now and
again, but hitherto it has been the self-consciousness of
an artist with severe critics at his shoulder. It has
become self-satisfaction. The critics have put a giant's
robe on him, and he has not flung it off. He dismisses
'Tom Jones' with a simper. Personally Thackeray 'scarce
appeals to us as the ideal gentleman; if there were
nothing else [what else is there?], perpetual nosing after
snobbery at least suggests the snob.' From Mr. Stevenson

one would not have expected the revival of this silly
charge, which makes a cabbage of every man who writes
about cabbages. I shall say no more of these ill-
considered papers, though the sneers at Fielding call
for indignant remonstrance, beyond expressing a hope that
they lie buried between magazine covers. Mr. Stevenson
has reached the critical point in his career, and I should
like to see him back at Bournemouth, writing within high
walls. We want that big book; we think he is capable of
it, and so we cannot afford to let him drift into the
seaweed. About the writer with whom his name is so often
absurdly linked we feel differently. It is as foolish to
rail at Mr. Rider Haggard's complacency as it would be to
blame Christopher Sly for so quickly believing that he was
born a lord.

The key-note of all Mr. Stevenson's writings is his indifference, so far as his books are concerned, to the
affairs of life and death on which other minds are chiefly
set. Whether man has an immortal soul interests him as an
artist not a whit; what is to come of man troubles him as
little as where man came from. He is a warm, genial
writer, yet this is so strange as to seem inhuman. His
philosophy is that we are but as the light-hearted birds.
This is our moment of being; let us play the intoxicating
game of life beautifully, artistically, before we fall
dead from the tree. We all know it is only in his books
that Mr. Stevenson can live this life. The cry is to
arms; spears glisten in the sun; see the brave bark riding
joyously on the waves, the black flag, the dash of red
colour twisting round a mountainside. Alas! the drummer
lies on a couch beating his drum. It is a pathetic picture, less true to fact now, one rejoices to know, than it
was recently. A common theory is that Mr. Stevenson
dreams an ideal life to escape from his own sufferings.
This sentimental plea suits very well. The noticeable
thing, however, is that the grotesque, the uncanny, holds
his soul; his brain will only follow a coloured clue. The
result is that he is chiefly picturesque, and, to those
who want more than art for art's sake, never satisfying.
Fascinating as his verses are, artless in the perfection
of art, they take no reader a step forward. The children
of whom he sings so sweetly are cherubs without souls. It
is not in poetry that Mr. Stevenson will give the great
book to the world, nor will it, I think, be in the form of
essays. Of late he has done nothing quite so fine as
'Virginibus Puerisque,' though most of his essays are gardens in which grow few weeds. Quaint in matter as in
treatment, they are the best strictly literary essays of
the day, and their mixture of tenderness with humour

suggests Charles Lamb. Some think Mr. Stevenson's essays
equal to Lamb's, or greater. To that I say No. The name
of Lamb will for many a year bring proud tears to English
eyes. Here was a man, weak like the rest of us, who kept
his sorrows to himself. Life to him was not among the
trees. He had loved and lost. Grief laid a heavy hand on
his brave brow. Dark were his nights; horrid shadows in
the house; sudden terrors; the heart stops beating waiting
for a footstep. At that door comes Tragedy, knocking at
all hours. Was Lamb dismayed? The tragedy of his life
was not drear to him. It was wound round those who were
dearest to him; it let him know that life has a glory even
at its saddest, that humour and pathos clasp hands, that
loved ones are drawn nearer, and the soul strengthened in
the presence of anguish, pain, and death. When Lamb sat
down to write he did not pull down his blind on all that
is greatest, if most awful, in human life. He was gentle,
kindly; but he did not play at pretending that there is
no cemetery round the corner. In Mr. Stevenson's exquisite essays I look in vain for the great heart that pal-
pitates through the pages of Charles Lamb.

The great work, if we are not to be disappointed, will
be fiction. Mr. Stevenson is said to feel this himself,
and, as I understand, 'Harry Shovel' will be his biggest
bid for fame. It is to be, broadly speaking, a
nineteenth-century 'Peregrine Pickle,' dashed with Meredith, and this in the teeth of many admirers who maintain
that the best of the author is Scottish. Mr. Stevenson,
however, knows what he is about. Critics have said
enthusiastically - for it is difficult to write of Mr.
Stevenson without enthusiasm - that Alan Breck is as good
as anything in Scott. Alan Breck is certainly a masterpiece, quite worthy of the greatest of all novelists,
who, nevertheless, it should be remembered, created these
rich side characters by the score, another before dinner-
time. English critics have taken Alan to their hearts,
and appreciate him thoroughly; the reason, no doubt,
being that he is the character whom England acknowledges
as the Scottish type. The Highlands, which are Scotland
to the same extent as Northumberland is England, present
such a character to this day, but no deep knowledge of Mr.
Stevenson's native country was required to reproduce him.
An artistic Englishmen or American could have done it.
Scottish religion, I think, Mr. Stevenson has never understood, except as the outsider misunderstands it. He
thinks it hard because there are no coloured windows.
'The colour of Scotland has entered into him altogether,'
says Mr. James, who, we gather, conceives in Edinburgh
Castle a place where tartans glisten in the sun, while

rocks re-echo bagpipes. Mr. James is right in a way. It
is the tartan, the claymore, the cry that the heather is
on fire, that are Scotland to Mr. Stevenson. But the
Scotland of our day is not a country rich in colour; a
sombre grey prevails. Thus, though Mr. Stevenson's best
romance is Scottish, that is only, I think, because of his
extraordinary aptitude for the picturesque. Give him any
period in any country that is romantic, and he will soon
steep himself in the kind of knowledge he can best turn to
account. Adventures suit him best, the ladies being left
behind; and so long as he is in fettle it matters little
whether the scene be Scotland or Spain. The great thing
is that he should now give to one ambitious book the time
in which he has hitherto written half a dozen small ones.
He will have to take existence a little more seriously -
to weave broadcloth instead of lace.

109. GEORGE MOORE ON STEVENSON FROM 'CONFESSIONS OF A
YOUNG MAN'

1888, 284-7

George Moore (1852-1933) was an Anglo-Irish novelist,
dramatist, and autobiographer. These objections to
Stevenson are developed in Moore's review of 'The Master
of Ballantrae' (No. 119) and of Yeats's 'The Secret Rose'
(No. 161). For Moore's later revised assessment of
Stevenson, see the preface to his 'Lewis Seymour and Some
Women' (1917), vi-viii, where the early travel writings in
particular are praised. Moore also wrote to Colvin in
1917 to thank him for his edition of Stevenson's letters,
which, he said, 'have given me the very greatest pleasure,
revealing Stevenson to me even more perfectly than
"Travels with a Donkey", "An Inland Voyage", "Men and
Books", etc.' (E. V. Lucas, 'The Colvins and Their
Friends' (1928, 145). Moore continued to believe, however, that fiction was 'outside his talent'. See the summary of Moore's views on Stevenson in Rupert Hart-Davis,
'George Moore: Letters to Lady Cunard' (1957), 95.

I will state frankly that Mr. R. L. Stevenson never wrote
a line that failed to delight me; but he never wrote a

book. You arrive at a strangely just estimate of a
writer's worth by the mere question: 'What is he the
author of?' for every writer whose work is destined to
live is the author of one book that outshines the other,
and, in popular imagination, epitomises his talent and
position. What is Shakespeare the author of? What is
Milton the author of? What is Fielding the author of?
What is Byron the author of? What is Carlyle the author
of? What is Thackeray the author of? What is Zola the
author of? What is Mr. Swinburne the author of? Mr.
Stevenson is the author of shall I say, 'Treasure Island,'
or what?

I think of Mr. Stevenson as a consumptive youth weaving
garlands of sad flowers with pale, weak hands, or leaning
to a large plate-glass window, and scratching thereon
exquisite profiles with a diamond pencil.

I do not care to speak of great ideas, for I am unable
to see how an idea can exist, at all events can be great
out of language; an allusion to Mr. Stevenson's verbal
expression will perhaps make my meaning clear. His
periods are fresh and bright, rhythmical in sound, and
perfect realizations of their sense; in reading you often
think that never before was such definiteness united to
such poetry of expression; every page and every sentence
rings of its individuality. Mr. Stevenson's style is over
smart, well-dressed, shall I say, like a young man walking
in the Burlington Arcade? Yes; I will say so, but, I will
add, the most gentlemanly young man that ever walked in
the Burlington. Mr. Stevenson is competent to understand
any thought that might be presented to him, but if he were
to use it, it would instantly become neat, sharp, ornamen-
tal, light, and graceful; and it would lose all its original richness and harmony. It is not Mr. Stevenson's
brain that prevents him from being a thinker, but his
style.

Another thing that strikes me in thinking of Stevenson
(I pass over his direct indebtedness to Edgar Poe, and his
constant appropriation of his methods), is the unsuitable-
ness of the special characteristics of his talent to the
age he lives in. He wastes in his limitations, and his
talent is vented in prettinesses of style. In speaking of
Mr. Henry James, I said that, although he had conceded
much to the foolish, false, and hypocritical taste of the
time, the concessions he made had in little or nothing
impaired his talent. The very opposite seems to me the
case with Mr. Stevenson. For if any man living in this
end of the century needed freedom of expression for the
distinct development of his genius, that man is R. L.
Stevenson. He who runs may read, and he with any knowledge

of literature will, before I have written the words, have
imagined Mr. Stevenson writing in the age of Elizabeth or
Anne.

110. ANDREW LANG, FROM AN UNSIGNED ARTICLE, MODERN MEN:
MR. R. L. STEVENSON, 'SCOTS OBSERVER'

26 January 1889, i, 264-6

Lang (1844-1912) was a poet, mythologist, classical scholar, and historian, as well as a prolific reviewer. The
chief body of his work on current literature appeared in
a monthly causerie for Longman's entitled At the Sign of
the Ship, but his reviews also appeared in the 'Academy',
'Saturday Review', 'Morning Post', 'Illustrated London
News', etc. Lang's friendship with Stevenson developed
from the time both frequented the Savile Club and he was
to become one of the band of staunch supporters of Stevenson's work. This article on Modern Men was the first in a
series initiated by W. E. Henley, then editor of the
'Scots Observer' (later the 'National Observer'). An
assessment of a later date is found in Lang's 'Essays in
Little' (1891), 24-35.

... The deserved popularity of this writer is all the
more remarkable and satisfactory, because he was praised
by critics long years before the general public heard of
his name. The public and the critical are but seldom of
the same mind; when they do agree, their unanimity is
wonderful. As an illustration of our author's popular
success, it is told how a small American lad was once
induced or compelled to read 'Rob Roy' - a romance by one
of our forgotten old novelists. On finishing this fable,
the American youth remarked that it was 'not bad, and
rather like Stevenson.' This is, indeed, the general verdict of boyhood, and the man who has boys of his party can
afford to sneer at reviewers. But Mr. Stevenson has the
reviewers too, and it was the 'Spectator' [R. H. Hutton,
unsigned review, 11 August 1888] which found it possible
to equal 'The Black Arrow,' on the whole, with 'Ivanhoe.'
A humble critic who has found 'The Black Arrow' not more,
but rather less, readable than le dernier de Monsieur W. D.

Howells, can only congratulate Mr. Stevenson. *Non equidem invideo*; but a man may be really envious when he remembers how kindly Mr. Matthew Arnold spoke of Mr. Stevenson's work, and how 'Kidnapped' was the last novel which Lord Iddesleigh read, and that it charmed him greatly on almost his latest day of life.

The combination of all these verdicts - from the not wholly disinterested 'boom' of the American journals to the honest liking of schoolboys, and the admiration of poets and statesmen - has made for Mr. Stevenson a splendid and worthy popularity. But his earliest, and, as it were, his esoteric admirers may perchance feel a little hurt and jealous. 'We admired him,' they say, 'when he did his first things - things as good as he has ever done - his Night with Villon, his Sieur de Malétroit's Door; and we are discomfited by your howling, barbarous devotion to his boys' books and his moral romance.' Human nature is thus constituted, and the present reviewer is conscious of the temptation to be exclusive. But the merit of Mr. Stevenson's boys' books is too great for the present writer. He cannot pretend to sulk off with his 'Inland Voyage,' and to turn his back on 'Kidnapped' and 'Treasure Island.' No; they are popular, but they are very good for all that; though, as to being impeccable - as to being on a level with 'Quentin Durward,' or 'Ivanhoe,' not to speak of 'Old Mortality' - the idea is absurd. I speak frankly, because Mr. Stevenson's writings have an almost unholy attraction for me. 'Magazine day' was a festival of one's nonage; for many years the birthday of the new serials has been no more cheerful occasion than one's own. But now I can rejoice again in the advent of 'Magazine day,' and slink off to some quiet corner with the last number of 'The Master of Ballantrae.' One has not been so eager since 'The Virginians' came out, in an age almost prehistoric. Except 'The Black Arrow,' there is nothing of his but it delights me: in verse or prose, this author holds one with his glittering eye, and cannot be shaken off. Now it is the exquisite happy charm of the manner, in which you can see that the author is happy too, and is applauding himself in his heart, like a literary Little Jack Horner. Now it is the originality of the matter; often it is the combination of manner and matter, of imagination, of observation, of *finesse*, of delicate labour, that wins you, and makes you read a passage twice over, even when you are pining to learn the end of the story. Yet, with all this granted, one cannot pretend that Mr. Stevenson is to be equalled with Scott, with Thackeray, with Poe even, or with Hawthorne. His best pieces, like the quarrel in the heather, and the rival

pipers (in 'Kidnapped'), are, indeed, as good as good
things of Sir Walter's, though they are good in a different and more reflective, often a more didactic, always a
more self-conscious way. But as to greatness of the whole
piece, as to variety and copiousness of humour, comparison
is mere cruelty.

'Then why compare?' a reader will ask. Merely to
remind people that there have been greater periods of
romantic literature than ours, and that it is possible to
puff ourselves up too hugely over the good thing which we
undeniably possess. Mr. Stevenson himself has criticised
Scott's weak points, and has passed remarks on Fielding
which exert a gentle astonishment. He is strong where
Scott is weak - in genius for style, and in sedulous
attention to style.... But whereas Scott, in the best
sense of the word, is *genial*, Mr. Stevenson has occasional
humours as of a literary changeling. He has a liking for
the strange and sinister in human nature - not a liking of
sympathy, of course, but a liking begotten of some touch
of similar quality in his own genius. You can see that he
takes pleasure in psychological experiment, and not only
studies the conduct of man as he finds it, but as it might
be in rare and unusual combinations. You watch him, as it
were, in his laboratory, throwing odd, unholy ingredients
into the caldron where mortal passions and emotions are
seething. He himself seems almost as curious as his
reader, and as uncertain of the result. From this double
interest of the spectacle - the artist's temperament and
the artist's results - comes a great part of his charm,
his enigmatic attraction. Yet all this aspect of his work
is so well hidden, so far from conspicuous, that the
simple can read him without even suspecting the double
problem.

Probably Mr. Stevenson really reached the large public,
for the first time, by a double problem, by the romance of
'Jekyll and Hyde.' It had a large palpable moral - its
weak point - which attracted the favourable consideration
of the clergy, and made the fortune of the book. Yet, in
spite of its one truly alarming scene, what defects there
are in the allegory! Dr. Jekyll is rather a worse kind of
fellow than Mr. Hyde; the doctor has a dreadful bedside
manner, an unctuous false *bonhomie*, which are not the
faults of the other partner. Of the two, Mr. Hyde, perhaps, is really more of what we commonly call a gentleman
in his truculent sincerity. What became of whatever was
good in Jekyll when Hyde was prowling about, psycholo-
gists have not discovered. Yet, if the allegory is to
hold water, there should have been another figure of goodness all compact: Jekyll with no touch of Hyde. But when

did an allegory ever yet hold water?

Perhaps these remarks may seem inclined towards the heresy of a great work. 'Why does not Mr. Stevenson do a great work? Why does he scatter the small change of his wealth?' some people ask. It is an open secret that the author's physical condition is very unlike that of Scott - Scott of the mighty arms which moved the wonder of the Ettrick Shepherd. That, no doubt, is the real reason which may prevent Mr. Stevenson from giving the world such a masterpiece as 'Esmond.' But why should everybody clamour for great works? A recent pamphlet has a dreadful prophecy that Mr. Stevenson's Great Work will be a blend-ing of Mr. Meredith and Tobias Smollett. May it not be so! Mr. Stevenson has no success in drawing women, and, when he does attempt it, the influence of Mr. Meredith is only too apparent. The Countess in 'Prince Otto' is a Meredithian countess; nay, wherever a girl appears in 'The Black Arrow,' one hears the voice, not of nature, but of Mr. Meredith. It is enough that Mr. Meredith should be witty and ingenious in his own elaborate and artful manner. If Mr. Stevenson ever succeeds, where most men fail, in drawing a woman, one may hope that she will not be in Mr. Meredith's school. Indeed it is certain that Mr. Stevenson can only succeed when he is himself, as he invariably is when he is dealing in verse or prose, with everything but womankind. Men, nature, beasts, children, may well be enough for his art; and as to the women folk, it were better that they should be lay figures, like Rowena, than artful Meredithian maids and matrons.

Let us leave Mr. Stevenson alone, and not pester him with advice, not even with injudicious and perilous encouragement. His impulses will guide him right. There is an unfinished window in his palace, as in Aladdin's, the window that should be painted with the effigy of a Becky Sharp, a Beatrix Esmond, a Di Vernon, a Jeani Deans. Let not the window be finished and adorned with a copy.

Perhaps it is much more curious that Mr. Stevenson, remembering childhood as he does with the fresh memory of genius, has never in prose drawn a child - such a child as little Rawdon Crawley, or Henry Ashton. His hero in 'Treasure Island' is a delightful young miracle, but not a child like the Dream Children of 'A Child's Garden of Verse.' But we have no right to ask everything even from so various a humourist, so accomplished a wielder of style, so keen an observer, such a master of the terrible, so winning a teller of tales, so vivacious a critic. As Partridge observed, on an occasion which Mr. Stevenson, as a moralist, may deplore, *non omnia possumus omnes!* (1)

Note

1 Virgil, 'Eclogues', viii, 63: 'We cannot all of us do
   all things.'

'The Wrong Box'

June 1889

'The Wrong Box' was the first of three novels on which
Stevenson and Lloyd Osbourne, his step-son, collaborated.
According to Osbourne's account (Balfour, 'Life', ii, 34),
he wrote entirely on his own a work first entitled 'The
Finsbury Tontine' and later changed to 'The Game of
Bluff'; Stevenson then revised and improved this work,
leaving the essentials of the story unchanged (but see
LS, iii, 104). Scribners offered $5,000 for the manu-
script on condition that Stevenson's name be placed first
and that they be given the rights for both England and
the USA, though they eventually settled for US rights
alone for that sum. Longmans secured the rights in England and the book was published in both countries in June
1889. Few favourable reviews appeared aside from those in
the 'Scots Observer' (27 July 1889), the 'Scotsman' (No.
112), and the New York 'Critic' (6 July 1889). E. T. Cook
dismissed it in an unsigned review in the 'Athenaeum'
(27 July 1889), saying it would

> try the faith of his most ardent admirers.... If there
> are readers who can get through more than a quarter of
> the small volume and find it amusing they must be won-
> dered at and not envied.... To have aided in the pro-
> duction of a book three-fourths of which consist of
> tedious levity is, indeed, not a thing to be proud of.

(As the 'Scots Observer' noted (24 August 1889), the
'Athenaeum' was playfully ridiculed at one point in the
novel (ch. xv).) Mrs Oliphant ('Blackwood's', August
1889) called 'The Wrong Box' ('a very wrong box indeed')
a 'silly and vulgar story' and expressed the view that
while Stevenson's versatility might be admirable it was
carrying matters a trifle too far when he undertook 'to
show us how he can climb a greased pole and grin through

a horse-collar'. Devoted followers of Stevenson, especially those of a less sombre turn of mind than Mrs Oliphant, were inclined to regard the novel as another
instance of the variety of his talents. For the very
devoted, knowledge of it came to be a distinguishing
badge. As Kipling said ('Something of Myself' (1937),
108), it qualified one for Eminent Master R.L.S.:

> Even to-day I would back myself to take seventy-five
> percent marks in written or viva-voce examination on
> 'The Wrong Box' which, as the Initiated know, is the
> Test Volume of that Degree. I read it first in a small
> hotel in Boston in '89, when the negro waiter nearly
> turned me out of the dining-room for spluttering over
> my meal.

111. FROM AN UNSIGNED REVIEW, MR. R. L. STEVENSON IN THE
WRONG BOX, 'PALL MALL GAZETTE'

19 June 1889, xlix, 3

The preface to this somewhat remarkable book is as
follows: -

> 'Nothing like a little judicious levity,' says
> Michael Finsbury in the text: nor can any better
> excuse be found for the volume in the reader's hand.
> The authors can but add that one of them is old enough
> to be ashamed of himself, and the other young enough
> to learn better.

We do not know who Mr. Osbourne is, but as he 'is young
enough to learn better' there is hope that he may improve.
As for Mr. Stevenson, who 'is old enough to be ashamed
of himself,' we are very glad to hear it. He ought to be
ashamed of himself. There may be 'nothing like a little
judicious levity,' but when the whole point of the levity
turns upon the effort first to lose and then to find a
corpse, it is doubtful whether the excellence of the
object altogether justifies the choice of so repellent a
subject. Some years ago [1884] Mr. Stevenson contributed
to an Extra Christmas number of this paper a weird story
under the title of The Body Snatcher, but we can hardly
think that the success of that little tale warranted a

return once more to 'a deader' as a leading element in a
work of fiction. The story of 'The Wrong Box' is a
broadly farcical one. Various characters, more or less
cleverly drawn, play a kind of ghastly game at hide and
seek with a dead man's body; first of all it is stowed
away in a barrel, and then it is concealed in the interior
of a Broadwood piano. The whole of the fun of the tale
turns upon the attempts of the unfortunates who find the
corpse in their possession to palm it off upon their
neighbours. The only thing that can be said in favour of
the plot is that it is run through with sufficient rapidity to prevent the olfactory nerve discovering the
whereabouts of the concealed carcase....

The story is not worthy of the creator of 'Dr. Jekyll
and Mr. Hyde,' but if the difficulty about the corpse
could be surmounted, it might possibly furnish the ground-
work for a very amusing piece of the farce-masquerading-
as-comedy order, which used to form the staple fare at the
Criterion. We must, however, enter our forcible protest
against the funereal fun of a story which has as the
pivot on which the whole plot turns the buffeting from
pillar to post of a corpse. The notion quite too un-
pleasantly suggests reminiscences of luckless Juliet's
vision when she pictures herself playing ball with the
bones of her ancestors. We fear Mr. Stevenson's voyagings
have not had a beneficial effect on his genius. Church-
yard humours of this description have no real popularity
anywhere, in any modern civilized country, with the doubtful exception of some of the professedly 'funny' columns
of the lower class American newspapers.

112. AN UNSIGNED REVIEW, 'SCOTSMAN'

24 June 1889

Mr Robert Louis Stevenson's power and place in literature
is so peculiar and personal to himself that some surprise
will be felt at first sight of the title page of his new
story, 'The Wrong Box.' It bears the name of a collaborator, Mr Lloyd Osbourne. What Mr Osbourne's share in the
story may be it is hard to determine. The rich fancy
everywhere displayed in the work, the extraordinary dash
and brilliancy of the style, and the curiously eccentric

conduct of the narrative are all qualities already identified with former stories that bear the name of Mr
Stevenson alone. It is a story in the delightfully crazy
manner of the 'New Arabian Nights' - a farcical romance.
It is like the Gaboriau romance in structure - a succession of startling incidents and situations that might, if
the author so willed it, go on for ever. It is based
upon a supposed murder, and the story follows the strange
adventures of a corpse in a water butt. A crowd of fan-
tastical characters, all near enough to human nature to
ensure a warm interest, individualised with a fine skill,
and yet impossible enough to be thoroughly romantic, pass
before the reader, like the figures in a carnival procession - all feather-brained and striking the funniest
attitudes of mind and body. The effect is original and
striking. The book is, as the authors put it in a brief
preface, 'a little judicious levity.' It is so far away
from life that there must be many readers who will not see
the joke; and to these the book will seem a mere soap-
bubble, gaily coloured, sparkling, and empty. To the
other, and probably larger class of readers, it will
yield the rich enjoyment of watching the play of as fine
a fancy as ever drew men's thoughts aside from everyday
cares. It is not a very surprising book for Mr Stevenson
to have written after all he has written. But it is as
good as any one of the 'New Arabian Nights,' and every
one who reads it will have his memory warm with merry
thoughts and pictures.

'The Master of Ballantrae'

September 1889

113.   STEVENSON, FROM LETTERS TO COLVIN, HENRY JAMES,
E. L. BURLINGAME, AND W. H. LOW

1887, 1888, 1889

(a) From a letter to Colvin dated by him 24 December 1887

... [I] have fallen head over heels into a new tale, 'The
Master of Ballantrae'. No thought have I now apart from
it, and I have got along up to page ninety-two of the
draft with great interest. It is to me a most seizing
tale; there are some fantastic elements; the most is a
dead genuine human problem - human tragedy, I should say
rather. It will be about as long, I imagine, as 'Kidnapped'.... I have done most of the big work, the
quarrel, duel between the brothers, and announcement of
the death to Clementina and my Lord - Clementina, Henry,
and Mackellar (nicknamed Square-toes) are really very fine
fellows; the Master is all I know of the devil. I have
known hints of him, in the world, but always cowards; he
is as bold as a lion, but with the same deadly, causeless
duplicity I have watched with so much surprise in my two
cowards. 'Tis true, I saw a hint of the same nature in
another man who was not a coward; but he had other things
to attend to; the Master has nothing else but his
devilry.... (LS, iii, 35-6)

(b) Letter to Henry James dated by Colvin March 1888

My novel is a tragedy; four parts out of six or seven are
written, and gone to Burlingame [see (c) below]. Five

339

parts of it are sound, human tragedy; the last one or two,
I regret to say, not so soundly designed; I almost hesitate to write them; they are very picturesque, but they
are fantastic; they shame, perhaps degrade, the beginning.
I wish I knew; that was how the tale came to me however.
I got the situation; it was an old taste of mine: The
older brother goes out in the '45, the younger stays; the
younger, of course, gets title and estate and marries the
bride designate of the elder - a family match, but he (the
younger) had always loved her, and she had really loved
the elder. Do you see the situation? Then the devil and
Saranac suggested this *dénouement*, and I joined the two
ends in a day or two of constant feverish thought, and
began to write. And now - I wonder if I have not gone too
far with the fantastic? The elder brother is an INCUBUS:
supposed to be killed at Culloden, he turns up again and
bleeds the family of money; on that stopping he comes and
lives with them, whence flows the real tragedy, the noc-
turnal duel of the brothers (very naturally, and indeed,
I think, inevitably arising), and second supposed death of
the elder. Husband and wife now really make up, and then
the cloven hoof appears. For the third supposed death and
the manner of the third re-appearance is steep; steep,
sir. It is even very steep, and I fear it shames the
honest stuff so far; but then it is highly pictorial, and
it leads up to the death of the elder brother at the hands
of the younger in a perfectly cold-blooded murder, which I
wish (and mean) the reader to approve. You see how daring
is the design. There are really but six chapters, and one
of these episodic, and yet it covers eighteen years, and
will be, I imagine, the longest of my works. (LS, iii,
48-9)

(c) Letter to E. L. Burlingame dated by Colvin April 1889.
Burlingame was the editor of 'Scribner's Magazine'.

I am quite worked out, and this cursed end of 'The Master'
hangs over me like the arm of the gallows; but it is
always darkest before dawn, and no doubt the clouds will
soon rise; but it is a difficult thing to write, above all
in Mackellarese; and I cannot yet see my way clear. If I
pull this off, 'The Master' will be a pretty good novel or
I am the more deceived; and even if I don't pull it off,
it'll still have some stuff in it. (LS, iii, 114-15)

(d) Letter to W. H. Low (see No. 54e) dated '(about) 20th
May 1889'. Serial publication of 'The Master of Ballan-
trae' in 'Scribner's Magazine' ran from November 1888 to
October 1889.

I have at length finished 'The Master'; it has been a sore
cross to me; but now he is buried, his body's under
hatches, - his soul, if there is any hell to go to, gone
to hell; and I forgive him: it is harder to forgive
Burlingame for having induced me to begin the publication,
or myself for suffering the induction. (LS, iii, 122)

114. AN UNSIGNED REVIEW, 'PALL MALL GAZETTE'

14 September 1889, xlix, 3

The writer of this review would appear to be William
Archer, judging by the reference - found in nearly all his
comments on Stevenson - to optimism and pessimism. Ste-
venson mentions this review in his Note to 'The Master of
Ballantrae'. In telling the story through the voice of
Mackellar, he says,

> I was doubtless right and wrong; the book has suf-
> fered and has gained in consequence; gained in relief
> and verisimilitude, suffered in fire, force and (as
> one of my critics has well said) in 'large dramatic
> rhythm.' The same astute and kindly judge complains
> of 'the dredging machine of Mr. Mackellar's memory,
> shooting out the facts bucketful by bucketful'; and I
> understand the ground of his complaint, although my
> sense is otherwise. The realism I love is that of
> method; not only that all in a story may possibly have
> come to pass, but that all might naturally be recorded
> - a realism that justifies the book itself as well as
> the fable it commemorates.

Mr. Stevenson has done it at last: in 'The Master of Ballantrae' he has produced something very like a classic.
Readers who have done Mr. Stevenson the injustice of
following the Master's career in monthly instalments, may
be inclined to cry 'Oh, oh!' and shrug their shoulders.

'Able work,' they may say, 'and even subtle, but scrappy
and lacking in form.' That was our own impression until
we came to read the book through at a sitting, when we
found it no less nicely proportioned than skilfully sustained. The one quality to which it can lay no claim is
cheerfulness. It must be admitted that for a militant
optimist, Mr. Stevenson indulges in singularly gloomy
fantasies. Perhaps he wishes to promote true Mark-
Tapleyism among his readers by putting them through
imaginative experiences under which there is some merit
in being jolly. 'The Wrong Box' (to go no further back)
was the grimmest of farces; 'The Master of Ballantrae,'
or, as it might be called, the Doom of the Duries, is the
saddest of tragedies. This is not a reproach; on the
contrary, it is because Mr. Stevenson has here shown himself a truly tragic artist that we hold this book to be by
far his finest achievement in the way of fiction. Moreover he gives the reader fair warning by taking for his
second title 'A Winter's Tale' - 'A sad tale's best for
winter.'
     The element of adventure in 'The Master of Ballantrae'
is of no great importance. It bulks largely enough to
make the book attractive even to boy readers, be their
age fifteen or fifty; but Mr. Stevenson has done as well
before in the same line, and perhaps better. The strength
of the book lies in the combined subtlety and poignancy of
its spiritual drama. We have here delicacies of analysis
that Mr. Meredith has scarcely surpassed, flashes of the
keenest imaginative insight. It would be hard to name two
characters in fiction more vigorously designed or more
carefully developed than James and Henry Durie. There is
nothing so difficult as to draw a fascinating scoundrel.
The scoundrelism is easy enough; it is the fascination
that is apt to come scant off. In James Durie Mr. Stevenson has invented a new villain, and has drawn him with a
distinction of touch and tone worthy of Vandyke. He is
appallingly vivid to us, and fascinates us much as he
fascinates the worthy Mr. Mackellar through whose eyes we
see him. He is no mere unscrupulous adventurer of the
Barry Lyndon order, and still less a vulgar criminal. He
may rather be called a polished professor of wickedness
as a fine art. Mr. Henry, again, is a pathetic figure, if
ever there was one, whether in the long-suffering and
somewhat 'dour' magnanimity of the first part of his history, or in the relaxation of all his faculties after the
crisis. No less true and touching are the slow agonies of
disillusionment through which the proud heart of Alison
Graeme is made to pass, and the irony of the punishment
that follows upon her obstinate blindness. Old Lord

Durrisdeer, too, is drawn with unfailing felicity, a quite
original character, yet one whom Scott would not have
disowned. How finely conceived are the initial relations
of these four personages to each other! With what swift-
ness of psychological penetration, what terseness of
dramatic utterance, are the gradually developing phases
of the situation displayed! Scene after scene thrills the
imagination and engraves itself on the memory.

Besides the Durie family there are practically but two
characters in the book. One of these, the Chevalier
Burke, is spirited but conventional. The other, Mr.
Ephraim Mackellar, is touched with a quiet humour which
relieves in some measure the gloom of the tragedy. Mr.
Mackellar figures as the narrator of almost the whole
story; a device by which much is gained but something is
lost. The style, admirable in all essentials of force,
colour, and economy, shows now and then a too obvious
striving after quaintness. Mr. Mackellar does not write
like an eighteenth-century Scotchman, but rather like a
nineteenth-century imitator of Mr. Stevenson who has out-
done his original in the search for verbal surprises.
Moreover, so scrupulously is the fiction of Mr. Mackellar's
authorship kept up that his narrative is apt to assume the
appearance of a niggling mosaic of fragmentary reminiscences. In the whole book, there is scarcely one continuous scene of any length, moving with a large dramatic
rhythm. We seem always to hear the dredging-machine of
Mr. Mackellar's memory at work, shooting out the facts
bucketful by bucketful; and this imparts a certain sense
of laboriousness to the narrative. There are one or two
passages which strike us as less successfully realized
than the rest. The chief of these is the conversation
between Mackellar and Lord Durrisdeer on the night of the
duel, in which the worthy steward's tact and his lord-
ship's patient self-possession seem almost more than
human. A blemish of a different order, to our thinking,
is the manner of the Master's death. It is, in effect, an
inadmissible plunge into the supernatural. Mr. Stevenson
may have come across reports of such cases of suspended
animation; but for the purposes of fiction all phenomena
not generally acknowledged to be explicable under ascer-
tained laws must be accounted miraculous. We take somewhat similar objection to the scalping of the treasure-
seekers. It is a violet irruption of a force not properly
accounted for within the limits of the story. But these
are trifling flaws, if flaws they be, in a work of singular power and beauty.

115.   ANDREW LANG, AN UNSIGNED REVIEW, 'DAILY NEWS'

5 October 1889

E. J. Mehew has identified this review as Lang's on the
basis of parallels between it and his comment on Stevenson
in 'Essays in Little' (1891) and elsewhere. In several
places Lang refers to the pleasure Matthew Arnold and Lord
Iddesleigh received from Stevenson's work (B, 5088). See
Introduction, p. 26.

By a great many people a new story of Mr. **LOUIS STEVENSON'S**
is expected with more interest than any other novelty in
literature. It has hitherto been the author's rare fortune to conciliate adverse parties of readers, those who
like adventure and incident merely, and those who care for
style and for study of character. Mr. **STEVENSON** is not
among the authors who write too much and with too feverish
speed; he scarcely takes **SCOTT'S** advice to go on striking
while the iron is hot. Readers have a personal concern
moreover in his development, and in his wanderings of
which he keeps them advised. Not often does a romance
wing its way to us from Wakiki, from 'the loud shores of a
subtropical island.' In the development of Mr. **STEVEN-
SON'S** genius there have been so many phases that people
naturally ask themselves 'What next?' He became known
first as a writer of essays, unusually finished, and
unusually eclectic in style; reminiscences of many an
author, of Sir **THOMAS BROWNE,** of **ADDISON'S** circle of
THACKERAY, floated up here and there among moralisings
which were audacious with youth, and with the high intellectual spirits that no sickness could tame. Then Mr.
STEVENSON gave the world the maddest of modern romances,
where the characters of the pavement seemed to sail down
Tigris rather than Thames, and to be denizens of Bagdad,
not of London. Next he produced a story, the most elaborate of his works, in which recollections of **GEORGE SAND**
and of Mr. **GEORGE MEREDITH** had a hand; he puzzled as much
as he pleased us with the vagaries of Prince **OTTO.**
Presently he turned to a new audience, that of boys, and
his 'Treasure Island' showed us a man of the first literary talent, dealing delightfully with the old materials of
'Kingston and Ballantyne the Brave.' *Ut placeas pueris*
appeared to be his ambition, and yet he pleased statesmen
and poets - Mr. **MATTHEW ARNOLD** and Lord **IDDESLEIGH.**

'Kidnapped' was another venture in the same seas, the
fairy seas that break round Mull and Coll. The book was,
in a sense, unfinished; the adventures were less coherent
than in 'Treasure Island.' Less agreeable to boys, but the
pictures of Highland and Lowland character, the sketch of
the rival pipers, and of CLUNY with his cards in his mountain den, were not less true and vivid than pages in
'Waverley' and 'Rob Roy.' The simplicity, the enjoyment
of SCOTT, were not there; the Highlanders were observed
with equal accuracy, but in a very different temper. Now
Mr. STEVENSON has returned to Scotland, just after the
Forty-five, but his tale wanders from land to land like
its author.
    It would be audacious to prophesy for 'The Master of
Ballantrae' the success of 'Treasure Island.' Not here is
the buoyant and boyish spirit of adventure, the hero is
a worn, and wily, and wicked man of the world. The temper
is more akin to the temper of M. ZOLA than of SCOTT; it is
a study in the darkest hues, a study of courage and wit,
and grace, all wasted and bemired; of honour and justice
wrecked and ruined; of loyalty compelled to be true to an
object which is overthrown, and gradually sunk in madness,
and debauchery, and despair. A tale of fraternal hatred,
of insult and outrage from brother to brother, of what a
woman's and a man's heart might be forced to endure, is
told by an old, pedantic, faithful family servant, who
confesses himself a physical coward, and in heart a murderer. Other incidents are narrated by an Irish adventurer, a BARRY LYNDON without his force, but with a kind
of hare-brained goodness of heart, and capricious unconscious humour. It is not possible that such a story
should delight the young as the artless and impossible
adventures of the boy JEM HAWKER delighted them. Here is
a hidden treasure that comes to naught; here is a shivering magical Hindoo servant, trying the art of suspending
animation in the frozen forests of Canada. 'Good way in
India; here, in this dam cold place, who can tell?' One
is involuntarily reminded by SECUNDRA DASS of JOS SEDLEY'S
shuddering Hindoo attendant in 'Vanity Fair,' and of the
picture where he looks chill and lost in the wilds of
Brompton. Certainly the adventures in the 'Master of Ballantrae' are not on a level with Mr. STEVENSON'S other
doings in romance. There is one exception. The scene
between the two brothers, where long hatred breaks out in
a blow; the duel by candle light in the dark garden, the
disappearance of the Master after 'the sword hilt dirled
on his breast-bane' - all that is admirably conceived and
convincingly narrated.
    But here comes in one of Mr. STEVENSON'S difficulties.

He sets himself to tell this piece of passion and romance
in the words of his old pedantic, faithful family servant. How to shape MACKELLAR'S homespun for superior
flights, as he phrases it, that is the problem. Naturally
he knows better than we that such a narrator would not
record his impressions thus; that he would not give as
pictures: 'a windless stricture of frost had bound the
air; and as we went forth in the shine of the candles,
the blackness was like a roof over our heads.' In that
duel the story culminates. Briefly, it tells of the
hatred between two sons of a Scottish house; one a perfectly accomplished fiend, the other, a dour, honest,
narrow, and honourable gentleman. The lookers on are the
aged father, a wonderfully delicate study; the wife of
the younger brother; the Irish adventurer; and MACKELLAR,
the steward, with so much moral courage on occasion, and
so tremorous a nerve in physical danger. He 'hath a great
scene,' as SHAKESPEARE says, when he awakens the wife, who
has married one brother and probably loved the other, with
the news of the fraternal duel. All these gloomy characters are drawn with a curious care and minuteness; little
incidents, as the throwing of the coin through the window,
are living before the eyes. The style is so artful that
it even absorbs our attention too much in itself. The air
is always heavy and charged with storm, except here and
there - when the Irish chevalier speaks - there is no
relief. We watch by the broken brain of the younger
DURISDEER, by the spirit that long suffering has turned to
an insanity of hatred and terror, with a cruel impatience
and regret. Such is this remarkable, elaborate, melancholy, and almost hopeless book. What remains of all the
gallantry, the beauty, the devotion? The brave, the
accomplished, the much-enduring Master lies forgotten in
the northern wilderness; his fraternal enemy beside him.
These are the fortunes of a little Scottish Theban line;
ETEOCLES and POLYNICES are here, but where is ANTIGONE,
and where the hope that goes with the passing of OEDIPOUS?
It is a very modern gloom that broods over the roof-tree
of DURISDEER. Mr. STEVENSON, like the character in Mr.
MORRIS'S old prose tale, has 'painted the judgments of GOD
in purple and yellow.'

116.   FROM AN UNSIGNED REVIEW, 'DUNDEE COURIER'

11 October 1889

Mr Stevenson tells us in his essay - A Gossip on Romance -
that a tale, to be a success, must prove so absorbing,
that we shall be 'rapt clean out of ourselves' during the
perusal. This entrancing quality belongs to most of Mr
Stevenson's own works, which enjoy here and in America a
popularity ranging from the enthusiasm of boys, who almost
transfer their allegiance from R. M. Ballantyne in the
younger author's favour, up to the gratification of the
scholarly ex-Premier, whom one of Mr Stevenson's 'dyna-
mitards' calls 'the truculent Gladstone!' Everything from
this writer's pen is interesting and enjoyable (anybody
can see that it was not he but his collaborateur who wrote
'The Wrong Box,' with which is name is so discreditably
associated). His genial humanity, his keen eye for the
picturesque in men and manners, his fine sensibility to
delicate impressions of sense, and his power of conceiving
interesting types of character, which he brings before the
mind's eye in vivid portraiture - these are some of the
causes of his peculiar readableness. And then the literary style! It is probably the most highly-finished style
of any living novelist. It is at once polished and
forceful, delicate and sinewy: and everywhere you find a
grace of sentence, an aptness of phrase, and a pervasive
distinction of manner, which he has largely gained from
his French masters Dumas and Molière, and from the classic
English models, all of which he has so assiduously studied. Mr Stevenson's style is thus a most eclectic one,
and, indeed, in his 'Memories and Portraits' he has
frankly confessed how he has played the sedulous ape to
many a famous writer. The result, however, of this conscious labour by which he has acquired his style is that
occasionally the artificiality is obtruded, and you miss
(in his tales) the breezy naturalness of Scott, or (in
his essays) the spontaneousness of Lamb's quaint manner.
The art is sometimes finicking, and you feel that the
author is posturing. But, in the main, Mr Stevenson makes
delightful reading. Considered all round, 'The Master of
Ballantrae' is probably this author's best work of fiction. It has all the interest of plot and incident to be
found in 'Treasure Island' or 'Kidnapped,' while it is
more mature in literary expression, and deals with deeper
passions in human life. Bloody fights like those of
'Treasure Island' are merely tragedy of the vulgar sort -

are, indeed, not tragedy at all in the proper sense
(though considerably above Mr Rider Haggard's ceaseless
cataracts of gore), and such adventures appeal only to
those primitive instincts not yet wrought out of us,
which Mr Andrew Lang seems so delighted to recognise as
being strong in himself, and which he seems so eager to
foster. But now Mr Stevenson makes an advance in this
narrative of the hapless history of the ancient Scottish
house of Durrisdeer. A domestic tragedy, evolved almost
entirely from within, was surely never so skilfully dis-
closed by author's pen. Two brothers Durie (James, the
'Master,' and Henry, his brother) dwelling perforce in
the same country mansion, and hating each other with a
dark intensity, which was the blacker for the mutual love
of early boyhood, rivals also in love of the ward, who
formed another of the family circle, and she driven by
circumstances to wed the one she did not love - these form
ample material for a moving drama. The plot is too complicated to be suitably sketched; enough that there is no
lack of strong incident, varied scene, and dramatic dialogue. There is, moreover (to a much greater degree than
hitherto) characterisation of a subtle and striking kind.
If ever there has been a 'deep villain' depicted in the
pages of a novel, it is James Durie, the Master of
Ballantrae; and a strangely-mingled composition too.
Fascinating in his person, he was a consummate master of
all the arts that please - handsome in figure, brilliant
in talk, graceful in every gesture he might make. He was
gallant and generous, imperious and exacting. 'I have a
kingly nature,' he would say, yet no profitable policy was
so mean but he would stoop to it. 'I never failed to
charm a person when I wanted' - yet he could be a tiger on
occasion. None so pat with an insinuating compliment,
none so stinging with a poisonous innuendo. 'I never knew
a woman,' said he to his brother Henry, and alluding to
Henry's wife, 'who did not prefer me.' He could play at
ingratiating hypocrisy or ingenuous insolence with equal
aplomb. A gentleman-adventurer, versed in the ways of
Court and camp, acquainted with 'East' and 'West,' he
failed to avert the ignominious death by which, despite
his lying arts and audacious scheming, he at length so
miserably perished. The other personages are delineated
with the same vivid force - the reputable, trusty, astute
Ephraim Mackellar, the honest, unselfish, and notoriously
abused Henry; my old Lord Durrisdeer, wrapped up in his
knavish, captivating son, and partial to a fatuous
degree; Alison Graeme, faithful in the end, and the more
devoted because so blind and imprudent at the first; and
the jaunty, amusing Colonel Burke, of the Emerald Isle.

One must not omit to mention the thrilling description of
the midnight duel between the brothers. This chapter
should stand as one of the most powerful and touching in
the annals of romance. Enthusiasm, however, for an author
must not blind the critical judgment. Mr Stevenson is a
trifle over-rated. The pleasure afforded by his books
elicits extravagant praise. The reigning school of criticism (Imperial Cockneyism, as Mr Robert Buchanan (1) dubs
it) is more concerned about the polish and brilliance of a
book than about its depth and truth, the nobility of its
inspiring *motif,* and its moral and spiritual power. And
it is nothing short of ridiculous to hear reviewers speak
of 'great literature' in certain current connections.
Fine as Mr Stevenson's work is, he must penetrate more
profoundly, and aspire more loftily, and develop more
expansively, ere he can assume a position among the larger
gods of literature.

Note

1 Buchanan (1841-1901), poet and novelist, is now most
   often recalled for his controversial remarks on his
   contemporaries in The Fleshly School of Poetry,
   'Contemporary Review', October 1871.

117. W. E. HENLEY ON 'THE MASTER OF BALLANTRAE' AS A
'MASTERPIECE IN GRIME', UNSIGNED REVIEW, 'SCOTS OBSERVER'

12 October 1889, ii, 583-4

Stevenson remarked on this review in a letter (February
1890) to Charles Baxter, the manager of his business
affairs and one of his best and oldest friends:

> I believed 'The Master' was a sure card: I wonder why
> Henley thinks it grimy; grim it is, God knows, but sure
> not grimy, else I am the more deceived. I am sorry he
> did not care for it; I place it on the line with 'Kid-
> napped' myself. We'll see as time goes on whether it
> goes above or falls below. (LS, iii, 158)

'The Master of Ballantrae' is one of the gloomiest, or
rather the grimiest, of stories. There is not a noble nor
a lovable character in the book: the narrator is a poltroon; the hero is a devil in human shape, while his arch-
enemy sinks into a vindictive dullard; the one woman in
the story is morbidly enamoured of her husband's brother;
the chief scene is a scene of fratricidal strife; the
supernumeraries are a choice assortment of smugglers,
pirates, murderers, and mutineers; than the plot there is
nothing uglier in Balzac; and the whole thing is a triumph
of imagination and literary art. But it is not pleasant
reading. There is wit, but it is cold, cruel, even brutal;
there is humour, but it is black, corrosive, bitter as
gall. The story, which turns on the unnatural hatred of
two brothers, would in the hands of a weaker writer simply
shock and repel. Told as Mr. Stevenson tells it, it
throws a sombre fascination over the reader from the first,
and holds him enchained to the close. The author has done
nothing cleverer; he has never before gone so deep; his
narrative has never been more masterly in its concision,
vividness, and energy. Every situation is boldly faced;
every incident fitted with consummate skill into the
framework of the plot; not a single descriptive touch is
wasted. The book shows how thorough a Scot Mr. Stevenson
is: beneath all that fascinating, many-coloured web which
he has woven of wild romance and capricious fancy and
extravagant fun, the hard, gloomy, uncompromising side of
the Scottish intellect asserts itself. In 'The Master of
Ballantrae' the spirit which animated the old Scottish
theologians and preachers and soldiers - the severe, un-
flinching, pleasure-hating spirit to which the race owes
so many of its defects and so much of its fibre - seems
to have entered into the Kingdom of Romance, and made part
of that Kingdom its own. But 'The Master' is a romance
which differs from the romances of Sir Walter as a black
marble vault differs from a radiant palace.
    There was grim enough humour in 'Treasure Island,' but
the grimmest passages therein are a symphony in rose-pink
compared to the narrative of the Master's wanderings,
where Mr. Stevenson seems actually to gloat over pictures
of frenzied atrocities and bestial revellings. The ruf-
fians who mutinied under Long John - even Pew and Israel
Hands - are sober, cleanly, almost respectable mariners,
compared to the raving, loathsome miscreants who formed
the crew of the *Sarah*. And what a contrast there is between 'The Master' and 'Kidnapped': 'Kidnapped,' so rich
in character and mellow humour and kindly feeling and
rousing, open-air adventure; so fiery and throbbing with
the glory of comradeship, so breezy with the air of the

Highland hills, so full of the scent of the heather! What
a contrast between the scene in which Alan Breck's sword
flashes in the round-house - and will flash till the love
of the heroic in literature lies dead - and the midnight
duel between the brothers James and Henry Durie! The one
is kindling, gladdening, brilliant, ringing with steel,
pulsing with the love of battle, charming in its fiery
fierceness: the other is as sinister, black, and ghastly
as a scene in Webster. But the scene - the candles burning steadily in the windless, frosty air of the midnight
wood, the trembling steward watching the duel to the death
of the two brothers - is no more to be forgotten than
Webster's work.

The characters are irresistibly life-like. James
Durie, the Master of Ballantrae, is one of Mr. Stevenson's
strongest creations. The figure is hardly human. It
seems touched with lurid flickerings from the Pit. It has
the superhuman cunning, the malignity and mockery, the
exquisite delight in evil of a fiend. Insidious, false,
murderous, with a veneer of sensibility and a heart rotten
with egotism, taking a feline delight in torturing his
victims, an artist in deceit, endowed with a diabolic
charm, alternately the polished gentleman and the fleering
scoundrel, vain, insolent, and insatiably greedy, - it
would be hard to conceive a more hateful character than
the Master of Ballantrae. Yet, so sure is Mr. Stevenson's
insight, so delicate his art, this incarnate rascal is not
without traits which redeem him from the ranks of the impossibly wicked. He has wit and courage; he is full of
resource; and in the brave fight which he makes for his
life with the band of desperadoes in the wilderness he
enlists the sympathy of the reader. Henry Durie is an
admirable foil to the villain. A man of deep feelings,
but with no charm of manner, he is doomed to play a heavy
part; he endures in silence; his passion smoulders while
his brother's flares out in vindictive sarcasm or the
coarsest taunts. He yields to the Master's exactions 'in
a kind of noble rage'; but in the end he shows himself as
iron-hearted, as relentless in revenge as he had been
patient in suffering, devising and compassing his tormen-
tor's death with a dogged, gloating, implacable ferocity
which is almost as repulsive as the Master's flouting
truculence and glee in the infliction of torture. Most
excellent is the portrait of the steward, MacKellar, a
type of Scot caught in the life; and the Chevalier Burke,
the Irish solider of fortune, though not a striking
success, is very far from a failure. He is a more conventional figure than the other actors in the story - his
analogues have swaggered through a hundred tales - but his

talk is a genuine Irish mixture of blarney and bravado, and
he is an admirable teller of a story. His account of his
meeting with Ballantrae by night in the Indian Garden
reads exactly like a passage in the 'New Arabian Nights.'

The story, as has been said, is infinitely clever. But
it leaves an unpleasant impression; it leaves, as the
saying is, a bad taste in the mouth of the reader. A book
of villainy and gloom all compact can never rank with the
highest works of art. There should be light as well as
shadow in a tale. The story leaves you in the end with an
impression of unreality. You feel as if you had awakened
from a sinister dream; not as if you had been watching a
little corner of the life of the world. You have been
excited, nay thrilled; you have been carried away by the
marvellous narrative gift of the writer; but you have
neither been elevated nor moved to laughter or tears.
You have an impression as if you had emerged from a black
labyrinth lit with infernal fires and echoing with infernal laughter. With all its cleverness, its strength and
subtlety, and constructive and narrative perfection, the
book is not one such as wins and holds the favour of the
many. The world of readers will never take it to their
heart as they have taken the stories of Long John and
Alan Breck, or even the story of Prince Florizel. It is
a masterpiece, but a masterpiece in grime. Of the style
it is needless to say one word. Of the title this may be
said: that it should have run 'The Master of Durrisdeer.'
In naming his book Mr. Stevenson has committed a blunder,
strange, indeed, in a Scotsman.

118. AN UNSIGNED REVIEW, 'GLASGOW HERALD'

17 October 1889

This story has been for several months before the public
in the pages of 'Scribner's Magazine.' It must be confessed that the construction of the work does not well
adapt it to the publication in sections, and that those
who have only followed it from month to month in a spas-
modic fashion are not likely to appraise it so highly as
those who read it first as a symmetrical whole. But even
in its complete form, we are unable to join in the chorus
of adulation with which the book has been received in certain quarters. It is the fashion to applaud everything

that Mr Stevenson does, not always because it is excellent, but because it is done by Mr Stevenson. And we gladly admit that what he does is generally good, and sometimes excellent. Now, 'The Master of Ballantrae,' while in some respects one of the most remarkable stories he has ever published, is by no means a satisfying book. It is as superior to 'The Wrong Box' as good is to bad, but it is not superior to 'Kidnapped.' It is not even so good as 'Kidnapped' in dramatic movement and in scenic display. Its great fault is its pervading gloom - and it is a serious fault in a romance. There is not a relieving gleam of humour in the whole narrative, and one feels oppressed with the atrabiliar atmosphere, whether the scene before us happen to be Durisdeer or the American wilds. There is not lacking a large spicing of adventure, but somehow it has the taint of unreality. The wanderings of 'The Master' in the earlier chapters have a vagueness that does not excite our interest and emotions like the wanderings of David Balfour and Alan Breck. The Master himself, while an unsatisfactory study, is perhaps the most remarkable figure Mr Stevenson has yet drawn. The contrast and conflict between the Master and his younger brother constitute the *motif* of the story, but we confess it wearies us. The fraternal enmity is too terrible, unnatural - the strain of misery is too far prolonged. The reaction and revulsion occur before the climax is reached; and the climax is too theatrical and artificial. Next to the figure of the Master, that of Ephraim Mackellar, the narrator of the story, is the most effective, and we recognise in it a clever conception skilfully developed. The mingled pawkiness and simplicity, business shrewdness and sentimental loyalty, moral courage and physical cowardice, of the worthy steward make up a fine study. The interjection of the figures of the Chevalier Burke and Secundra Das, the mysterious Hindu, do not add either to the intelligibility or symmetry of the narrative, although Secundra comes in useful for dramatic effect. The Chevalier is represented as an Irishman; but he seems more like a Highland adventurer of a very familiar type trying to speak with a brogue. Now all this does not mean that 'The Master of Ballantrae' is not a clever, an interesting, and a striking book; it simply means that we do not regard it as so worthy of abject worship as some persons have declared it to be. No doubt each work of every fictionist should be judged on its own merits, and as an imaginative creation it really does not matter whether 'The Master of Ballantrae' is or is not superior to other products of the same writer. But for ourselves, while we might be inclined to

re-peruse 'Kidnapped,' we have not the slightest desire to
see 'The Master of Ballantrae' again. And we fancy the
majority of our readers will be of our thinking.

119. GEORGE MOORE, REVIEW, 'HAWK'

5 November 1889, iv, 489-90

See headnote to No. 109. 'Hawk: A Smart Paper for Smart
People' was a weekly edited by Augustus M. Moore, George
Moore's brother.

So unanimous have been the journals of culture in their
praise of Mr. Stevenson's genius, especially as manifested
in his new book - and so perturbed is the public mind by
the oracular utterances regarding the great store future
generations will set upon it, and the high place it will
one day take among English classics - that I am almost
constrained to apologise for the unseemliness of a perverse taste which refuses to accept even as excellent that
which others are agreed to praise as sublime. My difficulty is certainly not inconsiderable; a man, not to say a
critic, may very well write himself down an ass before he
well knows where he is; and yet it seems sure when one
considers it that all cannot be right with a book of
adventure in which no very decided story is told. Of
course I am aware that it is ridiculous for me to decry
a book that the 'Spectator,' the 'Saturday Review,' the
whole of Bedford Park, and all the aesthetics of Clapham
and Peckham Rye have in oecumenical council decided is to
live for ever. For plea of my condemnation of a work
already canonized and enthroned amongst the Immortals, I
will again suggest to its many erudite admirers that it
is, perhaps, after all only a story of adventure with the
story left out. In making this suggestion, I feel like
the child in Hans Andersen's tale of the lying weavers who
persuaded the King and his court that they were supplying
them with garments of magical lightness when they had only
persuaded them to walk about naked. When the child said:
'No father, the King and his court are walking about
naked,' everybody recognised the truth and the weavers
were stoned out of the town.

As naked of story as the King and his court were of
clothes, 'The Master of Ballantrae' seems in my eyes. No
doubt diligent searching would reveal the workings of the
plot - diligent searching will discover the departure and
arrival of a train in 'Bradshaw' - but it does not strike
me as being any part of my critical duty to follow up the
various zigzag lights which flickered across the pages.
Suffice it to say for the condemnation of the book, that
the story - if there is a story - is involved in many disjointed narratives. The author fails to set forth his
scheme as he did in 'Treasure Island,' as Defoe did in
'Robinson Crusoe,' as did, indeed, every writer who has
written a book of adventures that has outlasted a generation. I have read all but the last thirty or forty pages
- these the very strictest sense of critical duty could
not induce me to toil through - without receiving one distinct impression concerning either 'The Master of Ballantrae,' his sons, the steward, Mr. MacKellar, their aims,
or their achievements. Never does Mr. Stevenson grasp his
story and do his will of it. His claim upon it is that of
a white, languid hand, dreamily laid, and fitfully attempting to detain a gallant who would escape; ineffectively
the hand is laid on the lappet and on the sleeve. The
hand is long and delicate, somewhat epicene; and fingers
are long and weak; the skin is pallid and relieved by the
brilliancy of numerous rings.

Some three or four scenes, however, fix themselves upon
my mind. I remember the pirate vessel and its captain,
and this captain Mr. Stevenson has characterised very
skilfully, but merely from the outside. It is a clever
'make-up': just such a one as a clever actor would invent;
and the life on board is also excellently well invented.
But nowhere any breath of design, nor are we held under
spell of any imaginative impulse, creative or descriptive.
We float on a painted ocean in a painted boat, among a
little wretchedness of cardboard and tinsel. The thing is
a toy - a pretty daintily conceived toy, equivalent in
artistic value to a Savoy opera or a view of Bedford Park
on a fine day. Indeed, I utterly fail to see in what this
portion of the book is better than similar scenes
described again and again by Captain Marryat. A memory of
'Percival Keene' rises, and if I remember rightly the
blunter narrative is, in all those qualities through which
the tooth of time cuts slowest, superior to the dilettan-
tism before me.

As soon as we are quit of the pirate vessel the story
is taken up by another person, and we drift into a mist
of vapidities, we wade through dry deserts of barren
artificialities, until at last we fall in with an oasis in

the shape of a duel between two brothers. And upon my
word the scene is very nicely done. Yes; it is very nice
in the modern and in the original sense of the word. So
nice is it, so beguiling is the art that there are times
when it seems that Mr. Stevenson is rising to the situation, and is really investing his subject with some passion and dignity. But hardly has the impression entered
the mind than it is destroyed by some more than usually
irritating trick of phrase.

Again the story becomes a doll, and the author a doll-
maker; an eyelash is added, and a touch of carmine is laid
on the corner of the lips.

The duel done with, we drift again into vain seas of
speech where windless sails of narrative hang helpless
and death-like, and vague shapes, impersonal as unimagined
hosts, people the gloom; and through the sepulchral
weariness, the self-conscious style sounds like a fog
horn. Suddenly, when the soul of hope is well nigh dead
within us, comes another incident; whence it comes and to
what scheme of life it belongs I know not, but it is a
rift in the darkness.

Mr. Stevenson tells how some people took a path by
night, which led through a wood and 'debouched' upon the
high road. He describes with admirable picturesqueness
the departure of a carriage, how it descended into the
vale, mounted the succeeding hill, and stopped on the
summit, and one of the travellers took out one of the
lamps and waved it for a farewell sign. This third incident was the last that arrested my attention. But dulness
is not a provable quantity; what one finds dull, another
may declare to be bright and entertaining; bad writing is
more demonstrable, and to the task of making good this
accusation, I will now apply myself.

We know from Euclid that before even the simplest proposition can be proved, it is necessary to presuppose the
acceptance of certain truths, self-evident, because the
human mind cannot think them otherwise than as they are
stated. Now I submit that the statement that two straight
lines cannot enclose a space, is not more self-evident
than that the first excellence of a writer is the power
to press in a paragraph that which might be easily expanded in a column. As corollary to the axiom, I will add
that matter and form cannot exist independently of each
other. To deny this is equivalent to saying that something may be created out of nothing. If this premiss be
granted, I ask how is it possible to admire the following
passage: -

Not that I ever lost the love I bore my master.

But, for one thing, he had the less use for my
society. For another, I could not but compare the
case of Mr. Alexander with that of Miss Katharine;
for whom my lord had never found the least attention.
And, for a third, I was wounded by the change he
discovered to his wife, which struck me in the nature
of an infidelity. I could but admire, besides, the
constancy and kindness she displayed. Perhaps her
sentiment to my lord, as it had been founded from the
first in pity, was that rather of a mother than a
wife; perhaps it pleased her - if I may say so - to
behold her two children so happy in each other; the
more as one had suffered so unjustly in the past. But
for all that, and though I could never trace in her one
spark of jealousy, she must fall back for society on
poor neglected Miss Katharine; and I, on my part, came
to pass my spare hours more and more with the mother
and daughter. It would be easy to make too much of
this diversion, for it was a pleasant family, as
families go; still the thing existed; whether my lord
knew it or not, I am in doubt. I do not think he did;
he was bound up so entirely in his son; but the rest
of us knew it, and in a manner suffered from the knowledge. [From ch. vi, The Master's Second Absence]

This seems to me as bad a page of English as I ever
read; but let my opinion be waived, it is well-known that
I am no judge of nice and delicate things. I will ask,
however, Mr. Andrew Lang, the entire Savile Club, all the
aesthetes of Clapham, and even those living in the far-
thest limits of Peckham Rye, to put their hands over their
heart and say if the quoted page is not lacking in those
qualities which go to make a good page of prose - clearness of vision and strength of outline. I challenge all
these judges to say that it is not, if I may be permitted
to make a bull, miniature painting on a large scale -
a maudlin design, stippled with a camel-hair brush on a
sheet of ivory a yard and a half square. Anything more
limp and insipid I cannot imagine. But if the quoted
passage can be described as being vigorously and excellently drawn, then the book will most assuredly become an
English classic, for it would be easy to point to a vast
number of pages that differ in nowise from it.
    As the form, so the matter. A little pirate vessel
that might, with a naughty boy for crew, scour the shores
of the Serpentine, robbing the nursemaids and slapping
the children in perambulators - an art having nothing in
common with the realistic imaginings of Defoe, or the
hyperbolical dreamings of Hugo.

On p. 55 [ch. ii] Mr. Stevenson says: - 'Twice we
found women on board; and though we have seen towns
sacked, and of late years some very horrid public tumults,
there was something in the smallness of the numbers, and
the bleak, dangerous sea surroundings, that made these
acts of piracy far more revolting.' This is intended, I
presume, to flutter the suburban dovecots, to cause a
little thrill in the drawing-rooms, to cause the maidens'
eyes to be cast down, to cause mamma to pause and then,
with a sigh of relief, to continue her reading. It might
have been left out she thinks but she concludes there is
nothing sufficient to justify a letter of reproach to Mr.
Mudie. I mention this so characteristic does it seem to
me of the taste and moral tone of our time.
   Mr. Stevenson's book is representative of the little
morbid hankering after taste so prevalent in these days.
It is as pretty as a drawing-room that has been recently
re-decorated and arranged, according to the latest canons
of fashion. I say recently decorated, because the style
seems to me to betray the writer who does not think as he
writes; but who elaborately translates what he has first
written out in very common language into an artificial
little tongue which he takes to be gentle; and through
the emendations we often read the original text, as
happens in inadequate translation from a foreign language.
Here are a few examples: 'It so *befell* that I was intimately mingled with the last years and history of the
house.' 'Teach stood like one stupid, never thinking *on*
his pistols.' 'The captain had not a guess *of* whether we
were drifting.' In his desire for elegance, Mr. Stevenson, seems to have here strained grammar not a little:
'All would *redound* against poor Henry.' 'And sometimes
repenting my *immixture* in affairs so private.' 'But we
decided at last to *escalade* a garden wall.' 'The thought
of a man's death - of his *deletion* from the world.' 'I
had moments when I thought of him as a man of pasteboard -
as though, if one should strike smartly through the *buck-
ram* of his countenance,' &c. These seem to me merely
calculated niceties of phrase, and not sentences born of
the context, as are those of the great masters - the
beautiful organ fugues of De Quincey, the violoncello
obligatos of Ruskin, the brass-like vehemence of Carlyle's
strident sonorities blown of cornet and double bass.
   'The Master of Ballantrae' is the weakest piece of writing of Mr. Stevenson's with which I am acquainted. The best
is A Night with Villeon [A Lodging for the Night: A Story
of Francis Villon]. In this story, for the space of some
ten or twelve pages he is strong, picturesque, and, what
he never is elsewhere, original. In all his other work he

suggests to me a sort of gracious attendant to Edgar Poe –
a Ganymede limned by some eighteenth century artist in the
pseudo classic draperies of that century. 'Treasure
Island' is a very sweet elongated version of 'The Gold
Bug,' and Mr. Stevenson never seems to tire of the recom-
position of that sombre tale of America's greatest genius,
Wilson William [William Wilson].

I have said that my judgment of this book stands in
absolute contradiction to that of all other critics,
intelligent and stupid, obscure and famous. Time alone
can decide between us. Had I more space at command, I
should probably quote the well-known instances how the
succeeding generation has rejected the judgment of the
preceding – consigning to oblivion the writers its predecessor most prized and cherishing those which it regarded as the least worthy. Contemporaneous criticism,
whether it be made of praise or blame, is poor stuff
indeed; all is unstable except genius, and genius is not
immediately recognizable even by the most capable and best
intentioned; its attributes have always remained undefinable. Yet there is a sin which the future pardons less
easily than any other – vacuousness and affectation for
the sincere is the kingdom of the future, and it seems to
me impossible to deny that 'The Master of Ballantrae' is
in exceeding degree vacuous and insincere.

120.   J. A. SYMONDS, FROM A LETTER TO H. F. BROWN

19 November 1889

From 'Letters of J. A. Symonds' (1969), iii, 410–11.
See headnote to No. 22.

I cannot say that I agree with you about 'The Master of
Ballantrae'. It has all Stevenson's power of style – but
the story is decrepit – does not go on four legs. There
is no reason assigned for the domination of that shadowy
and monstrous person, the Master, over his family. The
best thing in the book is the old steward's character. I
regard the book as an inartistic performance; feeble in
what it has been praised for – psychological analysis;

silly in its episodes of pirates and Indians, which
Stevenson does with a turn of the wrist and a large daub
of blood.   There is nothing in it so human as the dis-
agreement between Alan Breck and David Balfour on the
moor.

121. M. O. W. OLIPHANT, FROM THE OLD SALOON, 'BLACKWOOD'S
MAGAZINE'

November 1889, cxlvi, 696-702

Stevenson refers to this and a review of 'The Wrong Box'
in LS, iii, 151:

> Talking of 'Blackwood' - a file of which I was lucky
> enough to find here [Samoa] in the lawyer's - Mrs.
> Oliphant seems in a staggering state: from 'The Wrong
> Box' to 'The Master' I scarce recognise either my
> critic or myself.   I gather that 'The Master' should do
> well, and at least that notice is agreeable reading.

Mrs Oliphant had dealt harshly with 'The Wrong Box'.

... if we were then in a 'Wrong Box' with Mr Stevenson,
and almost angrily conscious of the fact that he had
deluded us by the loan of his name into that undignified
and unworthy exhibition, we are proportionately grateful
and joyful now to find him in his right mind, in a piece
of work which would do credit to any name.   Perhaps it is,
however, inappropriate to use the word joyful in any connection with the 'Master of Ballantrae'; for a tale of
more unmitigated gloom, with less admixture of any con-
solation human or divine, it has seldom been our lot to
read.   That it should have held the careless reader, who
loves adventure it is true, but still more loves sunshine and cheerfulness and a happy ending, through the
hard ordeal of serial publication, is a testimony to the
power of sheer genius and literary force such as we have
never known the like of.   We can but stand aside and
compliment the subscribers of the high-toned and valorous
American magazine in which this wonderful triumph has been
achieved.   They have shown that the writer of fiction, if

he be but strong enough, need think of none of the conventional requirements with which smaller hands are compelled
to recommend their art, and that neither a love story, nor
a heroine, nor a cheerful picture of human life, nor
indeed anything that can be called a picture of human life
at all, is necessary to him who has the power, and who has
attained such a sway over his audience as Mr Stevenson
has secured. We know nothing since the days of 'Caleb
Williams' which has equalled this achievement; nor indeed
do we know that Godwin's book, though it has become a
classic, actually mastered the interest of his contemporaries so as to be sought for by high and low, as this
book is. And in its first manifestation as a story published in parts it is entirely unique.

When Thackeray announced 'Pendennis' as a novel without
a hero, he was but playing with our credulity, and banter-
ing, as he loved to do, a faithful public, which indeed
did not at once believe in him, which was often mystified
and troubled in its growing faith, yet among which there
was always a remnant which understood what that great
genius would be at, and took his professions of cynicism
at their true value. Mr Stevenson makes no professions
of cynicism. It is perhaps one of the peculiarities of
an age which is no longer that of Thackeray, that such
professions are unnecessary, and that we are at present at
liberty to think as we please of our fellow-men without
attributing that bad opinion to any philosophical theory
or system. Fiction, like the other arts, is following new
laws, and we are reminded on all sides that one cycle is
over and another has begun to describe the unfailing round
which separates the ages.... Let us then with humility
study the art of fiction upon its new lines, and see what
is given us by the new school.

We have no sooner written these words, however, than we
cancel them; for Mr Stevenson can never be the founder,
or even leader, of a new school. There is nothing in his
art which can confer a new impulse. He may be copied, it
is true; but as the chief thing in him to be copied is
genius, and that is a thing incommunicable, we doubt
whether his imitators will ever attain any importance. It
is not that we should not all be the better of studying
that fine, transparent, and marvellously lucid style which
once was full of all manner of exquisite caprices and
mannerisms, as is the fashion of youth, but now has
settled down to its work as an incomparable medium for the
telling of a terrible story, self-corrected of all the
prettinesses which were becoming to lighter subjects, but
would be totally out of place in such as this - but only
that no mere style could commend the astonishingly painful

fables in which Mr Stevenson is most strong, without that
grip of power which must exist in the hand which exercises
it, and which no training can confer. To make such a
blood-curdling tale as that of Dr Jekyll and Mr Hyde the
model of a common art is impossible; the Thing, which is a
sort of horror far more potent than ever was that hideous
Frankenstein which once so much impressed our weak-minded
grandfathers, has been done - by sheer force of power, and
perhaps an awful moral suggestion in us, that something
true lies beneath the dreadful tale. But to attempt to
copy it would be much like the attempt, with a turnip and
a white sheet, to emulate the achievements of a real ghost
- a thing calculated to bring both ghosts and men about
the rash masker's ears. Mr Stevenson may teach his contemporaries an old but never worn-out lesson, that there
are more things in heaven and earth than have been yet
dreamt of by any philosophy, and may lead them to search
over again for themselves into the endless complications
of human relationship when stripped of all the glosses of
conventional representation, and even of natural feeling;
which will be partly good and partly bad, as most human
impulses are. For, after all, the conventional has, or it
could not continue, a certain commonplace of truth in it,
and natural feeling exists in the most curious persistency
even in hearts from which it seems banished; so that, on
the whole, whatever divergences may be permitted to an
original genius, the common bread-and-butter view is the
one most to be trusted, the more absolutely true. And
unless he could transmit that grip of which we have
spoken, which takes hold on us as with a hand of iron,
and no more will let us go than the Wedding Guest was let
go till the marvellous tale had come to an end, it will
never be in his power to form a school or to shape a new
development of fiction. To copy Dickens was not difficult, though it is an industry which has fallen very
low; and to copy Thackeray was possible, though the
results can scarcely be said to be desirable. We hesitate
- it is perhaps a weakness - to place Mr Stevenson on the
line with these two names. But it would be less possible
to copy him than either of these, and we hope that nobody
will try.
     There is something in the 'Master of Ballantrae' which
reminds us of what has always appeared to ourselves a
singularly ingenious suggestion made in one of his stray
pages of criticism (which were often so admirable) by the
great Christopher North, (1) whose countenance, formed
like Mars to threaten and command, looks down upon us from
the place of honour in this sanctuary where once his wit
sparkled and his wisdom flowed. He was 'under canvass' in

his old age, disporting himself less actively than his
wont upon the moors, or in the shallows of the brown and
golden Highland stream, when, in the evening after the
labours of the day, he began to discuss Shakespeare with
his companions. We are not aware whether these late
chapters have ever been republished. And there, not
without a flavour about, through the blue peat-smoke, and
the scent of the rustling heather, of a certain steaming
compound which had perhaps too much prevalence (in literature) in those days, the Professor gave forth his theory
of a certain thread of meaning which he thought he had
found in some of those great dramas which are our pride
and boast. Probably it was no more than a notion struck
out on the moment - one of those wandering lights that
gleam across the mind with a sort of dancing reflection
from the great light of poetry when we gaze into it, and
feel the dazzle mount into our brain. It was this - that
Shakespeare chose a certain relationship to form his tale
upon, contrasting it in different manifestations, the
good and the bad, the feeble and the strong, so as to
show that side of human nature in all its phases. No
doubt, in the special example given there might be some
truth in the idea - Hamlet and Laertes being, as the
critic showed, placed in a position almost entirely similar, both with a father's murder to avenge; while in the
case of Lear, the unnatural daughters Regan and Goneril
were contrasted not only with the too gentle Cordelia,
but with Edgar the slighted son, whose devotion to his
father was so undeserved - so that both sides of that
problem of human guilt and virtue, hesitation and promp-
titude, were set before the spectator. That Shakespeare's
mind might have found some thread of intention such as
this to form a fantastic guide through the necessary evo-
lutions of a plot, with that love for an ingenious pretence which belongs to the poet and the child, is possible
enough: although his subject became far too great for it,
and no one now would think of finding any balance to
Hamlet, the noblest of poetical conceptions, in the shallow cavalier with his conventional impulse of revenge, who
is the protagonist according to this interpretation. But
Wilson's suggestion is nevertheless a fine bit of literary
perception, and very pleasing to the fanciful reader.
     The 'Master of Ballantrae' follows in some degree this
theory of construction. It is a story of the relationship
between two brothers, kept with great austerity of purpose
wholly within the lines of its selected ground, but without any contrasting group of beings more happily inspired
to relieve the reader's mind - a characteristic which
increases the intensity of the tale. The brothers

themselves are indeed contrasted in a remarkable way,
especially in the beginning of the story; but there is no
Edgar to make us aware that hatred is not the rule of
family life, or that relentings of the heart may still
come in, however desperate may be the impulse of fraternal
opposition. From beginning to end the two brothers of
Durrisdeer hate each other with boundless and unchangeable
animosity. There is no relenting on either side, - even
less perhaps on that of the virtuous and otherwise tender-
hearted brother than on that of the reprobate. We are
made indeed to feel that his utter odiousness, falsehood,
and selfishness have been revealed with such pitiless dis-
tinctness, that Henry hates the incarnation of every evil
quality in James, whereas the other only hates his
brother's person and the advantages of position which are
in his eyes stolen from himself. The better hater in this
way is the better man, who feels nothing but bitter disappointment when he finds that he has not as he thought
killed the Master, not alloyed even with a grain of satisfaction that his has not been the hand to shed his
brother's blood. We are not, indeed, even when most
carried on by the stream of events and excited by the
sombre occurrences and wonderful pictures of the story,
allowed at any time fully to approve, much less to entertain a thorough sympathy for the virtuous brother. No one
in the group, indeed, except perhaps the teller of the
tale, the subdued yet distinct personality of Ephraim
Mackellar, the steward, secretary, and *doer* of the house,
attracts our sympathy. The old lord is a pathetic figure,
and the unfortunate lady who stands between the two
brothers has traces of sense and spirit did it suit the
narrator to keep her less determinedly in the background,
but we can fix no affection on either. And the servants
in the house, the country people, the dim society in the
background, gentlemen and clowns, are all alike detestable. There is no generosity or kindness among them. Not
one, until there comes into the house the keen-sighted
spectator Mackellar, whose wits are marvellously sharpened
(as always occurs in fiction) by the fact that he is bound
to see through and record everything, does justice to
Henry. He is always pushed aside by his own family, slan-
dered outside, his every act misconstrued. This is perhaps one reason why the atmosphere of the book is so
gloomy. There are abundance of beautiful sketches of
Durrisdeer and the surrounding country. But in the story
itself the sun never shines, the air is lowering and omi-
nous, a constant consciousness of calamity, of wrong and
injustice, brooding over the house.
    In the midst of this gloom, however, the two prominent

figures revealed to us are masterly. The family has
secured itself by an expedient not unusual, though very
undignified, among the gentry of England and Scotland at
the period, one son going 'out' with Prince Charles, the
other keeping allegiance with the Government, so that
whoever won, the race might be safe, and its lands and
titles. This is how, though Henry becomes Lord Durrisdeer, his elder brother is still Master of Ballantrae.
The elder brother, however, is the rebel not from any
chivalrous principle nor faith in the Jacobite cause (for
which neither of them would seem to have cared the least),
but for vanity and restless ambition which prompted him to
run the risk - great as it was - with a hope of self-
aggrandisement not to be obtained in any other way. The
very key-note is thus struck in a sordid tone. In other
instances when this expedient was resorted to, we have
always been accustomed to believe that some sort of political principle, some tradition of loyalty to the fallen
race, was in the background; whereas, according to Mr
Stevenson, there was here none. The Master of Ballantrae
is thus, even when he risks his life for it, without faith
or principle, a mere interested adventurer. He is afterwards a vulgar traitor betraying his friends to the
Government, sucking the very life-blood of his family by
a pretence of danger which no longer exists for him, - a
pirate on the seas, by land a *chevalier de l'industrie*,
living by his wits wherever he goes, betraying everybody
that trusts him: he is full of taunt and intolerable mockery, a man with the gift of driving others almost mad with
his tongue, as well as of putting a remorseless knife into
them with the greatest coolness if they happen to come in
his way. This monster is, however, the most charming and
delightful of men. He is gay and polished and debonair;
he has every social gift, and, in addition to everything
else, a perception of character and of goodness, a sense
of what is noble and generous, which is difficult to realise as existing together with so many bad qualities.
Thus, when Ephraim Mackellar, in a sudden madness of
impatience with the smiling devil before him, makes a
wild thrust at him to push him overboard, the Master so
comprehends and respects his sudden exasperation as to
bear no malice, but laughs, and declares that he likes
him all the better; even while Mackellar, full of miserable compunctions, cannot forgive himself for the frenzied
impulse. We have had many gay prodigals before who
injured and swindled all their belongings, yet never lost
the power of charming and deceiving. It is indeed quite a
common character in fiction. But there is something in
the Master's charm which is original, as is his depravity.

It deceives nobody, for he becomes odious and the most
intolerable of burdens even to the father who spoilt him,
and the woman who loved him; but, on the other hand, the
good Mackellar, who detests him cordially, finds a variety
and companionableness in the fellow-traveller whom he is
forced to accompany which almost makes up to him for the
horror of a wintry voyage. This paradox has in it a
strange humanity which raises it infinitely above the
usual haunting spectre of the wicked son.

We are compelled to doubt, however, whether anything
so odious as the Master could have retained in his down-
fall and deterioration any such reality of original
brightness – and this not by an effort or for a purpose
of evil: for he captivates Mackellar when it is entirely
useless to do so, not with the object of making a tool of
him, but in mere – to use such a word – wantonness of
good-nature and pleasure in pleasing. 'You could not have
been so bad a man if you had not had all the machinery of
a good one,' says Ephraim, not with Mr Stevenson's usual
felicity of phrase; but the mixture of this curious fascination and of a strain of never quite extirpated noble-
ness in what is, taking it altogether, the most odious
character in modern fiction, is one of the most remarkable
conceptions of a ruined angel which has ever been given to
the world.

Henry, the good brother, is scarcely less remarkable in
his way, though he is less attractive. He is, to start
with, 'a good solid lad,' without the qualities of the
elder son, the family backbone and stand-by sacrificing
everything to keep up its credit and save its honour, but
so self-restrained in his Scotch *dourness*, and so little
apt to show his better side, that not even those who are
most deeply indebted to him recognise his worth; and no
one, indeed, except the clear-sighted steward, fully
understands either the noble integrity and generosity of
his character, or the sufferings which he bears so un-
complainingly. We think Mr Stevenson errs in making Henry
so completely misunderstood. He despises the commonalty
too much to give them a chance of showing how the race,
sooner or later, always does recognise a good man. We
cannot think it is possible that an upright and honourable
person, however *dour*, could have completely escaped the
perceptions of his neighbours, and remained through all
the years of his manhood, the victim of a general misconception. Henry is, indeed, unspeakably *dour*. He is magnanimous in every act, but in feeling never relents,
always regarding his brother with remorseless antipathy.
The shock of disappointment which is his only feeling when
he ascertains that he has not killed him in the wild,

sudden duel which takes place between them in the dark
shrubbery in the dead of night, by the light of two candles which flare on steadily over the ghastly scene, the
pool of blood, the fallen body - is utterly unlike anything which we remember in fiction. It may be true to
nature in such exceptional circumstances, though stubborn
prejudice insists in our bosom that he should have been in
some degrees relieved as well as disappointed by his failure. Hatred, however, grows between the two by every
meeting, along with, on the side of the innocent, a certain horror of belief in the wicked Master as in a man
who walks the world protected by his infamy, - a man whom
nothing can kill, in diabolical armour, sustained by all
the powers of darkness. Henry's deterioration under this
fixed idea, the madness produced in him by his brother's
persecution, the horrible way in which his imagination and
every thought are chained to the movements of his enemy,
is deeply tragic, though so painful that we would fain
struggle against it, and declare it to be impossible and
untrue. In this respect Mr Stevenson must bear the brunt
of his own singular tragic power, - for our heart revolts
at the remorseless purpose which enfolds the good man in a
web of such despair. The two brothers are thus brought at
the end of their protracted struggle almost to an equality
in guilt as well as misery for it is Henry who at last in
his madness hires the villanous crew who drive his brother
to desperation; and they die together in a supreme horror,
in the intense and unyielding hatred which unites them
like love.
     Ephraim Mackellar the steward, the excellent, scrupu-
lous, timid, all-observant, and all-understanding retainer, is so good and so true that we almost regret the
absorbing interest which makes it well-nigh impossible to
do justice to him. And we observe that there are some
critics who give a high place to the Irishman, the Chevalier Burke, who interposes a chapter or two of his experiences to clear up points on which Mackellar could not be
informed, and whose description of the pirate and the
horrible scenes on board is admirably effective; but these
are usually critics who cannot disabuse themselves of the
idea that Mr Stevenson's book must be a book more or less
for boys. We trust that this sombre tragedy will for ever
do away with that delusion. It is very strong meat for
men, - too strong, we fear, for many gentle readers to
whom its almost unbroken gloom, and the struggle of these
spirits in pain from the first word to the last of their
story, will prove a reversal of all they look for in fiction - the soothing, the repose, the mild excitement, the
happy end. Here all is uncompromising, tragic, and

terrible, a deadly struggle all through, ending in a scene
which for impressive horror has few equals in anything we
know.   Mr Stevenson scarcely unbends enough to permit his
fascinated reader here and there a laugh.   Humour is subdued, and fun is not in this winter's tale.   He does not
intend to cheer our hearts, but to congeal our blood.   And
we can well conceive that to a young reader, who has perhaps a long and ghostly corridor to traverse with his
candle ere he (or she) gets to bed, after that last vision
of the Master's waxen countenance with the week's beard
which has grown in his living grave, there will be awful
possibilities of that face gleaming out upon him as he
goes, from the next dark corner, which will add to the
story a fearful delight.

We must add that the Scotch of Mr Ephraim Mackellar is
a pleasure to hear.   With scarcely an apostrophe from
beginning to end, with no broken dialect or words *estro-
piés*, the purity of a grave and dignified language which
is English with a difference, has never been more admirably exemplified.   The writer never for a moment loses his
nationality; but it is not by letters cut off, or apos-
trophes added, that he makes it visible.   The construction, the flavour of his language, the individuality of
idiom and form, are infinitely more characteristic than
any amount of eccentric spelling or provincial broken
words.

Note

1   John Wilson (1785-1854), author and professor of moral
    philosophy at Edinburgh, figured as 'Christopher North'
    in his Noctes Ambrosianae, which he contributed to
    'Blackwood's Magazine'.

'Ballads'

December 1890

122. R. H. HUTTON, UNSIGNED REVIEW, 'SPECTATOR'

3 January 1891, lxvi, 17-18

On Hutton see headnote to No. 48.   For Stevenson's comment
on this review, see No. 126a.

There is something wanting in Mr. Stevenson's work as a
poet, and we believe it to be that idealising gleam of insight which gives wholeness of effect, and especially
satisfying finish of effect, to the subjects treated.
There is not one of these ballads which does not leave the
reader with a sense of disappointment, or even of want.
And yet now and then Mr. Stevenson seems to pass from the
mere vivid narrator of life and action into the poet.
Only he never sustains the poetic glow for long together;
and, what is more, he never binds the whole ballad together by the significance (romantic or otherwise) which
he gives to its whole drift and the impression it leaves
behind.   For example, in The Song of Rahero: a Legend of
Tahiti, which is the first ballad in the book, there is
plenty of vigour, plenty of movement, plenty of keen external vision, but there is no wholeness uniting the
separate parts; - the hero of the concluding part being
the cunning and cruel trickster of the opening part, and
having no concern at all with the intermediate part.   Then
the wholesale butchery of which the King Hiopa is guilty,
is left quite unaccounted for by the mere thirst of one
woman who has no special relations with him, for wreaking
vengeance on a particular act of selfish cruelty which

369

involved only one person. Indeed, Mr. Stevenson gives us
no notion at all why the mother of the murdered lad gains
so much influence over the chief of an alien tribe as to
persuade him to devise a plan for burning a clan of no
less than eight hundred persons, - men, women, and children, - one great holocaust. Doubtless such acts of reckless butchery are committed amongst men in the stage of
civilisation or barbarism in which Tahiti was at the time
of the legend; but then, they are not proper subjects for
a poem until they are in some adequate way made intelligible by being connected with the recognised passions of
men. And Mr. Stevenson shows us no such connection,
except in the case of the one woman who incites King Hiopa
to his treacherous and sweeping deed of massacre. Perhaps
the finest and most truly poetical passage in this little
volume of ballads is that in which the mood of Támatéa's
mother changes from that of despair at her son's murder to
that of thirst for vengeance: -

[Quotes from the Song of Rahéro, part ii: 'But the mother
of Támatéa arose with death in her eyes' to 'Carrying
death in her breast and sharpening death with her hand'.]

That is fine poetry, and the passage describing the pause
before the burst of the hurricane is worthy of Scott, or
even of Homer; but then there is very little, perhaps
nothing else, in the book equal to it. For the most part,
Mr. Stevenson is content with the outward adventure he describes, and passes over the motives and passions of men
so lightly, that there is no wholeness, no singleness of
conception, in his ballads. The Feast of Famine is very
inferior even to The Song of Rahero, not only in this but
in all other respects. The tale is not so lucidly told,
and the close of it is feeble and ineffective. The only
fine passage, indeed, is the description of the fanatic
priest and his vigil.
    Again, in Ticonderoga, the well-known legend in which a
Stewart pledges his word to a Cameron to give him protection against the avenger of blood, and afterwards finds
that the blood to be avenged is that of his own brother,
and that he himself should have been the avenger, but none
the less is faithful to his word, and thereby kindles the
anger of the dead brother, who presents himself to him in
sleep, and assures him that at Ticonderoga he himself
shall die, and meet once more the spirits of the kindred
whom he has offended by adhering to his pledge, Mr. Stevenson disappoints us profoundly. He makes the whole
ballad turn on the riddle and mystery of the name, -
which proves eventually to be the name given by the Red

Indians to one of the American villages in which the
English troops have to encounter the hostile Indian
tribes.   But that is a very thin subject for a ballad.
Surely the mere fact that at that time the name was unknown, and supposed to be revealed by the presence of a
disembodied spirit, would not have filled the denounced
Stewart with so much dread that he would have mused on
nothing but the name, which is what is here described.
Surely he would have had something to say to himself as
to the merits of the controversy with his dead brother,
and would have asserted not only his own right, but his
obligation to keep the promise he had made, even though
it did imply his surrender of the function of the avenger.
Yet Mr. Stevenson never even touches on this aspect of the
question, and makes the whole significance of the ballad
turn on the mystery of a name.   Heather Ale: a Galloway
Legend, is, again, either a very poor theme, or is so
treated as to become a poor theme for a ballad.   Christmas
at Sea is better, and strikes us as having real power in
its way; but on the whole, Mr. Stevenson's ballads have
disappointed us.   He does not give any poetical integrity
to his subjects.   The action, when action is described,
is vigorously and vividly described; but the adventure
overpowers the motive, and the resulting effect is one of
adventure pieced together in verse.   And seeing how high
Mr. Stevenson can rise into the region of poetry when he
has mused sufficiently on his theme, this is necessarily
a disappointment to the reader.

123.   A. C. SWINBURNE, FROM A LETTER TO LADY JANE
HENRIETTA SWINBURNE

4 January 1891

From 'The Swinburne Letters' (1962), ed. Cecil Y. Lang,
vi, 2.

If you don't know the legend of Ticonderoga, I think you
will be as much excited by it as I, who consider it one of
the very best supernatural stories on record, and not
badly told this time in verse.   I also like the close of
the last poem, Christmas at Sea - and the Pacific Island
stories are at all events new and curious.

124.   COSMO MONKHOUSE, REVIEW, 'ACADEMY'

31 January 1891, xxxix, 108-9

William Cosmo Monkhouse (1840-1901) was a civil servant,
poet, and critic whose literary and art criticism appeared
in the 'Magazine of Art' (when Henley was its editor), the
'Saturday Review' and the 'Academy'.

One is tempted to believe that Mr. Stevenson was not quite
in earnest, if in earnest at all, when he wrote and published the first two of these remarkable ballads.   It is
not because the versification is so very indifferent, for,
despite the delightful sparrow-flights in 'The Children's
Garden,' and many noble verses in 'Underwoods,' it was
always evident that his mastery of metre was imperfect and
not unlikely to break down on a longer and more exacting
exercise.   But in these ballads there are infelicities of
expression and defects of style which it is hard to
believe that the author of 'Kidnapped' could have allowed
to remain in any work of his, whether in prose or verse,
except by way of a joke.   It is not, in a word, the technical imperfections nor even the defective music that is
most astonishing in these ballads, but the fact that one
of the finest literary instincts in the world should fail
its possessor so often and in passages of so great importance.

   For instance, Rahèro, the hero of the first ballad,
wakes to the fact that his treacherous enemies have set
fire to the banqueting house in which they are sleeping
off the effects of a debauch, and that he is the only one
of his tribe who is not stupefied by drink and smoke.   He
immediately tries to find and wake his family, and Mr.
Stevenson can find no fitter phrases than these to describe the way he did it: -

   Rahèro stooped and groped. *He handled his*
     womankind;
   But the fumes of the fire and the kava had
     quenched the life of their mind.

Scarcely more elegant is the description of one of the
sacred spots in the island:

> And now was he come to a place Taiárapu,
>   honoured the most,
> Where a silent valley of woods debouched on
>   the noisy coast
> Spewing a level river. There was a haunt of
>   Pai.

Nor less surprising in the work of such an author is the number of involved and 'squinting' constructions, such as

> Strong in the wind in his manhood;

or

> To bind what gods unkindly have sundered into
>   one;

or

> The holiday village careened to the wind and
>   was gone from view
> Swift as a passing bird; and ever as onward it
>   bore,
> Like the cry of the passing bird, bequeathed its
>   song to the shore.

But of all the errors of literary judgment which Mr. Stevenson commits in these unfortunate poems none is more frequent and marked than the introduction of fine words in the midst of the otherwise homely texture of his verse. This is sometimes unhappy enough in narrative passages, as when he writes of the 'emulous crowd' and the 'sedulous fisher,' or tells us that 'copious smoke was conceived; but it becomes absolutely ludicrous when it occurs in the passionate exclamations of savages. Hiopa has a vision in which the roof-tree of his enemies 'decays and falls on the empty lodge, and the winds *subvert deserted walls*,' and the Mother of Támatéa, in the exultation of her revenge, apostrophises the fire as the '*debited* vengeance of God,' bids her enemies 'hark, in your dying ears, the song of the conflagration'; and tells them that '*the smoke of your dissolution* darkens the stars of night.'

But Rahéro is a finer poem than the Feast of Famine which follows, and it has no little interest as a contribution to folklore. Rahéro, savage though he be, is of the stuff of which legendary heroes are made. A man who, escaping from a conflagration in which every man, woman, and child of his tribe except himself have been burnt alive, can instantly plan how to begin it all over again,

is no common person. To kill a fisherman on the shore and
make off with his boat and his wife is, so to speak, the
work of a moment for such a man as Rahèro. This is really
the core of the legend, and is the only part of it in
which Mr. Stevenson's imagination has been seriously
interested. The verse in which this last adventure is
described is certainly not free from flaw, but it is full
of life and strength, and does much to redeem the rest of
the ballad. As he gets into the boat the fisherman's
wife mistakes him for her murdered husband and speaks to
him, but

[Quotes from The Song of Rahéro, part iii: 'Never a word
Rahéro replied' to 'And sure he was none that she knew,
none of her country or clan'.]

Here, at least, the scene is fully felt and the verse
is sustained by the force of uninterrupted passion.
Faults the passage has; but, if all the rest were equal
to it, there would not have been so much reason to regret
the valuable time which has been wasted on the composition of this ballad. But in any case there would have
been sad waste, for Mr. Stevenson should have a higher
ambition than to be the Walter Scott of Tahiti or even
the Homer of the Cannibal Islands. Besides these tales of
the South Sea, the volume contains Mr. Stevenson's spirited ballad of Ticonderoga, reprinted from 'Scribner's,'
and two short poems, one of which, Christmas at Sea, is
in Mr. Stevenson's best manner, and altogether delightful.

125.   EDMUND GOSSE, FROM A LETTER TO G. A. ARMOUR

31 January 1891

From 'Life and Letters of Sir Edmund Gosse' (1931),
ed. Evan Charteris, 225.
    In April Stevenson wrote to Gosse asking for his opin-
ion of the 'Ballads' (see No. 126b). To my knowledge
Gosse was never to express that opinion to him. The
'South Sea Letters', actually entitled 'The South Seas',
were to appear serially (February-December 1891) in 'Black
and White' and the New York 'Sun'. George Alison Armour
was an American bibliophile and patron of letters.

What do you think of Stevenson's 'Ballads'?   I confess we
are all disappointed here.   The effort to become a Polynesian Walter Scott is a little too obvious, the inspiration a little too mechanical.   And - between you and me
and Lake Michigan - the versification is atrocious.   Nor
is his prose above reproach.   There has been a good deal
of disappointment among the few who have read the
approaching 'South Sea Letters'.   The fact seems to be
that it is very nice to *live* in Samoa, but not healthy to
write there.   Within a three-mile radius of Charing Cross
is the literary atmosphere, I suspect.

126.   STEVENSON, FROM LETTERS TO H. B. BAILDON AND EDMUND
GOSSE

Spring 1891

(a) From a letter to Baildon dated by Colvin spring 1891.
H. Bellyse Baildon had been Stevenson's schoolmate at
Edinburgh and was later a lecturer in English literature
at the University of Vienna and subsequently at Dundee
College; he afterwards wrote 'Robert Louis Stevenson.
A Life Study in Criticism' (1901).

... Glad the 'Ballads' amused you.   They failed to entertain a coy public, at which I wondered; not that I set
much account by my verses, which are the verses of Prosa-
tor; but I do know how to tell a yarn, and two of the
yarns are great.   'Rahéro' is for its length a perfect
folk-tale: savage and yet fine, full of tailforemost morality, ancient as the granite rocks; if the historian, not
to say the politician, could get that yarn into his head,
he would have learned some of his A B C.   But the average
man at home cannot understand antiquity; he is sunk over
the ears in Roman civilisation; and a tale like that of
'Rahéro' falls on his ears inarticulate.   The 'Spectator'
[No. 122] said there was no psychology in it; that interested me much: my grandmother (as I used to call that able
paper, and an able paper it is, and a fair one) cannot so
much as observe the existence of savage psychology when
it is put before it.   I am at bottom a psychologist and
ashamed of it; the tale seized me one-third because of its
picturesque features, two-thirds because of its astonishing psychology, and the 'Spectator' says there's none.   I

am going on with a lot of island work ['The South Seas'],
exulting in the knowledge of a new world, 'a new created
world' and new men; and I am sure my income will **DECLINE**
and **FALL** off; for the effort of comprehension is death to
the intelligent public, and sickness to the dull.   (LS,
iii, 246-7)

(b) Stevenson, from a letter to Gosse dated April 1891.
For Gosse's opinion of the 'Ballads' see No. 125.

By the by, my 'Ballads' seem to have been dam bad; all the
crickets sing so in their crickety papers; and I have no
ghost of an idea on the point myself: verse is always to
me the unknowable. You might tell me how it strikes a
professional bard: not that it really matters, for, of
course, good or bad, I don't think I shall get into *that*
galley any more. But I should like to know if you join
the shrill chorus of the crickets. The crickets are the
devil in all to you: 'tis a strange thing, they seem to
rejoice like a strong man in their injustice. (LS, iii,
262)

'Across the Plains'

April 1892

The twelve essays collected in this volume had appeared earlier in the following periodicals:

Across the Plains ('Longman's Magazine', July and August 1880)
The Old Pacific Capital ('Fraser's Magazine', November 1880)
Fontainebleau ('Magazine of Art', May and June 1884)
Epilogue to 'An Inland Voyage' ('Scribner's Magazine', August 1888)
Random Memories: The Coast of Fife (as Contributions to the History of Fife, 'Scribner's Magazine', October 1888)
Random Memories: The Education of an Engineer ('Scribner's Magazine', November 1888)
The Lantern Bearers ('Scribner's Magazine', February 1888)
A Chapter on Dreams ('Scribner's Magazine', January 1888)
Beggars ('Scribner's Magazine', March 1888)
Letter to a Young Gentleman ('Scribner's Magazine', September 1888)
Pulvis et Umbra ('Scribner's Magazine', April 1888)
A Christmas Sermon ('Scribner's Magazine', December 1888)

127.   STEVENSON, FROM LETTERS TO COLVIN AND ADELAIDE BOODLE

1887, 1888, 1891

(a) From a letter to Colvin dated by him December 1887. Shortly after Stevenson's arrival in the USA in 1887, he accepted Scribner's offer of $3,500 for twelve magazine

articles. These appeared in 'Scribner's Magazine', one
each month, during 1888; nine of the twelve essays were
reprinted in 'Across the Plains'. 'Smith opens out' is
quoted from Burns's Holy Fair: 'Smith opens out his cauld
harangues.' The Rev. George Smith was Stevenson's great-
grandfather on his mother's side; according to Colvin this
line was quoted 'against Stevenson himself, in his didactic moods ... when [friends] wished to tease him' (LS,
iii, 34).

I get along with my papers for Scribner not fast, nor so
far specially well; only this last, the fourth one (which
makes a third part of my whole task), I do believe is
pulled off after a fashion. It is a mere sermon: 'Smith
opens out'; but it is true, and I find it touching and
beneficial, to me at least; and I think there is some fine
writing in it, some very apt and pregnant phrases. Pulvis
et Umbra, I call it; I might have called it a Darwinian
Sermon, if I had wanted. Its sentiments, although parson-
ic, will not offend even you, I believe. The other three
papers, I fear, bear many traces of effort, and the un-
genuine inspiration of an income at so much per essay, and
the honest desire of the incomer to give good measure for
his money. Well, I did my damndest anyway. (LS, iii, 34)

(b) From a letter to Miss Adelaide Boodle, dated by Colvin
April 1888. Miss Boodle had been a friend and neighbour
of the household at Skerryvore. She was asked to keep an
eye on the house and to report on it from time to time.
In her correspondence with Stevenson, she is referred to
as the Gamekeeper and he as the Squire.

I wrote a paper the other day - Pulvis et Umbra; - I wrote
it with great feeling and conviction: to me it seemed
bracing and healthful, it is in such a world (so seen by
me), that I am very glad to fight out my battle, and see
some fine sunsets, and hear some excellent jests between
whiles round the camp fire. But I find that to some
people this vision of mine is a nightmare, and extin-
guishes all ground of faith in God or pleasure in man.
Truth I think not so much of; for I do not know it. And
I could wish in my heart that I had not published this
paper, if it troubles folk too much: all have not the same
digestion, nor the same sight of things. And it came over
me with special pain that perhaps this article (which I
was at the pains to send to her) might give dismalness to
my *Gamekeeper at Home*. Well, I cannot take back what I
have said; but yet I may add this. If my view be anything
but the nonsense that it may be - to me it seems self-

evident and blinding truth - surely of all things it makes
this world holier. There is nothing in it but the moral
side - but the great battle and the breathing times with
their refreshments. I see no more and no less. And if
you look again, it is not ugly, and it is filled with
promise.
    Pray excuse a desponding author for this apology....
(LS, iii, 54-5)

(c) From a letter to Colvin dated 25 November 1891.
Colvin, speaking of the essays in 'Across the Plains', had
said, in a note appended to that volume, 'the lights seem
a little turned down'.

I agree with you the lights seem a little turned down.
The truth is, I was far through (if you understand Scots),
and came none too soon to the South Seas, where I was to
recover peace of body and mind. No man but myself knew
all my bitterness in those days. Remember that, the next
time you think I regret my exile. And however low the
lights are, the stuff is true, and I believe the more
effective; after all, what I wish to fight is the best
fought by a rather cheerless presentation of the truth.
The world must return some day to the word duty, and be
done with the word reward. There are no rewards, and
plenty duties. And the sooner a man sees that and acts
upon it like a gentleman or a fine old barbarian, the
better for himself. (LS, iii, 311-12)

128. AN UNSIGNED REVIEW, 'SCOTTISH LEADER'

14 April 1892

The question is not one of the oldest in criticism, and
at anyrate it is one that the critic is often tempted to
ask himself - Will Mr R. L. Stevenson take his definite
and final place in English literature as a writer of
essays or of novels? As a poet we may more summarily dispose of him, for the 'Underwoods' and the 'Child's
Garden of Verses,' bright though they are, and fragrant
enough, have yet no kinship of species with Sappho's high
Pierian flower. It is in the field of prose - not necessarily a kitchen garden - that Mr Stevenson's real work

has been done, and under his culture certainly that field
is as far as may be from a mere place of pot herbs. Im-
passioned prose, as De Quincey called it, imaginative
prose, or fanciful, as it may be termed more properly -
this is what the author of 'Virginibus Puerisque' and
'Treasure Island' has given us. But is it the one or the
other of these books that marks its author's true strength
and vocation? - is it among the romancers, with Scott and
Dumas, that Mr Stevenson will stand, or among the essayists, the pleasant prattlers and gossips of literature,
with Montaigne and Addison and Lamb? Is the volume of
sketches (reprinted most of them) which has just been
issued under the title of 'Across the Plains' by Messrs
Chatto & Windus, more significant of the writer's merits
than, say, 'The Master of Ballantrae'?

Everywhere of course in Mr Stevenson's work the imaginative quality is conspicuous, and in his novels not seldom
it rises to the rank that is loosely yet intelligibly
enough termed creative. Long John Silver and Alan Breck
are figures quite as vivid in their way as Dirk Hutteraick
and D'Artagnan, nor are there many scenes more animated
than that of the fight, for example, in the round-house in
Captain Elias Hoseason's ship. To a certain section of
the public, perhaps the 'Strange Case of Dr Jekyll and Mr
Hyde' appears the most characteristic work of Mr Stevenson
and the most brilliant, but the author himself probably
would not be much flattered by the reasons which that
highly respectable class of his readers would give. To
them it seemed that in Mr Stevenson they had found an unexpected moralist, as in Dr Jekyll certainly they had discovered a very obvious moral, and a tale which, as
Mr Henry James said of 'Madame Bovary,' might without
impropriety be printed as a Sunday School tract. As
moralist, however, Mr Stevenson is no more all-compelling
than he is as poet, and among his imaginative creations
the duplicate doctor will hardly outlive that tale of the
wanderings of David Balfour. After all, however, one, or
even two, good novels do not necessarily make a novelist,
par excellence; it has to be shown also that they so domi-
nate and eclipse the rest of his work as to make fiction-
writing the feature of that which first catches and last
keeps our regard. Thackeray wrote poems, yet in the
record of English literature he is not a poet, but a
novelist. Lamb, too, wrote poetry, yet he is an essayist
once for all. Indeed, nearly every man of any imaginative
and literary power tries all these three kinds of literature, and his definite and abiding place in letters is
determined by the proportion of merit and of bulk too (for
bulk indirectly is not insignificant) which these different kinds receive in treatment at his hands. Mr Stevenson
is at the least as versatile as most men of like eminence

in his craft, and if one thinks that on the whole and in
the long run he shows and endures as an essayist rather
than a novelist, the reason must be that while his fiction
is sound and brilliant beyond all question, the best part
of his work, nevertheless, and the most part, has been
done in the region of desultory imaginative prose.

In the essays now published there is much to justify
the conviction of those who hold this belief, much to
refresh the admirers of 'Virginibus Puerisque' and 'Memories and Portraits,' and to confirm them in their admiration. The opening sketch, which gives its title to the
volume, is an account of Mr Stevenson's experiences in an
emigrant train between New York and San Francisco, and
affords perhaps one of the best examples of the author's
egotistically gossipping style. A delightful egotist is
Mr Stevenson - as entertaining in a way as Montaigne himself, although he is quite the antithesis of Montaigne in
his self-consciousness. Always there is a deal of deliberate posing in the personal talk of the voyager along the
canals of Northern France, and on the moorlands of the
Cévennes. Mr Stevenson may have been as limp as possible
in that shed on the quays of New York; he may have been as
disreputable as he pleased before the Commissary of
Châtillon-sur-Loire, but in his account, at least, of
these experiences he seems as carefully draped in his
shabby garments as ever Chatham was in his bandages and
flannel. To make a literary effect is his object above
all things - or that at least is the impression which the
reader carries away from him - and to achieve that end one
feels that the writer's own personality is freely and
studiously utilised. What justifies it all is, of course,
that about the effect there is nothing vulgar; an air of
delicate mockery saves everything, and we close the book,
knowing that Mr Stevenson, to give us a charming essay,
has been exploiting and exaggerating himself, and laughing
at himself, too, and at us all the time.

To make a literary effect - that is Mr Stevenson's
object, and he avows it in the most un-English fashion,
and utterly without shame. That the matter of literature
is all-important, and the manner of it only secondary and
trivial by comparison, that the aim and the duty of an
author is to improve his readers, to inform and educate
them, and only in a side way as it were, and a casual, to
delight - this has been the creed for the most part of the
British literary man. Mr Stevenson's theory is almost the
direct reverse of this. To him words are what colours are
to the painter, and the handling of them in literary fashion is essentially a kind of decoration. The meaning, of
course, is not unimportant, an author must not talk nonsense, nor must he speak commonplace if possible - but at
least he must not speak it in a commonplace way. For that

after all is the main thing – to utter thoughts which
maybe have been uttered a thousand times before, in a
manner which is new and striking, to speak common things
in a way of your own, *proprie communica dicere*, to
acquire, in short, a style. With a style the literary man
is fairly well equipped, even though he have no science
and no philosophy to speak of, for in the first place he
has the technique of his craft, and then in the second he
has learned so much else in acquiring that technique. For
a style is not acquired without long study, that takes a
man all over the field of literature, and that, besides
supplying him with a fund of erudition, gives him also the
liberality of mind that such studies traditionally confer.

Such, at least, seems to be Mr Stevenson's doctrine,
and in the practice of it he has certainly acquired a distinct and notable style of his own. There is no doubt of
it, Mr Stevenson is one of the stylists of English literature – perhaps not one of the great stylists, not one of
the heavy weights, if a vulgar metaphor may be allowed for
a moment, but a stylist rather of wonderful lightness and
grace. One does not put him beside such various masters
of their art as Landor and Newman and Ruskin, nor along
with Browne and Hooker and the other worthies of old time.
To be a great stylist, after all, one must have great
thoughts – and Mr Stevenson's thinking for the most part
is merely ingenious and graceful. At times the ingenuity
becomes mere smartness, it is true; at times the grace is
touched with affectation, yet the former are the essential
qualities of his style, the latter only the occasional
defects. As an example of the observant power that has
so much to do with Mr Stevenson's imaginative force, as
indeed it has to do with all imagination, and not less as
an instance of his skill in verbal effects, the following
sentence that describes the coast of Caithness is perhaps
as representative as any that could be culled: – 'The
plateau broke down to the North Sea in formidable cliffs,
the tall outstacks rose like pillars ringed about with
surf, the coves were over-brimmed with clamorous froth,
the sea-birds screamed, the wind sang in the thyme on the
cliff's edge; here and there small ancient castles top-
pled on the brim; here and there it was possible to dip
into a dell of shelter, where you might lie and tell yourself you were a little warm and hear (near at hand) the
whin-pods bursting in the afternoon sun, and (farther off)
the rumour of the turbulent sea.' Of this same kind of
writing we have had much from Mr Stevenson already, yet
hardly any example that will surpass this. More unusual
in him are the imaginative pages of Pulvis et Umbra, an
essay that strikes a higher tone than any perhaps that has
come hitherto from its author's pen. There may be differ-

ence of opinion about the perfect taste of the passage in
which Mr Stevenson gives a poetically ingenious interpretation of the spring of life on our planet - some thinking
perhaps that it too much recalls Burke's tape-worm metaphors - but there can be little dispute about its power.
'This stuff,' so runs the passage, 'when not purified by
the lustration of fire, rots uncleanly into something we
call life; seized through all its atoms with a pediculous
malady; swelling in tumours that become independent, sometimes even (by an abhorrent prodigy) locomotory; one
splitting into millions, millions cohering into one, as
the malady proceeds through varying stages.... Meanwhile
our rotatory island, loaded with predatory life, and more
drenched with blood, animal and vegetable, than ever
mutinied ship, sends through space with unimaginable
speed, and turns alternate cheeks to the reverberation of
a blazing world, ninety million miles away.' In his prefatory letter Mr Sidney Colvin makes a half apology for
these and other sentences on the last pages of the book as
'written under circumstances of especial gloom and sickness,' when Mr Stevenson sailed for the South Sea. If so,
one can only say that wisdom, like the gloom and sickness
are not unjustified of their children. After all, however, it is not mainly in such flights that we recognise
that Mr Stevenson with whom a score of delightful volumes
have made us familiar. It is in the 'Random Memories'
rather of Bob Brown and the bleak moors of Caithness, and
the nights of desperate literary toil in Anstruther, in
the pictures of the bandit-like boys at North Berwick, and
the beggar who talked about 'Keats - John Keats, Sir,' and
the other 'fine poets.' In these and the hundred other
sketches like them Mr Stevenson has added to our literature a wealth of dainty vignettes which, even if all his
more ambitious pictures were forgotten, would suffice to
give him an honoured place.

129. WILLIAM ARCHER, FROM MR. STEVENSON'S NEW BOOK, 'PALL
MALL GAZETTE'

20 April 1892, liv, 3

This review in letter form should be read in conjunction
with Archer's earlier assessment of Stevenson (No. 52).

My dear Stevenson,
     On this eleventh of April, eighteen hundred and ninety-
two, I sit baking in the sun in a Surrey garden, gay with
crocus and hyacinth and japonica. The copses around are
all a-quiver with song; I can distinguish a score of different notes, though, except the unwearying lark, I cannot
name one of the singers. I avoid the shade, scant as yet,
of the great elm trees. The sun stings my skin, and
throws the silhouette of my pencil, black as its own lead,
upon my paper. For the moment I do not envy you your
Samoa. Rather I can fancy you saying to yourself, a
little wistfully, 'Oh to be in England, Now that spring
is there.' Nor do I so much as usual begrudge the Samoans
your bodily presence; for here has my Editor, the god of
Congruity surely inspiring him, placed in my hands the
latest sheaf of your discoursings, so that all morning I
have had in my ears the echo of your voice, the homely
cadence of your Lothian speech, and have rejoiced in your
beautiful buoyancy of spirit, your incomparable art of
finding the right, the vital, the electric word. Our
relation has been from the first - since before we ever
set eyes on each other - one of harmony in discord, and I
shall presently have to resume one or two of the disputa-
tions of our old *Noctes Skerryvorianae*; when you would
pace the long drawing-room up and down, a cigarette between your fingers and your arm in its (I hope long-
disused) sling; (1) I, meanwhile, quiescent in body on
the low divan, and revelling in the intellectual gymnastic
of coursing, so to speak, your nimbler wit. But before
coming to matters of contention let me tell you of a few
of the passages in this new book which sing to my very
soul. First, and very near the beginning, in your account
of your old unhappy emigrant-journey Across the Plains,
comes that just and admirable celebration of the beauties
of American nomenclature. 'None can care for literature
in itself,' you say, 'who do not take a special pleasure
in the sound of names;' and then you go on to point out
that, among many other picturesque and beautiful words,
'the names of the States and Territories themselves form
a chorus of sweet and most romantic vocables.' Truly;
but when you mention as examples Delaware, Ohio, Indiana,
Florida, and half a dozen others, how can you find it in
your heart to omit the two most beautiful of all - Ala-
bama, with its Homeric sonority, and the simple, touching,
melodious Maryland? A little further on, I recognize with
delight the poet of the 'Child's Garden' in your account
of the story which made Ohio the favourite home of your
imagination.... Masterly in its very obviousness is your
etching of the vast plain of Nebraska, with 'the line of
railway stretched from horizon to horizon, like a cue

across a billiard-board;' and I don't know that you have
ever done a prettier piece of wording than this picture of
the Pacific rollers on the beach of Monterey.... I welcome your Random Memories, your Lantern-Bearers (that
ingenious, unconvincing plea for the realism of idealism),
your Chapter on Dreams (why should that thrilling dream-
romance be 'unmarketable'?), and your arrantly Socialistic
reflections on Beggars, which (the portraits apart - a
trifling reservation) might have been written by Bernard
Shaw. I begin to suspect you of being a Fabian in disguise; or rather I perceive you, beyond all question, to
be a Fabian *malgré lui*.

    And now, behold! I have left no space for the promised
disputation. It matters the less, since on second
thoughts I find that I don't want to dispute with you but
to congratulate you on having come over to my side. In
Pulvis et Umbra you have told - in a large, summary,
bravura style indeed, but still with all desirable sincerity - that very half of the truth about life which you
have hitherto, as I think immorally, veiled in a mist of
phrases. It is quaint and delectable to find, but a few
pages removed from this outburst of biological pessimism,
your boyish jibe at Swift (dated thirteen years ago) as
'a kind of leering, human goat, leaping and wagging its
scut on mountains of offence.' I don't pretend that there
is any inconsistency between the two utterances. The
stoical moral you draw is the clear negation of the cynicism of Swift. But the Dean, besides being a great literary artist (and that should exempt him from sheer con-
tumely 'even from the youngest'), was a seer, a recorder
in immortal types and symbols, of a certain side of the
truth. If he was unhappy enough to be blind to certain
other sides, is that a reason for calling him names? Is
it not boyish to 'hate cruelty cruelly'? I am sure you
have grown humaner, even towards misanthropy, since 1879.
But this is really a digression. What I wanted to do was
to express my cordial acceptance (a few phrases and for-
mulas apart) of the philosophy of Pulvis et Umbra. Your
point, I take it, is that the 'origin of good' is quite as
profound a mystery as the 'origin of evil' and much more
edifying and inspiriting to contemplate. Why, certainly;
and though this is, in the last analysis, an indictment,
not a defence, of Nature, it is an excellent rejoinder to
the misanthropic pessimist. You admit in effect that life
is a very bad business, and then urge that man is heroic-
ally, admirably, astoundingly, successful in making the
best of it. Quite so; I admire, I applaud his heroism as
much as you do. But allow me to suggest that this is a
very different philosophy from that 'aggressive optimism'
which declares life a good in itself, and treats as cow-

ardly, impious, almost criminal, the confession that it is
not all beer and skittles. Let us make the best of life
by all means; but I don't think (nor, as it now appears,
do you) that the best way to make the best of it is to go
about telling each other half-truths until we're blue in
the face, and abusing, with sectarian rancour, those who
hint at the other halves.

Need I say, my dear Stevenson, that in speaking of
'sectarian rancour' I had no utterance of yours in my
mind? Your philosophy has never failed in sweetness, any
more than in light. (Of course you remember that we owe
to Swift the juxtaposition of 'these two noblest things'?)
I could even find it in my heart to regret the deeper insight, the higher sincerity, of such a paper as this
Pulvis et Umbra, since they remind us of a time when, as
you wrote to Sidney Colvin, you 'were very far through.'
Fortunately, if you 'came none too soon to the South Seas,
where you were to recover peace of body and mind,' you at
least did not come too late. If, among other things, you
have recovered your 'aggressive optimism,' I shall be the
last to complain. Yes, human life, with the universe for
its background, makes a brave spectacular drama, and,
though I reserve the right of rational criticism, I have
no mind to hiss it, and am in no hurry to quit the
theatre. And to me, as to countless others, the world
seems ever so much better and brighter for the knowledge
that somewhere, even though it be 'at the back o'beyont,'
you have taken a new lease of life on more favourable
terms, and that still, despite the interposing hemisphere,
your art can ever and anon bring us face to face. - Ever
yours sincerely,

William Archer

Note

1 The sling used by Stevenson to help prevent haemorrhage
   of the lungs.

130. RICHARD LE GALLIENNE, FROM A REVIEW, 'ACADEMY'

14 May 1892, xli, 462-4

Le Gallienne (1866-1947), poet and essayist, reviewed in
the 'Star' under the signature 'Log-roller'. He was one

of the original members of the Rhymers' Club along with
W. B. Yeats, Ernest Rhys, Lionel Johnson, and others. Le
Gallienne here praises Stevenson as a stylist; later in
'The Romantic '90s' (1925), 104-5, he was to speak of
Stevenson and Pater as the outstanding models of the time
for aspirants in the art of prose. This review was re-
printed in 'Retrospective Reviews' (1896), i, 113-27.

... Mr. Stevenson's final fame will be that of an essayist, nearest and dearest fame of the prose-writer. Nearest and dearest, because the largest amount of selfish
pleasure enters into the writing of essays, approaching,
as it does, as nearly as possible to writing merely for
writing's sake - as the lyric-poet just sings for singing's sake: the joy in the mere exercise of a faculty.
In the essay no octave-spanning architecture has to be
considered, with a half-heart that would fain be at the
floriation of niche and capital. Such *magnum opus* is,
one supposes, the greater work, certainly it is bigger;
but the essayist cannot but feel the essential and somewhat jeering limitation of the greatest monuments of art,
monuments which attain their air of majestic completion,
simply by a roof, which shuts out the stars. The essayist
is essentially a son of Shem, and his method is the wayward travel of a gipsy. He builds not, but he pitches his
tent, lights his fire of sticks, and invites you to smoke
a pipe with him over their crackling. While he dreamily
chats, now here now there, of his discursive way of life;
the sun has gone down, and you begin to feel the sweet
influences of Pleiades.

At least, so it is with Mr. Stevenson, the Stevenson we
care for most. And it seems certain that it is so he
would be remembered of us: for this new volume of essays
abounds in continual allusions to the joyous practice of
the literary craft, plainly confiding to us that the pleasure of the reader and the writer in their 'Stevenson' is
mutual. One of the great charms of Fontainebleau for Mr.
Stevenson appears to have been its sympathetic environment
for the young 'stylist.' 'Style' as the end and aim of
existence was in the air, not only in the ardent chatter
of young artists, but in the very dignity and grace of the
woods themselves. Only in such a place and in such company, of his fellow-craftsmen, may the young artist hope
to be understood, hope to preserve his temperament un-
spoiled of Polonius.

For art is, first of all and last of all, a trade.
The love of words and not a desire to publish new discoveries, the love of form and not a novel reading of
historical events, marks the vocation of the writer
and the painter. The arabesque, properly speaking,
and even in literature, is the first fancy of the
artist: he first plays with his material as a child
plays with a kaleidoscope; and he is already in a
second stage when he begins to use his pretty counters
for the end of representation. In that he must pause
long and toil faithfully: that is his apprenticeship;
and it is only the few who will really go beyond it,
and go forward, fully equipped, to do the business of
real art - to give life to abstractions and significance and charm to facts. In the meanwhile, let him
dwell much among his fellow-craftsmen. They alone can
take a serious interest in the childish tasks and pitiful successes of these years. They alone can behold
with equanimity this fingering of the dumb keyboard,
this polishing of empty sentences, this dull and literal
painting of dull and insignificant subjects. Outsiders
will spur him on. They will say, 'Why do you not write
a great book? paint a great picture?' If his guardian
angel fail him, they may even persuade him to the
attempt, and, ten to one, his hand is coarsened and his
style falsified for life. [From Memories of Fontaine-
bleau]

The business of real art - 'to give life to abstractions
and significance and charm to facts.' The latter half of
this simple and suggestive statement is especially applic-
able to Mr. Stevenson's own work, particularly in the case
of such books as the 'Travels with a Donkey,' and 'The
Inland Voyage.' Nothing could be more commonplace than
the 'adventures' which supply the theme, nothing less so
than Mr. Stevenson's account of them. Looking ahead, sometimes, the road seems straight and uninteresting enough.
Nothing in sight promises anything. So we are often
inclined to feel when, slowly but surely, some well-worn
fact, which we had ignored as quite unpromising, begins
opening out beneath the eye of Mr. Stevenson's meditative
imagination like a morning flower. He sees everything as
if it had never been looked on before. Nothing has, so to
say, gone cold for him. For him there is no such thing as
merely *hard* fact. Each fact is a sensitive centre of
infinite interests. And he makes us aware of this with a
simplicity so natural that we are apt to forget that his
record is anything more than a record of actual fact, that
it is, as Mr. Pater would say, 'the transcript of his sense

of fact rather than the fact' itself. The expression
which his themes thus take on is not that of mystery or
wizardry, as in Coleridge or Miss Christina Rossetti; it
is rather, to use a phrase of Mr. Stevenson's own, that of
a 'solemn freshness': born, I should say, of a constant
habit - a co-operation between the philosophic and the
poetic instincts - of relating particulars to generals.

[Le Gallienne comments first on Stevenson's travel essays
then turns to 'the essay pure and simple, where the talk
pursues its wayward round about a given theme'.]

   Mr. Stevenson has never touched a home-spun theme to
finer issues than in The Lantern-Bearers. His power,
referred to above, of transfiguring facts into symbols,
is here seen in its triumph. The strange passion of small
boys for a bull's-eye is the humble text for a large and
literally illuminative discourse on that poetry - more
difficult than anything in Browning - other people's
poetry; and on the true realism, which 'always and everywhere is that of the poets.' He describes how when autumn
nights began to set in, half a dozen of 'the fellows' used
to meet on the links equipped with bull's-eye lanterns
fastened to their waists, but carefully swathed in buttoned great coats. 'When two of these asses met, there
would be an anxious "Have you got your lantern?" and a
gratified "Yes!" That was the shibboleth.' Why they
carried them they hardly knew. True, they would now and
again crouch inside some hollow of the links, and revealing the blazing eye in their centres, 'delight themselves
with inappropriate talk.'

   But, 'the essence of this bliss was to walk by yourself in the black night; the slide shut, the top-coat
   buttoned; not a ray escaping, whether to conduct your
   footsteps or to make your glory public: a mere pillar
   of darkness in the dark; and all the while deep down
   in the privacy of your fool's heart, to know you had
   a bull's-eye at your belt, and to exult and sing over
   the knowledge.'

   Realism would describe these youngsters as little

   boys very cold, spat upon by flurries of rain, and
   drearily surrounded, all of which they were; and their
   talk as silly and indecent, which it certainly was ...
   but ask themselves, and they are in the heaven of a
   recondite pleasure, the ground of which is an ill-
   smelling lantern.

Thus in depicting life at large, 'To miss the joy' - that
is, the lantern - 'is to miss all.' 'To find out where
joy resides, and give it a voice far beyond singing,' that
is at once the true poetry and the true realism.

In Pulvis et Umbra, Mr. Stevenson starts in one of
those strange fantastic moods of low spirits, when, like
Hamlet, we ask ourselves, 'What is this quintessence of
dust?'; when the familiar countenance of life changes to
an unmeaning fantastic visage, just as sometimes in reading a familiar English word will take on a more gibberish
aspect than the remotest Welsh, and won't come right again.
In such a mood Mr. Stevenson ponders on the truth that man
was made of the dust of the earth. He takes it literally.
He sees dust full of strange fertility, swelling up and
taking shape, becoming flowers and beasts and men - man
'grown upon with hair like grass,' 'fitted with eyes that
move and glitter in his face, a thing to set children
screaming.' He sees all these various lives living on the
murder of each other - a circumstance which in his dream
seems more quaint than terrible. Then the aspect of this
'monstrous spectre,' man, 'the disease of the agglutinated
dust,' begins to wear a kindly, though still more comical,
aspect. This mere sport of winds, this fortuitous concord
of atoms, actually imagines that such a chance-child as he
owes duties to an unseen something and to his neighbour;
he has a conscience, cherishes a 'duty.' Not only man,
but 'the whole creation, groans in mortal frailty, strives
with unconquerable constancy.' And, with the hearty laugh
that comes of the contemplation of this odd spectacle, the
sickly, spectral vision takes a better meaning -

> Surely not in vain
> My substance from the common earth was ta'en.
>   [FitzGerald's 'Rubáiyát', I, lxi]

The strong reminiscence of the style of Sir Thomas
Browne in this Pulvis et Umbra essay is appropriate to the
quaint vision which is its theme, and is blent with Mr.
Stevenson's own individual style no less successfully than
Lamb used to blend such rich old colours in his own
wonderful writing. In these two essays, and in similar
essays in 'Virginibus Puerisque,' Mr. Stevenson reminds us
of the old prose masters in another quality than their
Latinisation. He has the same high solemnity of accent,
stirring one's heart by groups of simple words, wherein
one seeks in vain for the secret of the magic. We have no
writer of nobler English than Mr. Stevenson at present
among us. Occasionally, one admits, the art peeps out a
little, but it serves to remind us that we are in the

hands of a writer who will not willingly give us less than his highest.

And then the all-pervading manliness, blowing like the breath of pinewoods through all Mr. Stevenson writes, the real feeling of *camaraderie* set up between him and his reader, and the still untroubled sanity of his simple philosophy of life. These are the root-qualities beneath all his charm of expression. Mr. Sidney Colvin, who has seen the book through the press, expresses the fear, in a prefatory letter to Mr. Stevenson, that the tone of the later essays (those of which I have been writing) may be found 'less inspiriting' than Mr. Stevenson's wont. Surely Mr. Colvin is needlessly disquieted. It is true one feels in them the struggle of faith with experience, but it is a struggle in which faith is no less victorious, if just a little wearied, than of old.

One word concerning that Letter to a Young Gentleman who proposes to embrace the Career of Art [No. 103]. It is a manly protest against that literary commercialism which has recently been somewhat blatant. But if litera- ture is ill-paid, asks Mr. Stevenson, 'the wonder is it should be paid at all. Other men pay, and pay dearly, for pleasures less desirable.' Literature, like virtue, is its own reward. A view in which, undoubtedly, there is a large measure of truth; for, when the writer grumbles about poor pay, he must not forget that he did his work not to please the public, but himself. In fact, the practice of art - like the practice of prayer - is simply the indulgence of one of the higher appetites. But in a sort of fakir zeal for cutting himself with knives, Mr. Stevenson goes on to deduce from the pleasure in the pro- duction of literature the essential unmanliness of litera- ture as a profession.

> To live by a pleasure is not a high calling: it involves patronage, however veiled; it numbers the artist, however ambitious, along with dancing girls and billiard markers. The French have a romantic evasion for one employment, and call its practitioners the Daughters of Joy. The artist is of the same family, he is of the Sons of Joy, chose his trade to please himself, gains his livelihood by pleasing others, and has parted with something of the sterner dignity of man.

Is not 'a romantic evasion' delicious? In blunter English the artist is a spiritual prostitute. At the first blush the position has the attractiveness of all half-truths. But, really, it is perhaps hardly true at all. For the

essence of prostitution is not in the pleasure, but in the
sale; and Mr. Stevenson admits that the artist (when he
does his real things, that is when he *is* an artist) works
first to please himself, sings, writes, paints, because he
must, would do so were there never a buyer in the world.
The idea of sale is but a second thought. In some cases,
doubtless, it becomes a second nature. But by that time
the man has ceased to be an artist, and is out of the
question. Take such a case as Montaigne's. No writing
relies more for its charm on its personal revelation than
his, and yet we know that he proposed to himself 'no other
than a familiar and private end.' Whether or not his
vanity really had an eye to publication does not matter.
Certainly he did not write to sell himself. In fact the
artist, consciously or unconsciously, is a sort of Narcis-
sus, and he writes books and paints pictures as so many
mirrors of his own darling individuality; to give to
others, but chiefly to himself, to enjoy 'the taste of
himself.' If either is of the Children of Joy, the writer
or the reader, it is surely the reader; his is the barren
pleasure, certainly not the writer's - often no little
prolific. Yet one can quite understand the fascination
which this 'Daughter of Joy' theory has for Mr. Stevenson
as a man of letters. It is, of course, the fascination of
suicide.

[The following paragraphs were added to the review when it
was reprinted in 'Retrospective Reviews' (1896).]

   Let us consider a moment that question of 'a more manly
way of life,' for on this question of manliness a good
deal of cant is abroad. Whether, properly speaking, the
question of comparative degree enters into the quality or
not, I am not sure. Personally I feel that there can be
no question of 'more' or 'most' manly. A calling is
either manly or unmanly, and there we leave it. It is
true that thews and sinews and the open air may enter more
into one than the other, but it yet remains to be proven
that such are the essential components of manliness. One
may surely, like Whitman, be 'enamoured of growing out-of-
doors,' without stigmatising as mannikins those who must
grow within doors. The business of the 'soldier and the
explorer' would seem to be Mr. Stevenson's ideal of a manly
way of life. They have, he says, 'moments of worthier
excitement' even than the artist's, 'but they are purchased
by cruel hardships and periods of tedium that beggar language.' What about those other hardships which Carlyle
declared made the history of letters more sickening than
the Newgate Calendar? And as for those moments of worthier

excitement, has the man of letters no nobler excitement in
the pursuit of his craft than the small peddling, technical triumphs of phrase on which Mr. Stevenson alone
insists? What of the seasons, not few, of his highest
work, when quite literally *laborare est orare* - when Mr.
Stevenson wrote the Lantern-Bearers, for example? To make
the comparison between the soldier and writer equal, you
must put them both either on a technical or an ideal basis.
Mr. Stevenson would appear to put the writer on the technical and the soldier on the ideal basis, unless those
'moments of worthier excitement' refer to some particularly neat sabre-stroke or particularly happy shot with
his Martini. And I can't help thinking that the worthi-
ness of the soldier's excitement depends a good deal on
his conception of why he is fighting. The mere passion
of fighting for fighting's sake, the mere lust of slaying
'Fuzzy-Wuzzy,' may be more manly than the splendid idealism, the enthusiasm of humanity, the brave battle with
adverse fates, which often has given us the classics of
literature, but if it be so - well, hurrah for petti-
coats!

Then, as to the pleasure given by the writer to the
reader. Does the comparison with the dancing girl and the
billiard marker cover the field? Surely it but applies to
the skirts of it - especially, it may be thought, as
regards the dancing girl. But Mr. Stevenson, it will be
remarked, is generalising, not particularising - and certainly not distinguishing. 'Pleasure' surely means anything, and nothing is gained by pretending that there is
any serious analogy between the pleasure of the ballet and
billiards, and the pleasure derived from fine literature.
If, too, the question of the 'barrenness' of the pleasure
of art, which has become a catchword since The Kreutzer
Sonata, be raised - is an emotion necessarily barren because it does not persaude us to go right away and break
the sixth and seventh Commandments? ''Twas the manner of
primitive man,' we know; but really we have other ways of
utilising our emotion. And if march-music does not lend
valour to our arm, it may to our thought - which is better.
Besides, if this theory of barrenness hold, we must never
look at a sunset, a flower, a woman, or any object which
inspires in us those thoughts that do often lie too deep
for - blows.

Finally, there is this fundamental weakness in the
theory: it ignores the necessity of evolution. It was as
inevitable that there should be men of letters as that
there should be cavemen. Here they are in the process of
the suns, and why not make the best of them? After all,
they have done a good deal for us. Manly or not, they

have often made us better men.

Let us clear our souls of cant - even of this cant of manliness - and remember that the manliness of an occupation is not in its being outdoor or indoor, or in the amount of physical strength we put into it. It is impossible to insist too much on the distinction between what is merely male and what is manly. This, of course, is platitude unashamed; but he who combats sophistry must not be afraid of platitude. Sophistry, too, proves often but inverted platitude. In the present instance, for example, what is more obvious than that art, like every other human activity, has its prostitutes? There is the platitude. Mr. Stevenson simply ignores the limits of its application, and says that all artists are Sons and Daughters of Joy. And so we get the sophism.

131.   STEVENSON, FROM A LETTER TO RICHARD LE GALLIENNE

28 December 1893, LS, iv, 247-8

The 'triumphant exposure' refers to Le Gallienne's comment on a passage in Stevenson's Letter to a Young Gentleman (No. 103). For the passage, see p. 313 for the exposure, p. 391. This letter is reprinted, with some additions, in Le Gallienne's 'The Romantic '90s' (1925), 106-9.

... I [have] to thank you ... for a triumphant exposure of a paradox of my own: the literary prostitute disappeared from view at a phrase of yours - 'The essence is not in the pleasure but the sale.' True: you are right, I was wrong; the author is not the whore, but the libertine; and yet I shall let the passage stand. It is an error, but it illustrated the truth for which I was contending, that literature - painting - all art, are no other than pleasures, which we turn into trades.

And more than all this ... I have to thank you for the intimate loyalty you have shown to myself; for the eager welcome you give to what is good - for the courtly tenderness with which you touch my defects. I begin to grow old; I have given my top note, I fancy; - and I have written too many books. The world begins to be weary of the old booth; and if not weary, familiar with the

familiarity that breeds contempt. I do not know that I am
sensitive to criticism, if it be hostile; I am sensitive
indeed, when it is friendly; and when I read such criticism as yours, I am emboldened to go on and praise God.

You are still young, and you may live to do much. The
little, artificial popularity of style in England tends, I
think, to die out; the British pig returns to his true
love, the love of the styleless, of the shapeless, of the
slapdash and the disorderly. There is trouble coming I
think; and you may have to hold the fort for us in evil
days.

'The Wrecker'

June 1892

'The Wrecker' was the second of three novels Stevenson and
Lloyd Osbourne wrote in collaboration. Why, after 'The
Wrong Box' was so badly received, did Stevenson return to
collaboration with Osbourne? Stevenson appears to have
been confident enough of himself to believe that collaborations would not place his reputation or future earnings
in any real jeopardy. He also enjoyed collaboration with
Osbourne, found it a pleasant change from his usual practice and, on the whole, easy and recreational, though 'The
Ebb-Tide' proved an exception in this respect. He also
felt it beneficial to Osbourne, whose talents he thought
promising. With 'The Wrecker' (as no doubt with the other
collaborations) there was a strong economic incentive; it
was undertaken with the aim of purchasing a schooner on
which Stevenson and his family could live and travel while
engaging in trade with the natives. An economic advantage
of collaboration was that any earnings would be safe from
the pirates since Osbourne was an American citizen and
therefore protected by US copyright laws, though this was
not a consideration after the International Copyright Act
came into effect in July 1891. Finally, 'The Wrecker' and
'The Ebb-Tide' offered Stevenson an opportunity for
experiment and this, no doubt, is what justified the
collaborations on artistic grounds.

'The Wrecker', unlike 'The Wrong Box', proved to be an
extremely profitable and popular book. It was serialized
in 'Scribner's Magazine' (August 1891 - July 1892), for
which the authors received $15,000 (Furnas, 'Voyage',
360), and subsequently published in book form in June 1892
by Scribners in the USA and by Cassell & Co. in England.
Writing to Colvin in November 1893, Stevenson expressed
his pleasure with sales, indicating that they had 'already
in little more than a year out-stripped "The Master of
Ballantrae"' (LS, iv, 240). Stevenson was at first disappointed at sales in the USA and, judging from a letter
sent him by our Burlingame (B, 4154), had suspected Scrib-

ners of unfair dealings. Low sales were not at that time
owing to unauthorized editions since the International
Copyright Act had come into effect, and indeed once it had
Stevenson asked for 'The Wrecker' a 15 per cent rather
than the 10 per cent royalty earlier agreed upon. Whether
sales were at first low because the book was a collaboration is uncertain; but sales were soon to pick up and had
not declined noticeably by the turn of the century when
Osbourne reported the novel had 'always been in excellent
demand, rivalling "Kidnapped", "Master of Ballantrae", and
"Catriona", and still continues to earn £200 a year with
unvarying regularity' (Balfour, 'Life', ii, 34).
     Stevenson's explanation of his modest intentions in the
Epilogue to the novel gave the clue to reviewers, whether
they looked on 'The Wrecker' favourably or not. Those who
reacted favourably pardoned the careless design and
praised it as a perceptive account of life and manners.
The 'Scotsman' (11 July 1892) thought it the best book
Stevenson had yet produced and that it represented a new
method and a new concern in that its 'motives and sources
of interest are drawn from the life of today'. The
'Saturday Review' (16 July 1892) expressed the opinion
that it surpassed all his earlier work except 'Master of
Ballantrae', chiefly on the grounds that it evidenced 'an
amount of original observation of men and things that we
do not find in his former works of fiction'. William
Archer in an unsigned review in the 'Pall Mall Gazette'
(14 July 1892) noted that the novel might have been made
more compact and otherwise improved in design, but not
without a loss of freshness and spontaneity. The 'Spectator' (No. 133) praised the novel for its drawing of
character and the vivid impressions it offered of life in
France and the USA. The reviewer for the 'Daily Chronicle' (2 July 1892) felt Stevenson had transformed an
adventure story into an 'organic whole', a 'masterpiece
of fine art' in spite of its 'zigzagging manner'. On the
other hand, less sympathetic reviewers, such as E. T.
Cook, writing in an unsigned review in the 'Athenaeum'
(6 August 1892), thought the Epilogue made a very poor
case for the novel and objected to the mass of irrelevant
detail and the ignobility of the characters. Others as
well objected to the faulty design, the low types, and to
the carnage aboard the *Flying Scud* (ch. xxiv), which, as
Mrs Oliphant said ('Blackwood's', October 1892), left the
reader 'with the scent of sickening blood and disgust in
his nostrils rather than a sublime horror in his mind'.
Mrs Oliphant also deplored the public's indiscriminate
admiration of all of Stevenson's productions and accused
him of a 'mischievous curiosity' to see just how far his
public would go in accepting inferior work.

132.   STEVENSON, FROM LETTERS TO HENRY JAMES, COLVIN, AND
CHARLES BAXTER

October, November 1891

(a) Letter to James dated by Colvin October 1891

'David Balfour', second part of 'Kidnapped', is on the
stocks at last; and is not bad, I think. As for 'The
Wrecker', it's a machine, you know - don't expect aught
else - a machine, and a police machine; but I believe the
end is one of the most genuine butcheries in literature;
and we point to our machine with a modest pride, as the
only police machine without a villain. Our criminals are
a most pleasing crew, and leave the dock with scarce a
stain upon their character.
  What a different line of country to be trying to draw
Adela [Adela Chart from James's The Marriages], and trying
to write the last four chapters of 'The Wrecker'!
Heavens, it's like two centuries; and ours is such rude,
transpontine business, aiming only at a certain fervour
of conviction and sense of energy and violence in the
men; and yours is so neat and bright and of so exquisite
a surface! Seems dreadful to send such a book to such an
author; but your name is on the list. And we do modestly
ask you to consider the chapters on the *Norah Creina* [ch.
xii] with the study of Captain Nares, and the foremen-
tioned last four, with their brutality of substance and
the curious (and perhaps unsound) technical manoeuvre of
running the story together to a point as we go along, the
narrative becoming more succinct and the details fining
off with every page. (LS, iii, 297-8)

(b) From a letter to Colvin dated 16 or 17 November 1891

'The Wrecker' is finished, that is the best of my news; it
goes by this mail to Scribner's and I honestly think it a
good yarn on the whole and of its measly kind. The part
that is genuinely good is Nares, the American sailor; that
is a genuine figure; had there been more Nares it would
have been a better book; but of course it didn't set up to
be a book, only a long tough yarn with some pictures of
the manners of to-day in the greater world - not the
shoddy sham world of cities, clubs, and colleges, but the
world where men still live a man's life. (LS, iii, 304)

(c) From a letter to Charles Baxter dated November 1891.
Baxter and Stevenson were close friends, especially during
their years together at Edinburgh University when they
were extravagant pranksters and drinking companions.
Later Baxter became Stevenson's business and literary
agent.

... I believe 'The Wrecker' is a good yarn of its poor
sort, and it is certainly well nourished with facts; no
realist can touch me there; for by this time I do begin
to know something of life in the XIXth century, which no
novelist either in France or England seems to know much
of. (LS, iii, 309)

133. J. ST LOE STRACHEY, FROM AN UNSIGNED REVIEW,
'SPECTATOR'

23 July 1892, lxix, 132-3

John St Loe Strachey (1860-1927), journalist and nephew
of John Addington Symonds, was a contributor to the
'Saturday Review', the 'Standard', 'The Economist', and
other periodicals. In 1896 he became the editor of the
'Cornhill' and in 1898 the editor and proprietor of the
'Spectator'.

Mr. Stevenson's admirers may be divided into two classes,
- those who like and those who do not like 'The Wrong
Box.' The former class will declare 'The Wrecker' one of
the happiest and most entertaining of his romances, while
the latter will probably place it among his less successful books. The skeleton of the story is a tale of the
sea, full of shipwreck, murder, and sudden death; but
interwoven with this narrative of the strange and fateful
things that happen 'to the suthard of the line' - that
region of romance where the rules that govern this work-a-
day and prosaic world of ours are overridden and set at
naught - are a series of studies of men and manners in
Paris, in Edinburgh, and in San Francisco. In these
studies, Mr. Stevenson shows a power of humorous and
didactic delineation which, though very different in
style and manner from that of Dickens, is yet, by its

freshness, its bonhomie, and its ability to hold the
reader spell-bound over the most prosaic details, suggestive of Charles Dickens. Many of the characters and the
incidents described are, we fully believe, destined to
make an impression on the English-speaking world comparable to that produced by the creator of Mr. Micawber.
Especially is this true of Pinkerton. Mr. Stevenson has
drawn in him a 'type' which is characteristically American, - the pushing business-man, whose heart is as true
and his nature as generous, as his mercantile transactions
are shady, and who joins an intense love of his country,
and an eager desire for culture, with a willingness to do
almost anything but hurt a woman or injure a friend, in
order to further a bogus speculation or to advertise a
worthless 'product.' Mr. Henry Adams, one of the ablest
of living historians, has pointed out that the key-note of
the typical American character is an intense belief and
hope in regard to the future of America, and has shown how
to this belief and to this hope is to be ascribed the
American tendency to cat-sprawl, to bluff, to talk big,
and to exalt a collection of mud huts into a city. The
American is so sure of the greatness that awaits him and
his, and lives so much in his speculations of the future,
that the unimportant fact that the future as yet wants
realisation is forgotten and put aside. But to make his
dream complete, the American wants the American man of
enterprise to be the cleverest, the best, the most chivalrous, as well as the richest, on the face of the earth.
Hence he is for ever thinking of how 'to build up the
type,' to get culture, and to make the American worthy of
his noble heritage. This alert, eager, boisterous spirit
has been caught and transferred to his pages by Mr.
Stevenson with an art that is beyond admiration. Without
losing a point of humour, he has contrived to paint a picture which cannot be said to be exaggerated, and which is
throughout sympathetic and attractive. Even when Pinkerton is engaged in his most objectionable speculations, and
is practising his worst barbarisms and vulgarities, our
hearts warm to him; and at his worst, every woman-reader
will call him 'a dear,' and every man 'a capital good
fellow at bottom.' He first appears before us as an art-
student in Paris, where he is hopelessly trying to become
a painter, not because he has any turn for art, but
because he thought his country needed more culture, and
his soul burned within him to bring her the gift which
would best help 'to build up the type:' -

[Quotation from ch. iii: 'Pinkerton's parents were from
the Old Country ...' to '"If we fail, like these old

feudal monarchies, what is left?"'.]

Pinkerton's account of his reasons for taking to art are
too good not to be given. He gave them to Loudon Dodd,
his American friend, the hero of the novel, who represents
the opposite type of American humanity, - the hyper-
sensitive, over-cultivated type so familiar to us in the
novels of Mr. Henry James and Mr. Howells: -

> 'Was it an old taste?' I asked him, 'or a sudden
> fancy?' - 'Neither, Mr. Dodd,' he admitted. 'Of
> course, I had learned in my tin-typing excursions to
> glory and exult in the works of God. But it wasn't
> that. I just said to myself, "What is most wanted in
> my age and country? More culture and more art," I
> said; and I chose the best place, saved my money, and
> came here to get them.' [From ch. iii]

As may be imagined, Mr. Pinkerton does not succeed as an
artist, and is soon in San Francisco helping 'to build up
the type' by speculating wildly in everything, from
brandy to agricultural implements, and in his spare time
organising picnics on a commercial basis, buying up old
wrecks, and running a variety of mad enterprises with the
zeal of a saint and the energy of an election agent.
While Pinkerton is thus engaged, he generously invites to
join him the shy, retiring Loudon Dodd, an artist to his
finger-tips, and possessed with that intense horror of
publicity and vulgarity which is to be found in the cultivated American who has been left on the world by the
bankruptcy and death of his father. Loudon Dodd, in
spite of the shame and agony which are often occasioned
him by Pinkerton's vagaries, is devoted to Pinkerton, and
Pinkerton worships Loudon Dodd, as a person of his type
always worships an artist and man of cultivation. As may
be imagined, the juxtaposition of the two men leads to
some exceedingly humorous situations. When Loudon Dodd
arrives at San Francisco to join his friend, he finds the
whole city placarded with advertisements announcing a
lecture on 'Student Life in Paris, Grave and Gay, by H.
Loudon Dodd, the Americo-Parisienne sculptor.' The
'knotted horrors of Americo-Parisienne,' and the huge
posters with his portrait, make poor Dodd almost expire
with vexation; but finding it would break Pinkerton's
heart to protest, and that he cannot get him to understand
the depth of his objections - 'If I had only known you
disliked red lettering,' was as high as he could rise -
Dodd gives in, and consents to read the lecture which has
been written for him by a local pressman, Harry Miller.

After that, Dodd is gradually drawn into the vortex of
Pinkerton's schemes, miserably protesting, but seldom able
to do so effectually, because of the latter's feelings,
and of his childlike devotion to his friend. Besides,
Pinkerton supports Dodd, and how could he be so unchival-
rous as to wound the man who cheerfully works to help
him....

[Before] quitting Mr. Stevenson's book, we must mention
the wonderful picture of the old Scotch jerry-builder.
Mr. Stevenson is always happy in Scotland, but he has
seldom done anything better than old Uncle Adam, with his
talk of 'stuccy,' of 'plunths,' of the advisability of not
paying too much attention to the theory of strains, and of
how Portland cement will go a long way if it is properly
sanded. There is also in the book an admirably drawn 'low
attorney,' one Bellairs, and one or two excellent sailors.
Judged, however, as a whole, the book is not altogether
satisfactory. The character-drawing, and the impressions
of American and French life are excellent; but the sensational story on which they are somewhat inartistically
superimposed, though good enough as a piece of sensationalism, somehow seems out of place. Here, too, we must make
a protest against the shambles business in the last chapter.
It is quite unnecessarily brutal. Still, in spite of
any and every defect that can be urged against it, the
book is in the fullest sense a delightful one, and will
give three or four hours of pure enjoyment to thousands
of men and women. Those who have not yet read it are
indeed to be envied, almost as much as the man who has
never read 'Treasure Island.'

134. LIONEL JOHNSON, REVIEW, 'ACADEMY'

6 August 1892, xlii, 103-4

Johnson (1867-1902) began reviewing after leaving Oxford
in 1890, contributing to the 'Academy', 'Pall Mall Gazette', National Observer', 'Daily Chronicle', etc. He was
associated with W. B. Yeats, Richard Le Gallienne, Ernest
Rhys, and others as a member of the Rhymers' Club. This
review was reprinted in 'Reviews and Critical Papers by
Lionel Johnson' (1921), ed. Robert Shafer, 40-5.

In one of his early essays, Mr. Stevenson played with the
charming fancy, that the conduct of life depends upon
skill in literature: not indeed wholly, but in a great
measure. It is no light task, he insisted, to communicate
your precise sense of things, in set phrase, to another
man: the choice of words, the nicety and exactitude of
them, may fail to impress your companion, as you would
have him impressed. All speech, all intercourse by word
of mouth or by 'hand of write,' is so much practice of the
literary art; and human converse is thus encompassed with
peril.

> The world was made before the English language, and
> seemingly upon a different design. Suppose we held
> our converse not in words, but in music, those who have
> a bad ear would find themselves cut off from all near
> commerce, and no better than foreigners in this big
> world. But we do not consider how many have 'a bad
> ear' for words, nor how often the most eloquent find
> nothing to reply. [From 'Virginibus Puerisque', iv,
> Truth of Intercourse]

From the first this whimsical commonplace has powerfully
influenced Mr. Stevenson; it has made of him an aesthetic
casuist, anxious about the veracity of his least word, its
minutest tone and accent. Be it a story, a piece of criticism, an essay in ethics, a personal reminiscence, or a
private adventure, each of his words is positively tremu-
lous with its desire to tell the truth. Since the whole
of life is a continuous and coherent affair, he refuses
to isolate literature in a secluded palace of art or book-
worm's study: he wants to know life upon all sides, and he
wants to express it upon all sides by the use of words.
Thus it is that his choice of an adjective, his composition of a phrase, or his disposition of incidents, is for
him an exercise in good conduct: a trial of truthfulness.
We live in a very rich, full world: our behaviour in it,
and our attitude towards it, expressed in words, comprehend all matters of belief and conduct. Of modern
writers, only Mr. Pater shares with Mr. Stevenson this
fine anxiety not to play life false by using inaccurate
expressions. He also, whether he write essays or imaginative studies, or more formal narratives, shows this care
for the truth, as he apprehends it. To Mr. Pater an
Italian church or a French landscape, an ancient liturgy
or a classical rite, is a thing with definite values of
its own, a thing with claims and rights, towards which he
has duties; a shipwreck or a walking tour, an American man
of business or a French artist, is the same to

Mr. Stevenson. The one is more meditative, more learned,
more gentle, than the other; but both are men who feel the
pathos, the heroism, the living significance of things -
Virgil's 'sense of tears in mortal things' and Browning's:

> How good is man's life, the mere living! how
>   fit to employ
> All the heart and the soul and the senses for
>   ever in joy!

It is curious to reflect that many critics have found in
Mr. Pater and Mr. Stevenson - two intensely practical,
humane, and sympathetic writers - little more than unreal
eclectic profundities, intricacies, and extravagances.

'The Wrecker' contains, as it were in solution, all
the perfections of Mr. Stevenson: upon the face of it, it
has all the stirring romance of adventure which we enjoyed
in 'Treasure Island'; it displays two characters with all
the impressive fidelity which made Alan Breck and the
Master of Ballantrae so wonderful; it includes episodes
and sketches, varieties of life, such as those in the two
books of travel, in the 'Silverado Squatters,' and many
single essays; it has much of that fantastic humour which
adorns the 'New Arabian Nights'; it provides us with more
of those brilliancies of moral sentiment, already so
characteristic of Mr. Stevenson. The result is a delightful and imperfect book - a *satura*, a *farrago*, in which
every reader can come upon something to his taste, and no
reader feels satisfied throughout. The writers explain
how it all came about, in an ingenious epilogue or apology: they determined, one moonlit night in the Pacific,
to write a story about the tale of a wreck, often the
occasion of a rascally romance in commerce.

> Before we turned in, the scaffolding of the tale had
> been put together. But the question of treatment was,
> as usual, more obscure. We had long been at once
> attracted and repelled by that very modern form of the
> police novel or mystery story, which consists in begin-
> ning your yarn anywhere but at the beginning, and
> finishing it anywhere but at the end; attracted by its
> peculiar interest when done, and the peculiar difficul-
> ties that attend its execution; repelled by that
> appearance of insincerity and shallowness of tone,
> which seems its inevitable drawback. [From the Epi-
> logue to 'The Wrecker']

They determined, by a more artistic method, by a gradual
approach to the story, making the chief character familiar

from the first among many various scenes, to give an air
of reality to the central mystery. To this end the story
flies from Muskegon to Edinburgh, from Edinburgh to Paris,
from Paris to San Francisco, before the puzzle of the
wreck in the Pacific is introduced: and, to solve that
puzzle, the story flies from San Francisco to Dorsetshire
and to Barbizon, where the answer is given. The answer
takes us to Australia, the Pacific, and San Francisco once
more. I do not know that courtesy compels me to accept
for literal truth the author's explanation: but it is more
convincing, at least, than Poe's account of his evolution
of the 'Raven,' in his essay upon the Philosophy of Composition. To Mr. Stevenson's method are due at once the
charm and the defect of 'The Wrecker.' The charm lies in
single episodes: the bohemian life of art in Paris, the
bohemian life of commerce in San Francisco, the splendid
voyage to the Pacific islands, the search for treasure
upon the abandoned ship: and in certain characters,
Pinkerton, the tactless and romantic speculator; Nares,
the brutal, philosophical, and cordial seaman. But the
central facts of the story are obscured by the very means
employed to make them plausible and natural. The story
begins and ends with some lack of symmetry and rounded
form. The last details are told by Mr. Stevenson, *propria
persona*, in a letter of dedication to a friend. It
reminds us of Scott's intricate prefaces, introductions,
and involved machinery for getting his main story under
weigh. Pleasant in themselves, these contrivances do but
embarrass the story which they are meant to serve. In
the present case, the difficulties of the narrative are
pardonable enough, for they help us to realise that
variety and richness of life which Mr. Stevenson never
wearies of praising.

It may be objected to this story, that it contains
episodes of brutal violence, murder, and blood-shedding,
which its author presents with a certain callousness, if
not with a certain gusto. But Mr. Stevenson himself sup-
plies an answer by his constant trust in human nature.
To him every man has some nobility, and we are all
incomprehensible together. Captain Nares was full of
barbarity, vanity, ill-conditioned humours; but

> he won me to a kind of unconsenting fondness. Lastly,
> the faults were all embraced in a more generous view:
> I saw them in their place, like discords in a musical
> progression, and accepted them, and found them pictur-
> esque, as we accept and admire, in the habitable face
> of nature, the smoky head of the volcano, or the per-
> nicious thicket of the swamp. [From ch. xii, The
> *Norah Creina*]

The world is a pageant of vices and of virtues, to be
endured by all means, to be enjoyed if may be. Our vices
have something good in them, and our virtues are not all
pure. Dodd, the narrator of the story, is grossly ungrateful to his strange, lovable comrade, Pinkerton: he
writes him pages of penitence.

> Wonderful are the consolations of literature! As soon
> as that letter was written and posted, the conscious-
> ness of virtue glowed in my veins like some rare vin-
> tage. [From ch. v, Down on My Luck in Paris]

In the thick of a dangerous storm Nares was happy:

> Well, there's always something sublime about a big deal
> like that; and it kind of raises a man in his own
> liking. We're a queer kind of beasts, Mr. Dodd.
> [From ch. xii, The *Norah Creina*]

Bellairs, a 'shyster,' or disbarred lawyer, with qualms of
conscience, goes to blackmail an unfortunate man. Dodd
comments: 'I used to wonder whether I most admired or most
despised this quivering heroism for evil.' Mr. Stevenson
feels to the full what Mr. Watson has expressed in four
lines:

> Momentous to himself as I to me
>   Hath each man been that ever woman bore;
> Once, in a lightning-flash of sympathy,
>   I *felt* this truth, an instant, and no more.
>   [Epigrams, xxii]

But with Mr. Stevenson this truth is always present; and
it has preserved him from that easy contempt for whole
classes of men, which so many brilliant living writers
love to express. It is instructive to compare Mr. Stevenson's praise of a free, natural life of work under sun and
wind and rain, with Mr. Kipling's praise of a strenuous,
rapid, active life - the one so simply honest and exhilar-
ating, the other so merely bitter and exasperating. The
two writers have something in common: Mr. Stevenson makes
us interested in such things as a 'deep-water tramp, lime-
juicing around between big ports, Calcutta and Rangoon and
'Frisco and the Canton River': Mr. Kipling in such experience as 'loafing from Lima to Auckland in a big, old, condemned passenger-ship turned into a cargo-boat and owned
by a second-hand Italian firm.' Yet the interest roused
in us by Mr. Stevenson is very different from that roused
by Mr. Kipling: it is the difference between the truth of

poetry and the truth of science. Behind Mr. Stevenson's
writing there is a soul and a heart; behind Mr. Kipling's
a good memory and a keen eye. A detail, recorded by Mr.
Stevenson, has always some human interest; it betokens
more than quick observation and mechanical experience. It
means that Mr. Stevenson has been true to his pleasant
boast: that he has never found life wholly dull and vapid;
that his sympathy with all forms of life and all ways of
men has made him alert to notice the little details which
go to compose them. This is a brave book, as confused as
the 'Iliad,' as adventurous as the 'Odyssey,' and with no
little of the heartening morality common to both.

'Island Nights' Entertainments'

April 1893

Three previously published stories were brought together in this volume:

The Beach of Falesá (entitled Uma, 'Illustrated London News', 2 July - 6 August 1892)
The Bottle Imp (New York 'Herald', 8, 15, 22 February, 1 March 1891; 'Black and White', 28 March, 4 April 1891)
The Isle of Voices ('National Observer', 4, 11, 18, 25 February 1893)

Of these three stories Stevenson thought most highly of Beach, chiefly on the basis of its realistic portrayal of life and character in the South Seas. It was also a tentative venture into new territory for him in that it dealt with the passional relations of man and woman in a way no earlier work had. He was disappointed that editors objected to the false marriage contract that deceived Uma into believing she was legally married to Wiltshire (ch. i). The 'Illustrated London News' omitted the marriage contract; Stevenson insisted it appear in the reprinting, but in the edition by Cassell & Co. the phrase in the contract 'for one night' was changed to 'for one week', though it is difficult to know what purpose was served by the change (LS, iv, 11, 45, 96). These reactions confirmed Stevenson's view that if he were to treat adult love he could do so only in a way that would be unacceptable to the public:

> with all my romance, I am a realist and a prosaist, and a most fanatical lover of plain physical sensation plainly and expressly rendered; hence my perils. To do love in the same spirit as I did (for instance) D. Balfour's fatigue in the heather ... there were grossness - ready made! (LS, iv, 48)

In Beach he had not dealt directly with passion, but still
they objected and their reaction embittered him: 'Since
the Beach, I know nothing, except that men are fools and
hypocrites; and I know less of them than I was fond enough
to fancy' (LS, iv, 101).   Generally, large sales were
not expected for volumes of short stories and Stevenson
was surprised to learn that 'Entertainments' sold well,
far better than had 'The Merry Men' (LS, iv, 236).

135.   STEVENSON ON THE BEACH OF FALESÁ, FROM LETTERS TO
COLVIN

1891, 1892

(a) From a letter dated 29 April 1891.   The High Woods of
Ulufanua was the title first given to The Beach of Falesá.

I have taken up again The High Woods of Ulufanua.   I still
think the fable too fantastic and far-fetched.   But, on a
re-reading, fell in love with my first chapter, and for
good or evil I must finish it.   It is really good, well
fed with facts, true to the manners, and (for once in my
works) rendered pleasing by the presence of a heroine who
is pretty.   Miss Uma is pretty; a fact.   All my other
women have been as ugly as sin, and like Falconet's horse
(I have just been reading the anecdote in Lockhart),
mortes forbye.   (LS, iii, 264-5)

(b) From a letter dated 5 September 1891

I have a whole world in my head, a whole new society to
work, but I am in no hurry; you will shortly make the
acquaintance of the island of Ulufanua, on which I mean
to lay several stories; the Bloody Wedding, possibly the
High Woods - (O, it's so good, the High Woods, but the
story is craziness - that's the trouble) - a political
story, the Labour Slave, etc....   I have just interrupted
my letter and read through the chapter of the High Woods
that is written, a chapter and a bit, some sixteen pages,
really very fetching, but what do you wish? the story is
so wilful, so steep, so silly - it's a hallucination I
have outlived, and yet I never did a better piece of work,
horrid, and pleasing, and extraordinarily true; it's six-

teen pages of the South Seas; their essence.... Golly,
it's good. I am not shining by modesty; but I do just
love the colour and movement of that piece so far as it
goes. (LS, iii, 286-7)

(c) From a letter dated 28 September 1891

Since I last laid down my pen, I have written and re-
written The Beach of Falesá; something like sixty thousand words of sterling domestic fiction (the story, you
will understand, is only half that length); and now I
don't want to write any more again for ever, or feel so;
and I've got to overhaul it once again to my sorrow. I
was all yesterday revising, and found a lot of slack-
nesses and (what is worse in this kind of thing) some
literaryisms. One of the puzzles is this: it is a first
person story - a trader telling his own adventure in an
island. When I began I allowed myself a few liberties,
because I was afraid of the end; now the end proved quite
easy, and could be done in the pace; so the beginning
remains about a quarter tone out (in places); but I have
rather decided to let it stay so. The problem is always
delicate; it is the only thing that worries me in first
person tales, which otherwise (quo' Alan) 'set better wi'
my genius.' There is a vast deal of fact in the story,
and some pretty good comedy. It is the first realistic
South Sea story; I mean with real South Sea character and
details of life. Everybody else who has tried, that I
have seen, got carried away by the romance, and ended in
a kind of sugar candy sham epic, and the whole effect was
lost - there was no etching, no human grin, consequently
no conviction. Now I have got the smell and look of the
thing a good deal. You will know more about the South
Seas after you have read my little tale than if you had
read a library. As to whether any one else will read it,
I have no guess. I am in an off time, but there is just
the possibility it might make a hit; for the yarn is good
and melodramatic, and there is quite a love affair - for
me; and Mr. Wiltshire (the narrator) is a huge lark,
though I say it. But there is always the exotic question,
and everything, the life, the place, the dialects -
trader's talk, which is a strange conglomerate of literary expressions and English and American slang, and Beach
de Mar, or native English, - the very trades and hopes and
fears of the characters, are all novel, and may be found
unwelcome to that great, hulking, bullering whale, the
public. (LS, iii, 292-3)

(d) From a letter dated 31 January 1892. In The Beach of

Falesá (ch. i) the native girl, Uma, is led to believe her marriage to Wiltshire is legal by the use of a false wedding contract. It is uncertain who refused The Treasure of Franchard; it was published in 'Longman's', April-May 1883.

The Beach of Falesá I still think well of, but it seems it's immoral and there's a to-do, and financially it may prove a heavy disappointment. The plaintive request sent to me, to make the young folks married properly before 'that night,' I refused; you will see what would be left of the yarn, had I consented. This is a poison bad world for the romancer, this Anglo-Saxon world; I usually get out of it by not having any women in it at all, but when I remember I had The Treasure of Franchard refused as unfit for a family magazine, I feel despair weigh upon my wrists. (LS, iv, 11)

(e) From a letter dated 17 May 1892

I think you seem scarcely fair to Wiltshire, who had surely, under his beast-ignorant ways, right noble qualities. And I think perhaps you scarce do justice to the fact that this is a place of realism à *outrance*; nothing extenuated or coloured. Looked at so, is it not, with all its tragic features, wonderfully idyllic, with great beauty of scene and circumstance? And will you please to observe that almost all that is ugly is in the whites? I'll apologise for Papa Randal if you like; but if I told you the whole truth - for I did extenuate there! - and he seemed to me essential as a figure, and essential as a pawn in the game, Wiltshire's disgust for him being one of the small, efficient motives in the story. Now it would take a fairish dose to disgust Wiltshire. (LS, iv, 45-6)

136. A. T. QUILLER-COUCH, FROM MR STEVENSON'S LATEST, 'SPEAKER'

15 April 1893, vii, 428-9

<hr>

(Sir) Arthur Quiller-Couch (1863-1944) was a frequent contributor of stories and literary causeries to the 'Speaker' as well as the assistant editor at the time of its founding in 1890. It was Quiller-Couch who wrote, on

Colvin's request and after Arthur Conan Doyle had refused,
the concluding chapters of 'St Ives'. Portions of this
review were reprinted in 'Adventures in Criticism' (1896),
162-7.

... The 'New Arabian Nights' were in many respects a
parody of the Eastern book. They have, if we make a few
necessary allowances for the difference between East and
West, the same, or very near the same, atmosphere of gallant, extravagant, intoxicated romance. The characters
have the same adventurous irresponsibility, and exhibit
the same irrelevancies and futilities. The Young Man with
the Cream Cakes might well have sprung from the same brain
as the facetious Barmecide, and young Scrymgeour sits helpless before his destiny as sat that other young man while
the Barber, malign and inexorable, sang the song and
danced the dance of Zantout. Indeed Destiny in these
books resembles nothing so much as a Barber with fore-
finger and thumb nipping his victims by the nose. It is
as omnipotent, as irrational, as humorous and almost as
cruel in the imitation as in the original. Of course I
am not comparing them in anything but their general presentment of life, or holding up The Rajah's Diamond and
trying to make it stand as a good tale beside Aladdin. I
am merely pointing out that life is presented to us, in
Galland and in Mr. Stevenson's first book of tales, under
very similar conditions - the chief difference being that
Mr. Stevenson had to abate something of the supernatural,
or to handle it less frankly.

    But several years divide these 'New Arabian Nights'
from the 'Island Nights' Entertainments'; and in the
interval our author has written 'The Master of Ballantrae,'
and his open letter on Father Damien. This is to say that
he has grown as an artist, and grown even more in his
understanding of the human creature and serious speculation on this creature's duties and destinies. He has
travelled far, on shipboard and in emigrant trains; has
passed through much sickness; has acquired property and
responsibility; has mixed in public affairs; has written
'A Footnote to History,' and sundry letters to 'The
Times'; and even, as his latest letter shows, stands in
some danger of imprisonment. Therefore, while the title
of his new volume would seem to refer us once more to the
old Arabian models, we are not surprised to find this
apparent design belied by the contents. The third story,
indeed, The Isle of Voices, has affinity with some of the
Arabian tales - with Sindbad's adventures, for instance.
But in the longer Beach of Falesá and The Bottle Imp we
are dealing with no debauch of fancy, but with the prob-

lems of real life.

For what is the knot untied in the Beach of Falesá? If
I mistake not, our interest centres neither in Case's
dirty trick of the marriage, nor in his more stiff-jointed
trick of the devil-contraptions. The first but helps to
construct the problem, the second seems a superfluity. The
problem is (and the author puts it before us fair and
square), How is Wiltshire, a fairly loose moralist with
some generosity of heart, going to treat the girl he has
wronged? And I am bound to say that as soon as Wiltshire
answers that question before the missionary - an excellent
scene and most dramatically managed - my interest in the
story, which is but half-told at this point, lags woe-
fully. As I said, the 'devil-work' chapter strikes me as
stiff, and the conclusion but rough-and-tumble. And I
feel certain that the story 'itself is to blame, and neither the scenery nor the persons, being one of those who
had as lief Mr. Stevenson spake of the South Seas as of
the Hebrides, so that he speak and I listen. Let it be
granted that the Polynesian names are a trifle hard to
distinguish at first - yet they are easier than Russian
by many degrees - and the difficulty vanishes entirely as
you read the Song of Rahéro, or the 'Footnote to History.'
And if it comes to habits, customs, scenery, etc., I protest a man must be exacting who can find no romance in
these after reading 'Typee.' No, the story itself is to
blame.

But what is the human problem in the Bottle Imp?
(Imagine Scheherazadé with a human problem!) Nothing
less, if you please, than the problem of Alcestis -
nothing less, and even something more; for in this case
when the wife has made her great sacrifice of self, it is
no fortuitous god, but her own husband who wins her
release, and at a price no less fearful than she herself
had paid. Keawe being in possession of a bottle which
must infallibly bring him to hell-flames unless he can
dispose of it at a certain price, Kokua, his wife, by a
stratagem purchases the bottle from him, and stands committed to the doom he has escaped. She does her best to
hide this from Keawe, but he by accident discovering the
truth, by another stratagem wins back the curse upon his
own head, and is only rescued by a pretty artifice of the
story-teller.

Two or three reviewers have already given utterance
upon this volume; and they seem strangely unable to determine which is the best of its three tales. I vote for The
Bottle Imp without a second's doubt; and, if asked my
reasons, must answer (1), that it deals with a high and
universal problem, whereas in The Isle of Voices there is
no problem at all, and in the Beach of Falesá the problem
is less momentous and perhaps (though of this I won't be

sure) more closely restricted by the accidents of circumstance and individual character; (2) as I have hinted, the
Beach of Falesá has faults of construction, one of which
is serious, if not vital, while The Isle of Voices, though
beautifully composed, is tied down by the triviality of
its subject. But The Bottle Imp is perfectly constructed
as well as admirably written: the last page ends the tale,
and the tale is told with a light grace, sportive within
restraint, that takes nothing from the seriousness of the
subject. Some may think this extravagant praise for a
little story which, after all (they will say), is flimsy
as a soap bubble. But let them sit down and tick off on
their fingers the names of living authors who could have
written it, and it may begin to dawn on them that a story
has other dimensions than length and thickness.

Mr. Barrie, in the little book of portraits which he
called 'An Edinburgh Eleven,' and published in 1889 [see
No. 108] has a remark upon Mr. Stevenson which was perfectly just at the time. 'The keynote of all Mr. Stevenson's writings,' he said, 'is his indifference, so far as
his books are concerned, to the affairs of life and death
on which other minds are chiefly set. Whether a man has
an immortal soul interests him as an artist not a whit:
what is to come of man troubles him as little as where man
came from. He is a warm, genial writer, yet this is so
strange as to seem inhuman. His philosophy is that we are
light-hearted birds....'

All very true at the time, but (as I think Mr. Barrie
will be quick to admit) not quite so true today, and
hardly likely to be true at all in a year or two. For the
'Master of Ballantrae' has been published since, and
'Across the Plains,' and with these two books it is no
longer child's-play.

137. A. B. WALKLEY, REVIEW, 'BLACK AND WHITE'

13 May 1893, 572

Arthur Bingham Walkley (1855-1926) was a literary and
dramatic critic whose work appeared chiefly in the 'Star',
the 'Speaker', and 'The Times'.

Mr. Robert Louis Stevenson's new book, Island Nights'
Entertainments is something very much more than a new

book. Fine - as any book of Mr. Stevenson's must be - as
a piece of literature, as a work of art, it is greater
than these; as the whole, according to Euclid's axioms, is
greater than its part. It lifts you clean out of the
atmosphere of books and bookish things, and casts you
headlong into the thick, the very mellay, of life itself,
and squeezes you so tight against nature that the breath
is well-nigh out of your body. As you read you become (I
swear) sun-burned and weather-beaten. The book is like a
sea trip or a practice with the dumbbells; it strings up
your muscles and renews your blood. Mr. Stevenson's case,
as it seems to me, is almost unexampled in the history of
the humaner letters. Here is a man who from his youth up
has saturated himself with literature, first a student and
then a master of classic prose, who has loved art passionately like a mistress, a born author, and who yet counts
literature and art as nothing beside life itself, life at
first hand, the life according to nature, the life of a
free man under the wide heavens, the life of the 'noble
savage' running 'wild in woods.'

I say - off-hand, and reserving the right to contradict
myself if provoked - that this case is unexampled. Someone will be sure to instance 'unabashed Defoe.' But,
though Defoe was a man of letters with a keen joy in life
at first hand, it was not the life Mr. Stevenson's soul
loveth; it was not the life according to nature. Life for
him meant commerce with men; he had no passion for sea,
and valley and mountain - as any reader of 'Robinson Crusoe' will soon discover for himself. Mention Thoreau and
George Borrow, and you will be getting, as the children
say, 'warmer.' But these men were nature-lovers, 'noble
savages,' first and always, and literary artists only now
and then, as it were, by a sort of happy accident. Their
great concern was to live their 'natural' lives, one of
contemplation, the other of action; their expression of
these lives in literature was - if the pedantry may be
passed - more or less of a *parergon*; they would have been
virtually the men they were had they never written a line.
But Mr. Stevenson, with all his lust for life, lives for
literature. The conception of him as existing without
writing is simply unthinkable. Perhaps the nearest case
to his is Pierre Loti's. But here, again, I would distinguish. Loti approaches life and nature as a dilettante,
he seeks from it a variety of exquisite sensations, so
that his books are, in their essence, egoisms, personal
confessions, records of moods and emotions. Not so Mr.
Stevenson's, which are objective and dramatic. Add that
Loti is the son of his own works, I mean that he is a
self-taught writer; he invented his own style - as the

White Knight invented his own helmet: he declares that he
has never read the classics of his own land. Now,
Mr. Stevenson's style is a growth from genuine classic
tradition; it was learnt in the schools; it is not a
thing apart, but the latest and, as some think, the most
perfect stage in the evolution of English prose.

Even in such a narrative as that of The Beach of
Falesá, the first and by far the most considerable of
the three tales making up the present book, which narrative purports to be told by an illiterate trader in the
South Seas, Mr. Stevenson's characteristic style, with its
reminiscences of Sir Thomas Browne and other deliberate
archaisms, is to be detected in every page. 'I took the
glass, and the shores *leaped* nearer, and I saw the tangle
of the woods and the breach of the surf, and the brown
roofs and the black insides of houses peeped among the
trees.' That 'leaped' is true Stevenson: no South Sea
trader would have thought of it; nor would he have used
such seventeenth-century English as 'our desires thus
jumping together,' nor have hit upon so vividly picturesque a figure as 'the want of her took and shook all
through me like the wind in the luff of a sail,' or as
'the blood spread upon his face like wine upon a napkin.'

Nevertheless, though these may seem instances to the
contrary, when I said that Mr. Stevenson's method is objective and dramatic, I meant it. Bating an occasional lapse
into Stevensonian English, John Wiltshire, the narrator of
the present tale, has his own language, the straightforward language of an unlettered Englishman mingled with
sailor slang and South Pacific lingo; while his thoughts,
his ways of looking at life, are all his own. He is not
the mouthpiece for Mr. Stevenson's views, the cultivated
artist masquerading in flannel pyjamas, but himself –
'just a trader,' as he says, 'just a common, low-down,
God-damned white man and British subject.' He has the
narrow prejudices of his set. He doesn't like mission-
aries. 'No trader does; they look down upon us, and make
no concealment; and, besides, they're partly Kanakaised,
and suck up with natives instead of with other white men
like themselves.... When I saw the missionary step out of
his boat in the regular white uniform, white duck clothes,
pith helmets, white shirt and tie, and yellow boots to his
feet, I could have bunged stones at him.' Nor has he any
man-and-a-brother views about Kanakas or niggers.

But he is a splendid fellow, a tall man of his hands,
with his head screwed on straight, and his heart in the
right place. This heart of his is 'true to Poll,' as a
sailor's should be. Poll is a native girl, Uma, a sort of
Polynesian Madame Chrysanthème, a charming specimen of the
Eternal Feminine from the South Seas – Mr. Stevenson is

not usually fortunate with his female characters, but this
one is altogether delightful - whom Wiltshire betrays by a
mock marriage, celebrated by a grinning black before a
drunken old sea-dog, thus: -

> This is to certify that Uma, daughter of Fa'avao,
> of Falesá, Island of - , is illegally married to Mr.
> John Wiltshire for one week, and Mr. John Wiltshire is
> is at liberty to send her to hell when he pleases.
>   JOHN BLACKAMOOR,
>   Chaplain to the Hulks.

Her goodness shames him into repentance for his trick, and
he makes her into his 'old lady' ('the proper name of a
man's wife') for better and for worse, by the help of the
first missionary to hand. Then strange romantic things
happen to him, and happen, as the immortal Captain Nares
would say, 'thick.' He unmasks a villainous wife, who
nearly succeeds in murdering him, spends a night of blood-
curdling adventure in the bush, and ultimately does justice, with cold steel, upon his enemy. To tell this part
of the story in detail would be to give Mr. Stevenson
away. I will only hint, just to whet your curiosity, that
there is dynamite in it, and a collection of bogeys made
fearsome by luminous paint, and much wallowing in gore
(... 'with that I gave him the cold steel for all I was
worth. His body kicked under me like a spring sofa...the
blood came over my hands, hot as tea....') After the riotous, exuberant, exotic life of this story, the two others
of the book, 'The Bottle Imp' and 'The Isle of Voices' -
tales of Polynesian thaumaturgy - leave one comparatively
cold. But 'The Beach of Falesá' is worth a king's ransom.

138. LIONEL JOHNSON ON STEVENSON AS A PROBATIONARY
CLASSIC, FROM A REVIEW, 'ACADEMY'

3 June 1893, xliii, 473-4

On Johnson see headnote to No. 134. Though 'Island
Nights' Entertainments' was the occasion for this essay,
it offers comment on Stevenson's work in general rather
than on that particular volume, which indeed it altogether
neglects to mention. The essay was reprinted in 'Post
Liminium' (1911), 106-11.

... Two Scotchmen, the immortal Scott and the admired
Mr. Stevenson, have done wondrously in endearing Scotland
to us. Scott displayed the romance of the great past, and
led us into a splendid company of fighters and saints and
singers, nobles and beggars and burghers, in old Scotland,
old England, and old France: the tragedy and comedy of
life in its variety. Burns is for Scotchmen: only they
can really know his power; others can and must admire,
but without a perfect appreciation. Scott belongs to all
the world: romantic revivals abroad, religious revivals at
home, have derived much of their inspiration from his
benignant and refreshing genius. But Scott's travels were
mostly of the mind and the imagination; he seldom left the
heather without regret. Mr. Stevenson is a wandering Scot
in the literal sense. Thinking of his twenty-five volumes, dated from all parts of the earth, we cannot but
praise and thank the courageous spirit of a writer whose
wanderings, so often made in search of health, have issued
in books of a cheerfulness and zest and zeal, so sane and
indomitable and strong. With infinite pains and a minute
delicacy of skill, his art, the consolatory companion of
his wanderings, has taken us on an enchanted journey from
the rivers and woods of France to the seas and islands of
the Pacific. Addison, with unfailing grace and humour,
with the serenest and the surest power, has enshrined for
us the ways of Queen Anne's London; he touches upon high
life and upon low, upon humours of the court and of the
coffee-house, upon the critic, the politician, the gallant, the great lady, the honest citizen; - his pages
contain it all, he concentrates in them all that bygone
London. Travel, for most men of his kind and taste,
meant a decorous ramble round the courts and great cities
of Europe: a conscious pursuit of culture at a stately
pace. But now, all the round world is known, we put
girdles round the earth in the manner of Puck. *Colonial,
imperial, federal*, are words much in the mouths of our
politicians, and our men of arts and letters fly from
China to Peru, and all manner of nations wrangle together
over vast African regions and islands of the Southern
Seas. Well, our leisurely Addison would find it a bustling, arduous, complicated theme for art. How shall he
portray French peasants and Kanakas, Californians and
Chinese, San Francisco and Fontainebleau, Samoa and the
Hebrides, yet preserve his sureness of hand, his clearness of sight, his grace and moderation and repose? A man
may pitch his tent or sling his hammock wherever he choose
in the four continents, or upon the great seas; catch a
little local colour, pick up snatches of native dialect,
learn something of national habits and racial ways, and

produce his probably unimportant work in its season. Now, as in 1830, to quote the pleasant malice of Merimee, the watchword is ever 'point de salut sans la couleur locale.' When these romances have some charm, it is commonly the charm of strangeness and nothing more: an excellent charm indeed. But that is not enough to hold us captive.... A story does not live only because it treats of Floren- tines or Red Indians or Russians or Arabs. Art is, of course, independent of time and place: we are equally at home with Clytemnestra and Uncle Toby, Dido and Hester Prynne; we require, and in them we find, the 'one touch of nature,' the common humanity. But even that is not all; we want to find the artist displaying his human sympathies and knowledge and insight in a special, proper, personal way of his own. We have heard so much of late about the impersonality of art! It is very true; but take two of the most impersonal artists in the world, any great pair of Flauberts, and you will find them dealing with the same things, the same scenes, characters, situations, with infinitely various results; the two men are two, and they are men. Briefly, any story can please that is written by a man about men and women; that reveals a man, with a definite sense of things, an apprehension of his own, writing about other men of whatever age or race, so as to make men of all ages and races interested in them.... They who fulfil our conditions are classics. Of no living man, and of no lately dead man, can we say that he is classic: simply because the judgment of other ages, and often of other races, has not been passed upon him. But some living men are probationary classics, classics on approval: such is Mr. Stevenson. In him I find a modern Addison, with the old graces and the old humours. True, he is definitely 'romantic': he loves the stir of adven- ture, the whole business of the whole world: he is an ardent enthusiast for tasting many kinds of life. But he has no fierce, feverish brilliance and rapidity; not like those vague persons who have been called 'unattached Christians,' he is full of attachment to humanity, and is not satisfied with making hasty, clever, soulless sketches of mankind. Wherever he goes, he learns to know and love the heart, the soul, the true and active nature, of the country and the country men. As Addison with his London folk, so Mr. Stevenson with all the people under heaven known to him: they can never and nowhere be so strange to him, so marvellous or so repulsive, but he will make friends with them, try to read their hearts, and picture them as naturally as the folk of his own Lothians. Addi- son, Steele, Montaigne, Lamb, Browne, each in his way and measure, was thus friendly with the world. 'I am averse,'

said Browne, 'from nothing: my conscience would give me
the lye if I should say I absolutely detest or hate any
essence but the Devil; or soe at least absolutely abhor
anything, but that we might come to Composition.' This
temper is most commonly shown by your leisurely essayist,
your writer of wayward genial disquisitions, your pleasant
and generous moralist. Mr. Stevenson has shown it in his
various essays, in 'Virginibus Puerisque,' in 'Memories and
Portraits,' in 'Men and Books,' in 'Across the Plains'; as
also in 'Travels with a Donkey,' in 'An Inland Voyage,' in
the 'Silverado Squatters,' records of pleasing experiments
in residence and travel; as also in 'A Child's Garden of
Verses,' where the grown man is still a perfect child.
This temper prompts and inspires him to handle matters of
actual practical concern, political, social, religious, as
when he champions the memory of Father Damien, or exposes
the calamitous misgovernment of Samoa, or turns the dynamiter into effective ridicule. But in all these examples
of his art Mr. Stevenson is largely his own master, he is
to himself 'both law and impulse'; for all the niceties of
design and style demanded for such books, they leave their
composer a wide freedom; novels, romances, stories do not.
In these he must sternly suppress and limit many fancies,
desires, impulses; there are temptations to overcome,
seductions to withstand. In a word, he must reconcile his
own personality with the impersonality required by his
art; and who will affirm that Mr. Stevenson has not
succeeded? He has succeeded very largely by style, by 'a
fine sense of his words.' As Newman puts it:

> while the many use language as they find it, the man of
> genius uses it indeed, but subjects it withal to his
> own purposes, and moulds it according to his own pecu-
> liarities.... We might as well say that one man's
> shadow is another's as that the style of a really
> gifted mind can belong to any but himself. It follows
> him about as a shadow. His thought and feeling are
> personal, and so his language is personal.

The style of Mr. Stevenson, like all good styles, owes
much to other good styles: he constantly reminds us of
Thoreau, Hazlitt, Browne. But one of its original and
pervading elements is an artful mastery and adaptation of
a Scotch habit of speech, his own birthright: a mingling
of its terms and graces and humours with the less homely
and statelier language of literary English. His David
Balfour surely speaks for him, saying of the 'vulgar'
English, 'Indeed, I have never grown used to it, nor yet
altogether with the English grammar, as perhaps a very
critical eye might here and there spy out even in these

memoirs.' 'Kidnapped' is a Scotch book in the Lowland
tongue, the speech of old Mackellar; but something
indefinably, pleasantly Scotch, a somewhat deliberate
sententiousness and slow elaboration, all very delightful,
hangs around Mr. Stevenson's every page. This is an age
of very individual style: no one could mistake a page of
Mr. Meredith, or of Mr. Pater, or of Mr. Hardy; and a page
of Mr. Stevenson is no less unmistakable. Whether he describe a coil of rope, or a bad conscience, or a sword-
thrust, his language alone will make the thing his own,
apart from any peculiar interest or insight in his position towards it. And so, all the world over, the least
familiar things come home to us, and convince us, and
charm, because told in a language that all his readers
have learned to know and most have learned to love. And
with style the whole mind of the writer comes in power
upon us; all his attitudes and apprehensions. Beautiful
as is 'Rosamund Gray,' it is not Lamb: one work of Mr.
Stevenson differs from another in merit, but they are all
his. Burney asked Johnson, whether he did not think Otway
frequently tender. 'Sir, he is all tenderness!' So, of
Mr. Stevenson shall we say that he is all cordiality, all
sympathy, all comprehension? It is hard to find the exact
expression for that power of reaching through the externals to the interior of things: of discerning in and by
the outward aspects and manners of men their very selves
and natures. Mr. Stevenson so wins upon us by his minutely appropriate style, that we cannot fail to see what
he would be at: what it is in these peoples and places -
Scotch be they, or Samoan, that touches him, rouses his
human interest and concern. *Mentem mortalia tangunt*, (1)
and not always to tears alone. Mr. Stevenson is full of
the movement, the animation of life. With no forced
phrases, no calculated recklessness or brutality of speech,
he takes us, not into the landscape and setting of men's
lives, but into their secret. He writes, to outward
view, with no eye but for his own pure personal pleasure;
not with an eye to an astonished or shocked or captivated
public. By touches of that unique style, he brings the
ugliest and coarsest things into the pale of beauty, and
gives to all the rough lives and places of the world the
consecration, not of a brutal or of a silly sentiment, but
of an honest and sincere humanity.

Note

1 Virgil 'Aeneid', i, 462. 'Sunt lacrimae rerum, et
   mentem mortalia tangunt': There are tears for human
   affairs, and mortals' sorrows touch the heart.

139.   EDMUND GOSSE, FROM A LETTER TO STEVENSON

7 July 1893

From 'Life and Letters of Sir Edmund Gosse' (1931), ed.
Evan Charteris, 229.

I have finished reading for the third time your 'Island
Nights' Entertainments.' When I read these stories first
I was a little puzzled by the exotic air of them - not
exceedingly attracted, I must say. But I read them a
second time, and the charm fell upon me, and now a third
time, and I am tempted to think them your best work, or
a bit of it. The writing was never more delicately right,
more rare without preciousness, more picturesque without
loss of nature. I include all three stories, although I
believe I think the 'Beach of Falesá' the most heroic performance of the three - the most difficult to carry
through.

'Catriona'

September 1893

140. STEVENSON ON 'CATRIONA', FROM LETTERS TO COLVIN

1892, 1893

(a) From a letter dated February 1892

... I have a confession to make. When I was sick I tried
to get to work to finish that Samoa thing ['A Footnote to
History']; wouldn't go; and at last, in the colic time, I
slid off into 'David Balfour', some 50 pages of which are
drafted, and like me well. Really I think it is spirited;
and there's a heroine that (up to now) seems to have
attractions; *absit omen*! David, on the whole, seems
excellent. Alan does not come in till the tenth chapter,
and I am only at the eighth, so I don't know if I can find
him again; but David is on his feet, and doing well, and
very much in love, and mixed up with the Lord Advocate and
the (untitled) Lord Lovat, and all manner of great folk.
And the tale interferes with my eating and sleeping. The
join [with 'Kidnapped', to which it was a sequel] is bad;
I have not thought to strain too much for continuity; so
this part be alive, I shall be content. But there's no
doubt David seems to have changed his style, de'il ha'e
him! And much I care, if the tale travel! (LS, iv, 17)

(b) From a letter dated 2 March 1892

Since I last wrote, fifteen chapters of 'David Balfour'
have been drafted, and five *tirés au clair*. I think it
pretty good; there's a blooming maiden that costs anxiety
- she is virginal as billy; but David seems there and

alive, and the Lord Advocate is good, and so I think is an
episodic appearance of the Master of Lovat. In Chapter
XVII. I shall get David abroad - Alan went already in
Chapter XII. The book should be about the length of
'Kidnapped'; this early part of it, about D.'s evidence in
the Appin case, is more of a story than anything in 'Kidnapped', but there is no doubt there comes a break in the
middle, and the tale is practically in two divisions. In
the first, James More and the M'Gregors, and Catriona,
only show; in the second, the Appin case being disposed
of, and James Stewart hung, they rule the roast and usurp
the interest - should there be any left. Why did I take
up 'David Balfour'? I don't know. A sudden passion.
(LS, iv, 19)

(c) From a letter dated 9 March 1892

All the time 'David Balfour' is skelping along. I began
it the 13th of last month; I have now 12 chapters, 79
pages ready for press, or within an ace, and, by the time
the month is out, one-half should be completed, and I'll
be back at drafting the second half. What makes me sick
is to think of Scott turning out 'Guy Mannering' in three
weeks! What a pull of work: heavens, what thews and
sinews! And here am I, my head spinning from having only
re-written seven not very difficult pages - and not very
good when done. Weakling generation. It makes me sick of
myself, to make such a fash and bobbery over a rotten end
of an old nursery yarn, not worth spitting on when done.
Still, there is no doubt I turn out my work more easily
than of yore; and I suppose I should be singly glad of
that. And if I got my book done in six weeks, seeing it
will be about half as long as Scott, and I have to write
everything twice, it would be about the same rate of
industry. It is my fair intention to be done with it in
three months, which would make me about one-half the man
Sir Walter was for application and driving the dull pen.
Of the merit we shall not talk; but I don't think Davie is
without merit. (LS, iv, 25-6)

(d) From a letter dated April 1893

Tod Lapraik [ch. xv] is a piece of living Scots: If I had
never writ anything but that and Thrawn Janet, still I'd
have been a writer. The defects of D.B. are inherent, I
fear. But on the whole, I am far indeed from being displeased with the tailie. One thing is sure, there has

been no such drawing of Scots character since Scott; and
even he never drew a full length like Davie, with his
shrewdness and simplicity, and stockishness and charm.
Yet, you'll see, the public won't want it; they want more
Alan! Well, they can't get it. And readers of 'Tess [of
the d'Urbevilles]' can have no use for my David, and his
innocent but real love affairs.
     I found my fame much grown on this return to civilisa-
tion. *Digito monstrari* is a new experience; people all
looked at me in the streets of Sydney; and it was very
queer. Here, of course, I am only the white chief in the
Great House to the natives; and to the whites, either an
ally or a foe. It is a much healthier state of matters.
If I lived in an atmosphere of adulation, I should end by
kicking against the pricks. O my beautiful forest, O my
beautiful shining, windy house, what a joy it was to
behold them again! No chance to take myself too seriously
here. (LS, iv, 167)

141. A. T. QUILLER-COUCH, FROM FIRST THOUGHTS ON
'CATRIONA', 'SPEAKER'

9 September 1893, viii, 268-9

In his opening remarks Quiller-Couch mentions Barrie's
earlier judgment (see No. 108) that the masterpiece
expected of Stevenson is long overdue. This review was
reprinted in 'Adventures in Criticism' (1896), 168-76.

... 'Is, then, the great book written?' I am sure I
don't know. Probably not: for human experience goes to
show that The Great Book (like The Great American Novel)
never gets written. But that a great story has been
written is certain enough: and one of the curious points
about this story is its title.
     It is not 'Catriona'; nor is it 'Kidnapped.' 'Kid-
napped' is a taking title, and 'Catriona' beautiful in
sound and suggestion of romance: and 'Kidnapped' (as
everyone knows) is a capital tale, though imperfect;
and 'Catriona' (as the critics began to point out, the
day after its issue) a capital tale with an awkward
fissure midway in it. 'It is the fate of sequels' - thus

Mr. Stevenson begins his Dedication - 'to disappoint those
who have waited for them;' and it is possible that the
boys of Merry England (who, it may be remembered, thought
more of 'Treasure Island' than of 'Kidnapped') will take
but luke-warmly to 'Catriona,' having had five years in
which to forget its predecessor. No: the title of the
great story is 'The Memoirs of David Balfour.' Catriona
has a prettier name than David, and may give it to the
last book of her lover's adventures: but the 'Odyssey' was
not christened after Penelope.

Put 'Kidnapped' and 'Catriona' together within the same
covers, with one title-page, one dedication (here will be
the severest loss), and one table of contents, in which
the chapters are numbered straight away from I. to LX.:
and - this above all things - read the tale right through
from David's setting forth from the garden gate at Essen-
dean to his homeward voyage, by Catriona's side, on the
Low Country ship. And having done this, be so good as to
perceive how paltry are the objections you raised against
the two volumes when you took them separately. Let me
raise again one or two of them.

(1.) 'Catriona' is just two stories loosely hitched
together - the one of David's vain attempt to save James
Stewart, the other of the loves of David and Catriona:
and in case the critics should be too stupid to detect
this, Mr. Stevenson has been at the pains to divide his
book into Part I. and Part II. Now this, which is a real
fault in a book called 'Catriona,' is no fault at all in
'The Adventures of David Balfour,' which by its very title
claims to be constructed loosely. In an Odyssey the road
taken by the wanderer is all the nexus required; and the
continuity of his presence (if the author know his business) is warrant enough for the continuity of our interest
in his adventures. That the history of Gil Blas of San-
tillane consists chiefly of episodes is not a serious
criticism upon Lesage's novel.

(2.) In 'Catriona' more than a few of the characters
are suffered to drop out of sight just as we have begun
to take an interest in them. There is Mr. Rankeillor,
for instance, whose company in the concluding chapter of
'Kidnapped' was too good to be spared very easily; and
there is Lady Allardyce ; a wonderfully clever portrait;
and Captain Hoseason - we tremble for a moment on the
verge of re-acquaintance, but are disappointed; and
Balfour of Pilrig; and at the end of Part I. away into
darkness goes the Lord Advocate Prestongrange, with his
charming womenkind.

Well, if this be an objection to the tale, it is one
urged pretty often against life itself - that we scarce

see enough of the men and women we like. And were it not
better, perhaps, to be grateful for a tale, as for a life,
which teaches us to desire the better acquaintance of the
folk we meet? And here again that which may be a fault in
'Catriona' is no fault at all in 'The Adventures of David
Balfour.' Though novelists may profess in everything they
write, to hold a mirror up to life, the reflection must
needs be more artificial in a small book than in a large.
In the one, for very clearness, they must isolate a few
human beings and cut off the currents (so to speak)
bearing upon them from the outside world; in the other,
with a larger canvas, they are able to deal with life more
frankly. Were the 'Odyssey' cut down to one episode - say
that of Nausicäa - we must round it off and have everyone on the stage and provided with his just portion of
good and evil before we ring the curtain down. As it is,
Nausicäa goes her way. And as it is, Barbara Grant must
go her way at the end of Chapter XX.; and the pang we feel
at parting with her is anything rather than a disparagement of the author.

(3.) It is very certain, as the book stands, that the
reader must experience some shock of disappointment when,
after 200 pages of the most heroical endeavouring, David
fails after all to save James Stewart of the Glens. Were
the book concerned wholly with James Stewart's fate, the
cheat would be intolerable: and as a great deal more than
half of 'Catriona' points and trembles towards his fate
like a magnetic needle, the cheat is pretty bad if we
take 'Catriona' alone. But once more, if we are dealing
with 'The Adventures of David Balfour,' - if we bear
steadily in mind that David Balfour is our concern - not
James Stewart - the story becomes not only tolerable, but
surprisingly natural and just. Then, and then only, we
get the right perspective of David's attempt, and recog-
nising how inevitable was the issue when this stripling
engaged to turn back the great forces of history.

It is more than a lustre, as the Dedication reminds us,
since David Balfour, at the end of the last chapter of
'Kidnapped,' was left to kick his heels in the British
Linen Company's office. Five years have a knack of making
people five years older; and the wordy, politic intrigue
of 'Catriona' is at least five years older than the rough-
and-tumble intrigue of 'Kidnapped'; of the fashion of the
'Vicomte de Bragelonne' rather than of the 'Three Musketeers.' But this is as it should be; for older and
astute heads are now mixed up in the case, and Prestongrange is a graduate in a very much higher school of
diplomacy than was Ebenezer Balfour. And if no word was
said in 'Kidnapped' of the love of women, we know now

that this matter was held over until the time came for it
to take its due place in David Balfour's experience.
Everyone knew that Mr. Stevenson would draw a woman
beautifully as soon as he was minded. 'Catriona' and her
situation have their foreshadowing in The Pavilion on the
Links. But for all that she is a surprise. She begins to
be a surprise - a beautiful surprise - when in Chapter X.
she kisses David's hand 'with a higher passion than the
common kind of clay has any sense of;' and she is a
beautiful surprise to the end of the book. The loves of
these two make a moving story - old, yet not old: and I
pity the heart that is not tender for Catriona when she
and David take their last walk together in Leyden, and
'the knocking of her little shoes upon the way sounded
extraordinarily pretty and sad.'
    It remains just now to add that Mr. Stevenson twice, at
least, introduces the word 'damned' with surprising
effect. I know no better (though seemingly trivial) test
of a classic than the manner of his 'damns'. 'David Balfour' is a very big feat - a gay and gallant tale.

142. T. WATTS-DUNTON, UNSIGNED REVIEW, 'ATHENAEUM'

16 September 1893, 3438, 375-7

On Watts-Dunton see headnote to No. 82.

Difficult and in many ways unsatisfactory as is the autobiographical method of fiction, it has certain unquestionable advantages over the historic method. One of these
is that the personality of the narrator as an eye-witness
of the incidents lends a unity of impression to material
that in itself may sometimes be without unity, and sometimes even perhaps without congruity. The very fact that
the adventures come to a hero of a well-delineated temper
acts as a sort of plot, for the plot is the hero's own
life unfolded in a literary medium by himself. Had these
same adventures been recorded by the historic method, this
lack of unity would have been apparent. This very lack
of unity, this absence of any sign of a constructed plot,
will often lend an organic vitality to a story which
nothing else could lend. In the story of which the volume

before us is the conclusion the value of the autobiographical method in its power of fusing disparate and even incongruous material is strikingly seen. In 'Kidnapped' the
struggle of the hero, David Balfour, was with the machinations of a wicked uncle of the approved fairy-story type.
In 'Catriona' David's struggle is mainly with a gang of
murderous conspirators called the Whigs, myrmidons of the
Duke of Argyll, who, having determined to get rid of a
political foe by judicial murder, cause David to be kept
prisoner on the Bass Rock because he is an inconvenient
witness - the one person, indeed, whose testimony could
prove the entire innocence of the accused whom Whiggery
has determined to send to the gallows.

By the historic method material so disparate as that
contained in the story and its sequel could hardly have
been held together, howsoever skilfully the working
characters might be kept revolving round the hero as
centre; but by the use of the autobiographic method the
hero's own personality prevents that solution of continuity which is so fatal to a work of art. That the villain
of the piece is in the first part the murderous uncle,
while in the second it is the composite ogre Whiggery, is
true. But no matter; it is the hero, David Balfour, who
suffers from the machinations of both, and as his experiences are recorded by himself his life-story is the plot.
Indeed, it might be even maintained that this very drifting from one villain to the other aids the illusion; for
in real life such shiftings go on to the very end of the
chapter. And Whiggery is as good a villain as another.
In modern times - that is to say, ever since the tragic
mischief of drama ceased to be Fate - the villain has been
a very important personage in a story, more important
sometimes than even the hero himself. The hero, as in
many of Scott's novels, may be a perfectly 'washed-out'
'walking gentleman,' but so long as he makes a good foil
to the villain, he may be a success. This is so even in
the highest poetry. For instance, when Macbeth rushes,
dagger in hand, into the chamber of the walking gentleman
Duncan, to murder him in his sleep, we hold our breath to
be sure, but it is on account of the Macbeth interest, not
on account of the walking gentleman interest; and when
there comes the terrible knocking at the gate, it is not
in the smallest degree our sympathy with the walking
gentleman Duncan, who is lying dead, that arrests for the
moment the pulsations of our hearts, but our sympathy with
the picturesque villain who has lifted assassination into
high poetry. And an uncle makes a very good villain.
Indeed, from the crime of the murderer of the children in
the Tower - nay, from the murder of the babes in the wood

down to the wickedness of Ralph Nickleby and on to the
latest novel at Mudie's - the wicked relative has triumphantly held his place as the best of all villains.
Properly he should be a baronet, but a duke or a money-
lender will do. But in 'Kidnapped' the machinations of
the uncle were frustrated; he became harmless for further
villainy, and otherwise as contemptible almost as Count
Fosco appeared when his murders turned out to be only
hypothetical and he stood before the world as a mere
swag-bellied bird-fancier.

If the story of David Balfour was to be continued - as
no hero could reach his goal *per saltum* (if he could and
did there could be no story, for the hero has to be
baffled at every turn) - another villain was indispensable. But who was to baffle David now that the uncle was
placed *hors de combat?*

As the scene of the story is Scotland and the time
Jacobite, the answer to this question is obvious enough.
The villain must be Whiggery. True, the hero was himself
a Whig; but that, as the crafty novelist knew, merely
adds piquancy to the hero's impeachment of the ogre Whiggery. When it can be said of the villain of any story,
'Out of his own mouth is he condemned,' the triumph of the
novelist is complete. As Mr. Stevenson's story is told
through the mouth of a dramatic character, it would be
out of place to make inquiry here as to what are his own
views of that question between Whiggery and Jacobitism
which burned once so fiercely, and which is again being
revived in a fashion that can only be called comic.
Having set himself to tell the story of a Whig gentleman,
entangled, through a series of misadventures and mistakes, as a Jacobite in the machinations of Argyll and his
henchmen, what the novelist had to do was to realize the
situations as completely as his power of imagination would
allow. But here presents itself a question that has been
discussed in these columns in days gone by. What is the
present state of the historic conscience in this country?
From the artistic point of view it may be laid down as an
axiom that the more vigorous the power of any imaginative
writer of seeing and presenting the physiognomic details
of any dramatic action, the more careful has he to be in
selecting any particular dramatic action for treatment.
If, for instance, either Boccaccio or Keats had shed upon
the story of Isabella the full electric light of his
imagination - a light such as would illuminate all the
physiognomic details of the great culminating situation of
the story - the subject would have been found to be un-
suited to artistic treatment, for the simple reason that
art must never actualize such horrors as those of the

mutilation of the corpse and the festering head. And the
same, perhaps, was to be said of that other Italian story
treated by Tennyson in The Lover's Tale. Now is the same
canon to be applied to the demands of the historic conscience? That the harm done by unconscientious manipula-
tions of the truths of history or of contemporary life is
in exact relation to the force of the imagination at work
upon them, is manifest. It is Thackeray's enormous command over realistic details that makes his impeachment of
Marlborough so cruel. And even in fiction dealing with
the other levels of life, it would seem that the power of
seeing and presenting the physiognomy of any dramatic
situation in its minutest details may be so great as to
give an undue importance to the situation selected for
treatment, resulting in a picture of human life that is
altogether erroneous.

Art is, of course, nothing more than a skilled and
imaginative selection from nature's _répertoire_, which is
infinite. An ordinary dramatist taking the story of
'Hedda Gabler,' for instance, and using the same incidents
and situations as Ibsen uses, would really have left upon
our minds a truer impression of Scandinavian life and
morals than has been left by Ibsen. The illusion called
up by a dramatist of less realistic power than Ibsen
commands would be only partially accepted as representing
Scandinavian life. The work of such a dramatist would be
taken to be a story, more or less fanciful, told by action
and dialogue, and nothing more than such a story. But
Ibsen's play, owing to the marvellous realism of easy dialogue, seems to be 'a square cut out of real life,' and
the spectator, led away by realism and forgetting how
impossible it is for _any_ artistic picture to be actually
'a square cut out of real life' - forgetting that art is,
and must always be, a mere matter of selection - goes away
with the impression that the days and nights of Scandinavian married ladies are occupied not in the true business
of life, but with love thoughts about men who are other
women's lovers and husbands, while all the men, even to
the judge upon the bench, are mainly intent upon seducing
their friends' wives.

Now in the story before us the ogre Whiggery commits
the very foulest crime that it is possible for any villain
to commit. Of all forms of murder, judicial murder is at
once the most diabolical and the most mean. Moreover, it
strikes at the heart of civilization itself. The vast
strength of the judicial system of a community such as
ours is the outgrowth of a surrender of the rights of the
natural man that is equally vast, and to keep that power
irresistible and inviolable is the most sacred duty that

citizens can recognize. In the cobweb texture of a circu-
lating library story the imagination at work is of so
feeble a kind that the Duke of Argyll might, on insuffi-
cient evidence or on none, be charged with the crime of
judicial murder without any serious outrage being committed upon a dead man whose name is part of history, for
it is only the poor novel-spinner's fun. Only a partial
illusion is gained, and perhaps only a partial illusion is
sought, by ordinary story-tellers; but to this category
Mr. Stevenson does not belong. He is a novelist of quite
extraordinary imaginative power, exercising an extraordinary command over those physiognomic details which give
vitality to a dramatic picture. Perhaps, indeed, at his
best he is comparable with only one novelist, and that one
the greatest of all - Walter Scott. In Scott's time the
demands of the historic conscience were not recognized as
they are now. In our time history has become not only
more scientific, but also more conscientious than it was
in his. Now, unless there is full documentary evidence of
Argyll's having been guilty of such infamy as he is
charged with, is a writer of great imaginative power,
armed evidently with an unusual knowledge of the time,
justified in using a well-known historical character for
the development of a story?

There is no doubt, however, that Mr. Stevenson has here
given us a novel of extraordinary fascination. Upon him,
if upon any one of Scott's successors, has the mantle of
the Wizard fallen. We can give him no higher praise; for
if the final cause of art is to add to man's narrow stock
of true delights, Scott's work is more precious than that
of any other writer, proseman or poet, of the nineteenth
century. When Joubert said of latter-day literature, 'It
hurts,' he in two words uttered a criticism that might be
expanded into two volumes. We live in times so transitional, so overshadowed by a future whose possibilities
for ill and for good can only be vaguely dreamed of, that
literature in a general way simply *must* 'hurt.' Hence
art - when, like that of Scott, it is able and willing to
add to the enjoyments of life - able and willing to make
it seem a delightful thing to live - becomes more precious
to the soul of man than any of those profundities and
attempted solutions of enigmas which Carlyle found - thank
Heaven! - to be altogether wanting in the 'Waverley
Novels.'

To say, then, that a writer of our day has a share, and
a large share, of the master's geniality is to offer him a
great meed of praise. It is difficult to think that
scenes so fresh as these, scenes as full of the enjoyment
of life for its own sake as Scott's, were written by a

recluse who, according to his own account, is in the habit
of sitting 'late into the night,' 'toiling to leave a
memory behind him.' Perhaps, however, Scott's matchless
geniality of tone - the inevitable efflorescence of a
matchless geniality of constitution and a matchless freedom from the greed of fame - had this drawback, that it
was the cause of that slovenliness of style which has been
so often commented upon. Slovenliness can certainly not
be charged against Mr. Stevenson's style. Its occasional
self-consciousness is about the only fault in the book.
As to his characters, Scott himself might have been proud
of them all; but the heroine Catriona is beyond all praise.
As fascinating as Miranda and Mignon, to whom she is in
some sort akin, she throws a halo of heroism as well as
of beauty over the book from her first appearance to the
last page. Her adventures in Holland with David, especially during the walk to Leyden and during their sojourn
under one roof as brother and sister, are to be ranked
among the choicest passages in fiction. Indeed, it would
be hard to match anywhere, and impossible to surpass, such
writing as that ... where the delightful simplicity of
the girl's nature is rendered by a marvellous delicacy of
touch. Her mind has been deeply disturbed by certain
harmless passages between David and her friend Barbara: -

> 'Did you kiss her truly?' she asked. There went
> through me so great a heave of surprise that I was
> shook with it 'Miss Grant!' I cried, all in a dis-
> order. 'Yes, I asked her to kiss me a good-bye, the
> which she did.' 'Ah, well,' said she, 'you have
> kissed me too, at all events.' [From ch. xxiv, Full
> Story of a Copy of Heineccius]

And the nobility of her nature is delineated with an equal
success when her eyes became opened to the relations between David, her father, and herself. Barbara is an
almost equally successful delineation of a piquant character of the Beatrice type. Her only fault is that in certain portions of the story she rises to such a pitch of
winsomness as to become a somewhat threatening rival of
even Catriona herself. And, of course, it is always a
dangerous thing to set up rivals to either the hero or
the heroine of any story. Although it was manifestly
impossible to keep her style of raillery from suggesting
at times that of Beatrice and at times that of Diana
Vernon, she is a real addition to our gallery of piquant
and beautiful girls. Among other characters there is a
splendid profile of the son of the notorious Simon, Lord
Lovat. And Alan Breck, when he does reappear, is worthy
of himself.

143.   'CATRIONA' AND THE DAEMONIC, FROM AN UNSIGNED
ARTICLE, 'GLASGOW HERALD'

23 September 1893, 7

... As was to be expected, the critics are puzzling their
heads over such questions as whether 'Catriona,' following
in the wake of 'Kidnapped,' though at a distance of ten
years, is another proof of the mistake committed by
authors in attempting 'sequels,' and whether Mr Steven--
son's self-exile to Samoa has favourably or prejudicially
affected his genius. On one point, indeed, there seems to
be substantial agreement. Mr Stevenson has not in
'Catriona' produced the book which, according to Mr Barrie
in his 'Edinburgh Eleven' [No. 108], he will yet write.
We are told on all hands that the Stevenson who has given
us 'Catriona' is a very different man from the Stevenson
who wrote 'Treasure Island.' The elder Stevenson has not
the élan, the youthful gaiety and Dumas insouciance of the
younger, and yet he does not show any of the special
literary virtues which we are in the habit of associating
with middle-age. Such criticism may be, however, a trifle
unjust. Genius cannot be pushed; certainly it ought not.
Besides, it is too soon to prophesy. The George Eliot who
wrote 'Middlemarch' is by no means the same as the George
Eliot who gave us the romance of Adam Bede and Mr Gilfil's
love story; nor is the James Payn who has produces scores
of novels during these later years that are full of man-
of-the-worldliness quite the same as the James Payn who
wrote 'Lost Sir Massingberd.'
     But there is one feature in the literary transformation
or evolution of Mr Stevenson which may, to judge from the
portrait of the chief villain in 'Catriona,' be authori-
tatively pronounced upon. That is the steady degradation
of the diabolic in his work. There was no scoundrel to
speak of in 'Kidnapped;' Hoseason, and even the very
wicked uncle, scarcely deserve mention. The true predecessor of James More, the father of Catriona, is the
Master of Ballantrae. But what a contrast between the
two! The Master of Ballantrae is a bad - a horribly bad -
man. But there is an undoubted fascination even about his
badness. You feel yourself in the presence of one who,
under other and conventionally happier circumstances,
might have been a Cæsar Borgia or even a Bonaparte. But
what of James More or Drummond or M'Gregor - let him be
known by whatever alias sounds least unpleasant? Can the
degenerate son of Rob Roy, even if we accept as accurate

the statements made to his prejudice by Scott, have sunk
so low as to be a hypocrite, a sponger, a traitor, and, in
spite of his physique, a coward? 'Shame of Appin,' his
daughter styles him. 'Stinkin' brock?' exclaims Alan
Breck, even more energetically, when he ascertains that he
has been betrayed. It is not that James More is badly
drawn. He is drawn only too well. With the exception of
the altogether delightful Barbara Grant, he is perhaps the
best portrait in 'Catriona.' But he is depressingly disgusting, a moral nightmare. Even when he is in his coffin,
you feel towards him as David Balfour himself did, after
James gave his son-in-law and his daughter his final
benediction. '"I have never been understood." said he,
"I forgive you both without an afterthought;" after which
he spoke for all the world in his old manner, was so
obliging as to play a tune or two upon his pipes, and
borrowed a small sum before I left. I could not trace
even a hint of shame in any part of his behaviour; but
he was great upon forgiveness: it seemed always fresh to
him. I think he forgave me every time we met, and when
after some four days he passed away in a kind of odour
of affectionate sanctity, I could have torn my hair out
for exasperation. I had him buried; but what to put upon
his tomb was quite beyond me, till at last I considered
the date would look best' [from Conclusion]. One can
understand David Balfour tearing his hair out - Pecksniff
was a gentleman compared with James More - but it is not
easy to understand his running the risk involved in marrying the daughter of such a man.

In considering the deterioration of the dæmonic in
literature, of which James More is such an appalling
example, let us remember what exactly that dæmonic is.
Goethe when in search for a religion stumbled upon it,
and thus described it: - 'It was not divine, for it
seemed unintellectual; nor human, for it was no result of
understanding; nor diabolic, for it was of beneficent
tendency; nor angelic, for you could often notice in it a
certain mischievousness. It resembled chance, inasmuch as
it demonstrated nothing; but was like Providence, inasmuch
as it showed symptoms of continuity. Everything which
fetters human agency seemed to yield before it; it seemed
to dispose arbitrarily of the necessary elements of our
existence.' Add to this that Goethe had Napoleon in his
mind when he wrote this passage, that he attributed the
possession of the dæmonic influence to such different persons as Byron and the Duke of Weimar, that he said of
Mephistopheles he is 'too negative a being,' and of himself, 'It does not lie in my nature, but I am subject to
its influence,' and you can come as near an understanding

of the dæmonic as is possible. 'Magnetic' must not be
confounded with 'demonic.' The late Mr James Blaine (1)
was a magnetic man; the First Napoleon was not only
Goethe's but the world's dæmonic man. When Goethe first
came across Napoleon and each proclaimed the other to be
emphatically 'a man,' he fully deserved the description.
Contemplating the later period of the conqueror's active
career, nearly eighty years after it has come to a close,
one may not be quite disposed to say of that career as a
whole that it was 'not diabolic, for it was not of beneficent tendency.' Finally, at all events, Napoleon's
influence was wholly malefic. So long, however, as he
was merely France's Avenging Angel - a messenger of Satan
(if you will) sent to buffet the rest of Europe for venturing to interfere with the internal politics of his
(adopted) country, he was her dæmonic man, her Man of
Destiny. As such he will live in history. The true dæmonic man of literature is not necessarily therefore a bad
man any more than Napoleon was a bad man when he first
influenced Goethe's imagination. He is - rather let us
say he ought to be - a man of very varied gifts, endowed
with a strong will, and, above all, with a belief that he
is a kind of Providence sent to do a special work, and
quite resistless so long as his work is unaccomplished.
The dæmonic man has not figured much in British literature
till this century, not even in the highest. Hamlet had
some of his elements, and had his chance of playing the
part on a small stage. But he threw that chance away, for
reasons best known to himself - and Shakespeare. The reason for this, no doubt, is that dæmonic men have not
figured much - if at all - in our actual history. Our
great men - our Chathams, Nelsons, Wellingtons - were men
of passion perhaps, self-confidence, and ambition, but
quite explicable on ordinary psychological principles, and
had nothing weird or uncanny about them. Cromwell is our
nearest approach to the dæmonic man; according to Carlyle
and the Carlylians, he is really dæmonic, whereas Napoleon was diabolic. But with the advance of historical
science even Cromwell is being explained as - may one
say? - the incarnation of Duty permeated by Religion,
just as Wellington was the incarnation of Duty pure and
simple. As a consequence, therefore, one does not find
dæmonic men in British literature which preceded the Napoleonic era. In the old fiction, in Defoe, in Fielding,
in Smollett, even in Richardson, there are plenty of men
with strong wills and strong passions, who influence
others by means of these. But none of them, strictly
speaking, can be said to be dæmonic. Even Scott, who,
as we know, not only lived in but was affected by the

Napoleonic era, was too healthily conventional in his
views of ordinary life to take much interest in the dæmonic man or to present him on his stage. Perhaps the nearest approach to anything of the kind is Henbane Dwining,
the strong-willed, sceptical, unscrupulous, but not cowardly, apothecary in 'The Fair Maid of Perth' who bends
the commonplace vengeful villain Ramorny to his will.
Henbane is a dæmonic man distinctly inclining towards diabolism, like Napoleon himself in the later years of his
reign.
     It would probably be going too far to say that it was
Charlotte Brontë who introduced the dæmonic man (in a
stunted condition) into British fiction. But it is not
too much to say that in Rochester he obtained costumes
and a staging not altogether unworthy of him. Of late it
has become a fashion to sneer at Rochester. Even Mr
Leslie Stephen says of him, 'I must admit that, in spite of
of some opposing authority, he does not appear to me to be
a real character at all except as a reflection of a certain side of his creator.... Get him besides any man's
character of a man, and one feels at once that he has no
real solidity or vitality in him. He has, of course,
strong nerves and muscles, but these are articles which
can be supplied in unlimited quantities with little expense to the imagination.' No critic - certainly no
living critic - is more deserving of respect than Mr
Leslie Stephen. Yet this estimate of Rochester strikes
me as superficial.... Rochester has his weaknesses and
worse; his endeavour to marry Jane without informing her
of the fact that he has already a wife alive, although
mad, is almost incredibly wicked - worse than even an
offer to make her his mistress would have been. But
almost from the first he is a strong, attractive, and
more than magnetic personality. Jane Eyre succumbs to
him, and in every sense considers him her master; and
although she flees from him lest she should allow her
passion to carry her away into 'sin,' she is unaffectedly
glad to return to him when she has a legal right to do so,
and when, thanks to misfortune, the angelic has triumphed
over the diabolic in his nature. 'Jane Eyre' caused a
great outcry when it appeared, and that mainly because the
Mrs Grundy of the time could not stand - or would not
understand - the dæmonic man, who bent his energies to
conquer a fluttering little governess much as Bonaparte
set himself to conquer Russia. But Mrs Grundy has had
to put up with a good deal since the publication of 'Jane
Eyre,' and may have to put up with a good deal more. The
other day I stumbled upon 'The Shadow of Desire,' published in America, and evidently written by an American.

This author - Irene Osgood (2) she is styled - evidently
has a 'purpose' of her own. Yet I find this passage in
it. 'Before she could cry out or make any resistance, he
had caught her in his arms again, and with one hand on her
throat, held her head back. She closed her eyes almost
fainting, for he was kissing her again. His thick sensuous lips were pressed against her delicate ones'.... She
had never dreamed of such kisses before, and she gave
back kisses hot and fast until her heart almost ceased to
beat, and she lay like a dead thing, overwhelmed by this
new and strange sensation.' 'She' in this scene is Mrs
Ruth Bronson, who is represented as animated by 'a great
pure love' for her (second) husband. She does not care
two straws for the man, Will Dunston by name, to whom she
'gives back kisses hot and fast.' On the contrary, when,
having killed Bronson in a duel, Dunston - not unnaturally
perhaps when one thinks of these kisses - comes and
demands Ruth, she drives him away like a fury, and, after
taking a convenient attack of madness, marries a third
husband who has 'desired' her longer than either Bronson
or Dunston. But Dunston has 'voluptuous red lips' with
'sensuous curves.' His fascination, in fact, is a 'subtle
animal magnetism.'

The descent from Rochester to the Master of Ballantrae,
James More, Mr Hardy's Alec D'Urberville, and Miss Osgood's
Will Dunston, though steady and perhaps 'inevitable' -
everything is 'inevitable' in these days of the New Fatal-
ism - has been by no means rapid. It has reached us
through 'Guy Livingstone,' Ouida, and Miss Braddon. (3)
The hero-villains of fifteen years ago, though wicked and
generally able to work their wicked will with women, were
on the whole companionable, given not only to murder and
seduction, but to camaraderie, stimulated by brandy and
soda. They are not dæmonic in the strict sense of the
word, but they are not unmitigatedly diabolic. But the
Master of Ballantrae and his successors are of the essence
of diabolism; they have not even what the cynic terms redeeming vices. There will, I have no doubt, be a reaction
against this degradation of the dæmonic; I am not quite
sure that it has not already commenced. In an almost forgotten story, 'Fortune's Fool,' by Mr Julian Hawthorne -
that Mr Julian Hawthorne who might have fought for the
empire of the uncanny in humanity with Mr Stevenson himself had he been equally industrious - there is a more
powerful being of the fascinating order than the Master of
Ballantrae himself. But even Brian, although he squeezes
the very soul out of Tom, his victim, and Sancho Panza,
has some qualities that are akin more to the angelic than
to the diabolic. Then Detectivism, whose high priest is

Dr Conan Doyle, still reigns in our midst, and Detectivism
is distinctly non-diabolic; the great discoverer of crime
- even although he has a weakness for locking stable doors
when the steed has been stolen - is a Michael, not a
Satan. Nay, in the hands of such an artist as Dr Doyle,
there is something Goethean, dæmonic, Providential about
him. Let us not be too downcast. We live in times of
moral anarchy, it is true; but it is anarchy *plus* Sherlock
- or should we now rather say Mycroft? - Holmes.

Notes

1 James Gillespie Blaine (1830-93) was US secretary of
   state under presidents Garfield and Harrison; in 1884
   he was himself an unsuccessful candidate for the presi-
   dency.
2 'The Shadow of Desire' (1893) was one of a number of
   melodramas written by Irene Osgood (Mrs Robert Har-
   Harborough-Sherard) (1875-1922).
3 'Guy Livingstone' (1857) was a novel by G. A. Lawrence
   (1827-76), the hero of which was an officer in the Life
   Guards and a libertine. Ouida (Marie Louise de la
   Ramée) (1839-1908) was the author of numerous novels,
   chiefly about fashionable life, but her 'A Village Com-
   mune' (1881) won Ruskin's praise for its authentic view
   of peasant life. Mary Elizabeth Braddon (1837-1915)
   gained recognition with 'Lady Audley's Secret' (1862).

144. EDWARD BURNE-JONES, FROM A LETTER TO SIDNEY COLVIN

1893 (?)

From Colvin, 'Memories and Notes' (1921), 57.
   (Sir) Edward Burne-Jones (1833-98) was the English
painter and designer.

Have you read 'Catriona'?... You didn't tell me, and if
you had you must have talked of it, for it is a wonder,
and every page glitters, and I can't make out why the
Speaker doesn't read it to the House of an evening - much
better for them to listen to it than to each other's

nonsense. I am right glad he has made a woman at last,
and why did he delay? this one is so beautifully made.
Oh, he's a miracle of a lad, that boy out there in the
Cannibal Islands; I wish he would come back and write
only about the Borderland.

145. HENRY JAMES, FROM A LETTER TO STEVENSON

21 October 1893

From 'The Letters of Henry James' (1920), ed. Percy
Lubbock, ii, 207-9

My dear Louis,
    The postal guide tells me, disobligingly, that there is
no mail to you via San Francisco this month and that I
must confide my few lines to the precarious and perfidious
Hamburg. I do so, then, for the plain reason that I can
no longer repress the enthusiasm that has surged within me
ever since I read 'Catriona.' I missed, just after doing
so, last month's post, and I was infinitely vexed that it
should not have conveyed to you the freshness of my rapture. For the said 'Catriona' so reeks and hums with
genius that there is no refuge for the desperate reader
but in straightforward prostration. I'm not sure that
it's magnanimous of you to succeed so inconsiderately –
there is a modesty in easy triumph which your flushed muse
perhaps a little neglects. – But forgive that lumbering
image – I won't attempt to carry it out. Let me only say
that I don't despatch these ineffectual words on their too
watery way to do anything but thank you for an exquisite
pleasure. I hold that when a book has the high beauty of
that one there's a poor indelicacy in what simple folk
call criticism. The work lives by so absolute a law that
it's grotesque to prattle about what *might* have been! I
shall express to you the one point in which my sense was
conscious of an unsatisfied desire, but only after saying
first how rare an achievement I think the whole personality and tone of David and with how supremely happy a
hand you have coloured the palpable women. They are quite
too lovely and everyone is running after them. In David
not an error, not a false note ever; he is all of an

exasperating truth and rightness. The one thing I miss in
the book is the note of *visibility* - it subjects my visual
sense, my *seeing* imagination, to an almost painful under-
feeding. The *hearing* imagination, as it were, is nourished like an alderman, and the loud audibility seems a
slight the more on the baffled lust of the eyes - so that
I seem to myself (I am speaking of course only from the
point of view of the way, as I read, *my* impression longs
to complete itself) in the presence of voices in the darkness - voices the more distinct and vivid, the more brave
and sonorous, as voices always are - but also the more
tormenting and confounding - by reason of these bandaged
eyes. I utter a pleading moan when you, e.g., transport
your characters, toward the end, in a line or two from
Leyden to Dunkirk without the glint of a hint of all the
ambient picture of the 18th century road. However, stick
to your own system of evocation so long as what you positively achieve is so big. Life and letters and art all
take joy in you.
    ... If it hadn't been for 'Catriona' we couldn't, this
year, have held up our head. It had been long, before
that, since any decent sentence was turned in English.
We grow systematically vulgarer and baser. The only blur
of light is that your books are tasted....

                                                    H.J.

146. STEVENSON, FROM A LETTER TO JAMES

December 1893, LS, iv, 249-50

_____

My Dear Henry James,
    ... Your jubilation over 'Catriona' did me good, and still
more the subtlety and truth of your remark on the starving
of the visual sense in that book. 'Tis true, and unless I
make the greater effort - and am, as a step to that, convinced of its necessity - it will be more true I fear in
the future. I *hear* people talking and I *feel* them acting,
and that seems to me to be fiction. My two aims may be
described as -

    1st. War to the adjective.
    2nd. Death to the optic nerve.

Admitted we live in an age of the optic nerve in

literature. For how many centuries did literature get
along without a sign of it? However, I'll consider your
letter....   R.L.S.

147. EDMUND GOSSE, FROM A LETTER TO STEVENSON

13 November 1893

From 'Life and Letters of Sir Edmund Gosse' (1931), ed.
Evan Charteris, 231-3.

My dear R.L.S., -
    It is rather late in the day to thank you for the gift
of 'Catriona,' but I can't set to do anything else before
getting that off my mind. We were down in Devonshire
when it came out, and the family pestered me so much
about it that I bought a copy the very day it was published, for the sake of peace. When we were half through
it, for we read it aloud in full conclave, o' evenings,
your gift came, which we have kept in silver paper and
lavender for posterity and great occasions. The whole
family knew its 'Kidnapped', so the audience was prepared. I think we were all too much excited with the
story to criticize. When we cooled down, and I had time
to think it over again in our professional way, it was
borne in upon me, as the holy say, that 'Catriona' is
about the best - the sanest and truest - bit of narrative
you have done.
    I have one criticism to make, which is purely personal
to myself, and which you will very likely pooh-pooh. To
me the charm of your writings is yourself, is the personal
accent. Now, in no book of yours is the dramatization so
complete as in 'Catriona'. David seldom betrays himself -
he is consistently and persistently the brave, honest,
priggish, moral Scot that you intend him to be. And that
is well enough, and vastly proper from the novelist's
point of view. But you - to my thinking - were pre-
eminently sent into God's earth to be an essayist, the
best in my humble opinion (without one soul to approach
you) since Lamb. To me you always seem an essayist writing stories rather than a born novelist. That may or
may not be sound judgment, but, given that that is my

conviction, you see how I resent that a book of yours should extinguish the essayist altogether....

We have been hearing of your visit to Honolulu, which I suppose is true? I say that, because the gossip-columns of the newspapers pullulate with gossip about you that cannot be true, such as:

'All our readers will rejoice to learn that the aged fictionist L. R. Stevenson has ascended the throne of Tahiti of which island he is now a native';

or

'We regret to announce the death, in Cairo, of the well-known author, Mr. Stevenson.'

or

'Mr. Stevenson is now in Paris.'

or

'The vineyards which are cultivated in the island of Samoa by Mr. Stevenson, have been visited by desolating storms; the gifted romance-writer fears that he will, this season, export none but elderberry wine.'

'Mr. R. L. Stevenson, who is thirty-one years of age, is still partial to periwinkles, which he eats with a silver pin, presented to him by the German population of Samoa.'

We are quite disappointed if the newspapers pass a single day without a paragraph of this kind, and I am sorry I do not know how your future biography is to be compiled from the enormous mass of conflicting material. Since Byron was in Greece, nothing has appealed to the ordinary literary man as so picturesque as that you should be in the South Seas. And I partly agree....

Your affectionate friend,
E.G.

148.   GEORGE MEREDITH, FROM A LETTER TO STEVENSON

25 January 1894

From 'Letters of George Meredith' (1970), ed. C. L. Cline, iii, 1152-3.

... Here, as all who love you, I among them, rejoice to see your name is the name most commonly printed in the

newspapers, as relating to the small English world of
Letters, I mean. I don't remember in the whole course of
my literary life any name in England that has been treated
so affectionately, as well as respectfully, but this has
its disadvantages for us, though it may not touch you, for
about every other month we are harassed by news of your
being ill, of your being chased out of the Island, of I
don't know what. - Then comes the contradiction to be
succeeded by another rumour.... Let me tell you of
'Catriona': the girl herself is an excellent study of a
Celtic damsel; she is truly painted, and I like her, and
there an end, but give me Barbara Grant and rather than
fifty Davids, I would have old Preston Grange. Scenery
generally excellent, very salt, bleak, and cordial.
Always delighted to meet Alan Breck on any terms. As for
the writing I say nothing more than that I trust it may be
the emulation of young authors to equal it....

149. VERNON LEE ON 'CATRIONA' AS A 'MASTERPIECE OF CON-
STRUCTIVE CRAFT', FROM ON LITERARY CONSTRUCTION,
'CONTEMPORARY REVIEW'

September 1895, lxviii, 404-7

Violet Paget (1856-1935), novelist and critic, wrote under
the pseudonym Vernon Lee. The extract below was reprinted
in her interesting critical study 'The Handling of Words'
(1923), 1-7.

The craft of the writer consists, I am convinced, in
manipulating the contents of his reader's mind, that is
to say, taken from the technical side as distinguished
from the psychologic, in construction. Construction is
not only a matter of single words or sentences, but of
whole large passages and divisions; and the material which
the writer manipulates is not only the single impressions,
single ideas and emotions, stored up in the reader's mind
and deposited there by no act of his own, but those very
moods and trains of thought into which the writer, by his
skilful selection of words and sentences, has grouped
those single impressions, those very moods and trains of
thought which were determined by the writer himself.

We have all read Mr. Stevenson's 'Catriona.' Early in
that book there is a passage by which I can illustrate my
meaning. It is David Balfour's walk to Pilrig:

> My way led over Mouter's Hill, and through an end
> of a clachan on the braeside among fields. There was
> a whirr of looms in it went from house to house; bees
> hummed in the gardens; the neighbours that I saw at
> the doorsteps talked in a strange tongue; and I found
> out later that this was Picardy, a village where the
> French weavers wrought for the Linen Company. Here I
> got a fresh direction for Pilrig, my destination; and
> a little beyond, on the wayside, came by a gibbet and
> two men hanged in chains. They were dipped in tar, as
> the manner is; the wind span them, the chains clat-
> tered, and the birds hung about the uncanny jumping
> jacks and cried. [From ch. iii, I Go to Pilrig]

This half-page sounds as if it were an integral part
of the story, one of the things which happened to the
gallant but judicious David Balfour. But in my opinion
it is not such a portion of the story, not an episode
told for its own sake, but a qualifier of something else;
in fact, nothing but an adjective on a large scale.
Let us see. The facts of the case are these: David
Balfour, having at last, after the terrible adventures
recorded in 'Kidnapped,' been saved from his enemies and
come into his lawful property, with a comfortable life
before him and no reason for disquietude, determines to
come forward as a witness in favour of certain Highlanders, whom it is the highest interest of the Government to
put to death, altogether irrespective of whether or not
they happen to be guilty in the matter about which they
are accused. In order to offer his testimony in what he
imagines to be the most efficacious manner, David Balfour
determines to seek an interview with the Lord Advocate of
Scotland; and he is now on his way to his cousin of Pilrig
to obtain a letter from him for the terrible head of the
law. Now if David Balfour actually has to be sent to
Pilrig for the letter of introduction to the Lord Advocate, then his walk to Pilrig is an intrinsic portion of
the story, and what happened to him on his walk cannot be
considered save as an intrinsic portion also. This would
be true enough if we were considering what actually could
or must happen to a real David Balfour in a real reality,
not what Stevenson wants us to think did happen to an
imaginary David Balfour. If a real David Balfour was
destined, through the concatenation of circumstances, to
walk from Edinburgh to Pilrig by that particular road on

that particular day; why, he was destined also - and could
not escape his destiny - to come to the gibbet where, on
that particular day, along that particular road, those two
malefactors were hanging in chains.

But even supposing that Stevenson had been bound, for
some reason, to make David Balfour take that particular
day the particular walk which must have brought him past
that gibbet; Stevenson would still have been perfectly
free to omit all mention of his seeing that gibbet, as he
evidently omitted mentioning a thousand other things which
David Balfour must have seen and done in the course of his
adventures, because the sight of that gibbet in no way
affected the course of the events which Stevenson had
decided to relate, any more than the quality of the por-
ridge which David had eaten that morning. And as it happens, moreover, the very fact of David Balfour having
walked that day along that road, and of the gibbet having
been there, is, as we know, nothing but a make-believe on
Stevenson's part, and so there can have been no destiny at
all about it. Therefore, I say that this episode, which
leads to no other episode, is not an integral part of the
story, but a qualifier, an adjective. It acts, not upon
what happens to the hero, but on what is felt by the
reader. Again, let us look into the matter. This beginning of the story is, from the nature of the facts,
rather empty of tragic events; yet tragic events are what
Stevenson wishes us to live through. There is something
humdrum in those first proceedings of David Balfour's,
which are to lead to such hairbreadth escapes. There is
something not heroic enough in a young man, however
heroic his intentions, going to ask for a letter of
introduction to a Lord Advocate. But what can be done?
If adventures are invented to fill up these first chapters, these adventures will either actually lead to something which will complicate a plot already quite as complicated as Stevenson requires, or - which is even worse
- they will come to nothing, and leave the reader disappointed, incredulous, unwilling to attend further after
having wasted expectations and sympathies. Here comes in
the admirable invention of the gibbet. The gibbet is, so
to speak, the shadow of coming events cast over the
smooth earlier chapters of the book. With its grotesque
and ghastly vision, it puts the reader in the state of
mind desired: it means tragedy. 'I was pleased,' goes on
David Balfour, 'to be so far in the still countryside;
but the shackles of the gibbet clattered in my head....
There might David Balfour hang, and other lads pass on
their errands, and think light of him.' Here the reader
is not only forcibly reminded that the seemingly trumpery

errand of this boy will lead to terrible dangers; but he
is made to feel, by being told that David felt (which perhaps at that moment David, accustomed to the eighteenth-
century habit of hanging petty thieves along the roadside
might not) the ghastliness of that encounter.

And then note how this qualifier, this adjectival episode, is itself qualified. It is embedded in impressions
of peacefulness: the hillside, the whirr of looms and hum
of bees, and talk of neighbours on doorsteps; nay, Stevenson has added a note which increases the sense of peacefulness by adding an element of unconcern, of foreignness,
such as we all find adds so much to the peaceful effect of
travel, in the fact that the village was inhabited by
strangers - Frenchmen - to whom David Balfour and the Lord
Advocate and the Appin murder would never mean anything.
Had the gibbet been on the Edinburgh Grassmarket, and
surrounded by people commenting on Highland disturbances,
we should have expected some actual adventure for David
Balfour; but the gibbet there, in the fields by this peac-
ful foreign settlement, merely puts our mind in the right
frame to be moved by the adventures which will come slowly
in their due time.

This is a masterpiece of constructive craft: the
desired effect is obtained without becoming involved in
other effects not desired, without any debts being made
with the reader; even as in the case of the properly
chosen single adjective, which defines the meaning of the
noun in just the desired way, without suggesting any further definition in the wrong way.

Construction - that is to say, co-ordination. It means
finding out what is important and unimportant, what you
can afford and cannot afford to do. It means thinking
out the results of every movement you set up in the
reader's mind, how that movement will work into, help, or
mar the other movements which you have set up there
already, or which you will require to set up there in the
future. For, remember, such a movement does not die out
at once. It continues and unites well or ill with its
successors, as it has united well or ill with its predecessors. You must remember that in every kind of
literary composition, from the smallest essay to the
largest novel, you are perpetually, as in a piece of
music, introducing new *themes*, and working all the themes
into one another. A theme may be a description, a line of
argument, a whole personage; but it always represents, on
the part of the reader, a particular kind of intellectual
acting and being, a particular kind of mood. Now, these
moods, being concatenated in their progression, must be
constantly altered by the other moods they meet; they can

never be quite the same the second time they appear as the
first, nor the third as the second; they must have been
varied, and they ought to have been strengthened or made
more subtle by the company they have kept, by the things
they have elbowed, and been - however unconsciously -
compared and contrasted with; they ought to have become
more satisfactory to the writer as a result of their stay
in the reader's mind....

'The Ebb-Tide'

September 1894

In spite of the favourable reception given 'The Wrecker',
Colvin continued to warn Stevenson about the damage col-
laborative work would have on his reputation and future
sales, and he was especially distressed when he saw the
first chapters of 'The Ebb-Tide'. These chapters, chiefly
if not exclusively the work of Osbourne, Colvin thought
very inferior work; he suggested the book run serially in
England and the USA but that it not be republished in book
form. He held to this opinion even when he saw the two
final chapters, written solely by Stevenson, and judged
them to have been 'done with astonishing genius' (B, 4256).
The story was published in 'Today, a Weekly Magazine
Journal' (11 November 1893 - 3 February 1894) and in the
USA in 'McClure's Magazine' (February-July 1894). Once
Colvin was aware of Stevenson's determination to go ahead
with book publication in spite of his advice, he only
hoped that publication would be delayed until after sub-
scription sales to the Edinburgh Edition, which he and
Charles Baxter had planned together, were well under way
(B, 4291). S. S. McClure secured the book rights in the
USA and the book was published by Stone & Kimball, a
Chicago firm, in July 1894; William Heinemann published
the book in England on 21 September (see McKay, 'Some
Notes on Robert Louis Stevenson', 36). Colvin was
relieved to find the reviews not so bad as he had feared.
Still, the objections that he and Stevenson had foreseen
were in fact made. Reviewers generally agreed that
Stevenson should not have again produced a work in collaboration with Osbourne; they found the ending, in spite
of the power of the writing, to be weak and puzzling.
The 'Standard' (15 September 1894) remarked on how frequently Stevenson's hand 'fails to do him justice at the
end of a story', though in this instance the failure was
linked to the basic uncertainty of intention apparent

throughout the work - 'uncertainty, a wavering between
flippancy and gravity in handling the most solemn matters'. There were other comments on the unevenness and
disjointed quality of the work. 'The Times' (15 September 1894) objected to the 'fanciful aspect of the second
half'. The 'Saturday Review' (22 September 1894) noted
that a number of scenes, however brilliant by themselves,
appeared to have been 'designed independently of the end
in view, and tend towards no tremendous culmination' - in
short the novel was 'by no means a model of design nor a
good example of the art of cumulative construction'.
Perhaps what most startled and displeased reviewers - and
their comments are an echo of those on 'Master of Ballantrae' - and was the complete absence of 'romance', the
unrelieved presence of harsh and unpleasant realities, of
the horrible and the grotesque. The 'Speaker' (29 September 1894) characterized it as

> strong with a strength that is almost, if not abso-
> lutely, savage. There is a directness of speech which
> startles the ordinary reader, and a vivid force of
> character painting that astounds him.... Of grace,
> virtue, beauty, we get no glimpse. All we have in
> exchange is a picture of the fag-ends of certain use-
> less and degraded lives.

Stevenson was inclined to agree with the judgment on the
characters and he himself described them as a 'troop of
swine'. Still, he was pleased with the book in certain
respects, and, upon reading it in its serial form, put
aside his usual modesty and declared it 'excellent'. He
seems to have been assured that in spite of the terrible
labour over the book with respect to style - a labour un-
equalled since 'Prince Otto' - it was a success and he was
given confidence that he would succeed with a similar
style he was then using in the opening chapters of 'Weir
of Hermiston'.

150. STEVENSON, FROM LETTERS TO COLVIN, EDMUND GOSSE,
AND HENRY JAMES

1893, 1894

(a) From a letter to Colvin with entries dates 16, 21 and
23 May 1893

I can't think what to say about the tale, but it seems to
me to go off with a considerable bang; in fact, to be an

extraordinary work; but whether popular! Attwater is no
end of a courageous attempt, I think you will admit; how
far successful is another affair. If my island ain't a
thing of beauty, I'll be damned. Please observe Wiseman
and Wishart; for incidental grimness, they strike me as
in it. Also, kindly observe the Captain and *Adar*; I
think that knocks spots. In short, as you see, I'm a
trifle vainglorious. But O, it has been such a grind!
The devil himself would allow a man to brag a little after
such a crucifixion! And indeed I'm only bragging for a
change before I return to the darned thing lying waiting
for me ... where I last broke down. I break down at every
paragraph, I may observe; and lie here and sweat, till I
can get one sentence wrung out after another. Strange
doom; after having worked so easily for so long! Did ever
anybody see such a story of four characters?...
    This forced, violent, alembicated style is most abhor-
rent to me; it can't be helped; the note was struck years
ago on the *Janet Nicoll*, and has to be maintained somehow;
and I can only hope the intrinsic horror and pathos, and
a kind of fierce glow of colour there is to it, and the
surely remarkable wealth of striking incident, may guide
our little shallop into port....
    I am discontented with 'The Ebb-Tide', naturally;
there seems such a veil of words over it; and I like more
and more naked writing; and yet sometimes one has a longing for full colour and there comes the veil again.
(LS, iv, 174-7)

(b) From a letter to Colvin, entry dated 5 June 1893

This tale is devilish, and Chapter XI. the worst of the
lot. The truth is of course that I am wholly worked out;
but it's nearly done, and shall go somehow according to
promise. I go against all my gods, and say it is *not
worth while* to massacre yourself over the last few pages
of a rancid yarn, that the reviewers will quite justly
tear to bits. (LS, iv, 184)

(c) From a letter to Edmund Gosse, dated 10 June 1893

Yes, honestly, fiction is very difficult; it is a terrible
strain to *carry* your characters all that time. And the
difficulty of according the narrative and the dialogue
(in a work in the third person) is extreme. That is one
reason out of half a dozen why I so often prefer the
first. It is much in my mind just now, because of my last
work, just off the stocks three days ago, 'The Ebb-Tide':
a dreadful, grimy business in the third person, where the

strains between a vilely realistic dialogue and a narrative style pitched about (in phrase) 'four notes higher'
than it should have been, has sown my head with grey
hairs; or I believe so - if my head escaped, my heart has
them. (LS, iv, 189)

(d) From a letter to Henry James, dated 17 June 1893

It seems as if literature were coming to a stand. I am
sure it is with me; and I am sure everybody will say so
when they have the privilege of reading 'The Ebb-Tide'.
My dear man, the grimness of that story is not to be
depicted in words. There are only four characters, to be
sure, but they are such a troop of swine! And their behaviour is really so deeply beneath any possible standard,
that on a retrospect I wonder I have been able to endure
them myself until the yarn was finished. Well, there is
always one thing; it will serve as a touchstone. If the
admirers of Zola admire him for his pertinent ugliness
and pessimism, I think they should admire this; but if,
as I have long suspected, they neither admire nor understand the man's art, and only wallow in his rancidness
like a hound in offal, then they will certainly be disappointed in 'The Ebb-Tide'. Alas! poor little tale,
it is not *even* rancid. (LS, iv, 193-4)

(e) From a letter to Colvin, dated 23 August 1893. At
the head of this letter Colvin wrote as follows: 'On a
first reading of the incomplete MS. of 'The Ebb-Tide',
without its concluding chapters, which are the strongest,
dislike of the three detestable chief characters - or
rather two detestable and one contemptible - had made me
unjust to the imaginative force and vividness of the
treatment.' This letter was apparently written shortly
after Stevenson received Colvin's favourable comment on
the novel.

Your pleasing letter re 'The Ebb-Tide', to hand. I propose, if it be not too late, to delete Lloyd's name. He
has nothing to do with the last half. The first we wrote
together, as the beginning of a long yarn. The second is
entirely mine; and I think it rather unfair on the young
man to couple his name with so infamous a work. Above
all, as you had not read the two last chapters, which seem
to me the most ugly and cynical of all.

[These remarks, from the same letter, were written at a
later date:]

Since you rather revise your views of 'The Ebb-Tide',
I think Lloyd's name might stick, but I'll leave it to
you. I'll tell you just how it stands. Up to the discovery of the champagne, the tale was all planned between us and drafted by Lloyd; from that moment he has
had nothing to do with it except talking it over. For we
changed our plan, gave up the projected Monte Cristo, and
cut it down for a short story. My jmpression - (I beg
your pardon - this is a local joke - a firm here had on its
beer labels, 'sole jmporters') - is that it will never be
popular, but might make a little *succès de scandale*.
However, I'm done with it now, and not sorry, and the
crowd may rave and mumble its bones for what I care....
   Hi! stop! you say 'The Ebb-Tide' is the 'working out
of an artistic problem of a kind.' Well, I should just
bet it was! You don't like Attwater. But look at my
three rogues; they're all there, I'll go bail. Three
types of the bad man, the weak man, and the strong man
with a weakness, that are gone through and lived out.
(LS, iv, 229-30, 231, 233)

(f) From a letter to Colvin dated February 1894.
Stevenson speaks here of the serial version of 'The Ebb-
Tide', which appeared in 'To-Day', 11 November 1893 -
3 February 1894, and in the USA in 'McClure's Magazine',
February-July 1894.

When [the mail] came and I had read it, I retired with
'The Ebb-Tide' and read it all before I slept. I did
not dream it was near as good; I am afraid I think it
excellent. A little indecision about Attwater, not much.
It gives me great hope, as I see I *can* work in that con-
stipated, mosaic manner, which is what I have to do just
now with 'Weir of Hermiston'. (LS, iv, 266-7)

151. FROM AN UNSIGNED REVIEW, 'SATURDAY REVIEW'

22 September 1894, lxxviii, 330

... We are not of those who profess to apportion to Mr.
Stevenson and to Mr. Osbourne their respective shares in
the present venture. One must be very young and cocksure
to do that. Nor shall we ascribe any weakness or defect
that may be noted in 'The Ebb-Tide' to Mr. Stevenson's
collaborator - an easy way of judgment, perhaps, yet one

that seems to us not merely rash, but of dubious fair-
ness. And thus must such a proceeding appear, we can but
think, to all readers except the young and confident
person who would have you imagine he knows all about the
deed of partnership. The question of interest that will
occur to the reader who takes up this volume - 'Is this
romance, in spirit and in style, Stevensonian?' - will
receive an instant and unhesitating answer. There are few
pages - there is, certainly, not one incident of the
narrative - which do not clearly reveal the creative
genius and literary craftsmanship of Mr. Stevenson. The
book is, in short, intensely Stevensonian. Whether it is
to be classed with 'Kidnapped' and with 'Treasure Island'
is another matter. This, also, with some judges is possible; and, though we should dissent from this verdict, we
would not treat it with disrespect. With regard to the
question of collaboration, we think that the views of the
majority of readers may be summed up in the conclusion, it
is better to have Mr. Stevenson and another than not to
have Mr. Stevenson at all.

It is in what concerns the 'story' that 'The Ebb-Tide'
differs most from the romances that are solely Stevensonian. As a story, it is decidedly inferior to the works we
have cited. All through the narrative there is a recur-
rent suggestion of the undeveloped. In force of delineation, in subtlety of revelation - both of character and of
the motive springs of action - and in piquancy of dialogue, the book is as characteristic of Mr. Stevenson's
art as any that he has set his name to. The suggestion
of the undeveloped is a radical weakness in the story,
since it inevitably brings with it to the imaginative
reader processes of development that must have raised the
story to the first rank of fiction, yet are absolutely
neglected. Brilliant as are the successive incidents of
the narrative of the voyage that forms the first part,
The Trio, there is something inoperative, something of
sterility, when looked at collectively and retrospect-
ively from the final scene of the story. They have not
the air of inevitableness. They seem to have been
designed independently of the end in view, and tend towards no tremendous culmination. Like 'The Wreckers,' the
story is a romance of the South Seas. The scene opens at
the Tahitian town of Papeete, and introduces three beach-
combers, who are reduced to the final stages of destitution - literally 'on the beach,' as the expressive local
term has it. The wretched estate of these men, who have
missed the flood-tide of their affairs, is set forth with
inimitable power and effect. The trio is composed of a
Yankee skipper, John Davis; Robert Herrick, an Oxford man,
who has sunk through utter want of moral tone; and Huish,

a London clerk, whose vileness is mitigated by a cheerful
courage and a Cockney humour which recalls the immortal
Bailey in 'Martin Chuzzlewit'.... Chance, and bitter
necessity, make these worthies fast comrades; and by a
stroke of luck they are put in charge of the schooner
Farallone, whose officers have died of smallpox. The
Yankee skipper schemes to steal the vessel and share the
cargo of Californian champagne with the others. The
horrors of that voyage with the drunken captain and clerk,
and the scared Kanakas who form the crew, are thrillingly
depicted. Herrick vainly remonstrates with the skipper
for 'stealing,' as he calls it, his 'profits,' and drinking the champagne which had cost him his 'honour.'
    And so they sail until they sight a 'new island,' of
which an exquisite description is given, which introduces
the fantastic element of the story in the person of the
owner of the island, one Attwater, who makes up the 'Quar-
tette.' This person, mystic, fatalist, evangelist, is a
most striking and original conception. He magnetizes the
weak and vacillating Herrick, and confounds the Yankee
skipper and the malignant and vicious Huish by the sheer
force of his personality. The scene in which he reveals
to Herrick the full significance of that worthy's degradation is exceedingly impressive. Indeed, throughout this
second portion of the book Mr. Stevenson's imagination is
freely at work. Yet it must be owned that the final scene
falls somewhat flat. It is strong in the horrible and the
grotesque, but the grotesque is not of the kind that intensifies the horror. No one, we think, who takes up 'The
Ebb-Tide' will put it away until the last page is reached,
so irresistible is the charm of the vivid and picturesque
narrative. But the story is by no means a model of design
nor a good example of the art of cumulative construction.

152.   RICHARD LE GALLIENNE, FROM A REVIEW, 'STAR'

27 September 1894

See headnote to No. 130. This review was reprinted in
'Retrospective Reviews' (1896), i, 146-9.

A loyal admiration may occasionally, I trust, permit
itself a loyal faultfinding. Messrs. Stevenson and

Osbourne's new romance, 'The Ebb-Tide', demands loyalty
in both directions. 'Part I.' seems to me good sound
adventure. It holds us with the true Stevensonian spell,
a tale 'of marvellous oceans swept by fateful wings.'
But when we turn from it, in breathless expectation, to
'Part II.,' the change is abrupt and painful. The spell
seems suddenly to have failed, and the more we read of the
insufferable, impossible Attwater, prig and pearl-fisher,
university man and evangelist, expert alike with his Bible
and his Winchester, the unreality increases. Even the
three men whose fortunes had fascinated us in 'Part I.'
seem to lose their humanity so soon as the Farallone
glides into the still waters of the coral-island lagoon,
where the six-foot-four Attwater, a sort of beautiful
Frankenstein, lives as elegantly as though his address
were Park-lane - superintending his pearl-fishers, wearing
clothes of the best West-end cut, drinking the best of
wines, and talking with the purest of university accents.
In the self-conscious atmosphere of this fairy island none
of the men, who up till now have borne themselves with a
certain vigor and individuality, seem any longer able to be
themselves. The little Cockney alone preserves something
of his original character, and, wicked as it may be, and
insufferable little cad as he doubtless was, it was, I
confess, a great disappointment to me that he wasn't able
to throw that vitriol at Attwater - mean, no doubt, as was
the form of his contemplated revenge. With the discharge
of Attwater's Winchester the last flicker of interest in
the story abruptly dies. Herrick, who has all through
been the least alive of the three, has become little more
than a lay figure, and the sea-captain Davis a grotesque.
Conceive a rough, drunken, unprincipled, and yet a sort
of manly sea-dog (with a soft place in his heart for his
wife and children, it is true) suddenly converted into a
canting milksop, saying his prayers ostentatiously on the
beach and calling upon his companion 'to come to Jesus.'
It is difficult to understand Mr. Stevenson's intention in
this. Did he get a little tired of his story, and determine, in a whimsical mood, to wind it up in a spirit of
pure farce - just as once, the reader may remember, he
mischievously let the sawdust out of his Prince Florizel
of Bohemia?

I have another fault to find with 'The Ebb-Tide' - the
extreme self-consciousness of some of the writing, and the
stilted style of some of the conversations. These latter
are mainly in the mouths of Robert Herrick, another university man fallen on evil days and harboring with strange
bedfellows, and, of course, Attwater, who always talks

like a book - one of Mr. Meredith's. When Herrick is discussing with his mates a description of the supposed
island given in 'Findlay,' he says 'it's rather in the
conditional mood'; and even at the beginning of the story,
when the three beach-combers are sleeping out in the
misery of their destitution, and the Cockney clerk calls
for a yarn, Herrick talks about the Arabian Nights and
'the Freischütz,' as though his companions were Bodley
Head poets. It is a pretty dream story he tells all the
same. When things seem at their worst, he takes a pencil
and writes a phrase from the Fifth Symphony on the wall of
the ruinous old calaboose where they are all three taking
shelter, adding a tag of Latin underneath. 'So,' thought
he, 'they will know that I loved music and had classical
tastes.' There is surely an air of unreality about this?
And Robert Herrick's very name is against his being quite
alive. A name so indissolubly connected with a poet so
well known as Herrick cannot be applied to anyone else
without the new bearer of it being overshadowed by the
personality of his original. However, we mustn't forget
in dealing with Mr. Stevenson's Herrick that it is romance
he is writing, and that the gentleman who has come down
in the world, and is driven to house with thieves and
vagabonds, but still keeps a Virgil in his pocket, has
always been a legitimate figure in romance.

Apart from Herrick's occasionally stilted talk, and
particularly Attwater's - who, however, is so unnatural as
a whole that, so to say, it would be still more unnatural
if his talk were not so, too - Mr. Stevenson himself, if I
may venture to say so, is a little too consciously the
literary artist here and there in this new book. If the
book were anything but a book of adventure, one would not
mind so much. I am far from missing the charm of a
certain air of literary self-consciousness in its right
place, but in dealing with rough seamen and perils upon
the high seas this literary daintiness strikes a somewhat
incongruous note; just as some of Mr. Hardy's stilted
writing seems so out of color in the midst of his Wessex
Arcady. And, by the way, would a rough seaman like Davis
say 'I love you' to another man? Wouldn't he express
affection for a comrade in some blunter idiom.

However, the first part of 'The Ebb-Tide' is as thrilling a piece of narrative as Mr. Stevenson has written; and
one or two of the situations - such as that where Huish
and the captain drink champagne all day long in the cabin,
and leave the ship to look after itself; or the moment
when the fraud in the champagne cargo is discovered - are
as dramatic as anything Mr. Stevenson has done.

153. AN UNSIGNED REVIEW, 'SPEAKER'

29 September 1894, x, 362-3

We do not wonder that the critics have been puzzled by the
latest story bearing the name of Mr. Stevenson. After
turning from the pages of 'David Balfour,' with their
inimitable distinction of style and tone, it is undoubtedly a woeful disappointment to have to descend upon those
of 'The Ebb-Tide.' As a Stevenson book, we take it, 'The
Ebb-Tide' must not be counted. It certainly has no claim
to a place with those romances which are already ranked
among the classics of our tongue. But, if we can get rid
of the commanding presence of Stevenson pure and simple,
and judge Stevenson *plus* Osbourne, unaffected by natural
prejudices, we shall find 'The Ebb-Tide' to be a very
remarkable book. It is strong with a strength that is
almost, if not absolutely, savage. There is a directness
of speech which startles the ordinary reader, and a vivid
force of character-painting that astounds him. There is
not so much as the shadow of a woman cast upon the story.
In this respect Mr. Stevenson and partner faithfully copy
Mr. Stevenson alone. Of grace, virtue, beauty, we get no
glimpse. All that we have in exchange is a picture of the
fag ends of certain useless and degraded lives. Three
miserable creatures, whose wickedness or weakness has
caused them to fall away from civilisation, and who have
reached a depth of abject woe hardly known even to the
occupants of an English casual ward, are the heroes of the
tale. It would be difficult to find any creatures less
heroic. Herrick, the University man, who carries his tattered Virgil in his pocket to remind him of what he once
was, is merely weak, not wicked, but his weakness is of
that despicable sort which forfeits not only the respect
of others, but self-respect as well, and makes a man an
outcast and a pariah. Captain Brown is merely a villain
of the melodramatic order, who will drink and lie and
steal with the worst of men, but who is not without a
certain degree of physical courage and a maudlin tenderness for the children he has deserted. It is the last
person of the trio - Huish, the Cockney clerk - who has
the individuality that arrests attention. But what an
individuality it is! If the purpose of the authors had
been to show us of what unutterably loathsome material the
dregs of modern civilisation consist, they could not have
done so more effectually than by giving us this portrait
of Huish. He is a Cockney born and bred, with the little

narrownesses and vulgarities of his class, and that terrible sharpness of intuition which sometimes disconcerts
the wisest. He talks the slang of Whitechapel, and knows
the latest of music-hall ditties; but he remembers also
the hymns he learnt in the Sunday-school, and can use
them with blasphemous effect when he chances to be in the
mood. Of conscience, honour, loyalty, he knows less than
the beasts that perish. Compared with his degradation,
the state to which his two companions have fallen seems
almost an exalted one. We do not pretend to know whether
Mr. Stevenson or Mr. Osbourne is responsible for this
picture of Huish, but in its terrible force and intensity
there is more than a touch of genius. It is the story of
these three outcasts, from the moment when they are found
starving on the beach at Papeete until, a few weeks later,
Huish is shot dead by the man whom he has tried to murder,
that is told in 'The Ebb-Tide.' But though the story it-
itself is full of exciting incidents which crowd on each
other at times with a breathless haste that recalls 'The
Wrecker,' it is not the mere plot that interests the
reader, but the picture of this human wreckage, the inevitable doom of Huish, and the faint suggestion of better
days for his two companions. This is not the Stevenson
we love, but it is something to be read and remembered,
nevertheless.

154. I. ZANGWILL IN DEFENCE OF 'EBB-TIDE', REVIEW,
'CRITIC' (NEW YORK)

24 November 1894, xxii n.s., 342-3

Israel Zangwill (1864-1926), author, philanthropist, and
leader in Jewish affairs. Zangwill's reputation as a
writer was established with 'The Children of the Ghetto'
(1892). His reviews and comments on books and literary
matters appeared in a column in the 'Pall Mall Magazine'
called Without Prejudice and in the 'Critic' in a column
entitled Men, Women and Books.

To judge by the reviews and the advertisement columns, a
great new novel is published every week. It is depress-
ing to be told by the same reviewers who discover these

great new novels that Mr. Stevenson's new romance, 'The
Ebb-Tide,' is badly constructed, a mere random series of
adventures, sliced out of a chain of heterogeneous episodes that might have gone on forever. In reality, the
story is so symmetrical that it is perhaps the best constructed of all Mr. Stevenson's books, and it might therefore seem surprising that critics could be found blind to
so striking a unity as the book manifests. But the reason
why they have failed to recognize it is easily discover-
able. It is not constructed on what I have called the
parlor-game formula, to which the stock British novel
invariably reduces itself; the said formula being, as in
the parlor-game of 'Consequences,' entirely connected with
the recontre of the hero and the heroine under peculiar
circumstances, and with their ultimate union in the bonds
of matrimony. As, to start with, Mr. Stevenson dispenses
with a heroine altogether, it is plain that the acutest
vision can detect no trace of the stereotyped form in 'The
Ebb-Tide.' The poor critics! Mr. Stevenson has really
set them too hard a task. To abolish the petticoat, and
yet expect them to discover the coherency of his composition! Why, *cherchez la femme* is their first thought in
hunting for a scheme! They have yet to learn that a
story, short or long, is merely the evolution of an idea,
that (*pace* Lord Chesterfield) it has no necessary connection with marriage or even with women, and that, when the
author has developed his theme, his task is completed.
What that theme is need not be clearly stated on the first
page. Often it is part of the plot interest of the story
to keep its point secret till the last page. Then, however, the conclusion is a flash-light upon all that has
gone before. This is exactly the case with 'The Ebb-
Tide.' The theme is not formally stated, and the book
ends so abruptly that if the reader closes it and writes
a review of it instead of reviewing it, he is likely to
fall into the error of supposing his author to be a fool
rather than himself. Let us examine the texture of 'The
Ebb-Tide' by the light of these remarks, and by the flash-
light thrown on the whole book by the abrupt close. It
begins with the picture of three men in the South Seas.
They are 'on the beach,' which is equivalent to sleeping
on the Embankment, as, according to Mr. David Christie
Murray, (1) himself and so many other lights of the day
have done in their time. These three men have come by
very different routes to this common lodging-house of
poverty à *la belle étoile*. One of them is a University
man, who has fallen lower and lower through want of backbone. Another is a captain who has lost his ship through
drunkenness, and the last of the trio is a cockney cad of

the most brutal type. It was a conception of genius to
unite in a desperate adventure these strange bed-fellows
whom misery has made acquainted.

The theme of the book, then, is the inter-relations of
these three curiously-assorted characters during their
joint criminal enterprise; and it is supplemented by their
individual relations to a fourth man - for whom General
Gordon might well have been the model - with whom the
course of their adventure connects their lives. When the
adventure is over, when the mutual relations of the quar-
tette have been exhausted, when the interaction and revelation of character are complete, the book is finished, and
the author wisely lays aside the pen. He has taken the
affairs of his men at the ebb-tide, he has shown to what
fortune it led on, he has exhibited his characters in
every light, and turned them inside out - and so *voilà
tout*. There are two species of novels, the novel of
character and the novel of adventure. Mr. Stevenson loves
adventure, but he is also a student of character (using
character almost in its technical theatrical signification
of 'highly colored'). And so it has naturally occurred to
him to combine the two species in one, and to have flesh
and-blood figures acted on by incidents, and reacting on
them, instead of lay figures buffeted about by the winds
of romance. In the preface to 'The Wrecker' (likewise
written in collaboration with Mr. Lloyd Osbourne) he
explained that his idea was to interest the reader in his
personages preliminarily to their embarking on the adventure with which the book was really concerned. But in
that book he was only groping for the true method, for
'The Wrecker' is merely a novel of character and a novel
of adventure pieced together, so that one may put one's
finger on the seam.

It is only in 'The Ebb-Tide' that he has struck the
true method and achieved a true unity, and fused character
and adventure intimately from the first page to the last.
The varying turns of his characters' fortunes are cunningly contrived to lay bare their hearts and souls, and
the result is, not only an enthralling romance, but a
subtle study of the psychology of blackguardism in divers
shades and degrees; a study which is convincing except in
the case of Huish, the cockney, whose desperate courage in
the latter stages has at least not been sufficiently 'prepared' in the original introduction of him, though, for
the rest, he is the most vivid figure of all. This little
masterpiece - for, by virtue of its construction, its
beautiful English, its virile force, and its creation of
four new characters, 'The Ebb-Tide' is nothing less -
strikes several of the dominant notes which have haunted

Mr. Stevenson's later work, apart from the deserted
islands and the hidden treasures which have always fascinated him and his readers. One of these *Leit-motifs*, as
one might almost call them, is the intense interest in
villains, whose more genial side our broadly human artist
delights to exhibit, dwelling, though not in the spirit of
Mr. Gilbert, upon the coster's innocent *penchant* for
basking in the sun after he has finished jumping on his
mother. Another of these later *Leit-motifs* is the illustration of the social possibilities of the most despised
human individual, when he is the only companionable being
in peculiar and perilous circumstances. The disreputable
'shyster' in 'The Wrecker,' when he was the sole companion
in misfortune of his contemptuous enemy, was discovered to
have a pleasing fondness for sentimental poetry; and in
'The Ebb-Tide' the University man and the Captain find the
intolerable Cockney endurable, if only from the primitive
human instinct of gregariousness. There is here quite a
field to be worked by story-writers in search of stories.
One might develop the relations of the most incongruous
couples isolated together on desert islands - say one of
'the souls' and a 'suburban' corn-factor, an impressionist
artist and a Royal Academician, a minor poet and a prize-
fighter, a czar and a nihilist, a dramatist and a critic.
How each would cling to the other in their joint loneli-
ness! - for the dread of solitude is the touch of nature
that makes the whole world kin. Yet another of Mr. Stevenson's *Leit-motifs* is the romance of the modern, which
exists this very day contemporaneously with type-writers
and county-councils, though it would have been a greater
achievement to have found it here at home and not gone
questing to the South Seas for it as for a buried treasure.

The treasure lies here, under our eyes, at our very
feet. Every alley and byway is swarming with romance.
The great dramas of life are working themselves out under
every roof in the most prosaic of streets. Never was
there more romance than to-day, with its ferment of problems and propaganda, its cosmopolitan movement, its contrasts of wealth and poverty, its shock and interactions
of populations and creeds, its clash of mediaeval and
modern. The ends of the ages meet in every Atlantic
liner. It will be an eternal pity if a writer like
Stevenson passes away without having once applied his
marvellous gifts of vision and sympathy to the reproduc-
tion and transfiguration of every-day human life, if he is
content to play perpetually with wrecks and treasures and
islands, and to be remembered as an exquisite artist in
the abnormal.

Note

1 Murray (1847–1907), a novelist and journalist, wrote a
   series of articles describing a tour through England in
   the disguise of a tramp.

'Weir of Hermiston'

May 1896

155. STEVENSON, FROM A LETTER TO CHARLES BAXTER

1 December 1892, LS, iv, 138-9

On Baxter see No. 132c. 'The Justice-Clerk' was the early
title given to 'Weir of Hermiston'. 'Braxfield' refers
to Robert Macqueen (1722-99), Lord Braxfield, the 'Hanging
Judge'.

... I have a novel on the stocks to be called 'The
Justice-Clerk'. It is pretty Scotch, the Grand Premier
is taken from Braxfield - (Oh, by the by, send me Cock-
burn's 'Memorials') - and some of the story is - well -
queer. The heroine is seduced by one man, and finally
disappears with the other man who shot him.... Mind you,
I expect 'The Justice-Clerk' to be my masterpiece. My
Braxfield is already a thing of beauty and a joy for
ever, and so far as he has gone, *far* my best character.

156. ARNOLD BENNETT ON 'WEIR OF HERMISTON'

21 May 1896

From 'Journals of Arnold Bennett' (1932), ed. Newman
Flower, i, 206.

Stevenson's 'Weir of Hermiston, An Unfinished Romance',
appeared yesterday. Chap. VI. 'A leaf from Christina's
psalm-book' contains about forty pages of the subtlest,
surest, finest psychological analysis that I can remember.
I am quite sure that there exists nowhere a more beautiful
or more profoundly truthful presentation of the emotional
phenomena (both in the man and in the woman) which go to
the making of 'love at first sight'. On p. 178 [ch. vi]
Stevenson, with secret pride I swear, says: 'Thus even
that phenomenon of love at first sight, which is so rare
and seems so simple and violent, like a disruption of
life's tissue, may be decomposed into a sequence of accidents happily concurring.'... Yes, it may, by a Stevenson; perhaps by a Meredith; but by none else of modern
writers. 'Weir of Hermiston' is as far beyond anything
that Hardy, for example, could compass, as 'The Wood-
landers' is beyond 'In the Shadow'. Which is to say
much! The mere writing of 'Weir of Hermiston' surpasses
all Stevenson's previous achievement.

157. JOSEPH JACOBS, UNSIGNED REVIEW, 'ATHENAEUM'

23 May 1896, 3578, 673

Jacobs (1854-1916) was an author, journalist, and editor,
as well as a prominent leader in Jewish affairs; he is
identified as the reviewer in the 'Athenaeum' files.

Stevenson's 'Weir of Hermiston' certainly promised to be
the best of his novels; yet it is impossible to tell how
the promise would have been carried out. Mr. Colvin has
gone so far as to say that he knows no work in the literature of romance more masterly or of more piercing human
interest or of more concentrated imaginative vision. This
can only be taken as an *ex parte* statement.
    The fact is that the development of the story does not
reach a point at which Stevenson would have competed with
the great masters of romance. His theme was to have been
that of Brutus condemning his son, the Brutus in this
particular instance being the hanging Lord Braxfield,
known in Scotch gossip. This was to have been led up to
by a tale of seduction and murder, and followed by the

breaking of the gaol in which the condemned hero is confined. As the story at present exists it breaks off
before seduction or murder, condemnation or rescue. Under
these circumstances it is impossible to say what increase
of mastery Stevenson had obtained during the last weeks of
life in the delineation of the acuter phases of human passion.

Of the hanging judge, however, we see enough to feel
confident that he would have proved a masterpiece. The
coarse dignity and power of the man are brought out sufficiently well in the prologue to make one feel confident
that the scene of the trial, if it could have been given
some show of *vraisemblance*, would have been effective.
But could it? Such a violation of the decencies of justice as the condemnation of a son by his own father would
no more have been possible in Scotland than anywhere else
in modern times. Stevenson was aware of this difficulty,
and was casting about for a mode of overcoming it. It
would seem as if the Brutus in the modern version only
directed his son to be arrested on the capital charge.

The weakness of the book consists in its villain, 'the
young fool advocate,' who was to have seduced the heroine
and to have been slain by the younger Hermiston. But he
is too facile and flimsy a rogue to impart tragic intensity to any part of the plot hinging on him. It would
have taxed all Stevenson's ingenuity to have preserved our
respect for his heroine if she had become the victim of
such a plaster Mephistopheles.

It would, indeed, have been the heroine that would have
taxed Stevenson's powers to the utmost. He had evidently
braced himself up to prove to the world that he could draw
a woman. But the very elaborateness of the effort arouses
our doubts. Nearly fifty pages - about one fifth of the
whole fragment - are devoted to the first glances and
meeting of the lovers. This does not look like mastery.
A greater artist would have produced his effects with
fewer lines. Indeed, the whole book promised to be of
unusual length for Stevenson if it had been carried out on
the same scale as the preliminaries. Greater power is
shown, however, in the few touches which make the
heroine's mother stand out for us and live. Another
female portrait almost equally successful is that of the
elder Kirstie, the heroine's aunt and the hero's retainer,
who is attached to him with a devotion the complex elements of which are indicated with masterly skill. Yes,
Stevenson could draw a woman, but it was only when the
fires of her womanhood had burnt down. To him woman
remained throughout the eternal puzzle. The very last
page of the book before us contains the sentence, 'He saw

for the first time the ambiguous face of woman as she
is.' The words might apply to Stevenson as much as to his
hero. But the great masters of romance know something
more of woman than that.

But if he knew not woman, how well he knew men, young
or old! Take, for instance, this passage, in which Stevenson tells in his own way how in spring a young man
turns to love: -

> Brightnesses of azure, clouds of fragrance, a
> tinkle of falling water and singing birds, rose like
> exhalations from some deeping aboriginal memory, that
> was not his, but belonged to the flesh on his bones.
> His body remembered; and it seemed to him that his body
> was in no way gross, but ethereal and perishable like a
> strain of music; and he felt for it an exquisite ten-
> derness as for a child, an innocent, full of beautiful
> instincts and destined to an early death. [ch. vi]

Or, again, take this picture of Lord Hermiston standing before the body of his wife: -

> Dressed as she was for her last walk, they had laid
> the dead lady on her bed. She was never interesting in
> life; in death she was not impressive; and as her hus-
> band stood before her, with his hands crossed behind
> his powerful back, that which he looked upon was the
> very image of the insignificant. 'Her and me were
> never cut out for one another,' he remarked at last.
> 'It was a daft-like marriage.' And then, with a most
> unusual gentleness of tone, 'Puir bitch,' said he,
> 'puir bitch!' [ch. i]

The whole man is there.
Stevenson has been scarcely so successful with the
'Four Black Brothers of the Cauldstaneslap,' who were to
have become the deities of the machinery of the tale. So
far as we have them, none of them lives except Dandie the
poet. The story of their ride after their father's murderers is largely spoilt for us by the mixture of Scots
and English in which it is written. Indeed, the whole
book carries the licence of the 'kail-yard' to an
extreme. We can scarcely have half the book before us,
yet already the glossary, which is eminently necessary,
deals with over a couple of hundred words. Lord Hermiston objects to 'palmering about in bauchles.' He talks
a little 'sculduddery' after dinner. We have 'ettercaps'
and 'carlines,' scraps of Scots 'ballants,' and, in short,
the book is not for the Southron.

But it is perhaps unreasonable to judge this fragment
as if it had been presented to us in what would have been
its final form.   There can be little doubt that Stevenson,
with his fine literary tact, would have reduced the dialect and shortened some of the preliminaries if he had
had time to complete the book.   But Stevenson's friends
have made such exaggerated claims for it that one is
called upon to judge it from the standpoint of the highest, and to indicate its failings when so judged.   That it
indicates a further stage towards maturity in Stevenson's
art can be willingly granted.   That the handling of character is as firm as in any other part of his work is
equally obvious.   'Weir of Hermiston' intensifies our
regret at the early loss of its author.   It promised to
be - it might have been - his masterpiece.   Even as it
is, it is a masterly torso.

158.   A. T. QUILLER-COUCH, REVIEW, 'SPEAKER'

6 June 1896, xiii, 613-14

Colvin's editorial note appeared in 'Cosmopolis', May
1896, following serialization of the novel there from
January to April; the note was reprinted in English and
American editions of the novel.

In the first paragraph of his Editorial Note upon 'Weir
of Hermiston' Mr. Colvin informs us that this fragment of
a tale holds 'certainly the highest place' among Stevenson's writings.   In the last paragraph he talks of 'the
seizing and penetrating power of the author's ripened art
as exhibited in the foregoing pages, the wide range of
character and emotion over which he sweeps with so
assured a hand, his vital poetry of vision and magic of
presentment.'
    It seems to me that Mr. Colvin had already sufficiently
proclaimed his opinion of 'Weir of Hermiston' in his Epilogue to the 'Vailima Letters' - 'The time was now ripe -
had only the strength sufficed - for his career as a
creative writer to enter upon a new and ampler phase.   The
fragment on which he wrought during the last month of his
life gives to my mind (as it did to his own) for the first

time the full measure of his powers; and if in the
literature of romance there is to be found work more
masterly, of more piercing human insight, or more concentrated imaginative vision and beauty, I do not know it.'
Very likely not: and the tribute was at least appropriately spoken. But I think the appropriateness disappears when we find this opinion dogmatically asserted
in an appendix to the published fragment. 'Certainly the
highest place,' says Mr. Colvin; and obviously believes he
has put the matter beyond question.

But come, now. Not even in the opinions of the good
and great does certainty, constant and absolute, reside.
And I would respectfully ask if this oracular attitude of
Mr. Colvin's be altogether wise. Is there no danger of
its rousing a mild and wondering resentment among those -
I will not attempt to compute their numbers, but they
cannot be wholly negligible - who have not yet enjoyed
a course of critical instruction at Mr. Colvin's feet,
and are quite unprepared to be lifted so complacently on
Mr. Colvin's avuncular knee? And is there no danger that
some reflection of this mild resentment may be extended
to the book itself? I hope, indeed, that I over-estimate
this danger. For, in truth, 'Weir of Hermiston' appears
to me a very splendid fragment of romance, and one that
to a great extent justifies Mr. Colvin's eulogiums - had
they only appeared elsewhere.

But 'certainly the highest'? We are speaking of a
fragment, be pleased to remember: and this fragment
should be considered not as something complete in itself,
but as that for which Stevenson intended it, a portion of
a work to be hereafter completed. Considering it thus, I
confess that it seems to contain elements of weakness -
of weakness over which it is quite possible that Stevenson would have triumphed, but I hardly think we do wisely
in assuming that he would have triumphed as a matter of
course. Let us pass the main difficulty of the plot -
the practical difficulty which Mr. Colvin admits he
cannot solve - of getting Lord Hermiston to preside at
his son's trial. It seems that Stevenson meant Hermiston,
like an old Roman, to pass sentence on his only son: and
this was to be the great 'situation' of the book: 'but I
am assured on the best legal authority of Scotland that
no judge, however powerful, either by character or office,
could have insisted on presiding at the trial of a near
kinsman of his own.' It is therefore not easy to see how
Stevenson could have brought his tale into line with fact
unless at considerable cost to the climax.

This difficulty, however, lies outside the written
fragment, on which alone we are trying just now to build

our prophecies of a story that will never be completed.
Now one of the first things to be noted of the written
fragment is that it exhibits a method of narrative which
is very unlike the method of 'Kidnapped' or of 'The Master
of Ballantrae,' or (for that matter) of 'The Ebb Tide.'
Mr. Colvin would say that in 'Weir of Hermiston' Stevenson's career as a creative writer was entering upon a new
and ampler phase. Well, he had at all events begun to
amplify his method of narrative. He would seem to have
reconsidered the position once taken up in an essay (if I
remember), that the first rule of narrative is to make
every sentence help forward the tale; or at least to be
inclining to a more liberal interpretation of his own
teaching. The characters of 'Weir of Hermiston' do not,
as of old, spring up and take shape and grow in the rush
of talk and incident, but are elaborated beforehand and
placed upon the stage in almost every case with a formal,
and sometimes with a very lengthy introduction. Even the
unfortunate Mrs. Weir is prefaced with a list of ancestors whom she did not resemble; while Weir himself and
Kirstie and the four brothers of Cauldstaneslap sit for
their portraits (like the Australian cricketers) before
they begin to play. Nor is this all. In places, as in
the opening of the magnificent eighth chapter, we have
moralising, naked and unashamed. There is no challenging
its beauty; Stevenson's moralising was always beautiful;
but he used to print his moralising and his romantic
stories in separate books. Nor am I venturing to breathe
a complaint against his new method. I simply point out
that for Stevenson it *was* a new method, and that we
should be cautious therefore of predicting its immediate
success in a long and sustained story. Throughout his
career he was experimenting ceaselessly, and he never set
his hand to an experiment of greater interest; but that it
was an 'assured hand' (in Mr. Colvin's phrase) I must,
after reading the fifty pages devoted to showing how
Archie and the younger Kirstie fell in love at first
sight, take leave to doubt.
   There are elements of danger, too, in both the young
men. Archie stands more than once on the verge of prig-
gery, if he do not overstep it; and Frank Innes is surely
a trifle inadequate. A meddling fool may serve to set
great events in train, but this particular fool is doomed
to seduce Kirstie while the image of Archie is yet vivid
in her heart. There lay the *crux* of the book. Had that
point been passed, and passed triumphantly, Mr. Colvin's
'prave orts' might have been accepted without a murmur.
But, after all, it is the business of a work of art to
cope with the difficulties of its own creating and 'Weir

of Hermiston' never arrived at its great test. Who will
deny that only consummate art could have made the seduction of Kirstie convincing or even tolerable? Given such
a Frank Innes how many men of all that have written fiction could have made it convincing or even tolerable? Can
you name three? No. This story had still to be tested
before it could hold 'the highest place among its author's
writings.'
    I declare I will not utter another word of doubting.
As it is, I dare say some idiot will arise and assert that
this *causerie* was written in a spirit of detraction. Why,
sir, were the book as naked as 'Castle Dangerous,' he
that would spy upon it must (as Stevenson once observed)
wear the name of Ham. But it is, on the contrary, a rich
and beautiful fragment: how beautiful, an unofficial
admirer or Stevenson might even now be trying to say, had
not Stevenson's editor and official admirer considered it
within his province to forestall criticism with that
oracular Note. 'Weir of Hermiston' *might* have been Stevenson's masterpiece; but in any case it would have had
some pretty stout rivals.

159. J. ST LOE STRACHEY, FROM AN UNSIGNED REVIEW,
'SPECTATOR'

13 June 1896, lxxvi, 843-5

On Strachey see headnote to No. 133. The 'Spectator'
files identify him as the reviewer.

... [Though] there is so much good drawing of character
and so many artful and stimulating situations in the book,
the story is somehow or other not the success it ought to
be. It is like those pictures in which the drawing, the
colour, and the intention are alike excellent, and yet the
work as a whole is disappointing. Whether, if Mr. Stevenson had lived, he would for the first time in his career
have conquered this difficulty of composition, and have at
last brought a story to perfection, it is of course impossible to say. It is conceivable that he might have done
so. If he had, he would have produced a novel as great as
anything in Scott, for of the stuff of which great novels

are made, here is enough and to spare. The parts of the
tale are as near perfection as may be. We fear, however, that he would have failed in this drawing together
of the material, this co-relating of the parts to the
whole, this interfusion of a general harmony. It is,
indeed, this quality of harmoniousness which is lacking
in 'The Master of Ballantrae', in 'Catriona', and in all
Mr. Stevenson's other novels. That it is also lacking in
'Weir of Hermiston' is, we suspect, an essential, not an
accidental, defect. But to say that this last work of a
man of rare genius is not perfect is not to condemn it.
It is full of a thousand things that stir the fancy and
spur the imagination. The words, as in every great work
of literature, are brimming over with meaning, and hurry
us along in a torrent of eager and excited interest....

160. E. PURCELL, FROM A REVIEW, 'ACADEMY'

27 June 1896, xlix, 521-2

On Purcell see headnote to No. 21.

Those who have studied the play of literary reaction are
listening with foreboding, though without surprise, to
the chorus of adulation which has greeted Stevenson's
last fragment. It is the last, and it is a fragment.
The last-born - the little Benjamin, dearest to a father's
eye, regarded with most favour by friends and family -
with compunction we read into it all the concentrated
merits of its predecessors which perchance we had under-
valued. And a fragment, too: what scope that affords for
panegyric of an unwritten masterpiece! I can remember
quite distinctly the blank looks and secret grumbling of
staunch admirers as 'Edwin Drood' and 'Denis Duval' were
sapping their faith: the sense of relief, mingled with
remorse, when the tension was snapped; the revulsion of
feeling which inspired the comfortable doctrine that a
feeble opening was only a foil to the problematical
splendour of the later pages that would have been.
    Further, the fame of Dickens and Thackeray lacked the
support of the grandest advertising agency the world has
yet seen. Caledonia, stern and wild enough upon occasions

to little sinners like Keats and Byron, has ever been to
each poetic child of her own not only a fit nurse, but a
most partial, indulgent, and boastful one. Stevenson
began auspiciously by being born a Scot. True, he rather
derogated at first by canoeing and donkey-driving in
stupid foreign lands, apparently destitute of 'gowans' and
'rowans,' and by writing essays and wonder-stories in
strictly English English. Then came his first Scotch
tale: a glorious cake, well stuffed with plums - delicious
dialect words, and lots of lovely Scotch names of places.
Names, names, names - why, the first column of a North
British Railway Guide is divine music to the Caledonian
exile's ear. For the exile is the real fugleman. I hear
that in Edinburgh they affect genteel indifference to
'braes' and 'cuddies' and 'puddocks': nay, I suspect that
they secretly prefer to see their books spiced with scraps
of French and Italian. But I know as a fact that when the
Scotch critic in London or Oxford, on glancing down a
first-cut page, lights on one or two such Masonic pass-
words as 'brig' or 'burn,' 'howe,' or 'toon,' all that is
'stern and wild' in him melts at once into a dulcet recep-
tivity. And should he see in print but one cherished
topographical name - the Brig o' Guddlepuddock or the Kirk
o'Cuddyclavers - he feels that he has discovered another
mastermind. Is this an abuse? No: merely a picturesque
and healthy Celtic survival. But, all the same, nostalgia
is not criticism.

Now there is the grossest assurance, affrontery, downright impudence in the Scotch argument that you and I
cannot appreciate or criticise Scotch genius because we do
not exactly know what 'puddocks' are, and have never gone
there to identify them. Remoteness of time and place,
difference of language, strangeness of environment are
allowed to be no bar to our grappling with Hesiod, or
Hafiz, or Dante, or Tourgenieff; but the divine Ploughman!
and the inimitable Shepherd! and the wizardly Sir Walter!
- impossible! All this is just disgusting conceit veiled
under flimsy mysticism. 'Waverley' is just as easy to
criticise as 'Père Goriot,' 'Kidnapped' as 'Treasure
Island'; for true criticism is cosmopolitan....

A minute criticism of the few first chapters of an
unfinished work would be both futile and unfair. Far
more to the purpose is it to protest against the extravagance which has proclaimed these chapters as Stevenson's
masterpiece, and to point out the reason why. It is this.
All the leading reviewers who have started this exaggeration - the smaller men merely follow their lead - are
probably Scotch by birth or sympathy. Their patriotism
and nostalgia is fired to frenzy by the thought that their

country employed Stevenson's last thoughts; and, as Mr.
Colvin concludes, 'surely no son of Scotland has died
leaving with his last breath a worthier tribute to the
land he loved.' That is all: compliment to be paid back
with interest.

'Weir of Hermiston,' so far as it went - and like Mr.
Colvin I shrink from divining the sequel - is not
superior, not even equal, to the author's best work. Of
course, every year he gained more facility, more concen-
tration, more experience. But his inherent deficiencies
he never made up. And here, even in the first chapters -
the later ones in places seem disjointed and unrevised,
and, I infer, had not been printed (1) - there is unusual
abruptness and want of unity. In fact, they seem rather
to promise a series of powerful character-sketches, strung
together by a thin, conventional, tragic story. But
powerful they are, many of them. By far the finest is
that of the weak, devoted wife. Next the Four Brothers.
The 'Hanging Judge' is excellently interpreted; but, after
all, given Braxfield as a model and the 'elder Brutus
tragedy' as a *motif*, the treatment was obvious and inevitable. And had Stevenson thought of him, there was another
judge of that period of whom he could have made more. The
elder Kirstie is a fine creation, but there is something
morbid which jars a little in the powerful chamber scene.
Some, it seems, think the niece a failure; her airs and
graces, of course, appear to us just old fashioned enough
to be vulgarly genteel, but I must think her a very living
being. The hero, so far, is an anachronism for the
assumed date, 1814. If the Four Brothers and old Hermiston are put forty years too late, young Weir is equally
too early. He is clearly painted partly from Stevenson's
student-self, partly from some college friend; and so far
he has not impressed us. One of the best critics, when
old Weir says a remark is 'merely literary and decorative,' defies us to find another modernism. They abound
in thought and phrase.

Rich as it is in those perfections of which Stevenson
was a supreme master, 'Weir of Hermiston' would never have
been a great novel, for a great novel he could never have
written. Many years ago I pointed that out in these
columns, and hinted at the reason. A stranger, he wrote
to tell me that I had divined his secret. We discussed
at some length this and kindred matters. He knew, he
owned, success was impossible, but he *must* go on trying.
In the only letter I have preserved I find one sentence
which to those who have deeply studied him means everything; to others it is but a phrase. 'Ethics,' he wrote,
'have ever been my veiled mistress.' He could see that

without a firm, strong, undoubting (albeit, ignorant or insolent), moral standpoint, no great, grasping novel could be achieved. What he would not see was that great literature is not all great novels; that though the stately galleon, with its noble lines and steady stride, is indeed admirable, the graceful shallop, the saucy frigate, and the storm-loving Greenlander are equally in their way masterpieces. To the end he fought against conviction - 'Mind you,' he says, 'I expect my "Justice Clerk" to be my masterpiece.' Yet, I doubt if he was ever deceived as to the result. The great novel never emerged, but in its stead what a roll of successes, and in such various styles! Why complain? Great novelists we have had, but only one man who could give us the Isle of Voices, of all his gems the fairest, rarest, most imperishable. His fame must not be hurt by hysterical patriots; some one should protest, and distasteful as it is, I claim to do so, and for this reason. When I had reviewed 'Virginibus Puerisque' in the 'Academy,' Mark Pattison, who had reviewed it, I think, in the 'Athenaeum,' (2) as we talked it over, approved my youthful enthusiasm, and surprised me by the immense importance he attached to the book and the new author. My faith in Stevenson was primitive, was spontaneous, and has never wavered. Not all his present idolators can say as much.

Notes

1 None of the chapters had been printed before Stevenson's death.
2 The 'Athenaeum' review was by Arthur John Butler (No. 18).

161. GEORGE MOORE ON YEATS AND STEVENSON, 'DAILY CHRONICLE'

24 April 1897

The following extract is from a review of Yeats's 'The Secret Rose'. Quiller-Couch responded in defence of Stevenson in the 'Speaker' (No. 162); Moore answered shortly afterwards in the 'Daily Chronicle'; whereupon Quiller-Couch returned to the defence again in the

'Speaker' (22 May 1897).

This book teaches many things. Its first lesson is that
Stevenson is not the only man who ever lived who wrote
English prose; and at the present time a more welcome
truth could hardly be whispered in the world's ear, for
many are surely tired of the lapwing cry, 'Stevenson and
So-and-so and So-and-so and Stevenson.'...

About ten years ago I read a story by Stevenson. I
forget which, nor does it matter - it was in a volume
entitled 'The Merry Men.' I was struck by the unexpectedness of every epithet; but while admiring the extraordinary epithet, I remembered the ordinary one, and was much
exercised by the ingenuity with which the latter had been
avoided, and what still further increased my wonderment
was that in every instance the extraordinary epithet and
turn of phrase was an improvement upon the ordinary.
Every sentence held a fresh surprise, and my admiration
waxed until I happened upon a man who stopped a clock with
an 'interjected finger' [from Markheim]. At this I cried,
'Halt.' Now I see, I said, that this man's style is but a
conjuror's trick - a marvellous trick, but a trick. He
spins one plate, two plates, three plates; he goes on
throwing up plates until a dozen are whirling in the air.
He throws up the thirteenth, and, lo! one comes down
crashing.... 'This man,' I said, 'is saying the ordinary
things in very neat language; but ordinary thoughts are
better expressed in ordinary language.... He translates.
... He picks the common words out and sticks in rare
words.... A delicious take in.... Very like modern
cabinet-making: an ordinary mahogany chest of drawers is
inlaid with satin-wood and lo, it becomes at once eighteenth century!'

All Stevenson is in that unfortunate 'interjected
finger'; he imagined no human soul, and he invented no
story that anyone will remember; his whole art consisted
in substituting rare words and new turns of phrase for
old and familiar epithets and locutions. The 'interjected
finger' pointed the way, and having to speak about Stevenson soon after, in a book I was then writing, I said: 'He
is the best-dressed young man that ever walked in the
Burlington Arcade.... He makes every thought sparkling
and clear, but he deprives it of all mystery, of all
romance.... Romantic! He's about as romantic as Voltaire, and would have been a much greater writer if he
had lived in the reign of Anne.'

'The Secret Rose' teaches truths still more essential

than that Stevenson wrote with the brain of a boy and the
imagination and perceptions of the meticulous eighteenth
century. It teaches a lesson sadly needed at the present
moment - that romance comes from within and not from
without. Murder is deemed romantic, and reviewers recommend So-and-so's last romance because 'the sword is
rarely if ever sheathed during the long course of the
narrative.' Since the days of Stevenson massacre has
succeeded massacre, and always in the name of romance,
and writers have been found to follow popular taste with
the meekness of mummers. Stevenson's conception of life
has been mixed with bog-water and kneaded by the literary
agent, but, at best, it was a trivial conception; it was
never higher than that of a blithe noble-hearted boy, a
boy who prefers a raft to a boat, and hopes to be one day
a pirate captain on the Spanish Main. To such superficial
conception of life Stevenson brought his talent for literary marquetry, and a public, jaded by the unromantic
moralities of positivism, accepted eagerly books that were
at least free from geological theology. To this was
added the fascinating theory that books might be beautifully written, though they contained no more thought than
might be swallowed by an urchin of six. The public was at
once interested, the public always is interested in
tricks - tricks are fertile, and tricks may be learnt.
A man stops a clock with an inserted finger. Open the
Thesaurus, look out 'inserted,' and among the equivalents
you will find 'interjected.'

Some will think that I might have praised Mr. Yeats's
'Secret Rose' without having given up so much space to
depreciating Stevenson. Very likely, but we all have our
own way of doing things, and it is my belief that the time
has come to remind the world that great literature cannot
be composed from narratives of perilous adventures. The
narratives of the ancient writers were declarations of
their philosophical faiths. Stevenson is the leader of
those countless writers who perceive nothing but the
visible world; and these are antagonistic to the great
literature, of which Mr. Yeats's 'Secret Rose' is a survival or a renaissance....

162. A. T. QUILLER-COUCH, AN ANSWER TO MOORE, 'SPEAKER'

1 May 1897, xv, 484-6

See headnote to No. 161. This article was entitled The
Moral Idea.

In last Saturday's 'Daily Chronicle' appeared a review, by
Mr. George Moore, of Mr. W. B. Yeats's new book, 'The
Secret Rose'; and on the ground that 'it is only by comparison that we perceive merits and defects' Mr. Moore
took occasion to insert into that review certain stric-
tures upon Stevenson's prose. They seem to me to prove
that Mr. Moore has a pretty firm hold on one end of a
stick: and I am ready to admit that a stick can be
flourished with most effect from one end. And yet, after
all, a stick has usually two ends.
     For the moment Mr. Moore has allowed his intellect and
his affections to be captivated by the beauty of the
'moral idea' in fiction. It is a great thing to find an
English critic captivated by any idea, and certainly the
peculiar beauties of the moral idea have stood in peculiar
need of recommendation to English writers and readers for
a very long while. At the same time I trust that Mr.
Moore will not allow it to grow into a monomania; for my
present purpose is to show (1) that the presentment or
development of a moral idea is by no means the single end
of literature in general, or of fiction in particular, and
(2) that to deny 'moral ideas' to Stevenson is to betray
either a limited acquaintance with his writings or a lack
of sympathy so profound as to nullify any attempt to grasp
his intentions.
     Let us first consider Stevenson's alleged want of moral
ideas. 'About ten years ago' Mr. Moore read a story by
Stevenson - he 'forgets which, nor does it matter'; but it
was in a volume called 'The Merry Men' - and his reading
led him to the conclusion that all Stevenson's art lay in
clothing ordinary ideas, or no ideas at all, in extremely
rare language. 'A delicious take in.... Very like modern
cabinet-making: an ordinary mahogany chest of drawers is
inlaid with satin-wood, and lo! it becomes at once
eighteenth-century!' Mr. Moore alighted on a sentence in
which a man stops a clock with an 'interjected finger';
and he now finds himself able to assert that 'all Stevenson is in that unfortunate "interjected finger"; he

imagined no human soul, and he invented no story that
anyone will remember: his whole art consisted in substituting rare words and new turns of phrases for old and familiar epithets and locations.'

Were any such accusation even near the truth, I can
assure Mr. Moore than he would not be counting me to-day
among Stevenson's warmest admirers. That Stevenson had
tricks of style all must allow: that the inexperienced
might be led to value him by these tricks and grace-notes,
may also be granted. But I think I state no singular case
in saying that while I have grown to admire these tricks
less and less, I have grown to like Stevenson more and
more. Marry, for why? Well, for several reasons, and
among them because his writings, taken as a whole, are
filled with a sound and honest philosophy of life. This
is precisely what Mr. Moore denies. 'The narratives of
the ancient writers,' says he, 'were declarations of their
philosophical faiths. Stevenson is the leader of those
countless writers who perceive nothing but the visible
world.' Mr. Moore forgets which story he read: but he
thinks it worth while to remember that he dropped the book
and was afterwards moved, as a result of his brief study,
to say of Stevenson: 'He is the best-dressed young man
that ever walked in the Burlington Arcade.... He makes
every thought sparkling and clear, but he deprives it of
all mystery, of all romance.... Romantic! He's about as
romantic as Voltaire, and would have been a much greater
writer if he had lived in the reign of Anne.'

I feel obliged to suggest that Mr. Moore might with
profit resume and extend his study of Stevenson. To save
trouble he might begin with the volume he dropped, 'The
Merry Men.' It contains two stories (at least) which I
fancy he must have overlooked - Will of the Mill and
Markheim. Will of the Mill is born in a valley through
which a river runs and a high road. Along the high road,
year after year, post-chaises and waggons and pedestrians,
and once an army 'horse and foot, cannon and tumbril, drum
and standard,' go hurrying from one busy stage of the
world's theatre to another. Will watches them pass, and
dreams of the mysterious world beyond his valley and longs
to see it. But he is a slow countryman, and dallies with
the wish year after year. He ends by keeping an inn, in
the parlour of which he sits and listens to the talk of
more initiated spirits; and as procrastination begets
timidity, when the time comes he shirks even the adventure
of marriage, and poorly disappoints the honest girl who is
ready for him. So he lives and vegetates; but there is
one adventure, one voyage, that no man may shirk. There
arrives at length a passenger who tells him this, and

that the time has come. The passenger's name is Death;
and with him at length Will of the Mill sets forth upon
his travels. Call this an allegory, a mystery, what you
will; I ask, does it not contain a 'moral idea'? Is it
not built upon the moral idea that excess of cautious
wisdom is a disease of the soul, paralysing manhood? Take
Markheim, in which a man, red-handed from a murder,
reviews his past, interrogates his 'other self' in a
vision, and so, having a way of escape from the law but no
way of escape from himself, surrenders to the police.
Consider this extract from the talk of Markheim's spiritual visitor: -

'Murder is to me no special category,' replied the
other. 'All sins are murder, even as all life is war.
I behold your race, like starving mariners upon a raft,
plucking crusts out of the hands of famine, and feeding
on each other's lives. I follow sins beyond the moment
of their acting; I find in all that the last consequence is death; and to my eyes the pretty maid, who
thwarts her mother with such taking graces on the
question of a ball, drips no less visibly with human
gore than such a murderer as yourself.'

You may call this a straining of the moral insight, if
you choose; but only in wantonness of depreciation can you
talk of it as the writing of a man 'who perceived nothing
but the visible world.' Take 'The Master of Ballantrae';
here you have a longer story broad-based upon a moral
idea. For the tragedy of that book does not of course
reside in the Master and his wickedness, but in the
gradual (and to my thinking, most subtly revealed)
deterioration of the honest brother whom he persecutes.
Take 'Dr. Jekyll and Mr. Hyde': it is the downright
deliberate allegorising of a moral idea - the idea of two
natures contending in a man. Remove that idea, and the
story crumbles into a heap of nonsense. Again, is there
no moral idea in the study of 'Kirstie' in 'Weir of Hermiston'? - no moral idea in the over-darkened 'Ebb-Tide,'
that tale of varied depravity and its varied rewards? -
no moral idea in The Bottle Imp? - if not, there is no
moral idea in the story of Alcestis. These tales stand,
I admit, at various removes from life, as we observe life.
But each has its informing lesson, and the lesson of each
is sought in the heart of man.
     At the same time, we must admit that Stevenson's fancy
was capricious; and often enough he told a story out of
sheer caprice, and left morality behind him. But his
Essays redress the balance, and his Poems. Here let me

quote from a lecture delivered by Professor Raleigh before
the Royal Institution in May, 1895: -

> His genius, like the genius of Nathaniel Hawthorne,
> was doubly rich, in the spirit of romance and in a wise
> and beautiful morality. But the irresponsible caprices
> of his narrative fancy prevented his tales from being
> the appropriate vehicles of his morality.... Hence his
> essays, containing as they do the gist of his reflec-
> tive wisdom, are ranked by some critics above his
> stories. (1)

The majority of Stevenson's poems and practically the
whole body of his Essays depend upon moral insight for
their origin and their justification. It is from the sum
total of his work that we deduce his philosophy; and finding it, as we think, a full one, we have surely some reason
to complain of a critic who on a confessedly imperfect
acquaintance with his writings assures the world that the
man had no moral insight at all. Should Mr. Moore retain
his opinion after a perusal of 'Across the Plains' and
'Songs of Travel'; and should he still cling to his
admired phrase, 'The best-dressed young man that ever
walked the Burlington Arcade'; well - I shall be sorry,
but at least we shall have a little more ground on which
to build a compromise.

But, to leave Stevenson for the moment and come to the
general question. The moral idea is a mighty fine thing
in literature, and I feel almost jealous of Mr. Moore's
devotion to it. But is it the one and only essential of
great literature, or even of great fiction? I submit
that there is such a thing as *truth of temperament*, and
that this too may be worth Mr. Moore's attention. The
Essays of Michael, Lord of Montaigne, are scarcely inspired by moral ideas; but they have undeviating truth of
temperament, and have found it a fair preservative of man's
esteem. I search 'Much Ado About Nothing' and 'As You
Like It' in vain for moral ideas; but truth of temperament
informs them both, and they are still reckoned among the
triumphs of literature. Is it for moral ideas or for
truth of temperament that we value Jane Austen? Scott -
Mr. Moore (I seem to remember) can find little to admire
in Scott. He appears to be studying literature just now
through a single eye-glass. A second glass might correct
his observations. I believe that by that second glass he
would discover quite unsuspected beauties in quite a large
number of authors. And what better could befall a critic?

Note

1 (Sir) Walter Raleigh's lecture was published in 'Robert
   Louis Stevenson' (1895).

'St Ives'

October 1897

163. STEVENSON, FROM LETTERS TO COLVIN AND R. A. M.
STEVENSON

1893, 1894

(a) From a letter to Colvin dated 23 August 1893

I am deep in 'St. Ives' which, I believe, will be the next
novel done. But it is to be clearly understood that I
promise nothing, and may throw in your face the very last
thing you expect - or I expect. 'St. Ives' will (to my
mind) not be wholly bad. It is written in rather a funny
style; a little stilted and left-handed; the style of St.
Ives; also, to some extent, the style of R.L.S. dictating
'St. Ives' is unintellectual, and except as an adventure
novel dull. But the adventures seem to me sound and
pretty probable; and it is a love story. Speed his wings!
(LS, iv, 230-1)

(b) From a letter to R. A. M. Stevenson dated by Colvin
17 June 1894. Robert Alan Mowbray Stevenson (1847-1900),
a painter and art critic, was R. L. Stevenson's cousin
and the 'Spring-heel'd Jack' of his essay Talk and Talkers;
he was recognized by W. B. Yeats and others as a brilliant
conversationalist. From 1889 to 1893 he was professor of
fine arts at University College, Liverpool; following this,
he was the regular art critic for the 'Pall Mall Gazette'
and a contributor to the 'Magazine of Art' and the 'Portfolio'. His best known work of criticism is 'The Art of
Velasquez' (1895).

My work goes along but slowly. I have got to a crossing
place, I suppose; the present book, 'St. Ives', is
nothing; it is in no style in particular, a tissue of
adventures, the central character not very well done, no
philosophic pith under the yarn; and, in short, if people
will read it, that's all I ask; and if they won't, damn
them! I like doing it though; and if you ask me why!
After that I am on 'Weir of Hermiston' and 'Heathercat',
two Scotch stories, which will either be something different, or I shall have failed. (LS, iv, 287)

(c) From a letter to Colvin dated 18 June 1894

I must not let you be disappointed in 'St. I.' It is a
mere tissue of adventures; the central figure not very
well or very sharply drawn; no philosophy, no destiny, to
it; some of the happenings very good in themselves, I
believe, but none of them *bildende*, none of them constructive, except in so far perhaps as they make up a kind of
sham picture of the time, all in italics and all out of
drawing. Here and there, I think, it is well written; and
here and there it's not. Some of the episodic characters
are amusing, I do believe; others not, I suppose. However, they are the best of the thing such as it is. If it
has a merit to it, I should say it was a sort of delibera-
tion and swing to the style, which seems to me to suit the
mail-coaches and post-chaises with which it sounds all
through. 'Tis my most prosaic book. (LS, iv, 289)

(d) From a letter to Colvin dated by Colvin September 1894

I have been trying hard to get along with 'St. Ives'. I
should now lay it aside for a year and I daresay I should
make something of it after all. Instead of that, I have
to kick against the pricks, and break myself, and spoil
the book, if there were anything to spoil, which I am far
from saying. I'm sick of the thing as ever any one can
be; it's a rudderless hulk; it's a pagoda, and you can
just feel - or I can feel - that it might have been a
pleasant story, if it had been only blessed at baptism.
(LS, iv, 314)

164.   JOSEPH JACOBS, FROM AN UNSIGNED REVIEW, 'ATHENAEUM'

16 October 1897, 3651, 518-19

On Jacobs see headnote to No. 157.   The 'Athenaeum' files
identify him as the reviewer.

This is a rattling, touch-and-go tale of adventure of a
somewhat ordinary type, yet relieved by some fine but
slight studies in characterization.   That it will not add
to Stevenson's reputation is clear from this description,
as well as from his own doubts about the book already published to the world in the 'Vailima Letters.'   Whether it
was altogether wise of his executors to publish it admits
of some doubt; yet, after all, it will not lower, if it
will not enhance, his reputation; and it is, of course,
far above the average trade novels that pour forth in such
increasing floods from the press.   Perhaps the most remarkable (and significant) thing about the book is the skill
with which Mr. Quiller Couch has supplied the last six
chapters, which both in style and briskness of treatment
bear an astonishing resemblance to the preceding thirty.
It was a dangerous and difficult task that Mr. Quiller
Couch undertook, and to some it might seem of disputable
taste.   But he has come out of the ordeal triumphantly,
and for once a patch has proved to be not altogether a
botch....
    [But] the fact is, this book bears the mark of a fagged
mind on almost every page of it.   It is largely reminiscent of other works of the same writer.   The interview
which the heroine's brother has with the hero resembles
closely a scene in 'Beau Austin.'   The escape from
Edinburgh Castle has its counterpart in a similar escape
in 'The Black Arrow.'   The villain viscount is a faint
copy of the Master of Ballantrae.   The counting up of the
treasure recalls the last pages of 'Treasure Island.'
The fight with the drovers is a similar incident to the
attack by Cluny's men in 'Kidnapped.'   Rowley's flageolet
takes the place of the penny whistle of the carrier in
'The Wrong Box,' while the friendly relations of the hero
with that burly villain Burchell Fenn had previous existence in the pages of 'The Wrecker.'   And so throughout the
majority of incidents recall similar passages in Stevenson's earlier books, and prove that while he was occupied
in writing 'St. Ives' his mind had lost its power of

fresh combination. That the loss was only temporary that
vigorous fragment 'Weir of Hermiston' is more than sufficient proof.

Little fresh as are the incidents, they are even less
well considered and connected. The story is practically
of an escaped military prisoner who travels from Edinburgh
to his uncle's place in the south, and then returns to the
northern capital. The motive for the return is supposed
to be an invincible desire to see the loved one, but the
coxcomb tone in which the fair one is wooed does not make
this return at risk of death any the more probable.
Stevenson may possibly have felt this, as he props up the
motive with a somewhat trumpery charge of assault in which
others might be implicated for the hero's sake. But even
this is only brought in as an afterthought, for it could
not have been made the principal motive, or else the
attractive power of love would have been so much diminished. When St. Ives gets to Edinburgh again, where he
is wanted for an alleged murder, really the result of a
duel, he naturally falls into great dangers, from which he
ultimately escapes by the most mechanical of methods, a
casual balloon that wafts him away to the Bristol Channel.
Altogether the book, regarded from the point of view of
plot, is a panorama of improbabilities.

Nor on the character side is there much to attract.
We have already referred to the unconvincing nature of the
hero's position as an Anglo-Scotch Frenchman. The heroine
is somewhat of a lay figure. More care has been taken
with the villain, but he is after all merely a lath that
is not even painted to look like iron; and in the relations of the hero, either to heroine or villain, there is
nothing inevitable, nothing that could not be otherwise.

Yet unsatisfactory as the book is, both in construction and characterization, it has an interest of its own
to the student of Stevenson's art. Previous to this book,
his studies in characterization were somewhat forced, and
he had clearly to content himself with but a few figures
on the stage. He characterized 'with deeficulty.' But
here at last he began to show himself a compeer of the
masters in that quality in which they specially proved
their mastery. What distinguishes Fielding, Scott,
Dickens, Thackeray, and even Charles Reade to a certain
extent, is the ease and fecundity with which they create
minor characters. It is possible they crowd their can-
vases too much, but the total result is to produce that
effect of bustling life which it is the peculiar function
of the novelist to reproduce. Here in 'St. Ives' Stevenson
for the first time came to his own in this respect; it is
crowded with subordinate figures, the majority of them

alive and some of them uproariously kicking. There is
Major Chevenix, the hero's rival, a dry stick, but a
gentlemanly. The heroine's aunt, Miss Gilchrist, is
crabbed and caustic, but good-natured at bottom. Rowley,
the boy valet, is scarcely the success that the pains
devoted to him would warrant, but he is certainly alive.
One of the minor characters, a French colonel who had
broken parole in order to reach the death-bed of his only
daughter, sounds a note of almost tragic intensity. But
whether it be a postboy demanding blackmail, or a runaway
bride who is sorry she has run away, or an attorney's
clerk who has touches of patriotism, or an Edinburgh buck
who is professor of nonsense in an imaginary university –
whether they are portrayed in few or in many lines –
almost every character introduced has the tang of individuality.

Stevenson must have felt some of this increased capacity
himself, for he has been so greatly daring as to introduce
as one of his minor characters no less a person than Walter
Scott himself. The passage in which he appears is short
and slight, but may be here quoted as an instance of perhaps the most characteristic thing about 'St. Ives,' the
evidence it gives of the capacity of indicating character
by a few traits:

[Quotes ch. x from 'Our encounter was of a tall, stoutish,
elderly gentleman' to 'And when I applied to Sim for
information, his answer ... told me, unfortunately,
nothing'.]

The incident is slight enough in all conscience, but
every touch tells, and the whole impression is one of
life. It is, perhaps, worth while mentioning that the word
cigar is here spelt otherwise than in the rest of the book
book, where it has the old spelling *segar*. There are also
some anachronisms of fact and tone.... These discrepan-
cies would doubtless have been removed if Stevenson had
lived to revise the proofs, but no amount of revision
could have made up for the want of cohesion in the plot,
the inefficient colouring of the chief characters.

It is needless to say that in speaking in these somewhat slighting terms of 'St. Ives' we are judging it by a
high standard. Whether destined to be classic or no,
there is no doubt that Stevenson's work stands out markedly from the ruck of machine-made fiction, and this very
book with all its faults shows that he was slowly maturing
to a mastery of his art which might have raised him to an
equality with the greatest of the past.

165. JOHN JAY CHAPMAN ON STEVENSON'S SHAM ART

1898

From an essay entitled Robert Louis Stevenson, in 'Emerson
and Other Essays', 217-47.
    Chapman (1862-1933), the American essayist, poet, and
reformer, visited the Stevensons in Bournemouth in 1885,
having been given a letter of introduction by Henry James
(B, 4923). In his autobiographic Retrospections, Chapman
tells of having, during that visit, sat up for several
nights in a cottage neighbouring Skerryvore at work on a
tragic story.

> Will you believe it? I read this story aloud to
> Stevenson and his wife, and was so excited about it
> that they almost seemed to think there was something
> in it.... I found the story years afterward and
> destroyed it. It was feeble and extravagant trash.
> This was before the days of Stevenson's fame, but he
> afterward came to America and felled the whole city
> with his success.... Why did I not look him up and
> thank him for his early kindess to me? Was this shy-
> ness or ingratitude? I don't know. (M. A. DeWolfe
> Howe, 'John Jay Chapman and His Letters' (1937), 51)

One reason Chapman did not welcome Stevenson is that at
the time he was undergoing a crisis following the self-
mutilation of his left hand. James mentioned this incident to Stevenson in a letter dated October 1887, a month
after Stevenson's arrival in the USA (B, 4939).
    In a letter to Mrs C. Grant LaFarge, 11 August 1896,
Chapman expressed his feelings about Stevenson with
greater bluntness than in this essay:

> Stevenson's manner of writing is the last form of
> whipped up literary froth, very well done.... [He] is
> a bad influence because he's so highly artificial. He
> struts and grimaces and moralizes and palavers and
> throws in tid bits of local color, fine feeling,
> graceful ornament, O my, ain't he clever - the rogue -
> hits you in the mid-riff - don't he - so beautiful -
> did you catch that - how smartly he led up to that
> anecdote - how well he lays in his Scotch pathos - his
> British patriotism - his nautical knowledge - and such
> light diet! I swear I am hungry for something every
> time I lay down Stevenson - give my rye bread, give me

notes to Dante, give me a book about the world....
It's sham literature. It's all of it sham.... I feel
Stevenson sweating in every line. I feel an echo in
every syllable.... It is the tradition and sentiment
of literature, the secondary traits, catchwords, and
paraphernalia of writing.... His popularity is a good
sign perhaps as showing a certain knowledge and appro-
bation of the literary forms of the past - very widely
spread, but it's a bad influence. ('Chapman and His
Letters', 115-16)

In the early eighties, and in an epoch when the ideals of
George Eliot were still controlling, the figure of Stevenson rose with a sort of radiance as a writer whose sole
object was to entertain. Most of the great novelists were
then dead, and the scientific school was in the ascendant.
Fiction was entering upon its death grapple with socio-
logy. Stevenson came, with his tales of adventure and
intrigue, out-of-door life and old-time romance, and he
recalled to every reader his boyhood and the delights of
his earliest reading. We had forgotten that novels could
be amusing.

Hence it is that the great public not only loves
Stevenson as a writer, but regards him with a certain
personal gratitude. There was, moreover, in everything
he wrote an engaging humorous touch which made friends
for him everywhere, and excited an interest in his fragile
and somewhat elusive personality supplementary to the
appreciation of his books as literature....

The quality which every one will agree in conceding to
Stevenson is lightness of touch. This quality is a result
of his extreme lucidity, not only of thought but of intention. We know what he means, and we are sure that we
grasp his whole meaning at the first reading. Whether he
be writing a tale of travel or humorous essay, a novel of
adventure, a story of horror, a morality, or a fable; in
whatever key he plays, - and he seems to have taken
delight in showing mastery in many, - the reader feels
safe in his hands, and knows that no false note will be
struck. His work makes no demands upon the attention.
It is food so thoroughly peptonized that it is digested as
soon as swallowed and leaves us exhilarated rather than
fed.

Writing was to him an art, and almost everything that
he has written has a little the air of being a *tour de force*.
Stevenson's books and essays were generally brilliant
imitations of established things, done somewhat in the

spirit of an expert in billiards. In short, Stevenson is
the most extraordinary mimic that has ever appeared in
literature.

That is the reason why he has been so much praised for
his style. When we say of a new thing that it 'has
style,' we mean that it is done as we have seen things done
before. Bunyan, De Foe, or Charles Lamb were to their
contemporaries men without style. The English, to this
day, complain of Emerson that he has no style.

If a man writes as he talks, he will be thought to have
no style, until people get used to him, for literature
means *what has been written*. As soon as a writer is
established, his manner of writing is adopted by the
literary conscience of the times, and you may follow him
and still have 'style.' You may to-day imitate George
Meredith, and people, without knowing exactly why they
do it, will concede you 'style.' Style means tradition.

When Stevenson, writing from Samoa in the agony of his
'South Seas' (a book he could not write because he had no
paradigm and original to copy from), says that he longs
for a 'moment of style,' he means that he wishes there
would come floating through his head a memory of some
other man's way of writing to which he could modulate his
sentences.

It is no secret that Stevenson in early life spent much
time in imitating the styles of various authors, for he
has himself described the manner in which he went to work
to fit himself for his career as a writer. His boyish
ambition led him to employ perfectly phenomenal diligence
in cultivating a perfectly phenomenal talent for imitation.

There was probably no fault in Stevenson's theory as to
how a man should learn to write, and as to the discipline
he must undergo. Almost all the greatest artists have
shown, in their early work, traces of their early masters.
These they outgrow.... It is noticeable, too, that the
early and imitative work of great men generally belongs to
a particular school to which their maturity bears a logical relation. They do not cruise about in search of a
style or vehicle, trying all and picking up hints here and
there, but they fall incidentally and genuinely under
influences which move them and afterwards qualify their
original work.

With Stevenson it was different; for he went in search
of a style as Cœlebs in search of a wife. He was an
eclectic by nature. He became a remarkable, if not a
unique phenomenon, - for he never grew up. Whether or not
there was some obscure connection between his bodily
troubles and the arrest of his intellectual development,

it is certain that Stevenson remained a boy till the day
of his death....

To a boy, the great artists of the world are a lot of
necromancers, whose enchantment can perhaps be stolen and
used again. To a man, they are a lot of human beings,
and their works are parts of them. Their works are their
hands and their feet, their organs, dimensions, senses,
affections, passions. To a man, it is as absurd to imitate the manner of Dean Swift in writing as it would be to
imitate the manner of Dr. Johnson in eating. But Stevenson was not a man, he was a boy; or, to speak more
accurately, the attitude of his mind towards his work
remained unaltered from boyhood till death, though his
practice and experiment gave him, as he grew older, a
greater mastery over his materials. It is in this attitude of Stevenson's mind toward his own work that we must
search for the heart of his mystery.

He conceived of himself as 'an artist,' and of his
writings as performances. As a consequence, there is an
undertone of insincerity in almost everything which he has
written. His attention is never wholly absorbed in his
work, but is greatly taken up with the notion of how each
stroke of it is going to appear....

It seems to be a law of psychology that the only way in
which the truth can be strongly told is in the course of
a search for truth. The moment a man strives after some
'effect,' he disqualifies himself from making that effect;
for he draws the interest of his audience to the same
matters that occupy his own mind; namely, upon his experiment and his efforts. It is only when a man is saying
something that he believes is obviously and eternally
true, that he can communicate spiritual things.

Ultimately speaking, the vice of Stevenson's theories
about art is that they call for a self-surrender by the
artist of his own mind to the pleasure of others, for a
subordination of himself to the production of this
'effect' in the mind of another. They degrade and be-
little him. Let Stevenson speak for himself; the thought
contained in the following passage is found in a hundred
places in his writings and dominated his artistic life.

'The French have a romantic evasion for one employment,
and call its practitioners the Daughters of Joy. The
artist is of the same family, he is of the Sons of Joy,
chose his trade to please himself, gains his livelihood
by pleasing others, and has parted with something of the
sterner dignity of men. The poor Daughter of Joy carrying
her smiles and her finery quite unregarded through the
crowd, makes a figure which it is impossible to recall
without a wounding pity. She is the type of the

unsuccessful artist.' [Letter to a Young Gentleman, No. 103]

These are the doctrines and beliefs which time out of mind, have brought the arts into contempt. They are as injurious as they are false, and they will checkmate the progress of any man or of any people that believes them. They corrupt and menace not merely the fine arts, but every other form of human expression in an equal degree.... The doctrines are the outcome of an Alexandrine age. After art has once learnt to draw its inspiration directly from life and has produced some masterpieces, then imitations begin to creep in. That Stevenson's doctrines tend to produce imitative work is obvious....

[Here Chapman deals at length with the models in evidence in Stevenson's work. He decides that his most natural and direct style is found in his travel writings, especially those in 'Across the Plains'.]

The reason why Stevenson represents a backward movement in literature, is that literature lives by the pouring into it of new words from speech, and new thoughts from life, and Stevenson used all his powers to exclude both from his work. He lived and wrote in the past. That this Scotchman should appear at the end of what has been a very great period of English literature, and summarize the whole of it in his two hours' traffic on the stage, gives him a strange place in the history of that literature. He is the Improvisatore, and nothing more. It is impossible to assign him rank in any line of writing. If you shut your eyes to try and place him, you find that you cannot do it. The effect he produces while we are reading him vanishes as we lay down the book, and we can recall nothing but a succession of flavors. It is not to be expected that posterity will take much interest in him, for his point and meaning are impressional. He is ephemeral, a shadow, a reflection. He is the mistletoe of English literature whose roots are not in the soil but in the tree.

But enough of the nature and training of Stevenson which fitted him to play the part he did. The cyclonic force which turned him from a secondary London novelist into something of importance and enabled him to give full play to his really unprecedented talents will be recognized on glancing about us.

We are now passing through the age of the Distribution of Knowledge. The spread of the English-speaking race since 1850, and the cheapness of printing, have brought in primers and handbooks by the million. All the books of the older literatures are being abstracted and sown

abroad in popular editions. The magazines fulfil the same
function; every one of them is a penny cyclopedia. Andrew
Lang heads an army of organized workers who mine in the
old literature and coin it into booklets and cash.

The American market rules the supply of light literature in Great Britain. While Lang culls us tales and
legends and lyrics from the Norse or Provençal, Stevenson
will engage to supply us with tales and legends of his
own - something just as good. The two men serve the same
public.

Stevenson's reputation in England was that of a comparatively light weight, but his success here was immediate. We hailed him as a classic - or something just as
good. Everything he did had the very stamp and trademark
of Letters, and he was as strong in one department as
another. We loved this man; and thenceforward he purveyed
'literature' to us at a rate to feed sixty millions of
people and keep them clamoring for more.

Does any one believe that the passion of the American
people for learning and for antiquity is a slight and
accidental thing? Does any one believe that the taste for
imitation old furniture is a pose? It creates an eddy in
the Maelstrom of Commerce. It is a power like Niagara,
and represents the sincere appreciation of half educated
people for second rate things. There is here nothing to
be ashamed of. In fact there is everything to be proud
of in this progress of the arts, this importation of culture by the carload. The state of mind it shows is a
definite and typical state of mind which each individual
passes through, and which precedes the discovery that
real things are better than sham. When the latest Palace
Hotel orders a hundred thousand dollars' worth of Louis
XV. furniture to be made - and most well made - in
Buffalo, and when the American public gives Stevenson an
order for Pulvis et Umbra - the same forces are at work
in each case. It is Chicago making culture hum.

And what kind of a man was Stevenson? Whatever may be
said about his imitativeness, his good spirits were real.
They are at the bottom of his success, the strong note in
his work. They account for all that is paradoxical in his
effect. He often displays a sentimentalism which has not
the ring of reality. And yet we do not reproach him. He
has by stating his artistic doctrines in their frankest
form revealed the scepticism inherent in them. And yet
we know that he was not a sceptic; on the contrary, we
like him, and he was regarded by his friends as little
lower than the angels.

Why is it that we refuse to judge him by his own utterances? The reason is that all of his writing is playful,

and we know it. The instinct at the bottom of all mimicry
is self-concealment. Hence the illusive and questionable
personality of Stevenson. Hence our blind struggle to
bind this Proteus who turns into bright fire and then into
running water under our hands. The truth is that as a
literary force, there was no such man as Stevenson; and
after we have racked our brains to find out the mechanism
which has been vanquishing the chess players of Europe,
there emerges out of the Box of Maelzel a pale boy.

But the courage of this boy, the heroism of his life,
illumine all his works with a personal interest. The last
ten years of his life present a long battle with death.

We read of his illnesses, his spirit; we hear how he
never gave up, but continued his works by dictation and in
dumb show when he was too weak to hold the pen, too weak
to speak. This courage and the lovable nature of Stevenson won the world's heart. He was regarded with a peculiar tenderness such as is usually given only to the young.
Honor, and admiration mingled with affection followed him
to his grave. Whatever his artistic doctrines, he
revealed his spiritual nature in his work. It was this
nature which made him thus beloved.

166. W. E. HENLEY AGAINST THE 'SERAPH IN CHOCOLATE, THE
BARLEY-SUGAR EFFIGY', 'PALL MALL MAGAZINE'

December 1901, xxv, 505-14

This was a review article of Balfour's 'Life of Robert
Louis Stevenson' (1901). Among the many responses to the
article were two unsigned items: The Candid Friend,
'Academy', 23 November 1901, and Literary Leprosy,
'Saturday Review', 30 November 1901. Andrew Lang's com-
ments appeared in Literary Quarrels, 'Morning Post', 16
December 1901.

Mr. Graham Balfour has done his best; and his best should
rank decently among official biographies. He is loving,
he is discreet, he has much knowledge.... As to Mr.
Balfour's tact and piety (a most serviceable blend), there
cannot be two opinions: he has written lovingly of his
dead cousin, and, according to his lights, he has written

well. I mean, he has done his best for the Stevenson of
legend and his best for the Stevenson of life. So far as
I can see, he does not distinguish the one from the other:
his predilections are all with rumour and report; and if
they be not, at least he can govern his tongue. On the
whole, I may congratulate him on his result....

Yet I am discontented, dissatisfied, still looking for
more. I daresay the feeling is personal; that I cannot
judge equably, for I know too much. So be it. 'Tis a
fact that, recalling what I can recall, I can only take
Mr. Balfour's book as a solemn and serious essay in that
kind of make-believe in which the biographee (if one may
use so flippant a neologism in so august a connexion) did
all his life rejoice, and was exceeding glad. I read;
and as I read I am oppressed by the thought that here is
Lewis Stevenson very much as he may well have wanted to
be, but that here is not Lewis Stevenson at all. At any
rate, here is not the Lewis Stevenson I knew....

For me there were two Stevensons: the Stevenson who
went to America in '87; and the Stevenson who never came
back. The first I knew, and loved; the other I lost touch
with, and, though I admired him, did not greatly esteem.
My relation to him was that of a man with a grievance;
and for that reason, perhaps - that reason and others - I
am by no means disposed to take all Mr. Balfour says for
gospel, nor willing to forget, on the showing of what is
after all an official statement, the knowledge gained in
an absolute intimacy of give-and-take which lasted for
thirteen years, and includes so many of the circumstances
of those thirteen years that, as I believe, none living
now can pretend to speak of them with any such authority
as mine. This, however, is not to say that Mr. Balfour's
view of his famous cousin is not warranted to the letter,
so far as he saw and knew. I mean no more than that the
Stevenson he knew was not the Stevenson who came to me
(that good angel, Mr. Leslie Stephen, aiding) in the old
Edinburgh Infirmary; nor the Stevenson I nursed in secret,
hard by the old Bristo Port, till he could make shift to
paddle the *Arethusa*; nor the Stevenson who stayed with me
at Acton after selling Modestine, nor even the Stevenson
who booked a steerage berth to New York, and thence
trained it 'across the plains,' and ended for the time
being as a married man and a Silverado squatter; though I
confess that in this last avatar the Stevenson of Mr.
Balfour's dream had begun, however faintly and vaguely,
to adumbrate himself, and might have been looked for as a
certainty by persons less affectionate and uninquiring
than those by whom he was then approached. Mr. Balfour
does me the honour of quoting the sonnet into which I

crammed my impressions of my companion and friend; and, since he has done so, I may as well own that 'the Shorter Catechist' of the last verse was an afterthought. In those days he was in abeyance, to say the least; and if, even then, *il allait poindre à l'horizon* (as the composition, in secret and as if ashamed, of 'Lay Morals' persuades me to believe he did), I, at any rate, was too short-sighted to suspect his whereabouts. When I realised it, I completed my sonnet; but this was not till years had come and gone, and the Shorter Catechist, already detested by more than one, was fully revealed to me.

I will say at once that I do not love the Shorter Catechist, in anybody, and that I loved him less in Stevenson than anywhere that I have ever found him. He is too selfish and too self-righteous a beast for me. He makes ideas for himself with a resolute regard for his own salvation; but he is all-too apt to damn the rest of the world for declining to live up to them, and he is all-too ready to make a lapse of his own the occasion for a rule of conduct for himself and the lasting pretext for a highly moral deliverance to such backsliding Erastians as, having memories and a certain concern for facts, would like him to wear his rue with a difference. At bottom Stevenson was an excellent fellow. But he was of his essence what the French call *personnel*. He was, that is, incessantly and passionately interested in Stevenson. He could not be in the same room with a mirror but he must invite its confidences every time he passed it; to him there was nothing obvious in time and eternity, and the smallest of his discoveries, his most trivial apprehensions, were all by way of being revelations, and as revelations must be thrust upon the world; he was never so much in earnest, never so well pleased (this were he happy or wretched), never so irresistible, as when he wrote about himself. Withal, if he wanted a thing, he went after it with an entire contempt for consequences. For these, indeed, the Shorter Catechist was ever prepared to answer; so that, whether he did well or ill, he was safe to come out unabashed and cheerful. He detested Mr. Gladstone, I am pleased to say; but his gift of self-persuasion was scarce second to that statesman's own. He gave himself out for the most open-minded of men: to him one point of view was as good as another; Age's was respectable, but so was Youth's; the Fox that had a tail was no whit more considerable than the Fox whose tail was lost. *Et patati, et patata*. 'Twas all 'as easy as lying' to him, for 'twas all in the run of his humanity. But in the event it was academic; for where he was grossly interested, he could see but one side of the debate; and

there are people yet living (I am not one of them) who,
knowing him intimately. have not hesitated to describe him
in a word of three letters, the suspicion of which might
well make him turn in his grave. And yet, I do not know.
He ever took himself so seriously - or rather he ever
played at life with such a solemn grace - that perhaps,
after all, he would scarce stir where he lies for the
dread vocable. For he was a humourist and a thinker, and
could he hear it, he would certainly smile, fall (like
the Faquir of story) to considering himself umbilically,
and, finding in the end that he had fairly earned it, go
back to sleep, with a glow of satisfaction for that this
part also had been well played. No better histrion ever
lived. But in the South Seas the mask got set, the
'lines' became a little stereotyped. Plainly the Shorter
Catechist was what was wanted. And here we are: with
Stevenson's later letters and Mr. Graham Balfour's estimate.

'Tis as that of an angel clean from heaven, and I for
my part flatly refuse to recognise it. Not, if I can help
it, shall this faultless, or very nearly faultless, monster go down to after years as the Lewis I knew, and
loved, and laboured with and for, with all my heart and
strength and understanding. In days to come I may write
as much as can be told of him. 'Till those days come,
this protest must suffice. If it convey the impression
that I take a view of Stevenson which is my own, and which
declines to be concerned with this Seraph in Chocolate,
this barley-sugar effigy of a real man; that the best and
the most interesting part of Stevenson's life will never
get written - even by me; and that the Shorter Catechist
of Vailima, however brilliant and distinguished as a
writer of stories, however authorised and acceptable as a
artist in morals, is not my old, riotous, intrepid, scornful Stevenson at all - suffice it will.

For the rest, I think he has written himself down in
terms that may not be mistaken, nor improved, in a fragment of an essay on morals printed in the Appendix to the
Edinburgh Edition. 'An unconscious, easy, selfish
person,' he remarks, 'shocks less, and is more easily
loved, than one who is laboriously and egotistically unselfish. There is at least no fuss about the first; but
the other parades his sacrifices, and so sells his favours
too dear. Selfishness is calm, a force of nature: you
might say the trees are selfish. But egoism is a piece
of vanity; it must always take you into its confidence; it
is uneasy, troublesome, searching; it can do good, but not
handsomely; it is uglier, because less dignified than selfishness itself. But here,' he goes on, with that careful

candour which he so often has, 'here I perhaps exaggerate
to myself, because I am the one more than the other, and
feel it like a hook in my mouth at every step I take.
Do what I will, this seems to spoil all.' This, as it
seems to me, describes him so exactly that, if you allow
for histrionics (no inconsiderable thing, remember!), you
need no more description. It was said of him, once, that
when he wrote of anything, he wrote of it with such an
implacable lucidity as left it beggared of mystery. This
is what he has done in this passage; and who runs may read
him in it as he was. 'Tis to this anxious and uncloi-
stered egotism of his that we are indebted for so much good
writing in the matter of confession and self-revelation....
'Tis to this that we are indebted for the prayers, the
supplications for valour, the vocalisings about duty
(which the most of us do as a matter of course), by which
that part of the world which reads Stevenson - (and that
part of it which does not is happily the smaller) - has
long been, and is still being, joyously edified....

[Henley here elaborates upon Stevenson's egotism and
recalls instances of his ingratitude to him for various
personal and professional favours.]

I have said nothing of Stevenson the artist in this
garrulous and egotistic pronouncement on his official
'Life;' for the very simple reason that I have nothing to
say. To tell the truth, his books are none of mine: I
mean, that if I want reading, I do not go for it to the
Edinburgh Edition. I am not interested in remarks about
morals; in and out of letters I have lived a full and
varied life, and my opinions are my own. So, if I crave
the enchantment of romance, I ask it of bigger men than
he, and of bigger books than his: of 'Esmond' (say) and
'Great Expectations,' of 'Redgauntlet', and 'Old Mortality', of 'La Reine Margot' and 'Bragelonne,' of 'David
Copperfield' and 'A Tale of Two Cities:' while, if good
writing and some other things be in my appetite, are there
not always Hazlitt and Lamb - to say nothing of that
'globe of miraculous continents' which is known to us as
Shakespeare? There is his style, you will say; and it is
a fact that it is rare, and in the last times better,
because much simpler, than in the first. But after all,
his style is so perfectly achieved that the achievement
gets obvious: and when achievement gets obvious, is it not
by way of becoming uninteresting? And is there not something to be said for the person who wrote that Stevenson
always reminded him of a young man dressed the best he
ever saw for the Burlington Arcade? Stevenson's work in

letters does not now take me much, and I decline to enter
on the question of its immortality; since that, despite
what any can say, will get itself settled, soon or late,
for all time. No; when I care to think of Stevenson it
is not of 'R.L.S.' : R.L.S. 'the renowned, the accomplished, Executing his difficult solo:' but of the
'Lewis' that I knew, and loved, and wrought for, and
worked with for so long. The successful man of letters
does not greatly interest me: I read his careful prayers,
and pass on, with the certainty that, well as they read,
they were not written for print; I learn of his nameless
prodigalities - and recall some instances of conduct in
another vein. I remember, rather, the unmarried and
irresponsible Lewis: the friend, the comrade, the *char-
meur*. Truly, that last word, French as it is, is the only
one that is worthy of him. I shall ever remember him as
that. The impression of his writings disappears; the
impression of himself and his talk is ever a possession.
He had, as I have said elsewhere, all the gifts (he and
his cousin, he and Bob) that qualify the talker's temperament: - 'As voice and eye and laugh, look and gesture,
humour and fantasy, audacity and agility of mind, a lively
and most impudent invention, a copious vocabulary, a right
gift of foolery, a just inevitable sense of right and
wrong' (this though I've blamed him for a tendency to
monologue, and a trick of depending too much on his
temperament). And I take leave to repeat what I've said
elsewhere, that those who know him only by his books -
(I think our Fleeing Jenkin, were he alive, would back
me here) - know but the poorest of him. Forasmuch as he
was primarily a talker, his printed works, like those of
others after his kind, are but a sop for posterity; - 'A
last dying speech and confession (as it were) to show
that not for nothing were they held rare fellows in their
day.'
      A last word. I have everywhere read that we must
praise him now and always for that, being a stricken man,
he would live out his life. Are we not all stricken men,
and do we not all do that? And why, because he wrote
better than any one, should he have praise and fame for
doing that which many a poor, consumptive sempstress
does: cheerfully, faithfully, with no eloquent appeals to
God, nor so much as a paragraph in the evening papers?
That a man writes well at death's door is sure no reason
for making him a hero; for, after all, there is as much
virtue in making a shirt, or finishing a gross of match-
boxes, in the very act of mortality, as there is in
polishing a verse, or completing a chapter in a novel.
As much, I say; but is there not an immense deal more?

In the one case, the sufferer does the thing he loves best
in life. In the other, well - who that has not made
shirts, or finished match-boxes, shall speak? Stevenson,
for all his vocalisings, was a brave man, with a fine,
buoyant spirit; and he took the mystery of life and time
and death as seemed best to him. But we are mortals all;
and, so far as I have seen, there are few of us but strive
to keep a decent face for the Arch-Discomforter. There is
no wonder that Stevenson wrote his best in the shadow of
the Shade; for writing his best was very life to him.
Why, then, all this crawling astonishment - this voluble
admiration? If it meant anything, it would mean that we
have forgotten how to live, and that none of us is prepared to die; and that were an outrage on the innumerable
unstoried martyrdoms of humanity. Let this be said of
him, once for all: 'He was a good man, good at many
things, and now this also he has attained to, to be at
rest.' That covers Sophocles and Shakespeare, Marlborough
and Bonaparte. Let it serve for Stevenson; and, for ourselves, let us live and die uninsulted, as we lived and
died before his books began to sell and his personality
was a marketable thing.

167. G. K. CHESTERTON AGAINST THE UNJUST DISPARAGEMENT
OF STEVENSON

1902

From The Characteristics of Robert Louis Stevenson,
'Robert Louis Stevenson', 19-34.
    Chesterton (1874-1936) was a Catholic apologist, cri-
tic, novelist and poet. This essay was first published in
the 'Bookman' (London), October 1901, and was first reprinted, with an essay by (Sir) William Robertson Nicoll,
in the second of the 'Bookman Booklets' (1902). It was
reprinted again as the second of the 'Bookman Biographies'
(1903), and later as one of the 'Little Books for Bookman'
(1906). The 'Bookman' was a popular illustrated literary
magazine founded and edited by Nicoll; because of the wide
interest in Stevenson he was frequently treated in its
pages.
    Chesterton was long a champion of Stevenson and his
book-length study of him (1927), which develops certain
of the views presented here, offers some of the most

interesting comment on Stevenson that we have.   See Introduction, p. 43.

All things and all men are underrated, much by others,
especially by themselves; and men grow tired of men just
as they do of green grass, so that they have to seek for
green carnations.   All great men possess in themselves
the qualities which will certainly lay them open to censure and diminishment; but these inevitable deficiencies
in the greatness of great men vary in the widest degree
of variety.   Stevenson is open to a particularly subtle,
a particularly effective and a particularly unjust disparagement.   The advantage of great men like Blake or
Browning or Walt Whitman is that they did not observe the
niceties of technical literature.   The far greater disadvantage of Stevenson is that he did.   Because he had a
conscience about small matters in art, he is conceived
not to have had an imagination about big ones.   It is
assumed by some that he must have been a bad architect,
and the only reason that they can assign is that he was
a good workman.   The mistake which has given rise to this
conception is one that has much to answer for in numerous
departments of modern art, literature, religion, philosophy, and politics.   The supreme and splendid characteristic of Stevenson was his levity; and his levity was the
flower of a hundred grave philosophies.   The strong man
is always light: the weak man is always heavy.   A swift
and casual agility is the mark of bodily strength: a
humane levity is the mark of spiritual strength.   A
thoroughly strong man swinging a sledge-hammer can tap
the top of an eggshell.   A weaker man swinging a sledge-
hammer will break the table on which it stands into
pieces.   Also, if he is a very weak man, he will be proud
of having broken the table, and call himself a strong man
dowered with the destructive power of an Imperial race.
This is, superficially speaking, the peculiar interest
of Stevenson.   He had what may be called a perfect mental
athleticism, which enabled him to leap from crag to crag,
and to trust himself anywhere and upon any question.
His splendid quality as an essayist and controversialist
was that he could always recover his weapon.   He was not
like the average swashbuckler of the current parties,
tugged at the tail of his own sword.   This is what tends,
for example, to make him stand out so well, beside his
unhappy friend Mr. Henley, whose true and unquestionable
affection has lately taken so bitter and feminine a form
[No. 166].   Mr. Henley, an admirable poet and critic, is,

nevertheless, the man *par excellence* who breaks the table instead of tapping the egg. In his recent article on Stevenson he entirely misses this peculiar and supreme point about his subject.

He there indulged in a very emotional remonstrance against the reverence almost universally paid to the physical misfortunes of his celebrated friend. 'If Stevenson was a stricken man,' he said, 'are we not all stricken men?' And he proceeded to call up the images of the poor and sick, and of their stoicism under their misfortunes. If sentimentalism be definable as the permitting of an emotional movement to cloud a clear intellectual distinction, this most assuredly is sentimentalism, for it would be impossible more completely to misunderstand the real nature of the cult of the courage of Stevenson. The reason that Stevenson has been selected out of the whole suffering humanity as the type of this more modern and occult martyrdom is a very simple one. It is not that he merely contrived, like any other man of reasonable manliness, to support pain and limitation without whimpering or committing suicide or taking to drink. In that sense of course we are all stricken men and we are all stoics. The ground of Stevenson's particular fascination in this matter was that he was the exponent, and the successful exponent, not merely of negative manliness, but of a positive and lyric gaiety. This wounded soldier did not merely refrain from groans, he gave forth instead a war song, so juvenile and inspiriting that thousands of men without a scratch went back into the battle. This cripple did not merely bear his own burdens, but those of thousands of contemporary men. No one can feel anything but the most inexpressible kind of reverence for the patience of the asthmatic charwoman or the consumptive tailor's assistance. Still the charwoman does not write Aes Triplex, nor the tailor 'The Child's Garden of Verses.' Their stoicism is magnificent, but it is stoicism. But Stevenson did not face his troubles as a stoic, he faced them as an Epicurean. He practised with an austere triumph that terrible asceticism of frivolity which is so much more difficult than the asceticism of gloom. His resignation can only be called an active and uproarious resignation. It was not merely self-sufficing, it was infectious. His triumph was, not that he went through his misfortunes without becoming a cynic or a poltroon, but that he went through his misfortunes and emerged quite exceptionally cheerful and reasonable and courteous, quite exceptionally lighthearted and liberal-minded. His triumph was, in other words, that he went through his misfortunes and did not become like Mr. Henley.

There is one aspect of this matter in particular, which it is as well to put somewhat more clearly before ourselves. This triumph of Stevenson's over his physical disadvantages is commonly spoken of with reference only to the elements of joy and faith, and what may be called the new and essential virtue of cosmic courage. But as a matter of fact the peculiarly interesting detachment of Stevenson from his own body, is exhibited in a quite equally striking way in its purely intellectual aspect. Apart from any moral qualities, Stevenson was characterised by a certain airy wisdom, a certain light and cool rationality, which is very rare and very difficult indeed to those who are greatly thwarted or tormented in life. It is possible to find an invalid capable of the work of a strong man, but it is very rare to find an invalid capable of the idleness of a strong man. It is possible to find an invalid who has the faith which removes mountains, but not easy to find an invalid who has the faith that puts up with pessimists. It may not be impossible or even unusual for a man to lie on his back on a sick bed in a dark room and be an optimist. But it is very unusual indeed for a man to lie on his back on a sick bed in a dark room and be a reasonable optimist: and that is what Stevenson, almost along of modern optimists, succeeded in being.

The faith of Stevenson, like that of a great number of very sane men, was founded on what is called a paradox - the paradox that existence was splendid because it was, to all outward appearance, desperate. Paradox, so far from being a modern and fanciful matter, is inherent in all the great hypotheses of humanity. The Athanasian Creed for example, the supreme testimony of Catholic Christianity, sparkles with paradox liks a modern society comedy. Thus, in the same manner, scientific philosophy tells us that finite space is unthinkable and infinite space is unthinkable. Thus the most influential modern metaphysician, Hegel, declares without hesitation, when the last rag of theology is abandoned, and the last point of philosophy passed, that existence is the same as nonexistence. Thus the brilliant author of 'Lady Windermere's Fan,' in the electric glare of modernity, finds that life is much too important to be taken seriously. Thus Tertullian, in the first ages of faith, said 'Credo quia impossibile.'

We must not, therefore, be immediately repelled by this paradoxical character of Stevenson's optimism, or imagine for a moment that it was merely a part of that artistic foppery of 'faddling hedonism' [see No. 6]

with which he has been ridiculously credited. His optimism was one which, so far from dwelling upon those
flowers and sunbeams which form the stock-in-trade of conventional optimism, took a peculiar pleasure in the contemplation of skulls, and cudgels, and gallows. It is one
thing to be the kind of optimist who can divert his mind
from personal suffering by dreaming of the face of an
angel, and quite another thing to be the kind of optimist
who can divert it by dreaming of the foul fat face of Long
John Silver. And this faith of his had a very definite
and a very original philosophical purport. Other men have
justified existence because it was a harmony. He justified it because it was a battle, because it was an inspiring and melodious discord. He appealed to a certain set
of facts which lie far deeper than any logic - the great
paradoxes of the soul. For the singular fact is that the
spirit of man is in reality depressed by all the things
which, logically speaking, should encourage it, and encouraged by all the things which, logically speaking,
should depress it. Nothing, for example, can be conceived
more really dispiriting than that rationalistic explanation of pain which conceives it as a thing laid by Providence upon the worst people. Nothing, on the other hand,
can be conceived as more exalting and reassuring than that
great mystical doctrine which teaches that pain is a thing
laid by Providence upon the best. We can accept the agony
of heroes, while we revolt against the agony of culprits.
We can all endure to regard pain when it is mysterious;
our deepest nature protests against it the moment that it
is rational. This doctrine that the best man suffers most
is, of course, the supreme doctrine of Christianity;
millions have found not merely an elevating but a soothing
story in the undeserved sufferings of Christ; had the sufferings been deserved we should all have been pessimists.
    Stevenson's great ethical and philosophical value lies
in the fact that he realised this great paradox that life
becomes more fascinating the darker it grows, that life is
worth living only so far as it is difficult to live. The
more steadfastly and gloomily men clung to their sinister
visions of duty, the more, in his eyes, they swelled the
chorus of the praise of things. He was an optimist because
to him everything was heroic, and nothing more heroic than
the pessimist. To Stevenson, the optimist, belong the most
frightful epigrams of pessimism. It was he who said that
this planet on which we live was more drenched with blood,
animal and vegetable, than a pirate ship. It was he who said
that man was a disease of the agglutinated dust. And his
supreme position and his supreme difference from all common optimists is merely this, that all common optimists say

that life is glorious in spite of these things, but he
said that all life was glorious because of them. He discovered that a battle is more comforting than a truce. He
discovered the same great fact which was discovered by a
man so fantastically different from him that the mere name
of him may raise a legitimate laugh - General Booth.

He discovered, that is to say, that religious evolution
might tend at last to the discovery, that the peace given
in the churches was less attractive to the religious
spirit than the war promised outside; that for one man who
wanted to be comforted a hundred wanted to be stirred; that
men, even ordinary men, wanted in the last resort, not life
or death, but drums.

It may reasonably be said that of all outrageous comparisons one of the most curious must be this between the
old evangelical despot and enthusiast and the elegant and
almost hedonistic man of letters. But these far-fetched
comparisons are infinitely the sanest, for they remind us
of the sanest of all conceptions, the unity of things. A
splendid and pathetic prince of India, living in far-off
æons, came to many of the same conceptions as a rather
dingy German professor in the nineteenth century; for
there are many essential resemblances between Buddha and
Schopenhauer. And if any one should urge that lapse of
time might produce mere imitation, it is easy to point out
that the same great theory of evolution was pronounced
simultaneously by Darwin, who became so grim a rationalist
that he ceased even to care for the arts, and by Wallace,
who has become so fiery a spiritualist that he yearns
after astrology and table-rapping.

Men of the most widely divergent types are connected by
these invisible cords across the world, and Stevenson was
essentially a Colonel in the Salvation Army. He believed,
that is to say, in making religion a military affair. His
militarism, of course, needs to be carefully understood.
It was considered entirely from the point of view of the
person fighting. It had none of that evil pleasure in
contemplating the killed and wounded, in realising the
agonies of the vanquished, which has been turned by some
modern writers into an art, a literary sin, which, though
only painted in black ink on white paper, is far worse
than the mere sin of murder. Stevenson's militarism was
as free from all the mere poetry of conquest and dominion
as the militarism of an actual common soldier. It was
mainly, that is to say, a poetry of watches and parades
and camp-fires. He knew he was in the hosts of the Lord:
he did not trouble much about the enemy. Here is his
resemblance to that Church Militant, which, secure only in
its own rectitude, wages war upon the nameless thing which

has tormented and bewildered us from the beginning of the world.

Of course, this Stevensonian view of war suggests in itself that other question, touching which so much has been written about him, the subject of childishness and the child. It is true, of course, that the splendidly infantile character of Stevenson's mind saved him from any evil arising from his militarism. A child can hit his nurse hard with a wooden sword without being an aesthete of violence. He may enjoy a hard whack, but he need not enjoy the colour harmonies of black and blue as they are presented in a bruise. It is undoubtedly the truth, of course, that Stevenson's interest in this fighting side of human nature was mainly childish, that is to say, mainly subjective. He thought of the whole matter in the primary colours of poetic simplicity. He said with splendid gusto in one of his finest letters: 'Shall we never taste blood?' But he did not really want blood. He wanted crimson-lake.

But of course, in the case of so light and elusive a figure as Stevenson, even the terms which have been most definitely attached to him tend to become misleading and inadequate, and the terms 'childlike' or 'childish,' true as they are down to a very fundamental truth, are yet the origin of a certain confusion. One of the greatest errors in existing literary philosophy is that of confusing the child with the boy. Many great moral teachers beginning with Jesus Christ, have perceived the profound philosophical importance of the child. The child sees everything freshly and fully; as we advance in life it is true that we see things in some degree less and less, that we are afflicted, spiritually and morally, with the myopia of the student. But the problem of the boy is essentially different from that of the child. The boy represents the earliest growth of the earthly, unmanageable qualities, poetic still, but not so simple or so universal. The child enjoys the plain picture of the world: the boy wants the secret, the end of the story. The child wishes to dance in the sun; but the boy wishes to sail after buried treasure. The child enjoys a flower, and the boy a mechanical engine. And the finest and most peculiar work of Stevenson is rather that he was the first writer to treat seriously and poetically the æsthetic instincts of the boy. He celebrated the toy gun rather than the rattle. Around the child and his rattle there has gathered a splendid service of literature and art; Hans Andersen and Charles Kingsley and George Macdonald and Walter Crane and Kate Greenaway and a list of celebrities a mile long bring their splendid gifts to the christening. But the

tragedy of the helpless infant (if it be a male infant -
girls are quite a different matter) is simply this, that,
having been fed on literature and art, as fine in its way
as Shelley and Turner up to the age of seven, he feels
within him new impulses and interests growing, a hunger
for action and knowledge, for fighting and discovery, for
the witchery of facts and the wild poetry of geography.
And then he is suddenly dropped with a crash out of
literature, and can read nothing but 'Jack Valiant among
the Indians.' For in the whole scene there is only one
book which is at once literature, like Hans Andersen, and
yet a book for boys and not for children, and its name is
'Treasure Island.'

168. FRANK SWINNERTON ON STEVENSON AS A WRITER OF THE
SECOND CLASS

1914

From 'R. L. Stevenson', 202-9. This book-length study of
Stevenson was widely read at the time of its publication
and was several times reprinted. Swinnerton (1884-   )
recalls the antagonism expressed towards it by reviewers
and supporters of Stevenson in 'Swinnerton: An Autobiography' (1936), 137, 286; and in 'Background with Chorus'
(1956), 182-4. The extract below is from the concluding
pages of the book. See Introduction, p. 42.

... The fact which all must recognise in connection with
Stevenson's work is the versatility of talent which is
displayed.... Quite obviously one cannot contemplate it
without great admiration. When it is remembered also that
it is the product of a man who was very frequently (though
not, as is generally supposed, continuously) an invalid,
the amount of it, and the variety, seems to be impossible.
Yet it is possible, and this fact it is which finally
explains our attitude to Stevenson. We think it marvellous that he should have been able to write at all, forgetting, as we do, that 'writing his best was very life
to him.' We do forget that; we ought not to forget it.
We ought not to forget that Stevenson was a writer. He
meant to be a writer, and a writer he became. He is known

chiefly in these days as a writer; and in the future he
will be still more clearly seen as a writer. The weaknesses of his work will be realised; to some extent his
writing will fall in popular esteem; but he will be less
the brave soul travelling hopefully and labouring to
arrive, and more the deliberate writer. When other men
sing and walk and talk and play chess and loiter, Stevenson wrote. In his life there is no question that he sang
and walked and loitered and talked and played chess; but
when he could do none of these things he could write.
Writing was as the breath of his body; writing was his
health, his friends, his romance. He will go down into
literary history as the man who became a professional
writer, who cared greatly about the form and forms of
expression. The fact that he concentrated upon expression
left his mind to some extent undeveloped, so that he could
express very excellently perceptions more suitable to his
youth than to his maturer years. It made his earlier
writing too scented and velvet-coated. But it enabled him
him, when his feeling was aroused, as it only could have
been in the last years of his life, to write at great
speed, with great clearness, an account of the political
troubles in Samoa and in particular of German diplomacy
there, which seems to us still valuable – not because the
facts it records are of extreme significance, but because
at the end of his life Stevenson was at last to be found
basing his work upon principles, really and consciously
grasped, from which the incidental outcome was of less
importance than the main realisation. Where he had
hitherto been shuttlecocked by his impulses, and tethered
by his moralism, he became capable of appreciating ideas
as of more importance than their expression. If he had
been less prolific, less versatile, less of a virtuoso,
Stevenson might have been a greater man. He would have
been less popular. He would have been less generally
admired and loved. But with all his writing he took the
road of least resistance, the road of limited horizons;
because with all his desire for romance, his desire for
the splendour of the great life of action, he was by
physical delicacy made intellectually timid and spiritually cautious. He was obliged to take care of himself, to
be home at night, to allow himself to be looked after.
Was not that the greatest misfortune that could have be-
fallen him? Is the work that is produced by nervous
reaction from prudence ever likely to enjoy an air of real
vitality? In the versatility of Stevenson we may observe
his restlessness, the nervous fluttering of the mind which
has no physical health to nourish it. In that, at least,
and the charming and not at all objectionable inclination

to pose. He was a poseur because if he had not pretended
he would have died. It was absolutely essential to him
that he should pose and that he should write, just as it
was essential that he should be flattered and anxiously
guarded from chill and harm. But it was necessary for the
same reason, lest the feeble flame should perish and the
eager flicker of nervous exuberance be extinguished. That
Stevenson was deliberately brave in being cheerful and
fanciful I do not for one moment believe; I think such a
notion is the result of pure ignorance of nervous persons
and their manifestations. But that Stevenson, beneath all
his vanity, realised his own disabilities, seems to me to
be certain and pathetic. That is what makes so much of
the extravagant nonsense written and thought about Stevenson since his death as horrible to contemplate as would be
any dance of ghouls. The authors of all this posthumous
gloating over Stevenson's illnesses have been concerned to
make him a horribly piteous figure, to harrow us in order
that we should pity. How much more is Stevenson to be
pitied for his self-constituted apostles! We shall do ill
to pity Stevenson, because pity is the obverse of envy,
and is as much a vice. Let us rather praise Stevenson for
his real determination and for that work of his which we
can approve as well as love. To love uncritically is to
love ill. To discriminate with mercy is very humbly to
justify one's privilege as a reader.

It is sufficient here to maintain that Stevenson's
literary reputation, as distinct from the humanitarian
aspect of his fortitude, is seriously impaired. It is no
longer possible for a serious critic to place him among
the great writers, because in no department of letters
- excepting the boy's book and the short-story - has he
written work of first-class importance. His plays, his
poems, his essays, his romances - all are seen nowadays
to be consumptive. What remains to us, apart from a
fragment, a handful of tales and two boy's books (for
'Kidnapped,' although finely romantic, was addressed to
boys, and still appeals to the boy in us) is a series of
fine scenes - what I have called 'plums' - and the charm
of Stevenson's personality. Charm as an adjunct is very
well; charm as an asset is of less significance. We find
that Stevenson, reviving the never-very-prosperous romance
of England, created a school which has brought romance to
be the sweepings of an old costume-chest. I am afraid we
must admit that Stevenson has become admittedly a writer
of the second class, because his ideals have been superseded by other ideals and shown to be the ideals of a day,
a season, and not the ideals of an age. In fact, we may
even question whether his ideals were those of a day,

whether they were not merely treated by everybody as so
much pastime; whether the revival of the pernicious
notion that literature is only a pastime is not due to his
influence. We may question whether Stevenson did not make
the novel a toy when George Eliot had finished making it
a treatise. If that charge could be upheld, I am afraid
we should have another deluge of critical articles upon
Stevenson, written as blindly as the old deluge, but this
time denouncing him as a positive hindrance in the way of
the novel's progress. However that may be, Stevenson
seems very decidedly to have betrayed the romantics by
inducing them to enter a *cul-de-sac*; for romantic literature in England at the present time seems to show no
inner light, but only a suspicious phosphorescence. And
that fact we may quite clearly trace back to Stevenson,
who galvanised romance into life after Charles Reade had
volubly betrayed it to the over-zealous compositor.
    Stevenson, that is to say, was not an innovator. We
can find his originals in Wilkie Collins, in Scott, in
Mayne Reid, in Montaigne, Hazlitt, Defoe, Sterne, and in
many others. No need for him to admit it: the fact is
patent. 'It is the grown people who make the nursery
stories; all the children do, is jealously to preserve
the text.' That is what Stevenson was doing; that is what
Stevenson's imitators have been doing ever since. And if
romance rests upon no better base than this, if romance
is to be conventional in a double sense, if it spring not
from a personal vision of life, but is only a tedious
virtuosity, a pretence, a conscious toy, romance as an art
is dead. The art was jaded when Reade finished his voci-
ferous carpet-beating; but it was not dead. And if it is
dead, Stevenson killed it.

169. MAURICE HEWLETT, THE RENOWN OF STEVENSON, 'THE
TIMES'

13 April 1922

Hewlett (1861-1923), was novelist, poet, essayist, and
author of, among other works, 'The Forest Lovers' (1898),
which brought him wide popularity, 'The Queen's Quair'
(1904), and 'The Song of the Plow' (1916). Hewlett wrote
John Freeman that the latter's Robert Louis Stevenson
('London Mercury', April 1922) had prompted his own

article but

> the opinion which I hung upon your peg had been mine
> for years. I kept it back because I didn't want to
> hurt Colvin, and rather wish even now that I had gone
> on keeping it back - because he *is* hurt. He told me
> he was preparing to attack the pair of us, and I
> replied with soft words.

A month later Hewlett was still attempting to repair
Colvin's injured feelings and prove to him that no conspiracy against Stevenson was afoot:

> Please, my dear Colvin, don't be afflicted with what I,
> or Freeman, think proper to say about Stevenson.
> Neither of us can possibly matter, or can have any
> effect whatever upon Stevenson or his memory.... I had
> always thought him overpraised and that such excess
> really obscured his excellence. When I found Freeman,
> unknown to me, saying so, I took up my own little
> parable. That's really all. You mustn't look round
> and say, *Nous sommes trahis*, because two writers have
> the same idea. Freeman and I are not partners in
> 'crime'. ('The Letters of Maurice Hewlett' (1926),
> ed. Laurence Binyon, 239)

That which always happens to a man, whom local renown and
the zeal of his friends have tilted out of his place in
the scheme of things is upon the point of happening, it
seems, to the gracious memory and solid worth of Robert
Louis Stevenson. Literary specific gravity is beginning
to operate; and so it always will, but whether late or
soon will depend upon the period of inflation. Unless
that has taken place early in a career (as in some living
instances it has done), the figure of the dead will glow
in the embers of the altar-fire for rather more than a
generation.
    It happened so to Browning and Carlyle; it had happened
before them to Byron. In the cases of Sir Walter Scott
and, after him, of Dickens, where the present fame was so
excessive that a pyre took the place of an altar and heca-
tombs of a handful of incense, the glow endured for twice
that time, and indeed is not quenched yet: but theirs were
two of the very rare sort where a man's works become
classics in his lifetime - a sort so rare that except
Pope, and in a smaller way Gibbon, I can recall no other
examples of it in our history. With Stevenson it has been

very much as it was with Browning, that death super-
vened upon a rising popularity. His estimation continued
to grow on, and was enhanced by the praises of those who
had not known until they lost him how warmly they were
concerned in his fame.

Two of them in particular [Colvin and Lang] were
responsible for what followed the birth, that is, of what
Mr. Freeman in a current review calls the Stevenson Myth.
I don't know that something portentous of the kind can be
denied, though I don't know either why it should be called
a myth, unless because Mr. Freeman wishes to euhemerise
it. Something undoubtedly took place after Stevenson's
death to sky the balance; he was had in a different estimation altogether. His works became apparently classics.
Two collected editions of them appeared, and at this hour
a third is being added to them. I am not at all in his
publishers' secrets, but I should say that, since his
death, the sale of his books rose steadily until somewhere about 1912, and has since then begun perceptibly to
decline. But that is mere guesswork.

His, then, is a more curious case than that of Tennyson, whose fame was well-established long before his
death, and yet enormously increased by the universal loss
which that event proved to be. It was a loss felt personally, as the loss of Dickens had been, the same in kind
though less in degree. I was 10 years old when Dickens
died: I remember the sort of hush which fell upon our
house and village, and no doubt upon the whole country.
People went about looking seriously at each other, saying
'Charles Dickens is dead.' An illustrated newspaper - I
think there was only one then - had a two-page drawing,
called 'The Empty Chair.' That was the death of a king
of men. Tennyson's made less of a stir, certainly:
Stevenson's in 1894 had been almost nothing.

He had been largely read, undoubtedly. 'Treasure
Island,' 'Jekyll and Hyde,' and 'Kidnapped,' any one of
them, I dare say, had gone as wide as 'Robert Elsmere' or
the sugared sentiments of William Black: but not one, I
will engage, so generally as 'Lorna Doone' - a novel
which, for certain qualities in it, will see several more
generations out, which has, in fact, done for itself what
nothing of Stevenson's has done yet, that is, imprinted
itself upon a countryside. With those three exceptions,
the work of Robert Louis was only known to amateurs of
literature, who prized 'An Inland Voyage' and its companion, the Cornhill Essays, and the 'New Arabian Nights,'
more highly than any of the popular three. I daresay
that, at 33, I was fairly typical of my kind. Well, in
1894 I had not read the popular three. I had, on the

other hand, the 'Voyage' and 'Travels with a Donkey' pretty well by heart. I knew all the Cornhill Essays, and still possess a tattered yellow-back copy of the 'New Arabians,' which used to travel about with me wherever I went. That delightful burlesque apart, I admired, and still admire, his tale of Villon in old Paris, A Lodging for the Night, and thought, as I still think, The Pavilion on the Links the best melodrama of that day - hardly bettered since.

After his death, after the first collected edition, after the Letters and the biography, the public became aware that the glamour resident in every act of Stevenson's life was latent also in every paragraph of his writing. There can be no doubt about that; few writers have so few slipshod passages. The glamour was there because he felt it himself. He loved his poses, admired his own gestures, revelled in the game he was playing, a new one in every book. Born writer and good writer as he was, he played every time at being a better. He made himself an expert (that was his inspiration) in the rules of the *genre*, whatever it was. So far as the *manner* of the thing went, he was hardly ever off the mark, and if he could but have been more interested in the *matter* (which in novels means the people of the tale) he would have been a great novelist. But they were never real enough to him. They didn't live; so they don't. You can't get round them because he couldn't get inside them. He tells you about them, puts them in this light and that; but they themselves elude you.

I said the other day, somewhere, that he had only added two characters to the population: 'Theophilus Godall, the princely tobacconist, and the Chevalier Burke, who is Barry Lyndon done right instead of wrong. (A Barry Lyndon could not have been cruel, as Thackeray made out. It was against nature.) That, I maintain, is true. If desire could have made a man live Alan Breck would have lived. But does he? He does not. Scott was Stevenson's master; Ephraim Mackellar is Jedediah Cleishbotham, with Dominie Sampson worked over him. Alan Breck is a pure Scott creation too. But other influences came to bear, some incongruous, some a clear gain. Smollett, Defoe, Dumas, and Thackeray all came in, and of those Dumas was the most profitable mine, spurring Stevenson into unflagging vivacity. Here, however, we have a reason for the want of vital juices in the persons of Stevenson's tales, that he was too much occupied in making them like their originals. I remember a letter in which he says that his characters would take the bit in their teeth.... Yet the bit which they took had been of some other maker's adjustment,

neither original sin nor original virtue of the author's.
     But what delightful reading they are, how easy, how
graceful, how plausible; with what a dewy sparkle of wit;
with what art worked over, with what zest worked out!
It is impossible to help loving and serving such a writer,
by doing at least half the work for him; and what more, in
the long run, can a writer want?   I hold that the partnership with Mr. Lloyd Osbourne was unfortunate.   'The Wrong
Box' is not fine enough for Stevenson; it trenches on the
vulgar and the mean, as the adventures of a corpse in a
grand piano are bound to do.   That was never Stevenson's
vein.   His was for whimsy, not clowning.   Typical of his
happy gaiety are The Treasure of Franchard and Providence
and the Guitar, and none the less so for the moral in
them.   There are some wonderfully good things in 'The
Wrecker,' and some very bad things, too.   Invention tired
at the end, and let it all down into the dust.   'Weir' was
a return, and might have been as good as 'Ballantrae.'
     His occasional essays are too long for my taste, and
have too much sack to the bread.   The more he had to tell
you, the more facts to marshal and to illuminate with his
fancy, wit, and sympathy, the better he was.   I have
always seen in him a historian who had missed his turning.
His account of the persecution of the Camisards, his
'Footnote to History,' his 'Life of Fleeming Jenkin,' and
the 'Critical Essays' ['Familiar Studies of Men and
Books'] are solid, good and ingenious work.   More than
that, they make live.   On them and his burlesques, so far
as I understand the matter, his fame will presently rest.
Meantime the resolving process has begun.   Specific
gravity has begun its priestlike task. Stevenson will
sink for a while, then rise up into his place.

170.   LEONARD WOOLF, THE FALL OF STEVENSON, 'NATION AND
THE ATHENAEUM'

5 January 1924, xxxiv, 517

Woolf (1880-1969) was active in literature and politics;
he was co-editor of the 'Political Quarterly' from its
founding to 1959 and literary editor of the 'Nation and
the Athenaeum' from 1923 to 1930.   He was associated with
the Bloomsbury group and married Virginia Stephen in 1912;
together they established the Hogarth Press.

We catch a sad glimpse of the struggle of successive
generations and of Colvin's devotion to the Stevenson
cause in a letter Gosse wrote Colvin (25 April 1924)
answering his queries about Woolf and what might be done
to counter the influence of the growing number of critics
determined to slight Stevenson; Gosse wrote:

> Leonard Woolf has been writing several loud articles
> in ... the 'Nation,' of which he is the Literary
> Editor. He is the son-in-law of our old friend Leslie
> Stephen, having married Virginia. I have never had any
> communications with him, but I don't think he is an
> 'idiot,' rather a perverse, partially educated alien
> German, who has thrown in his lot violently with Bol-
> shevism and Mr. Joyce's 'Ulysses' and the 'great sexual
> emancipation' and all the rest of the nasty fads of the
> hour. It is no use for us to strive with such a man.
> He would only redouble his sarcasms and jibes. What he
> hates in R.L.S. is radically what we love - the refine-
> ment, the delicacy, the beauty. You cannot argue with
> a type like that. You can only let it pass by, and, on
> the next possible occasion, say once more that R.L.S.
> was a beautiful writer and a beautiful soul. (National
> Library of Scotland)

The article does show a lack of knowledge of Stevenson's
reputation. The fall in popularity, as we have seen, did
not occur immediately after the death nor was it strange
for Rawlinson to come to the conclusion that 'as an
essayist Stevenson will probably live'. Gosse, St Loe
Strachey, Le Gallienne, and others had maintained this all
along. Woolf answered some of the many objections of
correspondents ('I was really astonished at the number and
vehemence of the people who protested against what I
said.') in another article on 19 April 1924. The article
appearing here was reprinted in 'Essays on Literature,
History, Politics, etc.' (1927), 33-43.

There has never been a more headlong fall in a writer's
reputation than there was in Stevenson's after his death.
The consumptive Scotsman who walked down Bond Street in
a black shirt, a red tie, a velvet jacket, and a smoking-
cap, and who finally retired to live and die on a coral
island in the South Seas, was just the man to captivate
the taste of the romantic 'nineties. Mr. Gosse is almost
the sole survivor of the inner circle of - somewhat
quarrelsome - admirers who helped to create the Stevenson

legend. The climax of the legend was that Stevenson not
only wore a velvet coat, had flashing eyes, and was a
brilliant talker, but was also a great writer, a great
novelist, a great essayist, a great thinker, and a consummate artist in words. That romantic age in which
Andrew Lang, Mr. Gosse, Henley, and Sir Sidney Colvin were
prophets swallowed the legend whole, asked for more, and
got it. Stevenson seemed to have been permanently placed
in a very high niche among the greatest of writers when
the younger generation began to read 'Plays Pleasant and
Unpleasant.' The effect was appalling: the velvet coat
suddenly lost its romance; the name 'Tusitala' roused no
more emotions than did such monosyllables as 'Shaw' or
'Wells'; and ill-mannered young men began to say that the
rhythm of Stevenson's great passages was spoiled for them
because they could always hear the machinery grinding out
the tune. Never has there been a swifter or greater flow
of that terrible tide which inevitably sweeps in and cuts
off one generation from the next, making it impossible
for the sons to understand the enthusiasms of their
fathers and leaving a few poor embittered survivors stranded high and dry on the further shore.

Well, even metaphorical tides have a habit of ebbing
and flowing; and when a writer's reputation has been
plunging steadily downhill for thirty years, it has
usually gone too far, and it is time for a revival. Is
there going to be a resurrection of Robert Louis Stevenson? To judge from the publishers' lists, which are good
barometers of literary reputation, Stevenson's resurrection is already beginning. The first ten volumes of the
Tusitala Edition of his complete works have just been
published.... At the same moment, Miss Rosaline Masson
produces a new 'Life of Robert Louis Stevenson,' contain-
ing a certain amount of new material and adorned with a
large number of photographs. Thirdly, Mr. H. G. Rawlinson, of the Indian Educational Service, has edited, with
introduction and notes, 'Selected Essays of Robert Louis
Stevenson.' I cannot believe that the simultaneous
appearance of all these books is fortuitous; it is rather
the first ebb in the tide which carried us all so far
from the velvet coat and Tusitala.

The publication of these books has given me an opportunity
of rereading a good deal of Stevenson: 'Treasure Island,'
'Kidnapped,' The Body Snatcher, and some of the famous
essays. There was more pleasure in the rereading than I
had expected. If Stevenson is not the great writer whom
they thought him to be thirty years ago, and whom Miss
Masson apparently still thinks him to-day, he is better

than his present reputation among 'highbrows' would lead
one to suppose. The worst thing about him is his literary
style. Mr. Rawlinson, after apologizing for it and pointing out its most glaring faults, comes to the strange conclusion that 'it is as an essayist that Stevenson will
probably live.' As an essayist Stevenson is already dead,
and I do not believe that anyone will ever be able to
resurrect him in the essay. The reason is that in that
form of writing a false literary style tells most fatally
against a writer, particularly when, as with Stevenson, he
has nothing original to say. It is astonishing how
drearily thin and artificial the famous Aes Triplex and
Pulvis et Umbra, for instance, are when one reads them
again. Stevenson had no style of his own; as he said himself, he played the 'sedulous ape' to great prose writers,
and the consequence is that his essays have the same flavour as those which brilliant undergraduates send in for
University prizes. I will quote a sentence or two in
which he seems to me to be at his best, and I think that
most people will agree that they do not reach a higher
level than that of any first-rate journalist: -

As for the innumerable army of anaemic and tailorish
persons who occupy the face of this planet with so much
propriety, it is palpably absurd to imagine them in any
such situation as a love-affair.

Our race has never been able contentedly to suppose
that the noise of its wars, conducted by a few young
gentlemen in a corner of an inconsiderable star, does
not re-echo among the Courts of Heaven with quite a
formidable effect.

Do the old men mind it, as a matter of fact? Why,
no. They were never merrier; they have their grog at
night, and tell the raciest stories, they hear of the
death of people about their own age, or even younger,
not as if it was a grisly warning, but with a simple
childlike pleasure at having outlived someone else; and
when a draught might puff them out like a guttering
candle, or a bit of a stumble shatter them like so much
glass, their old hearts keep sound and unaffrighted,
and they go on bubbling with laughter, through years of
man's age compared to which the valley of Balaklava was
as safe and peaceful as a village cricket-green on
Sunday.

Stevenson was quite a good imitator of great writers,
but he was not a great writer or artist himself. His ear

for verbal music was not fine, and his phrases are rather
laboured. He is, indeed, at his best where he is sufficiently interested in his subject to forget about his
style. He can then write good, plain, honest English
which makes no pretensions to be great literature. This
is the case in 'Treasure Island' and in some of his other
stories. I must have read 'Treasure Island' many times,
but, when I read it again last week in the Tusitala
Edition, it still carried me along with it, and was
thoroughly entertaining. It is pre-eminently a day-dream
type of story, and Stevenson always remained a typical
day-dream writer. He appeals to the child or to the
primitively childish in grown men and women. There is
nothing against him in that; a good story is rare, and
personally I hope that I shall never grow too old to
enjoy one. 'Treasure Island,' 'Kidnapped,' 'The Master
of Ballantrae' are all good stories, and the more Stevenson forgets himself and his style in them and becomes
absorbed in telling the tale, the better they are. And
there is one other form of writing in which occasionally
the same thing happens to him. He wrote one really good
essay, the essay on Samuel Pepys in his 'Familiar Studies
of Men and Books.' There again the character and story of
Pepys caught his attention, and he forgot to think about
his words and periods; the result is a vigorous, subtle
study of an extremely interesting person.

Select Bibliography

EHRSAM, THEODORE G., and DEILY, ROBERT H., 'Bibliographies of Twelve Victorian Authors'. New York: Octagon Books, 1968.

FURNAS, J. C., 'Voyage to Windward. The Life of Robert Louis Stevenson'. London: Faber & Faber, 1952. The most authoritative biography; the chapter Dialectics of a Reputation traces the response to Stevenson from the time of his death.

HAMMERTON, J. A., 'Stevensoniana'. Edinburgh: John Grant, 1910. A miscellaneous collection of anecdotal and appreciative commentary by Stevenson's contemporaries.

McKAY, GEORGE L., 'Some Notes on Robert Louis Stevenson, His Finances and His Agents and Publishers'. New Haven, Conn.: Yale University Press, 1958. This modestly titled pamphlet contains a wealth of information.

McKAY, GEORGE L., 'The Stevenson Library of Edwin J. Beinecke', 6 vols. New Haven, Conn.: Yale University Press, 1951–64. Catalogue of the immense collection of Stevenson materials at the Beinecke Library, Yale University; especially useful for its listing of unpublished letters by Stevenson and others in which opinions are expressed on his works and his critics.

PRIDEAUX, W. F., 'A Bibliography of the Works of Robert Louis Stevenson'. London: Frank Hollings, 1917.

Select Index

The index is divided into two parts: I Robert Louis Stevenson: Works; II General Index.

II GENERAL INDEX

THE CRITICAL HERITAGE SERIES

GENERAL EDITOR: B. C. SOUTHAM

Volumes published and forthcoming